BEING A
WELL WOMAN

BEING A WELL WOMAN

Miriam Stoppard, MD MRCP

Holt, Rinehart and Winston

New York

For Tom

Being a Well Woman was conceived, edited and designed
by Dorling Kindersley Limited, 9, Henrietta Street, London WC2E 8PS

First published in the United States by
Holt, Rinehart and Winston, 383 Madison Avenue,
New York, New York 10017.

Published simultaneously in Canada by Holt, Rinehart and
Winston of Canada, Limited.

Originally published in Great Britain under the title *Everywoman's Life Guide.*

Library of Congress Cataloging in Publication Data

Stoppard, Miriam.
Being a well woman.

Includes index.
1. Women—Health and hygiene. 2. Women—Physiology.
3. Women—Diseases. I. Title.
RA778.S826 1982   613'.0424   82-3048   AACR2

ISBN: 0-03-060606-1

First American Edition

Printed in the United States of America

1   3   5   7   9   10   8   6   4   2

ISBN 0-03-060606-3

Author's Acknowledgment

Several good things have happened as the result of being asked by Peter Kindersley and Christopher Dorling to write *Being a Well Woman*. Meeting Amy Carroll, my editor, has meant a great deal to me. Our collaboration started well and grew into one of the happiest working relationships I've known. I am indebted to her.

Dorling Kindersley staff have given me valued support and *Being a Well Woman* bears their stamp as much as mine: Debbie MacKinnon initiated the design and supervised artistic production; Denise Brown was responsible for the artwork and design content; Fiona MacIntyre assisted Amy Carroll on the editing side.

Being a Well Woman is dedicated to my husband, not just because his pride in my achievement makes work easier, but because his loving encouragement makes everything better and anything possible.

CONTENTS

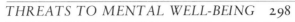

INTRODUCTION

ON BEING FEMALE

You start being female the moment you are conceived. With the union of the ovum (which is always genetically female because it contains X chromosomes) and an X sperm, a female child is created. Men produce two kinds of sperm: X sperm, which are genetically female, and Y sperm, which are genetically male. If the ovum combines with an X sperm to make an XX fetus, it will be a girl. If, on the other hand, the ovum combines with a Y sperm, the fetus is XY, a boy. You can see from this description that the basic sexuality of the human race is dependent on the X sperm from the ovum, and is only modified by the addition of an X or a Y contribution from the sperm. One could, therefore, draw the broad conclusion that the human race is, at root, female.

With this perspective, it is possible to look at the intra-uterine development of the sexes, particularly with reference to the genital organs, from a female point of view. Under the influence of the second X chromosome, the various female sex organs develop from special parts of the embryo, and form the clitoris, the labia, the ovaries and the uterus. All four organs are there, in different form, in the male: the influence of the Y chromosome has rendered the clitoris somewhat larger (the penis), the labia a quite different shape (the scrotum), and, although the uterus is virtually non-existent, every man has a vestige of the primitive uterine system, and the ovaries, which remain inside the body in women, descend to the outside and are carried in the scrotum. (This is because the production of sperm needs to be at a slightly lower temperature than the body's internal temperature to be efficient and healthy.) So the second generalization we may make is that human beings at the time of birth are modelled on a basically female anatomy.

After birth, being female is the consequence of two separate influences – one internal, the other external. The first is not within our control; rather it is determined by internally-secreted female hormones from the ovaries. This process begins in infancy and builds up to the *menarche*, when periods first start, and it includes associated signs of feminine sexuality such as development of the breasts and nipple buds (see p. 138). Even so, the female body responds to internal female hormones before there are any outward signs of it. These hormones to a large extent determine body size, body configuration, the length of bones, the size of muscles, etc., and also, to a certain extent, the female personality.

The second, much more important, influence is the behavior of parents, adults and peers towards girls, which gives them a very clear idea of what is expected in behavior and role playing. As a girl gets older, the environment, or the genetic-environment interaction, plays an increasingly important part in how she turns out. Research is showing that this effect may be the most important single factor in determining how a girl's personality develops, how she behaves, what her aspirations are, how ambitious she is, how assertive she is, and how determined she is to examine her options and exercise them

Even in the very early years, a girl's initial programming by adults in the environment around her will lay down the basic patterns of how she will handle her future life and problems. It is from childhood onwards that her expectations develop. This notion is an extremely important one because not only do we act on our expectations but others respond to them in a similar way. For instance, if you expect to be treated as an equal, the chances are that you will be. Certainly you will increase your chances of being treated as an equal if that expectation is implicit in your words, actions and inter-personal relationships. If a small female child is encouraged to be just as independent, just as adventurous, just as strong, just as resilient as a boy would be, she will grow up not only with those characteristics, but with the expectation that the people around her will honor them.

On the other hand, if a girl grows up believing that a display of helplessness is the best way to get herself through difficulties, nothing but problems can result. She may be unfortunate enough to learn helplessness by example from her mother or she may fortuitously discover helplessness for herself as a mode of behavior which brings results. But even in the latter case it is the fault of her parents for allowing this situation to develop. If a little girl finds that she can get her own way by wheedling things out of her father, and then using her father as leverage against her mother, she will be tempted to continue with this kind of manipulation as she grows up.

Further problems may result if a girl is not given consistent guidance on the way that she should behave: if her mother, on the one hand, feeds her information about independence, alternative options to marriage, a fairly free lifestyle, and an active career, but her father, on the other hand, tries to perpetuate the belief that a woman's place is in the home, that an expensive education is wasted on a girl, that there is no question of a university career. So it is not surprising that contradictory expectations from parents lead a girl to have a confused view of her role.

Society in general, and parents in particular, are by and large unaware of the effect that their behavior and expectations have on the subsequent development of their children. That parents respond to a girl child differently from a boy child, and that these differences have an effect on the gender appreciation of the child is well known. There are also differences in a mother's behavior when she *thinks* she is relating to a girl, from when she *thinks* she is relating to a boy.

It has been known for some time that mothers differ significantly in the way that they react to and stimulate female and male babies. In one experiment, mothers were presented with "actor" babies of about six months old, and were asked to play with each baby for ten minutes. They were given seven toys designated as masculine, feminine or sexually neutral.

One of the most dramatic findings was that the mother's behavior was strongly influenced by stereotypes about the baby's perceived gender and the type of play appropriate for that gender. The first toy that was offered when the baby appeared to be a boy was nearly always a hammer-shaped rattle. When the baby was perceived as a girl, the usual toy that was offered first was a soft pink doll.

There was also a difference in the way that mothers talked to boys and girls. For example, boys were given verbal encouragement to be vigorous and physically active. Girls on the other hand were praised for being clever, and for their attractiveness.

One of the most intriguing findings was the tendency of mothers to encourage physical activity when they thought the baby was a boy. So if the baby was active and mobile, the mother responded with the same kind of behavior, but if a baby dressed as a girl did the same thing, the mother responded with calming activity.

In a follow-up study done on older babies, it was noted that by the age of thirteen months, a baby's choice of toy reflects the same gender bias that was hinted at by his/her mother six or seven months earlier. Choice of toy is very similar for girls and boys, but they use them in different ways. Boys are much more physically active – they push, pull and bang their toys. Girls opt for much finer movements, like fitting objects together, or putting toys in particular places.

By the time a child is three, s/he clearly demonstrates at least a symbolic understanding of gender. This is exemplified by his/her accurate use of "he," "she," "her" and "him" and correct reference to his/her own gender. Intellectually, a child has the skill to sort objects into masculine and feminine categories. The pretend play of five-year-olds shows their understanding of adult gender roles, especially in games which relate to the family or to work situations such as hospitals with doctors (male) and nurses (female).

There are many more ways in which parents manipulate and produce sex differences. Parents discipline their children differently: girls are quite often made to suffer withdrawal of parental love and affection whereas boys are punished physically. (The sex differences can be accentuated by parents if disciplining boys more often falls to fathers than mothers, and vice versa.) The psychological effects of the withdrawal of love and affection are known to be deep and sometimes unforgettable. If girls tend to be disciplined more in this fashion than by straight physical punishment, it is logical to suppose that they would have an increased need for affection and be more dependent. Research has shown that children who are disciplined in this way tend to be less aggressive than those who receive physical punishments.

Girls are further molded by their parents because they are usually more protected, controlled and restricted than boys. They are not encouraged to be independent in the way that boys are. This lack of encouragement or opportunity for independence and autonomy takes its toll. In one long-term study, girls who had protective mothers were found to have more feminine interests during childhood and adulthood, and over-protection was found to have a feminizing influence on boys as they grew up. Fathers are quite a lot to blame for accentuating sex differences; they emphasize the masculine elements of behavior and achievement in their sons, while they nurture and protect their daughters.

There is no doubt that hormones play a part in producing such characteristics as aggression, and that these vary between individuals of either sex as well as between the sexes, but while differences in aggression between boys and girls are accepted as being natural, there is quite a lot in their initial programming which seems to make aggressive behavior acceptable in boys but not in girls. Aggression in girls is generally disapproved of, and very often they re-channel it into

more acceptable forms such as ambition. Physical aggression is felt to be more appropriate when displayed by boys and general acceptance encourages them to use it more, and to gain prestige and status through it. It would be much more sensible to teach that aggressive behavior is misplaced in everyday life and unattractive and unacceptable in either sex. A much more sane view of masculine aggression would be that it was an exaggerated form of competitive behavior, and that it is self-destructive and damaging to relationships – certainly when compared to the more civilized ways of women and girls, who tend to use verbal forms of hostility and aggression.

The media don't help. Even before boys and girls are literate, the sex roles are implicitly endorsed in books for infants. Little girls are seen as quiet, sweet, good and angelic, helping mother around the house. Boys are not expected to behave like this at all, and are very rarely seen in domestic situations. They are naughty, and that is assumed to come naturally to a boy. In brother and sister activities, the girl is usually a passive observer and a compliant playmate. The boy is dominant, commanding and active.

Later on, girls themselves perpetuate the myths that have been started in childhood. Romantic papers are packed full of love stories which show girls whose main aim in life is to find, catch and keep a man. They completely deny the role of girls as independent individuals with minds and interests of their own.

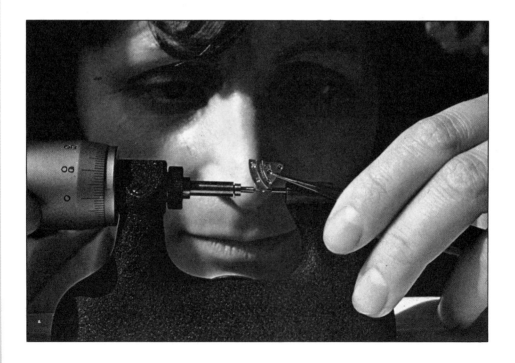

And then as girls get older, they (and men for that matter) are bombarded with the glossy guidelines of what all normal and good girls should aspire to: the looks of the latest female pop-star or film star; the mores of the ideal stay-at-home wife; the sole ambition of love and early marriage, tied up with ribbons, hearts, flowers and wedding bells. In fact, confirmation of the mother's first reaction to a baby dressed in pink, regardless of its real sex, is to hand it a soft, fluffy doll.

It is almost impossible to resist the exhortations of the advertisers. Like all human beings, girls who are growing up and women who are housewives want to fulfill and achieve their roles. Their roles, however, are increasingly defined by advertising. The advertisers have succeeded in presenting imagery which, in fact, is not based on reality as we know it, but women chase after it because they believe it reflects society's ideals. Even if women resist buying the advertised products, they do not fail to absorb the promotional images.

Once they are at school, girls notoriously under-achieve and this is because a lot of sex differentiation has already taken place by the time children show their abilities at school. By school age, boys are already more independent and adventurous, girls are more restricted, protected and aren't given much chance to stand on their own feet.

The way girls are treated is very important, since it is thought that there is a relationship between independence and intellectual ability, especially analytical thinking. This is the capacity to see problems in global terms, to apply general principles to them, and to use reasoning and analysis to solve them. This is particularly necessary in scientific and related fields. If a mother (or father) doesn't encourage independence and has poor expectations for her/his daughter, then the child is rarely given the opportunity to develop, to test and assess her abilities for herself. Very often she ends up under-estimating herself and is not confident of attempting things alone. She is dependent on the approval of other people to give her courage and self-esteem, and if she has been disciplined by the withdrawal of love and affection, she will be very concerned about the approbation of others, and this promotes her conformity and passivity. Several psychologists feel that early independence is the key characteristic to developing intellectual ability. Early independence encourages initiative, taking responsibility, and solving problems for oneself instead of relying on others.

Contrary to what one would hope, education goes on to emphasize stereotyped sex roles. In an American study, a questionnaire was used with women teachers to assess their sex-role ideals by getting them to describe what an adolescent girl student should be like. More than three quarters of them concurred with the stereotype for girls: they wanted them to be unassertive, dependent, submissive, emotional and concerned with their appearance.

Unless the gulf between "girls' subjects," i.e. the arts, cooking, needlework, typing and commerce, and "boys' subjects," i.e. science, math, geography, economics, woodwork, philosophy and logic, can be bridged, boys and girls will continue to be stereotyped. The labels of masculine and feminine must be neutralized. This means that the girls have to be taught the same subjects as boys, in the same way as boys are taught them. Curricula have to be organized so that it is possible for girls and boys to study all subjects, especially since most male ideals coincide with those that are considered socially most desirable.

More importantly, the jobs that the subjects lead to have to be seen to be suitable, acceptable, and accessible for both sexes. Until this happens, girls will continue to grow up with feminine role models that have love, marriage, a husband and children as more important immediate goals than anything else. They will continue to do this as long as school provides no connection between interests, experiences and activities out of school, and information, qualifications and opportunities offered inside school. Until these two polarized images of femininity are bridged, there can be no equality for women.

And what if equality did reign? What if the charter of the women's movement was ratified? A rather vague feeling, in the Sixties and early Seventies, that my emotions did not chime with my intellect about the more radical demands of the feminist movement has only hardened with time. What I had always felt, and am now absolutely convinced of, is that much of the politics of the feminist movement and the biology of the human female do not easily coalesce. It is a most uneasy communion. Where it is attempted, guilt and doubts about selfishness and self-indulgence are often the uncomfortable aftermath. It is simply not possible for most women to turn their backs on many of the activities for which they have a biological, an emotional and an intellectual need.

Where the radicals got it wrong was to propose that the two sides of a woman's personality, the biological and the political, are mutually exclusive: that to be the political feminist animal, to enjoy equal status with a man in every walk of life, to be given the same opportunities, to be viewed in the same ways, one had to reject the other, softer side of the feminine personality. This is not mandatory. To advocate it is naïve. It is biologically naïve and politically naïve.

Some of women's greatest strengths lie in their femininity, and to stifle this or deny this can only land women in a great deal of trouble. In the end they will be saddened and lowered by the schism because it is irreconcilable. The majority of women simply don't wish to operate like men. They are not happy while they are doing it, and if they feel pressured to do so, one of the inevitable results is a feeling of inadequacy and possibly a threat to mental well-being.

Women often fail to live up to radical feminist ideals not through any fault of their own, but because of their biology. Female hormones affect attitudes and behavior in a way which makes them indivisible. Recently, the charge of capital murder against two women in England was dropped on the grounds that they were not in control of themselves when they killed someone while suffering from premenstrual syndrome. In these cases, a judge and jury were sufficiently well convinced by medical testimony to believe that the two women could not be held responsible for their actions when going through the biological disarrangement of a monthly event experienced by all fertile women to some degree. How can we, on the one hand, be asking for equality in all walks of life, stating that we are trustworthy employees, claiming that we are decisive managers, reiterating that we are as capable of analyzing problems in a broad perspective as men while on the other we are claiming that a biological event, and a frequent one at that, is grounds for mitigation which is disallowable for men. It could be construed that we are asking for more than equality.

While one must applaud the fact that women's complaints are finally being taken seriously by the world at large, and the judiciary in particular, one might question whether they are grounds for preferential treatment. One might question whether it is a feminist issue at all. The real objective surely is to comprehend the biological functions of an individual well enough to have a sensitive and sensible grasp of a person's true responsibility for his or her actions. No un-prejudiced feminist would claim this as a privilege or right of her sex. It is the right of all human beings. Which brings me to what I consider to be the most important aspect of being female. It is not being a feminist and rejoicing in feminist victories, it is being human.

The only way to come to terms with biological and political forces is to weld them into a new philosophy and that is what seems to be happening now in the women's movement. In a new form of feminism, the lessons learned in the Sixties and Seventies are being absorbed into women's everyday lives. It is wrong, biologically and politically, to think that all women don't need men. Women were not necessarily meant to be dependent on men or live their lives with only one, but they were meant to interact with them, and just like men, women have to find a way of fulfilling their intellectual ambitions through work and their emotional needs through home and children. Neither of these things can be done *without* men; most women have to work at jobs with men, no woman can have children without men.

What women have to come to terms with is not the denial of men, but living lives which make no pretense at denying the desire for a home and children. It is time we called a truce to the female biology versus female politics war.

BEING A WELL WOMAN

Until recently women had a tendency to ignore their health – they were often meticulous about the health of their children and their husbands but neglectful of their own. Now they have realized that their health can be pivotal; certainly for the woman who has a family to look after – who would take over her responsibilities if her health suffered? And as more and more women enter professions, take up senior and managerial positions, and hold down responsible jobs, their health becomes important to themselves and their employers.

Economic as well as feminist arguments have led to improvements in women's health care and increased facilities for medical checks for women. Improvements in monitoring women's health exemplify preventive medicine at its best: regular Pap smears and breast examinations can save thousands of lives.

Being a well woman, however, is as much in your hands as the doctor's! Only you can make sure you eat a balanced diet, take enough exercise to keep fit, regulate your alcohol and drug intake, relax sufficiently to moderate stress, wear proper clothes and get regular checkups. It is up to you to be aware of danger signs – both in your physical and your mental well-being – and to take the necessary steps to bring them back to normal. This chapter can help you do that.

NUTRITION

Being fit means being healthy in all respects. The first priority is to eat a proper diet, and the second is to engage in as comprehensive an exercise program as possible.

Over the past ten or fifteen years, the concept of a balanced diet has gone through a radical change. It used to be thought that as long as our diet contained the minimum requirements of proteins, fats, carbohydrates, vitamins and minerals, then it could be topped up with any sort of food that would give us the energy we needed. Given this freedom of choice, most of us opted for a diet which is far too rich in protein, far too reliant on saturated fat, and far too full of refined carbohydrates. We eat too little fresh fruit and vegetables, grains, beans and other foods providing roughage. Moreover, we tend to fry food instead of grilling it, and when we do fry, we often use animal fat. Most of us eat an unhealthy diet which, in the long run, is hazardous to our health. Malnutrition used to mean being underfed, but now, in the Western world, malnutrition means being over-fed. Where once it used to be very rare, now it is very common.

The "new" balanced diet

Modern scientific research based on societies where the incidence of heart disease (the major 20th century killer) is low has produced a new definition of a balanced diet. The most significant changes affect our intake of protein, fats, carbohydrates, and fiber.

Protein needs 8–10% of total daily calories
Protein is the body's essential restorer. It is involved in most body processes but its main function is to build and repair body tissues. It is also indispensable in the formation of enzymes, amino acids and antibodies.

A healthy adult woman needs about 50 grams of protein each day; there is no nutritional advantage to eating more than this minimum daily requirement of protein. Proteins used to be described as "first class" (animal protein) and "second class" (vegetable) but we now know that there is nothing especially worthy about animal protein provided you take a variety of vegetable proteins: people in the Eastern world whose diet is much lower in animal protein than our own, are just as strong as we are and do not show signs of protein depletion. Therefore, our protein "allowance" can come from any source. Protein, in its most concentrated form, is found in lean meat but it is also available in nuts, grains and cheese.

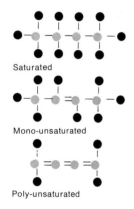

Saturated

Mono-unsaturated

Poly-unsaturated

Carbon   Hydrogen

There are three types of fat: saturated, mono-unsaturated and poly-unsaturated. Fat is made up of a combination of carbon and hydrogen atoms and saturation refers to the number of hydrogen atoms coupled to carbon ones.

Fat needs 5–10% of total daily calories
Fats, in both solid and liquid forms, provide the body with energy but have twice as many calories weight-for-weight as protein and carbohydrates. Some fat is essential to protect the body's vital organs, to assist in regulating body temperature, and for functions of the skin, but high-fat diets have been associated with cancer and heart disease.
Saturated fats are generally solid at room temperature and are found primarily in animal fat, dairy products, and in coconut and palm kernel oils.
Mono-unsaturated fats are usually liquid and are considered "neutral" in their effects on health. They are most commonly found in poultry, fish, margarine, and groundnut and olive oils.
Poly-unsaturated fats are usually liquid and have been found to reduce cholesterol in the blood and may be considered therefore the most "healthful". They are most commonly found in game, fish, and corn and safflower oils.
Cholesterol is a substance resembling fat. High blood cholesterol levels contribute in some way to the development of heart disease; eggs are very rich in cholesterol.

Fats now provide as much as 35% of our total caloric intake per day, but there is absolutely no reason why this proportion should be so high. Indeed, the American Heart Association recommends that less than 10% of our total daily calories should be derived from fat (of any kind).

Carbohydrate needs 65–80% of total daily calories
Carbohydrates are our major source of energy for growth and body maintenance as well as everyday mental and physical

endeavors. They are available as natural sugars and starches present in vegetables, grains, and fruits. Carbohydrates which are not used are converted to fat by the body.

Up until the last five or ten years, carbohydrates were always considered to be the arch villains of our diet; in fact dieters invariably deleted these foods first when weight loss was desired. Refined carbohydrates such as sugars and syrups should still be avoided but foods containing natural carbohydrate, such as fresh fruit and vegetables, or unrefined wholefoods, are extremely good for us since they provide a plentiful supply of energy along with minerals, vitamins and roughage. Foods which contain complex carbohydrates such as green and yellow vegetables, rice, potatoes, peas and beans, cereals and grains, should even be seen as the would-be dieter's greatest friend, because in addition to meeting energy needs they provide more protein with fewer calories, and may slow down the uptake of calories that leads to weight gain.

Certain plant carbohydrates, known as "complex" carbohydrates (cellulose, pectin in fruits, and lignum in woody plants), cannot be digested and leave a rough, fibrous residue as they pass through our digestive system virtually unchanged.

Fiber

For years fiber was thought to have little bearing on nutrition because it was not absorbed by the body, but recent medical research, however, has shown that a diet rich in fiber has much wider health implications than was first thought. At the simplest level, fiber is important because it holds water in the feces and makes the stools soft and bulky. This helps to make bowel action regular, makes the passage of the stool comfortable, and speeds up the movement of food through the intestines.

Fiber, therefore, helps to prevent and treat constipation and although we still do not know the precise mechanism, it is now believed that fiber in the diet reduces the tendency to develop conditions like colitis, appendicitis, diverticulitis and bowel cancer. It has even been suggested that we may be protected from some forms of heart disease, piles and varicose veins, if we increase the amount of fiber in our diet. This can be done very simply by adding two tablespoons of bran to our diet every day.

Vitamins and minerals

A healthy body requires other substances to keep it in good shape: **Vitamins** are manufactured by plants and are present in animals; they regulate metabolism and help convert carbohydrates and fat into energy. Some vitamins (A, D, E and K) – the fat soluble ones – are stored in the body, while water-soluble vitamins (B complex and C) have to be replaced daily. A shortage of vitamins can cause a deficiency illness such as rickets, beri-beri and scurvy, but sufficient vitamins are present in a good balanced diet to meet all normal needs.

Minerals are also essential for certain metabolic processes such as water balance, glandular secretions, nerve and muscle responses. We get our minerals from animals and plants which have extracted them from the earth; they must be replaced regularly. Minerals include sodium, potassium, calcium, iron, manganese, phosphorus, etc. They are present in sufficient quantities in all animal foods and in many plant foods, especially fresh green vegetables and fresh fruit. Women stand a slightly increased chance over men of becoming iron deficient or anemic, because of the regular blood loss of menstruation, and should pay attention to eating some foods high in iron content.

Water

Most of the human body consists of water and it is present, not only in the blood, but in the cells and tissues. It helps to remove waste products from the body in the urine. Water should be drunk daily – at least a pint a day in skimmed milk or natural fruit juices. The four types of drinking water are:

Hard water: contains calcium, magnesium and other salts;
Soft water: contains sodium, often copper, zinc and iron;
Distilled water: no minerals – all removed by a steam process;
Mineral water: natural, untreated water. Can be sparkling or still and contain various combinations of minerals, but usually less sodium than tap water.

DO'S AND DON'TS FOR HEALTHY EATING

Do	Don't
Eat less meat – not more than once a day. Reduce the frequency and serving size of beef, lamb and pork.	Eat sausage, frankfurters, spam, bologna, and other processed meats high in fat.
Select lean cuts of meat and remove all visible fat before eating.	Baste with fat or dripping, or add cream sauces and dressings.
Grill, bake or poach. Cook in non-stick pans and pour off excess fat.	Fry foods, especially mushrooms, onions and bread, which soak up fat.
Eat more poultry and fish.	Eat skin of poultry; it contains the most fat.
Eat low-fat cottage cheese and natural yoghurts and drink skimmed milk.	Eat large amounts of butter, cream, cream cheese, ice cream, whole milk and full fat cheese.
Use recommended oils high in poly-unsaturates (see p. 20).	Eat cakes, pastry and biscuits made with saturated fats.
Eat more vegetables, some every day, and raw, if possible. Include more pulse vegetables – beans, peas and lentils.	Overwash or cook vegetables in too much water, or for too long, or finely chop foods or soak in water.
Eat more fruit, at every meal. Eat wholemeal bread and cereals regularly.	Eat foods made with refined sugars or flours, or heavily sweetened foods.
Eat only 1 main meal a day and try to make the rest vegetarian.	Skip breakfast or eat a heavy meal in the evening.
Eat several small meals rather than 1 large meal.	Snack on salted nuts, potato chips or other cocktail snacks.

Is there anything especially worthy about "health" foods?

Yes there is when they are wholefoods; that is, unrefined and untreated. No there is not when they claim to be "natural" foods. A natural vitamin has nothing over a synthetic vitamin – they actually are the same chemical molecule and would have exactly the same effect in the body, so there is nothing to be gained in seeking out and purchasing natural foods. Indeed, few foods can be said to be natural. Almost all foods are treated in some way by the manufacturer before they reach your pantry. You can only be sure that a food is entirely natural if you grow it, harvest it, cook it and eat it yourself.

On the other hand, the health food craze has encouraged many good eating habits. It has encouraged the substitution of polyunsaturated fats for animal and saturated fats; it is attempting to teach people to increase the amount of fiber in their food with whole grains, cereals, beans and brown rice, and emphasizes the importance of fresh fruit and vegetables. It accents fresh, untreated foods. All of these are beneficial. It's really not important how you arrive at a healthy diet – if it's through health foods, that's a good thing. What is important is making the change.

Should I take vitamins to supplement my meals?

No one in the Western world, eating a Western diet, needs vitamin supplements; there is no need to take vitamins unless a well-balanced diet is unobtainable. However, for certain conditions your doctor may prescribe them. Many of the claims for vitamins are unproven, especially those such as taking vitamin E for youthfulness, and vitamin A (carrots) for good eyesight.

Can eating the right foods make you live longer?

Almost certainly. There is mounting medical evidence that fairly small changes in your diet can reduce the risk of several life-threatening diseases. Obesity itself is associated with diabetes, arthritis, back pain, chest troubles, dietary disorders and bowel complaints. Simply losing weight puts you into a lower risk category for these conditions. A diet containing large amounts of animal and saturated fat will put you in a higher risk category than necessary for heart disease once you have passed through menopause. High-fiber diets may protect you from heart disease, bowel cancer, and cancer of the breast.

Can eating the right diet slow aging?

Despite the extravagant claims made for various dietary regimens, I know of no way in which the basic aging process can be slowed. There is no doubt that certain people who lead a healthy life, eat a good diet, take regular exercise and pay attention to staying fit, are more mobile, more agile, more supple, stronger, more active and generally enjoy life more than those who are not. All this means is that they have kept their heart, lungs, muscles and joints in better condition and therefore capable of working more efficiently than those of their slower and lazier sisters. In no way, however, has their actual aging been slowed down.

Are there times when I should pay more attention to my diet?

Yes, when you are pregnant you should be careful about eating a really well-balanced diet, though there's no need to drink a pint of milk a day – eat yoghurt or cottage cheese or a little more meat. After menopause the bones tend to soften. Then you need calcium and vitamin D (cheese contains both).

Are some foods considered to be harmful to us?

Over the past decade, scientists have come forward with the hypothesis that certain foods may be so unwelcome in our diet that they constitute a risk. The primary, albeit controversial, reason being that they are associated with the development of heart disease. For instance, there is an undeniable relationship between salt intake and blood pressure – high salt intake contributes to the development of high blood pressure. The average American consumes 12 grams of salt a day; other nations get by very well on one gram or less per day and are also healthier. Recent studies in Belgium have shown that reducing the salt intake from 11 to 5 grams a day would drop the blood pressure several points. Under ordinary circumstances there is no real biological need to take in salt. You may as well limit it in your diet.

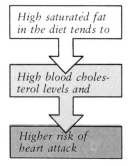

High saturated fat in the diet tends to

High blood cholesterol levels and

Higher risk of heart attack

Medical opinion is still divided about the relationship between cholesterol and saturated fat and the development of heart disease and strokes, but I believe the findings of controlled medical studies very persuasive as to its relationship (see left). There can be no harm in keeping fat intake low.

It's common knowledge that sugar causes tooth decay but much more importantly, it may contribute to the development of heart disease. When your blood-sugar level rises quickly it stimulates the pancreas to pump out insulin, and this in turn increases the liver's production of low density lipo-proteins which are associated with the development of atherosclerosis – in which the arteries are blocked off by fatty deposits in very much the same way as water pipes become clogged.

I've heard that eggs are a major source of cholesterol and a prime factor in heart disease. Is it therefore wise to eat them?

Egg yolk is very rich in cholesterol and most doctors working in the field of preventive cardiology recommend no more than two eggs per week for someone who is eating a "Western" diet rich in animal fat. On the other hand, the same experts would agree that there are many factors affecting heart health, fat being just one of them. If you are not under stress, eat a healthy diet, take regular exercise, are not obese and don't have high blood pressure, and there is no family history of heart disease, a diet containing more eggs a week will probably do you no harm.

Food groups Modern nutritional theory has led to a system of "food groups," which makes choosing a balanced diet easy as long as you remember to eat foods from each group every day. This system, outlined in the chart, opposite, allows you to choose from among various foods in order to receive the same vital nourishment.

FOOD GROUP SYSTEMS

Water and fluids – 3 to 5 glasses per day.

Food	Minimum daily requirements	Nourishment provided	Comments
High protein Meat, fish, poultry, game, offal, eggs, cheese, nuts, legumes	*2 servings* (each item = 1 serving) 3 oz meat, fish or poultry; 2 eggs; 4 oz cooked, dried beans, peas or lentils; 4 tbs peanut butter	Protein; fat; iron; A, D, B vitamins	Meat, fish and poultry have the highest concentration of high quality protein (with the best amino acids); grains and nuts contain incomplete proteins.
Milk and milk products Milk, cream, yoghurt, ice cream, cheese	*2 servings* (each item = 1 serving) 5 fl oz milk or yoghurt; 12 oz cottage cheese; 1 oz hard cheese	Protein; fat; calcium; D, A, B2 vitamins	Cream and cream cheese provide many calories and therefore energy, but they are low in protein. They are very high in animal fat.
Green/yellow vegetables Cabbage, kohlrabi, kale, mustard greens, spinach, brussel sprouts, green beans, celery, lettuce	*4 servings from among the 3 groups* (each item = 1 serving) 4 oz raw or cooked vegetables 6 fl oz juice; 1 orange; $\frac{1}{2}$ grapefruit; $\frac{1}{2}$ melon; 2 oz strawberries	Minerals including calcium, chlorine, chromium, cobalt, copper, manganese, potassium, sodium	All fruit and vegetables provide roughage and water.
Citrus fruits Tomatoes, oranges, grapefruit, strawberries, lemons, melons, papayas	1 large potato; 1 corn on the cob; 1 apple or banana; 4 oz cooked, canned or frozen cauliflower, carrots, peaches or pineapple	Vitamin C	
Other fruits and vegetables Potatoes, beets, corn, carrots, cauliflower, apples, bananas, pineapples, apricots		Carbohydrates; A, B, C vitamins	
Bread, flour and cereals Bread, biscuits, noodles, rice, breakfast cereals, oatmeal	*4 servings* (each item = 1 serving) 1 slice of bread; 2 in biscuit; 1 oz breakfast cereal; 4 oz cooked cereal, rice, noodles or spaghetti	Protein; carbohydrates; B vitamins; iron, calcium	Whole grain cereals and unpolished grains provide fiber. Avoid foods with refined flours or sugar as they provide few nutrients and have many calories.
Fats Butter, margarine, vegetable oils, fish oils, animal fats	1 or 2 tablespoons	Vitamins A, D	There is more vitamin D in margarine than in butter. Both provide many calories, and butter is also high in animal fat. Buy the margarine with polyunsaturated fats.

Calories and energy

Nearly all foods, with the exception of water, provide energy. The energy content of a food is measured in calories, or more accurately, kilo-calories. Fat is the richest source of energy and therefore provides the most calories per ounce – approximately 250. Protein is the second richest and provides approximately 100 calories per ounce. Carbohydrates provide 40 calories per ounce.

The body needs energy to do two things: first, to keep all the basic body functions going, e.g. the heart beating, lungs breathing, the digestive tract digesting (basal metabolism); second, to provide energy which is burnt up when muscles work during active exercise. The amount of energy used up in both of these processes varies from individual to individual – that is why our energy requirements vary. It also explains why some people can eat quantities of food without putting on weight, whereas others have to maintain a strict regime to keep their weight steady.

Below I have set out a sample diet for a woman doing light or moderate work (see opposite). As you can see, it includes a substantial breakfast and lunch, which are necessary to provide adequate energy for work. A heavy meal eaten in the evening results in excess energy being stored as fat.

SAMPLE BALANCED DIET

Total calorific value: 2200

Breakfast	Lunch	Afternoon
6 fl oz orange juice (96)	6 fl oz tomato soup (120)	tea (0)
$\frac{1}{2}$ oz cornflakes (54)	Cheese salad:	2 fl oz milk (36)
4 fl oz milk (72)	2 oz cheddar cheese (190)	$\frac{1}{4}$ oz sugar (28)
2-oz boiled egg (80)	1 oz lettuce (30)	
2-oz slice toast (wholemeal) (136)	2$\frac{1}{2}$-oz tomato (10)	**Total calories: 64**
$\frac{1}{2}$ oz butter (105)	1$\frac{1}{2}$ oz beetroot (18)	
tea or coffee (0)	1 tbs french dressing (60)	**Supper**
2 fl oz milk (36)	2-oz slice bread (136)	
$\frac{1}{4}$ oz sugar (28)	$\frac{1}{2}$ oz butter (105)	$\frac{1}{2}$ melon (58)
	5 fl oz fruit yoghurt (110)	3 oz roast beef (240)
	8 fl oz orange juice (128)	3 oz green beans (6)
Total calories: 607		4 oz roast potatoes (70)
	Total calories: 907	4 oz lemon sherbet (120)
		1 glass red wine (72)
		Total calories: 566
Mid-morning		
coffee or tea (0)		
2 fl oz milk (36)		
$\frac{1}{4}$ oz sugar (28)		
Total calories: 64		

Determining your average daily calorie needs

Your daily calorie needs, that which will maintain you at your "ideal" weight, depend very much on your age, your amount and type of activity and how much energy you expend doing it, and should be reflected in your daily diet. Below, you'll find some ways of determining it.

Height and weight charts

Most published charts have been constructed by insurance companies and have been found to be largely inaccurate. They don't really take into account body build, age, time of weighing, etc. I have set out more realistic low, average, and high weight ranges for the different heights. If you think you have a small frame you should weigh somewhere between the low to average; a medium frame can range either side of average, and heavy frames are definitely on the high side.

WEIGHT IN PROPORTION TO HEIGHT

Height		Low		Medium		High	
ft ins	m	lbs	kg	lbs	kg	lbs	kg
5 0	1.52	100	45.4	109	49.5	118	53.6
5 1	1.55	104	47.2	112	50.9	121	55.0
5 2	1.57	107	48.6	115	52.2	125	56.8
5 3	1.60	110	50.0	118	53.6	128	58.1
5 4	1.62	113	51.3	122	55.4	132	60.0
5 5	1.65	116	52.7	125	56.8	135	61.3
5 6	1.68	120	54.5	129	58.6	139	63.1
5 7	1.70	123	55.9	132	60.0	142	64.5
5 8	1.73	126	57.2	136	61.8	146	66.3
5 9	1.76	130	59.0	140	63.6	151	68.6
5 10	1.78	133	60.4	144	65.4	156	70.9
5 11	1.81	137	62.2	148	67.2	161	73.1
6 0	1.80	141	64.0	152	69.0	166	75.4

Rule of "16"
One easy way of estimating your average daily calorie needs is to multiply your "ideal" weight by 16. If you are 5'6" tall and of medium build your ideal weight is 129 lb (58.5 kg). Times this by 16 and you get 2,064. This is a rough guide only.

Activity and calories

Activity has a lot to do with our daily calorie needs, but "jobs" and recreations can range from sedentary to strenuous. Certain factors also influence energy computation:

Weight – *the heavier you are, the more energy you spend doing each activity*

Temperature – *both extremes of temperature can raise calories expended*

Gradient – *walking uphill, downhill or on sand uses more calories than on level ground*

Temperament – *as a rule, a relaxed person will use fewer calories than a tense person.*

Sedentary activities – 80 to 100 calories per hour
Reading, writing, eating, watching television or movies, listening to the radio, sewing, playing cards, typing, miscellaneous office-work, and other activities done while sitting quietly.

Light activities – 110 to 160 calories per hour
Preparing and cooking food, doing dishes, dusting, handwashing small articles of clothing, ironing, walking slowly, personal care, miscellaneous officework and other activities done while standing that require some arm movement; rapid typing and other activities done while sitting that are more strenuous.

Moderate activities – 170 to 240 calories per hour
Making beds, mopping and scrubbing, sweeping, light polishing and waxing, laundering by machine, light gardening and car-

pentry work, walking moderately fast, other activities done while standing that require moderate arm movement, and activities done while sitting that require more vigorous arm movement.

Vigorous activities – 250 to 350 calories per hour
Heavy scrubbing and waxing, handwashing large articles of clothing, hanging out clothes, stripping beds, other heavy work, walking fast, bowling, golfing, table tennis, volleyball, riding, roller skating, badminton, and fencing.

Strenuous activities – 350+ calories per hour
Swimming, playing tennis, running, bicycling, dancing, skiing, and playing squash.

MODIFIED CALORIE ALLOWANCE CHART

| Desirable weight | | Age | | |
lbs	kg	25	45	65
88	40	1750	1650	1400
99	45	1900	1800	1500
110	50	2050	1950	1600
121	55	2200	2050	1750
128	58	2300	2150	1800
132	60	2350	2200	1850
143	65	2500	2350	2000
154	70	2600	2450	2050
165	75	2750	2600	2150

This chart takes into account a range of "moderate" activities done at an average temperature of 68°F. If your activities call for little physical effort, or are sedentary, reduce the total by 25%; for light activity, reduce by 10%.

Calories and weight gain

Most authorities accept that a healthy adult woman needs between 2,000 and 2,500 calories per day. A person whose weight is steady is using up all the energy she takes in in the form of food. If she is using more energy than her diet provides, then she will lose weight. If she is using up less than her diet provides, then she will gain weight.

For every 3,500 calories we take in in excess of our needs, we will gain one pound in weight. The reverse also applies. For every 3,500 calories we use up in excess of what we take in in the form of food, we will lose one pound in weight. (That sounds easy enough what is difficult is to do it. A woman who normally eats 2,200 calories per day [see diet p. 26] must eat only 1,700 calories per day to lose just one pound per week; to lose two pounds she has to cut her daily intake to 1,200 calories – almost half.)

It is easy to see from the equation (left) that we can lose weight by either eating less or using up more energy. Sadly, the former is by far the more efficient and you should be wary of any slimming regime which claims to help you lose weight without limiting your diet. Exercising is a very inefficient way to lose weight because you would need to be fit and have a lot of time to do sufficient exercise to make a significant dent in your daily calorie intake. To lose only a pound a week (3,500 calories) you would need to exercise strenuously for at least an hour a day. Proper dieting gives you far better results in less time with less inconvenience.

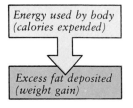

Energy taken in
(calories eaten)

minus

Energy used by body
(calories expended)

Excess fat deposited
(weight gain)

WEIGHT LOSS

First of all, how do you know if you are fat? Most doctors agree that if you are 10% above the ideal weight range for your height (see chart p. 27) then you are overweight. If you are 20% above what you should be, then you can be described as obese. On these criteria, almost half the adult population in America and Britain is overweight, and nearly half of these people are obese. We tend to get fatter as we get older, but at almost any age, more women are overweight than men. With very rare exceptions, you are fat because you are taking in more calories than you burn up – to accumulate excess fat, the energy you take in as food must exceed the energy that your body uses. There is no way round this unpleasant fact, and if you want to lose weight and then maintain it, you must reduce your food intake until it is less than, and then matches, the amount of energy that your body requires.

Factors affecting weight gain

Sexual differences

Women are born to be "fatter" than men. There are, of course, thin women but the average woman is at a disadvantage compared to all men. Women have a higher proportion of fat to muscle tissue than men; at age 20 a woman's body contains 25% fat to a man's 20%, at age 50 hers has 45% while his has 25%.

Men lose weight almost twice as fast as women do because they burn calories at a faster rate. Muscle tissue requires more energy to support it, hence more calories, than does fatty tissue. In addition, the female hormones estrogen and progesterone are natural fat converters; not only do they help to convert food into fat but they are also responsible for fluid retention.

Metabolism

This is individual to you and it determines your food needs. Undoubtedly some people need much less food than others. If you are one of these people, and you eat average or more than average amounts of food, you will almost certainly gain weight. Sadly your metabolism cannot be changed. If it is on the slow side you will have to curb your appetite. If you are one of the lucky ones, who have a rather high metabolic rate, you can probably eat whatever you like without putting on any weight. But take care. Whatever your metabolism is like, you will almost certainly need less food as you grow older and become less active; in fact, about 20% less calories at age 65 than at age 25.

Heredity and environment

Obesity tends to run in families, but it is difficult to know whether this is passed on genetically, or whether it is simply due to acquiring bad eating habits as a child – eating the wrong sorts of food, eating lots of sugary foods and drinks, eating between meals etc. The lifestyle that you grow accustomed to is also important. You tend to accept the lifestyle of your parents, and if this involves regular social eating and drinking and not taking any exercise, then your chances of putting on weight are increased.

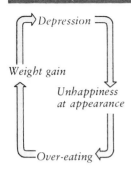

Depression

Weight gain

Unhappiness at appearance

Over-eating

Undoubtedly your psychological state can affect your weight because it may account for over-eating. Depression, anxiety and boredom are all states when you tend to turn to food for consolation, and this sets up a vicious circle.

Some women have problems with separating their own self-image from the image the media would have us accept as perfect, and this divergence may lead to the problem of compulsive eating, consequent weight gain and unsuccessful crash dieting. You will never have a healthy, balanced attitude to food if you're pursuing slimness because you've been brainwashed to believe it's attractive. You must believe it is. Once you do, dieting is easy. Another trap you must avoid is to believe all your problems can be laid at the door of your fatness and that they will disappear if you get slim. This is naive and can only lead to unhappiness and a great sense of resentment.

TYPES OF DIET

Type of diet and how it works	What you have to do	Good points
Calorie counting		
Between 1000–1500 calories/day. Keeps your calorie intake below your energy expenditure, therefore uses your own fat to provide calories of energy.	Add up calorie count of all foods each day and keep below limit by (a) following set menu (b) counting calories yourself. You need scales and a notebook.	It's flexible. You need not exclude any food. You can enjoy treats and eating out. Will fit in with family meals. Not expensive. You learn calorie values. You can keep it up when weight lost.
Low carbohydrate		
Between 1200–1500 calories/day. Reduces your carbohydrate intake, i.e. you are really just reducing the number of calories you eat by counting the carbohydrate units in foods.	Strictly limit foods containing sugar and starch and eat as much as you like of carbohydrate-free foods, e.g. meat, fish. You need a chart of carbohydrate values and you must record number of units eaten.	Simpler and easier than calorie counting. Diet is highly nutritious. Forms foundation of good eating habits. Very good if you want to lose a lot of weight. Whole family can join in.
High protein		
Unlimited calories if high-protein foods. Will only work if proteins provide fewer calories than you burn up. High weight loss claimed but mainly due to water loss not fat loss.	Eat lots of chicken and fish, exclude all carbohydrates, severely limit most other foods and liquids.	Is very satisfying: provides lots of vitamins and minerals. Often results in rapid weight loss.
Low fat		
Between 1000–1500 calories/day. Reduce your fat intake by counting fat units in foods and restricting them; 10 g fat = 1 fat unit.	Strictly limit foods containing fat. Eat as much as you like of fat-free foods, e.g., potatoes, pasta, bread. You need a chart of fat values.	Effective. Not expensive. Can be adapted for weight maintenance.
Crash diets and fasting		
Between 500–800 calories/day. You starve and therefore burn off your own fat to produce the calories you need.	Eat very little, e.g. 3 fruits/day but drink as much as you like of sugarless, milkless drinks & juices. Take multi-vitamin pill.	Effective. Fast, at least in first few days. Hunger often disappears after 2 days. May feel euphoric!

Slimming diets

There are as many diets as there are individual tastes which tends to suggest that none of them *per se* are successful. Any diet is successful only if you adhere to it and you don't slip back into bad habits once the weight is lost. There are many ingredients in the following diets, but by far the most important one is your own will power. Before you start on any diet, do check to make sure that it isn't too expensive, that it will fit in without too much difficulty to your routine, that it is not too rigid and allows you a few treats. All diets, regardless of name, work if they restrict calories.

Other aids to losing weight

Slimming aids

If you achieve the weight loss you desire but feel that your will power is at a low ebb, why not try some slimming aids. You can get appetite suppressants from your doctor as a short-term bridge to help you to grow accustomed to new eating habits.

Bad points

It can be a chore to weigh and record every food. You can miscalculate calories. It may be too flexible for you. You still have to choose a well-balanced diet.

Doesn't cater to all likes and dislikes. Too generous for some dieters. Limits fatty foods even though carbohydrate-free, e.g. cheese. Not good from health point of view if it limits fiber intake. Roughage can help slimmer by bulking the food and satisfying the appetite.

Badly balanced. Expensive. Too rich for some. May be too high in cholesterol for health. Too high in fat for health if fat not removed. Dangerous restriction of fluid.

Sweet foods and drinks must still be limited to lose weight. Alcohol must be limited.

Provides few nutrients. Elimination of protein from diet means body will start breaking down its own protein. Does not adapt to weight maintenance or encourage good habits.

Twenty-eight-year old Lesley Monk originally weighed 231 pounds, and her measurements were 45-34-48. With carefully-controlled dieting, however, she successfully slimmed down to an attractive 133 pounds, and her measurements are now 34-26-36.

Fiber bulking agents

You can try bulking agents, like methyl cellulose, which start to absorb water once they are swallowed. They swell up and fill the stomach, and manufacturers claim that this brings on a feeling of repletion which will reduce the amount of food you take at any meal. This claim, however, has not been substantiated as yet to any degree in scientific tests.

Exercise

This is an inefficient way to lose weight. Spot exercises can at best help you firm up muscles which underly your bulges, giving you a smoother outline. Isometric exercises, yoga and keep-fit exercises do little to help you lose weight, but you will no doubt feel a good deal less jaded after you have done them. Don't be fooled into thinking that machines which passively stimulate the muscles with electrical current will help you lose weight. They will not. Neither will massage: the masseuse may lose weight, but you will not.

No matter how keen you are to lose weight and get fit, you must realise that artificial aids like the belts shown on the right will not help you. To be successful you should work out a combined exercise and diet program which you know you can stick to.

Health spas

A short stay at a health spa will probably help you to lose a few pounds, particularly if you ask for a low calorie diet. It will also add reinforcement to your good intentions and will make you feel better rested and happier, but it can be quite expensive.

Support groups

If you need the support of others, why not join a diet group such as Weight Watchers. You will get lots of useful information on dieting, as well as continuing encouragement. Special diet sheets, weigh-ins, competitions for weight loss, and the opportunity for dieters to share their experiences are all covered.

Dieter's foods

If you are going to have to take care with weight maintenance for the rest of your life, you really should try to manage without recourse to special foods and regimens. However, if you must have these things, you can buy special dieter's foods, including low calorie soft drinks, low fat spreads and mayonnaise, low calorie jams, soups and crackers and artificial sweeteners.

Alternative therapies

If you really have an unconquerable weight problem, you might consult your doctor about trying hypnosis, acupuncture and psychotherapy, all of which claim successes. Remember there is absolutely no harm in being eclectic. Take advantage of all the sources of help that are available and choose those which suit you.

Are thinner people healthier?

As a general rule, the answer must be "yes" for the reasons already given. This does not mean that thin people do not have heart attacks, chest troubles and digestive disorders. Other things being equal, if you are thinner, you run less risk of getting them.

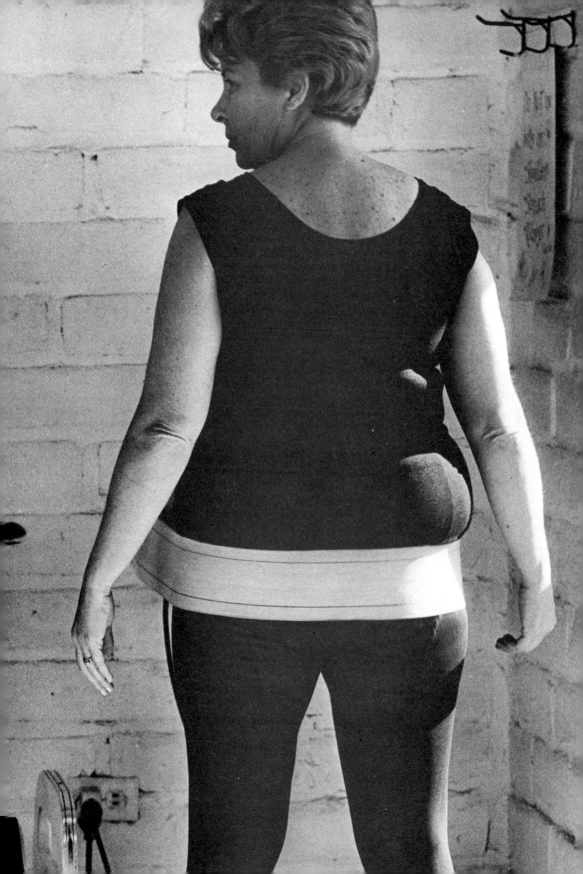

Can you ever really be too thin?

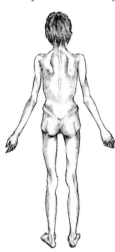

Yes you can, particularly if weight loss is due to self-imposed starvation, when it may be part and parcel of *anorexia nervosa*. This name implies that the appetite is lost due to a psychological disturbance. It is true that most anorexics are profoundly disturbed psychologically, due, in most cases, to a stress within the family environment, but quite often it is related to unhappy sexual experience during adolescence. Teenagers are the commonest sufferers and may allow their weight to fall as low as 66 pounds. When their weight drops below 100 pounds they usually stop menstruating and their skin may become covered in downy hair.

Bulimia nervosa is another eating disorder most commonly seen in twenty- to thirty-year-old women. Sufferers describe a repulsion from food but nonetheless eat. However, they are so guilty after taking food that they very often resort to vomiting or purgatives to get rid of it from their bodies. A quite frequent pattern of eating is a burst of compulsive eating followed by self-induced vomiting and then a period of starvation.

Anorexics attempt to retreat from adulthood and mature sexuality by returning their bodies to a pre-pubescent state.

"Mis-use" of food is only a symptom of such conditions; it is not the cause of the diseases. Treatment should therefore be aimed at finding out the psychological stress that is precipitating the attraction or revulsion. Psychiatric therapy should be sought and medical help, if necessary. The seriousness of these conditions should not be underestimated; if left untreated they can result in life-threatening disease.

What's the best way to lose weight?

The best way for *you* to lose weight is the way that suits you. No-one can lose weight and then maintain an ideal weight without finding a new eating pattern which they can live with easily most of the time. If you have incorrect eating habits you are going to have to correct them no matter how hard it is. There is no way other than using your will power to change your eating habits and keep them changed. It's hard enough to stick to any diet without choosing one which presents you with problems. If your passion is chocolate, don't choose a diet which completely excludes chocolate. If you like to eat little and often, don't opt for a diet that suggests going for long periods without food. If you favor vegetables, avoid the high-protein diet that includes lots of animal protein. If your predilection is to nibble, find a nibbler's diet. However, a diet will only work if it cuts down your calories.

Once I have lost weight, how do I stop putting it back on?

If you talk to any woman who has been fat but has lost weight and has managed to maintain her ideal weight, she will tell you that what made her avoid putting the weight back on was that she really wanted to stay slim. In other words, *thinking* slim really helps you to get and stay slim. Nearly all women describe how they went through a psychological barrier. On one side being fat was acceptable, and on the other side it was not. Usually they have had some sort of stimulus that helps them to crash the barrier – it may be a love affair, it may be the end of an affair. It may be a health risk, it may be as basic as self-disgust. Whatever it is, most women will state that they experienced a definite and palpable change in their state of mind. I believe you have to think yourself into this state before you can get slim and stay slim. See also, *Other aids to losing weight p. 31.*

What can I do to gain weight?

You are only underweight if you weigh less than 10% below your ideal weight for height. Even if you are, you may be quite fit and healthy, in which case don't worry about trying to gain weight. If you are substantially underweight there are two main reasons which commonly account for this. You may have a very high metabolic rate so that all the energy you take in as food is burned off rapidly, or you may not be eating as much as you think.

It's not easy to gain weight if you are naturally thin. Experiments with healthy youngsters have shown that they can eat two or three times their normal energy requirements and still do not gain weight. This is probably because they have the ability to burn off large amounts of energy even when it is greatly in excess of their needs.

The best thing to do is to recognize the fact that your body has its own system of weight control and it is very difficult for you to interfere with this from the outside. In addition, there is no reason for you to conform to statistics. Even though you are underweight you are probably at the perfect weight for your body, so you should accept that.

FITNESS

Being fit, to me, means being healthy in all aspects. It follows that the first prerequisite of being fit and healthy is to eat a healthy diet (see p. 20). The second is to marry your diet to as comprehensive an exercise program as your lifestyle will accommodate. You are fit if the following criteria can be applied to yourself:
- Your weight is within the ideal weight range for your height (see p. 27).
- You have a healthy heart and healthy lungs.
- Your muscles are strong and can see you through a period of sudden and sustained effort.
- Your body is supple and your joints are flexible.

The benefits of exercise

Exercise makes you feel good both physically and mentally. While exercise may be an inefficient way to lose weight over a short period, it's an excellent way of keeping your weight down over a long period. Walking an extra mile, only once a week, is five pounds less weight at the end of a year, so viewed in the long term, exercise is an excellent adjunct to diet for maintaining your ideal weight. Exercise, particularly strenuous exercise, can help the dieter because it suppresses the appetite. So it could be a good idea to do your exercises before the main meal of the day. Strenuous exercise lowers the plasma cholesterol and therefore protects the heart from developing atherosclerosis. Furthermore, exercise leads to a drop in blood pressure which is also good for your heart.

Research has shown that by taking up exercise you are moving yourself into a group of people who are likely to get a lot more out of life than the people who are not exercising. Results indicate that people who are physically active have a tendency to adopt other lifestyle habits that make them healthy and fit. They are likely to eat less, cope more effectively with stress, and may even give up smoking. The psychological rewards of exercise are legion. Most people who exercise strenuously will describe a period of palpable exhilaration when the exercises are over. This is partly self-satisfaction and partly a sensation of just feeling better. This feeling soon becomes addictive and you will find that you feel below par when you don't exercise. In addition, exercise *per se*, brings a feeling of calmness and relaxation. You can take advantage of this, if time allows, by retiring afterwards to a quiet room where you can practice relaxation, become aware of the sensations in your skin and muscles, appreciate the warmth and tingling, and savor the feeling of contentment. It is one of the most pleasant aspects of exercise.

Most people believe that they should exercise more but find it difficult to change sedentary habits. Good resolutions are repeatedly made and broken. Procrastination is common to us all because we are too busy and can't fit in a regular exercise routine. Other things take a higher priority and often we are just too lazy. But once you have begun to exercise and feel for yourself the very real physical and psychological benefits you will find that you jealously guard your freedom to exercise, so it's worth making a special effort to fit it into your life. If you need some convincing, try using some visual cues and imagery.

Practice these thoughts and images several times a day and use exercise cues as reminders. Take out a two week self-contract action plan to increase your weekend walking or any other form of exercise program.

POSITIVE IMAGERY DRILL

- You are looking at yourself in the mirror and see a vital, slim, healthy person.
- Fatty deposits are melting away from your arteries.
- Fat tissue is melting away from your paunchy, overweight abdomen.
- You are walking up a hill with cool fresh air going into your lungs; you feel fit and energetic.
- Your body feels warm and relaxed – you are experiencing the pleasant after-glow of exercise.

EXERCISE CONTRACT

- Look for opportunities for outdoor walking at the weekend. For example, take a 10 minute walk before dinner on both days.
- Look for opportunities for indoor or outdoor work during the weekend. For example, mow the lawn or do some vigorous household activity.
- Place exercise cues on various places in the home and at the office. For example, use the telephone, the refrigerator, television set, car steering wheel, desk, to remind you to exercise and to practice positive imagery.
- Practice positive imagery drill at least five times a day.

One of the good things about such a contract is that you can enlist the support of a helper, so your responsibilities are shared. Your helper should be able to: walk with you before dinner on Saturday and Sunday; exercise with you twice a week; encourage you at all times in your efforts; help you to review the results of your plan in two weeks' time.

Why the body needs to be exercised

Fitness is not only about feeling good but is necessary to keep the body in proper working order. Exercise helps the body in 3 ways:
● To maintain its mobility – the large muscles and joints must be moved through their complete range of movement so that you are able to twist, turn, move and stretch in any direction.
● To make the body strong with a built-in safety margin of extra strength, over and above our normal requirements, so that muscles and joints are not damaged when we have to make an extra effort.
● To "condition" our heart and lungs so that they can accommodate the body's need for extra oxygen when we undertake strenuous activities for 15–20 minutes at a stretch.

Testing for fitness

Before you can start on any exercise programme you must know how fit you are or rather *unfit* you are. You can do this very simply by finding out how your heart reacts to strenuous exercise. Your heart will respond to the body's increased need for oxygen by beating faster, and you can measure the rate by taking your pulse. The fitter you are, the less your heart rate increases because a fit heart pumps out more blood without being under stress. The chart below sets out optimum pulse rates at varying ages.

Fitness test
Run on the spot for 30 seconds, then take your pulse (count beats for 15 seconds then multiply by 4). This is your personal pulse rate after mild exertion.

When you exercise, your pulse should not go higher than the rate you have just calculated and the aim of the heart and lung exercises is to keep up this pulse rate for about 15 to 20 minutes of continuous exercising. The sort of pulse rate you should be aiming for is shown left.

Age	Pulse rate
15–19	146
20–24	142
25–29	138
30–34	134
35–39	130
40–44	126
45–49	122
50–54	117
55–59	113
60–64	109

When you first begin to exercise you should monitor your pulse rate every minute or so. If, when you take your pulse, the rate is higher than your personal rating then you should rest until your pulse rate comes down. Repeat this if you find that exercise increases your pulse beyond your personal rating. If you are very unfit you will probably find that you have to stop exercising quite often for rest periods. As the days go by you will find that you can exercise for longer periods without resting and that eventually you will be able to exercise continuously for 15 minutes without your pulse going above your personal rating.

Mobility exercises

These are aimed at loosening up all parts of the body. There is a great variety of mobility exercises and so-called exercise specialists who advocate their own brand of exercises. There is nothing especially worthy about any of them. Any will do as long as it puts your muscles and joints through a full range of movement. Any mobility program should include exercises for specific joints and muscle groups, i.e. shoulders, elbows, waist, hips, knees, ankles, spine and trunk.

Any variation on these exercises will do of course, and it's not necessary to find a special place or time in your house to do them. You can perform these exercises while you are going about the house or the office at any time of the day or night.

Spine stretch (10 times)
Stand with feet slightly apart; stretch up. Bend your knees, swinging your arms down and back. Stretch up again.

Side bends (10 times)
Stand with your feet apart and your hands on your hips. Slowly bend to one side, sliding hand down leg. Repeat on other side.

Arm circling (10 times)
Stand up straight, with your feet slightly apart. Raise your arms to shoulder height and circle them in each direction.

Toe-touching (10 times)
Stand with your feet apart and your hands at your sides. Bend down to touch your toes, keeping your legs as straight as possible.

Trunk rotation (10 times)
Stand up straight with your feet apart and your arms out at shoulder height. Swing arms round from side to side.

Ankle-touching (15 times)
Stand with your feet apart, arms out at shoulder height. Bend to touch your left ankle with your right hand, keeping your knees straight. Repeat on other side and continue whole movement, rhythmically.

Strengthening exercises

You should always begin this type of exercise by performing the easy version. Push-ups, which strengthen the arms and shoulders, can just be done with you standing up against a wall. You can then graduate to doing them against a table top, then on a chair seat, and finally, when your muscles are strong enough, you can do them on the floor. Similarly, you would start on straight leg raising, for the thighs and abdominal muscles, seated on a chair, then progress to sit-ups lying on the floor, and finally do V-sits with your heels on a chair. To exercise the leg muscles with knee bends, you would graduate from doing squats holding on to the back of a chair, to squats without a chair, then to jumps from the squatting position and finally star jumps.

Heart and lung exercises

The only way to exercise the heart and lungs efficiently is to increase the body's need for oxygen: the heart is called upon to pump more blood round the body faster and the demand on the lungs is to aerate the blood more efficiently by increasing the number of breaths taken per minute. To increase the workload of the heart and lungs to this point, it's necessary to strenuously exercise large muscle groups, particularly the legs, for several minutes. The only way to achieve this is to jog, run, cycle, swim or play a strenuous sport such as tennis, squash or football. Jogging and running may not be your predilection, and there may not be a heated swimming pool available, but there is no reason why you should not be able to accommodate this form of exercise in your own home several times a week if the only way you can do it is to run on the spot. This is good enough and you can make it more pleasant by watching television or by listening to your favorite music. If you have the money and your intention is firm, you might opt for a rowing machine or an exercise bicycle.

Whatever you do, choose a form of exercise which you enjoy and which doesn't disturb the domestic routine too much. Make it easy for yourself and for the others around you. If you can, get them to join you. When you are exercising, monitor your pulse rate as described, and if, after several weeks, you find that you can exercise continuously, try raising your pulse rate in steps of about five beats by gradually increasing the length or strength of your chosen exercises.

Guidelines on exercise

● Never start on any exercise program without finding out how fit you are (see p. 37 for your fitness test). If you are in doubt about your fitness, check with your doctor.
● Choose activities and exercises that you enjoy or you will never stick to your exercise program.
● Exercises should not be a chore; if they are, you are doing the wrong ones. Nor should they be physically punishing; if they are you are pushing yourself too hard.
● The best form of exercise is one which fits into your daily life: for example, taking the dog for a walk, cycling to work or to the stores, climbing stairs rather than taking the elevator, doing odd exercise while you are at the sink, bending down to cupboards, or just as you walk about.

• There is no need to spend a lot of money on expensive equipment. It's possible to do all your exercises effectively without buying a thing.
• Don't exercise on a full stomach. Try to spend a few minutes loosening up before beginning your strenuous exercises.
• Don't be over-zealous about increasing the length of your exercises too fast; always check on your pulse rate so that you reach the level of fitness suitable for your age slowly.
• Once you have reached your level of fitness, try to exercise regularly (3 to 4 times a week) to maintain it.

Alternatives to standard exercises

Dancing
Any form of dancing is excellent exercise. Disco dancing uses up about 600 calories an hour and if you get a bit breathless, all to the good. If you go disco dancing twice a week and you get breathless while you are doing it, you are probably quite fit.

Skating
Skating uses up 400 calories an hour and is also very good for your co-ordination. It encourages good posture, rhythmic movement and self-expression.

Isometrics
You do these exercises *without moving*. The muscles work against each other, or against immovable objects like a wall. Basically, isometric exercises are strengthening exercises and do nothing to improve mobility or to exercise the heart and lungs, but you can do them anywhere and they require no special equipment.

T'Ai-Chi-Chuan
This is an ancient Chinese ritual which combines meditation with slow graceful movement and claims to benefit the body and the mind in that it improves coordination, balance, concentration, self-awareness, inner peace and relaxation. According to devotees, it will promote better breathing and circulation of the blood, but you need a trained instructor to learn it.

Yoga
Yoga is a means of controlling the body and the mind. It necessitates daily practice of a series of postures, *not* exercises. The aim is to maintain each position for as long as possible. You can take up yoga at any age, regardless of your fitness, with a fairly certain knowledge that regular practice will give you a supple body and a more relaxed state of mind. It may even help you to deal with a smoking or drinking problem. If possible, you should start off yoga by attending a course of classes.

What is the best way to remain fit ?

Once you have become fit, staying fit is very easy and requires comparatively little time and effort (no more than 20 minutes, three or four times a week). The basic minimum for each of your exercise sessions would be:

- 5 minutes of mobility exercises or 2 minutes of mobility exercises and 3 minutes of strengthening exercises and
- 15 minutes of strenuous exercise which involves the legs, makes you pant and raises your pulse rate to your personal pulse rating. There is no one who can't fit this amount of exercise into her life. One exercise regime that would fit this bill is:
- Arm circling each arm, ten times;
- Side bends to each side, ten times;
- Trunk, knee and hip bend on each side, ten times;
- Head, arm and trunk rotating to each side, ten times;
- Alternate ankle reaching to each side, ten times;
- Running in place, jogging, exercising on a bicycle (indoors or out), walking briskly, swimming, playing a game of tennis or squash for 15 minutes.

Can exercise ever be harmful for me?

Only if you are unfit and exercise might strain your heart (see test p. 37); if you have a heart or chest condition which needs your doctor's attention; if you have a bone or joint disease – always check with your doctor if you are in any doubt as to your condition. Exercise is not harmful for healthy people, whatever their age, as long as they go slowly.

Are certain sports better than others for making you fit?

Yes, the so-called whole-body sports. Those that exercise all the muscles in the body – e.g. running, swimming, playing tennis, football, squash, etc. This is because they exercise the heart and lungs as well as the muscles and joints.

Can exercise cure certain complaints?

It would be very difficult to prove that exercise could "cure" defects and illnesses. However, it can undoubtedly help strengthen muscles and joints, which may ameliorate certain conditions, particularly if they are related to muscle tension. For instance, back strengthening exercises will help to tone up the muscles of the back, thereby keeping the spine in good alignment and protecting the spinal nerves which give rise to pain if damaged. They are also good for relaxing tense muscles, for instance, the muscles of the neck and shoulders (see head rolling, p. 43). In that exercise is relaxing, it can help you to cope with anxiety and stress.

What can I do to improve certain parts of my body?

It will take a great deal of spot exercising to remove fat from a localized part of the body such as the upper arms and thighs and you will probably give up before you can see any difference, so slowly is the fat lost. It is far more efficient to lose fat from certain parts of the body by an overall reduction of your weight. Diet is therefore quicker than exercise. However, exercises which tone up the muscles of, say, the abdomen and the buttocks will make those parts of the body firmer, and in doing so may improve the outline. You can capitalize on well toned muscles by keeping them contracted and held in whenever you remember during the day.

THE LAZY WAY TO EXERCISE

If the idea of doing strenuous exercise really doesn't suit you, try the ones below rather than give up altogether. Although they will not improve your heart/lung strength, they will improve your suppleness if done at least once a day. They can be done in various situations: some will gently stretch your muscles as you lie in bed, others while you are watching television, talking on the phone, or standing by a sink or kitchen table.

Keeping your feet flat, bend your knees and pull your feet as near to your buttocks as possible; breathe deeply. (10 times)

Starting from the position, left, clasp one knee to your chest, then lower it slowly until flat on the bed. (10 times each side)

If you have a headboard, stretch back and clasp it tightly. Hold this position for a few seconds. (10 times)

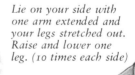

Lie on your side with one arm extended and your legs stretched out. Raise and lower one leg. (10 times each side)

Lie on your back with arms outstretched and knees bent. Roll your hips till knees touch floor. (5 times)

Stand with feet apart. Stretch out one arm and swivel around to stretch your waist. (5 times each side)

Steady yourself with one hand, then raise one leg to a right angle. Swing it back through 180°. (10 times each side)

Steady yourself, then stand on your toes, keeping a straight back. Squat down and hold for 5, then rise slowly. (5 times)

RELAXATION

The ability to relax is essential in today's world and will help you to be fit not only physically but, just as important, psychologically. Relaxation not only dispels fatigue and muscle aches, and makes certain discomforts (menstrual cramps, for instance) easier to bear, but it can also counteract the effects of stress and anxiety (see p. 299), and can improve your sleeping habits.

Relaxed women are better able to deal with problems and conflicts at home and at work, and find personal relationships easier to manage. Once relaxed, irritability and aggressiveness will dissipate and you will find you have energy to spare. Bear in mind, too, that if you are relaxed, energized and positive, these feelings will extend to people around you, so that you not only produce a better internal environment for yourself, but a better external one as well.

Relaxation can be achieved through a variety of techniques. In addition to exercises, which will relieve tension in the muscles, there are several forms of total body relaxation plus the more mechanical biofeedback.

Deep breathing

Proper breathing is an essential first step to being relaxed: most people breathe incorrectly – high up in the chest rather than from the abdomen. For your breathing to be more efficient, your abdomen should expand before your chest. Test your proficiency by standing naked in front of a mirror and monitoring your breathing, or by lying flat on the floor with your knees raised, one hand on the upper chest, the other on the top of the abdomen. If you are breathing properly, you should feel the abdomen rise at the start of the breath. Practice breathing until there is very little movement in the upper chest and plenty in the abdomen. Pay particular attention to exhaling; breathe out slowly with a slight sigh. Pause before inhaling and let the breath come in naturally.

EXERCISES FOR MUSCLE TENSION AND ACHES

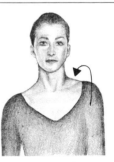

Back muscles (5 times)
Stretch arms above you. Slowly bend forwards and let your arms, neck and head flop down so that your fingers droop onto the floor; relax. Straighten up and repeat.

Neck muscles (5 times)
Bend your head forwards so that your chin rests on your chest. Slowly roll your head round and back, first clockwise, then counterclockwise.

Shoulder muscles (5 times)
Tense and relax your shoulder muscles by shrugging your shoulder, rotating it in a circle, backwards and forwards.

Centering An easy way to produce inner calmness when you are feeling tense and nervous is to concentrate on a point a few inches below your navel, your *center*. Even if you pause only for a few seconds to direct your thoughts, feelings and impulses to this spot, you will find that you will quickly recover your equilibrium and control.

Simple relaxation One of the easiest and simplest ways to relax is to lie down on the most comfortable sofa or bed that you have with a soft cushion and a warm cover. Now put on your favourite music, then lower the lighting. Close your eyes and say over and over again "relax, relax, relax." Then concentrate on each part of your body, starting with the toes, then the feet, then the ankles, then the knees, and ascend up the body until you deal with your face and forehead last. Try to make each part feel relaxed, loose and weightless. While you are doing this, slow down your breathing to about half speed and take deep breaths in and out. After ten minutes of complete relaxation you will find yourself calmed and refreshed.

Meditation Complete relaxation is only possible when we are free of the control of our thoughts, and yet it is impossible to stamp out all thought and any attempt to do so involves mental strain and effort. However, it is possible to permit thoughts to come and go and rouse only minimal response. Once you learn to free yourself from acting on or thinking about every thought or feeling that enters your head, you will feel more relaxed, alert and energetic and you will be able to create a personal space in your life freer from worrisome or negative thoughts and feelings.

Find a place where you can be undisturbed for at least 10 minutes twice a day. Make yourself comfortable in a chair or supported on the floor. Close your eyes and breathe deeply several times. Now focus your mind on a single activity: either the repetition of a word or phrase; concentration on a single image (such as a beautiful flower); or counting your breaths. You will notice that thoughts will enter your mind and interrupt your activity. When they do, do not pursue them, but gently focus again on your activity. Let the thoughts arise and pass through your mind without your being tempted to reflect on them.

The effects of meditation build up in time, and to be most effective it should be done regularly. If you need any positive reinforcement, remember, by being relaxed and in more control of your thoughts, you are improving the quality of your life.

Biofeedback If you are determined, you may be able to teach yourself to induce relaxation using biofeedback methods. For instance, you could train yourself to reduce your heart rate or your blood pressure by wearing a small electrical device wrapped round one of your fingers which registers your blood pressure or your heart rate on a small dial which you can carry around with you. By concentrating hard, you can bring down the blood pressure or pulse rate reading. Once you have learned to do this, by visualizing the read-out, you can jettison the biofeedback machine and impose your mind over matter any time you want to.

POSTURE

The benefits of good posture are immediate. Not only will you feel better, you will look measurably better. From the moment that you hold yourself correctly, you will look slimmer and more shapely than you did before. To prove it, do this very simple test. Take a tape measure, and without changing your posture from your usual one, measure your waist. Now hold your body erect, lift your rib cage up and pull your stomach in. Measure again. It will be at least two inches less than the first measurement.

Dramatic though this improvement is, there are more important ones, as far as your health is concerned, from having good posture: your muscles and joints are under less strain and can work more efficiently when your posture is good. Bad posture can also affect the workings of your internal organs. If you stoop and are round shouldered, your lungs can no longer work as a pair of efficient bellows. Indeed, as little as one third of their capacity is being used. Furthermore, if you are a smoker, you reduce the efficiency of your lungs and worse, if you get a cough or a cold, you increase the chances of it developing into bronchitis and possibly even pneumonia because the secretions tend to pool, stagnate and get infected.

If you slump you are not giving your digestive tract a fair chance. The stomach cannot grind up the food efficiently, pockets of gas may be trapped leading to muscle spasm and colic, and the movements of the intestine may not be as free as they should be.

Good posture is restful for the spine. When you are holding yourself properly the muscles of the back support the rather unstable spinal column, protect the bones from awkward movement and prevent the nerves from being compressed.

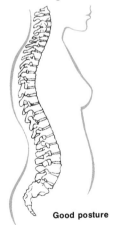 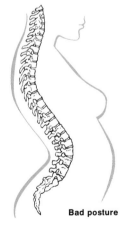

Good posture **Bad posture**

The most stable position for the spine (a pile of 24 tiny bricks stacked one on top of the other), when muscles and ligaments are not subjected to strain, is when the cervical and dorsal curvatures are maintained. (See diagram.)

Hold your shoulders straight and down (not back – women don't have strong enough muscles in the shoulders to stand at attention for any length of time without getting muscle aches). Hold your chin slightly up at a right angle to your neck and try to bring your ears over your shoulder.

Any posture which flattens out these curves, or reverses them, puts muscles, joints and ligaments under tension, and aches and pains are the inevitable result. Posture in the sitting and lying positions is therefore just as important as when standing, and considering that most of us spend a quarter to a third of the day lying in bed, a good supporting mattress is a wise investment.

HOW GOOD POSTURE PREVENTS BACK STRAIN

Good posture when you are lifting or carrying heavy weights or pushing and pulling heavy furniture is important, not only from the point of view of mechanical efficiency, i.e. it will take less effort if you put the leverage in the right place, but also from the point of view of protecting your bones, muscles and joints from strain, sprain and even tear. Here are some tips on how good posture can help you do heavy moving jobs safely.

Lifting a heavy object
To lift a heavy object (groceries or even a child), bend your knees and let the resilient muscles of the legs take the strain, not your back; hold the weight close to your body. Never bend down from the waist.

Moving a heavy object
Lean your back against the object and push it with your back and legs.

Bending down
Prevent strain by kneeling instead of stooping.

When should I pay attention to posture?

The hard answer is all the time if you are concerned about your health and fitness, your appearance and a long term insurance policy against muscle aches and pains.

But there are times when you should be most particular about your posture. Pregnancy is one. Your enlarging abdomen pulls your center of gravity in front of your pelvis. To counteract this, you tend to throw your shoulders back and this puts tremendous strain on the lower parts of the spine and the joints of the pelvis, which are slackening anyway in preparation for labor. You can do yourself a favor by not wearing high heeled shoes, which throw the body forward and therefore give the spinal muscles twice the amount of work to do, by resting on a supporting mattress whenever you can, particularly in the last trimester of pregnancy, and by making certain that all the seats you sit on regularly, particularly in your car, have good lumbar support to maintain the concave lumbar curvature of your spine. In the latter part of pregnancy, try to avoid long periods of standing, working in a stooped position, and carrying heavy bags. Don't be ashamed to ask for help if you need it.

Immediately after pregnancy it is also important to take pains over your posture, particularly if you want to regain your figure sooner. Your abdomen will flatten all the more quickly if you hold your rib cage upwards and inwards, and you will regain vaginal tone quickly if you practice your pelvic exercises (the contraction of pelvic muscles which is sufficient to arrest the flow of urine when you are emptying your bladder).

If you have had a back injury or a back complaint in the past, posture is doubly important to you because it will help to strengthen the muscles of the back which are prone to strain, and easily become sore and painful. The better your posture is, the stronger the muscles of your back will become.

CLOTHES

The choice of clothing is a very individual matter and it is not in the province of this book to tell you how to dress. However, there are a few things that I feel strongly about which can, and should, influence your choice of clothing. Certain medical complaints can be traced directly to both the fabric and specific items of contemporary clothing.

Clothes that are too hot can produce heat rashes, and chafing and bruising result not only from tight and elasticized clothing, but from pressure on delicate skin surfaces and in sensitive areas such as the genitals, underarms and breasts.

By the way, if you find any large patches of redness or sensitivity on your skin, this could be due to a reaction against the detergent you are using to wash your clothes. Try changing to "purer" soaps the next time you do the laundry.

Fabrics Starting in the 1940s and 1950s, there was a great movement towards synthetic fibers like nylon, orlon, helenca, polyester, etc. Synthetic fibers, however, are neither as flattering nor as healthy to wear as natural fabrics. On the whole, they do not absorb sweat efficiently, and this can lead to discomfort, sogginess of the skin and occasionally rashes. Vaginal infections are often caused by wearing nylon underpants that don't breathe.

When fibers are knitted, as in tights, they lose their elasticity, so when you first put on a pair of tights you will find that they accommodate you quite comfortably by stretching. If you then put on a tight pair of boots, your stockings will be pulled very tightly over the foot and by the time your toes have been squeezed for the best part of the day in this vise-like grip, they will be painful and tender. Indeed, tights are often as responsible as shoes for causing sore, aching feet, and they exacerbate vaginal problems such as infections and discharge.

Synthetic fibers can give rise to allergies of the skin because of the chemicals with which they are treated during manufacture and finishing. Some of the chemicals, like oxidants, are known by dermatologists to be potent sensitizers and in susceptible people give rise to allergic rashes.

*The case
for bras*

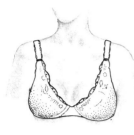

The fashion of the 1970s to go bra-less has done many breasts a good deal of harm. The only breasts that will not lose their shape without support are breasts which are small and lightweight. Medium-sized breasts weighing more than about half a pound put quite a strain on the suspensory ligaments of the breast when they have no independent support.

The suspensory ligaments are the only natural support which breasts have. Breasts can be thought of as entirely separate organs which are stuck on to the muscular chest wall. As the skin in which they are encased is infinitely elastic, it cannot be relied upon to support the breasts and help them keep their shape. Good firm chest musculature will only hold breasts high when the breasts themselves are young, small, firm and light. Once the breasts have started to slide down the chest wall, doing exercises for your pectoral muscles will do nothing at all to lift them back up again.

The suspensory ligaments are fine bands of inelastic tissue which run from the chest wall and through the breast tissue itself. If the ligaments were elastic we would have nothing to worry about because the breasts would bounce back after they had sagged. Sadly, ligaments don't behave like this. If they are stretched by heavy breasts, they stay stretched and they don't regain their shape. If you have breasts weighing over a pound or so, you will stretch the suspensory ligaments in a very short time, especially if you undertake regular exercise or play sports frequently. If the underside of your breasts dips down to touch the skin of your chest wall at all, then my advice would be to wear a bra, almost all the time, going without one only occasionally in the evening. And, moreover, it is absolutely essential that you wear a bra during pregnancy. Furthermore, once you have started to lactate you should graduate to a special nursing bra through which you can feed your baby without taking the bra off.

*The case
against girdles*

The best support for your abdomen and buttocks is firm, toned-up muscles. You can only achieve this if you exercise your muscles regularly and if you take pains to hold in your abdomen and keep it flat. I am against wearing girdles because I think psychologically and physically you tend to relax against them. You become lazy and forget to hold yourself properly and to keep your abdomen taut and firm. In plumper women they also produce unsightly bulges at their upper and lower edges and if they are very tight they may cause weals in the skin. Some of the fabrics used in girdles do not allow sweat to evaporate naturally.

*The choice
of shoes*

Good shoes are a good investment. If you like to wear high heels to improve the length of your ankle, then it is essential that you buy well-made shoes that have been fashioned on a well-balanced last. If not, you will find that your toes (mainly the big toe) take the whole weight of your body with each step (the equivalent of several tons) and a badly balanced heel will tip your body forward over your shoe. This makes good posture impossible and you will constantly have to correct your body position by over-using the muscles of the shoulders, back, waist, hips and thighs to bring

your center of gravity back into line. A badly-balanced shoe can therefore do you harm on two counts. First, the joint of the big toe may become so bruised and traumatized that it will swell to protect itself, and, if you go on wearing the shoes, will eventually lead to the development of a bunion. Second, you are a candidate for chronic backache if your back has to overwork every day to correct your posture.

When buying shoes, walk about the shop several times to see that your ankles, knees and hips do not have to take up an awkward position to maintain your balance. If the shoe pinches at all in the shop, do not buy it. It will pinch all the more once you get outside and have to wear it for any length of time. There is no ban on high-heeled shoes, but the higher the heel, the better balanced the last must be (and this usually means the more expensive the shoe is). A second equation is the higher the heel, the shorter the time you should wear the shoe.

Whenever you can, go barefoot or wear wooden exercise sandals. Broad, flat shoes like sneakers rest the feet. Synthetic materials for the uppers are not a good idea because they don't allow sweat to evaporate.

Do I need to wear special clothes during pregnancy ?

Until your stomach really begins to swell, about half way through the fourth or the fifth month, there is no need for you to buy special pregnancy clothes.

Psychologically you will probably feel better if you look close to your normal self during pregnancy. The familiarity of your own clothes will help you to feel less ungainly and large, and certainly more comfortable. Pregnancy is a bad time to start to wear any new style and whatever your taste, high-heeled shoes are really not a good idea, both from the point of view of balance, and therefore the safety of you and your baby, and the point of view of the extra work you are asking the muscles and joints of your spine and pelvis to do, which may result in aching legs and back.

SLEEP

When you go to sleep your body enters a state of semi-hibernation. Your body temperature drops 1°F(0.5°C) and your heart rate slows down. Your breathing becomes slow and shallow; digestive processes and movement of the stomach and intestines virtually stop at night. In contrast, movements of the skeletal muscles do not stop altogether. It would seem that muscles have to contract every now and then in order for them to rest and recover completely. During the night we move a good deal more than we think, most of us turning more than 20 times during our sleep.

Sleep patterns

Our need for sleep diminishes as we get older. A newborn baby may sleep anything up to 15 or 16 hours a day. By the time a child is eight or so, s/he probably doesn't need any more sleep than an adult. Most of us can function well on 6 or 7 hours of sleep daily. At seventy it's quite common to sleep only for about 2 hours during the night and to doze intermittently for the rest of the night. However, our need to sleep is not primarily a physical phenomenon. It almost certainly is a chemical and hormonal one. It's not a tired body that drives us to sleep, it's a tired brain. It's handy to think of the brain as a battery: 16 to 18 hours of wakefulness runs the battery down; it recharges during sleep.

When we are well rested, alert and wakeful, our brain cells are charged with granules containing chemicals necessary for efficient intellectual function. When we are tired, brain cells become depleted of granules. During sleep, the granules reappear.

Our bodies are governed by an internal clock. This clock has a regular 24 hour rhythm. For each of us the rhythm is slightly different, but it conforms to a general pattern. It is largely determined by the blood levels of the life-giving hormone, cortisol, which is secreted by the adrenal gland. At midnight, the blood level of cortisol is sinking rapidly to reach its lowest ebb between the hours of 2 and 4 a.m. Subsequently, the adrenals start to pick up and cortisol floods the body sufficiently to trigger off waking somewhere between the hours of 6 and 9 a.m. for most of us. Early morning people have an early cortisol peak. People who wake slowly and need a cup of coffee and the newspapers before they really get going and are a bit snappy in the morning, have a later peak. Be it early or late in the morning, most of us enjoy quite a cortisol kick, which makes us alert, active and energetic. Just after lunch there is a post-prandial dip in the plasma cortisol and this accounts for the drowsiness which many of us feel in the early afternoon. Towards the evening the cortisol picks up again and enables us to enjoy evening activities. As the clock moves towards midnight the cortisol starts to die away again and this is one of the triggers which makes us feel sleepy. Cortisol levels tend to stay up in those of us who are night people.

The brain has two centers which control sleep. The first, which sends us off to sleep, is sensitive to external factors like darkness, social and domestic cues, habits, other people saying that they are tired or going to bed, and internal cues like physical or mental tiredness. The second center keeps us asleep and is triggered by chemical reactions in the body and brain cells which occur towards the end of the day.

The red band, right, represents a woman with high cortisol levels in the morning. She will, therefore, be more alert and active early in the day. In complete contrast, the "black-band" woman finds it hard to wake up, but easy to stay awake late at night.

24.00 03.00 06.00 09.00 12.00 15.00 18.00 21.00 24.00

Dreaming Some scientists say that we sleep only to dream. They liken the brain to a computer which is sorting, sifting, analyzing and synthesizing information during all our wakeful hours. Just like a computer, the brain could "blow a fuse" if the circuits became jammed with redundant information. A computer clears its circuits electrically; the brain clears its circuits during sleep and it is thought that a clearing mechanism is dreaming.

This theory is supported by the fact that brain cells only manufacture the essential chemicals needed for intellectual functioning while we dream. When we are deprived of dreams, therefore, the brain cells are not given the opportunity to manufacture these essential chemicals. In sleep laboratories, volunteer subjects whose brain waves are being checked with electroencephalography tracings have been wakened each time the EEG showed the characteristic brain wave of dream sleep (rapid eye movement or REM sleep). Despite the fact that the volunteers were allowed to sleep quite peacefully when they were not dreaming and had the requisite 7 or 8 hours dreamless sleep, they awoke exhausted. If we want to wake in the morning feeling fully rested, it is essential that we dream. Hypnotics like barbiturates interfere radically with our dream cycles, which occur several times during the night, the first almost immediately after falling asleep, and the last just before we wake. With barbiturates, dreaming is almost abolished and this accounts in part for the hangover which follows the morning after you have taken a barbiturate sleeping pill.

Modern sedatives are related to tranquillizers and interfere very little with dreaming, which is why you can have a satisfactory night's sleep after taking one of these newer drugs. They also guarantee that you will be alert if you waken during the night.

Whether we remember our dreams or not, we dream, on average, four times a night and it is at this time that we are at the lightest level of consciousness, bar waking. Dreaming coincides with rapid eye movement (REM) sleep, so-called because the eyes can be seen moving rapidly from side to side.

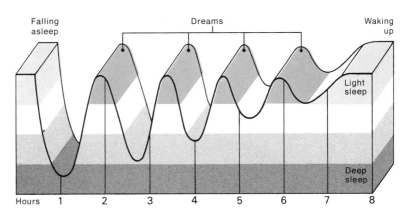

Insomnia Insomnia is going without sleep, and you may experience it as difficulty in getting off to sleep, waking a short time after you have dropped off to sleep, waking during the middle of the night, or waking in the early morning. Few of us lie awake for as long as we think and very rarely for the whole night or even several consecutive hours.

Causes of insomnia

Chronic insomnia is extremely debilitating. Everyone needs sleep and everyone should have sleep, so if you find yourself suffering from long-term insomnia, consult your doctor. Insomnia is nearly always related to a problem or a form of *stress* and it may be that talking your difficulties over with your doctor will help you to see them in a realistic light, and your insomnia too. It can be quite helpful to use sleeping pills in the short term to re-establish your sleeping habits, but you should never become dependent on them. It is wrong to use sleeping pills for long periods and if you find you cannot get a good night's sleep without a sleeping pill, then you should consult your doctor again and ask for further help.

It is not just stress and anxiety which can interrupt your sleep. By far the commonest cause is *resentment*. If you go to bed thinking about some injustice which happened to you during the day you will lie ruminating about your unfair treatment and you will start to think about ways of getting even. Your mind will start to race and it will be impossible to relax. Try to get your feelings sorted out before you go to bed.

A common cause of insomnia is *alcohol*. Alcohol is quite often taken late at night in an attempt to produce sleepiness. Indeed it does in the initial stages, and a couple of brandies last thing at night may get you off to sleep. However, as the alcohol level rises in the blood it produces an excitatory effect which may wake you and you will find that your mind is lively and racing. Furthermore, the little sleep you have had may blunt your further need for sleep and you may find yourself lying awake for quite a long time.

There is a fairly common form of insomnia during *pregnancy*. Despite the fact that most pregnant women can fall asleep as soon as they sit down during the day and feel utterly exhausted in the evenings, they quite often find that they are wide awake at bedtime or in the middle of the night. This is because their metabolism has to cope with the needs of the baby. The baby's body doesn't need rest nor does it need sleep. Indeed, it is actively growing and developing throughout the 24 hours; it doesn't know night from day, so the mother's metabolism has to match the baby's, and the normal braking system can't be applied.

Combating insomnia

If you find yourself lying awake, next to a snoring partner perhaps, don't lie there fuming and allow resentment to build up – take advantage of your insomnia and be constructive about it. Get out of bed, go downstairs, find yourself a book to read or do some job which you have been wanting to do for ages. It is never a good idea to lie in bed if you can't sleep. Getting up and engaging in some activity can often make you sleepy (see also *Hints to help you fall asleep*, opposite). Try and think positively about the few hours you have gained and make the best use of them.

How much sleep do I actually need?

Your need is individual to yourself; everyone needs a different amount of sleep. The amount of sleep you need is the number of hours you stay asleep if left undisturbed. On the rare occasions when we can indulge ourselves in this way we usually find that we sleep a couple of hours longer than our normal working day allows us. Most of us are at least two hours of sleep under par every day. It's not surprising, therefore, that we feel we are not functioning properly either physically or mentally and that we cannot cope with stress as' well as we would like.

As a general rule of thumb, our need for sleep runs in parallel with our growth rate, hence a baby who is growing very rapidly needs a lot of sleep. Women stop growing after the age of 23 and our sleep needs start to tail off from 7 or 8 hours a night by roughly an hour every decade until we may need only 4 hours in our sixties.

Why can some people exist on cat naps?

It is usually only old people who exist on cat naps, though the Mediterranean habit of a siesta is an awfully good idea. We tend to be of little use to anyone during the post-lunch dip and it seems sensible to take advantage of our normal physiology to sleep during this time and refresh ourselves for the late afternoon and evening. An hour of sleep between 2 p.m. and 4 p.m. is very energizing. This cat nap is one that we probably all need. The majority of us, however, cannot cat nap during the night until we are sixty or seventy years old.

What can I do about nightmares?

Nightmares are nearly always related to psychological stress. The cure for nightmares, therefore, is to deal with the situation that is causing stress. You may not be able to do this alone, so take a friend into your confidence, or go to see your doctor. If your nightmares are very traumatic, you may be helped by psycho-therapy or counselling.

HINTS TO HELP YOU FALL ASLEEP

● Arrange to do something quiet, relaxing and unexciting before you go to bed. Watching television, reading a newspaper or a book, taking the dog for a walk are all good ideas, so is a half-hour of yoga.
● Avoid coffee, tea or cola drinks, and tobacco after 4 p.m., and sweet snacks before bedtime.
● Make sure that the temperature of your bedroom is equable. You may have to open a window to allow air to circulate.
● Don't settle for a lumpy uncomfortable mattress, particularly if you have back trouble. Invest in the best mattress you can afford.
● Don't leave taps dripping or squeaky doors open to disturb you in the middle of the night; "bleed" any radiators that may be knocking.
● Wear loose-fitting pajamas or a nightdress, preferably made of cotton or other natural fibers as these are cooler and more comfortable.

● A hot bath last thing at night is soporific. It diverts the blood from the brain to the skin and makes you feel sleepy. So will a warm drink.
● Give yourself or have your companion give you a neck and back massage.
● Sex is probably the best hypnotic.
● Certain herbs such as camomile in a tisane, or hops in "sleep" pillows can be beneficial.
● Cut down on your hours of sleep.
● Once you are in bed and trying to go to sleep, try the following routine:
− starting at your toes, check your ankles, knees, hips, fingers, wrists, elbows, shoulders, torso, neck, face and forehead and make sure all your muscles are relaxed;
− slow down your breathing to deep breaths taken at half speed;
− try to make your mind a blank. Thinking of black velvet is a good idea.

MEDICAL CHECKUPS

It is important to achieve a sensible balance between practical monitoring of your body's health in all its aspects and being a hypochondriac. Some doctors make a case for not performing regular medical checks because they say that patients worry about them unduly, become obsessed about their follow-up and get upset about the result which, although it is outside of the normal range, is not one which the doctor feels is clinically important. Before you embark on any medical checkup, therefore, it is advisable to discuss your intention with your own doctor. Unless your doctor is completely unco-operative, you should not have any tests done without her/his agreement. In the best doctor/patient relationships, the doctor should agree with the need for the checkup and refer you to the appropriate specialist to have it done, if s/he cannot perform it.

You should be prepared to undertake almost all of your own regular health checks yourself (see pp. 77–80) and should rely on your doctor only for those checks which require a specialist's medical help. Even in these situations, you should take the initiative, you should not wait for your doctor to suggest a check up. If you want to, keep your own regular checkup chart so that you see when one is due or when one should be repeated, then go along to your doctor and remind her/him. Very often your own doctor is too busy to remember or to take the responsibility for your health. You should be prepared to take on that responsibility yourself and get the attention you want.

Before a test is done, ask for an explanation of what will happen to you, how the test will be done, and what the test is investigating. Make sure you know when the results will be ready and who will interpret the results. Ask your doctor if s/he would translate the results into a form that you understand. Don't be a Jonah and anticipate bad news, otherwise your medical checks will become a chore and you will become over-anxious about them and decide not to have them done which is self-defeating.

The aim of medical checkups is to prevent disease in the long term. They are an insurance policy for the future. It is possible that your own doctor may not subscribe to this view and may look askance at your request for regular medical checkups. Be prepared to discuss the subject openly and frankly with your doctor because her/his balanced view is valuable. If, knowing your family's medical history and your own medical history over many years, s/he feels that there is no indication for the tests, don't dismiss her/his reassurances; such views may be useful in tempering your own over-zealous interest in your health. Do remember, however, that it is your right as a patient to have regular medical checkups and if your own doctor won't arrange them, or won't put you in touch with someone who will expedite them, then it is also your right to find a doctor who will. You may come up against the obstacle that specialized medical checks, like mammography, are not available in the immediate locality, in which case you must be prepared to travel to have them done.

If you find that your doctor is quite unsympathetic to your request, and is somewhat dismissive about women's complaints in general, then you would be as well to change your doctor. What you are looking for is a doctor who understands female problems, is sympathetic towards them, and will give you the help that you require, if not from her/himself, then from a specialist to whom s/he will refer you. It is a sad fact that many doctors do not fall into this category, and you may have to look around for another one. If you feel that you have to leave a doctor because you don't get the attention you think you deserve, please do not do so without first discussing this with her/him, or writing to her/him. You will be doing other women a service if you let the doctor know that s/he has let you down in this respect and, who knows, you may change the way s/he approaches female problems in general.

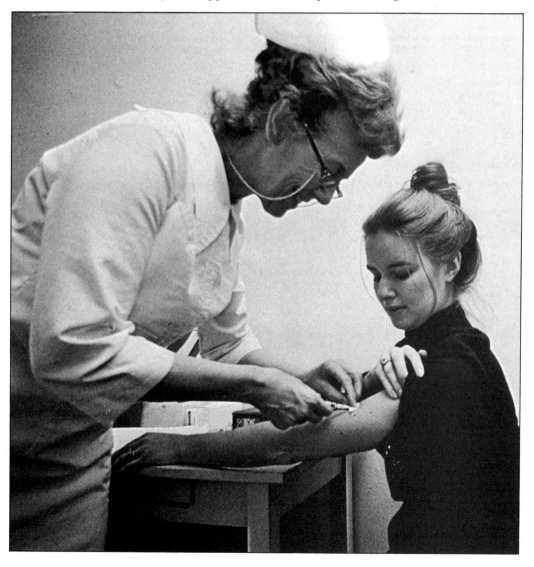

MEDICAL CHECKUPS

Name of test and purpose	When recommended	Age to begin
Chest X-ray		
To detect recent, current, and sometimes past, disease of the lungs	To check that the lungs are clear after a chest infection; if you spit blood; if you have chest pains; if you smoke; if you work in dusty conditions	From the age of 23 onwards
Blood pressure		
To check on the state of the heart and arteries	If you have a family history of high blood pressure, heart or kidney disease, stroke or diabetes; if you are overweight: if you had toxemia during pregnancy; if you're on the pill	From the age of 25 onwards
Complete physical examination		
To check on the general health of heart, lungs, brain and major internal organs	After a serious illness or surgery; if you are worried by a non-specific symptom	Rarely needed before the age of 30, unless there is a specified reason (see p. 80)
Internal examination		
To examine the pelvic floor, perineum and pelvic organs	If you have menstrual problems or a persistent complaint of the pelvis, vagina or perineum; if your mother took DES while carrying you, see p. 289)	Before you start any new contraceptive: if you are pregnant or have a pelvic inflammation
Cervical (Pap) smear		
To detect pre-malignant changes in the cervix	If you have inter-menstrual bleeding; irregular periods; or a positive family history of risk factors (see p. 280)	From the age of 16–20 onwards, or as soon as you're on the pill
Vaginal smear		
To detect pre-malignant changes in the vaginal cells	If your mother took DES while carrying you (see p. 289), or if you have a positive family history of risk factors (see p. 280)	From the onset of menstruation
Mammography		
To detect small breast lumps	If you fall into a high risk group (see p. 263), or if you have a positive family history	From the age of 30 onwards
Eye tests		
To detect defects in vision and glaucoma	If you have pain in the eye and it is red, especially if you are on the pill	From the age of 40 onwards; or if you have symptoms earlier; or if you are on the pill
Dental checkups		
To check on the general health of teeth and gums; to detect caries, and incorrect alignment	If you are pregnant; if your parents have poor teeth; if you have a rare dental disorder, like soft teeth	From the age of 2½ onwards

Frequency of follow-up	Who will arrange test and where	What the results will show	Who can interpret the results
Annually	Your doctor in a local hospital or mammography unit	Most diseases of lung tissue	A radiologist and your doctor
Annually	Your doctor In her/his office	If taken correctly and frequently (see p. 80) elevations in blood pressure may indicate a serious medical problem	Your doctor
Annually	Your doctor In her/his office	Gross disease of a major organ, and indications for further tests	Your doctor
According to your doctor or gynecologist	Your doctor or gynecologist in her/his office or a hospital clinic	Gross disease of a pelvic organ, and indications for further tests	Your doctor or gynecologist
Annually	Your doctor, a gynecologist or a family-planning clinic. In her/his office or a family-planning clinic	Early changes in the cells before they become malignant, and indications for further tests	A specialist in cytology who will send the results to your doctor
Annually, unless you have a chronic disease	Your doctor or gynecologist In a hospital cytology clinic	Early changes in the vaginal cells before they become malignant, and indications of further tests	A cytologist
Every 6 months if you are in a high risk group	Your doctor or a surgeon In a hospital X-ray department	Tiny breast lumps	A radiologist
Annually	Your doctor, ophthalmologist, optormetrist or optician In her/his office, a hospital clinic or an optician's office	Visual defects; early signs of increasing pressure on the eyeball, and indications for further tests	Your doctor, an ophthalmologist or an optician
Every 6 months	Your dentist or dental hygienist In her/his office	Early gum diseases or tooth decay	Your dentist or hygienist

Internal examination

It would appear from reading women's health books that women have a love/hate attitude to pelvic examinations. On the one hand there is a widely-held belief, particularly among American women, that having an internal manual examination sometime in the teen years, and then regular internal examinations thereafter is a magic recipe for good health. On the other hand, there are articles entitled "Surviving a Pelvic Exam" as though it were a horrendous experience to get through. Nothing could be further from the truth – a pelvic examination will probably cause discomfort but very rarely pain.

If possible, schedule the examination between periods (unless you are having bleeding problems). Don't disturb the vaginal area, especially by douching, 24 hours beforehand, and don't use spermicides if you have intercourse the night before (but do use another method of birth control).

Your doctor may recommend you have an internal examination if you have:

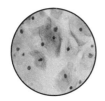

Normal cells

- Intermenstrual bleeding.
- Bleeding after intercourse.
- A vaginal discharge.
- If you suspect pregnancy and it's six weeks since your missed period (there's not much point in doing one earlier).
- An abnormal cervical smear.
- Painful intercourse.
- If you suspect venereal disease.
- Prior to going on the pill, having an IUD fitted, or using a diaphragm or cervical cap.
- If your mother took DES while she was carrying you (see p. 289).

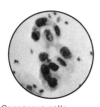

Cancerous cells

You have to undress for a pelvic examination and your doctor may ask you to lie on your back with bent knees spread apart or on your left side with your right knee bent up.

A speculum examination is a necessary part of a pelvic examination because, when the blades are opened, it allows the lining of the vagina to be directly seen by your gynecologist. The cervix can be examined and a cervical smear taken.

Most doctors, as a routine part of doing a cervical (Pap) smear test, perform a preliminary bimanual examination by placing one or two gloved fingers in the vagina and their other hand on the abdomen. The internal genital organs can be felt between the fingers of both hands. You should have an internal exam and Pap test once a year, but not more often unless you have symptoms referrable to the cervix, uterus, ovaries or tubes.

Cervical ("Pap") smear

Nowadays Pap smear is synonymous with cervical smear test. It is a test which has a high chance of detecting changes in cells before they become cancerous. To get at the cervix a speculum must be inserted into the vagina, then opened. Your doctor will scrape away a thin layer of cells from your cervix, smear them onto a glass slide, fix and stain them, then examine them under a microscope.

You should have your first Pap smear done between 16 and 20 years and thereafter annually, if possible, but certainly every 2 years. (See also *Smear tests* p. 281)

HAVING AN INTERNAL EXAMINATION

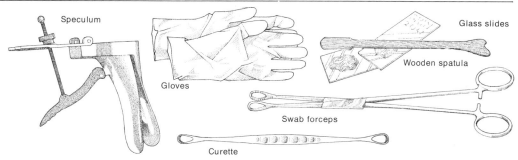

Speculum
Gloves
Glass slides
Wooden spatula
Swab forceps
Curette

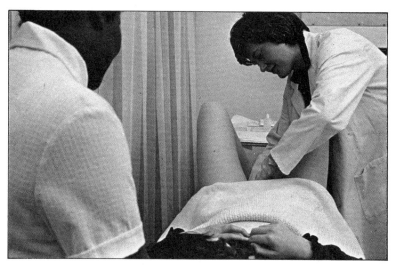

If you are aware of the importance of your health, and have a good and unembarrassed understanding of your own body, then you will know that there is nothing to fear from an internal examination. It is a painless means of assuring that the cervix and vagina are healthy, and is a regular gynecological procedure. If you should have any qualms or queries, don't hesitate to discuss them with your doctor.

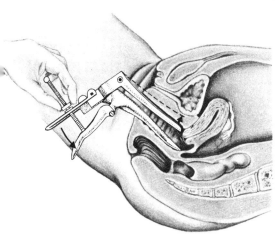

Speculum examination
With the speculum inserted and opened, both the cervix and the walls of the vagina are clearly visible. The speculum also facilitates the taking of smears.

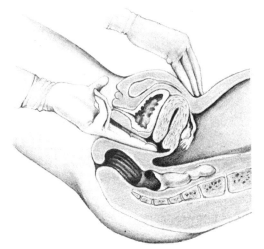

Bimanual examination
By placing the first and middle fingers inside the vagina and pressing down on the abdomen it is possible to feel the size, shape, position and tenderness of the uterus, ovaries and fallopian tubes.

DANGER SIGNS

What to note if you have:	What to ask yourself	What to do
Blood in sputum		
Color and quantity	Have I had a sore throat, cough, chest pain, or recent chest infection?	If there is a lot of blood, call an ambulance; otherwise make an appointment to see your doctor. Keep sputum to show doctor
Blood in vomit		
Color and quantity	Have I taken drugs? Have I eaten anything unusual, drunk a lot of alcohol or had indigestion recently? Do I have a duodenal ulcer?	If there is a lot of blood call an ambulance; otherwise make an appointment to see your doctor. Keep specimen of vomit to show doctor
Blood in stools		
Color and quantity of blood; color of stools; presence of mucus; any pain on passing	Do I have piles? Do I have a duodenal ulcer? Have I had stomach or abdominal pain? Have I recently had indigestion or an intestinal infection?	If there is a lot of blood call an ambulance; otherwise make an appointment to see your doctor. Keep specimen of stools to show doctor
Blood in urine		
Color and quantity of blood; any pain on passing	Have I had kidney or back pain; have I had a recent urinary infection?	If there is a lot of blood, call an ambulance; otherwise make an appointment to see your doctor. Keep a specimen of urine to show doctor
Bleeding after intercourse		
Color and quantity of blood	Do I have an unpleasant, itchy vaginal discharge? Are my periods regular? Could I be pregnant	Question your partner in case it is from him. See your doctor immediately
Inter-menstrual bleeding		
Color and quantity of blood	Am I on the pill? Could I be pregnant? Are my periods regular? Do I have a vaginal discharge that is smelly and itchy?	See your doctor immediately
Sudden heavy periods		
Quantity of blood; any clots	Have I had heavy periods before? Am I on the pill? Could I be pregnant?	If it doesn't stop, see your doctor as soon as possible
Lump in breast		
Size and shape of lump; consistency of skin (see p. 267)	When did I last do a breast examination; was it clear? Is there any discharge from the nipple?	See your doctor as soon as possible
Discharge from nipple		
Color and quantity of discharge; any blood. Tender nipple or breast	Have I just finished breast feeding? Am I on the pill? Am I feeling hot and feverish?	Take your temperature if you feel hot or your breast is tender. See your doctor as soon as possible
Sudden onset of indigestion		
Relationship to food; if alkalis bring relief	Do I have any pain elsewhere? Have I taken any drugs, alcohol or strange foods recently? Is there any change in my bowel habits?	If it persists for more than 3 days, see your doctor

What your doctor will do	What tests will be done	What it is likely to be
Question you about your chest. Examine your sputum and X-ray your chest	X-ray, throat swab, lab tests on sputum	If you are coughing, it's probably a small, burst blood vessel. It could be the aftermath of bronchitis or similar chest infection
Question you about food, your stomach and digestion. Examine your abdomen, look at your vomit and your stools. Possibly order a barium X-ray	Lab tests on stools, possibly on vomit; barium X-ray	The commonest causes are aspirin and other drugs, alcohol and duodenal ulcers
Question you about your stomach and intestines. Examine your abdomen and rectum (internally). Examine your stools. Possibly order a barium enema	Lab tests on stools; barium enema	The commonest causes are piles or severe diarrhea; it may occur with diverticulitis. Black, tarry stools occur when a duodenal ulcer bursts
Question you about your bladder, urine and kidneys. Examine your urine and arrange an intravenous pylogram (IVP)	Lab tests on urine; IVP	The commonest causes are cystitis or severe kidney infection
Question you about any blood or discharge, and about your periods. Examine your abdomen and breasts and give you an internal examination	Speculum examination; vaginal swab; Pap smear; pregnancy test	The commonest cause is a benign growth of the cervix, vagina or introitus; or your partner
Question you about any blood or discharge, and about your period. Examine your abdomen and breasts and give you an internal examination	Speculum examination; vaginal swab; Pap smear; pregnancy test	The commonest causes are minor menstrual irregularities or benign growths of the cervix, vagina or introitus
Question you about your periods. Examine your abdomen and breasts and give you an internal examination	Speculum examination; vaginal swab; Pap smear; pregnancy test	Out of the blue, the commonest cause is probably a miscarriage. If habitual, it is probably fibroids (see p. 235)
Question you about the lump. Examine both breasts and armpits	Mammography	The commonest cause is a benign cyst of the breast
Question you about the discharge. Examine both breasts, nipples and armpits	Mammography	The commonest cause is a benign cyst of the breast, or of the nipple ducts. This may happen when using the pill because of a change in hormone balance
Question you about food and digestion. Ask for a stool specimen for analysis. Try a course of treatment; order a barium X-ray	Barium X-ray; lab tests on stools	The commonest causes are starting to take medication for the first time or strange foods

61

DANGER SIGNS

What to note if you have:	What to ask yourself	What to do
Sudden onset of diarrhea, constipation, pipelike stools		
Color and shape of stools. Any mucus or blood – quantity and color	Have I started taking any drugs or different foods? Have I got a temperature; am I in pain?	Take your temperature; if it is raised, make an appointment to see your doctor. Keep specimen of stools to show your doctor
Onset of persistent headaches		
Position and frequency. Any related signs, e.g. pins and needles in the skin, flashing lights, nausea	Have I had shingles of the face, or toothache, recently? Does anyone in the family suffer from migraine? Have I been working hard or am I worried? Am I on the pill?	Take analgesics; see your doctor
Sudden pain in chest		
What makes the pain worse: breathing, coughing; or better: rest	Have my lower legs swollen recently? Am I on the pill? Do I have high blood pressure or bronchitis?	Take your temperature. If high, call your doctor or an ambulance, especially if you are breathless
Sudden onset of breathlessness		
What makes the pain worse: breathing, coughing; or better: rest	Have my lower legs swollen recently? Am I on the pill? Do I have high blood pressure or bronchitis?	Take your temperature. If high, call your doctor or an ambulance, especially if you are breathless
Sudden pain or tenderness of calf or swelling of one ankle		
Is the pain worse on pulling the toes up; how much swelling is there; is the other leg swollen?	Am I on the pill? Have I recently had a baby or surgery? Have I been in bed for a while?	Rest and put your leg on a stool. Call your doctor
Sudden onset of double vision		
Any other symptoms	Do I have headache? Do I feel nauseated? Do I have high blood pressure?	Lie down and wait an hour. Call your doctor immediately if it is still present, otherwise make an appointment to see her/him
Attacks of fainting		
Any other symptoms or feelings just before fainting	Do I bite my tongue when I faint; do I have any warning? Could I be pregnant?	Don't drive a car. Make an appointment to see your doctor

Vaccination Vaccination is true preventive medicine; once you are immunized against an infectious disease you do two things for yourself. In the first place you may prevent the infection ever taking hold in your body. If you are not so lucky, you are making certain that if your body is invaded by the bacterium, or the virus, then you will have the illness in a very mild form.

The principle behind vaccination is that exposure of your body to a bacterium or a virus in a dead or nearly dead form stimulates your body to produce specific antibodies to that germ. These antibodies circulate in your blood for a varying length of time. For instance, with smallpox, the level of antibodies will confer sufficient protection against the infection for about three years.

What your doctor will do	What tests will be done	What it is likely to be
Question you about food and digestion. Examine your abdomen and stools. Do a rectal examination. Try a course of treatment; possibly order a barium enema	Barium enema; lab tests on stools	The commonest causes are strange food, infection or diverticulitis
Question you generally. Give you a full physical examination. Take your blood pressure. Examine your eyes and your urine	None necessarily	The commonest causes are migraine, tension, headache, postherpetic neuralgia (related to shingles) and dental problems.
Question you, examine your chest, heart, sputum, blood pressure, chest X-ray; give you a course of treatment. If you are breathless, send you to hospital	Chest X-ray, sputum tests; investigations of legs and lungs to see if there are any clots	The commonest cause is bronchitis or tracheitis, as part of a virus or chest infection
Question you, examine your chest, heart, sputum, blood pressure, chest X-ray; give you a course of treatment. If you are breathless, send you to hospital	Chest X-ray, sputum tests; investigations of legs and lungs to see if there are any clots	The commonest cause is bronchitis or tracheitis, as part of a virus or chest infection
Question you. Examine your leg, give you a bandage; give you a course of treatment, if necessary	None necessarily; possibly regular blood tests	The commonest cause is deep vein thrombosis
Question you. Give you a full physical examination; take your blood pressure and examine the backs of your eyes	None necessarily	The commonest cause is migraine
Question you and give you a full physical examination	None necessarily: possibly a pregnancy test	The commonest cause is pregnancy, followed by epilepsy

Conversely, the level of cholera and yellow fever antibodies dies away sharply after about six to nine months. Once the level of antibodies against any infection is low, you need a booster.

Epidemiological studies have shown beyond doubt that when the number of vaccinated people in a community drops below a certain level, then the number of cases of infections begins to rise. For instance, the adverse publicity in the United Kingdom about the side-effects (encephalitis for example), associated with whooping cough vaccination in young children, led to a fall-off in the number of children who were vaccinated against this virulent illness. Within a short time there were epidemics of whooping cough in certain areas. Vaccination of this kind in small babies

63

VACCINATION CHART

Disease	When to have vaccination	How it's given	Side-effects	Where to get it	Duration	Booster
German measles	As a teenager (but *never* if you are pregnant)	Injection	None	Your doctor or health clinic	Life?	No
Smallpox	If you are going to an infected area. If you have been in contact with disease	Skin scratch or gun	Swelling at site. Sore, stiff arm, mild temperature, sore glands in armpit	Your doctor, or health clinic	3 years	Yes
Polio	Pre-school child	Orally, by drops on sugar lump	None	Your doctor	3 years	Yes
Tetanus	As a pre-school child. If you have deep wound, if working with manure	Injection	None	Your doctor or hospital emergency room	3 years	Yes
Tuberculosis	As a school child	Injection	Possibly sore arm	Your doctor or health clinic	Life	No
Measles	As a pre-school child	Injection	Swelling at site. Sore stiff arm. Mild temperature	Your doctor or health clinic	Life	No
Typhoid	When going to typhoid area; if in contact with disease during an epidemic	Injection	Sore arm, temperature	Your doctor	3 years	Yes
Cholera	When going to a country which requires it (telephone embassy)	Injection	Swelling at site. Sore arm. Temperature	Your doctor	6 months	Yes
Yellow fever	When going to a country which requires it (telephone embassy)	Injection	Swelling at site. Sore arm. Temperature	Your doctor	6 months	Yes

Certain parts of the world demand 2, even 3, different vaccinations and they may need a week or ten days between them, so warn your doctor in good time.

and young children is as much a protection of the community as the individual. By rigidly applying mass vaccination schemes, diphtheria, smallpox and tuberculosis have been completely eradicated from whole countries.

As adults, our main concern is to protect ourselves from infections which are endemic in communities abroad to which we travel. If you are going to have a vaccination, make sure that you consult your doctor, who will obtain the vaccines for you. S/he will also advise you on which vaccines you need for which countries and the period of time that can elapse between vaccinations, and s/he will provide you with the necessary vaccination certificate.

SMOKING

Light smoker: under 10 cigarettes per day
Moderate smoker: under 20 cigarettes per day
Heavy smoker: over 20 cigarettes per day

Smoking is never good for your health and some of the statistics relating smoking to disabling, and sometimes killer, diseases are quite staggering. In the present state of our knowledge I am at a loss to understand how people can ignore the indisputable fact that smoking is a causative factor in lung cancer, chronic bronchitis and heart disease.

● Women who use oral contraceptives and smoke, even moderately, are 12 times more likely to have a heart attack than women who do neither. Women who smoke heavily are 20 times more susceptible, even if they don't use oral contraceptives.

● Women smokers are 5 times as likely to get lung cancer as women who do not smoke; they get bladder cancer twice as often as non-smokers. In women who smoke and drink alcohol, tongue and mouth cancer develop 15 years earlier than in women who don't.

● More women smokers than non-smokers undergo early menopause, and the more a woman smokes, the earlier she is likely to experience it.

● Women who smoke while pregnant, even lightly, run twice the risk of miscarriage as nonsmokers; they produce children of lower birth weight and babies with an increased mortality rate.

● Children of mothers who smoke in pregnancy are shorter on average and tend to lag behind offspring of non-smokers in reading.

● 60% of mothers who lose babies to "sudden infant death syndrome" (SIDS) smoked during pregnancy or around the baby after birth.

If you smoke you are frankly mistreating your body. Even if you are otherwise quite healthy you are suffering without knowing it. Cigarette smoke interferes with the oxygenation of blood in the lungs: hemoglobin, the pigment in red blood cells which carries oxygen round the body, is converted to methemoglobin and can no longer transport oxygen efficiently.

Disease risks

Lung cancer was a rare disease until cigarette smoking became commonplace, but now it is quite common. At one time, the incidence of lung cancer in men was several times that in women and this could be directly related to the number of male smokers and female smokers, the ratio being something like seven or eight to one. Nowadays almost as many women as men smoke, and lung cancer occurs almost as frequently in women as it does in men. In fact, lung cancer is rising so fast in women it may overtake breast cancer as the number-one killer of women in the mid or late 1980s. Smokers, regardless of sex, are more likely to develop lung cancer than non-smokers and the risk of cancer increases directly in proportion to the number of cigarettes smoked.

The good news is that giving up smoking results in a corresponding reduction in risk. For lung cancer to develop from normal lung cells, there have to be several separate steps before a cancerous cell evolves and this may take several years. The initial irritant, or stimulus, causes changes in the cell nucleus and it multiplies. At this stage, however, the cell is not cancerous and will only go on to become so if the changes continue. If the initial stimulus is removed at an early stage, the multiplying process of the cell can be blocked and this has been confirmed experimentally. If smokers are able to give up smoking, they can reduce the risk of developing lung cancer.

The risk of heart disease among smokers is twice that among non-smokers. By the time you reach the age of 35 it is four or five times higher. The physiological effect of nicotine is that it narrows the coronary arteries which supply heart muscle with oxygen and nourishment. If you, or any member of your family, has any form of heart complaint, such as high blood pressure or angina, then it is mandatory that you give up smoking.

Lung cancer and heart disease can kill, but just as important is the debilitating effect of smoking where it leads to the development of chronic bronchitis. This causes a significant number of deaths each year in itself and additionally is often a contributing factor to deaths from many other disorders and surgery.

Cigarette smoke is irritating. The irritating effect is obvious if cigarette smoke gets in your eyes, where it can cause stinging due to the noxious chemicals it contains. Inhaled cigarette smoke will irritate the bronchial passages in the same way as our eyes. Our eyes become red and water. Our lungs do exactly the same. They produce excessive quantities of mucus in an attempt to bathe the inflamed bronchial membranes with a soothing balm.

The chemicals in cigarette smoke damage the fine hair-like processes (cilia) which line the bronchial passages. There are millions of cilia in constant movement over the lining of the bronchial tubes and their job is to waft foreign particles and mucus upwards to the back of the throat where they are coughed up and expelled. Cigarette smoke paralyzes cilia, leading to the stagnation of mucus and debris inside the lungs. Here it is ripe for infection should you get a cold, flu or bronchitis. Ironically, mentholated cigarettes damage cilia even more.

Chronic bronchitis, if it recurs winter after winter, eventually leads to chronic infection of the lungs with breakdown of lung tissue and loss of elasticity, inability to ventilate the lungs efficiently, and wheezing, shortness of breath on exertion and even the crippling disease of emphysema. In the advanced stage, emphysema may confine the sufferer to bed or a wheelchair.

Giving it up
It is salutary to remember that emphysema may have started off with a furtive cigarette in the school playground. If you haven't started to smoke, avoid it at any cost, and if you do smoke, do your utmost to give it up by whatever means you can.

Giving up smoking is difficult, and you may have a better chance of success if you have a dramatic health reason for doing it. Seeing someone with emphysema or in the terminal stages of lung cancer may be the drama that you need to inject yourself with to produce the necessary will power to give up smoking. If nothing else works, try hypnosis.

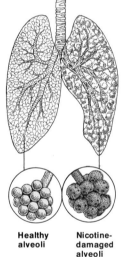

Healthy alveoli   **Nicotine-damaged alveoli**

*I really find it impossible to give up smoking completely. Can you
give me any help on cutting down?*

- Always smoke low tar cigarettes.
- Always smoke cigarettes with a filter.
- Smoke less than five cigarettes a day if you possibly can.
- Throw away a long stub.
- Do not inhale.
- Do not smoke in front of children.
- Do not offer cigarettes to your friends.
- Keep cigarettes as far away from you as possible so that getting one involves the maximum effort.

I don't smoke but people around me do. Can their cigarettes be dangerous to me?

A recent Japanese study has shown that there was a surprisingly high incidence of death from lung cancer in non-smoking wives of smoking husbands. "Passive" smoking can also result in severe headaches, allergic coughing and sneezing and extreme eye irritation.

Can my smoking affect my children?

Women who smoke during pregnancy have significantly more miscarriages and stillbirths, and surviving children have lower birth weights and develop more slowly both physically and mentally. Older children in a "smoking" household are more prone to respiratory illnesses such as bronchitis and pneumonia, and a large proportion undergo surgery for tonsil and adenoid conditions.

ALCOHOL

Like any drug that can make you feel good, alcohol is potentially addictive. What starts as social drinking easily progresses to taking a drink for the relief of anxiety or nervousness and then to habitual social drinking and taking a drink every time you become stressed. If you do not check your drinking at this stage, you can then go into the risky phase which is only one step away from the critical phase.

The risky phase begins to show itself when you become increasingly tolerant to alcohol and need to take more and more of it to achieve the desired effect. Once you begin to drink surreptitiously, then dependence on alcohol has developed.

You have entered the critical phase when you are unable to stop drinking and find yourself breaking promises and resolutions to do so. You avoid your family and friends and start to neglect your diet. Very soon you find that you have to take an early morning drink in order to start the day and you have to keep on drinking to get through it. It is now a dangerous addiction which can lead to disease and possibly even death. Furthermore, while alcoholism is a self-inflicted illness, its effect can go beyond the drinker, for it can result in the break-up of marriages, the alienation of children, dismissal from a job, and fatal injuries to the drinker and to others.

The effects of alcoholism on the body are dreadful. About 60% of chronic alcoholics suffer from fatty infiltration of the liver, and about 10% from cirrhosis of the liver. In both these conditions the liver is unable to function properly and the drinker constantly feels under par. Cirrhosis is a killer. The death rate from it went up by 30% between 1963 and 1973. Damage to the nervous system by alcohol is extensive and disabling. The first symptoms involve the nerves of the hands and the feet and cause tingling of the fingers and toes and cramps in the legs. Judgment begins to fail and one of the first indications is the inability to judge distances, and then coordination of hand, foot and eye deteriorate. In the later stages, the memory goes and brain damage is often permanent.

We can help ourselves and others to avoid the slippery slope to alcoholism by controlling our drinking.

● Be a good host and offer your friends more non-alcoholic drinks.

● Try to drink an equal quantity of water with your alcohol.

● Cut down on the aperitifs and on the liqueurs.

● Try to eat a snack while you drink.

● Skip a round of drinks when out, or order less than you would ordinarily, or even a non-alcoholic drink, and bear the few snide comments from your friends.

● Help to educate your children in good habits by maintaining a sensible attitude to drinking in the home (there is a high incidence of alcoholism in the children of alcoholics).

● Teach your children discrimination and to take everything in moderation.

● If you are pregnant, do your baby a service before it is born and don't drink heavily in pregnancy. If you do, you are putting your baby at risk. A German professor has estimated that 1 in 3 alcoholics will have a handicapped child. Make sure it isn't yours. See also *Alcoholism*, pp. 322–326.

DRUGS

Pharmaceutical technology is so advanced that almost anything you need is available in a pill or out of a bottle. Many drugs are freely available over the druggist's counter without recourse to your doctor for a prescription. We have become the generation of drug-takers; never before have so many diverse remedies been sought from bottles. Doctors here write millions of prescriptions for tranquillizers every year, and their availability has no doubt contributed to the dangerous easy-going attitude to medicines such as pain-killers, tranquillizers and sleeping pills.

Many drugs are needed, but very few for a long term. If your need for any kind of drug is chronic, then you should seek expert guidance from your doctor and you should not be prepared to accept repeat prescriptions over a long time. You should try to avoid long-term medication and only take medicines when you feel you really need them. There is nothing wrong with taking pain-killers, tranquillizers or sleeping pills under supervision for a

The majority of households have some form of medicine cabinet. Whatever drugs you are prescribed by your doctor, make sure that you take the full course, and throw out any excess tablets. Do not allow leftover medicine to accumulate, as shown in the photo on the right; if there are children in your household, lock the cabinet up for safety.

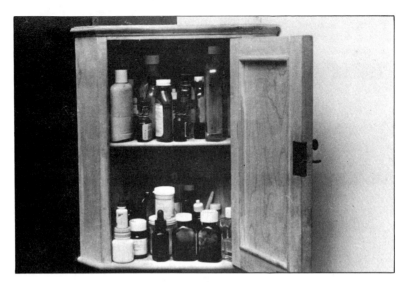

short time to form new habits, but if you find that you are having to take any medicine, even an antacid for longer than a week, you should consult your doctor.

One of the reasons for not treating drugs in a cavalier way is that they may produce side-effects, not only in you but in your developing baby should you become pregnant. The first twelve weeks of development are the most sensitive time for a fetus and you may innocently continue to take drugs during the first six weeks of your pregnancy because you are unaware that you are pregnant.

Drugs are often abused because they are not taken according to doctor's instructions. A course of pills should always be finished. This is particularly important with antibiotics where carelessness may be dangerous. If you do not take your tablets regularly, and for the full course, resistant strains of bacteria may develop and you may end up having a more serious illness than you had at the beginning. Furthermore, if antibiotics are used without just cause, there is a greater likelihood of resistant bacteria developing; you may then find yourself in the dangerous position of not having any antibiotics which can kill off resistant strains.

Analgesics   Most analgesics are powerful and effective, but because we resort to them so readily, we have a tendency to discount them as active drugs. They must, however, be treated with respect, if only because they can have side-effects which range from irritating to life-threatening.

When used correctly, aspirin is one of the most useful drugs known to medicine. It can be used in a variety of ways:
- As an ointment to get rid of hard skin.
- As a gargle with antiseptic properties.
- As a liniment for sore muscles.
- As an inhalant for inflamed bronchial tubes.
- As an analgesic tablet (always use the soluble form).

69

Aspirin is often used in high doses by doctors for its anti-inflammatory effect and is very useful in the treatment of rheumatoid arthritis and rheumatic fever. Its analgesic effects last for about 4–6 hours. The commonest side-effects of aspirin are dyspepsia, heart-burn and indigestion, and very rarely, it may irritate the lining of the stomach and cause bleeding. With very high doses you will get deafness and ringing in the ears, but this is temporary and subsides as soon as the blood levels fall. Aspirin is very dangerous in over-dose and may be fatal within a few hours because it disturbs the acid/alkali balance of the body.

Acetaminophen (trade names are Tylenol and Pabalate) This is somewhat weaker than aspirin as an analgesic, but many doctors feel it's worth sacrificing the analgesic effect because it is safer. It doesn't cause gastric irritation and therefore people suffering from peptic ulcers are free to take it. It is also safer than aspirin for infants and is available as a syrup. It is an excellent drug for lowering the temperature, and its effect lasts for about 4–6 hours.

Codeine is a very powerful analgesic which acts on the pain center in the brain. It also suppresses the cough center in the brain and therefore is commonly used in cough-medicines. It is capable of relieving all but the most severe pain for about 4–5 hours. The commonest side-effect with codeine is constipation because it slows down the movements of the bowel (it may be used as a treatment for diarrhea). You should not take codeine on a regular basis without consulting your doctor.

Sleeping pills

Old-fashioned hypnotics like chloral and barbiturates are still available as hypnotics, but their general use in the long term is to be deprecated. In the first place they produce side-effects, those of the barbiturates being the most dangerous. The most commonly used barbiturate sleeping pill is Nembutal which though short-acting (5–6 hours) is rapidly poisonous and in some susceptible people, as few as six tablets can be fatal. Barbiturates will make you sleep, but the quality of sleep that you enjoy in a barbiturate sleep is second-rate. Barbiturates do not permit dreaming and you may wake up with a hangover or feel quite exhausted after a night's sleep induced by barbiturate drugs. Often there is a "rebound" effect in which dreams become more intense, frequently run into nightmares, and disturb sleep.

Pharmaceutical advances have introduced safer and more physiologically acceptable sleeping drugs which interfere very little with sleep and dreaming, leave you alert and wakeful if you have to get up in the night to do something, but allow you to go back to sleep again and give you a good refreshing night's sleep. The most modern hypnotics are related to the tranquillizers. Many of them are not really sleep inducers. They send you off to sleep by calming the mind and making it ready for sleep.

Tranquillizers

Tranquillizers are among the most commonly prescribed types of drugs in America and are currently used by millions of people. The overwhelming majority of prescriptions for Valium, Librium and Miltown are written for women. The fact that so many women are

EFFECTS OF ALCOHOL ON DRUGS

Analgesics/narcotic
(Pethidine, Codeine, Pentazocine)

When used alone, either alcohol or narcotic drugs cause a reduction in the function of the central nervous system. When they are used together, this effect is even greater, and may lead to loss of effective breathing function (respiratory arrest). Death may occur.

Analgesics/non-narcotic
(Aspirin, Paracetamol, Phenacetin)

Even when used alone, some non-prescription pain relievers can cause bleeding in the stomach and intestines. Alcohol also irritates the stomach and can aggravate the bleeding, especially in ulcer patients. Alcohol may also increase susceptibility to liver damage from Acetaminophen.

Anti-alcohol preparations
(Antabuse, Calcium carbamide)

Use of alcohol with medications prescribed to help alcoholic patients stop drinking results in nausea, vomiting, headache, high blood pressure, and possible erratic heart beat, and can result in death.

Anti-coagulants
(Warfarin, Heparin, Dicoumarol)

Alcohol can increase the ability of these drugs to stop blood clotting, which in turn can lead to life-threatening or fatal hemorrhages.

Anti-convulsants
(Hydantoins, Valproate, Primodone)

Drinking may lessen the ability of these drugs to stop convulsions and may exaggerate blood disorder side-effects of the anticonvulsant.

Anti-depressants
(Imipramine, Amitryptilline, Mianserin)

Alcohol may cause an additional reduction in central nervous system functioning and lessen a person's ability to operate normally. Certain anti-depressants, in combination with red wines like Chianti, may cause a high blood pressure crisis.

Anti-diabetic agents/hypoglycemics
(Insulin, Chlorpropramide)

Because of the possible severe reactions to combining alcohol and insulin or the oral anti-diabetic agents, and because alcohol interacts unpredictably with them, patients taking any of these medications should avoid alcohol.

Anti-histamines/most cold remedies
(Phenergan, Chlorpheniramine)

Taking alcohol with this class of drugs increases their calming effect and a person can feel quite drowsy, making driving and other activities that require alertness more hazardous.

Anti-hypertensive agents
(Reserpine, Methyldopa)

Alcohol may increase the blood-pressure-lowering capability of some of these drugs, causing dizziness when a person gets up. Some agents will also cause a reduction in the function of the central nervous system.

Anti-infective agents/antibiotics
(Metronidazole, Chloramphenicol)

In combination with alcohol, some may cause nausea, vomiting, and headache, and possibly convulsions, especially those taken for urinary tract infections. Some are rendered less effective by chronic alcohol use.

Central nervous system stimulants
(most diet pills, Dexedrine, Caffeine)

Because the stimulant effect of this class of drugs may reverse the depressant effect of the alcohol on the central nervous system, these drugs can give a false sense of security. They do *not* help intoxicated persons gain control of their movements.

Diuretics
(Chlorthiazide, Frusemide)

Combining alcohol with diuretics may cause reduction in blood pressure, possibly resulting in dizziness when a person stands up.

Psychotropics
(Chlorpromazine, Haloperidol)

Alcohol with the "major tranquillizers" causes additional depression to central nervous system function, which can result in severe impairment of voluntary movements such as walking or using the hands. The combination can also cause a loss of effective breathing function and can be fatal.

Sedative hypnotics
(Barbiturates, Chloral, Diazepams)

Alcohol in combination further reduces the function of the central nervous system, sometimes to the point of coma or the loss of effective breathing (respiratory arrest). This combination can be fatal.

Sleep medicines

It is likely that non-prescription sleeping medicines, to the degree that they are effective, will lead to the same kind of central nervous system depression when combined with alcohol as the minor tranquillizers.

Tranquillizers, minor
(Diazepams, Nitralepam)

Tranquillizers in combination with alcohol will cause reduced functions of the central nervous system, especially during the first few weeks of drug use. This results in decreased alertness and judgment, and can lead to household and automobile accidents.

Vitamins

Continuous drinking can keep vitamins from entering the bloodstream. However, this situation changes when a person stops drinking.

Others

If you are taking any drugs which do not appear here, check with your doctor or pharmacist to be sure they are safe.

prescribed tranquillizers points to a bias on the part of doctors in their treatment of women as well as to the willingness of women to accept these habit-forming, and often debilitating, drugs as the answer to their problems.

The tranquillizer epidemic started in 1969 with the discovery of diazepams, which have a gentle tranquillizing effect, easily controllable with careful dosing. As many as one-third of all diseases have a psychological component related to stress (see p. 299) so the use of tranquillizers seemed medically quite justifiable. What is not justifiable is their long-term use for several years. They are undoubtedly habit forming but falsely treat the symptoms instead of the cause. Millions of women are fooled by the smoke screen of tranquillizers without attempting to discover and correct the root of their anxiety and stress.

Amphetamines Prescribed mainly for dieting, over 76% of these drugs are used by women. If taken over a short time, they suppress the appetite, relieve fatigue, and give the user a "lift." However, they are among the most grossly abused drugs, not only because they are too freely dispensed, but also because they are used for extended periods or in increased doses to those prescribed. Amphetamines are easily habit-forming and tolerance develops quickly. See also *Dependency/Addiction*, p. 317.

MENTAL FITNESS

We spend a great deal of time, energy and even money, thinking about and trying to do something about physical fitness. Unfortunately, the same does not apply to mental fitness and it should. To women, mental fitness should be as important, if not more important, than physical fitness. Why? Because there is no doubt that women, regardless of marital status, suffer from more mental illness than men: they outnumber men at psychiatric clinics, and they are more likely to have mental treatment in hospitals than men are. Women take more psychotropic drugs than men and are more frequently diagnosed by family doctors as suffering from mental health problems. The reason for these phenomena is twofold: first, our physical condition makes us more vulnerable – women are prone to psychological disturbances relating to hormonal behavior, not only monthly, but especially after pregnancy and childbirth, and we live longer to experience mourning, loneliness and the depression of old age. Second, the social status of women has meant that we frequently aren't given freedom of choice in our chosen lifestyles, which leads to frustration, and that no matter what lifestyle we choose, there are conflicts that can breed unhappiness such as balancing a family and a career, and even because marriage itself may be an ongoing mental trauma for us, much more than men.

This remarkable bombardment of mental trauma means that we must strive to maintain a basic state of mental health – so that we can take knocks and not go under; so that we can rise to emergencies and cope well with them; so that we are resilient enough to survive long-term, stressful situations; so that we can deal with possible loss of those closest to us.

Maintaining psychological equilibrium, however, requires a different sort of self-knowledge from physical fitness. It also requires supreme realism. It is essential that we realize our difficulties are not unique. We all go through periods of duress and, no matter how unpleasant, most of us survive. Adversity is normal, indeed it is a condition of living, and we must not overreact to it or feel that we've messed up our lives irretrievably and are failures because we're experiencing it.

When things go wrong, it is a natural reaction to think that we are to blame. But we should bear in mind that difficulties in our environment, over which we have no control, might be the major factor. Things such as bad housing, overcrowding, lack of money, loss of social standards, violence in society – are all factors we can do little about. Poverty is a particularly powerful exacerbating factor and, as with physical illness, mental illness is much commoner among poor people.

It is important, too, that we achieve a certain measure of emotional growth. Coming to terms with the way we feel about things, being able to work with our own emotions, as well as other people's, in a non-destructive but helpful, even affectionate, mood is a goal we should all try to achieve. Accepting ourselves for what we are and permitting ourselves a proper measure of self-esteem means that we can take responsibility for our own actions and seek and accept forgiveness from others, when necessary, without damage to our self-image. This process of independence is a long one and may even continue through life but it is necessary to seek out the goodness within ourselves.

Another effort to make is not to set our standards too high; it's not necessary and it can be a great strain. It is acceptable for anyone to give way now and then, to have a good cry, to pour out troubles to a friend, or to rant and rave to let off steam. Better that than burning out your fuse and becoming ill.

It is also possible to prepare for catastrophes, and the answer lies in yourself – you have to have the desire to cope and survive a bad time. If you practice on manageable "disasters" you'll find the major ones cause you much less stress, bearing in mind that once your mental fitness is jeopardized it will take time to come back to normal. There are, however, two ways in which you can control your body and mind immediately: relax (see p. 43) and breathe calmly and slowly.

Qualities of mental health

There is little doubt that mental health goes hand-in-hand with certain attitudes to life. These include:
● A proper emotional balance, whereby a full range of responses can be expressed according to the situation – neither too dramatically nor too grudgingly.
● A sense of realism, particularly about the sort of standards that should be set for oneself. An awareness of strong points and weak points, and the fact that everybody has them.

● Independence. There is also the recognition that everyone needs privacy and peace.
● Lack of self-pity. When faced with a problem, the problem itself is looked at, and not the person involved.
● A general attitude that problems are there to be solved and that nothing is hopeless.
● Close relationships with a few people, rather than superficial relationships with many.
● An inner sense of security rather than a reliance on controlling others.
● A preparedness to take on responsibility for one's own life. Blame is rarely placed on other people or events.

Achieving mental fitness

As with physical health, mental health doesn't just happen. It has to be worked on. Here are some guidelines you may find useful.
● First and foremost, eat well and exercise regularly. There really is a lot of truth in the saying "A sound mind in a sound body."
● Don't enter into any relationship where your partner does not have respect for your privacy. You must have some time in the day to do exactly what you want, when your preferences come first, and when the only person you have to please is yourself.
● Try to accept yourself as you are. You will be extremely unhappy if you are constantly striving to make yourself into a better person. Before you can accept who you are, you have to find out who you are, and that can be difficult and take a long time. One of the best ways to get insight into yourself, is to write a letter to an imaginary recipient about yourself and the way you feel about different things. You will find that you are putting down all sorts of important things which are otherwise difficult to state.
● Be reward-conscious and give yourself a treat, whenever you think you have accomplished something. A treat is energizing.
● Spend time with people you like, and who you are comfortable with – people who have similar interests to you. You will feel happier if you spend more time with that kind of person, and less time with people whom you don't like, regardless of duty.
● Try to give yourself the widest possible emotional spread – you will feel happier and better prepared to go through life's serious and worrying times. Don't forbid yourself to do something or feel something, simply because it is not grown up.
● Look hard at some of the "dangerous emotions" you may feel. Do you feel aggressive and angry? If you never do, then you are in trouble. It is perfectly legitimate to feel both of these emotions, despite the fact that you have been told they are wrong. To depress them entirely is dangerous. Guilt, on the other hand, does no good. It can destroy your self-esteem, and it may also stop you from doing things. If you are feeling persecuted, don't dismiss the feelings as self-delusion. They nearly always have a basis in something real, but you may be exaggerating them. Look around for the cause and try to deal with it.
● Start on a positive-thinking campaign. Decide that you are never again going to feel sorry for yourself. What you should really be trying to do, anyway, is to control your environment and

be able to affect it, not the other way around. You will never do this by thinking negatively. But don't set yourself unrealistic targets. Achievement brings the best possible sense of reward, so try to set targets that you can achieve in areas where you know you are good and likely to succeed. Never shrink from a problem or pretend it isn't there. One of the ways you will be better able to cope with life is to actually get yourself through a crisis. It is a great learning experience and you can always call on it in the future – "I've done it once, I can do it again."

● Establish your needs carefully. Even if you feel that you may want the support of a self-help group, or group psychotherapy, don't join the group unless you are very clear about the part you have to play and are willing to play it.

● Be active and get involved in doing things, be it for yourself, your partner, the children, the community, or the PTA. This is one of the best ways of staying mentally healthy. Not only does being active occupy your mind, but it actually may change your attitude towards problems and the way you handle them.

● Tell people what you want or you are very unlikely to get it. Once you have decided what your priorities are in life, make sure that everyone who is close to you and has to work with you knows what they are. If you do so, you will find that they start to work with you.

Recognizing mental ill-health

Not everyone, of course, finds it easy to stay on an even keel all the time. Here are some of the signs that you should be on the look-out for which suggest that your mental health may be impaired. All of us will notice them every now and then, but you should treat them seriously if they occur with any regularity or frequency.

● Emotions that seem to be out of proportion to what the situation warrants, whether uncontrollable, inappropriate or rigidly controlled.

● A feeling that the world is hostile and you cannot trust anyone.

● Difficulty in taking care of yourself and other people.

● Constant striving for perfection, and unpreparedness to accept weaknesses.

● Readiness to put important things off, lack of willingness to get up and do things, feelings of apathy, and non-interest.

● Increasing difficulty in communicating with people, where previously it was easy, or at least possible.

● Self-destructive or harmful behavior towards others.

If you find any of these things happening then you have to look at the pressures in your life to see whether or not your reactions are acceptable, and would generally be considered normal. If they are not, then you need help. Don't go on thinking that things will get better, they probably won't, so before they get serious, try to do some of the things listed above, and if you don't feel better within a short time, try and get advice and support. Even if you think the attitudes of psychiatrists and the conditions in our mental hospitals leave a lot to be desired, it is far better that you take advantage of what they can offer than you go under. (See also *Threats to Mental Well-Being*, p. 298.)

DAY-TO-DAY CARE

Your body is a beautiful, efficient machine built to a design that is beyond the skill of most engineers, so it is worth looking after it, checking it over regularly to make sure that it is in good working order, and doing regular repair and maintenance jobs whenever necessary. You will be repaid a hundredfold if you take a bit of time and trouble to *prevent* things going wrong, and if you deal with them early should they go wrong: you will be making the most of yourself, you will look better, and you will certainly feel better. As a bonus, you will be healthier.

Body maintenance can be overdone. Advertisements encourage us to use medicated shampoos, to cleanse our skins regularly and take make-up off every night. Physiologically, medically, and hygienically, there is no need to do any of these things. If your reason for doing them is an aesthetic one, that's fine, but I believe you, your skin and hair will be no healthier for having done them.

If you think something is not as it should be, you may be able to deal with it yourself or you may choose to seek some form of "alternative" remedy before orthodox medical treatment. There are several ways in which you can deal with the problem. In this chapter, I will tell you how you can help yourself with simple, effective, but harmless remedies; I will also outline what you should expect and try to get from orthodox physicians and specialists, and additionally, I will give the solutions that alternative treatment may offer to you.

SELF-EXAMINATION

By regular examination you should know most parts of your body very well. If you do, and examine yourself routinely, then you should detect whether or not there has been a change in your body as soon as the change occurs. The following guide will show you how to examine yourself. If you find something which was not there the last time you examined yourself, or even if you just feel uneasy about finding something, *consult your doctor immediately*. Your doctor is the only person who can assess whether the change you have noticed is indicative of anything serious, and s/he may be able to reassure you very quickly to the contrary. Always remember that self-examination is not a substitute for routine medical checks; your own self-examination should complement regular medical checkups (see p. 54).

BREAST EXAMINATION

Your regular breast examination should consist of two parts, observation and manual examination. You should be looking for dimpling of the skin over the surface of a lump; any change in the size, shape and color of your nipples; any discharge from the nipple.

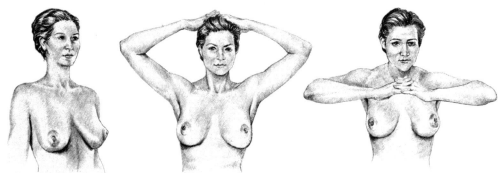

Take off your clothes to the waist, then stand or sit in front of a mirror. Look at each breast very carefully.

Raise both your arms above your head and turn from side to side so that your breasts are clearly outlined.

Bring your arms to mid-chest and lean forward. Examine each of your breasts in turn.

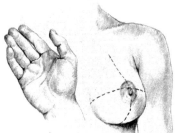

Lie on a flat surface, head on a pillow, shoulder slightly raised. With the flat of your hand and your fingers held straight, examine the four quadrants of each breast.

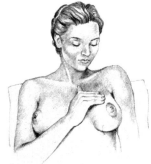

Start from the outside of the breast and move in a circular, clockwise direction. Use your right hand to examine the left breast. Keep your arm loosely at the side to examine outer parts.

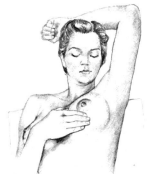

Examine the inner surface of each breast with the same movement. To stretch the breast tissue to make lumps easier to feel, extend the arm you are not using behind your head.

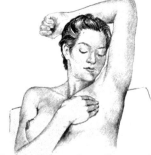

Feel for lumps along the top of the collarbone and in the armpit. This completes the examination on the left side. Now repeat procedure exactly for the right breast using the left hand.

Large or pendulous breasts are best examined with two hands. One underneath supports the breast, the other examines the top surface. Try to feel all the intervening tissue between your two hands. Reverse the procedure so that the palm of the top hand supports the breast and the bottom hand examines under-surface.

Breasts

Self-examination of the breasts is meant to detect lumps in the breast early – when they are less than 1 cm ($\frac{1}{2}$ inch) in diameter, if possible. You should examine your breasts about every 2–4 weeks; try to choose a time which easily becomes habitual, for instance after a bath or when you are undressing at night. If you find any sort of lump in your breast which worries you, consult your doctor at once, but remember, most lumps are not malignant. One word of clarification: all breasts become naturally lumpy in the week before menstruation. They also become heavy, enlarged, tender when squeezed, and the nipples may tingle. If you feel their consistency with your fingertips you will find that they contain small lumps similar to orange pips. These are swollen milk glands which enlarge in the second half of each cycle and shrink again when menstruation is over. They are perfectly normal and should not alarm you.

If you find any kind of a lump, consult your doctor immediately. Do not wait to see if it will disappear.

Freckles and moles

Most freckles and moles are of no consequence. Those that you should examine regularly are the ones that may be subject to regular friction: for instance, if they lie on your shoulder where your bra strap presses, in the middle of your back where your bra fastens, or on the side of your foot where your shoe rubs. If you have have a mole or freckle which is in one of the places above, consult your doctor about its removal *before* it gives any trouble.

Every two weeks you should look to see if any of the following have happened:
- If your mole has changed in shape, size or thickness;
- If your mole has changed in color;
- If there are any signs of redness around your mole;
- If there is any inflammation around your mole.

If you do spot any of these changes, go and see your doctor as soon as possible; s/he will probably refer you to a dermatologist for a specialist's opinion. This is largely precautionary, but a dermatologist will almost certainly advise removal of the mole or freckle by a small, painless operation to avoid future trouble.

Teeth and gums

Most dental trouble in the Western world is not due to bad teeth, but bad gums. It is exceptionally important to look to the health of both and to prevent disease, largely caused by the arch villain, plaque (see p. 114).

You can examine your own gums every morning by simply noticing whether they bleed on brushing. If they do, it probably means that you are not brushing properly, you are not brushing regularly enough, or you are not getting rid of plaque efficiently enough. Plaque leads to deposits of sharp, gritty, chalky material round the margin of the gums with the teeth. This irritates the gums, makes them swell so that the edges become soft and bleed when brushed. You should also check your toothbrush to make sure that it isn't too hard and that it has ideal characteristics (see p. 112). (You can use a disclosing tablet which you chew after you have brushed your teeth, to see whether or not your toothbrushing technique removes plaque; unless your teeth show up as spotless, you should change your technique.)

If your gums feel sore or tingle, or they appear red and swollen around their margins, it is possible that you have a gum infection. It is essential that an infection of the gums does not become chronic, so make an early appointment with your dentist (not your doctor) for her/his opinion and specific treatment. Do not resort to proprietary mouthwashes and medicated mouth tablets. They may even make the infection worse by creating resistant strains of bacteria and altering the natural flora of your mouth.

Discolored teeth do not always herald tooth disease, but check with your dentist anyway. If your teeth are over-crowded or grow crookedly, consult your dentist about having them straightened – this can be done simply and painlessly, in some cases with elastic bands! In addition to aesthetic reasons, it is worth considering straightening your teeth or even having one removed if they are too over-crowded – over-crowded teeth can trap food particles and thereby encourage decay.

Blood pressure

I am averse to recommending a self blood pressure test as it encourages hypochondria and neurotic anxiety and is usually of little value without medical supervision. A non-medically qualified person is unable to assess if a rise in blood pressure is serious – s/he may not be taking the blood pressure properly and may get inaccurate readings. Most people forget that a 15 minute rest period prior to taking blood pressure is necessary as the pressure may be raised simply by the excitement and the effort of taking it. Moreover, a single raised blood pressure reading, on its own, is completely without clinical significance, and a doctor would always want to check the blood pressure on several different occasions to ascertain that an elevated reading was not a mistake.

If you can make sure that you do not fall into any of these traps, that you can remain calm while taking your blood pressure, and calm if you find that it is elevated, then by all means take your blood pressure, but not more often than once a month. There is no real need for you to check your blood pressure more frequently than every three months.

Blood pressure is charted as systolic pressure over diastolic pressure. The normal diastolic reading is 80 mm of mercury so consult your doctor if you have consistent readings of 90 mm and above. A rise in the systolic pressure is much less significant than a rise in the diastolic. Systolic pressure is affected by excitement, nervousness, getting out of breath, lying down, etc. If you find a rise in the systolic pressure you should repeat your blood pressure check in two or three days time, taking care to observe all the precautions already listed. A rise of 10 mm of mercury in the systolic pressure, that is up to 130 mm, is not considered significant or worthy of special treatment by most doctors, unless you are pregnant. If your blood pressure varies between 120 and 130 I would simply suggest that you keep a check on it yourself. If, however, it is consistently at 130 or above, then by all means consult your doctor. You should inform your doctor of any rise in the systolic and diastolic pressures of more than 10 mm of mercury which is confirmed by two or three check readings.

Internal self-examination

While some women's groups advocate regular internal self-examinations as a form of preventive medicine in that they assume the average woman can learn to spot changes quickly, I feel that such examinations are difficult for most women, and that the results are generally unreliable. You can best keep track of the internal genitals by observing how they function, rather than how they look. Those internal examinations that are necessary are best carried out by a doctor (see p. 58).

CLEANSING

Many of us are still brought up on the slogan "Cleanliness is next to Godliness." As far as health and fitness go, there is no reason why cleanliness should have been given this divine description. There is nothing especially worthy about being dirty, but by the same token, there is nothing especially worthy about being clean. The health of the skin, hair, nails and orifices like the ears, nose, mouth, vagina and rectum will not be any more healthy for being obsessively cleansed; as we shall see they may be less healthy.

The hair and the skin have their own cleansing processes. The hair is cleansed and lubricated by sebum from the sebaceous glands. The skin gets rid of waste products both through sweat – it sheds millions of dead cells every day so that the surface is constantly renewed and repaired – and the secretion of sebum, which covers the skin with an "acid mantle," has antiseptic properties and repels bacteria. This natural cleansing system is so efficient that there would be hardly any need to touch the skin at all if we did not contaminate it with dirt and make-up.

Over-zealous cleansing may upset the delicate bacterial balance of the skin which is necessary for its health. Moreover, unless mild cleansing agents are used, the skin may be severely de-fatted. Fat, in the form of sebum, is a key to skin health, and its removal undermines the defense mechanisms of the skin, and will also lead to water loss because sebum is one of the best moisturizers known to science. It binds with water and holds water in the skin, thereby helping to keep the skin supple and well hydrated.

It's better to "under clean" than over clean. This applies particularly to parts of the body which are lined with delicate mucus membranes, like the mouth and the vagina. Both of these organs can take care of themselves unless they become infected. Under ordinary circumstances, you should not try to clean them (the mouth with mouthwashes, the vagina with antiseptic in your bath water), and the use of deodorants, particularly in the vagina, can be harmful. They, too, can destroy bacteria and upset the natural balance which maintains the vaginal secretions slightly on the acid side and which is absolutely necessary for its health, and for fertilization to take place. Purely on the level of aesthetics, the natural vaginal smell is preferable to artificial perfume. Moreover, this odor plays an important part in heterosexual relations as, at a biological level, many men would say it was attractive and you may become less attractive to your male partner if you camouflage it.

SKIN CARE

If I were allowed to take only one skin care product on a desert island with me it would be a moisturizer. The skin needs moisture. Moisture is being lost from the skin constantly as it permeates up from the lower levels and evaporates from the surface. The rate of evaporation is dependent on the humidity of the surrounding air; if the air is very damp then water is lost slowly. If it is very dry, or if there is a wind (which *per se* produces a drying effect), it will be lost more quickly. It is not a myth that damp climates, like the climate in the United Kingdom, are good for women's skin; dry, hot climates and dry, cold, windy climates are drying and ageing.

There are two ways of keeping the skin well hydrated. One is to put moisture in, the other is to stop moisture loss. The first is very difficult, and anything you buy to moisturize the skin can only do it transiently (no longer than 30 minutes). On the other hand, moisturizers which attempt to prevent water loss are much more efficient – the most modern ones have been formulated to resemble natural sebum (see p. 81) and these go some way in forming a barrier against water loss.

Skin structure
The outer covering is the epidermis, a relatively thin layer from which sweat glands and hair follicles emerge. Underlying and supporting the epidermis is the dermis. This contains blood vessels to nourish the skin.

Further down is the fatty subcutaneous layer which anchors the skin to the underlying muscles.

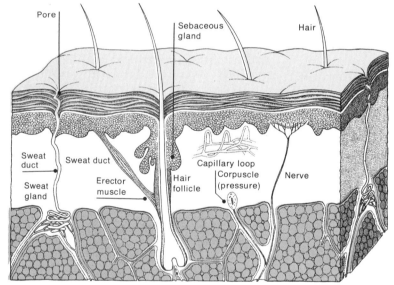

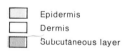

Epidermis
Dermis
Subcutaneous layer

Make-up   Make-up is very good for the skin, regardless of type – it is good for your skin even if you have acne. I used to shock the mothers of some acne patients in a hospital clinic by suggesting that the sufferers wear a fairly thick, well-pigmented stick make-up to cover their spots. There are two very good reasons for doing this: first, make-up does no harm to someone who suffers from blackheads or acne. It cannot block the pores (indeed, nothing but paint can block the pores). Second, it is very demoralizing for an acne sufferer to look in the mirror and see large, sometimes deeply-colored spots in her complexion so that a covering make-up is very good for morale. When you look good, you feel good.

When you feel good your acne stands a better chance of getting better. Make-up is also quite a good barrier against moisture loss and it prevents dust and grime getting into the skin. In a minor way it acts as a sunscreen, so it is always good to wear make-up when you go out in the sun.

The effect of sun

If you want your skin to stay young, then you should avoid exposing your skin to strong sunshine and never use a sun-bed with ultraviolet light. Most women chase a tan and there's no doubt that a tanned skin looks attractive, but a skin which has been tanned from the sun is a skin which has been aged by the sun. Therefore, if you must have a tan, get it out of a bottle. Fake tans, properly applied, can be almost as attractive as a tan induced by ultraviolet radiation; the difference is that the tan out of a bottle does not injure the skin. The tan from sunlight actually destroys skin because certain wavelengths in sunlight break up the collagen. Collagen is the skeleton of the skin and is responsible for its body, its plumpness and its suppleness. Healthy collagen, therefore, is synonymous with a youthful-looking skin. But collagen ages imperceptibly all the time. From starting off in beautiful elastic bundles, it snaps and breaks up until it resembles an old piece of elastic, and, so far as we know, there is no way of slowing down or correcting this process. Certainly cosmetic creams containing collagen can do absolutely nothing, as they simply cannot reach the collagen in the lower depths of the skin. Exposure to sunlight speeds up the process of collagen disintegration, so if you want your skin to be ten or fifteen years older than your actual age, do go ahead and sit out in the sun.

The dermis of skin contains an interweaving network of connective tissue proteins, or collagen. This allows the skin to stretch to accommodate body movement, or changes in shape and size.

If you must sit out in the sun, protect your skin with a sunscreening cream. If you smear one of these creams on your skin every two to three hours and make sure that all of it is covered, you will protect your skin from the harmful effects of ultraviolet radiation. The latest generation of sunscreens contains substances called *benzophenones*, which selectively absorb light of harmful wavelengths. The sunscreen index which is printed on the tube, gives you a good idea of how well the sunscreen will protect the skin. The higher the protection factor, the more efficient the sunscreen. If you go swimming, re-apply the cream.

Cleansing the skin

Plain soap and water are only good for greasy skins; the rest of us should avoid them. Greasy skins need de-fatting and as long as you don't use a vicious de-fatting agent, they will respond to regular and fairly frequent cleansing. For cleansing and taking off your make-up use a specially formulated soap or cleanser. When you clean your face (or the central greasy panel down your face if you have a combination skin) with soap and water, try using it in the following way: make a fine lather in the palms of your hands and then, with the fingertips of one hand, massage it into the skin. With circular movements, gently rub the lather on your skin as you would a cream. Leave for a minute, then rinse off. You can further de-fat the skin with an astringent lotion, but you can close up the sweat glands just as efficiently by splashing with cold water.

Beauticians and cosmeticians advocate taking your make-up off at night. If you feel cleaner and more comfortable doing this, by all means do so, but there is no health or beauty reason for doing this. In fact it is quite illogical. More rational would be to make your beauty routine coincide with the times when the skin is most active. The skin has a 24 hour clock and it goes through two growth spurts, the first is in the very early hours of the morning and the second, smaller one, is immediately after lunch. The best time for your beauty routine, therefore, is as soon as you wake up and early in the afternoon. There is no need to feel guilty any longer about going to bed with your make-up on.

Paradoxical though it may seem, water is a dehydrating agent. This is because water contains salts, e.g. carbonates. The more salt it contains, the more it absorbs water from your skin. Your hands may seem soft immediately after taking them out of water, but given a few minutes, you will find that they are dry, rough and scaly. The harder the water, the more salts it contains, the more drying it is.

The detrimental effect of water on the skin is increased if you add detergents to it because this strips the layer of protective fat from the skin. Soap has a similar effect and all but specially-formulated cleansing agents alter the pH (acid/alkali balance) of the skin. Detergents and soaps are highly alkaline, while the skin is acid, and for good health it should remain acid. Washing with an ordinary soap or a detergent alkalinizes the skin and it must then work hard to re-establish its acid status. Therefore, while a soak in a hot bath, with a liberal sprinkling of so-called bath salts, may be good for your nervous state, it's very bad for your skin. The longer you lie in your bath, the more dehydrated and alkaline it will become and the more vulnerable to roughness, dryness, scaliness and infection. So, take a shower instead whenever you can.

Don't apply a proprietary antiseptic to your skin, or add it to your bath water, unless you have an infection of the skin for which it has been prescribed. Antiseptics can irritate the skin and the delicate lining of the vagina, the mouth and eyes. They also upset the delicate balance of bacteria growing on the skin and in the vagina, a balance which is necessary for health.

Unwanted hair

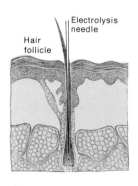

Hair follicle

Electrolysis needle

Electrolysis can permanently remove small numbers of facial hairs and hairs around the nipple. In the hands of a skilled person the process is painless. At each treatment session you will probably have twelve or fifteen hair follicles treated. A very fine needle, which has an electric current running through it, is applied to the hair root to burn and destroy it so that it never grows again. There should be no inflammation, swelling, infection or scarring after electrolysis treatment if it is properly done.

Unwanted facial hair, if it's sparse, can be disguised by bleaching. Hair can be removed from the legs and armpits with hair removing cream which dissolves the hair away at the level where it disappears into the skin. For the legs, to strip away new hair growth, apply liquid wax to the skin and remove it as a film when it's cooled.

Hair shouldn't be removed by shaving, except from the legs and armpits. It doesn't grow any thicker – that's a myth – but stubble looks unsightly and feels dreadful.

Excess hair all over the body nearly always has a hormonal cause and most teaching hospitals have a department in which this condition can be fully investigated. A complete hormonal profile is done under the guidance of an endocrinologist who will advise you whether or not treatment with hormone supplements will help.

Blemishes and spots

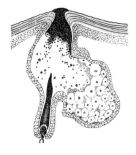

A blackhead is a mixture of sebum and keratin which forms a firm mass to block the hair follicle. It is black because keratin changes color on exposure to oxygen; the blackness has nothing to do with dirt. A blackhead can and should be removed. Make the skin soft and supple by leaning your head over a basin of steaming water and then gently, with your fingertips, not with your nails, squeeze out the blackhead. After it is removed, apply a thin smear of a simple antiseptic cream (available without prescription at any drugstore).

Ordinarily you should never be tempted to squeeze a spot in your skin. However, you can do so if you have a spot with an obvious head that ruptures easily. If you have to press hard, stop. Squeezing hard only spreads the bacteria into the lower levels of the skin and may make your spot larger and the lump harder.

Tips for taking care of the skin

● Try using two moisturizers at once. One should be a light fluffy cream which immediately sinks into the skin and transiently replenishes moisture; the other should be heavier and more greasy to act as a barrier against moisture loss.
● Don't sit out in the sun; wear a hat with a wide, shady brim and stay pale and interesting.
● If you must have a tan, get a fake tan.
● Forget those stories about make-up blocking the pores; wear make-up.
● Whenever you apply or remove make-up, use upward strokes. The force of gravity is constantly pulling your skin down; counteract this effect with your fingertips whenever you can.

Skin care myths

There are certain things which have gained popularity but which are entirely unnecessary for a healthy skin:
Oil This is not necessary for a healthy or supple skin. The only oil which is useful to the skin is natural sebum. All sorts of other oils, including the olive oil which is a component of many soaps, have no proven usefulness for the skin.
Massage In any of its varied forms, massage is not necessary for the skin, nor is exercising.
Deep cleansing Both deep cleansing and getting rid of dead cells are quite unnecessary.
Face packs These are quite redundant.
Rich food and coffee These are not detrimental to the skin. On the other hand, special diets are not especially useful.
Sleep This is not necessary for a healthy skin.

SKIN – SPECIAL NEEDS

The skin is the most extensive organ in the body: it protects, insulates and provides sensory information, and it is therefore essential to care for it correctly. As can be seen from the illustration, care for the skin varies according to the area of the body – compare, for example, the hardier areas like the feet with the more delicate vaginal areas.

Skin
Moisturize at least twice a day. Apply a light, fluffy moisturizer which sinks deeply into the skin and then a heavier moisturizer which traps moisture in the skin and prevents water-loss. Wear make-up – it's a barrier against water-loss and some of the harmful effects of sunshine. Avoid sunshine whenever you can but if you must go out in the sun, put on a sunscreen (see p. 83) every 2–3 hours.

Feet
Wear well-fitting, comfortable shoes. Vary the heel height during the day to give your feet a rest. Walk without shoes whenever you can. Wear wooden exercise sandals whenever you can. They are molded to the sole of the foot but allow the feet to spread freely. Weight is evenly balanced. The muscles of the soles of the foot are exercised as they grip the wooden base with each step. If you have trouble with your feet, invest in a regular pedicure. If shoes rub, they will cause hard skin callouses (corns), and blisters. Avoid shoes which do. Loose ones are the worst offenders. Blisters are caused by shoes which crush the toes together.

Vaginal area
Don't be obsessive but be meticulous about hygiene. Washing morning and night with ordinary soap and water is all that is needed. Don't use vaginal antiperspirants and deodorants. They may cause irritation and detract from your natural odor which is a sexual attractant.

Heels and soles
Remove hard skin, after a bath when it is softened, with a pumice stone or a special implement. Use hard skin-removing cream to keep your feet smooth. If you suffer from sweaty feet use an anti-perspirant talcum powder on your feet each morning and night and wash carefully with soap and water twice a day.

Knees
If you have to do a lot of kneeling and gardening you should wear pads, otherwise you may develop rough skin and callouses. Smooth them down with a pumice stone or a rough bath mitt.

Thighs
It is a secondary female characteristic to have a pad of fat at the top of the thighs. Even very skinny models have some fat there. If you are overweight this is the last area of fat (along with the fat on your upper arms) to disappear. The best form of cure is prevention. Try not to put on more than 20 lbs during pregnancy. Nothing other than general weight reduction will get rid of this pad of fat. It can't be removed by any kind of spot-reduction program. Massage will do no good at all, nor will exercise unless it is excessive. Plastic surgery is sometimes used.

Neck
As for face. Moisturize as often as you can. Always use upward stroking movements to counteract the downward drag of the force of gravity which helps to produce those sagging lines.

Breasts
Always treat them gently. Always wear a bra unless your breasts are light and small. You must wear a bra in pregnancy and when you are breast-feeding. Care of the nipples is especially important in pregnancy when you should make sure that they stay everted by the use of nipple shells if necessary.

Shoulders and back
Wash regularly and scrub with a bath mitt or loofah to cut down on oil and the tendency to get blackheads. Do not, however, scrub too hard otherwise you will simply stimulate the over-secretion of sebum.

Elbows
As for knees. Moisturize as often as you can to make the skin softer. Blanch the skin with preparations like lemon juice (this only has a transitory effect).

Abdomen
If you put on weight very quickly, and also during pregnancy, stretch marks may appear which vary from fine silvery lines, to rather unsightly pinkish red marks. Stretch marks are due to breakdown of collagen in the skin and you can do nothing to prevent them. If they are going to appear they will, and rubbing in oils and creams will not help. They usually fade to insignificance within a year of pregnancy, but if they are unsightly and remain so, it is possible to have them removed by plastic surgery.

Hands
Moisturize with hand cream or a barrier cream whenever you can remember, especially during the winter and after washing up. Only wear rubber gloves for dirty jobs if you wear cotton gloves underneath, soaked in hand cream. Otherwise your skin will be dried out by sweating inside the rubber gloves. Keep warm in the winter, and at the first sign of cold weather, by wearing gloves whenever you are outdoors. The best way of cleaning dirty nails is to bury them in a sponge that is filled with soapy lather. It's even better to prevent your nails getting dirty by wearing rubber gloves for dirty jobs (see p. 125) or scraping your nails on a cake of soap to fill the free edge. The soap under your nails can easily be washed out when you've finished the job.

Underarms
Wash morning and night if you can. Use a combined anti-perspirant/deodorant preparation morning and night to help prevent sweating and cut down odor. If you shave, do it carefully so that you don't break the skin; make sure it is after you have applied the deodorant and it has dried. Don't put deodorant on immediately after shaving or it will sting, and may cause a rash.

Will creams containing hormones, vitamins or collagen benefit my skin?

There is no evidence whatsoever that these ingredients and others such as avocado oil, cucumber extract, etc., are any more beneficial than simple moisturizing creams, nor are there any sound scientific grounds for preferring products which claim to be natural or organic, containing ingredients such as fruits, vegetables or herbs. Synthetic ingredients are just as efficient and, of course, if preservatives aren't present, the natural creams will sometimes separate or even go rancid, especially when exposed to the air or to heat.

Is there anything I can put on my skin to help prevent the formation of wrinkles?

Your skin is as unchangeable as the color of your eyes. The tendency to develop wrinkles, or to have a young-looking skin, is inherited from your parents. If your mother or your father has a good skin, the chances are that you will too. So far, there is nothing known to medical science that can be applied to the skin, or that can be taken by mouth, to prevent wrinkles. You should avoid anti-wrinkle creams that tighten up the skin because they tend to dry it out and, in any case, the tightening effect lasts only a few hours (see also p. 348).

Does smoking age the skin?

There is no real medical evidence to support all that has been written about the deleterious effects of smoking on the skin. However, one can argue against smoking from basic principles. Smoking causes an increased amount of methemoglobin (see p. 65) in the blood and this cuts down the blood's oxygen-carrying power, and, therefore, the efficient nourishment of tissues and the nourishment of the skin would be included in this general statement.

COMMON SKIN COMPLAINTS

*I have included alternative remedies only for completeness. Their inclusion doesn't constitute endorsement, or a belief that they are effective. Very few herbal remedies have been subjected to scientific testing. In the main, their efficacy is therefore anecdotal. For specific recipes please consult a herbal textbook.

SCABIES Infection with the acarus mite which results in an itchy rash affecting the finger clefts and the hands, wrists, elbows, ankles, feet and toes.

Cause The adult acarus mite burrows through the upper layers of the skin, then lays its eggs at the end of the burrow. The rash is infectious and passed on by contact.

Symptoms Itching, rash. With careful observation, the grey hairline burrow can be traced in the skin to a small greyish black speck which is the adult mite.

Investigation In a hospital dermatology clinic the "black speck" is extracted with a sterile needle and examined under the microscope to confirm the diagnosis.

Prevention All cases of scabies and contacts of diagnosed scabies must be treated promptly.

Treatment
Medical The doctor will give you specific treatment, usually a liquid which needs to be painted all over the body. Everyone in the family, and every contact, must be treated in the same way at the same time.

ACNE An oily skin with blackheads and a tendency to pustular spots. It's most common at puberty but there is an adult form which is often difficult to treat. It may leave scars if deep lumps appear after spots.

Cause Blockage of the sebaceous gland which eventually ruptures and releases sebum into the deeper layers of the skin where it is an irritant, causing inflammation which becomes invaded with skin bacteria. It has nothing to do with your diet.

Symptoms Greasy, spotty, unsightly skin.

Investigation Rarely done unless extremely severe, with disfiguring scars or unless acne persists through the twenties. Does not yield much useful information.

Treatment
Self Cleanse your skin meticulously. The aim of cleansing is to de-fat the skin. Acne is one of the few conditions in which soap and water are really useful. Bring your soap to a lather in the palm of one hand and, using it like a cream, massage it into the skin for two minutes, very gently. Never scrub or scrape, this simply spreads the bacteria across the surface of the skin and possibly into the deeper layers of the skin. When washing is complete, rinse off with warm water. Repeat the soap and water cleaning three times a day if you can, but at least morning and night. If you can, use an antibacterial cleanser. They can be bought over the counter and contain cetrimide. With the exception of creams containing hydroxyquinone, don't use proprietary acne preparations, but do use special acne creams available from your doctor. There is no need to avoid rich and fatty foods; there has never been any conclusive evidence that eating a special diet makes a significant difference to acne. If your morale is high, your acne will be better. You can do a lot to achieve this aim if you wear a thick textured make-up to cover up your spots. The sun is good for acne in that it makes the skin peel and this peeling action unblocks the sebaceous glands. So acne sufferers have almost the only kind of skin that should be exposed to the sun. Do not try sunshine or ultraviolet treatments without consulting your doctor.
Medical Your doctor may prescribe: special prescription cleansing lotions; special prescription antiseptic creams; special acne treatments which combine mild anti-inflammatory antiseptics/antibiotics.
Specialist The dermatologist has available an antibiotic regimen taken by mouth: Tetracycline tablets, 250 mg, one morning and night, which seem to have an inhibitory action on the bacterium which infects the sebacaous glands in acne. Special ultraviolet and sunlight treatments are normally successful only in mild cases. Minor surgical techniques which can abrade or scarify the skin, getting rid of unsightly scars. This is very often done in conjunction with a plastic surgeon and is by no means suitable for all cases of acne. Indeed, it is not usually considered for anything but severe cases.
Alternative Herbalists will almost certainly recommend special diets and special creams and possibly certain natural or herbal medicines to take by mouth, none of which are proven to work. Sage, plantain, verbascum and ground ivy are said to have useful astringent properties. Shepherd's purse has cleansing properties. Aromatherapists advocate the use of bergamot, camphor, cedarwood, juniper and lavender.

BROKEN VEINS Hairlike blood vessels running in the surface of the skin. Usually found on the cheeks, but quite often on the thighs and legs. Their continuity is broken because as we grow older the blood circulates through capillary vessels very slowly and tends to stagnate. In the cold the veins become blue.

Cause Inherited.

Treatment
Self Do not sit in direct heat or sunlight. Try to avoid exposing your skin to inclement weather or if you do, protect it with a good covering of make-up. Avoid spicy foods. Moisturize the skin over broken veins well. They tend to appear in delicate thin skin. Avoid marked temperature changes.
Specialist If you are really determined to get rid of your broken veins, a dermatologist may try electro-dessication which obliterates the broken veins with an electric current. No other treatment will remove broken veins.

WART Warts are usually well-defined lumps with rough surfaces which can be a pinpoint in size or as large as 1 in in diameter. The commonest site is the fingers and the hands; at the soles of the feet, where they grow inwards and produce painful *veruccae*, they are most troublesome and uncomfortable. Infectious warts in the genital and anal area are quite often difficult to eradicate.

Cause Hardly anything is known about the virus which causes warts. Those people who suffer from warts often have a sweaty skin. Some people seem to be entirely immune.

Symptoms When on the feet they cause pain, otherwise they are usually symptomless.

Investigation None if the diagnosis is obvious. If not, the wart may be excised or a small piece of it cut out for microscopic examination in a hospital clinic.

Treatment
Self Do not try patent wart cures. Go to your doctor for specific treatment and advice. Be meticulous about foot hygiene when you go to public swimming pools (where the virus is often picked up).
Medical Specific potent and effective wart cures. You will be given detailed instructions how to use them. Follow the regime to the letter, otherwise the wart may recur.
Treatment Recalcitrant warts can be burned off in a dermatologist's clinic with the use of carbon-dioxide, liquid nitrogen or electro-cautery. These treatments must only be used in the hands of experts, otherwise painful scars may result.
Alternative There is a multiplicity of wart cures for charming away warts and they do appear to respond. The connection, however, is fallacious. the charm is actually inside yourself. Research has shown that it takes about two years for your body to build up antibodies to the virus which causes your warts. They will then disappear of their own accord. Wart charms work when the charming coincides with the body's own production of antibodies.

89

DERMATITIS Red, dry, scaly patches in the skin, which frequently start in infancy, sometimes in the first year of life, and are sometimes accompanied by asthma. Many children improve markedly by the 7th year and the majority by the 14th. In childhood, dermatitis is usually confined to the face, wrists and the back of the knees. In adulthood, these sites remain affected but dermatitis may appear in patches on other parts of the body. It undergoes periods of activity and inactivity, is worse when you are overworked, overtired, anxious, stressed, or when you have an illness or an operation. During these times it may become very much worse, the skin may blister, weep, and eventually crust over..

Cause Tendency to develop dermatitis is called "atopy." The tendency is passed from your parents and carried in your genes. It cannot be removed. You can, however, prevent acute exacerbations by making sure you get enough sleep and avoiding stress and strain. Patients with dermatitis are more likely to develop skin allergies.

Symptoms Chronically itchy rash which may prevent sleep and may cause splitting and cracking of the skin.

Investigation Allergies should be excluded and correction of any obvious tension in the domestic or social background should be corrected if possible.

Prevention None other than avoidance of stressful factors.

Treatment
Self Avoid all contact with soap and water. Rub in simple emollient creams as often as you can: every hour or so to the hands and wrists, three times a day to your face, under your make-up, and on your body every night. These creams do not need to be expensive. Baby cream is as good as any. It's difficult, but try to avoid overwork, stress, strain and anxiety. Make sure you get the amount of sleep that you need. If you are going through a rough patch when you cannot sleep, ask your doctor to tide you over with some sleeping pills.
Medical Your doctor may prescribe potent anti-inflammatory creams to apply to your skin as sparingly as possible, 2–3 times a day. S/he may also give you tablets to take which will cut down the itching and will "tranquillize" the skin as well as you. If you are sleeping badly s/he may give you a course of sleeping pills.
Specialist The dermatologist has an array of creams and pastes to apply when your skin becomes recalcitrant to your own doctor's therapy. S/he may suggest that a stay in hospital, with intensive hospital treatment, will clear your skin and keep it clear for several months. If s/he does so, take his/her advice.
Alternative Burdock tea is claimed to clear all kinds of skin disorders if taken frequently. Chickweed and pennyroyal are claimed to improve skin disorders.

BOIL A localized, tender red swelling with a central collection of pus (core), usually starting as an infection in a hair follicle.

Cause Bacterial invasion of a hair follicle.

Symptoms Itching, soreness, pustule formation, crusting.

Investigation If large or recurrent, your doctor may take a bacterial swab to find the bacterium which is causing the infection, so that specific treatment can be given.

Prevention Resist picking at, or scrubbing, the skin. Don't squeeze spots that haven't developed into a pustule. Gently expel blackheads once they have formed.

Treatment
Self Apply hot salt water poultices (clean gauze soaked in a solution of 1 teaspoon of salt to a glass of warm water), to bring the boil to a head. Once the head is formed, break the skin gently with a sterilized needle or blade, and gently expel the pus. If small, apply a dressing of antiseptic cream (available at all drugstores over the counter). If large or recurrent, consult your doctor.
Medical Specific antibiotic cream to be applied 3–4 times a day under a light dressing. If recurrent, your doctor may give you an antiseptic to put in your washing water (never use otherwise), and an especially formulated soap containing an antiseptic. If boils are really a problem s/he may refer you to a specialist.
Specialist Full hospital investigation to find out the cause of your recurrent boils..
Alternative Special diets are recommended and the avoidance of rich and fatty foods. The following are given as remedies for "abscesses": cayenne (tonic), chamomile (strengthening, tonic), chickweed (cooling, reduces sweating), comfrey (draws a boil, heals skin).

MELASMA Flat, brown circular patches in the skin, most often on the face and sides of the neck, usually round, and often appearing in women taking combined contraceptive pills or in those who are pregnant.

Cause Not known for certain but it is thought to be caused by a sensitivity of the pigment cells in the skin (melanocytes) to increased circulating levels of the sex hormones, estrogen and progesterone.

Investigation None if the diagnosis is clear. If not, a small specimen of the skin may be removed and examined under a microscope.

Prevention None. The tendency to develop melasma is inherited.

Treatment
Self As the condition nearly always goes away within 9–12 months you should not attempt anything radical. Avoid sunlight and getting a tan because the brown patches will only turn darker and become more obvious. Whenever you go out in the sun, wear a shady hat and apply sunscreen cream every 2–3 hours.
Specialist In the hands of a dermatologist, bleaching creams may be tried. They should not be applied otherwise.
Alternative NB Old-fashioned bleaching agents like lemon juice etc., while recommended, will have no effect on this type of pigmentation.

ITCHING An irritation of the skin which is quite delicious to remove; a sensation which is impossible to resist and must be scratched.

Cause Inflammation, like dermatitis. Infections, like lice or scabies. Worry and anxiety. Chronic scratching.

Symptoms Itching, which may lead to further itching due to scratching. If the scratching continues the skin becomes thickened and scratching an ingrained habit.

Investigation Unrelieved itching of any sort should be investigated in a dermatology clinic.

Prevention Treating the underlying condition is the only prevention. Never continue to scratch your skin for longer than a few days without consulting your doctor.

Treatment
Self Apply a cooling lotion such as calamine. Never use an itch-relieving spray, which may contain sensitizing local anesthetics.
Medical Your doctor may prescribe creams containing tar or tar derivatives which are potent anti-itch substances. Anti-histamine tablets can do much to relieve itching, though they may make you sleepy (if they do, avoid driving a car and taking alcohol). A course of sleeping pills if the itching prevents sleep.
Specialist Sometimes it is necessary to use potent anti-inflammatory skin creams, though a dermatologist should supervise this therapy. They should only be used for a short time.
Alternative Sanicula is said to relieve rashes which itch.

ALLERGY A hypersensitivity to any substance which the body interprets as foreign. These substances are usually proteins, e.g. egg albumen, milk, fish. In the case of drugs, the drug attaches itself to a protein in the body.

Cause Precise reason for body recognizing the protein which has previously been accepted, as foreign, is not known. A general rule of thumb is that you can become allergic to anything at any time.

Symptoms Itchy rashes which are a response to a local allergy, e.g. the nickel under a watch or a necklace clasp, may be simply a red, scaly, irritating patch in the skin but if generalized they may produce nettlerash all over the body or sometimes angio-edema (swelling of the eyelids, face and lips). Possible difficulty in swallowing or breathing (if you experience these, get in touch with your doctor immediately).

Investigation Skin tests to find out the allergen. Exclusion diets to find a possible offending food.

Prevention As we do not have foreknowledge of what we may become allergic to, it is impossible to avoid development.

Treatment
Self Avoid the allergen once it is located. Use cooling lotions like calamine on the spots or swelling. Do not use proprietary creams which claim to relieve itching and contain a local anesthetic (read the label – a common one is benzocaine) as local anesthetics are potent sensitizing agents themselves and could make your allergy worse.
Medical A course of desensitizing injections which have a 50–50 chance of being successful. A course of antihistamines (be careful, they may make you sleepy for the first few days, so avoid alcohol and be careful when driving). If your allergy is very severe, your doctor may give you local anti-inflammatory steroid creams available only on prescription.
Specialist Further investigations particular to a dermatologist.
Alternative Acupuncture has been found to be effective in some cases.

BLISTERS Localized collections of fluid which may burst and release the liquid. Blisters vary in size from tiny pearly droplets (as in dermatitis, see p. 90) to large ones covering several inches of skin (as in severe burns).

Cause Commonest cause of blisters is friction, say from a tight or loose shoe, but they are also common as cold sores, shingles, burns and sometimes a reaction to drugs or damage to the skin by physical agents like strong sunshine.

Symptoms Soreness and tingling in the skin prior to the formation of blister.

Investigation If the cause is not obvious, investigations may have to be carried out in a hospital dermatology clinic.

Prevention For friction blisters, protect the skin by using special latex pads or two pairs of socks. Blisters of an infective origin can rarely be prevented. In the case of cold sores or shingles, the appearance of blisters may be aborted by the application of idoxuridine solution or ointment as soon as the skin begins to tingle, at half hourly intervals.

Treatment
Self A blister forms as a protective cushion when the skin is injured, so do not prick the blister immediately. If the blister bursts, keep the area dry and clean by covering it with a sterile dry gauze dressing. If the blister area scabs over, leave the scab to fall off itself.
Medical If the blister is thought to be of viral origin, your doctor may prescribe an idoxuridine preparation.
Specialist A specialist's opinion is only necessary if the blisters are part of a serious medical or dermatological condition.
Alternative Comfrey and shepherd's purse are said to aid skin healing in general. Herbalists suggest raw onions or potatoes and aromatherapists advocate camphor, chamomile and eucalyptus.

SENILE SPOTS Pigmented spots, flat, or raised circular brown spots in the skin, especially on backs of hands.

Cause Chronic, i.e. decades of exposure to sunlight. Don't forget that the backs of the hands are the areas of the body which are most exposed to daylight and sunlight. They appear at an earlier age in those countries where the number of sunshine hours is highest, e.g. Australia.

Investigation Usually none; only appropriate if the spot enlarges, becomes itchy, becomes more deeply pigmented.

Treatment
Medical No intervention unless any of the above pertain.
Specialist Surgical removal.

WHITEHEADS (Milia) Small, creamy white, raised, hard spots, usually in the skin around the eyes.

Cause Cysts of the sweat glands or sebaceous glands in areas where sebum secretion is low. The sebum collects inside the gland and becomes thick, hard and white. It does not burst as in acne.

Treatment
Self Sterilize a sewing needle. Cleanse the skin over the whitehead with a little antiseptic solution then prick the skin over the whitehead so that its surface is broken. Gently squeeze out the whitehead. Cleanse the skin with antiseptic solution. Whiteheads cause no trouble and if you are not concerned by their appearance, leave them alone.

CHILBLAINS Painful, itchy patches, which appear on any part of the body which is exposed to cold, worst in winter. In the cold, these reddish purple spots are sore and painful and on return to the warmth they become bright red and exquisitely itchy.

Cause There is a hypersensitivity of the blood vessels in the skin to cold. Initially they contract down, hence the soreness and purplish color, and then dilate up again when exposed to warmth, causing swelling and itching.

Symptoms Soreness and itchiness.

Prevention In cold weather make sure that the susceptible parts of your body are covered and warm. Wear warm socks, gloves, ear muffs etc.

Treatment
Self Wear as much warm clothing as you can find. If you suffer from cold feet, try thermal insoles inside your shoes or boots.
Medical Your doctor may be able to give you a cream containing nicotinic acid which will dilate the blood vessels.
Alternative No specific remedy but some agents are recommended by herbalists for improving the circulation. See varicose veins p. 135. Horseradish is said to redden and warm the skin (is a rubefacient).

HAIR

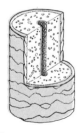

A thin protective outer layer surrounds the thicker cortex and the central core. The pigments of yellow, red and brown exist in the cortex and their proportions determine hair color.

That beautiful head of hair which you cherish, pamper, and are so proud of, is dead. Once you realize this, it becomes obvious that many of the exhortations put out by the media and advertisers to treat your hair with a multiplicity of creams, lotions and sprays, with the promise of putting new life into your hair, are patently untrue. You cannot enliven something which is dead. Only the tip of the growing hair root is alive, and it is buried deep within a hair follicle where it is nourished by capillary blood vessels. The main root is supplied with nerves (which are sensitive to distortion and this is why pulling the hair hurts). The nerve root buds off cells of keratin which are chemically strung together to form the hair shaft and which may be pigmented to various degrees, hence the differences in the color of our hair. Keratin scales are arranged very much like the feathers on a bird's wing: when your hair is in good condition, the scales lie smoothly on top of one another; when your hair is in bad condition, as it is after a chemical insult such as hair dyeing or bleaching, the keratin scales tend to curl up, and under a microscope look like ruffled bird feathers. You can see this quite clearly in the photographs below of a normal and a damaged hair.

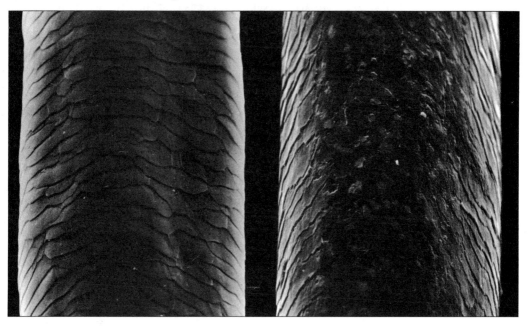

A perfect hair, with cuticle layer seen as being very smooth and very closed up along its length.

A severely damaged cuticle layer of hair which can be caused by over-exposure to alkaline products.

It follows, therefore, that the only way you can improve the innate quality of your hair is not by applying chemicals to the dead hair shaft, but by making certain that your inner health is good so that nourishment is brought to the hair root and that the newly-formed hair is of good quality. Such nourishment is guaranteed if you are eating a balanced diet and if you are not suffering an illness. Anyone living in the Western world and eating a balanced diet needs no supplements to ensure the health of the hair, but deficiencies of vitamins A and D are deleterious. It is claimed by some authorities that vitamin E is essential for the health of the skin and hair but this has never been scientifically proven.

Although clean hair may feel good, it is not healthier than hair which is not washed regularly. Unwashed hair may even be healthier, as the sebum which coats and lubricates the hair helps to keep these keratin scales smooth and flat and also acts as nature's own antiseptic on the hair. Over-zealous shampooing of the hair, therefore, is simply not logical. Furthermore, as the scalp and hair are self-cleansing under normal conditions, there is no need whatsoever for the so-called medicated shampoos, nor is there any justification for the claims made by manufacturers of these shampoos. They are quite unnecessary for the health of the hair and you can stop using them on yourself and your family now.

Antiseptics can cause allergies and at a basic biological level they can interfere with the natural balance of bacteria on the skin and hair which is necessary for their health.

Gray hair is just as strong and healthy as pigmented hair. All that happens when you get older is that the tiny organ in the hair root which is responsible for the deposition of pigment in the forming hair shaft ceases to work. This does not mean, however, that the keratin is second class. It's just as good as keratin produced in youth.

Hair-washing

The very best thing that you can do for your hair is to leave it alone. Left alone, the hair will look after itself and you will need to do no more than wash it every few days, according to how greasy it is and, your own personal taste.

The average head of hair needs washing about every three or four days. The best way to do it is as follows:

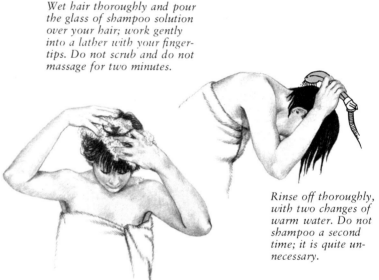

Wet hair thoroughly and pour the glass of shampoo solution over your hair; work gently into a lather with your finger-tips. Do not scrub and do not massage for two minutes.

Rinse off thoroughly, with two changes of warm water. Do not shampoo a second time; it is quite un-necessary.

Dissolve a dessert-spoonful of your shampoo in a glass of warm water and mix it well. This makes certain that the shampoo is distributed evenly through the hair.

Modern shampoos, chemically speaking, are detergents. Detergents exert their cleansing effect within about 30 seconds and can clean no more after that, even if they are applied for a second time. The maker's instructions which encourage you to shampoo twice are largely aimed at selling more shampoo. If you don't get a good lather the first time, it simply means that you have not distributed the shampoo efficiently through the hair, or you have not used quite enough.

Over-washing is deleterious to the hair and this includes over-zealous shampooing which takes into account shampooing more than once when you wash your hair, scrubbing, rubbing or massaging the head vigorously while shampooing. (When the scalp is wet it becomes soft and moist and hairs loosen up in their follicles. Too vigorous an action may loosen them completely.)

Shampoos　Always choose a mild shampoo. Probably the mildest shampoo you can find is a baby shampoo and what's good for a baby's hair can't be bad for a woman's hair. Many baby shampoos have the additional attraction of not stinging the eyes and they are usually cheaper. You need look no further. There is no evidence to show that shampoos with exotic ingredients have any more to offer than pure, simple baby shampoo.

On physiological and medical grounds, I am very attracted to the shampoos and conditioners which aim to restore and maintain the natural acidity of the scalp and hair. You have to be rather careful in examining the labels of hair products which claim to be "pH balanced" (pH is the scientific notation representing biological acidity, neutrality, or alkalinity. Neutral pH is 7.0, anything below it is acidic, anything above is alkaline. The skin's natural pH is between 3.5 and 5.5). Some manufacturers have jumped onto the bandwagon for pH-balanced products and simply add a weak acid to their shampoo or conditioner to bring it down to the skin's natural pH. You should be looking for a pH-buffered shampoo, so read the label to make sure that is what you are paying your money for. The same applies to conditioners that you might buy.

I am also in favor of "anti-oxidant" shampoos and conditioners, for purely chemical reasons, in that they help to rectify the harm which has been done by bleaches and dyes which act by oxidizing (liberating oxygen). This is exactly the same method which our grandmothers used to make whites whiter by spreading them out on the grass in strong sunlight, and, incidentally, is the way modern bleaches work.

The only time it becomes appropriate to use the plethora of hair cosmetics available, is when you insult your hair. An insult, albeit chemical, is a permanent, a dye, a tint or a bleach. All of these damage the hair but you can go some way to restoring it by the use of special shampoos and conditioners.

Permanents,　Permanents, even light ones, probably do more harm to the hair
dyes and tints　than anything else we put on it. They make the hair wavy and curly by first breaking the chemical bonds which hold the keratin scales together, and then fusing them in the curly or wavy shape. This is equivalent to melting down a gold bar and putting it into a mold to convert it to a new shape – it obviously cannot be good for the hair.

Dyes can either be chemical or vegetable and their effects are similar. They strip the hair and remove its natural color, or they give the hair new color by chemically binding a colored substance to the hair. However they do it, the process disrupts the normal physiology of the hair. Tints work in a similar way to dyes but the bonding of the color substance with the hair is not as strong and therefore the color tends to fade with washing.

Most of the chemicals used in perming, tinting and dyeing are strongly alkaline, and therefore disturb the hair's natural pH status. They also tend to distort the keratin scales, which curl up, and this makes the hair feel straw-like and very difficult to comb through. It is also why the effect of a conditioner is transient – it lasts, at the longest, the interval between shampoos, and sometimes not even as long as that.

Combing and brushing

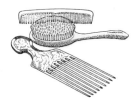

Rubbing and massaging the scalp in any way is not particularly good for it and this would include vigorous combing and brushing. The 100 brush strokes per side which our Victorian grandmothers used to advocate, did not do any good at all; in fact, all it did was to spread sebum down the hair and make greasy hair more greasy – sebaceous glands in the scalp respond to massage, brushing and rubbing by becoming more active. Increased sebum secretion will not improve the health of dry hair so, for most of us, the aim should be to tranquillize the scalp, not to stimulate it, and this applies particularly if you have a scalp complaint or even dandruff (which many people think to be abnormal but which is actually not). Massage, brushing and combing will only make the dandruff worse, so avoid stiff bristle brushes and fine combs; use soft brushes and wide-toothed combs.

Hair loss

A severe, generalized illness may show up in your hair: when your general health is undermined, so is the health of your growing hair, though it may not become apparent for several months. Hair growth goes in cycles; each individual hair grows for a period and then rests. At the end of the resting period it is shed. The length of these cycles varies from person to person, but because the hair grows 4 ins (10 cm) per year, and some women can sit on their hair, it is obvious that some growth plus rest cycles can last for several years.

Fortunately for us, adjacent hairs are not in the same part of the cycle at the same time. Therefore, though we lose up to about 100 hairs a day, they are from different parts of the scalp and we do not notice hair loss. A serious illness or a physiological event such as pregnancy may drive all the hairs into the resting phase at the same time. This means that they all may be lost around the same time, and this degree of hair loss can be quite frightening, as mothers who have lost a great deal of hair during the two years after a pregnancy will testify. The same can happen after a period of stress, anxiety or mental disturbance. Minor disturbances of hair growth can show themselves months later as lackluster hair, brittle hair, or hair that splits readily at the ends. There is very little that you can do about this.

Skin diseases which affect the scalp can also affect the health of the hair, and the most serious diseases are those which damage the hair follicle. If the follicles are permanently damaged, then hair growth ceases and will never restart. Only a trained dermatologist can tell you if the hair follicle is so badly damaged that hair loss is permanent and you should seek such an opinion before you go to a trichologist and waste money on hair restoratives when there is no chance of success. Under the supervision of a dermatologist it is sometimes possible to arrest the destruction of a hair follicle due to skin disease by the injection of potent steroids, but only your dermatologist can diagnose and treat these disorders.

Split ends   No matter how hard we try to do our best for our hair, the ends take a lot of punishment. First of all, they are the oldest, and if your hair is more than 12 inches long, then the tips are three years "dead." The ends also take the brunt of the force you use when you are brushing and combing, and are subjected to mechanical damage every day. They have been bleached and dried longest by exposure to the sun, and if your hair is permed or colored they may have been chemically assaulted many times.

It is not surprising, therefore, that they split. Split ends, *per se*, are nothing to worry about – you will only get problems when the split extends up the hair because then the ends will break off and your hair will become an uneven length. Even if your hair is unbleached, untinted, uncolored and unpermed, it's a good idea to have the ends, say, $1-1\frac{1}{2}$ ins (2.5–3.8 cm), trimmed off every twelve weeks or so, and if you do have chemicals of any sort put on your hair then the interval between trims should come down to six or eight weeks.

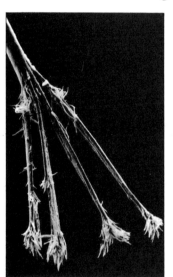

A severely split and damaged end of hair.

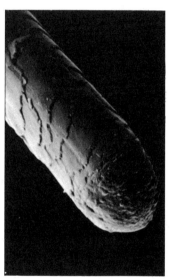

The end of a normal human hair.

A view of the cut ends of normal hair.

How can I keep my hair from "flying away" after shampooing?

Most tap water is alkaline due to the presence of salts, so after you have shampooed your hair you may find the static electricity makes it fly away and difficult to manage. Our grandmothers used to get over this by putting some lemon juice in the final rinsing water which made it acid and this reduced the static electricity.

Is artificial drying bad for the hair?

It's a good idea to give your hair a rest from any preparation or treatment every so often, even artificial drying. There is no reason why a hair dryer should do it any harm, but try letting your hair dry naturally in the sunshine in the open air once in a while – it's not just good for your hair, it's a very good feeling.

Can henna shampoo or rinses harm my hair?

Some natural hair cosmetics have stood the test of time and quite rightly. They have been subjected to the hardest test of all – millions of women over centuries – and have come through with flying colors. One of these is henna. There is hardly any hair, anywhere, which will not respond by being smoother, silkier, shinier and easier to manage after a henna treatment. This does not have to be expensive and it does not have to be performed in a hair salon. Very simple henna preparations are available at your local drugstore and most of them are effective.

Can hair dyes do me any harm?

It is not uncommon for the dye in hair tints and coloring to cause a skin allergy, which can be very severe, with weeping over the whole of the scalp, followed by crusting and scaling. This condition should be treated by a dermatologist.

In the United States, any hair dye which contains a coal tar derivative, 4-MMPD, has to carry a warning stating that laboratory tests on animals have shown that there is a possible link between this chemical and cancer.

COMMON HAIR COMPLAINTS

DANDRUFF Flaking of the skin of the scalp. Scales of skin pile up on the scalp, break loose and become lodged in the hair. It can be seen on the hair as small white flakes and may fall loose onto clothes.

Cause Dandruff is not infectious, nor is it abnormal. It is a variation of normal. Dead skin cells (in the shape of keratin scales) are being shed in their millions from the skin every day. They are rubbed off and lost without you noticing them. On the scalp, the presence of hair prevents the scales from being lost imperceptibly. They therefore tend to pile up and break off in visible flakes. The rate of turnover of the cells of the skin is affected by many factors, external and internal. Injury from sunburn (in the form of peeling) speeds up the turnover, so may inflammation of the skin (dermatitis), so may worry or stress. Skins vary in their individual reaction to these factors and even with individuals the rate may wax and wane. The presence of dandruff probably means that the scalp is in a sensitive state. It follows that one should do nothing to irritate it or make it more sensitive. The aim should be to soothe it; massage, rubbing, vigorous combing and brushing and the removal of individual scales with a fingernail can only worsen the condition.

Prevention Seborrhea, or even seborrheic dermatitis (dermatitis in an area of the skin where a lot of sebum is produced, e.g. ears, nasal folds, eyebrows, eyelashes, chest and shoulders) may underlie dandruff, and if your scalp is inflamed or if it weeps then you should consult your doctor for treatment of the underlying dermatitis. As your tendency to develop dermatitis is inherited, there is no way you can prevent this trait from showing.

Treatment
Self Wash your hair every 2–3 days, once only, with the mildest shampoo you can find, as described on p. 94. Use an anti-dandruff shampoo no more than once every two or three weeks. Do not use a medicated shampoo. The antiseptic may irritate your scalp and make your dandruff worse. Never over wash i.e. more than once, or scrub, or leave lather on the hair for longer than a minute or so. Never massage or vigorously brush and comb.
Medical If you have an underlying seborrheic dermatitis, your doctor may prescribe an anti-inflammatory steroid cream or lotion which is applied to the scalp in a special way. You make $\frac{1}{2}$-in partings all over your head and apply a thin smear of lotion or cream in each parting.
Specialist The dermatologist can only help you if you have an underlying seborrheic dermatitis – s/he may offer you more specialized treatment than your own doctor.
Alternative Salvia is said to specifically help dandruff. Drugstores carry herbal anti-dandruff shampoos of questionable value.

RINGWORM A fungal infection of the skin or scalp with irritating, circular, pink, scaly patches in the skin.

Symptoms Itchiness, soreness, sometimes weeping, very occasionally, with pustules.

Investigation Skin scrapings which are examined under a microscope, the diagnosis being confirmed by any strands of the fungus present.

Cause Fungus contracted from other people or animals, most commonly cats and mice.

Prevention Treat all cases and contacts promptly.

Treatment
Medical Specific anti-fungal cream, available only on prescription.
Specialist Nothing further to add as long as your own doctor can make the diagnosis. However, a dermatologist may make the diagnosis of ringworm when it is difficult to distinguish from other rashes.
Alternative Conserve of verbascum flowers is said to be useful in ringworm. Fluid extract of hydrastis.

LICE (Nits) An extremely itchy infection of the hair on the head, or pubic region.

Cause The head louse or the pubic louse. They are specific to human beings and they are passed on by contact. Adult lice lay eggs and cement them to the root of the hair.

Symptoms Itchiness.

Prevention All cases and contacts, particularly in the family, should be vigorously treated at the same time.

Treatment
Self There will be detailed instructions in the pack of anti-nit treatment that you buy, but generally this is the routine: follow the instructions on the package; when the treatment is complete, remove dead eggs from the hair with a fine metal or plastic tooth comb. If the itching does not subside immediately, repeat the treatment and the hair combing seven days later. Make sure you treat all members of the family and anyone in regular contact with the infected person.

EYES

Myths exist about what is good and bad for the eyes, as they do about any other part of the body. We were all chastised as youngsters for reading in a bad light, being told that it would strain our eyes. This is untrue. The eyes can't be strained by reading in a bad light, nor can they be strained by reading too much or by a lot of close work. The eyes are designed to see under all conditions. The eyes themselves have built-in mechanisms which make sight efficient at low-light intensities, over long periods, even when finely detailed work has to be done, so the eyes themselves cannot tire. The eyes are simply transmitters of light and light images through electrical impulses, and they can no more tire than an electric wire can tire of carrying a current.

It is the musculature of the eyes which may become fatigued. Each of the eyes has three pairs of muscles which work together to give us binocular vision: a pair of muscles of one eye works in an equal and opposite way to the other eye, so that both the eyes move together.

There are two important muscles inside the eye. One controls the size of the iris and is similar to the aperture in a camera, allowing different amounts of light into the eye; the other is the ciliary muscle which controls the size and shape of the lens. The lens is responsible for bending rays of light so that the image we are looking at falls exactly on the retina which, in turn, transmits the image to the brain. When we are doing very close work, the ciliary muscle has to contract quite a lot and this may tire it. Similarly, when we are working in exceptionally bright light, or we are in bright sunlight, the muscle of the iris has to constrict to prevent dazzle and may become fatigued.

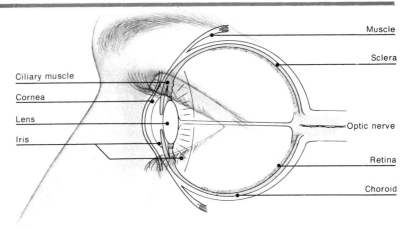

Light rays first pass through the transparent cornea which bends the rays through the first of the two chambers of the eye (the anterior chamber). At the back of this chamber are the iris and, just behind it, the lens. The colored iris controls the amount of light entering the eye; the lens focuses it onto the light-sensitive surface of the retina.

Tears

The eyes contain one of the most efficient natural antiseptic substances produced by the body – tears. Tears contain *lysozymes* which, as the word implies, "lies" or kills bacteria. Tears not only lubricate the eyes and help to keep the eyeball frictionless, they also irrigate, cleanse and sterilize the eyes.

Tears are being constantly secreted by the lachrymal glands which are situated in the outer and upper corners of the eye, underneath the upper eyelids. Tears are then circulated across and over the eyeball by a blinking action; having collected in the lower, inner corner of the eye they drain away through the pinpoint hole in the edge of the lower eyelid, down the tear duct and into the nose. (This is one of the reasons why your nose runs when you cry a lot.)

One of the most soothing things we can do for our eyes is to blink, and you will find this particularly beneficial in hot, dry atmospheres where the tears tend to evaporate from the surface of the eyeball, making it slightly dryer than normal, or if you have to stare very hard at something for long periods. Anything which interferes with our normal blink reflex (when the eyelashes are brushed we automatically close the upper lid), will reduce the circulation of tears across the eyeball and make the eyes sore.

Tears also have a protective action. Our eyes often water if we go into a smoky atmosphere or into a very cold wind. This is the eye's own way of trying to maintain itself at normal body temperature, to prevent noxious substances coming into contact with the conjunctiva (the outer covering of the eye), and also to sluice out any harmful particles which may enter the eye. The same happens when grit, dust or a foreign body get in the eye.

Eyelashes

Eyelashes are an essential part of the protective equipment of the eye. Their importance comes into perspective when the eyelashes grow abnormally. There is a condition when the eyelashes curve inwards as they grow, instead of outwards, and they scratch the surface of the eyeball, leading to sore, painful, red eyes which may eventually ulcerate. Under normal circumstances, the eyelashes act as a sieve for foreign bodies and also help to make a dust-proof seal when the eyelids are closed.

Skin around the eyes

This area is the subject of many beauty myths and high-pressure advertising advocating the use of special eye creams and uniquely formulated anti-wrinkle creams. The skin around the eyes is no different from the skin anywhere else in the body, except that it is rather thinner. In addition, it covers a hole: the hole being the orbit in the skull which surrounds the eye. Because there are few muscles underlying this skin, and not a lot of fat, it is not well supported and plumped out, and this means that it wrinkles very easily. Although it has been termed "delicate" by beauticians and cosmeticians, it is not delicate, nor does it need any special treatment. Anti-wrinkle creams are to be avoided, not only because their effect is transient, but also because many of them act by dehydrating the skin and causing it to contract (both effects should be avoided in skin which is on the thin side). No special eye cream can do more for the skin around the eyes than simple, good moisturizers and, as before, I would suggest using two. Apply your make-up on top of this and you will be doing all you can to preserve the bloom on the skin around your eyes. Nothing more complicated or more expensive will add to this.

Long and short sightedness

The eyeball tends to change shape as we get older. If it becomes too short, no matter how hard it tries, it projects an image which falls behind the retina, and the image is therefore blurred. If the eyeball becomes too long, the lens will throw an image in front of the retina. The first effect is associated with near-sightedness (*myopia*) and the second with farsightedness (*presbyopia*). Presbyopia is so common, as we reach the third and fourth decade, as to be accepted as a normal aging process, and it accounts for the need for reading glasses as we get older. Myopia can also be corrected by wearing spectacles.

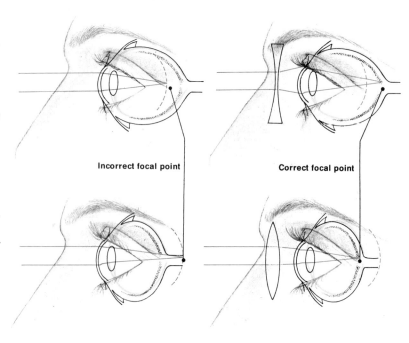

Myopia, or near-sightedness, arises when the lens focuses light rays from a distant source too far in front of the lens, resulting in a blurred image. It can be corrected by using a concave lens.

Presbyopia, or far-sightedness, results when light from a near object falls behind the retina. This can be corrected by using a convex lens.

Incorrect focal point

Correct focal point

Night vision

A good supply of vitamin A is necessary for night vision because it is the starting substance from which *rhodopsin* or "visual purple" is made. Visual purple is the pigment which is found in the lining of the back of the eye, the retina, and which helps us to see in the dark. Carrots are a good source of vitamin A. When I was a child I was encouraged by my mother to eat plenty of carrots because it would help me to see in the dark. This old wives' tale has an interesting origin. During the war, British pilots had a superior night-time bombing record than the German Luftwaffe. As a smokescreen for the British successes, the BBC broadcast to the Germans that the accuracy of the British pilots could be put down to the fact that their diet contained plentiful supplies of carrots.

Cleansing the eyes

The eyes are self-cleansing organs and they need no help whatsoever under normal circumstances. One of the best ways of cleaning out the eyes is to have a good cry, even though this may make the eyelids a bit puffy and red – this is because tears contain salts which make the tissues around the eye swell slightly. Nonetheless, the eyes are better off for having been thoroughly washed through by tears. Eye baths, eye washes and eye lotions are completely unnecessary and should never be used unless medically prescribed. Patent eye lotions which can be bought over the counter do nothing to improve your eyesight, eye comfort or the brightness of your eyes, despite their seductive claims.

Giving the eyes a good rub is a reflexive action which is both soothing and protective: it stimulates tear production, it promotes circulation of the tears around the eye, and it may dislodge microscopic particles of dust which irritate the surface. One of the drawbacks of complicated eye make-up is that it prevents women from periodically clearing the eyes in this way. However, rubbing too hard, pulling on the eyelashes, and using sharp instruments, irritate the eye and break down its natural integrity to repel invasion by bacteria and to maintain its health.

Foreign bodies in the eye

While holding this position, blink several times so that the lower lashes sweep the inner surface of upper lid.

Because the eye is such a sensitive organ and is very well supplied with sensory nerve endings, even a small foreign body which enters the eye feels very much bigger than it is. However, any foreign body can scratch the surface of the conjunctivae causing pain and possible ulceration and so should be removed as quickly as possible. You can attempt this yourself by pulling your upper eyelid over the eyelashes of the lower lid by grasping the eyelashes of the upper lid between the thumb and first finger and stretching the lid down over the lower lashes (see left), but, if this is not immediately successful, go straight to your nearest hospital emergency room, where it can be removed by experts. If your eye is weeping a great deal, do not wipe the tears away. This is the natural response of your eye and it is an attempt to flush out the foreign body from the eye and is very often successful. If the presence of the foreign body causes pain on blinking, then prevent blinking. You can do this very simply by taking a handkerchief folded into a small square and, with the upper eyelid closed, tape it over the eye socket so that the eye cannot be moved.

Glasses and contact lenses

Contrary to myth, starting to wear glasses does not make the eyes lazy, nor does it cause a deterioration in visual acuity; the two events are coincidental. Having to wear glasses is a signal that your eyesight is deteriorating and it will probably continue to do so whether you wear glasses or not; the glasses are not to blame.

Contact lenses are considered flattering by some women and necessary by others who play sports. There are two main kinds: hard lenses, which fit over the iris and retain their shape permanently and soft lenses, which cover a wider area of the eye and adjust their shape to the curves of the cornea. There exists a variety of types in both categories, including air-transmissible lenses, or semi-rigid lenses, which because of their relatively high gas permeability, can enhance both vision and comfort for hard lens wearers. Extended wear lenses, if approved by the F.D.A., can be worn for days at a time. Hard lenses are cheaper, more durable and produce better vision than soft lenses. Soft lenses are generally more comfortable to wear, but they are also friable, and, if worn for too long, they may encourage the growth of bacteria.

Sunglasses

Avoid strong, glaring sunlight for long periods. When I was a girl, we were told sunglasses were bad for us in that the eyes needed exposure to a certain amount of sunlight in order to "strengthen" them; recent medical research suggests that this belief is erroneous. Indeed, there is mounting evidence that prolonged exposure to strong sunlight may encourage the formation of cataracts (opacities over the eyes). So, if you go on vacation to a part of the world where the sun is very bright and glaring, or even if you find that the quality of the light on certain days makes you narrow your eyelids and constrict your pupils so as to cut down the amount of light entering the eye, or if you have to read in strong sunlight, wear protective sunglasses. Investing in a good pair of sunglasses, such as those which contain a pigment which darkens and screens the sun's harmful rays according to sunlight intensity, is a wise investment. Avoid cheap sunglasses.

COMMON EYE COMPLAINTS

BLEPHARITIS Inflammation of the rim of the eyelid.

Cause Seborrhea (too much sebum being secreted round each eyelash, or seborrheic dermatitis in a mild form), infection.

Symptoms Soreness of the margins of the eyelid, itching, scaling and possibly crusting. The eyes may be gummed together in the morning when you wake, or there may be a collection of pus or "sleep" in the inner corner of the eye.

Investigation Bacterial swab taken by your doctor.

Prevention Treatment of the pre-existing condition where there is a recognizable one.

Treatment
Self The best treatment is a simple household remedy: make a solution of a tablespoonful of salt, dissolved in a glassful of warm water. Bathe your eyes with an eye bath if you can, opening and blinking the eyes in the warm, soothing salt solution several times before throwing the water away. Repeat 5–6 times for each eye. If you do not have an eye bath, cotton wool soaked in the salt solution is almost as good.
Medical Your doctor may prescribe: an antibiotic eye cream to get rid of the infection; an anti-inflammatory eye cream to treat the underlying seborrheic dermatitis or a combination of the first two.
Specialist Referral to a dermatologist may help with treatment of an underlying seborrheic dermatitis. An ophthalmologist will not be able to add to this opinion as the cause is primarily in the skin, the eyelashes and their seborrheic glands.
Alternative Nothing more than general remedies for the health of the eyes, such as golden-seal.

CONJUNCTIVITIS Inflammation of the conjunctivas.

Symptoms Red, sore, stinging, itchy eyeball, watering of the eyes, sensitivity to light.

Cause Infection, glaucoma (increase of pressure within the eyeball), foreign body.

Investigation Bacterial swab taken by your doctor to locate the offending organism if the cause is infective.

Treatment
Medical If your doctor suspects an infection he will give you an antibiotic ointment or antibiotic drops. If there is an increase in pressure in your eyeball, s/he will prescribe eyedrops, and tablets to eliminate water from your body (diuretics). If there is a foreign body present in the eye which s/he cannot remove, s/he will refer you to an emergency room for expert attention.
Specialist Recalcitrant or recurrent conjunctivitis of infective origin may need a specialist's investigation to find a cause, and this can be done in a hospital department and laboratory. The same would apply for glaucoma, which does not respond to simple remedies.
Alternative As for blepheritis.

SORE/TIRED EYES Gritty feeling in the eyes and the need to blink.

Cause Lack of blinking due to concentration, tension of the muscles which control the movement of the eyeball, overuse of the ciliary muscle.

Symptoms Feeling of dryness, possibly itching and soreness of the eyes, tiredness after a lot of reading or close work.

Treatment
Self If you are undertaking close work, raise your eyes and look at the farthest object in the room. This automatically relaxes the ciliary muscles. At intervals, close your eyes and count up to 60. This rests the muscles of the eyeball. Blink frequently whenever you remember.
Alternative Cotton wool soaked in witch hazel and slices of cucumber laid on the eyes are both soothing remedies.

PINGUECULAE Horizontal bands of yellowish substance (fat deposits), spreading out from either side of the iris towards the corners of the eye.

Cause High blood cholesterol levels.

Investigation Full medical examination from your doctor, including examination of the heart, blood pressure, ECG and blood biochemistry (including blood cholesterol).

Prevention Eat a diet low in saturated and animal fat, and foods that contain cholesterol.

Treatment
Self Eat a low cholesterol diet with only small quantities of saturated or animal fat. Substitute polyunsaturated fats for animal fat.
Medical Pingueculae give any doctor a clue to the state of the patient's arteries. If there are deposits of fat in the eyes, there are almost certainly deposits of fat in the walls of their blood vessels, so making them more likely to suffer from heart or arterial disease. They alert the doctor to the need for immediate precautionary action such as advice about diet and examination to see whether or not the heart is under strain.

EARS, NOSE AND THROAT

The ears, nose and throat should be considered as one interconnecting system because, anatomically speaking, all three of them are connected by fine tubes and passageways. It is important to understand this because it explains why infection travels quickly from one part to another and why it is necessary to treat the symptoms in one part of the system quickly and thoroughly to prevent all three parts from becoming infected: if you suspect that you have an ear or throat infection, see your doctor immediately.

Ears The ear has three parts: the outer ear (the external auditory canal) which reaches up to the ear drum, the middle ear which contains tiny bones which transmit sound as sound, and the inner ear which contains our balancing organ and contributes to the mechanisms by which we keep our bodies upright, corrects their position if and when we veer from the upright position, and sends messages to the brain about the position of the body. As far as aural hygiene and day-to-day care go, we need only concern ourselves with the external auditory canal.

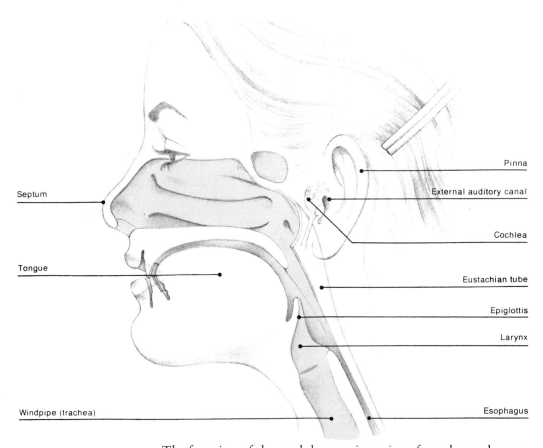

Pinna

External auditory canal

Septum

Cochlea

Tongue

Eustachian tube

Epiglottis

Larynx

Windpipe (trachea)

Esophagus

The function of the ear lobe, or pinna, is to funnel soundwaves towards the ear drum, and to do this effectively it must have a funnel-like shape. The skin which lines the external auditory canal is covered in fine hair and grease glands; the hairs prevent penetration of foreign bodies as far as the ear drum, and a rich production of grease, which when dry looks brown and waxy, coats the lining of the canal with a good thick layer of what is quite a powerful antiseptic substance to help prevent infection. If the lining of the canal is irritated by cleansing the ears with cotton swabs, or with a sharp instrument such as a hairpin or even a fingernail, or if the wax is removed, the sebaceous glands will respond by producing more wax.

If you think that your ears may be blocked with wax (and this is much rarer than people seem to think), do not try to remove the wax yourself but go and see your doctor, who can remove it easily, efficiently and painlessly by syringing out the ears with warm water. Under ordinary circumstances, insufficient wax is produced to block the external auditory canal. It is only if there is an underlying malfunction of the sebaceous glands that this occurs, and it is usually linked with chronic infection or chronic inflammation elsewhere in the ear, nose and throat area – for instance, chronic middle ear infection or chronic sinusitis.

Hearing loss A growing inability to hear sounds clearly – they may be blurred, muffled or distorted – is a positive indication of deafness.

There are two causes of deafness. The first is due to a sort of arthritis of the chainy bones which occupy the middle ear and which transmit sound waves to the nerve endings in the inner ear. When the joints between these tiny bones become stiff, the sound waves are transmitted inefficiently. The second is due to a deterioration in the sensitivity of the nerve endings in picking up sound waves and converting them to electrical impulses to be carried to the brain.

The distinction between a conduction and a nerve type of deafness can only be made by an ear specialist using special equipment. Only the conduction type of deafness can be prevented and that only when it is related to middle ear infections which must be treated rigorously and promptly and not allowed to become chronic. Such deafness is helped by hearing aids which can be fitted in the appropriate department of your local hospital, but you will need referral from your own doctor. The other type of deafness has no treatment.

There are some highly specialized, refined, surgical techniques which are aimed at improving the conduction of sound by the bones of the middle ear. These techniques are practiced at most teaching hospital ear departments and you can seek referral there by your own doctor if you have a conduction deafness.

COMMON EAR COMPLAINTS

VERTIGO Attacks of dizziness when you become unsteady on your feet, lose your balance and fall, often brought on by being in high places.

Cause In the absence of inner ear disease, the commonest cause of dizziness is violent movements of the head from side to side or backwards and forwards, causing the sensory organs in the inner ear to become confused about the position of the head and to send confusing messages to the brain and to make you feel dizzy. Messages from the eyes are instantaneous in that they are transmitted by electrical currents. Messages from the ears, however, lag behind those of the eyes because they are dependent on the movement of fluid. By the time the brain has received the message from the balancing organ about the position of the head, it has assessed and taken action on that same message from the eye and is on to the next.

Symptoms Dizziness, lack of balance, nausea, vomiting.

Investigation If the cause is not immediately obvious to your own doctor it should be undertaken by a specialist such as a neurologist or an ENT specialist.

Prevention In the case of motion- or sea-sickness, avoid travelling or take an anti-motion sickness tablet which damps down the sensitivity of the balancing organ prior to travelling.

Treatment
Self As for prevention, plus: close your eyes so that your brain only gets one set of messages about the position of your body, i.e. from the balancing organ. When on board ship, go to the lowest part of the ship where the movement is least. Do not eat a large, rich meal before travelling. Do not stand up quickly from a kneeling or crouching position or jump quickly out of a hot bath. This causes the blood to pool in the lower limbs, resulting in a relative shortage to the brain which will make you feel transiently giddy.
Medical Potent anti-vertigo remedies available only on prescription.
Specialist Not necessarily applicable unless the cause is serious neurological disease.
Alternative Coltsfoot, catnip, peppermint and eyebright are sometimes recommended, especially if headache is present.

EARACHE Pain in the region of the ear which may be of a sharp, throbbing or aching character and seems to be referrable to the ear. It may feel deep or superficial.

Cause An infection (usually an infected sebaceous gland) of the external auditory canal; an infection of the middle ear causing an increase in pressure in the middle ear; toothache; dental abscess; sinusitis; sore throat; or tonsilitis. These are just a few of the causes of earache and the point in listing them is to show that pain in any structure surrounding the ear may give rise to pain in it.

Symptoms Pain in the region of the ear sufficient to warrant treatment with pain killers to relieve the symptoms.

Investigation This can only be carried out by a doctor, so consult him/her if your earache persists for longer than 6–8 hours.

Prevention Do not fiddle with the external auditory canal. Always go to your doctor if you suffer from recurrent middle ear infection and make sure you take the full course of antibiotics even though your symptoms may subside before the course is finished.

Treatment
Self The application of a warm pad is sometimes soothing. To ease the pain, take two soluble aspirins dissolved in water, every 4 hours. Do not take any more than 3 doses without consulting your doctor.
Medical By examination, your doctor will be able to narrow down the cause of your earache and give you specific treatment which may involve: a course of antibiotic therapy taken by mouth; local antibiotic cream to be put in the external auditory canal; referral to a dentist to make sure that the pain is not being caused by a dental infection; referral to an ear, nose and throat specialist for an expert examination and opinion.
Specialist Unless the earache is recurrent, a specialist's treatment is unnecessary. In recalcitrant cases, where the cause is chronic middle ear infection due to bouts of tonsilitis, then a specialist may recommend a tonsillectomy.
Alternative As the underlying cause may be serious, alternative remedies should not be used until serious disease has been excluded. Alternative remedies include angelica, anemone, chickweed, hops.

TINNITUS A ringing or buzzing sound in the ears, occasionally accompanied by muffling of sound, dizziness and loss of balance.

Cause Several drugs can cause tinnitus (especially if the blood levels get higher), for example, aspirin, antibiotics such as streptomycin and erythromycin, and you should inform your doctor straight away if you experience these symptoms. A second cause of tinnitus which usually shows itself in middle age is Ménière's syndrome. This is due to a change in the amount of salt in the balancing organ.

Symptoms Ringing or buzzing in the ear, dizziness, loss of balance, nausea, vomiting.

Investigation Part of this can be done by your own doctor but s/he may feel it is necessary to refer you to an ENT specialist so that more complex investigations can be completed and the exact cause of your tinnitus can be found.

Treatment
Self If the tinnitus is drug-induced it is not always possible to prevent it. If you are suffering from Ménière's syndrome, you can help yourself by making sure that you stick to a diet which is low in salt.
Medical If the tinnitus is drug-induced, the doctor may quite rightly not wish to reduce your dose of drugs because the tinnitus is not necessarily a symptom of overdosage, but only that your dosing regimen has achieved the required levels of the drugs in your blood. This would be so in aspirin medication for rheumatic heart disease and for severe arthritis. If you are suffering from Ménière's disease this can be quite successfully treated using diuretics and drugs which alleviate dizziness.

Nose One of the most important functions of the nose is to moisturize inhaled air which, if dry, can be irritating to the bronchial tubes. Air is moisturized if the lining of the nose is kept well lubricated with mucus which is secreted by cells scattered throughout the lining. Drying out of the lining of the nose not only causes a prickly, itching sensation inside the nose, it is also detrimental to the air passages so that anything which dries out the nasal cavities is to be avoided. Fierce central heating is not usually sufficient to do this, but a long air flight, where the air is filtered and circulated, will quite often produce nasal discomfort due to drying out of the nasal membranes.

More than merely being anti-social, picking the nose may be harmful, especially if the tiny delicate area just inside the inner part of each nostril is damaged. In most people there is a bed of capillary blood vessels very near the surface of the skin, and if these are damaged the nose may bleed profusely. Remember, too, to avoid blowing your nose extremely hard (particularly if you have a tendency to nose bleeds), as forceful nose blowing may rupture the tiny blood vessels.

Mechanical intervention of the nasal cavities, just as with the external auditory canal, should always be avoided – foreign bodies should never be pushed into the nose even, as a playful act, as they may penetrate up into the nasal cavities (which reach as high as the eye) and be extremely difficult to remove. If a foreign body does get high into the nose, do not attempt to remove it yourself, but go immediately to a hospital emergency room.

COMMON NOSE COMPLAINTS

SINUSITIS Bacterial infection and inflammation of any or all of the three pairs of sinuses in the facial bones.

Cause Bacterial invasion, quite often superimposed on a viral infection such as the common cold or flu, which undermines the health of the lining of the sinuses and which is transmitted from the nose or the throat.

Symptoms Severe ache and tenderness over the affected sinus, i.e. just above the eyebrows, just on the cheek bones, on either side of the bridge of the nose, copious discharge from the nose and loss of resonance of the voice.

Investigation If recurrent, X-ray of the skull may show fluid levels which suggest a chronic infection and the presence of pus.

Prevention If you have a tendency to develop sinusitis every time you get a cold, then it is worth getting some special nose drops from your doctor which will facilitate drainage from the sinuses and therefore prevent the collection of fluid and secondary bacterial infection. You should never use these nose drops more often, or for longer, than your doctor tells you. You will prevent sinusitis becoming chronic by taking antibiotic therapy for the full course.

Treatment
Medical The sinuses, anatomically speaking, are sealed-off bags and it is very difficult to get high concentrations of antibiotics that will kill off bacteria into them. It is sometimes necessary, therefore, to take prolonged courses of antibiotics to completely eradicate the infection. Should your doctor prescribe such a course, make sure that you take it until all the tablets are used. If sinusitis is recurrent it may be necessary to refer you to an ENT specialist.
Specialist In an attempt to completely eradicate a chronic infection an otolaryngologist may suggest that you have sinus wash-outs which are just as the word suggests and are usually performed as an out-patient.
Alternative No specific remedy. Hyssop, fennel, coltsfoot and chickweed are said to "clear and relieve the respiratory tract".

COMMON COLD Viral infection of the nose and throat. Itchiness, prickling, dryness and soreness with running of the nose, soreness of the throat.

Cause The common cold virus.

Symptoms In addition to the local symptoms described above, generalized symptoms such as headache, aches and pains in the muscles and joints (particularly backache), headache and raised temperature.

Investigation None worthwhile.

Prevention Rarely possible.

Treatment
Self Treatment of the common cold is entirely symptomatic and you may as well do that yourself without bothering the doctor. Relieve your discomforts, aches, pains and high temperature by taking two soluble aspirin or other preferred pain-killer every 4 hours until your symptoms have abated. If the lining of your nose is very inflamed and breathing is difficult, use an over-the-counter cold remedy to relieve your blocked nose. Ease your sore throat by sucking lozenges according to the manufacturer's instructions, and no more often. If you are feeling really ill and have a high temperature, stay in bed. You do not need to take any food but make sure you take plenty of fluids, i.e. three pints in one day and more if your temperature is raised. Until your temperature has come back to normal, stay in a room where the temperature is fairly constant.
Medical Not necessary unless you have another underlying medical condition, e.g. diabetes, heart disease.
Alternative Vitamin C tablets: one, 3–4 times a day or cinnamon, ginger and marjoram infusions, oil of wintergreen and chamomile inhalants can unblock air passages.

NOSE BLEEDS Bleeding from the nose, usually precipitated by increasing the blood pressure in the head.

Cause Increased blood pressure in the head due to nose-blowing, coughing, vomiting, getting very angry; superficial blood vessels in the lining of the nose prone to rupture; picking the nose.

Investigations Examination by specialist to see where the superficial vessels are or if the hemorrhage is coming from a benign polyp.

Prevention Avoiding raising the blood pressure in the head whenever possible. Avoid picking the nose. Having any polyp in your nose removed surgically.

Treatment
Self When the nose bleed occurs, keep the head forward and down. Never put the head back; if you do so you will swallow the blood. Blood being a direct irritant on the stomach you will only make matters worse by precipitating vomiting. With the head in the forward and down position, an ice pack placed over the bridge of the nose may help. If you know that the hemorrhaging is coming from the delicate area just inside the nostril, squeezing quite firmly between the finger and thumb may be sufficient to staunch the flow of blood.
Specialist Removal of a polyp. Cautery of a small area of superficial blood vessels so that they are obliterated.
Alternative Yarrow, plantain and potentilla are said to have styptic properties (they staunch bleeding).

ANOSMIA Loss of the sense of smell, inability to savor the flavors of food. Your tongue may still be able to distinguish salts, sweet, sour and bitter tastes.

Cause You may be born with it or it may be secondary to a fracture of the skull involving the nasal bone and damage to the nasal nerves. It may be secondary to chronic sinusitis; smoking dulls the sense of taste.

Symptoms Food is bland and tasteless to the point where it may be impossible to distinguish chopped apple from onion.

Investigation Unless investigated immediately it is perceived, investigation is rarely fruitful.

Prevention Treat sinusitis promptly and rigorously.

Treatment
Self Be meticulous about taking courses of antibiotics for chronic sinus infections. Stop smoking.
Medical If the olfactory nerves are damaged there is nothing that can restore the sense of smell.

HAY FEVER The production of antibodies in the cells lining the nose and the eyes to a substance the body interprets as foreign, very often pollen and dust, producing inflammation in the nose and the eyes.

Cause An allergy to tree, grass or flower pollen, horse, cat or dog fur, house dust etc.

Symptoms Soreness, itching, redness and running of the nose and eyes, possibly with sneezing.

Investigation Should be undertaken by an allergist using skin-testing techniques to isolate the offending allergen.

Prevention Avoid the allergen.

Treatment
Self Using a course of desensitizing injections, at least 6 months before the appearance of a seasonal allergen, there is a 50% chance that your allergy will be cleared, so see your doctor if you feel it will help.
Medical A course of desensitizing injections; antihistamines from your doctor; local anti-inflammatory nose drops or sprays, available on prescription from your doctor.
Alternative Coltsfoot and golden-seal are said to be useful.

MOUTH, TEETH AND GUMS

The mouth is almost the dirtiest place in the body, bacteriologically speaking. However, so delicately balanced is this particular population, that we should resist all attempts to interfere with or change it. Even a slight imbalance can result in an over-growth of one species of bacterium; for example, when we suck too many antiseptic lozenges for a sore throat this suppresses certain species of bacteria and allows others to overgrow. The others might well be yeasts, and the result can be a nasty thrush infection of the mouth which may spread quickly down the rest of the gastrointestinal tract.

Yet again, I must reiterate the basic rule about hygiene in the body, certainly where delicate linings and membranes are concerned: leave well alone; do not wash, rinse, and swill out with antiseptic solutions to get rid of smells, tastes, and odors which we have been programmed to think of as bad, unwanted and unpleasant. A good rule to remember is that if you feel you need to use a proprietary remedy, say a mouth wash, for more than a few days at a time, than it's a doctor's or dentist's opinion you need and not something from a bottle.

Eating, drinking, chewing, swallowing and talking are all good for the mouth and there are several reasons for this. First, the presence of food in the mouth stimulates the secretion of saliva which, like tears, is a natural lubricant and cleansing agent; it helps to keep the surface of the mouth clean of debris. Secondly, any movement of the parts of the mouth, including the tongue, helps to get rid of the dead cells which are constantly being shed from the surface of the oral membranes. The lining of the mouth reproduces itself more rapidly than any other tissue in the body, except for the bone marrow (and the rest of the gastro-intestinal tract). New cells are constantly budded off and old dead cells sloughed away. If they are not removed efficiently by the actions of eating, drinking, chewing, swallowing and talking, then they tend to pile up. An example of this is a yellowish-brown furry tongue which has quite wrongly been taken to be an index of bad health or an upset stomach. It is not. It simply means that the cells from the surface of the tongue, which are normally removed and swallowed, have been allowed to collect.

To be healthy, the mouth has to remain moist and well-lubricated. If it dries out, as it does in a mouth-breather or in someone who breathes through the mouth throughout the night, then it not only smells rather unpleasant, but its health is undermined and bacteria are encouraged to multiply in abnormal numbers.

The health of the teeth is at least 50% dependent on the health of the gums; in the Western world, many more teeth are lost through gum disease than through tooth decay (see p. 114). Brushing the teeth regularly and frequently (at least twice a day) is the best possible way to maintain and protect the health of the teeth and gums.

Tooth brushing

There are fads and fashions in tooth brushing techniques, and over the years dentists have advocated several alternative methods. However, most dentists would agree that the single most important thing is that you choose a method which is suitable for you and which is efficient. At one time, a rolling action was propagated with a downward motion for the upper teeth and an upward motion for the lower teeth. This, however, was shown to be only about 50% as effective as the technique which is now generally recommended – a gentle, rapid, short, to-and-fro action in the horizontal plane. You should take care not to press too hard and not to see-saw the toothbrush backwards and forwards as this may damage the delicate gum margin.

TOOTHBRUSHES

The dental profession is fairly well united on the sort of toothbrush you should use and the frequency with which you should choose it. Here are some guidelines:

- The toothbrush should have a short handle so that it is easy to control, so that you know exactly where the head of the brush is and so that it doesn't waggle about in your mouth;
- The handle of the brush should be straight, without any bends in it, so that again you can direct the head accurately;
- The head of the brush should be fairly small and the bristles should be fairly short;
- Choose nylon bristle, not pure bristle, because it resists splitting and bending better than the natural material;
- Make sure that the heads of the bristles are absolutely flat. On no account choose a toothbrush with a serrated edge;
- The bristles should not be too hard; choose one labelled "Medium";
- If you brush your teeth twice a day, then buy a new toothbrush at least every six weeks, or as soon as the bristles become misshapen.

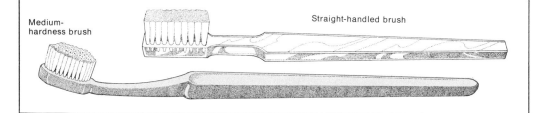

Medium-hardness brush

Straight-handled brush

Dental floss Using dental floss is an excellent adjunct to tooth brushing. It has to be used carefully so as not to damage the delicate margins of the gum. Use it as follows:

Wind a 4–6 in. length of floss around the first two fingers of each hand. Slide it gently down between two teeth, taking care to press it against the side of the tooth. (Do not see-saw it against the surface of the gum.) With a gentle, firm movement, swing it upwards, pressing against the side of the other tooth and removing any debris with it.

Tooth care Dentists are necessary for the health as well as the ill-health of the teeth and gums and you should visit your dentist every six months. S/he practices preventive as well as curative dentistry and can attack and treat tooth decay long before it gets to the stage where radical dentistry is needed. Your dentist can also advise on and recommend specialist treatment for teeth. Cosmetic dentistry may become necessary later on even if your early teeth were good.

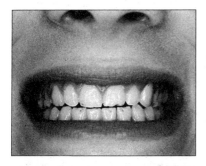
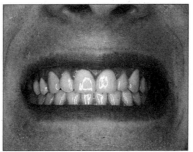

This patient's pitted and slightly decayed. teeth were greatly improved by cosmetic dentistry. To cap the teeth the outer layer of enamel was removed, and used as a mold for a porcelain crown which was then cemented into position.

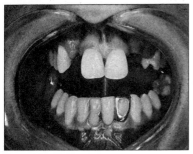
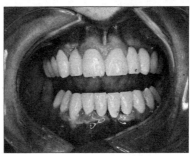

As this patient had no incisors, it was necessary to use a "fixed" bridge to hold the crowns in position. The bridge was anchored to the nearest strong teeth. Good dental care and regular hygiene would have prevented this being necessary.

Your hygienist, too, has an important part to play in keeping your gums healthy: s/he will expertly descale the teeth and remove any calcarius deposits from the gum margins which are often the start of gum disease.

Both calcium and vitamin D are essential for the health of the teeth, but not necessarily in the way that some people think. There are a lot of old wives' tales about them, one of them being that when you are pregnant your baby will remove calcium from your teeth, thereby undermining their health. This conception is completely untrue.

However, women should understand that they do determine the health and strength of their baby's primary teeth because they are being laid down in the baby's jaw while it is developing *in utero*. This means that all mothers must pay particular attention to taking plenty of calcium and vitamin D during pregnancy. It does not mean that they must drink a pint of milk a day (some doctors even advocate two), as there are many other excellent sources of calcium and vitamin D. Milk, however, is convenient, and you can take it in other forms, like custards or sauces. If, however, you hate milk and dairy products, simply consult a list of foods with high calcium content (see p. 25) and choose those for which you have a preference.

While it is a myth that your teeth suffer during pregnancy, your gums certainly do – one of the effects of the high level of circulating estrogen and progesterone which occurs during pregnancy is softening of the gum margins. Unless you pay meticulous attention to your diet and tooth brushing, this predisposes to the deposition of plaque, and for this reason alone, you should visit your dentist two or three times during pregnancy to make sure all is well.

Tooth decay

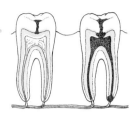

Bacterial decay initially destroys the tooth enamel. If left, this decay descends through the dentine and pulp layers, causing root abscess and severe pain.

There is unequivocal evidence to show that the sort of diet we eat affects the health of our gums and teeth, and that dental decay is caused in the main by sweet, sugary foods containing *sucrose*. Such foods include most refined foods and sweet drinks, sweets, chocolate and ice cream. If you want to have healthy teeth do not eat sweet, sugary foods or drinks between meals – within 20 minutes of taking such foods, damage to your gums and teeth has already begun.

If you can't avoid sweet things, try to brush your teeth immediately afterwards, and certainly before going to bed (and make sure you encourage these good habits in your children too). Dentists agree that "safe snacks" would include any fresh raw fruits or vegetables, potato chips, nuts or cheese. Cheese is a particularly useful and healthy food for the mouth, gums and teeth, as it stimulates the production of saliva and it is a very good way to end a meal. Saliva is alkaline and it shifts the pH of the mouth into the alkaline range to inhibit bacterial fermentation (which is the initial process that starts off tooth decay).

Fluoride

There is unequivocal evidence that fluoride, in all its forms, protects the teeth against decay and it is most effective if the flouride is actually in the teeth. By far the best way of taking fluoride, of course, is in drinking water, but there are few parts of the world where fluoride is added to the water and it's therefore up to you to make sure that you always use fluoride toothpaste and take fluoride in your diet or in the form of tablets.

A pregnant mother, however, cannot perform this service for an unborn baby. It used to be thought that if a pregnant mother took fluoride tablets every day then some of the fluoride would find its way into the baby's developing teeth; we now know that this is not so. The placenta is an extremely efficient filtering organ and it filters off the fluoride before it reaches the baby. However, as soon as your baby is old enough to take a fluoride tablet, then you should make sure that s/he has one each day and should continue to do so up to the age of 11. You will be doing your children an extra flavor if you get them to chew the tablets up and not swallow them whole. The chewing action crunches up the tablets and coats the teeth with a layer of fluoride and we know that a film of fluoride on the teeth makes them locally resistant to attack from tooth decay. The same applies to fluoride toothpastes, and it works for grown-ups, too. On a reassuring note, there is no evidence whatsoever linking fluoride with the development of cancer – an argument used by the anti-fluoride lobby.

Plaque

The arch villain of gum disease is plaque. Plaque is a thin film that forms over the teeth and is made up of bacteria and soft material which is formed from the saliva and the bacterial cells themselves. The formation of plaque is encouraged by eating or drinking sweet, starchy foods, particularly sweet snacks between meals.

Plaque starts off as a rather soft, sticky substance but, if not removed, may eventually become rock hard due to the incorporation of calcium. Inside it, bacteria thrive and multiply, producing acid which corrodes the outer protective enamel of the teeth. The bacteria are allowed to bore their way into the dentine of the teeth (which is sensitive and causes tooth ache) and if not arrested may eventually work their way through to the inner living part of the tooth, the pulp cavity.

Plaque is usually deposited around the lower parts of the teeth, at the gum margins. When it becomes hard and gritty it irritates the gums and they become soft and swollen. Pockets may form within which bacteria flourish and the gum margins may become chronically infected. The next step is *pyorrhea*, which is extremely difficult to eradicate. The gum margins become loose and puffy around the base of the tooth and they recede, leaving the tooth loose and unsupported. The best possible way of preventing plaque formation is attention to diet and careful, regular and frequent brushing.

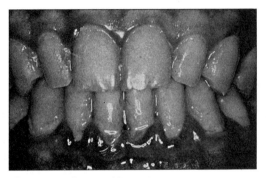

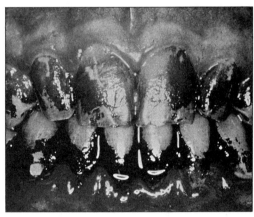

Plaque, usually invisible to the eye, shows up as dense areas of color when a "disclosing tablet" is chewed.

Smoking Somewhere down at the bottom of the list on the hazards of smoking would come the deleterious effect on the mouth. Smoking upsets the natural bacterial flora of the mouth, it causes unpleasant mouth odor and it stains the teeth, mouth, even the skin surrounding the lips, an unpleasant yellowish color. If you habitually hold a cigarette in your mouth in one position, for long periods at a time, the concentration of tars and heat may even produce inflammation and soreness of the tongue and lips, and possibly the formation of an ulcer.

Do drugs affect the teeth in any way?

Certain drugs can affect the health of the gums and teeth. Antiepileptic drugs, such as the hydantoins, can make the gum margins red, soft and swollen. If you are an epileptic and you are satisfactorily treated with hydantoin drugs, this is not something you can avoid, but you should be aware of it.

Tetracyclines, if taken by a pregnant mother, may be deposited in her baby's developing teeth and may stain the teeth a yellowish color. This does not mean that the teeth are any less healthy nor is there any way that the stain can be removed, but it is as well that you know about this.

What can I do about bad breath?

The usual causes are eating, drinking, bad teeth, infected gums, mouth ulcers, smoking and alcohol, but many people suffer from halitosis for no known reason.

Check with your dentist to make sure that your gums and teeth are in good health. Make sure that you do not go for long periods without eating or drinking, and if you smoke and drink, the answer lies with yourself.

Mouthwashes are to be avoided. The best you can do is to try to camouflage the odor by sucking mints or cachou. Chlorophyll sticks or tablets may also help.

COMMON MOUTH COMPLAINTS

GINGIVITIS Sore, red, swollen, inflamed gum margins.

Cause Nearly always infection, but may be due to taking hydantoin drugs (see p. 115).

Symptoms Sore, irritable, bleeding gums.

Investigation Your dentist or doctor may be able to make the diagnosis by examination or by a bacterial swab to isolate the infecting organism.

Prevention Regular, frequent and proper brushing of the teeth. Regular treatment of your teeth by hygienist and your dentist.

Treatment
Medical It is difficult to eradicate if the condition becomes chronic, so you should never allow this to happen. Your dentist may give you antibiotics, by mouth, in severe cases. If it is localized, a gingivectomy (cutting away the infected gum margin) may be suggested, followed by the use of dental sticks or dental floss to harden the gum margin.

PYORRHEA Chronic infection of the gums, with loosening and eventual loss of the teeth. Pockets form on the gums which harbor infection.

Cause Poor oral and dental hygiene.

Symptoms Sore, inflamed, puffy gums that bleed. Bad breath. Tooth decay.

Investigation Your dentist may take a swab to culture the infecting bacteria.

Prevention Careful tooth brushing (see p. 112). Regular visits to the dentist. Prompt treatment of any gum infections.

Treatment
Self Astringent mouthwashes, to be used only under dental supervision.
Medical Treatment with antibiotics as appropriate; gingivectomy to remove chronically infected pockets; removal of loose teeth.

COLD SORES Blisters caused by the herpes virus; related to the chickenpox virus. The affected skin (usually around the mouth, but nearly always below a line which can be drawn between the nose and the tip of the ear) becomes sore, blisters, then bursts and scabs over.

Cause The herpes virus is constantly present, lying dormant in the skin. It is awakened by an increase in the body temperature which may be due to ovulation (when the temperature may rise one whole degree) due to an infection such as a cold or flu or simply the sun.

Symptoms About 10–12 hours before the blister appears, the skin tingles, becomes sore and may feel hot or cold. The blister lasts for about 2 days and takes 10–14 days to disappear.

Prevention Avoid direct sunlight if you have a tendency to develop cold sores and wear a barrier cream. As cold sores are passed on by contact, avoid kissing.

Treatment
Self There is nothing available from a drugstore which can speed up the healing of a cold sore and it's a matter of your personal preference. Some people prefer to dry up the sore by the application of surgical spirit (but it stings like hell), others prefer to keep the skin soft by the applications of emollients such as vaseline so that the skin does not crack or bleed. Take your choice. Neither makes any difference.
Medical A substance called idoxuridine has been discovered to inhibit the growth of viruses and if it is applied to a cold sore early enough it may completely abort the development of the blister and the sore. Idoxuridine in a specially formulated ointment or solution is only available by prescription and should be applied every half hour or so as soon as the initial tingling symptoms in the skin appear. If it is not applied within the first 4–6 hours then it cannot exert its beneficial effect.
Alternative The following herbs have been recommended by herbalists: balm, centaury, chamomile, chickweed, comfrey and lavender. Myrrh is said to be a specific remedy for cold sores.

TOOTH ABSCESS Infection at the root of the tooth. Local collection of pus inside the jaw bone at the root of a tooth.

Cause The tooth is nearly always dead which means that chronic decay has penetrated to the pulp cavity, has killed the center of the tooth with its nerves and blood vessels and then tracked its way down the root of the tooth to the jaw bone itself. Having reached the jaw bone, which is hard and resistant, it can go no further and pus builds up, causing an increase in pressure which is exceptionally painful.

Symptoms Severe toothache. Swelling of the gum over the site of the abscess to produce a soft, tender, fluctuant lump (which is the collection of pus). Possibly swelling of the face and cheek overlying the tooth.

Investigation Visit your dentist immediately for an X-ray.

Prevention Meticulous hygiene in tooth brushing. Regular visits to your hygienist and dentist. Making sure you never neglect toothache but have dental decay treated early.

Treatment
Self Analgaesics, i.e. two soluble aspirin every four hours until you can reach your dentist.
Medical As soon as possible go to your dentist who will relieve pressure by releasing the pus. The dentist usually uses one of two ways to do this: s/he punctures the gum and allows the pus to drain out that way or s/he drills the tooth and allows the pus to drain out through the root and the dead shell of the tooth. (In a dire emergency, when there are no dentists available and you are suffering agony, you can release the pus yourself [if you are brave enough] by taking a sharp instrument which you have sterilized in a flame and nicking the gum over the fluctuant swelling.)
Alternative For toothache: oil of cloves, anemone, cayenne, chamomile, cinquefoil, hops and lavender are recommended by herbalists, and for abscess see "Boil," p. 90.

BLEEDING GUMS Bleeding of the gum margins when they are pressed with a finger, when you bite into hard foods such as an apple, and when you brush your teeth. The gum margins are usually red, swollen and possibly sore.

Cause The commonest cause is infrequent and inefficient brushing of the teeth. It may, however, be due to an infection of the gum margin, the worst of which is trench mouth.

Investigation Visit your dentist who may take a bacterial swab to see if the cause is infective.

Prevention Brush your teeth correctly, frequently and regularly, do not use mouth washes.

Treatment
Medical After excluding infection, your dentist will instruct you on how to brush your teeth correctly. If an infection is the cause, your dentist may treat it locally with antiseptic or anti-bacterial applications, or s/he may recommend that you have a gingivectomy (removal of the infected gum margin). S/he will also instruct you how to encourage the gum margin to grow back up between the teeth by gentle stimulation with dental sticks.
Alternative One specific remedy is myrica. The following are recommended for bleeding by some herbalists: baybery, bistort, stellaria, cinquefoil, nettle. For "sore gums," cayenne, myrrh and parsley.

APHTHOUS ULCERS Exquisitely tender ulcers of the mouth and tongue which may be a pinpoint or anything up to 1 in (2.5 cm) in diameter. They usually have a dirty yellow crater and a border which is red and inflamed.

Cause They may be the result of accidental chewing on the inside of the mouth, by a knock from a pencil or a fingernail. Quite frequently they arise from no obvious cause.

Symptoms Exquisite tenderness which prevents normal chewing, talking and swallowing; made worse by exposure to acids, e.g. vinegar.

Investigation None necessary unless very large, in which case seek reassurance from your doctor or dermatologist.

Prevention Don't fiddle with the mouth or put a sharp object in the mouth.

Treatment
Self Unfortunately, mouth ulcers take 10–14 days to heal and there is very little that you can do to speed this up. There are proprietary ulcer preparations available at your drugstore, but most of them contain local anesthetics to dull the pain. You should avoid these as local anesthetics can give rise to not just an allergy in the mouth but an allergy which may affect your whole body, and if you are unaware of this it may be dangerous the next time you have a local anesthetic injection at your dentist's.
Medical Unless the ulcer is extremely large, no medical treatment is indicated. If the ulcer is large your doctor may prescribe an antibiotic paint or specially formulated cream for use in the mouth.
Specialist Not necessary unless your doctor is in doubt about the diagnosis. While the cause of recurrent mouth ulcers is rarely found, a specialist may help in providing you with an efficient treatment which soothes your mouth and helps to clear them up.
Alternative The following are recommended for ulcers: angelica, burdock, coltsfoot and comfrey. Marsh mallow is said to be soothing to all mucus membranes.

VAGINAL AREA

Like many other orifices in the body the vagina is self-cleansing, especially when left alone but, unlike some other orifices, the vagina is helped by the force of gravity: fluids tend not to collect in the recesses of the vagina, but drain downwards under gravitational pull.

Under normal conditions, therefore, the vagina and the external vaginal area can remain quite healthy without any interference whatsoever. Indeed, if you think of this area as being in perfect ecological balance, you will understand the necessity *not* to interfere. As far as hygiene is concerned, the most that you should do is to wash the anal and vaginal area once or twice a day (more often if it is very hot), but underwash, and use a mild baby soap; never use an antiseptic soap. By underwashing I mean make the lather in the palms of the hands, wet the area with warm water and then gently rub the outer surfaces; never try to cleanse the inner surface of the vaginal area. There is absolutely no need. They are cleansed by the natural bathing process of the vaginal secretions – it's only the accumulation on the outside that needs removing.

Vaginal discharges

Discharge – normal discharge – is good for the vagina. All women have some vaginal discharge throughout the menstrual cycle though it may vary in its constitution during the first and second half of the month.

During the first half of the menstrual cycle, vaginal discharge is fairly scant but at, or near to, ovulation time it increases in quantity, is thin in consistency, transparent and stretchy. In fact it's very like the clear mucus secreted in the nose. Most, but not all, of this discharge comes from the cervix, whose glands respond to the high estrogen levels in the first half of the cycle by secreting mucus with the above characteristics. Vaginal glands respond in a similar way.

In the second half of the cycle, after ovulation has taken place and when progesterone levels climb, vaginal discharge changes its character. It becomes thicker, whiter, more jelly-like, stiffer and less stretchy. This vaginal discharge may stain clothing and leave a thick white or yellowish-brown deposit when it dries.

A good rule of thumb which will help you distinguish a normal from an abnormal vaginal discharge is that if it does not make you sore or itchy and if it does not have an unpleasant smell, then it is probably normal. (For abnormal discharges, see p. 120.)

The kind of secretions described, which appear on the outside as a vaginal discharge, are not just normal, they are good for the vagina. Vaginal health depends on the lining being kept moist and well lubricated by secretions from the millions of glands found in the cervix and the vaginal wall. What is more, the *introitus* (the areas surrounding the vaginal entrance and bounded by the labia majora), must also be kept moist and well lubricated to be healthy. If the vagina or the introitus dry out, they become itchy, sore and prone to infection. A pair of glands situated on either side of the labia minora (Bartholins's glands), constantly secrete fluid to keep the introitus moist and, along with the other glands of the vagina and the cervix, pour out secretions when you are sexually aroused to lubricate the vagina in preparation for penetration.

The vaginal secretions are acid. The vagina is only healthy if the secretions are acid (about as acid as dilute vinegar). If the acid balance of the vaginal secretions is disturbed, then the health of the vagina is in jeopardy.

This acidity is maintained by the bacterial population of the vagina which is in a very fine balance. The bacteria which populate the vagina produce lactic acid and it is this substance which keeps the vagina acid. If the numbers or types of bacterium in the vagina are disturbed, then this finely tuned acid balance may be lost and the possibility of invasion by unwanted bacteria, and yeasts such as thrush, increases, as does the chance of developing a vaginal infection. This is the basic reason why we should not interfere with the normal physiology of the vagina by over-zealous cleansing and the use of deodorants or antiseptics.

Menstrual hygiene
The two usual ways of absorbing menstrual loss are wearing an external sanitary napkin or putting a tampon inside the vagina. The sanitary pad can be attached to a belt which goes around the waist or attached, by means of an adhesive strip, to the inside of your panties. It has the disadvantage that it may chafe the upper thighs and may be seen under sports clothes or tight-fitting trousers. This only matters if you think the aesthetics are important. You should consider menstruation a normal function and it really shouldn't matter if others know that you are menstruating. The great advantage of a sanitary pad is that it provides a large surface area to absorb menstrual flow and for those women who have heavy periods there may be certain days where pads have to be worn because tampons simply cannot absorb the blood fast enough. Sanitary pads should be changed every four to six hours otherwise they do have an unpleasant odor.

Tampons are inserted into the vagina with your fingers or a specially designed applicator. Young girls should not attempt to use tampons until their periods are established and regular, around the age of 17 to 19, though there is no medical evidence for them not doing so if they wish to experiment. They should be warned, however, that if the hymen is intact and tough it will be ruptured by the insertion of a tampon and this may cause discomfort.

Tampons should be made of cotton and rayon; avoid any that are made from cellulose which claim that they can be left in the vagina for long periods between changes, or that are impregnated with any kind of chemical, for example deodorant. Tampons have the advantage of being convenient, inconspicuous and effective. Change them every 4–6 hours, last thing at night, and first thing in the morning. Occasionally at the end of a period a tampon may be forgotten and left in the vagina. Within 3–4 days this will lead to an offensive vaginal discharge. The vagina is self-cleansing and if the tampon is removed there is nothing that you should do yourself and you need not consult your doctor unless the discharge fails to clear up within 48 hours.

Tampons are a more aesthetic way of soaking up the menstrual flow and, despite the recent reports of several deaths from bacterial shock due to the wearing of tampons, they should not be discarded by women as part of an over-reaction to alarmist reporting. The makers of the tampon have performed very good studies which have shown why it is possible to suffer from bacterial shock when using their product. They also behaved in a very responsible way in advising women to discontinue using the tampon. The trouble was that the tampon was made of synthetic cellulose and the makers claimed that it was super-absorbable and could be left in the vagina for longer than the ordinary cotton tampon. What happened was that some women left them in for a very long time. Bacteria began to grow in them and the secreted bacterial toxins were then absorbed through the thin vaginal walls into the bloodstream of the wearer, giving rise to fatal shock from the bacterial toxins.

Menstrual extraction

In an attempt to make menstruation as short, painless, and convenient as possible, certain women's groups, in the early 1970s, designed a procedure of menstrual extraction. This involves inserting a cannula through the cervix into the uterine cavity and, by suction, extracting the whole of the crumbling endometrial lining into a collection jar. The extraction is usually done about the time when the period is due, or when menstrual blood loss has just started. There is a risk of infection with this procedure. Since full-length periods are natural and usually not too disruptive of a woman's schedule, there is little reason to alter the normal flow.

How can I tone up my vaginal muscles?

Not all of us, especially if we have had children, are blessed with snug, small vaginas. There is a post-natal exercise which is aimed at toning up the muscles of the pelvic floor and thereby toning up the vaginal walls themselves, and is worth practicing at any time. This is the exercise:
• Next time you go to the lavatory to pass urine, pull the muscles of the vagina upwards and inwards so that you stop the urine;
• Hold it to the count of five;
• Let the urine flow again for five seconds;
• Repeat the exercise to interrupt the urine flow.
Once you have learned to do this you can do it any time, whenever it occurs to you. Every woman should practice it at least once or twice a day.

Infections

Infections of the vagina most often ascend from the external vaginal area, and the tendency for this to happen increases if the urine is abnormal. If your urine is infected and it bathes the vaginal area each time you pass urine, then the infecting organism can possibly travel up the vagina. This chance is increased if your urine also contains sugar, as sugar encourages bacterial growth. Women suffering from diabetes find that they suffer more frequently from urinary tract infections, from vaginal infections and from *pruritis vulvae* (see p. 123), than do women whose urine contains no sugar. If you are diabetic, therefore, it is very important that you keep it under control with a proper diet and proper treatment, and that you attend to vaginal hygiene.

As already stated, a discharge which is odorless and non-irritating is probably normal. If your discharge is heavy, if it smells and if it irritates your skin, then it is probably due to an infection. The commonest infecting organisms are a yeast called *candida albicans* (which produces moniliasis or thrush), and *trichomonas* (which produces trichomoniasis). Both of them may be transmitted venereally, but thrush may be brought on by a monilia infection of the intestine, or even the mouth. In the former case, the yeast clings to the skin around the anus after the passage of feces and may then track its way to the vagina and cause a vaginal infection. The vaginal discharge with thrush is usually thick and white and makes the vaginal area sore and red. It may also spread to the thighs and cause a monilial infection of the skin. This shows itself as a fine, red, scaly rash, with small scattered spots which occasionally become infected and form pustules.

Moniliasis

This infection is rare in non-menstruating women – it is therefore a disease of the fertile years. It is more common in certain groups of women and these include:

● Women taking antibiotics. The number of (*monilia/candida*) fungi is normally kept in check by other bacteria. If an antibiotic kills them off, the fungus can overgrow.

● Women with diabetes. When diabetes becomes unstable, the presence of sugar in the urine provides a favorable medium for all organisms, and monilia can get out of hand like the rest.

● Women taking progestogens. The most common example of this is taking birth control pills containing a high dose of progestogen which seems to favor *candida* growth.

● Women with high internal progesterone levels e.g. pre-menstrual women, pregnant women.

Symptoms
The symptoms of moniliasis are a thick, white, curdy, vaginal discharge, soreness, irritation and itching of the vagina and pereneum. Quite often the skin becomes red and scaly and the rash may spread onto the inner sides of the thighs.

TREATMENT FOR MONILIASIS

Consult your doctor as soon as possible.	Ask for identification of the monilia by tests.
Refrain from intercourse until the infection is cleared.	Don't scratch; the fungus gets under your nails and you'll spread it.
Take a complete course of treatment; this may be for two weeks and may be in the form of suppositories and cream.	Don't use proprietary preparations bought over the counter; proper treatment is available only by prescription.
Go straight back to your doctor if the infection recurs – you may be re-infecting yourself from your anus and may need to take medication by mouth.	Don't use anything containing a local anesthetic; it may bring instant relief once or twice but it lasts a very short time and you may become allergic to it.

Trichomoniasis

Unlike moniliasis, *trichomoniasis* is worst just after menstruation and it affects both men and women. The organism lives in the vagina, cervix, urethra and bladder of women and in the urethra and prostate of men. It is most common in sexually active women, and 90% of their partners are infected too.

Symptoms

Men have few symptoms other than occasionally a discharge from the penis and burning on passing urine. Women on the other hand have an offensive yellowish vaginal discharge, soreness and itching of the vagina and perineum, and burning with urination. If the infection affects the bladder there may be the symptoms of cystitis (see p. 256).

TREATMENT FOR TRICHOMONIASIS

Both partners and all sexual contacts of the partners must be treated.
Flagyl, in a single 8 tablet dose by mouth or in a seven day course of one tablet, three times a day, is effective and mandatory. Douches, creams and suppositories are not enough.
Take Flagyl with meals to minimize gastric upset.

Don't take alcohol, you may get abdominal pain.
Don't take Flagyl if you're pregnant.
Don't take Flagyl for longer than a week – if you need a second course ask for a blood count (it occasionally affects blood cell production); you may experience a strange taste and your tongue may feel furry.

What factors predispose one to vaginal infections?

During periods of stress and at those times when you let your general physical condition run down, you are most vulnerable to vaginal infections. Being overweight also makes you more prone as less of the vulva is exposed to the beneficial drying effects of the air. Having a new sexual partner, or more than one, is also associated with increased likelihood of infection.

Is there anything I can do to prevent an infection from occurring?

Using a condom is the best protection against vaginal infections – not only with a new, or more than one, partner, but especially if you are being reinfected by your regular partner (see below). Practice good vaginal hygiene by keeping your vagina clean and dry: bathe carefully, wipe from front to back and avoid douches, hygiene sprays, bubble baths and bath oils. If you need extra lubrication during intercourse use a contraceptive foam or a cream or jelly which offers protection against infection – never petroleum jelly or vaseline, which are hard to remove and promote infection. Wear cotton underpants and avoid nylon pants, pantyhose and tight trousers which hold moisture in the vaginal area. Keep your weight down.

I have a very stable sex life with one partner yet I suffer from recurring infections which drive me mad; what can I do?

Quite probably you are being reinfected by your partner. Unless he is also treated, whether or not he shows any symptoms, the infection can be passed backwards and forwards continually. Gay women are just as likely to suffer from vaginal infections as they are spread by intimate sexual contact – skin to skin, mucus membrane to mucus membrane – which is not only limited to men and women. If your lover (male or female) has other partners, he or she may be passing their infections on to you. Reinfections are quite common in altered chemical conditions, especially for women who use birth control pills or those who have diabetes.

COMMON VAGINAL COMPLAINTS

VAGINITIS (senile) Inflammation of the vagina so that the vagina becomes dry, sore, itchy and prone to infection. Sexual intercourse becomes very painful; penetration is almost impossible.

Cause Senile vaginitis occurs just after menopause when the circulating levels of estrogen diminish. As described (see p. 425), estrogen stimulates the secretion of vaginal fluid which is thin, translucent, elastic mucus, especially designed to keep the walls of the vagina moist, well lubricated and healthy. When the estrogen levels in the blood diminish, the vaginal cells cease to secrete this nutritious, soothing fluid. The result is that the vagina begins to dry out. The upper layer of cells is no longer efficiently shed. The bacteria can no longer live in harmony as they did and the pH of the vagina is no longer held precisely in the acid range where it should be. This undermines the health of the vagina which is easily irritated and frequently becomes sore. The external part of the vaginal area may dry out and crack and become very itchy. Pruritis vulvae may start at this time.

Investigation Interview and internal examination by your doctor.

Prevention There is no doubt that hormonal replacement therapy with estrogens will relieve these symptoms, but as estrogens are potent drugs and in terms of treating the symptoms of senile vaginitis should not be thought of lightly, unless the symptoms are giving rise to really significant problems.

Treatment
Self Nothing other than hygiene as described above. In that soap and water dry out the skin, they should be used with care and not too frequently.
Medical The application of hormone cream containing sufficient hormones to have a local effect. Those bought over the counter do not have enough hormones to exert any effect at all; potent ones, therefore, are only available on prescription from your doctor and they may soothe the itchiness and the soreness of senile vaginitis. Estrogen-containing suppositories may do much to relieve vaginal symptoms and dyspareunia.
Hormone replacement therapy with estrogen, or estrogen plus progesterone supplement, may be given if the symptoms are severe.
Specialist Not indicated unless the condition fails to improve under the above treatment.
Alternative Herbalists recommend the following for use as a vaginal douche: marsh-mallow, yarrow and plantain.

PRURITIS VULVAE Chronic, irrisistible itching of the whole of the vaginal area, usually worst when hot or when in bed.

Cause Diabetes, trichomonas infection, moniliasis infection, urinary tract infection, psychogenic in origin. Those cases of pruritis vulvae which are thought to be psychogenic in origin are usually due to the itching stimulated by the act of masturbation.

Symptoms Itching, soreness and sometimes thickening of the skin in the vaginal area.

Investigation Exclusion of vaginal infections, urinary tract infection and diabetes.

Prevention Never scratch the vaginal area for any length of time. If you find yourself doing this for more than two or three days, consult your doctor. If not, you may find yourself in an unbreakable itch–scratch–itch cycle.

Treatment
Self None other than attention to normal hygiene but, if possible, avoid the use of soap and detergents, just use warm water.
Medical The application of soothing emollient cream which keeps the skin moist, soft and well lubricated. You should apply these creams every two to three hours. If there is a lot of inflammation, your doctor may give you a cream containing hydrocortisone. If he thinks there may be some infection present, he may give you a mild hydrocortisone cream which contains an antibiotic.
Specialist Not indicated unless treatment by your own doctor fails.

LICE Itchy infection of the pubic hair with the pubic louse *pediculosis pubis*, commonly known as "crabs."

Cause Pediculosis pubis.

Symptoms Itchiness and possibly a rash on the skin of the thighs.

Investigation Examination which reveals an adult louse or the eggs of the lice cemented firmly to the root of the hair so that they cannot be easily removed.

Prevention Avoid any known contact with pubic lice.

Treatment
Self As for nits (see p. 100). Be sure and treat all known contacts.
Medical Only needed if your own treatment proves ineffective.

PILES Small, soft swellings of the veins around the anal orifice.

Cause Are almost a "normal" occurrence in pregnancy, particularly in the latter three months when the size and weight of the baby presses on the veins which return blood to the heart. This may produce sufficient back pressure to make the veins of the rectum and the legs swell, so producing varicosities. These may be caused or worsened by any condition which increases the intra-abdominal pressure over the long term, e.g. a chronic cough, chronic constipation.

Symptoms Sore, itchy and sometimes painful swellings around the anal margin which may be made worse by the secretion of mucus which the rectum produces to protect its exposed lining. There may be bleeding on passage of the stool.

Investigation Clinical examination by your family doctor will confirm the diagnosis.

Prevention Varicose veins and piles are difficult to prevent if they are a consequence of pregnancy. Always make sure that you move your bowels regularly and that you keep the stool soft by including plenty of fiber in your diet. Never let a cough become chronic.

Treatment
Medical If piles are very minor they need no radical treatment but the soreness and itchiness may be relieved by the use of soothing emollient creams available from your doctor by prescription. Do not use proprietary preparations, most of which contain local anesthetics. These are potent sensitizing agents and the allergy may only become apparent when you react to a local anesthetic injection at the dentist.
Specialist Removal of piles can only be undertaken by a surgeon. S/he has two main options: firstly, injection with an agent which makes the pile solidify and shrivel. This is usually undertaken under a local anesthetic on an out-patient basis. Secondly, and for more serious prolapse or strangulated piles, the veins are actually stripped out. This is a major surgical operation; you will be admitted to the hospital and will be allowed to go home after about five days.
Alternative Herbal laxatives using lesser celandine or plantain leaves, pulped and applied locally.

ARMS, HANDS AND NAILS

There is very little that you can do about the overall shape of your arms, hands and fingers other than keeping your arms slim. It is genetically determined and is as much a part of you as the color of your eyes. There is no point in craving long, slender white fingers if yours are short and stubby. But there are certain things you can do to make sure that the health and hygiene of the hands are well taken care of.

Hand care

• Try to keep the hands warm and wear gloves whenever you go out in winter. The hands are one of the parts of the body farthest away from the heart, and by the time the blood has reached them, the circulation is rather sluggish and most of the nutrition has been absorbed from the blood. If the blood flow is slowed down even further by exposure to cold, then the nourishment of the hands suffers and this can lead to chapping of the skin around the fingertips and to soft, brittle nails which split easily. Some hands go "dead" on exposure to cold (Reynaud's phenomenon). They first go white and look dead, hence their common name of "dead man's fingers," but a short time later they go blue and then finally bright pink, when they tingle and may be painful.

● Just as important as keeping the hands warm during cold weather is keeping them out of water as much as possible, because water itself is dehydrating and gives the skin a tendency to crack. It is not just bad for the skin of the hands, it's also bad for the nails and cuticles – the nails become softened and split or crack, the cuticles also become soft and may tear easily. If they are chronically softened due to continuous soaking in water, they become subject to whitlows and monilia (thrush) infection (see p. 128). Keep them well moisturized with lots of hand cream, applied about twice as often in the winter as you would in the summer.

● For household chores it is worth protecting your hands with rubber gloves. Water, particularly hard water or water containing detergents, soap powders and alkalis, robs the skin of moisture (see p. 83). Always make sure, however, that your rubber gloves have a cotton lining. If not, the skin will sweat profusely inside the rubber and when the gloves are removed, you will find that your skin goes soft immediately, dries out very quickly, and becomes rough and scaly. Try not to wear rubber gloves for longer than five or ten minutes at a time. A trick I recommend is to wear a cheap pair of cotton gloves inside the rubber gloves and impregnate the cotton gloves with hand cream or hand lotion, so that every time you put on your rubber gloves, your hands will be given a beauty treatment.

Proper care of your hands and nails will ensure that they become an attractive asset to your general appearance.

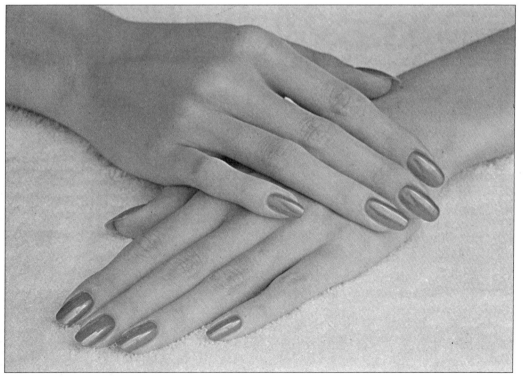

WEEKLY MANICURE

To keep the nails in condition, a regular home manicure done once a week should become part of your beauty routine.

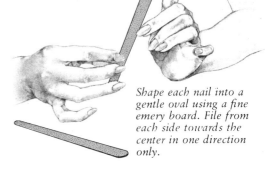

Shape each nail into a gentle oval using a fine emery board. File from each side towards the center in one direction only.

Soak your fingers in a bowl of warm soapy water for at least 3 minutes to soften the cuticles.

Apply cuticle remover all around the nail. Pad the end of an orange stick and use it to remove traces of cuticle from the nails and to push the cuticle down to the base.

Using a soft leather buffer, gently rub the nails from the tips to the cuticle.

Vigorously rub a small amount of hand cream onto your hands, but make sure you remove all traces from the nails.

Apply two coats of colored polish to the nails ending with a topcoat of colorless polish. Brush polish on in center of nail, then down each side.

To clean dirty nails
Impregnate a thick latex sponge with a soap solution and press your fingertips into it.

● For any really dirty job like gardening, always protect your hands and nails with special gardening gloves. This not only prevents your hands from being scratched or cut but also keeps them clean. If you don't, getting them clean may inflict more damage than gardening, as scrubbing and the use of strong cleaning agents roughens the skin, de-fats it and makes it prone to infection.

● If a dirty job does leave unsightly residues around the cuticles and down the fingernails, try a tip that a beautician gave me for cleaning them. Take a latex sponge (a make-up sponge is good enough), impregnate it thoroughly with soap and water and press your fingertips continuously into the sponge so that the soapy lather and the bubbles work the dirt and grime out of your fingertips and cuticles. A nail brush may be efficient but vigorous scrubbing with soap may tear the cuticle and will also soften up the nails.

Nails

Nails do not benefit from dietary supplements, like gelatin or cheese, but do from a weekly manicure (see left). All that part of the nail which we can see is dead. The only living part is the nail root buried behind and deeper than the lunula or half moon. The nervous habit of picking at the nails or the cuticle disturbs the nail root while it is growing, and this may lead to misshapen nails, to furrows, ridges and variations in thickness which may cause splitting when the nail finally grows out. Nail biting *per se* does not harm the health of the nails, but it is unsightly. It also causes the nails to grow twice as fast as normal (i.e. 3 mm a month instead of 1.5 mm). It also prevents the nails from performing the function for which they were designed – to protect the tender and very sensitive fingertips from injury.

Tennis elbow

Any movement which causes the elbow to be straightened out from a bent up position and is repeated for long periods of time, or is suddenly undertaken, will cause tennis elbow. Tennis elbow can, therefore, be caused by hanging curtains, cleaning windows or scrubbing floors – as well as by playing tennis. It is caused by sudden over-exercising of the muscles which extend the elbow, usually over a short period of time, and involves inflammation of the tendons which are inserted on the point of the elbow. Tennis elbow is characterized by pain on moving the elbow and exquisite tenderness over the point of the elbow. The mainstay of treatment is rest and, if persistent, it may be necessary to have physical therapy, ultrasonic treatment, and even hydrocortisone injections around the tendons. While certain serious traumatic injuries demand that parts of the arm be immobilized, it is detrimental to completely immobilize the elbow, the wrist and particularly the fingers for any length of time.

Do vitamin and mineral supplements improve the health of the nails?
The simple answer is "No." There is no medical evidence to show that vitamins or minerals like calcium or iron (unless an iron deficiency like anemia is present) will improve the strength of the nails or prevent brittleness and splitting of the nails.

127

COMMON HAND COMPLAINTS

GANGLION A soft, bubble-like swelling which may vary in size between a pea and a walnut on the back of the hands. It is attached to one of the tendons running to the fingers and moves with the tendon when the muscle contracts.

Cause A collection of fluid in the tendon sheath.

Investigation None usually necessary if the diagnosis is obvious. If not, minor surgical exploration may be necessary.

Treatment
Self An old-fashioned remedy, but a good one, is to place a large coin over the swelling and then a tight bandage or rubber band. The constant pressure disperses the fluid.
Medical If a cyst has formed it may be necessary to remove the cyst surgically. Your doctor will refer you to a hand specialist who can do this.
Specialist Surgical removal of the cyst.

WHITLOW A small tear in the nail fold which becomes infected, red, tender and swollen. Pus may form and track down to the nail plate and disturb nail growth.

Cause Prolonged exposure to water and detergents, which soften up the skin of the nail fold and the cuticles, thereby allowing bacterial entry.

Symptoms Exquisite soreness and tenderness, which may prevent movement of the whole finger. Pus may extrude from under the cuticle and the nail fold. The nail may lift off from its bed.

Investigation Bacterial swab.

Treatment
Self As for moniliasis. Do not attempt treatment with proprietary ointments, creams, lotions and antiseptics.
Medical Specific local treatment with antibiotic cream. If very severe, treatment with antibiotics by mouth. If the accumulation of pus is extensive, referral to the local hospital emergency room.
Specialist Under local anesthesia the nail fold and cuticle are scraped away, so allowing free drainage of pus. Daily dressings with antibiotic-impregnated gauze are necessary. Recurrent whitlows need investigation by a dermatologist to exclude the presence of a yeast or fungus which must be eradicated before the condition can be cured.
Alternative As for abscesses (see p. 117).

BRITTLE NAILS Soft nails which flake into several layers, or split very easily once they have grown beyond the tip of the finger.

Cause If there is no circulatory impairment, the cause is probably an inherited tendency.

Symptoms Inability to grow the nails beyond a certain length before they split and tear.

Investigation None indicated if the nails are otherwise normal. If pitted like a thimble, the condition may be a manifestation of psoriasis, so consult a dermatologist. If the nails are spoon-shaped and curl upwards at the edges, this may be due to an iron deficiency so consult your doctor.

Prevention Nail hardeners, or nail polish may help to prevent the edges from splitting.

Treatment
Alternative There is nothing known to medical science which will strengthen brittle nails. Eating gelatin is sometimes naively recommended but is without any basis.

MONILIASIS Infection of the cuticle and the nail bed with candida albicans or monilia (Thrush), a yeast. The edges of the nail and the cuticle become red, swollen and puffy.

Cause Constant immersion in water and detergents which softens the cuticle and prevents it from performing its protective function and pre-disposes to invasion of the nail bed by monilia.

Symptoms Soreness, pain and sometimes chronic infection of the skin surrounding the nail, plus thickening, yellow discoloration. flaking, cracking and splitting of the nail.

Investigation In a specialist clinic, samples of the nail may be taken, treated in a special way, examined under a microscope and the yeast cells found.

Prevention Do not expose the hands to immersion in water or detergents for long periods.

Treatment
Self As for prevention. Wear rubber gloves with cotton gloves underneath once the treatment has been brought under control. Do not do this until then as the monilia may infect the gloves and cause reinfection of the skin.
Medical Meticulous therapy with a specific anti-monilia agent, smeared on the nail and around the nail bed several times a day for as long as it takes to eradicate the infection. This may be several months.
Specialist In recalcitrant cases it may be necessary to consult a dermatologist for more specialized forms of treatment.

Are there any special exercises for my hands which will keep them supple and shapely?

No. If you have arthritis you should have special instruction about how to exercise your hands from your doctor and physical therapist. If your hands are normal, they are perfectly well exercised by the various tasks which we perform each day, and nothing extra is needed. Rubbing hand cream in vigorously will help improve the circulation and increase the blood supply to the base of the nails; it will also keep them smooth.

How can I stop biting my nails?

The only way to stop biting your nails is to become convinced that you really want to do it to improve their appearance, or simply as an act of will. I once took the rather heavy-handed action of telling one of my managers that he would not be appointed to a senior position until he had stopped biting his nails because no senior manager worth his salt would bite his nails. This stopped him. Seeing an improvement in your nails may help and you can do this immediately by giving your nails a coat of transparent nail polish which, of itself, almost defies intervention. As a last resort, of course, you can use false nails as camouflage.

What can I do to prevent spots and stains appearing on my nails?

Small red linear streaks (splinter hemorrhages) and small white spots appear in the nails as a normal variation of nail growth. Any small disturbance of the nail root will result in one of these minor changes. The nail takes about three to four months to grow out and the spot will grow out with the nail. There is nothing you can do about it. Yellow staining of the nails is sometimes due to the use of pink nail polish which contains a yellow dye as one of its constituents. This soaks into the substance of the nail and is also permanent. You can only wait for it to grow out or camouflage it with further coats of nail polish. If your favourite nail color leaves a yellow stain, one of the ways to prevent staining of your nails is to wear a base coat under the nail polish.

LEGS AND FEET

The hip, knee, ankle and toe joints take the weight of the whole body, and are therefore put under a great deal of strain whenever we are on our feet. You can help them to remain strong, stable, and disease-free if you make sure that the muscles that support them are in good trim. These muscles are the gluteal muscles of the buttocks, the thigh muscles, the muscles of the lower leg, the tendons around the ankle and the muscles of the feet, mainly the tiny ones in the soles.

Any housewife who does her own housework and shopping would find that she walked, on average, four or five miles a day were she to wear a pedometer. This is quite sufficient exercise for anyone, and certainly sufficient to keep the muscles of the buttocks and legs toned up. If, however, you lead a sedentary life, then you really should try to take some time each week to exercise your legs.

Walking is good: a two mile walk, taken at a pace that makes you slightly out of breath, three or four times a week, is quite sufficient. Better still, exercise on an exercise bicycle three times a week, for 20 minutes during each session; this not only keeps the muscles of the lower half of your body healthy and strong, it's also good for the heart and lungs.

It should be made clear, however, that no amount of exercise will change the underlying shape of your bottom or your thighs, calves or ankles. It is not difficult to increase the size of muscles by increasing the amount of work you ask the muscles to do, e.g. weight training, but it is impossible to change their shape so you will not get rid of a sagging bottom or a pad of fat on the outside of your thighs ("jodhpur" thighs) by exercising, not unless you exercise very hard for a very long time, and most people can't afford the time for this luxury.

Besides keeping the joints and muscles supple and healthy, exercise has another payoff. The muscles of the leg act as a pump when they contract and help to return the blood to the heart; this in turn prevents the pooling of blood and fluid in the lower extremities, so helping to prevent swelling of the ankles. Exercise also helps to support the veins of the leg and therefore mitigates against worsening of varicose veins, though it won't do anything about the underlying cause which is nearly always a deep-veined thrombosis (clot).

Foot care The feet are the extremities furthest away from the heart and the blood flow here is the most sluggish in the body so that nutrition of the tissues is at its lowest. In cold weather, the feet are the first to feel cold. Moreover, they are constantly over-worked and hardly ever allowed to rest. All of these factors mean that any injury, even a minor scratch of the skin, will take much longer to heal on the feet than anywhere else in the body. You should therefore take meticulous care of your feet by:
• Keeping them warm with socks and boots;
• Treating any minor injury meticulously and changing antiseptic dressings every day;
• Treating even a minor abrasion or a break in the skin with a simple antiseptic cream;
• Resting your foot whenever you can if it's been injured;
• When resting your feet, raise them on a stool or pile of cushions so that they are at a higher level than your trunk and, if possible, the rest of your body.
We should pay as much attention to the health, cleanliness and hygiene of our feet as we do to our hands – wash them at least once daily, morning and night if possible. Use a talcum powder, one which contains an anti-perspirant if you have smelly feet. If you can, wear socks and stockings made of natural fibers, like cotton and wool, which absorb sweat and which stretch and do not constrict the feet.

It is easy to damage the feet if you attempt to pedicure them yourself. If you have trouble with your feet, e.g. corns and callouses, or if your feet give you pain, regular visits to a chiropodist for a pedicure are a sound and wise investment. Never, ever, use a sharp instrument on the skin of your feet. You may inflict damage that will take weeks to heal.

Do your feet a favor and go shoeless whenever you can. A good tip is to take off your shoes as soon as you get home and wander around for as long as you can without anything on your feet. This is a rest cure in itself. A second alternative is to wear wooden exercise sandals whenever you can, and a third tip is to change your shoes as often as you can during the day, particularly if you are wearing high heels. So keep an extra pair of shoes at the office and in the car, and if you are at home, change your shoes to go shopping or when you go to pick the children up from school or outings.

Care of the feet is absolutely essential for people who suffer from diabetes. Because of the high level of sugar in the blood and tissues, minor injuries in diabetics can become rapidly infected and they therefore take much longer to heal. Attention to hygiene, regular visits to chiropodists and non-interference with a sharp instrument are essential. If you develop any kind of sore or ulcer on your legs and feet, consult your doctor immediately.

Quite a lot of damage can be done to your toes when you cut your toenails. Here are a few basic tips:

● Cut your toenails after a bath, when they are soft;
● Always cut the toenails straight across;
● Never cut the edges downwards at the sides, this only encourages ingrown toenails;
● Never cut them too short as this may damage the skin; cutting the toenails too short may also cause soreness and as your feet are constantly in use, this may take weeks to disappear;
● If while you are cutting your toenails you damage the skin, apply a simple antiseptic cream and a plaster for the next two or three days.

Whenever you wash your feet make sure that you dry gently, but thoroughly, between the toes. This minimizes the risk of fungal infection.

To prevent ingrown toenails, always cut the nails straight across, rather than at an angle.

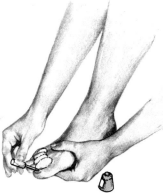

Put small pieces of cotton between your toes before you start to paint the nails. This separates the toes and prevents smudging.

PREVENTING FOOT PROBLEMS

Ill-fitting shoes produce corns, callouses and bunions. Corns are localized areas of hard, horny skin which develop from repeated rubbing or pressure. Callouses are large corns, and bunions are deformities of the point between the big toe and the foot. With the latter, a protruding knuckle forms a *bursa* (pouch) which can be extremely painful.

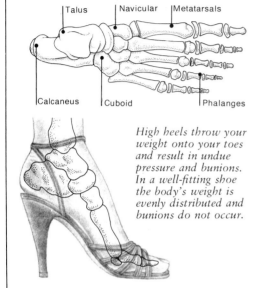

High heels throw your weight onto your toes and result in undue pressure and bunions. In a well-fitting shoe the body's weight is evenly distributed and bunions do not occur.

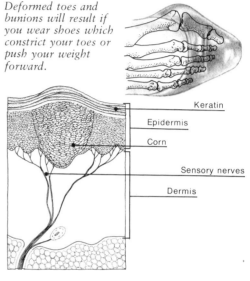

Deformed toes and bunions will result if you wear shoes which constrict your toes or push your weight forward.

Corns and calluses

Corns and calluses are caused just as often by loose fitting shoes as tight fitting shoes because it is friction which produces the callus. The skin responds to friction by producing what it believes to be a protective layer of dead cells which pile up, become thick and form a corn or a callus. So it is important when you are choosing shoes to make sure that they fit properly, and that means neither too tight nor too loose. If a corn starts to form, never wear the offending shoes again. Try to thin down the thickened skin with a pumice stone or with callus removing lotions. If the corn gets worse and becomes very thick, do not treat it yourself, but visit a chiropodist.

Support hose

You don't have to suffer from varicose veins to wear support hose – if you have a job in which you stand or walk a great deal, you will be helping the pumping action of the muscles of the legs if you wear support hose. They do not have to be heavy or thick; quite fine, aesthetically acceptable support hose can help a lot to prevent aching legs and swollen ankles.

What can I do about aching legs and tired feet?
- Do not stand for long periods of time if you can avoid it.
- Do not wear ill-fitting shoes.
- Go shoeless whenever you can.

- Change your shoes whenever you can.
- Wear exercise sandals whenever you can.
- When you sit down, put your feet on a stool.
- When you lie down, try to put your feet at a higher level than the rest of your body.
- At the end of the day, lie down flat on the floor and put your feet up against the wall so that the fluids can drain out of your legs and back into your body.
- If you do this with cold wet towels wrapped round your legs, the effect can be very soothing.
- Heat is soothing but not sitting with your feet in a hot mustard bath. This will only make swelling of the ankles worse. Lie down on your back, put your feet up against the wall and wrap them in a warm blanket.
- Wear support hose whenever you can.

Can I do anything about flat feet or fallen arches?

Once you have reached adulthood with flat feet then there is very little you can do, nor is there any need to do anything unless they cause you trouble. Flat feet rarely do cause trouble, other than a little aching at the end of the day, particularly if you wear badly fitting shoes. You should always try to wear shoes that give you good support around the arch of the foot by wearing laced shoes or shoes with a T-strap.

The sole of the foot has three arches, running in three different planes: lengthways, across and sideways, and fallen arches simply means that the muscles in the soles of the foot are slightly flatter than average; it does not mean necessarily that they are weaker. Only if fallen arches are spotted early, i.e. in early childhood, is it possible to do anything about them. Correction is not always orthopedically necessary; very often it is done for the sake of the parents who feel that, aesthetically, the child's foot would be improved in appearance. In this instance, your child can be given shoes with special built-up arches which will help to raise the muscles of the foot and also special exercises to do to strengthen the muscles of the soles of the foot. On the left is one which you might try if you find that the muscles of the soles of your feet are aching at the end of a hard day.

Stand on the thickest book you can find, with your toes protruding over the edge. Curl down your toes as tightly as you can and count to 10. Relax. Repeat the exercise 10 times.

You can really do this exercise almost anywhere. I personally find it quite a good exercise to do in bed without the aid of the book, simply by curling down my toes as hard as possible several times before going to sleep. It's also an excellent way of making sure that your feet, ankles and lower legs are relaxed before you go to sleep.

I often get cramps in my feet at night; what can I do about them?

An old-fashioned remedy is quite good: just before retiring drink a flat teaspoonful of salt in a glass of water. The rationale for this is somewhat tenuous but is based on the theory that cramps in the legs and feet can be caused by too little sodium in the body. Naturally, don't do this if you have high blood pressure. You can also wear socks while in bed as cold muscles often cramp up.

Are swollen ankles anything to worry about?

Not if the swelling goes down overnight. However, in pregnancy such swelling of the ankles may be an early sign of toxemia and high blood pressure. If this happens when you are pregnant, consult your doctor immediately, especially if you notice that your rings are getting tighter as well, as this may be a sign of accumulation of fluid.

Many women suffer from swelling of the ankles by the end of the day, especially in hot weather. In young, healthy women this is mainly because they are sedentary and the feet are in a dependent position. Because they are not walking about, the pumping muscle action of the legs cannot work to return the blood to the heart and so fluid tends to pool in the lower part of the legs and feet. If the swelling subsides overnight, there is really nothing to worry about. If it does not, you must consult your doctor as the cause may have something to do with your heart, your liver or your kidneys and you should have a checkup.

COMMON FOOT COMPLAINTS

INGROWN TOENAILS The upper, outer edges of the toenails (usually of the big toe), grow downwards and inwards and bite into the skin of the nail fold.

Cause There are a number of causes: the big toenail is usually small and the "pad" of the big toe is usually large and soft, and it curls round the toenail. When the toenails are cut, the predisposition to have ingrown toenails is increased if the edges are cut downwards instead of straight across. Shoes which crush the big toe will tend to bury the toe nail, making the tendency to grow inwards worse.

Symptoms Painfulness around the nail folds of the big toe. Tendency for the nail folds to become infected.

Investigation None necessary.

Prevention Never wear tight shoes. Never cut the edges of the toenails downwards, always cut them straight across.

Treatment
Self As above. If the toenail becomes sore or infected, consult your doctor.
Specialist There are two treatments for ingrown toenails, neither of which is infallible, and both are done by an orthopedist. Firstly, under local anesthetic, the toenail is avulsed, that is, removed. The nail bed is dressed antiseptically daily until the scab has fallen off and then it is better to leave the toe open to the air to heal completely. During this time, open-toed sandals should be worn. The nail then regrows. It may grow back again normally or it may regrow with the tendency to again become an ingrown toenail.

If the first treatment fails, then the only recourse the surgeon has is to destroy the root of the nail so that it can never grow again. It is not as bad as it sounds. It is not a painful operation and can be performed under local anaesthetic on an out-patient basis and the nail bed is not all that ugly without a nail.

BUNIONS Swelling, tenderness and deformity of the first joint of the big toe.

Cause Wearing very high heeled shoes for long periods, or pointed-toe shoes that crush the feet and push the big toe towards the little toe.

Symptoms Exquisite pain on walking and tenderness when handled.

Investigation None necessary.

Prevention A bunion only forms when the joint of the big toe is over-strained. When this happens, the joint produces a cushion of fluid which is held in a sac, a bursa, which surrounds the joint of the big toe. Prevention is therefore not to over-strain the big toe by not wearing high-heeled shoes for too long periods and by not wearing ill-fitting shoes.

Treatment
Self Rest the feet whenever possible as suggested above. Do not wear high-heeled shoes, do not wear ill-fitting shoes.
Specialist If the bunion is extremely severe and the feet become very deformed, it is possible to have surgical treatment from an orthopedic surgeon. The treatment is to completely excise the inflamed bursa and the joint which may become arthritic. In doing so, the orthopedic surgeon fixes the joint, so while it will be entirely painless it will be stiff and immovable. It will not bend. This does not mean that you cannot walk properly; you will, but you will not be able to stand on your toes.

ATHLETE'S FOOT Fungal infection of the toe clefts and toenails. Peeling and soreness of the skin between the toes, with thickening and splitting of the nails.

Cause Infection of the skin and toenails by a fungus.

Symptoms Soreness and itchiness of the toe clefts, which sometimes become infected.

Investigation Diagnosis confirmed by taking a small scraping of the skin from between the toes or a small specimen of the toenail and subjecting it to a special chemical treatment which makes the fungus obvious under microscopic examination.

Prevention Fungal infections rarely occur in people who have dry feet. It is nearly always sweaty feet which become infected with athlete's foot, so you should do the following if you have sweaty feet: wash morning and night and dry carefully; change your socks at least once a day, try to change them twice; use talcum powder between the toes – baby powder will do; try to wear socks and stockings made of natural fibers.

Treatment
Self As above. Do not use patent anti-fungal powders and creams.
Medical Specific anti-fungal cream, available from your doctor by prescription.
Specialist If the condition is recalcitrant to the treatment prescribed by your own doctor it may be necessary for a dermatologist to give you more specific treatment.

If the fungus affects the toenails it may be necessary to take the anti-fungal agent by mouth. This agent becomes impregnated into the toenail and kills off the fungus as it grows. As the toenails grow very slowly it may be necessary to take the tablets by mouth for up to nine months. Repeated checks of the toenails will be made until the dermatologist is sure that the fungal infection has been eradicated.
Alternative Nothing specific but herbalists recommend the following for fungal infections: balm, melissa and chamomile.

VARICOSE VEINS Bulging, dilated tortuous veins of the lower legs which may be accompanied by ankle swelling and later by ulcers over the inner aspect of the ankle.

Cause Deep vein thrombosis of the leg. May get worse during pregnancy due to the back pressure caused by the growing baby on the pelvic veins and thence on the veins of the legs.

Symptoms Occasionally, itching of the skin overlying the varicose veins, aching, tired legs, swelling of the ankles, and ulcers over the inner aspects of the ankles, due to stasis of the blood in the lower legs and poor nutrition to the tissues.

Investigation Rarely done if there is a history of deep veined thrombosis. If not, the veins of the legs can be shown up on a special kind of X-ray called a Venagram, performed in the hospital.

Prevention Prevention is not always possible as it may follow pregnancy or a surgical operation. One thing you can do is to avoid wearing garters.

Treatment
Self Wear support hose. Do not stand for long periods of time. Rest the legs in an upright position whenever possible. If you can, lie down on the floor, lean the legs up against the wall for half an hour and then put on your support hose. Treat any abrasions, bruises or minor infections of the lower limbs meticulously and take the precaution of consulting your doctor in case specific treatment is necessary.
Specialist If the veins are not severe they can be injected so that they thrombose up and eventually scar and shrivel. If the varicose veins are extensive, the second surgical procedure, which is performed by a cardiovascular surgeon, is to strip out the varicose veins of the leg. This is a fairly major operation and you will need to be in the hospital for a minimum of ten days.
Alternative Nothing specific, but it is believed by herbalists that the general circulation can be improved by: bayberry, cayenne, yellow gentian, holy thistle, horseradish and lobelia.

VERUCCAE Circular warts which may reach an inch in diameter. Instead of growing outwards, as they do on the fingers, they grow inwards and bury themselves deep into the skin of the soles of the feet because of the constant pressure of walking.

Cause A virus which causes warts. Its exact nature is not known but it is highly infectious and veruccae are nearly always picked up in public places where the feet are bare, e.g. swimming pools.

Symptoms Extreme tenderness on walking because of the pressure on sensitive nerve ends.

Prevention Meticulous hygiene in public places where the feet are bare, e.g. the use of footbaths at swimming pools.

Treatment
Self Do not try to treat veruccae yourself, always consult your doctor.
Medical Your doctor may provide you with specific anti-wart paints and instructions as to how to soak the feet, remove any dead skin over the wart, apply the wart paint and apply a dressing. This should be repeated at intervals.
Specialist If treatment by your own doctor does not work there are special wart clinics, run by dermatologists, where more radical treatment with liquid nitrogen, carbon dioxide snow, fuming nitric acid etc. can be used.
Alternative Veruccae can rarely be charmed away.

BEING SEXUALLY ACTIVE

Sexual behaviour, as well as attitudes and beliefs about it, is culturally determined and has traditionally been more rigidly regulated for women than for men. It is only recently that a woman's right to seek her own way of sexually expressing and fulfilling herself has been accepted. Years of perceiving their bodies as vehicles for reproduction have made it difficult for most women to think of themselves in a purely sexual sense.

A woman's sexual development is lengthier, more complicated, more vulnerable and more psychologically dependent than that of a man. Eroticism depends on self-acceptance and lack of fear. For many women too, feelings of affection are intimately bound up with any successful sexual act. But many girls and women are ambivalent about their bodies, feel insecure about personal relationships, and are unable to enjoy sex as a physical act rather than a psychological involvement.

It can take a long time for a woman to accept and celebrate her own sexuality. Unfortunately, due to their upbringing and perception of a woman's role, some women never really resolve their conflicts. Women ought to take pleasure in their femininity, but even at one of its earliest appearance – menstruation – the almost universal feeling is a negative one. This sexual anxiety is increased by fears of painful intercourse, pregnancy and childbirth.

A mature and fulfilling attitude to sex must spring from your whole body. To attract and make love to your partner as well as satisfy the needs of both of you, you must call upon your mind, your senses, and your internal rhythms, as well as your genital organs. Once you can express your feelings, sensations and perceptions with your body, you will have uncovered the key to successful and gratifying sex.

FEMALE ANATOMY

Human females and males are more anatomically and physically similar than most other species: the physical differences in stature, size and shape that can occur between two females are often far greater than the differences between men and women. The reproductive system and its hormones account for most anatomical variation between the sexes. Before puberty, girls and boys (except for their external genitalia) are very similar, although boys have longer forearms and girls usually more fat, but with puberty, secondary sexual characteristics appear as the result of the action of sex steroids. These developmental changes, however, in the skeleton, breasts, hair follicles and muscles, are really ones of degree, since the changes are mainly quantitative.

Secondary sexual characteristics

In the latter part of adolescence, usually well after menstruation has begun, a woman's body begins to take up the female shape. This is directly related to the secretion of the female hormones estrogen and progesterone. Your ultimate shape, be it curvaceous or boyish is dependent on two things: firstly the amount of estrogen and progesterone you produce, and secondly, the sensitivity of your body in reacting to those hormones.

These hormones are responsible for the following features, which are called secondary sexual characteristics and are the anatomical characteristics of your sex. They are not anything that you can get rid of, or should want to change, because they are the physical signals of your sex and are individual to you.

Breasts

The female breast, initially designed to nourish an infant, is far more highly regarded by society as a source of eroticism, a symbol of femininity, a determinant of fashion, and a measure of beauty. A major secondary sexual characteristic, the breasts are a symbol of feminine identity, forming part of the body image, and are important to a woman's self-esteem, as well as her sexuality. The "glorification" of breasts by society, the often unreal representations in magazines and newspapers, has left many women unhappy about their breasts to the point where they seek implants and injections to change their shape or may reject surgical treatment for breast problems. Each woman's breasts are unique in their size, shape and appearance, and there is no reason why they should conform to some idealized stereotype, or be the measure by which a woman is judged.

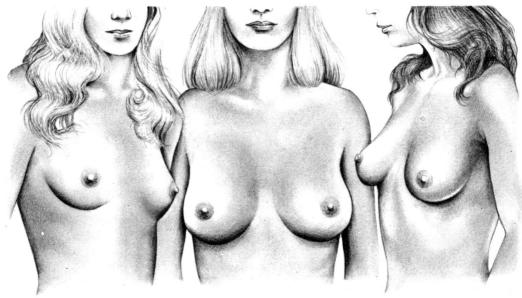

SECONDARY SEXUAL CHARACTERISTICS

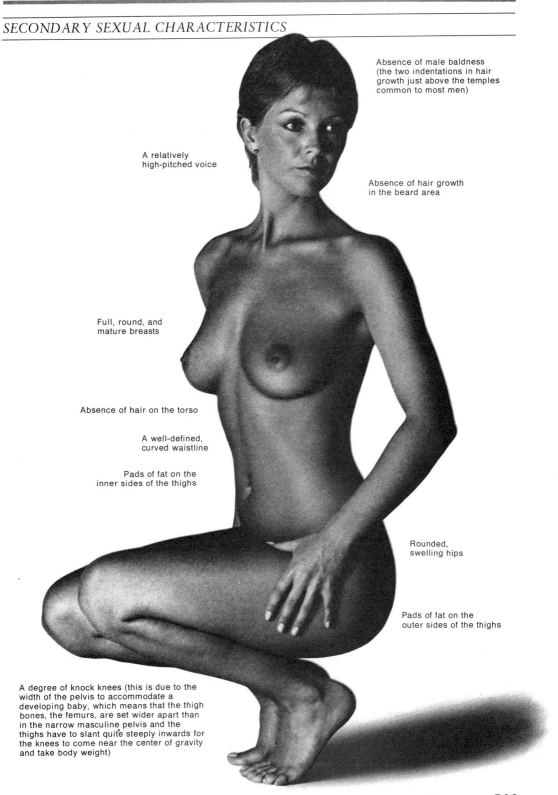

Absence of male baldness
(the two indentations in hair
growth just above the temples
common to most men)

A relatively
high-pitched voice

Absence of hair growth
in the beard area

Full, round, and
mature breasts

Absence of hair on the torso

A well-defined,
curved waistline

Pads of fat on the
inner sides of the thighs

Rounded,
swelling hips

Pads of fat on the
outer sides of the thighs

A degree of knock knees (this is due to the
width of the pelvis to accommodate a
developing baby, which means that the thigh
bones, the femurs, are set wider apart than
in the narrow masculine pelvis and the
thighs have to slant quite steeply inwards for
the knees to come near the center of gravity
and take body weight)

Breast development

The breasts, or mammary glands, are modified sweat glands and are really accessories to the major reproductive organs. They start to grow *in utero* from mammary buds when the fetus is about five months old, and at birth there is a nipple with rudimentary milk ducts already formed in the breast. Sometimes a newborn baby is born with precocious breast development: a high level of circulating female hormones in the mother's blood crosses the placenta and causes the baby's breasts to develop; they may even produce clear straw-colored colostrum for the first few days after birth, but quickly regress to flat discs.

At puberty, the breasts show the first signs of sexual development. In a small girl, the breasts consist only of a nipple projecting from a surrounding ring of pigmented *areola*. At about the tenth or eleventh year, the areola swells and becomes everted, and the nipple still projects from its center. After that, there is a fairly rapid increase in the volume of the breasts by the production of gland tissue and fat underneath the areola – this causes the nipple bud to become elevated on a sort of hillock. As the breast develops further, the areola becomes flattened over the breast tissue which takes up a circular, as opposed to a conical, shape.

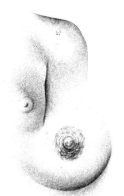

Breast anatomy

The size and shape of the breasts of mature women vary not only between individuals but at different times of each individual woman's life, i.e. during the menstrual cycle, pregnancy and lactation. Anatomically speaking, the breast extends vertically from the second to the sixth rib and horizontally from the border of the breast bone to a line drawn down from the center of the armpit. For descriptive purposes, the breast is divided into four quadrants (see p. 78) and from the upper and outer quadrant, there is a prolongation of breast tissue into the armpit itself known as the axillary tail of the breast. The deep surface of the breast is interwoven with the covering of the muscles of the chest, particularly the *pectoralis major*.

Lymph nodes situated near the armpit drain lymph from the breast to the armpit. The lymphatic drainage of the breast provides a useful background to how cancer of the breast may spread and also gives you the reasons why breast self-examination is as important as it is, and why you should do it in the way that I suggest (see p. 78).

The glandular tissue of the breast is supported in fat which is far and away the most substantial component of the breast. The milk-producing glands are grouped into lobes which radiate out from the nipple. Each lobe contains 15–25 milk ducts which usually open separately at the nipple. Just before a duct opens at the nipple, it widens out to form a swelling or ampula.

The breast has no definite surrounding wall and merges imperceptibly with the fat under the skin. Within the substance of the breast, the ducts are surrounded by fat and branching connective tissue which acts very much like a packing material and supporting framework.

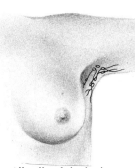

All cells of the body are bathed in fluid, and any excess tissue fluid, or lymph, drains away into the vessels of the lymphatic system. Along the system are clusters of cells called lymph nodes which play an important part in the body's system of immunity.

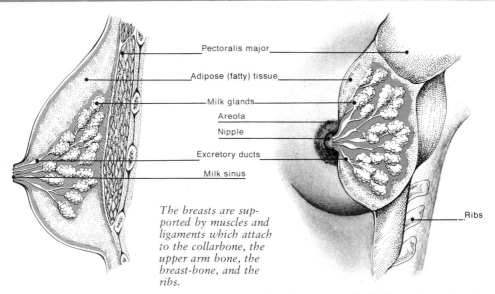

Pectoralis major

Adipose (fatty) tissue

Milk glands

Areola

Nipple

Excretory ducts

Milk sinus

Ribs

The breasts are supported by muscles and ligaments which attach to the collarbone, the upper arm bone, the breast-bone, and the ribs.

Breasts contain no muscle whatsoever (it follows therefore that no amount of exercise can improve the size or shape of your breasts). The height and shape of your breasts depends on a rather weak suspensory system – bands of fine ligaments called the *ligaments of crupa*, which are continuous with the deep coverings of the chest muscles, weave between the fat and lobules of the breast, and are attached to the skin. Ligaments are inelastic: once they are stretched they can never return to their previous short size and shape. It follows, therefore, that if you allow the ligaments of crupa to become stretched, your breasts will sag. This is why the fashion of going bra-less is deleterious to the shape of any breast except the smallest and lightest, and why it is absolutely necessary to wear a bra when you are pregnant and when you are lactating (see p. 48).

The skin over the breast is somewhat smoother, thinner and more translucent than the skin over the rest of the body. The areola skin is particularly thin, and contains sweat and sebaceous glands and hair follicles (a few hairs around the nipple area is not abnormal).

The nipple is conical or cylindrical in shape. Its pink color is due to the thinness of its skin and the browness due to pigmentation of the skin. It is soft or firm according to whether or not the muscle fibers contained in it are relaxed or contracted. Erection of the nipple with contraction of the muscle fibers is a sign of sexual arousal. Through the core of the nipple, milk ducts thread their way and open at its tip.

Body hair Sexual body hair usually appears around the eleventh or twelfth year, just after the breasts have begun to grow. Pubic hair first appears on the *labia majora* and then gradually spreads up over the *mons pubis* and forms a triangle. It may be another eighteen months or two years before the second batch of sexual hair appears in the armpits. There are specialized sweat glands in the

141

armpits which become active at about the same time. These are called *apocrine sweat glands*, and are slightly larger than the ordinary sweat glands which cover the rest of the skin and help to maintain body temperature. The apocrine sweat glands secrete sweat of a special kind, and it is the breakdown of this by the bacteria living in the armpit that causes body odor.

External genital organs

All the external structures of the reproductive system together are known as the *vulva*, or *pudendum*. In area this is bounded by the *mons pubis* anteriorly (at the front), the *perineum* posteriorly (at the back), and the *labia minora* and *majora* laterally (at the sides).

The vulva is highly sensitive to touch and is very erotic; it also serves to protect the vaginal and urethral openings.

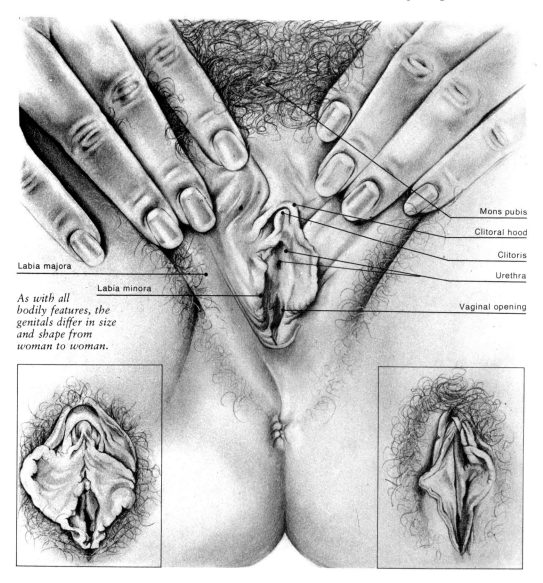

Mons pubis

Clitoral hood

Clitoris

Urethra

Labia majora

Vaginal opening

Labia minora

As with all bodily features, the genitals differ in size and shape from woman to woman.

Mons pubis
Also known as the *mons veneris* ("mountain of Venus"), it is a fatty tissue and skin covering for the *pubic symphysis* (the union of the two pubic bones). After puberty it is covered by pubic hair, normally triangular in area.

Labia majora (large lips)
Two lips form the outermost parts of the vulva. They are two-fold and normally lie together and so conceal the other external genital organs. They extend forward from the perineum and fuse at the front in the mons pubis. The outer surface is covered with pubic hair, the inner surface contains sweat and sebaceous glands. Estrogen-sensitive fatty tissue and erectile tissue lie underneath and encircle the vaginal opening.

Labia minora (small lips)
These two lips are delicate folds of skin which lie between the labia majora. At the back they fuse with the inner surface of the labia majora and form a skinfold. At the front, each splits into a fold which surrounds the clitoris. These folds form the *prepuce* which is equivalent to the prepuce in a man. Large numbers of sebaceous glands produce *sebum* which lubricates the skin and, in combination with the secretions from the vagina and sweat glands, forms a waterproof protective covering against urine, bacteria, and menstrual blood. There are wide variations in their size and shape and one is generally larger than the other: they may be hidden by the labia majora or project forward. During sexual excitement they become engorged, change of color and increase in thickness – sometimes as much as two to three times their diameter.

Vestibule
This is the area enclosed by the labia minora and contains the urethra, vagina and the two ducts of *Bartholin's glands*. These glands produce a few drops of mucus during sexual excitement which moisten the vestibule in preparation for intercourse.

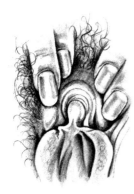

Clitoris
This structure, which gets its name from the Greek word "key" is analogous to the male penis and has exactly the same component parts in miniature. The clitoris is about 2–3 centimeters in length and is bent back on itself. The small head of the clitoris – the *clitoridis* (equivalent to the *glans penis*) – is covered by a sensitive lining which fits over the body of the clitoris. There are many receptive nerve endings in the clitoris which makes it the most erotically sensitive part of the genitalia for most females. During sexual excitement it becomes erect and doubles in size.

Hymen
Called after the Greek god of marriage, this is a thin membrane which guards the vaginal orifice. It is normally perforated during childhood when cycling, playing games, horseback riding, etc.

and this allows the escape of menstrual bloodflow. Thickness and rigidity are variable, but even so, perforation by an erect penis during first intercourse is rarely the painful experience which is mythically described. Many other mistaken ideas exist about the hymen: an intact one is not proof of virginity, neither is a ruptured one proof that intercourse has taken place; virgins are not precluded from wearing tampons.

Internal genital organs

In medical text books, the female genital organs are called the reproductive tract and consist of a pair of ovaries, the fallopian tubes, the uterus and the vagina. The uterus lies in the center of the pelvis with the bladder in front and the rectum behind, and is enclosed and supported in a double fold of ligament called the *broad ligament*.

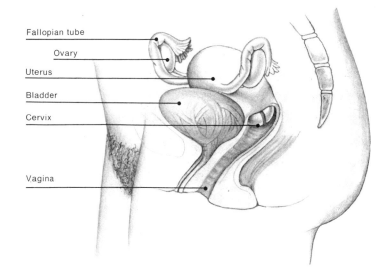

Fallopian tube

Ovary

Uterus

Bladder

Cervix

Vagina

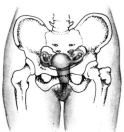

The internal reproductive organs shown on the left are encased protectively in the bones of the pelvic girdle.

Ovaries

The ovaries are two glands which produce ova (eggs) and sex hormones. They measure 3–4 centimeters in length, 2 centimeters in breadth and are about one centimeter thick and are flattened and bean-shaped. Their surface is pearly white but looks scarred and wrinkled. During a woman's fertile life they undergo monthly cyclical changes with the regular formation of cysts (follicles) which produce and liberate ova and secrete estrogen, followed by a regression of the follicle with the resulting production of estrogen plus progesterone. A woman is born with all the eggs she will have (approximately 400,000 are present at birth).

The position of the ovaries varies from woman to woman, but they nearly always lie near the sides of the pelvis with their long axes upright. The fallopian tubes hang over the ovaries so that when an egg is dropped it easily finds its way into the funnel-shaped end of this uterine tube.

Fallopian (uterine) tubes

Each fallopian tube (also known as an *oviduct*) is about 10 centimeters in length. Because it can be viewed from the outside via the uterus, the cervix and the vagina, it provides direct communication between the exterior and interior pelvis, a feature which is important for both surgical and X-ray purposes. The outer funnel-shaped end of the fallopian tube ends in a fringe made up of finger-like processes called *fimbriae*. The lining of the tubes is covered by cells which have mobile hair-like projections which are in constant movement, wafting towards the uterine cavity. They produce currents which transport the ova from the ovaries along the tubes and into the uterine cavity. If a fertilized egg fails to reach the uterus and becomes implanted in the fallopian tube, this can develop into an ectopic pregnancy. This condition is extremely serious as the tube does not permit much expansion and the tube can burst, causing severe bleeding and infection, if the embryo is not surgically removed. Ectopic implantation occurs in about 1 in 250 pregnancies.

Conditions of the fallopian tubes are described by the medical prefix "*salpinx*" which is the Greek word for tube: *salpingitis* (inflammation of the oviducts) and *salpingectomy* (removal of a tube) are examples.

Uterus

The uterus is a pear-shaped, hollow organ; the upper two-thirds are called the body, and the part which lies above the entrance to the fallopian tubes is called the *fundus*. The two horns which connect with the fallopian tubes are called the *cornua*. The lower one-third of the uterus is the cervix, which projects into the vagina.

The uterus is a muscular organ. It can stretch and swell to accommodate a full-term fetus, and then with its muscle fibers (which are the strongest in the human body, both male and female) expel it at delivery and then shrink back to its original size in six weeks.

The non-pregnant uterus is flattened from back to front and weighs anything between 50 and 100 grams. It measures about 8 centimeters in length, 5 centimeters in breadth and 2–3 centimeters in thickness. The uterine muscle or *myometrium* is 1 centimeter thick, so that the total length of the uterine cavity is about 7 centimeters.

The walls of the uterus are solid and made of muscle tissue, and enclose a cavity called the *endometrium* which undergoes cyclic changes during menstruation and forms the site for implantation of a fertilized egg. If it does not receive an egg, it sheds this lining.

The uterus is supported by elastic ligaments which give it a certain amount of flexibility (for instance to accommodate a full bladder). With advancing age and repeated childbirth they can lose their elasticity and allow the uterus to sag.

Quite commonly the uterus is deviated slightly towards the right side. When it is viewed from the side, however, it is usually bent forward on itself in a position which is called anteflexion at

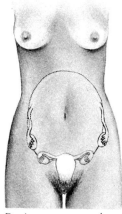

During pregnancy the walls of the uterus expand to five or six times their usual size to accommodate the fetus' body.

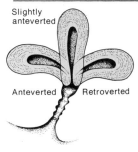

Slightly anteverted

Anteverted   Retroverted

an angle of about 90° with the vagina. However in about 20% of women the uterus bends backwards on itself in a retroflexed position. This is not abnormal and it does not make conception or pregnancy difficult.

Cervix

The upper part of the 2.5 cm-long cervix, which is the lower one-third of the uterus, is cylindrical, but the part which projects into the vagina is conical. The cervix contains much less muscle than the body of the uterus. The opening of the cervix into the vagina is called the *external os* (mouth) and the inside opening into the uterine cavity, the *internal os*. The lining of the cervix contains large, branched glands which produce copious quantities of mucus throughout the whole of the menstrual cycle. The quality and quantity of the mucus, however, varies according to the time of the month (see p. 180).

The appearance of the *os* differs according to whether a woman has had children, abortions, or neither; and its health.

The ringed area, far right, shows carcinoma in situ above the os. The close-up view, near right, shows the os of a normal cervix.

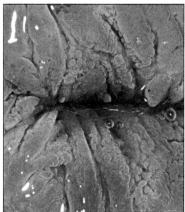

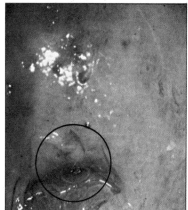

Normal   Pre-cancerous

Vagina

The vagina is a tube which measures about 8 centimeters in length. Its size is variable and so capable of distortion that any normal vagina can accommodate any size of penis with ease. When a woman stands erect her vagina is not vertical, but lies forwards and downwards from the uterus at an angle of about 70° to the horizontal. Usually, the front and back walls are in contact except at the upper end near the cervix. The cervix enters the vagina through the front vaginal wall (*anterior fornix*) and as a result, the back of the vaginal wall (*posterior fornix*) is longer than the front. This arrangement favors the passage of sperm into the cervix during intercourse because when a woman lies on her back, the opening of the cervix is not only directly exposed to semen, but is bathed by the pool of ejaculate which forms in the posterior fornix in which it rests. During intercourse, it is this posterior fornix which takes the brunt of penile thrusting and so protects the cervix from injury.

146

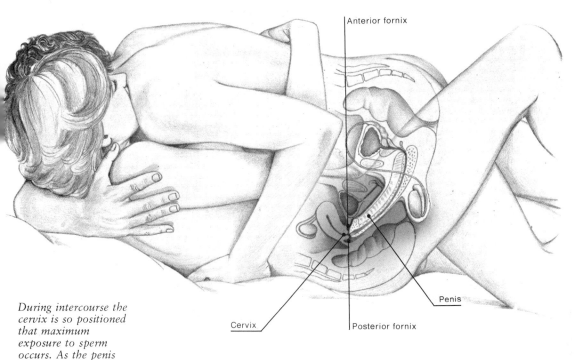

Anterior fornix

Penis

Cervix

Posterior fornix

During intercourse the cervix is so positioned that maximum exposure to sperm occurs. As the penis moves forward in the vagina the inner thighs and posterior fornix act as "shock absorbers."

The lining of the vagina is very thick and is thrown up into folds which run lengthwise and from side to side. The cells which line the vagina contain large quantities of the starch *glycogen*. Bacteria living normally in the vagina ferment the starch to produce lactic acid which makes the contents of the vagina naturally on the acid side. This is important for the health of the vaginal lining and for the ecological balance of the bacteria and yeasts which inhabit it. The upper layer of dead cells of the vagina is constantly being shed and, along with vaginal secretions, forms a normal vaginal discharge (see p. 118).

The vagina contains bundles of muscle which run down its length and it has a very rich blood supply which causes it to swell and become pink during sexual arousal. Vasocongestion during intercourse narrows the passageway and accounts for the gripping sensations felt by the penis. Two very strong muscles blend with the sides of the vagina about half-way down, and if these muscles are kept toned up by exercise (see p. 120) this helps to keep the vagina firm, tight and elevated.

There are very few sensory receptors for touch or pain located in the vagina; any sensations you may feel come from the urinary bladder or rectum. In fact, the upper part of the vagina is relatively insensitive. The lower third has some nerve receptors to touch and pain but these are scanty. The major erotic site for women is not the vagina but the clitoris (see p. 143).

The bladder lies in front of the upper half of the vagina and the tube leading from the bladder to the outside, the *urethra*, is embedded within the lower half of the front vaginal wall. The back wall of the vagina is very close to the rectum.

147

THE MENSTRUAL CYCLE

To my mind the cyclical changes which occur in the body on average every 28 days, but quite normally between 26 and 33, are misnamed. These changes result in menstruation, but there are many effects on other organs which are just as important and which are under-emphasized.

The basis of the menstrual cycle is regular changes in the pattern of female hormone secretion. The female hormones, estrogen and progesterone, are produced by the ovaries which are stimulated to manufacture them by a master hormone from the pituitary gland in the brain, and this in turn is supervised by releasing factors from a very deep brain center which can be influenced by emotional state. Hence menstruation can be disturbed by anxiety, by light and dark (menstruation sometimes ceases in women living in the Arctic circle where many of the winter months are lived in semi-darkness), and by time zone changes (jet-lag can result in disturbances of the menstrual cycle).

At the beginning of the hormone cycle, ie., immediately after menstruation begins, small quantities of estrogen are produced which gradually increase until they reach a peak just prior to ovulation, which occurs 14 days before the first day of your next menstruation. With the emission of an ovum, the remaining follicle, the *corpus luteum* – so named because it is yellow – begins to secrete progesterone which reaches its peak a few days prior to the onset of menstruation. The first half of the cycle before ovulation is termed the estrogenic phase of the cycle and the second half after ovulation, is the progestogenic phase. During the second half of the progestogenic phase, there is a small surge of estrogen secretion which dies away with the progesterone levels a few days prior to menstruation. These steeply falling levels of female hormones, and final withdrawal, result in the shedding of the uterine lining and menstrual blood flow.

The onset of menstruation

In many primitive cultures, and often in rural societies in the Western world, the onset of menstruation or the *menarche* is a mark that a girl is a woman and is ready to take up the duties and obligations of womanhood. There seems to be a trend for the menarche to occur earlier and earlier, so that every woman should have detailed knowledge of what happens during the menstrual cycle, not only for her own information, but so that she can educate her children in an accurate way free of myth and mystique. In America, the average age of the onset of menstruation is now 12.6 years. Only a century ago it was 15 years. There was an old belief that the menarche occurred earlier in girls living in hot climates, but scientific evidence does not support this myth; it is the daughters of better-off parents who are menstruating earlier than those who have poor parents. Most doctors now agree that the onset of menstruation depends on socio-economic status which influences diet and overall body weight.

Menstruation occurs about halfway through the growth sequence, and the changes which occur can be seen on the right.

9–10 years
The pelvic bones begin to grow and to take on a female shape. Fat is deposited on the breasts, hips and thighs.

10–11 years
Nipples start to bud and hair appears on the mons pubis.

11–13 years
Internal and external genital organs grow and develop, the vaginal wall starts to thicken; vaginal secretions may appear.

13–15 years
Pubic hair increases and appears in the armpits. Periods start but they may be irregular.

15–17 years
More fat is deposited on the hips, breasts and thighs. The periods now become regular.

17–18 years
By now bone growth is completed and adult height is reached.

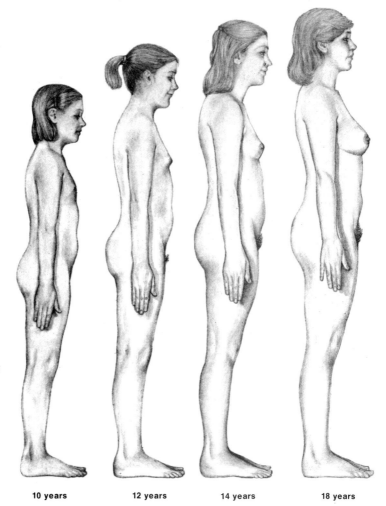

| 10 years | 12 years | 14 years | 18 years |

How the cycle starts

Your very first period represents the initial collaboration of four important organs of the body:
- The hypothalamus which is a very small part of the brain buried deep at its base.
- The pituitary gland which is connected to the hypothalamus anatomically and shares a common blood supply.
- The ovaries.
- The endometrium (the lining of the uterus).

For reasons which medicine does not yet understand, the hypothalamus begins to secrete chemicals called releasing factors about four full years before menstruation begins. These releasing factors pass to the pituitary through tiny arteries which connect it to the hypothalamus, where they cause the release of several hormones: *growth hormone* which causes the growth spurt that precedes the menarche; *follicle-stimulating hormone* (FSH) which stimulates the growth of egg follicles in the ovary and *luteinizing hormone* which causes rupture of an egg follicle and the release of the ovum. In other words it brings about ovulation.

149

CHANGES IN THE BODY DURING THE MENSTRUAL CYCLE

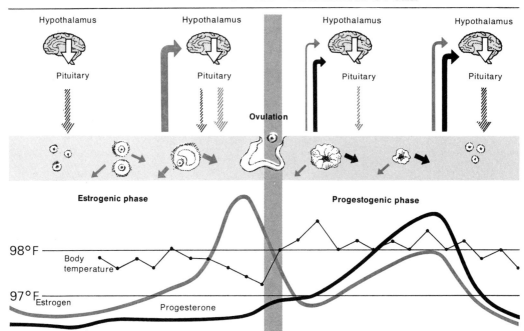

Estrogenic phase

Ovulation

Progestogenic phase

Body temperature

98°F

97°F

Estrogen

Progesterone

Estrogen
This stimulates thickening of vaginal wall. Vaginal moisture increases just before ovulation; blood levels 6 times higher than resting levels.

Progesterone
Relaxes all growth muscle (may cause constipation), increases skin sebum and raises body temperature.

Body Temperature
Rises about 1°F on ovulation. In people who are susceptible to cold sores, see p. 116, this rise in body temperature may be sufficient to excite the dormant cold-sore virus into activity, thus producing a cold sore.

1	2	3	4	5	6	7	8	9	10	11	12	13	14	15	16	17	18	19	20	21	22	23	24	25	26	27	28

Cervical mucus

Around ovulation, the mucus secreted by the cervical glands is thin, elastic and clear. This type of mucus is attractive to, and easily penetrated by, sperm and facilitates conception.

After ovulation has occurred, and under the effect of progesterone, the cervical mucus becomes thick, inelastic and opaque. It is hostile to and difficult for the spermatozoa to penetrate.

Breasts

The cells, of the milk glands and the ducts in the tissue thicken and grow.

The glands increase their sensory activity. In the week prior to menstruation, the glands may be so swollen that the breasts feel nodular and you may be able to feel individual glands – they will feel like orange pips. Breasts also become generally swollen, tender, heavy; nipples may tingle spontaneously and be sore to the touch.

Uterus/Endometrium

Bleeding   The endometrum starts to grow again from the stumps left behind after menstruation has taken place. Under the influence of estrogens from the growing egg follicles in the ovary, it grows very quickly, and it becomes very thick. Numerous new blood vessels find their way into the thickening endometrium, enriching the blood supply.

Many glands form and as the cycle progresses, they become large and tortuous until there is almost no space between them and the endometrium begins to break up. With the withdrawal of estrogen and progesterone at the end of the cycle, the secretory stage of the endometrium collapses and menstruation begins.

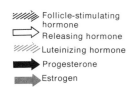

Follicle-stimulating hormone

Releasing hormone

Luteinizing hormone

Progesterone

Estrogen

The hypothalamus regulates the hormones secreted by the pituitary. 1) FSH is released, stimulating follicle growth. 2) The ovary releases estrogen, triggering the production of LH; ovulation occurs. 3) The follicles form the corpus luteum which releases estrogen and progesterone, stopping the flow of FSH and LH. 4) If fertilization doesn't occur, the levels of estrogen and progesterone fall; menstruation begins.

An age-old description of menstruation is that the uterus is weeping because pregnancy has not happened. Bleeding occurs because the endometrial lining crumbles. It becomes thick, and filled with glands in preparation for receiving a fertilized egg and is shed when conception does not occur. Menstruation, therefore, has a retrospective and a prospective function. Retrospectively, it is getting rid of the old uterine lining which was not used for a pregnancy. Prospectively, it is preparing itself for the whole cycle to begin again in case pregnancy should occur the following month. Like members of an obedient orchestra, various parts of our body respond in harmony to the directions of their conductor, the hypothalamus. There are more parts of the body taking part in this hormonal symphony than you may think.

I have drawn up an illustrated chart (see left) which shows you what is going on simultaneously in the organs of the body as you go through your menstrual cycle, so that you can see what is happening everywhere at any particular time. Remember, too, that all women are subject to mood changes during the cyclical hormone changes. The high levels of progesterone present in the week before menstruation, followed by blood levels plummeting to almost nothing, cause anything from minor irritability to a full-blown, premenstrual syndrome, see p. 236.

THE OVARIAN CYCLE

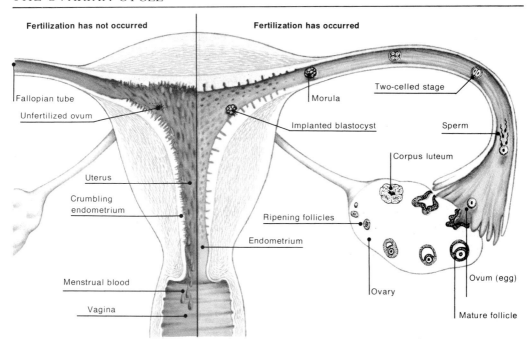

Fertilization has not occurred

Fertilization has occurred

Two-celled stage

Fallopian tube

Unfertilized ovum

Morula

Implanted blastocyst

Sperm

Corpus luteum

Uterus

Crumbling endometrium

Ripening follicles

Endometrium

Menstrual blood

Ovary

Ovum (egg)

Vagina

Mature follicle

Each month of your fertile life, one of your ovaries matures and releases an ovum, or egg. If it is not fertilized by sperm the endometrial lining breaks up and you will menstruate (left). If it is fertilized, it will multiply and eventually implant itself in the uterine wall where it will proceed to develop into a fetus (right).

There are some women, however, who bleed at the time of their regular menstrual period even after they are pregnant, as well as those who remain fertile even through menstruation.

The duration of the cycle The menstrual cycle starts on the first day of bleeding and ends the day before the next menstruation starts. The menstrual cycle, therefore, includes both those days when bleeding occurs and the interval between bleeding. The interval can be anything between 24 to 34 days but the average is 29. Even though you usually have a regular pattern, many women will find that their period is a few days out on either side if they have an illness; if they are overworked, tired, or worried; or if they travel through a time zone. In adolescence, menstruation tends to be irregular and the period between bleeding is usually longer. In the first couple of years after the menarche, periods may only occur two or three times a year and when they do they may be quite heavy. The blood is not always red, it may be dark brown or tarry.

Is there any truth in the many myths about menstruation?

Almost all societies have myths and rituals surrounding menstruation and many, like the Jews and the Moslems, have prayers for cleansing and purification following menstruation. Even now, in certain Western cultures, fruits like pineapples and raspberries are thought to be bad if eaten during menstruation. Washing the hair is believed by many to increase the menstrual flow or, as my mother used to say, "send the blood to your brain," or bring on a cold or even pneumonia. Others believe that menstruation is a cleansing process and if it does not occur, dangerous substances are dammed up inside the womb. None of these beliefs is true. A girl or woman can do exactly as she likes and take part in any activity: riding, swimming, working, walking, washing her hair, bathing, taking a shower, eating what she likes, dancing, driving and having sex.

When, after menstruation, do I become fertile?

If you count the first day of bleeding as day 1, you will ovulate approximately fourteen days later. A sperm is usually only capable of healthy fertilization for 36–48 hours. This means that for about two days prior to ovulation you will be fertile and there can be live sperm waiting to fertilize your ovum when it is dropped. It takes your ovum roughly forty-eight hours to travel down the fallopian tube and into the uterine cavity before it dies. It follows, therefore, that if you have intercourse in those forty-eight hours your ovum may become fertilized. This means that there are about four days in the month, two days before and two days after ovulation, when you are fertile. However, there are no hard and fast rules. Ovulation may be early or late. A new love affair may be such a huge emotional event that it may well upset your normal menstrual pattern anyway. If you travel over time zones and upset your biological clock, the hypothalamus may be affected and your periods become irregular for a short time. There really is not any time of the month when you may not be fertile – a small percentage of women even occasionally ovulate during menstruation. There is no such thing as an absolutely safe time. But undoubtedly for most women, fertility reaches its optimum on or around the 14th day after the first day of menstruation.

Can I control my menstruation?

Yes, with hormone pills, the most common of which is the oral contraceptive pill. If you have a very important engagement or an examination, or a good reason for not wanting to menstruate at the time you are expecting your period then go along and see your doctor and explain to her/him your predicament. S/he will be able to prescribe a short course of hormonal pills which will either bring on your period early or put off your period until after the expected date; neither of which should cause you any harm. If you are already on the combined "pill" you can completely suppress the menstrual period by taking two months of pills continuously. In other words, when you finish one pack go straight on the next day with a new pack so that you take the pills for two months consecutively, without a break. There is no evidence that you will come to any harm by doing this.

EROGENOUS ZONES

Though both sexes share erogenous zones, they are more important to the female. It has been known for some time, and research has confirmed it, that men are aroused by psychic stimuli, particularly visual ones, whereas women are usually aroused strongly only with physical contact and touch stimuli.

It's not by accident, therefore, that courtship or sexual foreplay begins by touching fingers or holding hands, and then proceeds to more intimate physical embraces, culminating in a high degree of skin contact during intercourse. Certain areas of the body, especially parts of the skin, are particularly sensitive sexually speaking. These areas are called erogenous zones. Exclusive of the external genital organs themselves, the most often quoted erogenous zones include the lips and buttocks for both sexes and, in women, the breasts and the nipples. Of the external genital organs, the glans of the penis and the region of the clitoris are particularly sensitive. The touching of these areas, particularly when accompanied by increasing intensity of emotions, leads to local and general bodily changes. The main local change is an increase in the blood supply which leads to swelling, pinkness and increased sensitivity. General body changes include an increase in the breathing rate, the pulse rate, blood pressure and sweating.

Beside the "primary" erogenous zones, there are secondary and even tertiary ones. Secondary zones would include all those which have sexual connotations derived from society or from the specific relationship between two people. Such zones would include the ears, eyelids, the upper legs, particularly the inner aspects of the thighs and any part of the skin which is normally covered.

The main reason why certain areas of the skin have become known as erogenous zones is because they are the most sensitive. Their sensitivity depends on the richness of their supply of sensory nerve endings, mainly the nerve endings which pick up touch (there are four types of nerve endings which distinguish between touch, pressure, pain and temperature). The parts of our body which have the richest supply of sensory nerve endings, are the lips and the skin surrounding the mouth, the fingertips, the areola and nipples, and all the external genital organs. It is these areas which pick up touch and translate it most acutely. In a sexual situation, the touch stimuli become sexual stimuli. An important, though secondary, factor affecting the rate of conversion of the touch stimulus to a sexual one, is the emotional involvement and intensity of the situation.

If the emotional component is very high, touch of almost any part of the body e.g. ankles, feet, neck, back, shoulders, arms, can become a sexual stimulus and this is why almost any part of the skin can be an erogenous zone, if it is touched by a sexually attractive and sexually desirable partner.

RE-THINKING SEX

As an emancipated 44-year-old woman with a medical background and no "mechanical" hang-ups about sex, I naively thought that I had my attitude towards books about sex fairly well taped. That was until I surveyed the large number of sex books on the market with the aim of giving my readers no less than these.

To my surprise I found myself stymied by instincts and emotions. Instinctively I felt that I could not attempt to simulate the average, even very good, sex book which you can buy in any book shop. I found I wasn't intellectually capable of treating sex like a car-owner's manual. Nor, to my surprise, was I *emotionally* capable of it.

All the time I was reading books on sex I found my intellect and my emotions were out of harmony. There was something wrong which I couldn't at first put my finger on. I found the books discomforting and disquieting. They made me uneasy; worse, they made me unhappy. While applauding the encyclopedic nature of some, the matter-of-fact tone of others, the highly personal view of yet others, I found myself thinking "This isn't how sex is in real life and if it isn't, what is?" And, "How can I write about it?" More important, "Do I have anything to offer?"

The reason I decided to write at all is that I think my view is more common than most sex books admit to, or would have the reader believe. That seemed important because readers of sex books, and particularly women who haven't been reading them for long, fall into the trap of setting up sex books as yardsticks. I know that's dangerous and I would like to counteract it.

Sex, of course, is recreational; it's fun, it's exhilarating, it's tranquillizing. But it is also beautiful, and it's about loving and caring – a view which I think has become obscured by our preoccupation with performance and fulfillment, to the extent that many people feel inadequate if they don't enjoy fellatio every night.

In coming to my point of view I undertook a journey of discovery about myself. This is an invitation for you to undertake your own journey. My aim is to pass on information about sex so that you can make up your own mind. It is also to clarify and demystify some attitudes, mainly propounded by sex books, which have become accepted conventions in recent years and which I think may be doing quite a lot of harm to a fair number of women. My hope is that it will lead you on a journey of self-discovery so that you can approach sex with a complete sense of ease.

Finding out about sex

Women don't necessarily need "how to" books about sex, glossaries of sexual terms, or physiological maps; after all, there are many women who succeed in their voyages of sexual discovery with the help of sympathetic partners, or who possess a lucky temperament and are prepared to initiate and experiment, and have the strength of character to know what they like and get it.

It is easy to see why they should succeed. It is not necessary to have physiological knowledge or information about the clitoris, as regards its position and function, in order to enjoy the sensation when it's stimulated; it's not necessary to know the meaning of the word to enjoy pleasant sensations. Everything exists independently of its name and tastes just as sweet. As for a catalogue of sexual positions, whoever wrote the books must have discovered them at least once naturally. No discussion of sex, no matter how good it is, can be a substitute for trial and error with a loving partner.

But there are circumstances when a chapter like this comes to the rescue: where error inhibits trial, when a partner is not sympathetic, and when a temperament is over-anxious rather than calm, over-emotional rather than rational. And, of course, there is the hypothetical, but nonetheless real, woman, who would be better off for solid information – one who has been conditioned into believing that only the missionary position for intercourse is decent, or who doesn't know that she has a clitoris to be stimulated, or that the clitoris fails to be stimulated in the missionary position, or who thinks it is wrong to touch herself and that her partner will be slighted if she does. . . . For such a woman, naming the clitoris doesn't bring it into existence, but it can bring it into her consciousness for the first time.

Why is this knowledge so important? The first reason is that good sex is very nice; it is nature's gift to every one of us and it's a shame and a loss if some of us don't know how to enjoy the gift.

Another reason why it is important, of course, is for procreation, and, occasionally, information about when, why, what, and where is crucial (it can be just as crucial in avoiding procreation).

But the most important reason is perhaps that sex affects most of us at our deepest level, that it has a place in our lives that is as much or more important than any other aspect of our relationships, be they long- or short-term. Beyond recreation and procreation, "sex" is the time, place, means, and language – on a level different from all others – of knowing someone else.

The experience of sex

Most sex guides make the subject of sex curiously different from life. In life you don't get the whole banquet spread out before you; in fact, one of the very good things about life is that there are surprises in store. I would hazard that the common experience of couples is that they do the same thing for quite a long time, quite contentedly, and then one day spontaneously do something else because they are *moved* to do it. Between loving partners sex has a sacramental role, a symbolic role. It is more than a mechanical act, and a "how to" approach to sex is as meaningless to true sexual communion as an instruction sheet on when to stand and when to kneel is to religious communion.

You may feel that I am coalescing "love" and "sexual fulfillment" too easily, too much. I feel that as long as you are aware that the one does not imply the other (a lifeguide, which is what this book is, is not a sex-guide) should recognize the connection between the two, as well as the distinction.

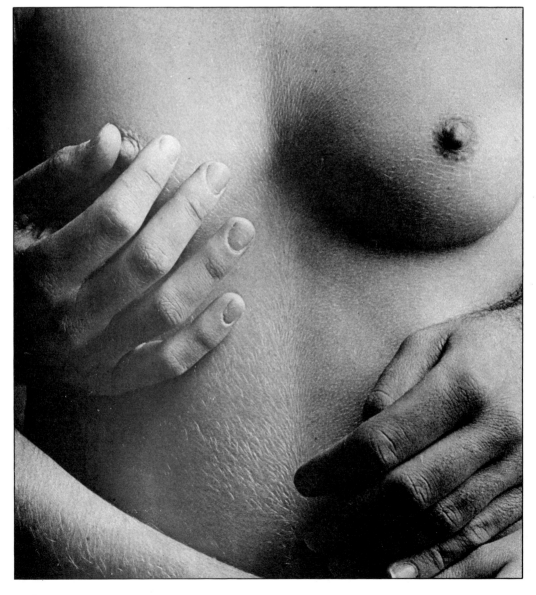

I am certain that fulfillment, happiness, maturity and morality in a sexual partnership are largely the result of equilibrium, much more than quality and very much more than quantity. In other words, it depends on two people being in balance. To use oral sex as an example: a couple that is moved in any sense to use their mouths are in equilibrium; partners who both only like cunnilingus are in equilibrium; partners who both only like fellatio are in equilibrium.

What disquiets me about much that is written about sex is that one's own need, or one's partner's need, for equilibrium is ignored, or worse still, it may be destroyed by the modern ethic to achieve more, faster. People very often feel they are being tested against a "successfully fulfilled" model, one that has as much reality as the famous average family, with the famous 2.3 children.

I believe that women, more so than men, shrink from a depersonalized approach to sex. Sex books, of course, were originally written for men, and in today's attempts to redress the balance, to procure for women what men had been enjoying for so long (and what women in perception or reality, had been going without), certain sexologists have done womankind a great disservice. In the last two decades women have been encouraged to go out and experiment, to achieve the ultimate orgasm, to take on a masculine persona, to sow wild oats, to play the field, to hop from partner to partner, and from bed to bed. Worse, this has been seen as synonymous with sexual liberation.

Women are, for the most part, biologically unable to behave like men; both on emotional and hormonal grounds it goes against the grain for most women to try to simulate men. The feminist movement has made a great number of women feel inadequate, undersexed, unable to perform, dissatisfied and unfulfilled because they cannot live up to the criteria of the so-called sexually liberated woman. In this one respect, the feminist advocates of sexual freedom have increased rather than decreased sexual frustration and have been responsible for more, rather than less, unhappiness. Women can't be men in any context, least of all the sexual one, and they should not try.

Therefore, my guide to sex is not about where to put your left elbow in the lotus position, or which is the best way to use a vibrator; it is about giving you a sense of informedness, a sense of security, and a sense of proportion so that you can make your own choices and your own discoveries.

Sexual behavior

Let's start off with the proposition that sex is natural and sex is good. Good sex is what makes you feel happy and satisfied and causes pain to no one.

Masturbation

Sexual awareness starts in the early teens with self-awareness and self-exploration. Two-thirds of girls masturbate by the time they are sixteen, and surveys have shown that four out of five girls believe that masturbation is not harmful, is acceptable, and very enjoyable.

For most girls, masturbation is the introduction to sex. It helps them to know how they function sexually; many girls experience their first orgasm through masturbation. It helps a girl to form preferences and may contribute to successful communion.

Masturbation may not only produce the most physically intense orgasm but can also evoke the greatest number of pelvic contractions. It can also bring the average woman to orgasm faster than any other type of sexual stimulation.

Homosexuality

Before graduating to a heterosexual partnership, many girls experience a homosexual encounter with another girl or woman. This does not mean that a girl will grow up with a preference for lesbian relationships. Many girls enjoy a homosexual friendship as part of learning about sex – it can be thought of as a trial run before she exposes herself to the hurdle of sex with a boy. It serves as an exploration to bolster her confidence and helps her to define what she really likes.

However, lesbian women prefer to have sex with their own kind and this sexual activity is as varied as anyone's – kissing, caressing, oral-genital stimulation, breast stimulation, mutual masturbation. Bisexuals enjoy sexual activity with both sexes.

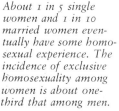

About 1 in 5 single women and 1 in 10 married women eventually have some homosexual experience. The incidence of exclusive homosexuality among women is about one-third that among men.

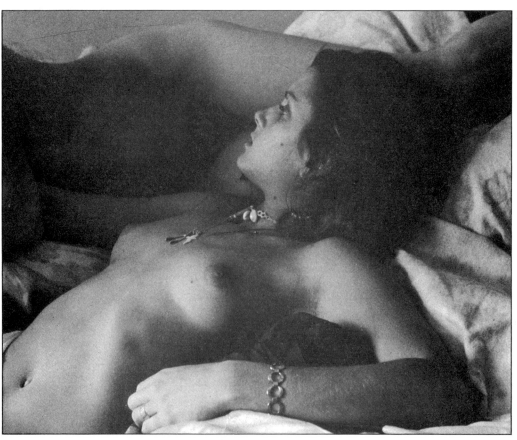

Foreplay

Sex is an escalating activity, starting off with touching and caressing, and going on to kissing and foreplay. Foreplay is much more important to women than to men. Men become sexually aroused by thoughts, by sights and by talking. Women are much less easily aroused by these things. In fact, they have a much narrower range of erotogenic·stimuli than men. The majority of women need physical stimulation of the breasts, of the clitoris and of the vagina to get them sexually aroused. What is more, the physical stimulation has to be continuous for sexual excitement to build. If stimulation is interrupted, the excitement can die completely and the woman has to start the climb to sexual excitement all over again.

In women, thinking gets in the way of sex so that a woman is most sexy when she feels the most and thinks the least. It is also true that they are more easily distracted during sexual foreplay than men; this is why women may find that they are listening for sounds, or even going over tomorrow morning's shopping list if foreplay is not successful.

There is an interesting biological supposition why this should be so. When the male first began to engage in sexual intercourse in a prone position he became vulnerable to attack. It was therefore necessary for someone to keep guard against predators. It was awkward to have a friend doing this for him so it fell to the lot of the female to keep watch. So that she could be an efficient and attentive guard, the clitoris became widely separated from the vagina so that it was not stimulated during sexual intercourse. While the woman was unexcited she could be on the alert for approaching enemies. This is a theory which was put to me by a professor of sexual medicine and while it may be of questionable validity, I find the irony attractive.

Oral sex

The majority of teenagers and adults engage in oral sex; indeed, among teenagers it is considered to be an act of greater intimacy than intercourse. A questionnaire survey done in America with teenagers revealed that boys enjoy all aspects of oral sex more than girls. Boys like using their mouth and tongue on a girl's vagina (*cunnilingus*) and enjoy having their penis kissed and orally stimulated (*fellatio*) more than a girl does, with either of these. This has been attributed to the double standard which is still prevalent in our society today – that it is not just acceptable, but applauded for boys to be freer and enjoy sex more than girls.

Oral sex is for many couples one of the most pleasurable and exciting forms of sexual activity. Fellatio and cunnilingus can be performed simultaneously, alternately, preliminary to intercourse, or can be used to produce orgasm.

Anal sex

Occasionally couples will experiment with anal sex – perhaps to satisfy their curiosity – but regular indulgence can lead to problems. Anal intercourse can evoke highly erotic responses similar to vaginal intercourse and, as the anus is tighter than a relaxed or overstretched vagina, it can create an added dimension to sexual excitement. Also, your partner can more easily stimulate your breasts, clitoris and vagina during penetration.

Be that as it may, the anus was not designed anatomically or biologically to accommodate the penis, and infections and injuries can result even with the most gentle lover. The penis must be well lubricated before insertion, with a cream or jelly (not saliva), and must never be reinserted into the vagina afterwards without being thoroughly washed as it will allow bacteria to infect the vagina. If anal intercourse is practiced regularly, for a long time, you may relax and dilate the anal sphincter to such a degree that you lose control of its function.

Fantasies

We nearly all of us engage in fantasies to do with sex. This starts in our early teens. Boys fantasize more than girls for the reason that they are more easily excited by sexual thoughts. Boys also use pictures, photographs, magazines, books, etc. to increase their sexual excitement during masturbation. Girls rarely do this. Girls' fantasies tend to be of a romantic nature, or related to their own sexual experience, rather than extravagant make-believe.

However, many mature women fantasize both during and prior to sex – they do so because it often enhances sexual enjoyment and it's a way of exploring and initiating sexual behavior. Fantasies and masturbation are closely connected – the one can very much increase the enjoyment of the other.

Sexuality Women can be spontaneously and honestly sexy, but this is more difficult for females than males. To be sexually arousable you must be sensitive to touch, be psychologically able to give of yourself and, in heterosexual relationships, be able to enjoy the entry of a penis into your vagina.

Some people believe that sexuality for the female is a developed ability – perhaps a learned pattern of lowered inhibitions. It is said that women reach their sexual peak in their late thirties and early forties – not because anything different is happening physically, but because it can take them this long to allow themselves to enjoy sex. But successful sexual activity leads, in turn, to more successful sexual activity. It appears that physiological responses to sexual arousal are basically identical in all women, it is psychological differences which determine whether a particular woman becomes sufficiently aroused sexually to be able to achieve an orgasm.

The greatest kindness a woman can do to herself is to enter sexual relationships believing that she is a completely equal partner. It is just and proper for a woman to initiate sexual overtures (indeed most men would welcome it) and to take the initiative in sexual union, and this can be exciting for both partners. A woman should also have sufficient self-assurance to ask if she is doing things the way her partner likes them done, to inquire if there is anything she is not doing which her partner has a preference for, and to encourage her partner to do the same

thing. She should never be afraid of being creative and of making suggestions to her partner. Any suggestion willingly received, no matter how outlandish it may seem, can improve sexual excitement for both partners. If you feel spontaneously moved to experiment then go ahead and suggest it, and always explain to your partner what you like best. Research has shown that nearly all men are concerned to please their partners and contrary to feeling embarrassed, they welcome being told. Don't hesitate.

Post-coital tristesse

This feeling is a mixture of sadness, remorse and guilt after a sexual liaison. It invariably follows an occasion where we know our motives for going to bed with someone were doubtful – after a party, in a strange town, when we felt a transient flash of attraction toward someone. We may gave had twinges of regret before going to bed, but defied our better feelings. PCT or PCR (post-coital remorse) is not uncommon, but seems to become less so as we get older, largely because we have the confidence to be discriminating and honest; honest both with ourselves and possible bed-partners. In any event, PCT is a self-limiting condition; once experienced, the natural inclination is to avoid it and not repeat the experience. While suffering it, there's only one way to handle it: tell your partner of your feelings and go.

More important, you should be honest with yourself and really examine if casual sexual relationships are something you wish to espouse. Most of us don't. Even if they're undertaken with full knowledge and by mutual consent of both partners, they are rarely fulfilling and invariably result in loss of self-esteem. Most women, though not all, require a loving, caring relationship within which to enjoy a satisfying sexual relationship, and simply cannot readily undertake "one-night stands" the way that many men do.

Choosing celibacy

After all this emphasis on sex, and having successful sex, it must be said that there is nothing wrong in not wanting sex at all. Sexual desire varies from none to a lot, and all variations are normal. There is absolutely nothing wrong with you if you don't want to have sex and don't have it. If you really don't want it, and are upset by having sex, be plain-spoken about it and let it be known. Sex is supposed to be a pleasure and not a burden. If it is onerous and distasteful, don't have sex and don't feel guilty about it.

ORGASM

During the last two decades one of the most dangerous rumors concerning women's sexuality has been that there is more than one kind of orgasm – vaginal and clitoral. There is not. All orgasms originate in the clitoris. Regardless of where a woman is stimulated, the orgasm starts in the clitoris and spreads backwards and upwards to the vagina and pelvis where it can be felt.

The clitoris can be stimulated in a variety of ways. Some women prefer that it isn't touched but is simply rubbed by the closed folds of the labia in a non-specific and general way. Others prefer that the clitoris is exposed and all of it, or a special part of it, is directly handled, rubbed or kissed. Yet other women find that indirect stimulation of the clitoris by the pressure of the man's body, or by the root of the penis as it enters the vagina, can be sufficient to bring the clitoris to orgasm.

What is certain is that there is no medical evidence to show two kinds of orgasm – one in the clitoris and one in the vagina. The orgasm starts in the clitoris and at the height of orgasm the physical sensation spreads to the vagina, whose wall contracts in small spasms. This peak of excitation also affects the muscles of the uterus, which contract in rapid spasms simultaneously.

The orgasmic experience

It is very difficult to put the sensation of an orgasm into words. It is different for every woman. The female orgasm is almost certainly more profound than the male one, though the majority of women are slower to come to orgasm than men. The process of female excitation involves many different parts of the body. As excitation increases, breathing becomes more rapid and the heart beats more quickly. The lips become pink, the pupils of the eyes dilate, the nipples become erect, the clitoris swells and, as the labia part, it becomes erect and exposed. As excitation climbs, the skin becomes flushed and pink, it begins to sweat, the breasts swell as they become engorged with blood and the labia, clitoris, vagina and pelvic organs enlarge, in very much the same way as the aroused penis does.

Many women describe that they go into a "plateau phase" of excitation which can be held for several minutes. They are aware that they are on the brink of orgasm; excitation and stimulation, if not interrupted, will be followed by orgasm when the woman allows herself to go over the brink. With further stimulation of the nerves to the clitoris, a crescendo of excitement is reached. This is the climax, or orgasm, and it may last several seconds. During orgasm the body may stiffen, muscles all over the body contract, and quite often the woman emits a scream – the so-called high pitched orgasmic scream – this may also last several seconds.

The muscles of the vaginal wall contract and relax very rapidly, as do the uterine muscles, and the glands of the vagina discharge a watery secretion which is the female equivalent of ejaculation, though not as obvious, not as profuse, and not as thick.

If you have cause to examine or wash yourself immediately after orgasm, you can feel that your labia and perineum are very swollen, so are the breasts, and it can take several minutes for the swelling to subside. It can also take several minutes for your breathing, heart-rate and blood pressure to return to normal.

After orgasm there is a great feeling of satisfaction, content-ment, tranquillity, happiness and sleepiness. There is also a feeling of closeness, loving and caring, and gratitude to one's partner.

Like anything else, orgasms differ (not only between individuals but in one individual at different times), and so do preferences. The majority of men need a respite before they can be sexually aroused and reach a climax again. The greater proportion of women are satisfied by one orgasm. Some women, however, can very rapidly go onto a second or third orgasm after the first and may feel cheated if they aren't completely satisfied. If you are one of these women be sure and tell your partner; most will enjoy obliging you.

The frequency which women seek an orgasm also differs. Some women are only happy if they are sexually satisfied regularly and frequently; others crave an orgasm much less. Some women don't require an orgasm at all. All of these are perfectly normal. All you have to do is to explain your preference to your partner. Not wanting an orgasm, of course, does not preclude sex. Many women find sexual communion in itself satisfying and rewarding. Despite not reaching a climax, they welcome sexual union because it is a natural consummation of their love for their partner and this may be sufficient in itself.

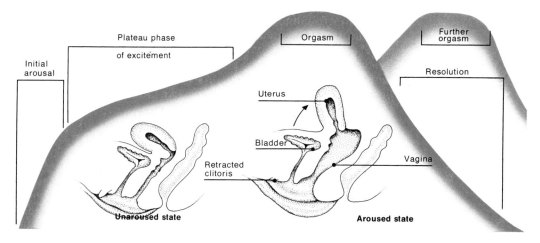

Are some women more likely to have orgasms than others?

Clinical evidence strongly suggests that women who approach sex in the following ways are more likely to have orgasms: they value sexuality for its own sake; they are interested in sex and actively seek to satisfy themselves; and they are uninhibited in sexual expression and value sexual interaction in and of itself.

Many women who don't have orgasms but who nonetheless enjoy sexual intercourse react more to the totality of the situation – its setting, timing, romantic overtones – and to the closeness, warmth and shared experiences with their partner rather than to the purely sexual aspects. These things are also appreciated by orgasmic women, but they are less important for their sexual gratification.

Why do women find achieving orgasm harder than men do?

I think the main reason is that women basically lack a sufficient level and length of arousal. Excitation must be significantly longer for a woman than a man, and be continuous as well. However, arousal can be "learned" and this depends on overcoming sexual inhibitions; getting sufficient stimulation – perhaps indulging in masturbation – and generally bulding up one's erotic responses.

Is every woman capable of having an orgasm?

Actual *physical* conditions which mediate against sexual enjoyment for women are rare: *vaginismus* – where the muscles surrounding the vagina close tightly whenever an attempt is made to insert something into the vagina, like a penis or tampon, does prevent intercourse, and *dyspareunia* – pain on intercourse – can be caused by several medical conditions such as endometriosis (see p. 290), pelvic infection, and, occasionally, a tipped uterus. However, both these conditions can be treated, vaginismus by relaxation and dilating techniques, dyspareunia by curing the underlying cause.

The most common factors precluding sexual pleasure are psychological attitudes and inadequate clitoral stimulation. If you feel resentment, anger, guilt, fear or shame you are not going to have successful sex, and even if you are wildly excited about your partner, unless you have sufficient, and in some cases, extended stimulation, it won't happen either. Remember, if you keep quiet and don't take responsibility for your pleasure, your partner may take it for granted that you are having as good a time as he is.

Is there anything I can do to achieve orgasm?

It is very difficult to generalize about what may be going wrong, but firstly it pays to cultivate a receptive and interested attitude to sex and sexual enjoyment. Secondly, you have to take an active role – not only in expressing and having your sexual preferences met, but in seeking out and experimenting with your bodily responses. Women can learn to have orgasms but, like everything else, this ability must be cultivated. Try to discover what makes you feel good and excited, and then by practicing continually – initiating and stimulating this response – you will, in time, become less inhibited, less fearful and more willing to "let go" and give yourself over to the experience. Once you achieve arousal to orgasm by any means – be it petting, masturbation, or intercourse – you should find it easier to do so again under similar circumstances.

SEXUAL PROBLEMS

Most sexual problems stem not from yourself or your own inadequacy or any "unnatural" or "abnormal" feelings that you alone may have, but from sexual disharmony with your partner: one partner likes the idea of something and the other is repelled. The other situation is that both like the idea but one believes it is perverse and is something which only happens in brothels. There can be difficulties if both partners find the passive role enjoyable and neither wants to take up the active role.

The commonest problem is that one partner feels the activity is distasteful and there are many sexual activities that somebody considers distasteful. Here are only a few: any position in intercourse where the male isn't on top; self stimulation of any kind including masturbation; oral sex of any kind; anal intercourse; too frequent sexual intercourse; sex with the lights on; sex with the lights off; touching your partner's genital organs with your hands; sexual intercourse anywhere but in bed; sexual intercourse with your clothes on; sexual intercourse naked; sexual intercourse.

By way of reassurance let me state what I believe about any sexual activity:

- You are not abnormal for wanting it.
- You are not abnormal for being repelled by it.
- You are not abnormally selfish for refusing it.
- You are somewhat selfish for insisting on it. (On the other hand, loving somebody may naturally and legitimately include the desire and the instinct to consume totally.)

The most important thing you can do if you come up against any kind of sexual problem is to talk about it. It goes without saying that the best person you can talk to is your partner but, if you find this hard to do, discuss it with your doctor or a friend. Once your problem is aired and shared you will feel better about it; and, you may get some useful advice. A problem which lies festering may eventually disenchant you with sex so that you avoid it. You and your partner may end up refraining from sexual activities altogether, or you may become bitter and resentful. Sex may become so divisive that it can end a relationship.

Given the Victorian attitude to sex – which was that it should never be discussed – it is not surprising that women, while plagued by doubts about many things which are easily explained, find it very difficult to voice their concern. If you are to solve your problems, however, this is the first step you must take. Society and the views of society are not going to solve your problems or make you happy; your own desires and your own happiness far outweigh the mores of the society in which you live.

It is also common for people to feel guilty about quite ordinary sexual practices; many parents pass on to their children doubtful wisdom learned from religious and political leaders. Most of us have heard from our childhood that "Sex is dirty." If we take too much notice of society, it can easily rob us of some of the most rewarding and satisfying experiences known to human beings and often because of some outmoded idea of what is right and what is good. The result is not that society suffers, but that you suffer. In this instance you should allow your head to be ruled by your heart, and follow what you believe to be fitting for your way of life, and practice what you and your partner enjoy.

The next thing to do is to forget some of the labels. Frigidity, nymphomania and impotence are vague terms; they don't have a precise meaning. However, once a woman is labelled frigid, or labels herself frigid, she may become anxious, inadequate, helpless and hopeless. Many of the words which describe sexual problems are meaningless and harmful, so don't use them.

The other important thing to remember is that no man is impotent and no woman is frigid. All men, given the time, the patience, and the counselling, can maintain an erection and control ejaculation. Similarly, a woman given sympathy, understanding, and gentle coaching through exploratory exercises by herself, and then with her partner, can not only enjoy sex, but can probably reach orgasm without too much difficulty.

If your partner doesn't excite you sexually, nothing is going to solve your problem and save the situation. No amount of sex counselling, sex therapy, experimentation and exercises are going to mend the rift between you if all love and feeling is gone.

Don't fall into the trap of using sex as an excuse or as a crutch. It just won't work. You can't always retrieve a broken marriage with sex just as you can't always rejuvenate a sexually dead relationship with innovation and experimentation. Trying sex on a swing, as one famous writer on sex has suggested, won't bring the fire to life if it has gone out.

Sex therapy

For couples who have sex problems that can't be resolved between themselves, sex counselling, sex clinics and sex therapy have a definite place and can be very successful. Seeking help from a sex clinic or therapist suggests that you have overcome many inhibitions – but if you have not, the first step is to try to rid yourself of any preconceptions about sex, including not being able to talk about it.

Most programs in sex clinics are slow, gentle and exploratory. They nearly always start with a long discussion about possible problems and then define the problem clearly. The counsellor will help you to talk openly and without embarrassment to your partner about all aspects of the problem, and to air any feelings and sentiments that you may have held back.

You will be encouraged to think positively. A program will be mapped out for you over the ensuing weeks. You will be told what is going to happen and what is expected of you. In going along to a sex clinic you are entering into a contract with your therapist; you are also entering into a contract with your partner. You owe it to your partner to carry out the program which your therapist suggests, not just willingly but enthusiastically.

A program will probably include advice about relaxing, about forgetting orgasms for the time being, and about losing your anxiety. You will be encouraged to go back to the beginning and find out how your body responds to sexual contact, even the simplest, such as the fingertip of your partner on your skin. You will be taught to concentrate on feeling, experiencing and enjoying every sensation that affects your body.

Your counsellor may suggest that you refrain from sexual intercourse for a few days or weeks, and practice exercises to tone up your "sexual muscles" (contracting and relaxing the vagina, squeezing your thighs together, etc.). Then you can go on to pleasure yourself, and to lying with your partner – touching, fondling and caressing each other.

Over the ensuing weeks of your program you will be counselled to experiment with ways of bringing yourself to orgasm, of allowing your partner to do so without penetration, and then to gradually graduate to orgasm during intercourse.

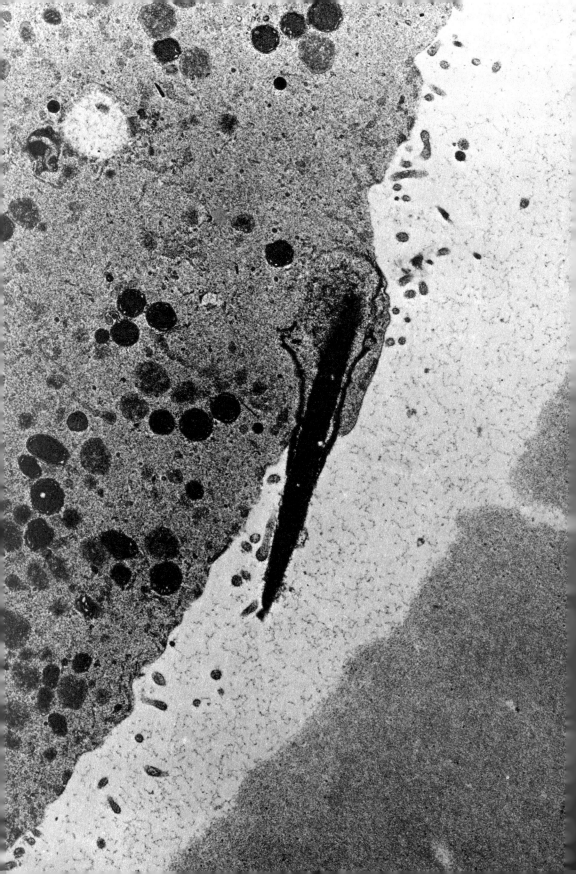

FERTILE LIFE

As with all other chapters in this book the subject is options. A discussion of fertility and its implications may not immediately strike you as being about choices, but it really is. There are choices to make and you can only be free to make them if you know what the options are. If you have sufficient knowledge about all the aspects and consequences of being fertile, you can decide what you really want and make informed judgements about how you go about achieving that.

Most of us take our fertility for granted. Many of us have been so well programmed by family and society that we consider the consequences of fertility such as pregnancy, childbirth and, possibly, abortion as inevitable. Of course they are not. Not if we manipulate fertility by family planning and contraception. Pregnancy, contrary to popular belief, need not be an occupational hazard of being female.

Almost one in ten women is concerned about the opposite of fertility; these are the women who find it difficult to conceive. More and more scientific endeavors have been directed towards solving this problem and although not everyone can be assured of having a child, there are conditions which can be treated so that successful conception is possible for many sub-fertile couples.

The information on pregnancy, labor and the post-partum period included here is not intended to be exhaustive. Many other books devote all their space to these subjects and this book is not competing with them. Rather, it puts pregnancy and other aspects of fertility into the broad perspective of women's lives and accents possible problem areas and solutions you might consider.

FERTILITY

Fertility is the ability to conceive and produce a child. As part of a chain of events, a normal egg must be met and penetrated by a normal sperm as shown opposite.

From the time that we begin to ovulate regularly, fertility for most of us is an ever-present part of our lives and one which the majority of us spend some time, thought and effort avoiding. There is now an epidemic of fertility. For our mothers and grandmothers before us, fertility was not omnipresent – before contraception was widespread, most women had one pregnancy after another, and while pregnant were infertile. By an act of nature, therefore, the majority of women avoided many of the unpleasant aspects of fertility, such as menstruation with associated dysmenorrhea, for most of their fertile lives.

It is interesting to hypothesize, therefore, that women might seek to return to this relative state of infertility by choice with the use of some "unnatural" or synthetic agent. Experiments being performed at Edinburgh University are already examining the effects of keeping women infertile for three months at a time (with prolonged courses of the oral contraceptive pill) and allowing only four menstruations a year. Why not extend these menstruation-less stretches for even longer? One ends up speculating that eventually it may be possible for a young girl whose fertility is established to be given some form of medication, possibly an injection, which renders her infertile until she personally decides that she would like a baby and therefore reverses this state by taking an antidote. The norm, therefore, would become infertility, and women would make an active decision to become fertile, not the other way around.

Age and fertility

Female fertility is fairly low immediately after puberty and reaches a peak about the age of 24; it begins to decline after the age of 30. Though it is rare for a pregnancy to occur after the age of 52, the medical literature reports that one Scottish woman had six successful pregnancies and one miscarriage after the age of 47. The effects of the mother's age on fertility are complex for the following reasons: ovulation is less frequent and the progestogenic phase of the cycle becomes irregular in the premenopausal years, the environment inside the uterus may be less favorable with advancing age, and even after fertilization, the ovum may stand a diminished chance of survival in older women.

The effects of age on men are less critical, fertility having been recorded at the age of 94 years. Fertility, however, is probably maximal around the age of 24 and declines thereafter. Though not the case with women, all forms of sexual activity in men decline from their early 20s onwards and it is accepted medically and scientifically, at least, that the degenerative processes of ageing actually begin before adolescence ends. Even as early as the third decade, ageing can be demonstrated in the testes.

The fertile couple

One important concept to understand about fertility is that it is not dependent on one individual alone – fertility is relative to each couple. The medical definition of fertility, therefore, depends on certain normal features in both the male and female partner of a couple and these include:
● Regular ovulation with the regular availability of a normal ovum for fertilization;
● A normal female genital tract, competent to transport and maintain ova, sperm and a fetus;
● Adequate insemination with the regular delivery of an adequate number of normal sperm to the upper vagina.
Certain fertility patterns are well established. In couples having intercourse without contraception, 8 out of 10 women will be pregnant within a year: 25% conceive within one month, 60% within six months, 75% within nine months and 80% in twelve months; 90% will have conceived after eighteen months. The number of conceptions becomes progressively smaller in time until finally there is left about 10% of couples who are involuntarily sub-fertile (see p. 172).

Likely occurrence of conception (%) for couples having frequent intercourse without birth control.

Factors affecting fertility Human beings are the only species that eat when they are not hungry, drink when they are not thirsty and have sex at any time. Most lower animals have a breeding season; most of us are probably of the opinion that we don't, yet the statistics from many countries suggest the opposite. The season may have a great deal to do with conception in human beings. There are peak months for conception, though they differ in different geographical areas. Further research has shown that in the northern hemisphere, at least, conception rate varies roughly with the temperature; as you move from warmer to colder climates, peaks swing from winter to summer. The conception peak usually occurs when the monthly average temperature is about 20°C(68°F) and in nearly all countries, the annual low point is around March. This finding prompted the statisticians to look for influences such as social conventions, and a glance at the calendar reminded them that March is the time of Lent and Easter. During this time religious considerations, particularly among Roman Catholics, impose a degree of self-denial. That may be yet another factor.

It is well known that animals can be made to extend their breeding season by several weeks if they are exposed to six or more hours of extra light a day. Some research carried out in southern England suggests that we may be subject to the same changes in our environment. A group of general practitioners examined the number of births month by month in relation to the daily hours of sunshine in their own practices. They found that irrespective of the time of year, conception is more likely to occur on those days when there is more than average sunshine!

Leaving aside these more speculative aspects of fertility, there are more basic biological factors which impinge on fertility. By far the most important factor is that a woman is fertile for only a few days of any month. These are the days around ovulation, which is generally in the middle of the monthly cycle, but for a woman who does not menstruate strictly every four weeks, it is more accurately 14–16 days before the start of a period, regardless of the length of the cycle. Some women, however, have been known to conceive while menstruating (see p. 152).

Can I actually tell if I am fertile?

No, you yourself can only tell if you are ovulating. This you can do by keeping a daily temperature chart and noting the rise in temperature which occurs around the middle of the cycle (see p. 180). If this happens regularly each month, then you are ovulating each month, but that tells you nothing about the normal transport of the ovum along the fallopian tubes to the uterine cavity, nor about the prospects of a fertilized ovum implanting successfully.

Can I tell if my partner is fertile?

No, there is no way that you or your partner on your own can tell without scientific investigation if he is fertile. Even if ejaculation is normal and the ejaculate looks normal to the naked eye, there is no way of knowing that it contains the right number or the right kind of sperm (see p. 175).

Is one partner more responsible for fertility than another?

If one partner has an obvious abnormality then, of course, he or she is more responsible than the other who has not. However, if investigation (see p. 174) of both partners shows that both are fertile but the union is childless, it is impossible to say that one partner is more to blame than the other. Fertility depends on two people being fertile together, and whereas a woman may be unable to conceive with one man, it may be quite easy for her to conceive with another, even though both men are equally fertile. We simply do not know what makes the crucial difference.

Are there any things I/my partner/we can do to improve our potential for fertility?

At the fertility clinic I worked in, there are a few tips which we used to give couples in the first two years of trying to conceive:

• Take your temperature daily, before you get up, and plot a chart to make sure you are ovulating and establish roughly when during your menstrual cycle you ovulate so that you can anticipate ovulation day. You can also use the cervical mucus and calendar methods (see p. 180) which will tell you when to have intercourse: the first two high temperature days are your fertile days.

• Abstain from sexual intercourse for 7–10 days prior to ovulation: abstinence increases your partner's desire and the number of spermatozoa in his ejaculate.

• Have a break; go away for a holiday; forget everything; relax, have a good time. Many couples have come back from a holiday if it is timed right (make sure it includes ovulation) with a pregnancy already begun.

If you possibly can, stop worrying about trying to have a baby. Anxiety is counter-productive. It is a well-known fact that once a couple stop worrying about having a child by, for instance, setting the wheels turning for an adoption, the woman conceives.

SUB-FERTILITY

Sterility and infertility are synonymous; the former, however, has connotations of irreversibility that make it threatening to most people. Sub-fertility is very often used interchangeably with infertility and this use of the word is acceptable unless there is an absolute bar to conception.

Approximately 1 in 10 couples in the United Kingdom are sub-fertile and are unable to have babies. The investigation of a couple's apparent infertility with its anatomical and hormonal convolutions, is long and difficult and it should start with an open, frank discussion with the family doctor. Couples must bring to any discussion about their sub-fertility, the willingness to be guided and to be realistic. Realism is paramount: in a survey of couples seeking help at an infertility clinic, 5% expected an immediate prescription for a fertility pill without any investigation; others were unwilling to involve their partners in any fertility investigation.

The first step in treatment is the acceptance that low fertility is not a matter of either partner exclusively, but of the couple as a unit (see p. 170). Fertility of a couple is the sum of the fertilities of the partners; the high fertility of one can, to some degree, compensate for the low fertility of the other. On the other hand, marginal fertility in both partners may result in sterility. This explains the paradox of a childless couple splitting up and *both* producing children without difficulty with a new partner.

Age and sub-fertility

In most Western countries, about 15% of marriages are childless; the figure for *sterile* marriages is somewhat lower. The 15% figure includes couples beyond the reproductive age and those who have deliberately avoided pregnancy. In a survey performed in England and Wales between 1900 and 1909, when very few couples used any form of contraception, nearly 12 out of every 100 couples were childless at the end of 10 years. The most important factor affecting fertility which came out of this survey was the woman's age at the time of her marriage. The older she was, the greater the chance that her marriage would be sterile.

Investigation of sub-fertility

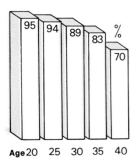

Age 20 25 30 35 40

Your chances of conception vary according to your age.

The time which one allows for involuntary sub-fertility depends very much on the age of the couple. In a young couple, in their early twenties, most clinics may suggest waiting two years; for couples in their thirties, one year would be considered adequate grounds for investigation, and it may be wise to investigate a couple in their late thirties after six months. In America, there is a predilection for pre-marital assessment of fertility: this is usually inadvisable since the necessary investigations may be hazardous and it is rarely possible to give an accurate prediction; the information is therefore liable to be misinterpreted or misused.

Traditionally, sub-fertility has been the concern of the woman and her gynecologist. However, the problem always requires the participation of a couple, and a doctor should learn of their mutual attitudes to childlessness since the cause of sub-fertility is equally likely to be found in either partner. While the initial assessment can be made by a well-informed doctor, sub-fertility is best managed by a team led by a gynecologist and a urologist. Today, assessment of fertility rarely requires more than a few months; on the other hand, subsequent management is necessarily slow since the opportunity to conceive is once every 28 days at the maximum, and after a year there have only been twelve or thirteen opportunities.

At the first interview, therefore, you will find that the need for patience is emphasized. You will be asked many questions relating to your gynecological history, general health and social life, and how you manage intercourse. Your partner will also be questioned on his medical history, and both of you will have a full physical examination with special emphasis on the genital areas.

If analysis of his semen and intercourse are satisfactory, especially if confirmed by a post-coital test, then your male partner can be excluded from further investigation. Problems of impregnation due to impotence will probably need careful and sympathetic treatment by a psychiatrist. However, the presence of too few sperm or the absence of sperm altogether will need further evaluation, and your partner may be asked to undergo special investigations and tests to track down a cause.

During all these laborious tests you must bear in mind the objectives in the investigation of your sub-fertility:
- To demonstrate the cause of sub-fertility and to deliberately avoid the implications of fault or guilt in yourself or your partner;
- To outline the chances for future childbearing, recognizing that this is always imprecise;
- To counsel you about the available alternatives;
- To offer any appropriate treatment.

It is important for you to understand this overall perspective and for you to realize that frequently there is no specific therapy that your doctor can offer you and in a way your doctor's role may be to help you to adapt to possible childlessness.

MALE EXAMINATIONS

Following your initial interview, you will almost certainly be asked to proceed immediately to the analysis of a semen specimen. The first sample may be collected after your first visit by masturbation, or arrangements can be made for two or three samples to be studied over the next few weeks. The following characteristics of the ejaculate will be investigated:
- The volume of the ejaculate, which should be 1–5 ml;
- The viscosity of the ejaculate, which should coagulate rapidly after ejaculation and then liquefy within the next 5–20 minutes;
- The general appearance of the ejaculate under the microscope, giving an impression of the size, shape, number and mobility of the sperm.

After this initial interview and the completion of at least two seminal analyses, you may be asked to engage in intercourse with your partner at a specific time, after which she will be examined in a post-coital test.

FEMALE EXAMINATIONS

In a post-coital test, secretions will be removed from your vagina and cervical canal and be examined microscopically and chemically. Other tests will include:
- Recording basal body temperature daily for 3 or 4 months;
- A biopsy of the endometrium, which is usually done about 7 days after ovulation to make sure that the endometrium has gone into the secretory phase and therefore to confirm that you have ovulated and that progesterone is being secreted normally;
- Examination of the cervical mucus and the vaginal cytology to confirm the above;
- Hormone assays, which usually test the level of blood progesterone or its urinary bi-product in the second phase of the cycle as an index of ovulation;
- Assessment of your genital tract by special X-rays to show up blockage in your fallopian tubes (this can be done by gas or with a dye which shows up on X-ray);
- Direct visualization of your pelvic organs using a fiberscope, which is passed through a very tiny hole at the top of the vagina. (The purpose of this maneuver can be three-fold: firstly, the surgeon can look around and make sure that everything appears normal; secondly, s/he can take biopsies [small specimens of tissue which can be examined microscopically], usually from the ovary; and thirdly, s/he can divide fine adhesions which may be blocking the tubes.)

CAUSES OF SUB-FERTILITY

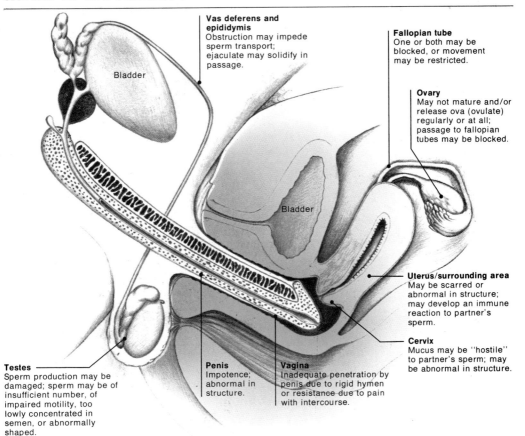

Vas deferens and epididymis
Obstruction may impede sperm transport; ejaculate may solidify in passage.

Bladder

Fallopian tube
One or both may be blocked, or movement may be restricted.

Ovary
May not mature and/or release ova (ovulate) regularly or at all; passage to fallopian tubes may be blocked.

Bladder

Uterus/surrounding area
May be scarred or abnormal in structure; may develop an immune reaction to partner's sperm.

Cervix
Mucus may be "hostile" to partner's sperm; may be abnormal in structure.

Testes
Sperm production may be damaged; sperm may be of insufficient number, of impaired motility, too lowly concentrated in semen, or abnormally shaped.

Penis
Impotence; abnormal in structure.

Vagina
Inadequate penetration by penis due to rigid hymen or resistance due to pain with intercourse.

Conditions that can be treated

Failure to ovulate
This can be treated by two kinds of fertility drug:
Gonadotrophin – stimulates the ovary to produce a mature ovum and to then advance to secreting progesterone so that the secretory phase proceeds successfully to menstruation.
Clomiphene – increases the pituitary gland's production of follicle stimulating hormone (FSH), so that the follicle gets a good start in its growth cycle. Your doctor will decide whether you are a case who is suitable for clomiphene treatment and in suitably selected cases, ovulation may be induced in 50–90% of patients. However, the number of pregnancies is lower.

Uterine and tubal disease
Endometriosis (see p. 290) can cause scarring of the fallopian tubes and uterus and makes the area hostile to the transport and implantation of ova. Doses of estrogens can simulate conditions which cause the endometrial implants to dry up (i.e. pregnancy).

Unless the cervix is infected, cauterization is rarely required and curettage of the uterus has not been found to be a very successful treatment. Blockage of the tubes due to adhesions may be eliminated during surgery: new techniques permit removal of a blocked segment and stitching of the healthy ends of the tubes together again. The high degree of skill required for such a surgical operation is usually only found at experimental surgical units or teaching hospitals.

Hostile cervical mucus

This may be due to poor sperm motility or to natural conditions in the vagina. Both can be improved by the administration of estrogen, which causes the mucus to become clearer, devoid of cellular debris, softer and thinner, so that maximum sperm penetration can be achieved.

In rarer cases a woman may be "allergic" to her partner's sperm in which case, using condoms during intercourse may reduce any antibodies she may have produced. Drugs may also be given to women whose mucus is hostile to sperm due to their higher male hormone level, in an attempt to reduce this.

The absence of sperm or too few sperm

Gonadotrophins or clomiphene may be used to stimulate production of sperm (as they stimulate ovulation in women), by acting on the testicles to produce sufficient testosterone, or on the pituitary gland to produce more FSH (follicle-stimulating hormone) and LH (luteinizing hormone).

Blockages due to obstructions in the epididymis and vas deferens can sometimes be cured by surgery, as can interference produced by a *variocele* (varicose vein in the testicle). *Variocelectomy* is one of the most effective methods of curing male infertility; it is likely to be used in 30% of couples having difficulty.

Artificial insemination (AI)

Artificial insemination using the husband's ejaculate (AIH) is indicated if the husband is impotent. In all other cases it is necessary to use semen from a donor (AID). This is a controversial topic and in most countries its legal status is uncertain. However, it is becoming more common and is likely to increase, particularly where a relaxed policy towards abortion reduces the number of infants available for adoption.

AID is only appropriate where there is no impediment to conception in the wife and, in these circumstances, four out of every five women can expect to conceive within six months of treatment. Arguments in favor of AID include the preference of many women to bear their own child rather than adopting a child of unknown parentage. Some couples view AID as a semi-adoption but with similarities between themselves and their child.

Psychological concerns have been raised about the effects of AID but this can be answered by the low divorce rate in couples who have used it; AID should always be safeguarded by careful selection and counselling. And while social concerns have been advanced about the effect of AID on marriage and the family unit, the most important concerns are those involving the legal uncertainties about the legitimacy and status of the child, and the culpability of the wife.

CONTRACEPTION

The advent of contraception separated sex from procreation and heralded liberation for women. Contraception is older than you may think: in 1882 the first diaphragm was invented.

When the wide choice of contraceptive methods became available, women were faced with two problems – one of honesty, and one of confidence. Before contraception was freely available, women could retreat behind their fear of becoming pregnant to avoid unwanted sex. Suddenly this option was no longer open and we had to learn to say "no" without feeling guilty. Contraception also meant that women had to come to terms with their own sexuality. Many women did not have the self-confidence to do so and shirked this responsibility to themselves. Some of us still have difficulties in coping with our sexuality.

However, the argument about whose responsibility contraception is has been settled – mainly through default. Both men and women now see contraception as a woman's responsibility, largely because it is women who are most affected by an unwanted pregnancy. In addition, most women would like to have the responsibility for contraception and the freedom to choose when to become pregnant (figures from the Pregnancy Advice Service demonstrate that many women who seek abortion have been using some kind of contraception; though some do only inconsistently, others are regular users. Such women often have to seek abortions because contraceptive methods have failed).

Deciding to use contraception

There are many reasons for using some form of contraception and one of the best is the benefits that it brings to you. Research has shown that the bigger the family, the more the mother's health will suffer with each baby and, just as important, the more each successive child suffers. However, the benefits are more than simply an improvement in your health – contraception will improve the quality of your life: it enables you to decide when to start your family, how large you want your family to be and how long to leave between your children, and this is to everyone's benefit. Contraception, whatever technique you decide on, is a means to an end. It is a means by which couples can plan their families according to their emotional, domestic and financial considerations and, probably most important, contraception is a means by which a woman can take the initiative and decide both if and when she is going to become pregnant. We acknowledge this initiative as a fundamental freedom to be enjoyed by all women.

Choosing a method

It is usually healthy people who use contraceptive devices and take contraceptive pills. Doctors and nurses are there to make sure there are no medical reasons against your using a particular method, so that you feel safe, secure and well motivated to use it. If you are healthy and physically normal, then the choice about the method should be yours and yours alone. Wherever possible, that "yours" should include your partner. You and your partner should discuss the benefits and disadvantages of all the methods

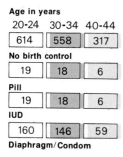

20-24	30-34	40-44
614	558	317

No birth control

19	18	6

Pill

19	18	6

IUD

160	146	59

Diaphragm/Condom

Number of live births (in 1,000s) per one million sexually-active women annually (in average effectiveness rates)

High effectiveness rates for any birth control method are an "ideal" measurement dependent on the method being used exactly right, all the time, with no mistakes. Average effectiveness rates, which take into account couples who don't use a method exactly as directed, are much lower. A comparison of the two will reveal the margin for error. Condoms, for instance, have been variously reported as being 97%–64% effective.

---

that are available and then be convinced that the one you have chosen is right for you both. If you are convinced about its rightness, you will have the best chance of making it effective and lowering the risk of a failure. Before you embark on any contraceptive method, you and your partner should also discuss any fears, possible side-effects, complications, problems or worries that you may have. Research has shown that where a man communicates with and shares more of a woman's daily activities, and also shares the responsibility for contraception, the man and the woman get more pleasure from making love. Usually such a man gives greater emotional support, and the couple seem to be happier and more loving.

Comments, opinions and horror stories from friends and relatives should be ignored when you are deciding on a contraceptive method; every woman reacts to her contraceptive differently and there is nothing to suggest that you will suffer either the side-effects or the benefits that your friends describe. Nor, indeed, is there any reason why a particular method should fail for you simply because it has failed for a friend. Research has shown that there may be many reasons why a method may fail, one of them being that pregnancy may be secretly desired by one partner who somehow takes the opportunity to make sure that the method fails.

Your *lifestyle* will have a great deal to do with your attitude towards contraception and the meticulousness with which you treat it. If you have decided that you wish to pursue your career through your twenties, which is your most sexually active time, then you will want to choose a method with the highest possible efficacy. In the United States over one million sexually active women end up each year having a legal abortion, and the chances are highest when the women are in their early twenties. Whether you are married or not, if you are involved in a caring sexual relationship you will want to protect your partner as well as yourself and your future children, from the physical and psychological traumas that sometimes follow an unwanted pregnancy. Perhaps even more importantly, if you are involved in a sexual relationship which is unloving, then it is vital for you to use an effective contraceptive method so that you do not find yourself pregnant at an inconvenient moment.

There may be *medical reasons* why certain methods are not open to you. For instance, if you have suffered from a deep-vein thrombosis of the leg it is unlikely that your doctor will allow you to use any kind of oral contraceptive pill containing estrogen. You may want to use an intra-uterine device (IUD), but if you have not had a pregnancy, or if you have had inflammation of your fallopian tubes, then your doctor will probably advise against you using the IUD because it may make you more susceptible to another infection and the IUD has a very small increased risk of giving it to you.

Your *age* is one of the most important factors in choosing a method of birth control because the incidence of certain risks peak at different ages. You will see that the risks associated with the pill increase as you get older, whereas the risks from intra-uterine devices remain constant (see pp. 185–187). The risk from abortion also increases alarmingly with age, whereas the diaphragm and condom have virtually no risk at any age.

One of the first problems that you or you and your partner may have to face is the *wide choice* of contraceptives that are available, and then you may have to make some concessions – what is the most reliable may not be medically suitable. A particular method may require premeditation, like the insertion of the diaphragm before you go to bed at night, or the carrying of a condom at all times, so there are aesthetic considerations, too. It is important to know the efficiency of the different contraceptive techniques because this is the only way you can compare the failure rates, and so choose the method which best fits your circumstances. You may find after using the chosen technique for some time that you or your partner do not get on well with it. While it is important to get things right at the beginning, do not be afraid to reassess things as you go along – there is no contraceptive method more calculated to fail than one with which you and your partner are disenchanted.

One of the conflicts that you may face is that basically you feel contraception interferes with your normal biology, and certainly the hormonal contraceptives do. There is, however, an array of methods available which interfere very little with the normal functioning of your body. All these various methods and devices can be shown to you and you can handle them and discuss their pros and cons with staff in a family-planning clinic.

Where to get advice

A family planning clinic is often the best place to find out about contraception as not every general practitioner can fit you with an IUD, for instance. In a progressive center the different contraceptive devices are on display; the statistics are available for your examination regarding the effectiveness, the failure rate, the possible side-effects, as well as advice on how you and your partner should go about co-operating in the use of the method. The staff are there to give you a sympathetic hearing, and answers and reassurance to your problems and questions.

Do not make a hurried decision. You and your partner should take your time over choosing a method and then once you have decided, put 100% enthusiasm behind using it.

Contraceptive worries

Despite the reassurances and the undoubted benefits of contraception, some of us continue to feel uneasy about using it and some of us never get around to using it at all. Some thoughts about contraception and the difficulties experienced by women are given below. If you recognize any that you have, be reassured that it is not unique to you – others have suffered it and have come to terms with it. Do not let your appreciation of this list end with reading it – act upon it.

● Sex should be romantic. It has to be spontaneous and unplanned. Using birth control seems too clinical, and sometimes unaesthetically messy.

- Using contraception may go against our inmost wishes; we may want a baby very badly but won't admit it to ourselves. We may even feel tempted to prove that we are fertile and get pregnant, thereby disproving the method of contraception.
- Contraception is a display of our own sexuality and we may feel embarrassed and even ashamed of it.
- With natural birth control methods, it may be difficult to abstain from intercourse during our fertile days, particularly if we feel that our partner will try to find sex elsewhere.
- We may have questions and anxieties about birth control and we don't know who to talk to to get reassurance.
- If we feel that a clinic or a doctor may be impersonal, sit in judgement or moralize, we may hesitate to go along to avoid embarrassment.
- Knowing that a pelvic examination is a necessary preliminary to the use of a contraceptive method, we may not seek medical help about contraception for fear of having a pelvic examination.

Natural methods (rhythm)

Three birth-control methods based on natural body cycles have proved effective under ideal conditions if followed properly. The three are the calendar method; the temperature method; and the cervical mucus method. They can be used separately but are more effective if used in combination.

Calendar method

Use the chart to calculate your fertile days. For example, if your shortest cycle was 25 days and your longest 30 days, then you are fertile from the 7th–19th day of your cycle.

Using the onset of bleeding as day 1 and the day prior to onset of next menses as the last day, mark down your cycles over the previous eight months. Find the shortest and longest cycles. Use the chart below to find your fertile days and avoid intercourse on those days. Recheck every month with the eight most recent menstrual cycles.

First fertile day	3rd	4th	5th	6th	**7th**	8th	9th	10th	11th	12th	13th	14th	15th	16th	17th	18th
Length of cycle	21	22	23	24	**25**	26	27	28	29	**30**	31	32	33	34	35	36
Last fertile day	10th	11th	12th	13th	14th	15th	16th	17th	18th	**19th**	20th	21st	22nd	23rd	24th	25th

Temperature method

This measures the basal body temperature, which drops and then rises prior to ovulation. Take your temperature each morning for five minutes before you get out of bed; if possible use a basal body thermometer. Record the temperature on a chart. It will drop 24 hours prior to ovulation and then remain elevated for three days. Avoid intercourse as soon as temperature drops and while it remains elevated.

Cervical mucus method

By being aware of changes in your normal vaginal discharge you can predict ovulation and unsafe days. There are four cyclic phases in this method:

Menstruation This obscures any discharge, so avoid intercourse in case you are one of the rare women who ovulate during menstruation.

Mucus, present at all times in the cervix, has cyclical characteristics dependent on hormone levels. At ovulation time, if viewed under a microscope, it reveals fern-like patterns when dry.

Early days Relatively "dry" days when there is usually no moisture or discharge but, if any, it is cloudy, sticky and thick. It may be safe to have intercourse unless you have a very short cycle. **Unsafe days** A more abundant, slippery and clear discharge heralds ovulation. Avoid intercourse as soon as you notice this change and until three full days after the "peak" effect of this discharge.

Relatively safe days From the fourth day after peak discharge day until the beginning of your period are your safest days for intercourse. The scant discharge will be cloudy, sticky and thick.

Advantages of the natural methods

All these methods are without medical risk and are inexpensive to use. They are also permitted by religious groups opposed to other contraceptive methods. By learning about your natural cycles you can become more in tune with your body, and this information is particularly useful in planning a pregnancy.

Risks and complications of the natural methods

These methods are all less effective, more complicated to use properly, and curtail lovemaking more than any other acceptable method. Women with irregular cycles, and those who have not kept track of their periods, find it difficult to calculate cycles. Travel and illness can affect temperature recordings; infections and sperm can mask mucus changes. There are no medical risks with these methods, only pregnancy, which, of course, can be medically unwise for some women.

DETERMINING FERTILE ("UNSAFE") DAYS

The 3 "natural" methods, if used in combination, will give a much clearer indication of ovulation, and thus the times to avoid intercourse (if a pregnancy is not desired); or, alternately, the times to have intercourse (if planning a pregnancy).

What you can record from external signs (menstruation, body temperature, cervical mucus) reflects the action of hormones on the uterus and ovary, which respond by maturing follicles and releasing ova and then progesterone and estrogen to continue the cycle.

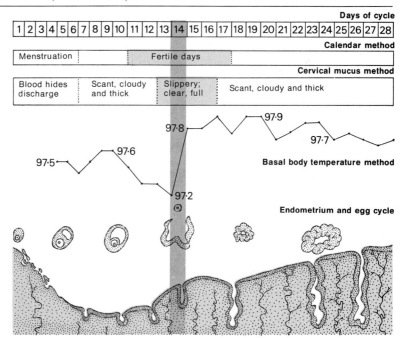

There is also a greater risk of birth defects in any pregnancy, as with these methods, older eggs or older sperms may be involved in fertilization. While this is a possibility for all couples, those using natural methods consistently put off intercourse to times outside the normal fertile period, and therefore run a higher risk of encountering abnormal eggs or releasing older sperm.

Using the natural methods successfully
- Always record the beginning of your period and any signs related to ovulation.
- Make sure you have your partner's agreement and support.
- If you are unsure about fertility on any day, avoid intercourse or use another form of birth control.

While I want to use natural methods, I find I feel the most amorous on unsafe days. What can I do?

Abstaining from intercourse doesn't mean abstaining from all sex. Oral sex, mutual masturbation and anal intercourse are all possibilities, even withdrawal (see below).

Is there anything wrong with using withdrawal on my fertile days?

If you don't mind the moderate risk of pregnancy and the psychological difficulties, withdrawal is a reasonably satisfactory choice. It can also be used in an emergency when other methods are unavailable. Make sure your partner withdraws well before orgasm and ejaculates well away from the vagina. It's a good idea to keep spermicidal foam handy in case of an accident. Don't repeat penetration unless the penis has been washed and make certain you attempt intercourse in a readily extractable position.

Diaphragm

Diaphragms are made with different types of spring rims. A cervical cap is similar to a diaphragm but is smaller, less elastic, and fits snugly on the cervix. This may be better for women with slackened muscles or bladder problems.

A barrier method of birth control, the diaphragm is a rubber dome mounted on a pliable metal rim. You insert it into your vagina where it fits over the cervix and prevents sperm entering the uterus. Used in conjunction with chemical spermicides, which you apply to the diaphragm prior to insertion and reapply after three hours while the diaphragm is still in place, it is a very reliable method of birth control.

In the course of an internal examination your doctor will measure you and select the correct-size diaphragm. When the diaphragm is fit and in place correctly, you should not feel it. Diaphragms should be checked for size every six months, as the vagina readily changes shape, and after childbirth, miscarriage or change in weight of more than 20 lb either way. After removing the diaphragm you should gently wash it in warm water, rinse, dry and store it in its case in a cool, dry place. Check regularly for tears and holes and replace yearly.

Advantages of the diaphragm
A diaphragm does not cause any physical, chemical or hormonal change in your body. It is nearly as effective as the pill and can equal the IUD and minipill in efficiency. Spermicides used with the device provide protection against vaginal and cervical infec-

To be effective, spermicidal jelly or cream must go inside the dome of the diaphragm, as well as on the outside and rim.

tions. The diaphragm does not interfere with breast milk production or future fertility. One other advantageous use is that it makes for neater lovemaking during menstruation – it can contain a normal menstrual flow of up to 12 hours.

Risks and complications of the diaphragm

There are no life-threatening complications and even less serious medical problems are extremely uncommon. Aside from rare allergic reactions to the latex or spermicide, the two main problems are ones of proper fit and/or proper use. Some women have such poor internal muscular support that they can't use a diaphragm; others claim that diaphragms are too "troublesome" to use regularly. For any woman over 35, or one who has intercourse less regularly, or is concerned about health risks, the minor inconveniences inherent in using a diaphragm are certainly outweighed by its advantages.

INSERTING A DIAPHRAGM

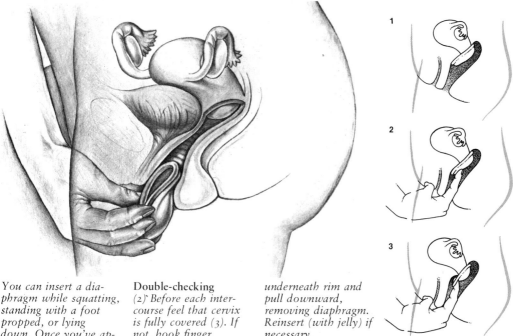

You can insert a diaphragm while squatting, standing with a foot propped, or lying down. Once you've applied spermicide, with one hand hold it dome side down, press in the sides and push it gently but firmly downward and back along the wall of your vagina. Tuck the nearest rim up behind bulge of pubic bone; the round end of the cervix must be fully covered (1).

Double-checking *(2) Before each intercourse feel that cervix is fully covered (3). If not, hook finger underneath rim and pull downward, removing diaphragm. Reinsert (with jelly) if necessary.*

Using the diaphragm successfully

● Advise your doctor or clinician if you feel your diaphragm is not fitting properly or if your weight has changed 20 lb up or down.
● Always check your diaphragm for holes or tears.
● Always insert it with spermicide; add more spermicide if intercourse does not take place within 3 hours and if additional intercourse is undertaken.
● Do not remove diaphragm until 6–8 hours after last intercourse. Clean at least once in 24 hours. Do not leave in indefinitely.

Is it possible to have oral sex if I use spermicides with the diaphragm?

While some partners find the taste of spermicides off-putting, they are medically harmless. You could delay inserting the diaphragm until after oral sex and just before intercourse.

While I like to use a diaphragm, how can I prevent it interrupting our lovemaking?

You should develop a routine for putting it in before you go to bed or show your partner how to insert it – many couples find this is a lot more fun than having the woman dash out of the room.

My partner claims that he "bumps into" my diaphragm and this causes him some discomfort. Can it really be so?

This occasionally happens with small diaphragms; see your doctor about the fitting of a larger one.

Oral contraceptives (birth control pills)

Currently the most effective reversible method of contraception, birth control pills contain synthetic estrogen and progestogen – hormones similar to those produced by the ovaries. These chemicals alter the body's hormonal balance so that the ovaries do not release eggs and pregnancy is prevented. A course of pills is normally taken daily for either 21 or 28 days; menstruation normally occurs every 28th day.

Pills can only be prescribed by a doctor or family-planning clinic and should only be given after a thorough gynecological checkup including a breast examination and a Pap smear (see p. 58). They are not recommended for women over 35, smokers, or anyone with a past history of a clotting disorder or heart disease.

Minipills

These contain no estrogen and have fewer side-effects (see below) than regular pills. While regular pills totally suppress ovulation, minipills do not, so that menstruation is determined by your own internal cycle. Menstruation, therefore, is likely to be less predictable than with the regular pill. Minipills do, however, prevent pregnancy, by partially suppressing ovulation and additionally by interfering with conditions in the cervix, uterus and fallopian tubes.

Minipills are slightly less effective than regular pills due to the absence of estrogen. They must be taken daily. The newer "low-dosage" combined pill may be a better solution for women concerned about large amounts of estrogen.

Advantages of the pill

Proper use of oral contraceptives ensures that you have the best chance of avoiding pregnancy with a temporary method. Pills do not interfere with intercourse and you are virtually free from cramps and heavy bleeding – periods are predictable, regular, light and painless. Iron-deficiency anemia is less common among pill users as loss of blood is halved.

Risks and complications of the pill

Serious complications of the modern low-dosage pill are rare but may include blood-clotting disorders, liver problems, skin cancer, gall-bladder disease and some eye problems (like the inability to wear contact lenses). More common side-effects include irregular bleeding, nausea, weight gain, increased susceptibility to yeast infections, headaches, breast tenderness and loss of libido.

Stop taking the pill and inform your doctor right away if you develop: shortness of breath; pain in the chest, abdomen or legs; vision changes; headaches; breast lump or severe depression.

Using the pill successfully
● Have regular checkups including internal examinations and Pap smears.
● Inform your doctor about your past and present medical history and any changes you notice while taking the pill.
● Take the pill with the least amount of estrogen possible, and certainly no more than 50 micrograms (mcg).
● Realize that pills are not a permanent answer to birth control and should be exchanged for another method before you're 35.
● Be aware that smoking increases your pill risks, so if at all possible, stop.

Will the pill affect my fertility?

In most cases normal menstruation returns spontaneously within 3 months after stopping the pill, but for 1–2 % of pill users, fertility is indeed delayed, especially if the women previously had irregular periods. Some women who have not had children before commencing the pill may be unable to conceive for reasons other than the pill, as fertility has not been proven.

Can the pill harm a fetus?

Certain abnormalities in the developing fetus have been attributed to the pill so that you should stop taking them as soon as you know, or suspect, you are pregnant.

Does the pill affect breast milk?

Both the quantity and quality of milk can be reduced and some traces of hormonal substances can be found in it (the effect on infants is undetermined). Another form of birth control is to be preferred if a further pregnancy is to be avoided.

Intra-uterine devices (IUD)

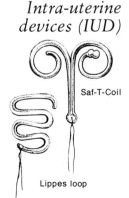

Saf-T-Coil

Lippes loop

These devices, also known as coils or loops, are small, 1–2 inch, flat, flexible objects made of plastic and/or copper which are inserted by a doctor into a woman's uterus. IUDs are second only to the pill in preventing pregnancies and work by making the womb environment hostile to embryo implantation. Once inserted, plastic devices can be left in indefinitely; ones containing copper should be changed every 2–3 years. While formerly, these devices were recommended for women who had previously had children, new designs can be worn by all women. After a pelvic examination, your doctor will determine what size IUD you need and then insert it using a hollow plastic tube containing the device; the inserter is then withdrawn leaving the IUD in its proper place. Most, but not all, women experience discomfort on insertion,

2 copper-wound
IUD's-top, Copper-7;
bottom, Copper T.
These must be replaced
regularly.

ranging from mild to unbearable. An IUD has a plastic string attached which is used to check that it has not been expelled. The IUD should only be removed by a doctor or clinician who will view it through a speculum and will pull gently on the string. This procedure is usually faster and less painful than insertion.

Advantages of IUDs
These devices are extremely successful in preventing pregnancy and once inserted they provide immediate and continued protection. You need not interrupt lovemaking or buy replacements (except bi-yearly) and they do not interfere with breast milk production or your natural hormonal balance. They also do not interfere with future fertility unless infection develops.

Risks and complications of IUDs
Most serious complications of intra-uterine devices are becoming exceedingly uncommon, but perforation of the uterus at the time of insertion or later migration, and rare pelvic infections have been reported. Pregnancy is complicated by the wearing of an IUD. Ectopic (tubal) pregnancy is more common in IUD users and pregnancy may end in spontaneous abortion. IUDs should be removed immediately if pregnancy is confirmed. Common side-effects include heavy periods and spotting. Some men experience discomfort during intercourse (the doctor can usually fix this by cutting the string). Expulsion is not uncommon so check your strings regularly. Occasionally the thread is drawn up into the cervix and your doctor or clinician should retrieve it.

INSERTING AN IUD

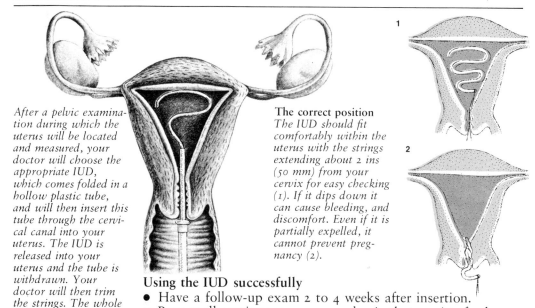

After a pelvic examination during which the uterus will be located and measured, your doctor will choose the appropriate IUD, which comes folded in a hollow plastic tube, and will then insert this tube through the cervical canal into your uterus. The IUD is released into your uterus and the tube is withdrawn. Your doctor will then trim the strings. The whole procedure takes about 5 minutes.

The correct position
The IUD should fit comfortably within the uterus with the strings extending about 2 ins (50 mm) from your cervix for easy checking (1). If it dips down it can cause bleeding, and discomfort. Even if it is partially expelled, it cannot prevent pregnancy (2).

Using the IUD successfully
● Have a follow-up exam 2 to 4 weeks after insertion.
● Report all continuous cramps and pain that persists for longer than 12 hours to your doctor.

- Check your thread regularly and inform your doctor immediately if you can't feel it.
- Continue to have regular checkups and get new devices as recommended.
- Report any abnormal vaginal discharges.

Can you wear tampons with IUDs?

Absolutely, the IUD can't be pulled out inadvertently or get tangled up in the tampon.

I've heard that IUDs can be used to end an unwanted pregnancy already in existence. Is this true?

Yes, it is, but it is obviously not an ideal contraceptive method. If a copper IUD is inserted up to 10 days after unprotected intercourse it has been shown to be highly reliable in preventing the pregnancy from continuing.

Vaginal spermicides (foam)

Used in conjunction with condoms or a diaphragm, spermicides are highly effective but should not be relied on as the sole medium. They work by providing both a mechanical and chemical barrier for sperm, the latter being the most effective. In foam form it comes in a can which is shaken then applied to the vagina via an applicator. It lasts for 30 minutes and must be reapplied if intercourse is extended or if new intercourse is undertaken.

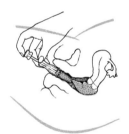

To be effective, spermicidal foam must cover the cervix completely.

Advantages of foam

Foam is immediately effective and doesn't alter your hormonal or physical condition. It is a useful back-up method and can repair the damage of a torn condom or failed withdrawal. It adds extra lubrication and provides some protection against sexually transmitted infections.

Risks and complications of foam

Outside of rare allergic reactions and unwanted pregnancies, there are no serious health risks with foam though recent research suggests that children conceived while spermicides were being used have a slightly higher chance of being abnormal. Non-medical problems arise when couples find it interferes with lovemaking.

Using foam successfully

- Do not use as your sole method of birth control.
- Keep foam handy and store away from heat.
- Always reapply for each intercourse, no matter how often.
- Give spermicide plenty of time to work; don't have a bath or use the bidet for 6 to 8 hours after last intercourse.

I want to use a vaginal spermicide but I don't like using foam. What do you recommend?

Creams, jellies, foaming tablets and suppositories are also available but the only one that comes close to foam in effectiveness is *cream*. Make sure the one you choose is meant to be used *alone*, as many creams must be used with a diaphragm or condom.

*Tubal
sterilization*

A highly recommended method of birth control for women who no longer want children, it permanently prevents further fertilization by interfering with the fallopian tubes. While other kinds of surgery result in sterilization (see hysterectomy, p. 293), they involve too many complications if sterilization is the only aim.

There are currently five different operations (see chart at right) which involve approaches either through the abdomen or vagina, and the tubes can be tied, clipped, sutured or cauterized (bound and sealed with a special instrument). While all procedures describe "tying" or "closing" the tubes, a portion of the tubes is also invariably removed. All procedures have the same failure rate (4 in 1,000 operations). You should discuss with your doctor/surgeon the best and safest procedure for you.

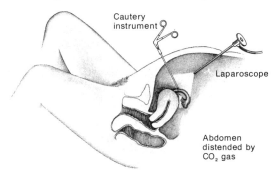

Cautery instrument

Laparoscope

Abdomen distended by CO$_2$ gas

Laparoscopy, using a specially illuminated telescope, closely examines the uterus, tubes and ovaries. It is used not only in performing certain tubal sterilizations, but reveals adhesions and evidence of ovulation for infertility diagnosis.

Advantages of tubal sterilization
While no tubal ligation method is 100% effective, it does have a higher efficiency rate than any temporary method and it is a permanent form of birth control. There should be no interference with your body's chemistry. As it is *permanent*, women who don't want or shouldn't have any more children don't have to worry further about birth control.

Risks and complications of tubal sterilization
Serious complications from tubal sterilization are rare; vaginal tubal ligation, however, has a slightly greater risk factor due to the greater risk of infection. As with all operations, complications due to anesthesia such as death or cardiac arrest must be taken into consideration, as should general surgical complications – the risk of infection and damage to internal organs.

If I change my mind about having more children, can I have my tubes opened?
The real answer is "no" although doctors have been experimenting with micro-surgical procedures which may make this possible in the future. Tubal sterilization is considered irreversible.

Will cutting the tubes interfere with my sex life in any way?
There is no hormonal or chemical change brought about by sterilization – eggs are still produced but can't be fertilized. If anything, not having to worry about birth control should make sex better.

METHODS OF TUBAL STERILIZATION

Operation	Description	Anesthetics and hospital care	Suitability	Side-effects
Laparoscopic tubal ligation ("band-aid sterilization")	Using a special instrument (laparoscope) inserted through a 1-inch (25-mm) abdominal incision, the surgeon views the tubes. Carbon dioxide gas is pumped in to lift the abdominal wall for a better view. A second small incision is made near pubic hairline and an electric cutting instrument is inserted to seal the tubes.	General anesthetic, possibility of local anesthetic with sedatives. Recovery time in hospital is about 2 days or less.	Not for women who have heart or lung problems or pelvic infection.	Occasional shoulder pain caused by irritation of abdomen by carbon dioxide gas used to inflate abdomen.
Laparotomy with post partum tubal ligation	Within 48 hours of full-term delivery or at time of Caesarean delivery, a 2–3-inch (50–75-mm) incision is made along curve of navel and tubes are lifted out and tied before incision is closed.	General, epidural, spinal or occasional local anesthetic. Normal hospital stay for delivery.	Suitable for most women post full-term delivery. The incision is quick healing and does not require further recovery time.	
Abdominal tubal ligation	A 5-inch (125-mm) incision is made in the lower abdomen, the tubes are closed off and the incision is sewn in layers.	General anesthesia with a stay of 5 days to a week – longer recovery at home.	Generally suitable for most women but especially for those who undergo additional abdominal surgery at the same time and for those women who have had previous surgery and may have scar tissue making other procedures difficult; all surgeons can perform.	Requires longer hospital stay with full recovery after 5–6 weeks.
Vaginal tubal ligation (culdoscopy or colpotomy)	Using a special instrument (culdoscope) inserted through a small incision in the back of the vagina, the surgeon views and then closes off the tubes before closing the incision. In colpotomy no special viewing instrument is used.	General or occasionally local anesthetic. Hospital stay of 2–3 days.	Not suitable for women who have heart or lung problems; pelvic, vaginal or cervical infections; or just after pregnancy. Minimal discomfort, a rapid recovery and no scar.	Has the highest risk of infection post operation. Intercourse must be avoided until 4–6 weeks after procedure.
Mini laparotomy	Similar to abdominal tubal ligation, a 1–1½-inch (25–38-mm) incision is made in the abdomen near the pubic bone. A special instrument (elevator) is used to move the uterus so the tubes can be grasped and closed. The incision is then stretched.	Local and occasionally general anesthetic. Hospital stay of several hours to 2 days.	Not for women who are very obese or have an abnormal uterus. Recovery is rapid and normal activities including intercourse, can be resumed after 1 or 2 days.	

I'm happily married and we don't want any more children. Is tubal sterilization to be preferred to vasectomy?

If you are satisfied that you have a stable permanent relationship and that neither you nor your partner want more children, then the preferred method of permanent birth control is vasectomy for the man (see p. 191). That is because it is a less complex procedure with fewer complications than tubal sterilization, and it costs less.

Male-only methods

Although most women feel they should take the responsibility for contraception, there are two reliable methods open to men. One is vasectomy, which is a permanent solution and should only be contemplated by couples who don't want or shouldn't have any more children. It is less complicated than female sterilization but should only be decided upon after careful consideration. The other is the condom. Condoms are readily available – to women as well as men. If you're between other methods, need a back-up or a change, or just want to be prepared – keep a supply handy. Some men always assume women are protected and don't bother to carry any.

The condom (sheath)

A popular and effective temporary method of birth control, it is one of the oldest available methods. Made of thin rubber and placed on the erect penis prior to penetration, it contains the ejaculation so sperm are prevented from entering the woman. Spermicidal jelly or cream should be used, not only for added protection in case of spilled sperm, but to add lubrication and prevent friction. A new condom should be used for each intercourse; on removal your partner should hold firmly onto the condom while withdrawing so that no sperm are lost. Condoms come in different shapes, colors, thicknesses, textures and some are lubricated and already covered with spermicide.

Advantages of the condom

As effective as the IUD if used properly, the condom is readily available, easy-to-use and can be worn by all men. In addition it provides protection against sexually transmitted infections and may protect women from cervical cancer (see p. 278). The slight loss of sensation men feel wearing it can be used to good advantage in the case of a man who ejaculates prematurely; his sensation can be slowed, giving his partner more time to reach a climax. Condoms are also used to desensitize rare allergic reactions to sperm that some women have which contributes to their subfertility. Condoms are the preferred method during and after reproductive tract infections, and as back-up for all other methods

Risks and complications of the condom

As long as the condom stays intact and no pregnancy results there are virtually no health risks. Aside from rare allergies to the latex or spermicide, most problems are non-medical. People vary in their reactions to its feel or smell, and some find that it interferes somewhat with lovemaking. A few men feel the loss of sensation is too great and some find it inhibits erections.

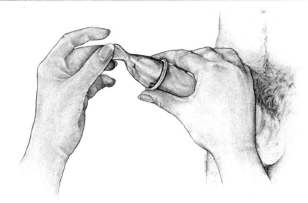

Helping your partner put on a condom may make him more enthusiastic about wearing one. Remember, if it doesn't have a reservoir end, pinch the tip to leave a little space for semen as you roll it on.

Using the condom successfully
● Use a new condom for each intercourse and inspect it beforehand for tears or holes.
● Make sure the condom is put on before the penis comes anywhere near the vagina.
● Withdraw the penis before erection subsides completely and hold on to the rim.
● Check carefully after use for tears.
● Don't use petroleum jelly or vaseline (which are irritating to the vagina) to lubricate, use water-soluble jelly only.

Vasectomy   This is a simple 15–20 minute procedure which is a permanent method of birth control for men. It can be done on an out-patient basis under local anesthetic. One or two ½-inch (13 mm) incisions are made in the scrotum and a portion of each of the vas deferens (the tubes which transport sperm from the testicles to the penis) is removed before it is tied and replaced in the scrotum. One or two stitches are made. During follow-up visits sperm counts are taken to ensure that there are no sperm present in the semen. Another form of birth control must be used until sperm counts are negative.

Advantages of a vasectomy
This procedure is nearly 100% effective and the risk of problems or complications are lower than for tubal sterilization. The recovery is rapid, and there is no change in hormone levels or the appearance or volume of semen. Sex drive is not affected.

Risks and complications of a vasectomy
There are occasionally minor problems such as blood clots under the incision, swelling or infection. Such problems clear up rapidly on treatment. Rarely, tubes grow together again so yearly sperm counts are recommended. By far the largest problems are psychological, as many men are adverse to having any surgery carried out on their genitals.

Why are other birth control methods necessary after vasectomy?
Sperm are stored in the prostate gland and seminal vesicles which are above the vasectomy site and it takes from 10 to 20 ejaculations to remove them.

Is there an injectable form of contraception?

Yes, there is a contraceptive injection containing female hormones which will stop you having your periods by inhibiting ovulation. However, a great body of medical research has not come out in favor of it. The efficacy of the injection depends on the constant and steady release of hormones from the injection site and this is not perfected. This means irregular bleeding may occur and the efficacy be capricious. Also there is the possibility of there being prolonged amenorrhea.

When should I start contraception after pregnancy?

Many women believe that it is impossible to conceive while they are breast-feeding a baby. It is certainly true that the hormones which stimulate milk secretion have an inhibitory effect on ovulation, but it is by no means 100% safe. In the United States statistics show that between 25–40 out of 100 women will be pregnant within one year if they rely on lactation as a method of contraception. However, there is no fixed time for the ovaries to get back to normal cyclical activity but as a rule of thumb, about half of all mothers will have ovulated by the fourth month after delivery, so start thinking about contraception, therefore, before you have your six-week post-natal checkup.

You may decide that you want to change your contraceptive from the method you were using before your baby, but do give it some thought before you go for your examination.

Do I need to use contraception if my periods are irregular?

If you are not menstruating, the chances are that you are not ovulating, but there is a small chance that you still are. The trouble is that you cannot be sure. In this situation there is only one thing to do if you wish to avoid pregnancy, and that is to use contraception.

What should I do if I have taken a risk and had unprotected intercourse?

You should consult your doctor, of course, who may be familiar with the post-coital pill. This is a hormonal preparation which can be used immediately after accidental intercourse, when pregnancy is suspected, to produce a chemical abortion. Indeed it has been called the "morning-after" pill. It is not in general use nor may your doctor approve of it. If you have any difficulty, consult your nearest family-planning clinic, which will be able to put you in touch with a specialist who has experience using this method of contraception. Bear in mind that if you do take this pill and you are pregnant but the fetus isn't aborted, it has been exposed to a large dose of hormones which may affect its development.

ABORTION

Legal abortion, I fervently hope, is here to stay for the following good reasons:

● Statistics from several programs for the study of abortion and the New York City Department of Health statistics, show

that voluntary legal abortion is improving women's physical and psychological health in that
– the infant mortality rate is decreasing;
– deaths associated with abortion are decreasing;
– hospital admissions for incomplete, usually illegal, abortions are decreasing;
– complication rates and mortality rates of legal abortion are decreasing;
– the mortality rate for early abortion is well below the mortality rate for full-term pregnancy and delivery.
• While women do have psychological difficulties coping with abortion, research has consistently shown that the psychological effects of legal abortion result in women feeling more happy than sad, and more relieved than depressed.
If tests have confirmed that you are pregnant and if you are considering abortion, there are only three options open to you and you should consider them and make your mind up quickly about what to do:
First, you can go ahead with the pregnancy and keep the baby;
Second, you can continue with the pregnancy, have the baby and give it to another family temporarily, i.e. foster it, or permanently, i.e. have it adopted;
Third, you can terminate the pregnancy by having a legal, medical abortion. On paper it looks easy, but for most women this is a very painful choice to make.

Feelings about having an abortion

A substantial number of women feel that it is morally, religiously and biologically wrong to interfere with a pregnancy in any way and therefore they are fervently opposed to abortion. Others are just as fervently in favor of abortion. Most of us are in-between, and most of us suffer a mixture of feelings when an unwanted pregnancy is confirmed. We may be fearful that our families, relatives and friends will find out and that we may be punished. We are fearful that we won't be able to decide what to do, and this indecision increases the circuit of anxiety. We are afraid that we will be alone in trying to decide what to do, and, of course, we are afraid of the prospects of motherhood. We may also be afraid of abortion, even though we know it is legal and safe. "Will it cost more than I can pay?", "Can I have it paid for by insurance?", "Will it be painful?", "Will I be punished by suffering post-operative complications?", "Will I be sterile afterwards", "I feel guilty now but will I carry around guilt feelings for the rest of my life?", "Will I regret what I have done and wish that I had had the baby?", "Will I fear sex and never be able to have a proper relationship with a man again?", "Will I become frigid?", "Will I ever be normal again?"

It is quite normal for you to feel all of these fears and to be in some instances, profoundly affected psychologically. You may even suffer a minor post-partum depression after the abortion has been done. For several weeks after the abortion, be prepared to feel depressed, withdrawn, tearful, inadequate, not able to cope well, and not able to make decisions properly. However, the reassuring news is that the majority of women feel relieved after an abortion although they may feel sad as well. You are going to have a fairly hard time and you need support, so establish it before you go into your abortion. Seek the help of a friend, make sure that your friend will stand by you and comfort you during and after the abortion. If this friend can be your doctor, that is even better; if it is one of your parents, you are very lucky; if it is your partner, you have the best of all worlds. Whoever you find, find someone because you are going to need him or her and you will pull through the post-abortion upset faster by having him or her close to you during this time.

Non-medical abortions

In the hands of a trained doctor, and in the sterile circumstances of a hospital and an operating room, an abortion is a relatively safe surgical procedure. However, there are many non-medical abortion methods which are used illegally. These are dangerous, inefficient and are based on nothing more than old wives' tales. You should remember that:
- There is no known chemical which when taken by mouth will safely and efficiently produce an abortion. Any substance for which such claims are made has to be taken in such large quantities that it will act as a poison;
- Hot baths, half a bottle of gin, jumping or falling from a great height will bring about an abortion only if you were going to lose the pregnancy in the first place;
- A sharp instrument poked into your uterus by someone who doesn't know what s/he is doing may well bring about an abortion, but it has a high chance of killing you at the same time, or at the very least, resulting in a hemorrhage which will require emergency transfusion, or a severe infection which may render you sterile for the rest of your life.

Spontaneous abortion

Abortion may be medically induced, or it may be spontaneous. In both instances it means that the growth of the developing fetus is stopped and it is expelled from the mother's body. Abortion has come to mean, to the lay public, medical termination of the pregnancy; a spontaneous abortion, which occurs without any intervention from the outside, has become known as miscarriage. To a doctor, however, miscarriage and abortion are synonymous.

Spontaneous abortions are much more common than is generally thought, though it is difficult to get accurate figures about frequency. Some go undetected when they occur, and many if detected, are unreported. In the first few weeks, even if they are detected, they are difficult to confirm and it may be that early miscarriages occur very frequently. It is said that up to a third of all first pregnancies miscarry, but nevertheless a normal second pregnancy usually ensues. The theory is that the womb needs a trial run in order to become fully developed.

Excluding early unrecognized miscarriages and those that are procured, spontaneous abortion occurs in something between 1 in 5 and 1 in 10 of all conceptions. As women get older, this figure probably rises.

RISKS OF ABORTION

Legal medical abortions occasionally result in complications which are set out below. You should bear all these risks in mind when you are considering abortion. However, at the present time, about 64 women die each year in the United States from an operation for an abortion. Before abortion was legalized, the number of women dying was nearly 300.

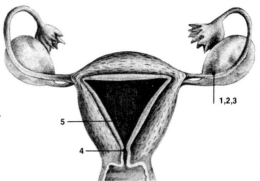

1. Infection of the fallopian tubes.
2. Blockage or adhesion of the fallopian tubes making subsequent conception difficult.
3. A slight risk of an ectopic pregnancy, i.e. one which occurs in the fallopian tube.
4. An incompetent cervical canal: the canal is stretched during the dilatation process, which is performed in most abortions done via the vaginal route, so that the cervix may be less competent in future and may possibly increase the risk of a spontaneous abortion.
5. Very rarely, the uterus may perforate and at worst this may mean that you have to have a hysterectomy.

The reasons for spontaneous abortion include ineffective implantation, failure of the fetus to grow normally after it has become implanted, and inadequate hormonal control of the pregnancy. Whatever the reason, most doctors believe that early spontaneous abortion is a good thing in that the embryo most probably was in some way not normal.

The vast majority of diagnosable miscarriages occur before the twelfth week in pregnancy. 50% occur during the second and third months. Similarly, four out of five terminations are done within the first 12 weeks. At this time it is a simple, straightforward procedure and can be performed under a local or general anesthetic according to how far advanced the pregnancy is.

Abortion procedure

Once your doctor has made certain that you are pregnant, s/he should discuss with you at some length whether you really want an abortion, and whether you have considered all the alternatives. Your doctor or counsellor will then make sure that you fulfill the requirements of the law and that you fully understand everything that is involved. If you are not given all the information about abortion, then ask for it. Be prepared to be questioned about yourself and your feelings and your thoughts about the abortion. Make certain that you know about any side-effects or complications that may occur. Think about getting psychological help and support, contraceptive advice and prescriptions for medicines that you may need after you have had your abortion.

Legal requirements for abortion

The United States Supreme Court made abortion legal throughout the country on January 22, 1973. The results of decisions in Roe v. Wade and Doe v. Bolton were as follows:
● During the first 12 weeks of pregnancy, there is no restriction,

qualification or prerequisite under state or federal law as to when, how or where an abortion is performed.

● During the second 12 weeks of pregnancy, the different states may impose requirements, such as that abortions be performed in a licensed hospital, designed to protect a woman's health.

● From 24 to 26 weeks a state may prohibit abortion if it chooses. While not affecting legality, regulations prohibit the use of federal funds for abortions, unless as a result of rape, incest or where the mother's life is in danger.

The time to have an abortion

There is no question that abortions are best performed before 12 weeks. After that time, and certainly after 16 weeks, it becomes not only more difficult, but more dangerous to procure an abortion through the vagina. After this time, an abortion is usually completed by injecting prostaglandins into the uterine cavity itself, which stimulates the uterus to contract. The abortion may take 12 hours and can be painful.

Only 1 in 100 abortions is undertaken after 20 weeks and nearly all of these are done because a very severe abnormality of the fetus has been discovered or because of extreme distress or illness of the mother. In these instances, abortion is performed by injecting a saline solution into the amniotic sac, which induces premature labor; and that terminates the pregnancy.

Where can I go for advice about abortion?

First go and see your family doctor (who should be well acquainted with your medical history), or go to an organization which specializes in giving help to people in your position. They offer a full, non-pressurized counselling service. You will have the opportunity to ask all the questions you want. You will be reminded about anything you have forgotten, all the various alternatives other than abortion will be discussed with you, and your personal domestic and financial commitments will be considered.

Do I need another person's consent for an abortion?

In most cases you will be required to sign a consent document beforehand, and some hospitals or clinicians may request that your husband or parent sign the form as well. They may make this a prerequisite for care, even though court decisions have upheld a woman's legal right to have an abortion without a parent's or a husband's consent. If you find such a request unacceptable, look for another doctor and/or hospital or center which is willing to perform your abortion without further consent.

Once I have decided that I want an abortion, where can I have it done?

Most major urban areas contain outpatient abortion clinics where the procedure can be carried out on a walk-in basis. Only a relatively few doctors will perform abortions in their offices and not all hospitals will be able to accommodate you. If you live in a rural or less populated area, you may have to travel to another

ABORTION METHODS

Vacuum (suction) abortion
(4–12 weeks of pregnancy)
The accepted technique for early terminations, it is usually carried out under a local paracervical block, or a general anesthetic. Using a series of dilating rods, the cervix is widened and an appropriate-sized vacuum tube (depending on length of pregnancy) is inserted. The tube is connected to a pump machine and is moved around your uterus until it has completely removed the pregnancy sac and the thick uterine lining. This procedure takes 3–5 minutes and is usually carried out on an outpatient basis. You are bound to experience some pain and strong cramps but most women are able to return home within an hour. Don't expect to be fully recovered for 1–2 weeks.

Dilation and evacuation abortion (D & E)
(13–24 weeks of pregnancy)
Similar to vacuum abortion, it is usually carried out for a more advanced pregnancy under general anesthesia. In addition to dilating rods and a vacuum pump, other surgical instruments are used to remove fetal and placental tissue, and drugs are administered to help the uterus contract afterwards. This procedure takes about 30 minutes and recovery is similar to vacuum abortion.

Dilation and curettage (D & C)
(up to 12–16 weeks of pregnancy)
In this procedure the uterus is dilated with rods under anesthesia as for a vacuum abortion and curettes (narrow metal rods with sharp, spoon-shaped ends) are used to scrape out the uterine lining. This procedure takes from 10–20 minutes and recovery is similar to the vacuum procedure. Occasionally, light bleeding or spotting may occur for a few days.

Saline or prostaglandin (amniocentesis) abortion
(15–24 weeks of pregnancy)
The only method which requires you to undergo labor, amniocentesis abortion should be done in a hospital. Saline (concentrated salt solution) or prostaglandin (a hormone) is injected into the amniotic sac surrounding the fetus and this induces premature labor. You will be given a local anesthetic prior to having a hollow plastic tube placed in the abdomen. The solution is inserted in the tube and the tube is withdrawn once the solution is in the abdomen, and some hours later labor will commence. Occasionally the cervix will be widened by using dilators, and drugs may be given to encourage contractions. The fetus is expelled relatively easily, followed shortly by the placenta. Hospital stay is $\frac{1}{2}$ day–2 days.

Because amniocentesis is carried out at an advanced stage of pregnancy it can be a very distressing procedure both physically and emotionally. You will experience labor and its accompanying discomforts and may expel a recognizable fetus at the end. Do seek help with emotional adjustment and try to have a close friend with you before and just after.

Hysterotomy
(15–24 weeks of pregnancy)
A rarely-used technique which is only recommended for women with specific medical problems who can't use saline or prostaglandin, or upon whom other methods have been unsuccessful, this is a major operation. The fetus is removed through an incision made in the abdominal wall and uterus. The physical recovery takes longer than with other methods and may involve substantial emotional trauma since the fetus is often born alive, but is too immature to live.

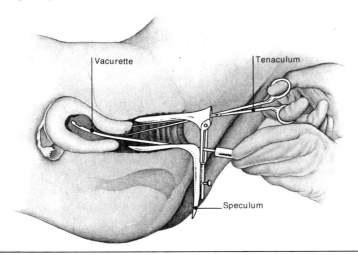

Vacurette

Tenaculum

Speculum

Vacuum (suction) abortion
With you under a local or general anesthetic, the doctor inserts a speculum into your vagina and uses a series of dilating rods to widen your cervix. Holding the cervix open with a tenaculum, s/he then inserts a vacurette, which is attached to a suction pump, to draw out any fetal material.

county, perhaps even another state. For assistance, you could get in touch with a local woman's crisis line, a woman's center or a chapter of the national Organization for Women, or Planned Parenthood.

* *How long will it take me to get back to normal after an abortion?*

If you have your abortion performed within the first 12 weeks of pregnancy, you will be physically back to normal within a week. Psychologically, however, it may take considerably longer for you to feel your usual self. The later it is done the greater the disturbance. Recovery varies from individual to individual. Most women however, take 3 to 4 weeks to get over the psychological effects of an abortion. Some take several months.

What should I do after the abortion?

- Rest for the remainder of the day after your abortion and do not undertake strenuous physical exercise for a minimum of three days afterwards.
- Keep an eye open for excessive bleeding, vomiting, fever, unpleasant vaginal discharge or severe abdominal pain and report them immediately to your doctor.
- Do not use tampons or douching for two or three weeks after your abortion.
- You may experience slightly heavier blood flow (just like a normal period with some menstrual cramps) on about the third day after your abortion. It should not persist, however, and if it does, contact your doctor.
- Have a post-partum checkup with your doctor within two weeks after the abortion has been done.
- Make sure that you start on some form of contraception as soon as you resume sexual activity.

How soon can I resume sexual intercourse?

Providing you are using contraceptives, you can resume relations in about 2 or 3 weeks if you feel up to it. Do not have intercourse any earlier than this, because you are somewhat more prone to having an infection introduced into the genital tract immediately after an abortion.

PREGNANCY

Having or not having children is a primary preoccupation of people today now that it is possible to control fertility. Most women grow up thinking that childbearing is expected of them; men also feel it is part of a need to prove sexual potency and virility. Together there is the desire to compete with other married couples and there may be the wish to fulfill the adult mother/father role. (Studies have shown that the need for such a role is particularly strong in working-class women for whom there may be no other function.) Some people desire children for the love and companionship they provide, and in many agricultural communities, children are required to help in the fields and act as security against old age.

Powerful external forces also exist which pressure couples towards children; the Roman Catholic Church is one which has taught that a marriage which is intentionally childless is unacceptable. The Catholic Church advocates large families, indeed the whole of the Judeo-Christian tradition shares the adage: "be fruitful and multiply and replenish the earth" (Genesis 1, V, 28). In the old days, barrenness was viewed as a curse or a punishment; even today, in many Muslim countries, childlessness is a tragedy and is a basis for divorce or for taking a second wife or concubine.

Secular pressures may be equally strong. Grandparents may encourage their children to raise a family. Much of Western society is child-oriented. The media presents the norm of a happy three- or four-child family and some sociologists have recognized the "idolatry of reproduction" or "the mania for childbearing" in contemporary society.

These forces are likely to be felt quite strongly by married couples who have opted to have no children. Those who intentionally make this choice, can expect to be regarded as selfish, emotionally immature or even abnormal. Even if you are unintentionally childless, you may meet the same attitudes, sometimes made worse by pity, so that you may feel yourself sexually inadequate, immature or incomplete. Not surprisingly, this may lead to marital pressures and conflict. It is very important for anyone associated with a sub-fertile couple to understand and sympathize with these influences.

On the other hand, there are motives which favor childlessness. One is the cost of raising children with the financial outlay necessary for food, clothes and education, coupled with the inability of most young mothers to earn before their children go to school. Children may frustrate career ambitions for both parents. Then there are the discomforts which accompany any young family: the noise, the mess, the time, the fatigue and the strain. In addition, having children puts stress on the mother's health and may destroy her figure, and in a growing minority of people, the threat of over-population or even cynicism about the future makes them unwilling to have children.

Deciding to be pregnant

Becoming pregnant should be the result of a choice – the choice to be pregnant. If you have chosen to have a baby, you and your partner will almost certainly feel happy, and your responses to becoming pregnant and being pregnant will be positive ones. If on the other hand, your pregnancy is unplanned, you have to make the decision whether to continue with it or not. If you decide to continue with your pregnancy you have made your first and most crucial decision. Many women feel ambivalent about being pregnant and it may take several months to be certain that choosing to be pregnant is right for you and your partner at that particular time. Some women never make the choice themselves; they let time decide. They feel that after several months their pregnancies are irrevocable, that they cannot end it, and that the decision has been taken out of their hands.

If you decide on having a baby, there are several things you can do before attempting, or achieving, pregnancy that make for a happier result. On the *social side*, discuss the matter fully with your partner so that you feel in basic agreement on how to and who will care for the child. Make plans for balancing work schedules and take a hard look at the many ways a child may affect your career goals. Children cost money so be sure you have the necessary medical coverage, insurance and funds for their equipment and up-keep. Check your work and state benefits relating to pregnancy and maternity leave.

From a *health point of view*, visit your gynecologist before you try to become pregnant to ascertain that everything is all right and that there are no contraindications (see genetic counselling). Have a test to see if you're immune to German measles; if not, discuss inoculation with your doctor. Have any medical or dental treatments completed, especially those involving X-rays or courses of drugs.

Stop using birth-control pills and substitute a non-chemical contraceptive for three months before you begin trying to conceive. Limit any drug or alcohol intake – both you and your partner. Eat a good diet, exercise daily and relax. Plan on conception taking about three to six months after you stop using birth control; couples over 30 may find it takes longer (see p. 170).

Genetic counselling

Some people run a higher risk of having abnormal children. These include couples who have already produced a child with a birth defect or genetic disease, women over 35, and those who have had two or more previous stillbirths or miscarriages. Certain ethnic groups are associated with specific genetic diseases: Greeks and Italians have a higher incidence of *thalassemia*, a blood disorder; similarly, Blacks are at greater risk from *sickle-cell anemia*; Eastern European Jews carry genes for *Tay Sachs* disease, a neurological condition. Couples from these groups and all cousins or other blood relatives who marry should consider genetic counselling. Your own doctor should be able to order any necessary medical or genetic tests or will recommend you to a specialist who can help. The doctor should discuss the results of any such tests and your options if a disability is disclosed.

"Older" mothers

As a general rule you should talk things over with your doctor before embarking on a pregnancy if you are over 40, especially if it is a first pregnancy. Age is not a preclusion to pregnancy and older women tend to have very little trouble during pregnancy and during delivery. They are given special attention and special care. A woman over the age of 35 having her first child is known as an "elderly primigravida"; she is likely to have a slightly longer labor than a younger woman. Roughly speaking, labor increases in length by about 1 or 2 hours for every 10 years of age.

There is also an increased risk of mongolism if either parent is over the age of 40. Interestingly enough, the fact that older women usually have older male sexual partners, and such men may be a factor in the higher incidence of birth defects in babies born to

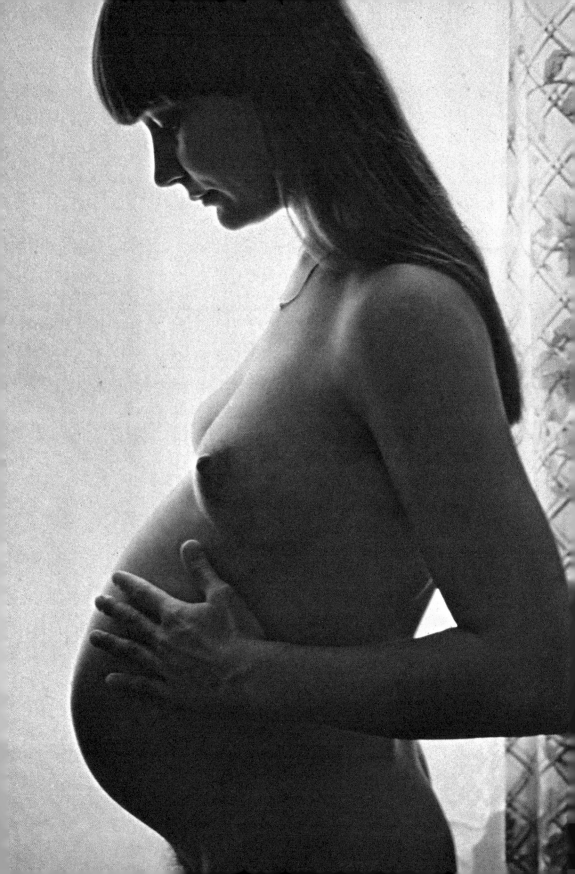

older mothers, has only recently been investigated. Some doctors estimate that at least 24% of babies born with Down's syndrome (mongolism) are conceived with defective sperm.

Most mothers over the age of 35 are given the option of having an amniocentesis performed (see below) which will show up the presence of major abnormalities in the fetus such as mongolism or spina bifida. If deformities are found you will probably be offered the option of an abortion. If your doctor balks at giving you the test, or an abortion, seek another opinion.

Never be put off starting a pregnancy because of your age, but do be meticulous about your prenatal care.

Rhesus auto-immunisation

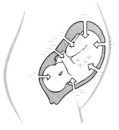

The danger in a rhesus situation is that antibodies from the mother cross the placenta to attack the baby's blood cells. This usually only causes problems after a second pregnancy

About 15% of white women and 1% of black women have a Rh negative blood group. If Rh positive blood enters the blood stream of an Rh negative woman she may produce antibodies. These antibodies are capable of killing Rh positive blood cells. When an Rh negative mother carries an Rh positive baby such antibodies may be formed when some of the baby's blood gets into the mother's circulation at the time of the delivery.

However, the potential for a problem usually only arises with a second Rh positive baby (the first one is hardly ever affected). During a second pregnancy, it is possible for maternal antibodies to cross the placenta to the baby and damage the blood cells. Even so, this may cause very little trouble. During subsequent pregnancies, however, levels of antibodies may rise and that is why all Rh negative women have tests done to ascertain antibody levels and a careful watch is kept on the baby's progress. Induction may be considered if the antibodies are high. Sometimes a complete blood transfusion has to be given to the baby

We now know how to prevent a Rh negative woman from making antibodies. An injection of antibodies from another person will prevent her forming her own.

Amniocentesis

Under a local anesthetic a hollow needle is inserted through the abdominal wall into the uterus and about $\frac{1}{2}$ ounce (24 grams) of amniotic fluid is removed. This fluid contains cells from the baby's body which, when studied by experts, provide information on its development.

This test will also reveal the sex of the baby but should never be carried out solely for this purpose as there is a 1–2% chance of the test causing the baby to abort. Ultrasound techniques which are used to locate the baby's exact position have reduced the earlier higher risk of this procedure. Amniocentesis can only be done after the 14–16th week of pregnancy and termination at this time is bound to be very distressing. However, for many older women who are worried about having babies with birth defects, amniocentesis has meant that they can attempt pregnancy with a much greater peace of mind.

Can you arrange to have a baby of the sex you want?

In the past when boys were more highly prized than girls, the ancient writings were full of helpful suggestions on how to have a

A baby's sex is determined at the moment of conception by the chromosomal make-up of the sperm fertilizing it. If the sperm carries a "Y," or male, chromosome the baby will be a boy. If it carries an "X" or female, chromosome the baby will be a girl.

boy, such as lying on your right side when you have intercourse, or holding the right testicle or nibbling the right ear. Biologically, however, only the father is responsible for the baby's. Men produce two types of sperm, y sperm which produce boys, and x sperm which produce girls. The woman's contribution to the new child, the ovum, is biologically sexless. By using information about the behavior of x and y sperm, you might be able to use the knowledge to get the baby of the sex you want:
- y sperm are smaller, faster, stronger and shorter-lived than female sperm;
- y sperm prefer a less-acid environment than female sperm; the normally acid conditions of the vagina, therefore, marginally favor female sperm.

A promising new technique called "sperm-separation," when used in combination with artificial insemination, does have a 75%–80% chance of producing a boy, but is only available in a few specialist centers.

With the caution that there is very little scientific confirmation of these suggestions you might try the following:

TO HAVE A FEMALE BABY

- Have intercourse up to 2 or 3 days before ovulation (male sperm will die, leaving only female sperm for fertilization).
- Do not abstain from intercourse, in fact have it fairly frequently. (This lowers the proportion of male sperm.)
- Douche the vagina with a weak vinegar solution – 1 part vinegar to 10 parts water (acid favors female sperm) before intercourse.

TO HAVE A MALE BABY

- Have intercourse on or as near ovulation as possible (the faster male sperm will reach the ovum before the heavy, slow female sperm).
- Don't attempt intercourse frequently (this increases the proportion of male sperm present in the semen).
- Douche the vagina with a solution of bicarbonate of soda – 1 teaspoon to 1 pint of water (making the vagina alkaline favors male sperm) prior to intercourse.

Pregnancy tests

If you wish to be in control of what happens during your pregnancy, your childbirth, and to your child after it is born, it is important for you to actively take on the responsibility of being pregnant and to get to know as much about what is happening to you and your baby as soon as you possibly can. One of the first things that you will have to find out is whether you are pregnant or not and this usually involves a pregnancy test. Some women, however, have a sixth sense and simply know that they are pregnant. As soon as the first period is missed, an observant woman may notice that her breasts hurt a little, that she is having to pass urine somewhat more frequently than she did before and that certain foods make her feel nauseated. She may even go off smoking or drinking coffee completely. All of these are well-known signs of pregnancy and besides these, many women know with a complete certitude that is difficult to verbalize, that they are carrying a child inside them.

Pregnancy tests you can do yourself
Any pregnancy test you do in your own home must be meticulously performed and you must follow the manufacturer's instruc-

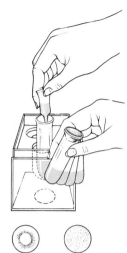

Positive   **Negative**

With a do-it-yourself pregnancy test, you add a small amount of a morning's first urine to the chemicals provided with the kit: shake and leave for 2 hours. You can then view the results in the mirror that comes with the kit.

tions to the letter. Done this way it can be as accurate as one done in a specialized laboratory, though great experience is needed to detect subtle changes. The tests are fairly cheap (approximately $10.00 and come in kit form. Tests vary, but they usually involve simple mixing of two component parts with a specimen of your urine and noting changes in the resulting liquid, either clarity or cloudiness or color transformation. Careful guidelines are given in the pack inserts as to how you should interpret the tests. If the result does not seem clear to you, or you are at all worried about the test, then go and see your doctor immediately. One word of advice; if you are scared of becoming pregnant, do not wish to have a baby and are anxious about the result of the test, it is far better to have the test performed properly in a scientific laboratory to give you a reliable result than to perform a test at home, perhaps inaccurately which may give you a false positive result and worry you even further, even though you can do the test earlier.

Laboratory pregnancy tests

The technology of pregnancy testing is now so advanced that a reliable result can be given on a small quantity of urine. It is based on the detection of a hormone which is excreted in the urine of a woman who has become pregnant, but only from about 14 days after the time she has missed her first period. The hormone is chorionic gonadotrophin (HCG). It is present in high concentration in the first specimen of urine that you pass early in the morning. Your doctor will ask you to collect a small specimen in a clean bottle or jar, and then it will be tested by mixing a small quantity with a detecting substance in a test tube or on a glass slide. The most accurate results are given by the test which requires this mixture to be left for two hours. This result is 90% certain. There is another test which gives a result in two minutes but this test is only 87% accurate. New radioreceptorassay tests (RRAs) are available which can detect very low levels of HCG in the blood in early pregnancy, even before the first period is missed. You can have one of these tests done at a family-planning clinic or a pregnancy advisory service and they will usually give you the result of the test on the same day. It is unwise to have the test done too early as the result may be equivocal. If you doubt the result of the test, have it repeated a few days later.

Calculating your expected date of delivery

As a general rule, pregnancy lasts 266 days from conception, or 280 days (9 calendar months and one week) from the *first day of the last period.* Don't forget that this represents an average and depends on you being able to remember exactly when your last period started (put it in your diary each month) and on having regular 28-day cycles. As many women have shorter and longer cycles than 28 days it is quite normal for babies to be born any time between 39 and 41 weeks from the first day of their mother's last menstrual period.

Some pregnancies *appear* to be much shorter or longer than this time and this usually means that the dates have been miscalculated or misjudged. Some women, for instance, experience a short bleed at their period time after they have conceived. If this is considered as the last period, the pregnancy would appear four weeks shorter than its actual length. Use the information below to find your delivery date.

EXPECTED DELIVERY DATE

Use this method to calculate your expected date of delivery bearing in mind it is based on regular 28-day cycles.

1. Note the first day of your last period – say September 12. Locate it on a calendar for the following year.	2. Subtract 3 months from that date, in this case you will be at June 12.	3. Add 7 days to this for your "due" date. In the example given the delivery date would be June 19.

Getting used to being pregnant

Even if your pregnancy is planned, you may find that it takes some getting used to. A lot of women don't like being "fat" and find the bodily changes associated with pregnancy unpleasant. Most of us worry about our babies being "all right" and about the changes a baby will make in our lives. Having a baby does involve a fundamental and substantial change in your life and lifestyle; you may think you know how you're going to feel before you are pregnant, but you don't, because once you are pregnant, your feelings will change and they will change again once your child is born. It's important for you to realize that you will change and you must not be frightened or surprised by the changes that will occur.

Here are some of the things you should do to assure yourself of a confident, secure and self-assured pregnancy:

Start thinking about yourself and your needs, about the baby and his or her needs, about your partner and what he will need. Make lists, timetables, charts, and prepare. You will be helped by a natural nesting instinct to gather things about you and to get organized, and you will find that this instinct increases until it reaches a peak in the third trimester of pregnancy.

Set about getting help. First you will need medical help and this is one of your rights as a pregnant mother, so you should not have difficulty in getting it. Second, and probably more importantly, you will need the help of a good supportive, positive friend. Your partner may do a great deal to fulfill your emotional needs during pregnancy, but I would suggest that you get the support of a female friend as well. Try and find one who already has children, if possible, one who had normal labors, normal deliveries, and healthy children, and who is finding motherhood a happy experience. With her, you can share your whole experience of pregnancy; you can compare notes, you can discuss your feelings and emotional changes, you can ask for advice and reassurance, and she will be someone you can simply talk to.

Get advice. The best person to get advice from is your own doctor, but get advice early because there are certain things you are going to have to do from the beginning to ensure your fitness, health and happiness and that of your baby's. You will need information about diet, about how much your weight should increase and when, about exercises you should and should not take, about clothing, about care of the breasts and the nipples, about taking drugs, about smoking, about alcohol, about warning signs that you should be on the lookout for, and about your rights as a pregnant mother. Don't miss out on a chance to do your best for yourself and your baby and get this information as soon as possible.

Read as many books on pregnancy as you can, attend prenatal classes so that you understand what is happening and what will happen, don't heed old wives' tales, and ask questions about anything that bothers you.

Be prepared to have some good feelings about your pregnancy (excited, creative, strong, energetic, loving, sensual, etc.), and some negative feelings (fear, I'm losing my independence, I'm exhausted, I don't want to give up my job, I don't like being shapeless), and some questions (What will it be like? Will the pain be unbearable? Will the baby be normal? Will I cope?). They are all usual and shouldn't cause you anxiety.

Involve your partner from the outset, discuss your feelings with him, share your fears, explain your moods, learn about pregnancy and childcare together, go to prenatal classes together, ask him to be present at the birth, take trouble with your appearance, go out with him as usual, have sex as usual for as long as you want (up to a few days before going into labor), allow him his freedoms as before and draw up ground rules based on equality for childrearing.

Tell any other children as soon as pregnancy is confirmed, put up a wallchart of progress through pregnancy and follow it through your own development, let them feel the baby kicking, encourage them to help with all preparations for the new baby, ask them to choose names. When the baby is born let your partner carry it and you remain free to embrace them; bring them presents from the new baby.

Involving your partner

Your partner was involved in the conception of your baby and as long as he remains with you, he should be closely involved in your pregnancy, your delivery and looking after your baby. This is not just a question of need, although you will need him, both emotionally and practically; it's a matter of shared love, shared responsibility and a shared workload. It's as well to get the groundrules clear at the beginning. You should expect and do everything you can to get equal sharing in all aspects of everyday life and work that may change as a result of you becoming pregnant and having a baby. This applies whether you opt to stay at home and look after your baby, or to return to work shortly after delivery. In either situation, you are working extremely hard and you need the help and support of your partner.

One of the best ways of getting this is to involve him in everything you do and in everything that happens to you. Most men, if encouraged, are as interested in what is going on as you are, but very often they are shut out and are made to feel that pregnancy and babies are nothing to do with them. There are a few men who really do feel this, but they are few and far between. Most men will take an interest in their pregnant partners, and the baby when it arrives, if they are encouraged and feel that they are sharing your experience. Your partner is more likely to help you with any onerous tasks in childrearing if he has been involved from the beginning.

Taking care of your own physical needs

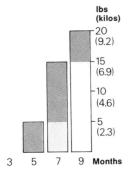

Weight gain in pregnancy should not exceed 20 lbs. (9.2 kilos), and should be distributed as reflected in the graph.

Diet
There are no special diets for pregnancy: there are no foods that you should avoid, there are no foods which are essential. Most old-fashioned diets for pregnancy included one or two pints of milk a day because it was erroneously thought that milk contained ingredients essential for pregnancy. You can get exactly the same nutrients from alternative foods to milk, particularly if you take an adequate and well-balanced diet (see pp. 20–26).

A balanced diet will give both you and your baby all the protein, carbohydrate, fat, vitamins and minerals that you need during pregnancy, and if you keep an eye on how much you eat, you will not put on more weight than you should. If you're in doubt about how much this is, see *left*.

During pregnancy there is no need whatsoever to take vitamin supplements yourself if you are eating a balanced diet. However, at the prenatal clinic you will almost certainly be given iron supplements which will include folic acid. This has been standard practice in prenatal clinics for several decades because it was found that women had a tendency to become anemic during pregnancy. However, the latest research has shown that this apparent anemia is a normal physiological response of the body to pregnancy, and iron supplements are probably not needed. Very few clinics, however, have discontinued the habit of giving iron, preferring to remain over-cautious. Folic acid is also usually given to guard against folic-acid deficiency, which used to be common in the second two trimesters of pregnancy.

Drugs

The fetus is going through its most sensitive phase of development in the first 12 weeks of its life. By the time it is 8 weeks old most of its vital organs have started to develop. It is during these first crucial weeks that the baby may be affected by foreign substances, including drugs and chemicals which may get into the mother's bloodstream. You should therefore avoid taking any drugs whatsoever, including any aspirin, during the first 12 weeks of your pregnancy. If, for instance, you are suffering from a debilitating condition such as pregnancy sickness, recurrent migraine headaches, or complete lack of sleep, then don't take anything for these conditions without consulting your doctor. S/he will know which of the drugs have been tried and tested and are suitable for pregnant mothers. All new drugs which come on the market have undergone testing in pregnant animals and there are many medicines of all types that are known to be safe in pregnancy. It is up to your doctor to supply you with them. If you find that you have unwittingly taken drugs when you were pregnant before you knew that you were, be reassured. Very few women come to harm because of this.

Smoking

The amount of medical evidence which now supports a causal relationship between ill health in your newborn baby and your smoking during your pregnancy is incontrovertible. You owe it to your developing child to give up cigarette smoking for the nine months that you are pregnant. Try and give up rather than cut down, whatever the cost. Many more premature and small for their age babies are produced by mothers who smoke. Other deleterious results of smoking on your baby would include a low birth weight, low resistance to and an increased risk of infection, respiratory disease of the newborn and the inability to breathe efficiently, and a high mortality rate.

Alcohol and addictive drugs

If you drink or take habit-forming drugs during pregnancy, your baby will be born with the need for alcohol and drugs. That is just for starters. If you drink excessive quantities of alcohol or take drugs chronically through pregnancy, your baby has an increased risk of being born abnormal, of being stillborn, or of dying shortly after birth. Research has shown that it isn't necessary to take large quantities of alcohol for there to be some effect on your baby – 2 to 3 drinks a day or the equivalent may be sufficient to produce such abnormalities as malformation and mental retardation (see p. 68). In addition, you will be making it difficult for your baby to get a good start in life because babies born to alcoholic mothers are not as able to suckle as normal babies, so take alcohol only in small quantities and do not take habit-forming drugs.

Checkups If you want to have a normal pregnancy and a healthy baby, the statistics show that the earlier you go to your doctor for your first prenatal visit, the higher the chance that you will get what you want. Good prenatal care is the nearest thing we have to real preventive medicine. Tests can be done to detect those mothers in whom complications may arise, so the treatment can be given early and the complications prevented. Prenatal supervision not only checks that all is well with mother and baby, but it gives you the opportunity of asking questions which will help to remove any mystique, ignorance, anxiety and fear of childbirth and infant care. You can have your first prenatal visit with your own doctor, or you can go directly to a prenatal clinic at a hospital. Whichever you choose, do it as soon as you suspect that you have become pregnant.

Your first prenatal visit will be quite a long one. It will be detailed in terms of questioning, and you will almost certainly be given an internal examination and urine and blood tests.

At your visit (and subsequent visits) you will be given a supply of iron and vitamin tablets and you will be booked into the hospital in which you will have your baby delivered. If you wish to

THINGS THAT WILL HAPPEN TO YOU DURING PREGNANCY

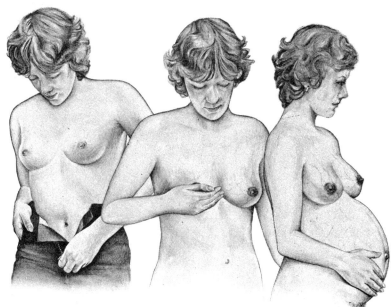

As your pregnancy progresses, your body will gradually change in shape. Your breasts will become larger, and have many dilated surface veins; your abdomen will swell – so much so, your naval may protrude – and stretch marks will appear.

First trimester

You will probably miss your first period.
Your breasts will become heavy, sore, tender and tingle.
You will need to pass urine more frequently than normal.
You may have a metallic taste in your mouth.
Fatigue and/or sleeplessness may be marked.

Your second period is missed.
Your breasts enlarge and the veins on the surface begin to show.
You continue to pass urine frequently.
Nausea and sickness may be present and not only in the morning.
You may go off certain foods, coffee and smoking.

The nipple area becomes brown and the tiny glands in the areola become prominent.
Nausea and sickness persist.
Weight gain may begin.
Your waistline starts to thicken.
Fatigue may be so great that you fall asleep whenever you sit down.

Second trimester

Nausea and sickness usually stop.
Your abdomen swells and your pregnancy can be seen.
You may feel your baby move from this time on – it feels like wind at first.
Breasts enlarge and surface veins dilate.
You may feel your uterus contracting from now on (goes hard for a few seconds) – these are Braxton-Hicks contractions.

Fluid (colostrum) clear and yellowish can be expressed from your breasts.
Pigmentation of the skin increases – particularly the line down center of abdomen (linea nyra); patches on face (chloasma); inner sides of thighs.
Palms of hands are pinker than normal.
Hair may start to grow or maybe fall out.

Abdominal skin becomes thin and stretch marks appear (you cannot prevent them or treat them) especially if you're blonde and it is your first baby.
Your navel is flush with the wall of your abdomen.
Cravings for certain foods may come on.
Weight gain is steady.

Third Trimester

Your baby's movements are frequent and clearly felt and seen.
Because your enlarging uterus presses on your stomach you may get indigestion and heartburn.
Your pelvic bones and ligaments are loosening in preparation for childbirth and you may get backache.

Your navel may protrude.
You may notice swelling of the ankles at the end of the day that goes down overnight.
Your ribs get pushed out by the growing baby and may be sore especially if the baby kicks in one direction.
You will be very tired at the end of each day.
Constipation may trouble you unless you eat plenty of roughage.

Your breasts are at their maximum size and colostrum may leak.
From 36 weeks onwards you may feel "tightening" as the baby's head engages in the pelvis, if it is your first baby this may not occur until just before labor.
You can feel parts of the baby.
Braxton-Hicks contractions are frequent.

have your baby at home or have a special preference as to where you would like to be delivered, you should have thought it out beforehand so that you can have a full discussion. If you decide on a hospital delivery you will be told who you should notify when you go into labor. You should also make it known whether you would like to have your partner present during your labor. Also, ask if there is a pamphlet which describes to you the services and benefits which are available to you as a pregnant mother.

Subsequent visits throughout pregnancy are routine. Your urine will be analyzed, you will be weighed, blood pressure will be taken and your abdomen will be examined. Other tests may be done to determine the baby's progress and general well-being. These include an *ultrasonic scan* – a painless procedure in which a transducer (a machine which picks up echoes of body tissues and transforms them into a visual picture) is passed over the abdomen to map out the baby's shape and position; *amniocentesis* (see p. 202); *AFP screening* – in which the mother's blood is tested for birth defects in the baby and possibly *fetoscopy* where a special instrument is inserted through the abdominal wall to view the baby.

Visits will be every four weeks up to 28 weeks and every two weeks to 36 weeks. From this time onwards, you will visit the pre-natal clinic weekly until the onset of labor.

MISCARRIAGE

There are many possible causes of miscarriage and several may be operating at any one time. Without special investigation it is rare to find a definite cause. Miscarriages are upsetting for most women who quite naturally suffer from feelings of inadequacy or failure and cast around for something or someone to blame. It may be a comfort to you to know that a miscarriage can be seen as a safeguard against having abnormal babies. By far the most frequent single cause of miscarriage is an abnormality of the developing fetus. Statistics show that between 50% and 75% of early miscarriages occur because of an abnormality of the embryo. The commonest causes of malformation are chromosomal abnormalities, then viral infections of the mother, for instance, German measles, and then certain drugs, in that order.

If you are healthy and strong and your growing baby is normal, there is very little that will disturb your pregnancy. Contrary to old wives' tales, pregnant women are impervious to fright, emotional upsets, accidents, purgatives, quinine and even operations. It has been recorded that curettage (scraping away the lining of the uterus) has been carried out inadvertently when a patient was pregnant and the pregnancy has continued normally.

There are, however, a few women who are prone to miscarriage and any of the above factors may precipitate miscarriage in them.

Miscarriages are described and named in different ways, according to the state that they have reached. Medically speaking, abortion and miscarriage are synonymous.

Types of miscarriages

Threatened abortion

This means that you have had some bleeding or spotting from the vagina and you may or may not have some abdominal pain. On examination your doctor may find that your cervix is closed and the probability is that if you rest and do not become anxious, everything will return to normal. Your doctor will almost certainly recommend bed rest and possibly give you a sedative and very little else.

Inevitable abortion

This means that your miscarriage has reached a point where it cannot be prevented. Instead of the bleeding stopping, it gets heavier and it is usually bright red in color. Your abdominal pains will get worse instead of better and within a few hours, you may pass the fetus, the sac which surrounds it, and the placenta, and quite a lot of blood. If your doctor is not present, try to save these products of conception in a receptacle so that your doctor may examine them as soon as possible.

An incomplete miscarriage

This means that your pregnancy is terminated, the fetus is no longer living but you have only passed part of the products of conception and some still remain behind in the uterus. These can cause infections. Your doctor will usually arrange for you to be admitted to the hospital for dilatation of the cervix and curettage of the uterine lining. You will probably be in the hospital no longer than three days and you will be back to normal in a week.

A complete miscarriage

This means that your uterus has expelled all of its contents. You will continue to bleed for several days as you usually do for a menstrual period. While your bleeding should diminish within three days, you should always contact your doctor to ascertain that your uterus is, in fact, empty. Moreover, it will be necessary for your doctor to determine your Rh type, if this hasn't been done before, to prevent possible complications with future pregnancies.

Missed miscarriage

This means that the fetus has died but the uterus has failed to expel it. Your doctor will usually recognize this condition because your uterus fails to grow as it should. Your doctor will probably have you admitted to the hospital for a D & C (see p. 197) or an induction of labor, depending on the stage of your pregnancy when the miscarriage occurs.

Recurrent miscarriage

There are a very few women who miscarry at an early stage each time they become pregnant and exhaustive investigations may not reveal a cause. The majority of these women can be successfully treated by an experienced obstetrician and can take a baby to term. About two-thirds of all women who have miscarried as many as three times go on to a normal fourth pregnancy without any special treatment. However, the more miscarriages a woman has, the less likely it is that they have occurred by chance – three consecutive miscarriages are now generally accepted as requiring special investigation and treatment; some women might prefer to be seen earlier.

Coping with miscarriage

Very few women miscarry without being emotionally disturbed. Some, if the pregnancy has lasted a few months, may go through a minor form of post-natal depression (see p. 228). Most of us who have suffered a miscarriage are beset by feelings of inadequacy, fear, guilt, sorrow and sometimes anger. You may feel so dejected that you believe you will never carry a baby to term and you may not want to become pregnant again. You will need the help and sympathy of your partner and the support of your doctor and friends. But the best possible medicine for a miscarriage is to try again. Your chances of becoming pregnant are the same as they were before you miscarried, and so are your chances of carrying a baby to term and delivering a normal baby.

If I have had a miscarriage, is it likely to recur?

The statistics on miscarriage are very encouraging. Roughly three-quarters of women who threaten to miscarry go on to produce a normal healthy child. Only about a quarter inevitably miscarry because they have a deformed embryo and, at most, 5 in 100 subsequently miscarry for other reasons.

CHILDBIRTH

Every woman remembers the birth of her first child. For the majority of women it is probably the most momentous event in their lives up to that time and subsequently it will be among the most memorable. Women approach childbirth in different ways, but all of us have certain feelings in common. Very few of us approach it with complete confidence. All of us harbor some fears – we know it's going to be painful and even though in the pre-natal classes we have been told how to cope with this pain and how to minimize it through relaxation, we still fear it. Without exception, all of us at some time during our pregnancies harbor the fear that our babies will not be normal. For the majority of women this fear increases in intensity and frequency in the last month or so of pregnancy. Most of us also have fears about how the actual childbirth will go – whether or not there will be complications, whether it will be very long, whether the baby will be in any danger, whether it will be necessary to resort to Caesarean section, even will I behave badly.

All of these fears are quite normal. Even after one successful childbirth, most women go into the second and subsequent ones with many of the same fears. Despite all this, most of us have perfectly normal labors, normal deliveries and normal babies. Having experienced childbirth with and without my husband, I am in no doubt about which I prefer. I found him very supportive.

He gave me courage and comfort during the most painful moments. He made it easier for me to bear the pain and he made me stronger. He witnessed our son's first moments of life and that drew us closer together. He expressed pride in my achievement and that added to my pleasure, and he shared the first embraces of our new baby and that bound us together as a family. But it's a matter of preference and many men feel strongly that they don't wish to be present at the birth of their children. Try and persuade your partner but don't pressure him. Make sure that you inform your doctor and your midwife in good time so that they can make the appropriate arrangements. Most maternity departments are happy to welcome fathers to the delivery room.

LABOR

No one knows why labor starts; what we do know is that the baby controls it. Just prior to the onset of labor, the baby gives a signal (probably a chemical or hormonal one) to the placenta, which starts to pour out a hormone setting labor in motion. The uterus responds by starting to contract regularly, though possibly infrequently at the beginning, and then with increasing force.

You can go into labor at any time and you are just as likely to have your baby during the night as during the day – the same number of babies are born in any hour of the 24.

When labor starts, your uterus is primed and ready for action. All the way through pregnancy it has been practicing with trial runs of weak, short-lived contractions which you can quite easily feel if you put your hand on your abdomen. Under your fingertips you will feel the muscles go hard and tight, but you will probably feel no discomfort. Many women experience these normal uterine contractions (Braxton-Hicks contractions) intermittently during their fertile life. For instance, they are evident at the beginning of menstrual periods when they may be painful, causing menstrual cramps or dysmenorrhea. Once labor is fully established, however, it becomes obvious that the largest and strongest muscle in your body is getting down to business. The contractions becomes strong and regular. At the beginning they are usually 15–20 minutes apart; they may be quite painful and they may last for about 40 seconds.

On average, labor lasts for 6–12 hours. Twelve hours is the usual length of labor with your first baby, though in 10% of women it lasts more than 24 hours and in 5% of women, it takes less than 3. The birth of the second and subsequent babies is usually easier, less painful and less exhausting than the first and lasts on average, 6 hours. Studies reveal that it takes about 150 contractions to deliver your first baby, 75 are needed for your second and third, and 50 for your fourth and fifth.

How will I know that labor is starting?

Labor may start merely as backache in the lower part of the back which may go on for 24 hours or more before anything further happens. The first sign is the onset of contractions which are powerful, regular, and of long duration.

The second sign is the rupturing of the membranes or breaking of the waters. Sometimes this can be a slow leakage, but nonetheless, is obvious, and at others it may be a gush of liquid from the vagina.

The third sign is a "show." A show is a small amount of blood-stained mucus – the plug of mucus which has become dislodged from the cervix. Quite frequently this sign of labor beginning is overlooked.

There is no need to get in touch with the hospital until you notice either of the second or third signs. As soon as you do, telephone the person you have been told to notify and tell them that you are on your way. If you have had a show, or if your waters have broken, do not wait for your contractions to become regular, strong and painful. Not all labors start this way. Many women do not have regularly spaced powerful contractions until they are well advanced through the first stage of labor. Quite a number have irregularly spaced contractions and their intensity and painfulness don't increase much as time goes on.

Induced labor

There are quite a few books around, particularly those written by feminist writers, which emphasize how to go about avoiding induction of labor. I question this attitude, based as it is on the premise that regardless of cost to mother and child, childbirth should not be interfered with. Yes, of course, childbirth is a natural process, and where everything is normal for mother and baby, it should proceed as a normal process with medical and nursing help performing only a monitoring and supporting role. But at least 5 in 100 women *need* an induced labor for sound medical reasons, and both they and their baby would be in jeopardy if labor was not started off artificially at a precise time.

Other than the medical reasons for induction, there are what are called social reasons which are largely a matter of hospital practice. Though the number is decreasing, there are hospital obstetric units which have opted for a high rate of induced labors. Doctors who supervise these departments have done so in the belief that induction is safe in their hands and that it reduces the risk of infant death. Another argument which is used in support of induction, which is usually started off very early in the morning, say 6 a.m., is that doctors and nurses can deliver patients during the day when they are fresh and alert and full hospital services and facilities are available to support them. The counter argument which is used to this statement is that during working hours, medical and nursing staff are over-worked in units where the induction rate is high.

If you are young (under 30 years of age) and your pregnancy is proceeding normally, the subject of induction will probably never be raised. If, however, you are an elderly primigravida, your obstetrician will consider the possibility of induction even though your pregnancy is proceeding normally, and even though the possibility of actually having to induce your labor is not great.

WHY INDUCTION IS CONSIDERED AND DONE

Leaving aside the social reasons for induction, and the fact that some hospitals have opted to induce the majority of labors because in their hands it is a safe and successful method of childbirth, there are clear medical reasons for considering induction.

● For elderly primigravidae. If you are over the age of 35 and pregnant for the first time, induction will always be considered. This is because complications such as placental insufficiency and toxemia are more common the older the mother, especially if it is the first pregnancy. Induction in this instance is performed as a safety precaution in an attempt to pre-empt complications for you and the baby. The date when you should come into the hospital for induction is usually discussed during your weekly visits in the last month of pregnancy. Please make sure that someone explains to you exactly what will happen during the induction procedure and what you, can expect.

● For second and subsequent labors in elderly mothers. Induction is considered and performed for the same reasons given above.

● For mothers with Rh incompatibility with a high level of antibodies. This is a medical necessity for induction at a time which can only be decided by your doctor according to the level of your antibodies and the health of your baby (see p. 202).

● For mothers with diabetes mellitus, especially if not well controlled. Early induction of labor can be carried out any time from the 36th week onwards according to the judgement of the obstetrician.

● For mothers with toxemia of pregnancy, with raised blood pressure, albumen in the urine and possibly even fits. This is a strong indication for induction of labor, especially if accompanied by placental insufficiency and fetal distress.

● For mothers with renal or heart disease, though the majority of women with heart abnormalities sail through pregnancy and have very easy labor.

● For mothers with high blood pressure, whether it has been running high for some time during pregnancy, or suddenly begins to rise towards the end of pregnancy. High blood pressure can deprive the baby of oxygen because placental function starts to fall away; the decision to induce labor will only be taken after careful monitoring of the baby's health.

You should therefore take the initiative with your obstetrician and raise the subject of induced labor and thrash the whole subject out with him or her until you have all the facts that you require and feel happy in your mind. If there is a strong medical reason or a medical necessity to induce your labor, you would be very unwise not to have it done. On the other hand, try and find out from your obstetrician just how necessary an induction is. If the necessity is questionable, then it is your right to seek a second opinion, and you should go ahead and do so if you feel strongly about it. There is no reason why you shouldn't suggest to your obstetrician that you try having a natural childbirth. You will almost certainly find him or her reasonable and they will agree to this, given that they can make a medical decision at any time if they feel induction is necessary.

If you happen to be enrolled at a hospital where labors are routinely induced, and you wish to have your baby naturally, then you can speak to the midwife or doctor concerned and ask to be transferred to a hospital where natural childbirth is encouraged.

Do I have to have induced labor?

No you do not, but I would suggest that you ignore strong medical advice at your peril. The overriding consideration of even the keenest advocates of natural childbirth should be to have a healthy baby at the end of delivery and a mother who is not debilitated. Dogma should not stand in the way of realism where childbirth is concerned. However, if you and your baby are quite normal and healthy, then you can exercise the option to find an obstetrician and a hospital unit where you can have the sort of labor that you want and this applies to any form of childbirth.

Are there any risks associated with induction?

Yes, there are, and in unskilled hands there are more. There are very few risks in, for instance, a university teaching hospital obstetric unit where induction is standard practice and where all the medical, nursing, and anesthesia staff are highly experienced. In one of these units there is no reason why an induced labor should not proceed normally or be any longer than normal or be any more painful than normal, or not culminate in a perfectly normal delivery.

Some of the complications of induction which have been recorded are as follows:

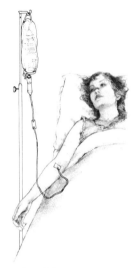

When labor is induced, synthetic oxytocin is intravenously given to encourage the onset of uterine contractions.

● The contractions of the uterine muscles are not always as smooth and as intense or as long as normal contractions. This, however, does not necessarily prolong labor. Induced labors are usually quite short, e.g. 8 to 10 hours as opposed to 12 to 14 hours for normal labor.

● If synthetic oxytocin is given through a drip into the arm, it is possible that the drip rate may get too high resulting in contractions of very great intensity and these can be painful. If the contractions are very prolonged, the blood supply to the baby can be temporarily interrupted. In a normal contraction, this happens anyway and experienced medical staff will adjust the drip rate to make sure this does not happen. Careful monitoring makes the uterine contractions fairly easy to control in experienced hands.

● An increase in blood pressure during induction has been reported.

● There is also the possibility of a higher rate of Caesarean section, forceps deliveries and episiotomies with induction, but this depends very much on the expertise and experience of the staff performing the induction and monitoring subsequent progress.

● A higher incidence of fetal distress has been reported, but again this reflects, to a certain respect, the care with which the fetus is monitored after induction. In good units, you and your baby are hooked up to a monitoring system which is displayed on oscilloscope screens. Medical and nursing staff can therefore spot any abnormalities as soon as they occur and can act appropriately.

What will happen if I have an induction?

The doctor will perform an internal examination to make sure that all is well. Then s/he will guide a pair of fine forceps through the neck of the cervix with a finger, nip a small piece of the amniotic sac between the forceps and rupture the membranes.

The doctor may then run a finger around the head of the baby to separate it slightly from the rim of the cervix. In doing so, s/he dilates the cervix slightly.

In most units, mechanical induction of labor is augmented with hormonal induction. This is done by either transfusing Pitocin or synthetic oxytocin (the hormone which is produced in your body which causes uterine contractions during labor) through a vein into your arm. Intravenous infusion may be started only after several hours if your uterus is not contracting regularly and at intervals of 10 to 15 minutes, or it may be started within 30 minutes of mechanical induction if that is the practice on the unit. By controlling the number of drops per minute that enter your vein, the staff can more or less control the frequency, regularity and intensity of your uterine contractions.

An alternative method of giving synthetic oxytocin (syntocinon) is in tablet form. These are placed between the gum and the side of the mouth and are sucked. The syntocinon is absorbed through the lining of the mouth. If you have ever had one you will find that if you suck hard you can increase the contraction rate, whereas if you stop sucking, it slows down. You are therefore in a position to control your labor yourself using a synthetic aid.

Within a couple of hours your labor should be well under way and your cervix dilating normally.

Other methods of induction

Acupuncture has been used successfully for inducing labor but there is hardly any proper medical research to support it.

Labour can be induced with a cervical vibrator which dilates the cervix. This can be extremely painful and is not well documented; it is not to be recommended.

It is claimed that a natural method of activating labor in some women is to stimulate the nipples. In a woman who is at full term, this will release oxytocin and is obviously completely safe as one cannot overdose oneself with this simple technique.

DELIVERY

A normal healthy woman delivering a normal healthy baby is involved in a natural process and it can and should proceed naturally, without intervention, if the mother is well motivated, well supported by other people around her, and relaxed. Childbirth can only be natural if these conditions prevail. If a woman is not well motivated to have her child naturally, then she may give up when the going gets tough and it nearly always does.

There is no such thing as labor which is entirely pain-free. It depends to a certain extent on the woman's pain threshold. Some women are prepared to bear more pain than others and will make an attempt to bear quite a lot of pain to be in full control of their labor and to deliver their baby naturally without the use of anesthetics or other pain killers.

Even well-motivated women gain from having sympathetic, enthusiastic, and encouraging people around them, particularly a supportive partner, which makes labor and delivery smoother, shorter and less painful.

Being relaxed can do a tremendous amount to reduce the amount of pain you feel and during your prenatal classes you will have been encouraged to do this in two ways: first, by the acquisition of information which gets rid of myths, legends and false fears and gives you the self-assurance to go into labor with self-confidence; and second, by perfecting the special exercises which help the muscles to relax for you during labor and those which allow you to control your respiration so that you breathe evenly and deeply, and in doing so, help you to reduce the pain.

Home versus hospital

Quite early on in pregnancy – it might even be at your first pre-natal visit – you will have to start thinking about whether you wish to opt for a home or hospital delivery. Rest assured that the ultimate choice is always up to you, no one can force you to do anything. However, you would be well advised to take account of some guidelines.

The following women are advised to have their baby in the hospital:
- Women who are having their first baby because the labor pattern is not established yet and it is impossible to tell whether you will have easy or difficult labors that require specialized support techniques which are only available in the hospital.
- Women who are having their first baby when over the age of 35.
- Women having their second or subsequent babies with a history of difficult or complicated labors.
- Twins or multiple births.

Before you take the decision to have your baby at home, and even if you feel strongly about it, there are some advantages to hospital confinement that you should bear in mind. The only way

HOSPITAL CONFINEMENT

- There are skilled medical and nursing personnel available for any emergency or complication, at any time of the day or night.
- You will be taught by nurses how to deal with the everyday care of your baby which can be quite scary with a first baby.
- There is a pediatrician on hand to examine your baby and reasssure you if you are concerned about anything.
- You will meet other new mothers on the hospital ward and compare and exchange notes which can dispel your fears and give you reassurance.
- You will be able to compare your baby to other newborn babies.
- Your anxieties, problems, difficulties and troubles can be shared with other mothers, e.g. difficulties in establishing breast feeding, the pain of a cracked nipple, the discomfort from stitches.

HOME CONFINEMENT

- You are in familiar surroundings.
- You are with your husband and family.
- You can have a friend or relative to help. If you get on well, mothers and mothers-in-law can be invaluable at this time.
- You don't worry about absence from your family.
- Your baby is always near you.
- You can do whatever you like to, with and for your baby, at whatever time you choose, For example, you can have the light dim and you can make sure you and the baby are quiet.
- You can establish what will be your domestic routine with your baby within a couple of days and s/he will become a member of the family immediately.
- If it's not your first baby you can introduce the new baby right away to siblings.
- You can have your own midwife to look after you.

to reduce the number of babies who die at birth because of oxygen lack is for doctors to recognize their suffering at the earliest possible time. To do this they need expensive monitoring equipment that is usually available only in a hospital.

There are compromises that you should consider. It is possible to have your delivery in the hospital and return home as soon as 6 hours after delivery, or you can stay in the hospital for 24 hours or 48 hours, 3 days, 5 days or a week. Discuss all these options with your midwife or doctor before you do go into the hospital, so they all know how you feel. Make certain you have come to a decision you are happy with.

Methods of delivery

Many women quite rightly feel that they want to be in charge of their delivery. After all, it's your labor, so you take the initiative and, within the bounds of medical safety, you decide what kind of delivery you would like and make sure you get it. If you find that medical and nursing staff are going to be obstructive during your prenatal time, then think seriously about changing the hospital where you will be having your delivery, or the doctor who will deliver you at home.

GIVING BIRTH

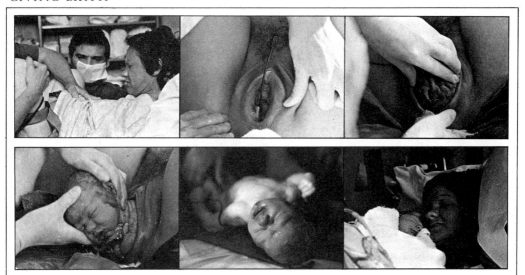

The first stage of labor is over once the cervix becomes fully dilated (10 cm) so that the cervix and vagina become one birth canal. During the second stage, the mother bears down during contractions in order to press the baby through the canal. When the widest part of the baby's head appears, and does not retract between contractions, it has "crowned" and the head will shortly emerge. Then the doctor or midwife will check to see that the umbilical cord does not obstruct the neck and may rotate the head so that the torso can be delivered more easily.

With a few more pushes, the baby emerges. Now delivered, the baby is checked, rapidly cleaned and given over to its parents to be welcomed and admired. In a few minutes' time, the placenta will be delivered to make up the third stage of labor.

In this sequence of a hospital birth, the mother is wearing an external electronic monitor around her abdomen to record her contractions and the baby's heart-beat. An internal monitor is inserted through her vagina to attach to the baby's head to record the pressure of contractions on it.

Natural childbirth

The major decision that you will have to make about the sort of delivery you choose is whether or not it will be natural or aided. A natural delivery involves no medical intervention and the administration of no type of anesthesia. I have great sympathy with women who feel that having a baby is probably the greatest biological event in their lives and who wish to experience every single second of it with an alert mind and body feeling and absorbing a multitude of sensations that accompany it, even though some of them may be extremely painful. Given that all aspects of pregnancy are medically normal, I would encourage every woman to consider having a natural childbirth.

Natural childbirth means that you will not only have your baby naturally, be fully conscious, but that you will be in a state to take the initiative throughout the whole of labor. However, it does not mean experiencing unnecessarily long and extremely painful childbirth. If you are fully informed and prepared for what is likely to happen through your reading and your prenatal classes, fear and tension will be avoided, you will give yourself the best possible chance of enjoying labor and you will know when you need to ask for help.

On the other hand I find most arguments in favor of suffering pain for its own sake dubious. Suffering pain is very unpleasant at the time and it is extremely debilitating and tiring. Even though you know you will have a brand-new baby at the end of delivery, pain can also be depressing. I have experienced both a painful and a painless labor and though the latter involved intervention with an epidural anesthetic, I am in no doubt which I prefer: the

TYPES OF DELIVERY

Name	Description	How to get it	Where delivered
Natural	Unaided and helped by relaxation and breathing techniques and self help control of pain.	At prenatal clinic and classes. Inform midwife in good time.	Home or hospital
Leboyer	Natural method devised by a Frenchman meant to mimic intra-uterine environment, i.e. dark, quiet, with heartbeat on audio etc.	Very difficult to get in U.S. unless you do it in own home, but you can ask for baby and lay it on your abdomen, etc.	Home or hospital
Induced	Artificial rupture of membrane and I.V. oxytocin. Fetal and maternal monitoring.	Ask at prenatal clinic and arrange with midwife or doctor. May be advised on medical grounds.	Hospital.
Forceps	If baby's head not descending. Normally can be aided by application of specially shaped metal forceps and gently pulled out – usually by obstetrician.	Only done if medically necessary.	Home or hospital
Vacuum extraction	Suction cup placed on head to aid descent. May be used instead of forceps.	Not commonly used in U.S. and U.K. Most common in Scandinavia and Holland. Only in special units.	Hospital.

painless one. However, there are many women who for good reason elect to have their babies naturally. That method is open to every one of us.

Types of anesthesia available

For those women who would prefer some form of pain relief during labor and delivery, there is quite a selection for you to choose from and you should make sure that you have discussed what drugs you may be given during labor with your midwife or doctor before you go into the hospital. Hospital-ward routine is pretty monolithic once it starts rolling, and if you have not expressed your preference prior to going into the hospital, it will be difficult for you not to feel that the initiative has been wrested from you and is completely in the hands of the medical and nursing staff who can give you any drugs they please when a rapid decision has to be taken. The drugs that you will be given fall largely into three groups:

Analgesics to relieve pain. In labor, pain relief is needed quickly and analgesics are usually given by injection.

Anesthetics to dull the conscious appreciation of pain. We nearly always lose some awareness of what is happening around us with these drugs and in large doses, of course, we lose consciousness. Many women who want to experience every second of childbirth find this unacceptable.

Others: sedatives to relieve anxiety and make you feel calm and sleepy; hypnotics which will actually send you to sleep; and tranquillizers which will make you feel relaxed, less worried, and possibly drowsy.

attendance	Pain (relief)	Length	Comments
dwife or doctor.	Can be very great.	On average up to 12 hours if normal.	Very good if you are well instructed. If labor is too painful you may require gas.
dwife or doctor.	Can be substantial.	As above.	As above.
dwife, doctor, esthetist and diatrician.	If with epidural or complete anesthetic relatively painless but only when delivery imminent.	On average up to 10 hours if normal.	Labor can be short, i.e. 6–8 hours and easy.
dwife, doctor, esthetist and iatrician.	Local anesthetic given before application.	Very quick, once applied.	With skilled hands an excellent method of shortening difficult labor and extricating baby.
ctor, midwife and esthetist.	Local anesthetic given before application.	Quick, once applied.	

All of these drugs, once in the mother's bloodstream, cross the placenta to the baby: all of them have some effect on the baby, always deleterious no matter how minor. A good answer would seem to be a form of pain relief that could be used locally to numb the pain of contractions while leaving the baby untouched and the mother in complete control of her senses. An epidural anesthetic fulfills these criteria. It anesthetizes the nerves that carry painful sensations from the uterus and birth canal to the brain (very much in the same way as a nerve from a tooth is anesthetized by a dentist) but in no way interferes with your awareness. If you arrange to have an epidural anesthetic, ask for it when labor becomes painful. The nurse will send for an anesthetist who will administer the anesthetic to you.

Episiotomy

An episiotomy is a cut which is made through the vaginal wall and the underlying muscle if the entrance to the vagina will not stretch sufficiently without tearing to allow the baby's head through. The baby's head is its largest diameter and once its head is through, the rest of the body does not stretch the vagina to the same extent.

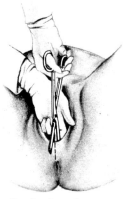

Cutting into the perineum to facilitate the baby's birth is a common practice in many hospitals, but one whose validity is being increasingly questioned.

The doctor and midwife usually use their judgement about whether an episiotomy is needed or not. Current research has revealed that contrary to accepted beliefs, tears heal quicker and with less pain than cuts. Episiotomies involve a greater risk of infection and do not prevent prolapse (see p. 290). Therefore, if you don't want one done, ask that it be placed in your notes that you are to be advised if and when the doctor considers it necessary.

An episiotomy is usually performed as the head is crowning, when the vagina is stretched to its maximum. Please make sure that you have discussed the episiotomy with your midwife while you are coming to full dilatation and make sure that you have the guarantee that you will be given a local anesthetic. Some midwives and doctors still have the primitive belief that at the height of a contraction, when you are suffering a great deal of pain, you will not feel the added pain of an episiotomy and are prepared to cut the perineum and the muscle without a local anesthetic to numb the pain. Insist that this does not happen.

Once the placenta has been delivered a doctor will stitch up your episiotomy. This must be done with great care to ensure the future integrity of the musculature of the vagina and rectum. It may take longer than you think because the stitching is usually done in layers, the muscles being stitched quite separately from the other tissues. The deeper stitches, and usually the superficial stitches, are made of soluble material which dissolves in 5 to 6 days and does not necessitate the rather painful procedure of having the stitches removed. On rare occasions, the stitches may dissolve before healing is complete.

The presence of stitches, however, always causes some discomfort so be prepared for it. The majority of women find that sitting down is painful and passing urine and feces may be uncomfortable. Sitting on a rubber ring will minimize your discomfort, as will an icebag in the crotch or a sanitary pad soaked in witch hazel placed over the incision.

AFTER-CARE

The time immediately after having a baby will almost certainly bring surprises and some feelings that you did not expect. You must realize that it is a period of adjustment to an enormous change. The time it takes for you to adjust physically, emotionally as well as practically to not being pregnant, to having a new baby to look after, and to coping with the various new tensions in your life, varies from woman to woman. You should be prepared to experience a mixture of feelings in the first few days after your baby is born, some of them ambivalent. You may feel somewhat frightened, a bit tearful and depressed, concerned about your ability to be a good mother, alternately exhilarated and despondent. These are all feelings which are normal and experienced by most mothers with a new baby. It should be reassuring to know that most mothers feel the same as you do, that most mothers cope quite well and you can too, and that your feelings are not entirely under your control. They are as much to do with the profound hormonal changes which are going on in your body (the tremendously high levels of circulating female and pregnancy hormones suddenly drop to a 100th or a 1,000th of their previous level. This drop affects your mood and your psychological balance and your emotional resilience) and the physical changes that are involved in bringing your body back to normal.

The first days after birth It is probably your emotions which concern you most. At first you may have a feeling of relief that it's over and done with, that you're through it, and you have a new baby and a comparatively flat abdomen. Then you may be besieged by a sensation of anti-climax, that the big event is over, and the future has a large question mark over it, so you may feel let down and introspective. Furthermore, you may wait for mother-love to be switched on and it doesn't come on. This is very common. The majority of women when questioned, confess that they have no special feeling for their newborn baby, nothing more than a person might feel for an unrelated defenseless tiny human being; there is no bonding, there is no feeling of kinship. The absence of maternal instinct may make you think you are abnormal or inadequate. You are, of course, neither. Mother-love is in your hormones and mother-love is switched on about the third day after birth (it may be growing before then but it is usually only on the third day that you feel a surge of love towards your new baby). This is because mother-love develops in parallel with lactation and seems to coincide with the regular secretion of oxytocin which is responsible for the milk let-down reflex. So if you don't feel mother-love immediately, don't worry. Wait for it to pour out with the milk. Incidentally if you have your milk suppressed with hormone supplement, mother-love still seems to appear at about the same time.

You are bound to be aware of the changes that are going on in your body. You will experience after-pains or uterine cramps which are usually strongest during the first three days after the baby's birth. They are fairly strong uterine contractions which are a normal and necessary part of uterine shrinkage following birth. They usually last a few minutes at a time, but if you find that they are frequent, severe and prolonged, ask the nurse or doctor for some medicine to relieve the pains.

Breast feeding

During the 72 hours after birth, the breasts secrete colostrum, a clear, nutritious straw-colored fluid which precedes the milk. Milk appears on the third day. All women, no matter what the size of their breasts, are equipped to breast feed their babies, and not having sufficient milk is rarely the real reason why a woman does not breast feed: the amount of milk you produce is a response to the amount of milk that your baby needs, and therefore that your baby takes. You will produce just as much as your baby needs to feed properly and be well satisfied. In the first three days after milk has appeared, it is important to stimulate the breasts to produce milk by drawing it off, and the best way to draw it off is to feed the baby. You should give your baby short periods (starting off with a minute, then going to two minutes, three minutes, etc.) on each breast, and feed your baby fairly frequently, say every three to four hours, or every two to three hours if your baby is very hungry. These frequent small feedings will encourage the breasts to produce sufficient milk for your baby, and prevent your nipples becoming sore and cracked. Letting the milk stagnate in the breasts inhibits further production. If you find that you are over-producing, you should draw it off with a breast pump. There is no point in breast feeding your baby if you hate every minute of it, nor is there any point in feeling guilty because you have been brought up to believe that you should breast feed your baby but can't or don't want to. You should have the self-confidence to decide how you want to feed your baby in whichever way makes you happiest.

BREAST FEEDING

Pros	Cons
Tailor-made food for baby	May have to feed often (every 2–3 hours) especially first 2 weeks
Baby protected against infection	Sharing of child care with father not easy
Convenient – can feed any time; always at right temperature; no need to sterilize	Siblings (and partner) may feel excluded
Baby rarely gains too much weight	Cannot be delegated (unless you use a breast pump and put milk in refrigerator to be given by bottle)
Stools not too runny or too dry	
Mother/child bonding can be rapidly made – "satisfying" to both	May get sore or cracked nipples which can be painful
Helps baby to learn how to establish relationships	
Baby learns to play at the breast – breast is first plaything	
May improve shape of breasts	
Good for the figure (return to pre-pregnant shape and weight more rapidly)	

BOTTLE FEEDING

Pros	Cons
May need less frequent feedings (3–4 hours) than breast	Food not ideal for baby
Father can share work-load and get to know baby	Inconvenient in terms of – making up – sterilizing – heating up from refrigerator
Can be delegated	Bonding between mother and child not as easy (if possible hold baby next to your bare skin and make eye contact during feedings).
You are free, i.e. can have time on your own or go back to work	
If you've gained too much weight in pregnancy you can go on reducing diet immediately (not impossible but not as easy when breast feeding)	

Breast feeding, when it is satisfactory to both mother and baby, facilitates the bonding relationship between the two.

Coping with exhaustion

You will probably find that you are pretty fatigued after delivery. Pushing a baby out uses up a lot of energy and you may find that you have aches and pains round the body where muscles have been used to perform an unfamiliar task. One of the reasons for opting for quite a long stay in the hospital is that it does allow you to catch up with your sleep. You can quite often nap during the day, even short snoozes can help to get rid of the sleep debt that you have built up in the month before delivery. Research has shown that in the four weeks prior to labor, women go without rapid eye movement (REM), or dream sleep. If they return immediately to a domestic routine or take full responsibility for night feeding of the baby, the backlog of REM sleep is never corrected. This will only make you feel more physically and mentally exhausted. Staying in hospital where the nursing staff will take over as many of your responsibilities as you choose, and where you do not have to think about domestic priorities, can be a heaven-sent opportunity for you to make up your sleep.

"Baby blues"

Traditionally, women become anxious and depressed on the third day after delivery, coincidentally with the onset of true lactation and the appearance of the milk let-down reflex (the flow of milk to the nipple when the baby suckles, or sometimes even when you hear your baby cry). Most women are irritable, tearful, subject to wild imaginings and fantasies, may have nightmares, lose their tempers easily and may even have temper tantrums. The majority of women get over these baby blues within a few days. If your depression continues into weeks, you should talk to your midwife, social worker or doctor about it and seek help (see p. 228).

During the first few days you may also have to cope with your surprise at the sight of your baby who may be covered with fine, downy, lanugo hair, whose body seems to be misshapen with stick-like limbs, whose very odd-shaped head may be swollen at one point due to the pressure of passing through the birth canal. Her/his skin seems to change color with frightening rapidity from blue, white to red; there are minor abnormalities here and there like birth marks, odd pigmented spots and moles, and generally your newborn baby may not seem very pretty.

As the first day passes into the second and the swelling on your baby's head begins to go down, and you've become used to the rapid color changes in the skin and the way the whole body goes into spasm at the sound of a loud noise, you are also having to cope with hospital ward routine and doctors and nurses who seemingly don't have your best interests at heart. The nurses may seem impatient with your attempts to feed your baby satisfactorily as they have to get the ward tidied up and on with their next job. It probably seems to you that they run the ward for their benefit rather than for that of the mothers and babies. Nursing staff have even been known to discourage women from breast feeding because it causes them too much trouble. If you and your baby are healthy and you want to breast feed, resist any pressure from the hospital staff to do anything else. Don't be put off by inflexible ward routine; ask to see the head nurse and explain to her the problems you are encountering and ask if you can have some help. If approached in this way, nursing staff are rarely un-cooperative; but if they are, persevere.

Changes in your body

It takes a woman's body nine months to return to normal after pregnancy and the greatest changes occur within the first six weeks after delivery. There is a drastic reduction in blood volume; the heart, the kidneys, the muscles, the joints, have to decelerate very quickly and the body has to repair itself. In doing this, the body experiences rapid tissue breakdown, which is called cataba-lism and is the equivalent to what happens during a period of convalescence after a major surgical operation. It takes time and you must be prepared for things to go fairly slowly. I remember very well waiting for my swollen ankles to go back into shape after the birth of my first son. I expected it to be almost instantaneous, but it took six weeks.

You are encouraged to be active within an hour or so of childbirth. You will be asked to have a bath, pass urine and move your bowels two or three hours after your baby has been delivered. There are very good reasons for this. It encourages the uterus to contract down hard and therefore minimizes the chance of a hemorrhage, it gets all the muscles and joints working again and, most important, it helps to avoid stagnation of the blood in the lower legs and pre-empts a deep-vein thrombosis.

Exercise and diet

We do need plenty of rest during the first six weeks after delivery, and we should be unscrupulous about getting it whenever we can, however we can, but we also need exercise, and in your prenatal class you will have been instructed in a course of post-natal exercises that you should do every day. While you should try to do this, I feel it's better to perform a few simple exercises as often as you can remember, say once every few hours for the first week or so. Here is the routine that I used to use:

For your back Put both hands in the small of your back and arch your back backwards 5–6 times. Rest.

For your abdomen Put your hands on your hips and pull your tummy in quickly and let it go. Repeat 10 times.

For your pelvic floor Pull your vagina upwards in a movement that will stop the flow of urine when you are emptying your bladder. If necessary, actually do this when you are passing urine to see how it feels and repeat the movement 10 times.

Even within a week you will be astonished at how much easier these movements become and how much fitter you feel. It's never too early to start thinking of diet and you will help yourself to recover your pre-pregnancy figure fast by not eating starchy foods but concentrating on high-protein foods such as meat, fish, eggs, low-fat cheese, skimmed milk, yogurt, fresh fruit and Vegetables, and by breast feeding. If you put on more than 20 pounds during pregnancy, every one of those pounds will still be there, probably in places where it's difficult to lose fat from, e.g. upper arms, thighs and abdomen. Start immediately by going on a sensible, well-balanced diet. Do not be over-ambitious and do not exclude foods that you really need, especially if you are breast feeding. There is no need to drink the recommended two to three pints of milk a day as long as you take plenty of fluid in the form of water or fruit juices.

Post-natal check Six weeks after delivery you should go to see your doctor for your post-natal check during which you will be asked about how you are coping, if you are feeling miserable or depressed, if you are suffering any discomfort or pain, if your blood loss is still continuing, if you are managing feeding, be it bottle or breast, if the baby is thriving. You will be given a full examination, including an internal examination to make sure that the uterus is shrinking satisfactorily and including examination of your breasts to make sure that all is going well, whether you are breast feeding or not. It's during the post-natal checkup that you should discuss contraception with your doctor because once you resume sex you must use a contraceptive method if you do not wish to become pregnant immediately. If you want to have an IUD fitted, it can easily be done as part of the post-natal check.

Resuming sexual relations The time at which women start to have sexual relations after pregnancy varies very much with culture and predilection. Many women find that their libido is low after pregnancy. Others, because they are eager to re-establish a relationship with their partner, may have quite a high sex drive, and it's perfectly normal and no harm will come to you if you have sex within seven days of delivery. The majority of women find it somewhat uncomfortable, and those that have had an episiotomy will probably find sex painful for several weeks. Indeed, the pain may prevent you from having sexual relations for three weeks or more. Discuss your feelings, both emotional and physical, freely with your partner so that he understands your motivations. Whatever you do, don't ignore sex completely because it's likely to be quite uppermost in your partner's mind. If you refrain from relations for too long it may increase any feelings of neglect and being shut out from you that he may have because of the baby.

Coping with the baby

Besides the happiness s/he brings, a new baby in the house, particularly if it is your first, causes drastic changes in routine and demands adjustment that can be uncomfortable for all members of the household. You may be surprised to find that it takes you some time to adjust to the idea of having a baby; of having a third person come between you and your partner; of having your relationship disturbed; of having to take care of a small defense-less human being; of the responsibilities that are involved, (physical, emotional and psychological); of the pitfalls that may beset you and of the difficulties you may have to overcome, both on your own behalf and for your new baby as well. Don't be foolish enough to think that everything will run smoothly, that there will be no crises and that you will feel overjoyed and happy most of the time. Your new baby will in turn delight you, make you feel fearful of her/his small size and frailty, and wear you down with frequent waking during the night and crying spells. You will constantly feel ambivalent as a person for the first few months. Any and all of the following feelings are quite normal in new mothers:

- You feel fulfilled in a way that you have never felt before.
- You feel inadequate because you think you cannot fulfill all your baby's needs.
- You love your baby very much.
- You feel resentful because you are tied to your baby and feel you have lost your freedom.
- Your baby has given your life new meaning and you feel enriched as a human being.
- You have become anonymous and lost your independence.
- Because of your baby you feel strong and can take on anything.
- You feel scared and afraid because you can't take care of, nor the responsibility for, this tiny new person – what if you drop the baby when you are bathing her/him?

Post-natal depression

Post-natal depression does not describe the feelings of anxiety, fearfulness and dejection which most women feel for a few days, or possibly a few weeks immediately after childbirth. It describes a psychological disturbance with severe depression which goes on for much longer and is a much more serious illness.

Most authorities believe that it has one of two causes:
- That it is the result of hormonal changes which occur at the time of delivery when high levels of female hormones in the blood suddenly plummet and the shock that this causes to the body.
- That it is the result of social stress.

The first cause can be treated by tapering doses of hormones which are given over a period of two to three months after delivery. Anti-depressants and tranquillizer drugs can be given in support of this basic hormonal treatment. Post-natal depression must always be taken seriously and handled by a psychiatrist who is experienced in treating the condition.

Social and emotional stresses are often associated with depression and they emphasize the need to involve your partner in your pregnancy as early as you possibly can, and to keep the channels of communication open no matter what happens.

Other factors which must be considered in the causes of postnatal depression have become apparent when cases of child abuse have been studied. These would include an abnormal pregnancy, or an abnormal labor or delivery, separation from the baby after childbirth, any other separation from the baby within the first six months of its life, illnesses of the baby in the first year of life, illness of the mother in the first year of life.

It's unrealistic to hope that we can turn out to be good mothers naturally without education, preparation, a good deal of determination and assistance. Unfortunately you can't be trained to be a good parent; there is not very much instruction available. There is certainly nothing that can prepare you emotionally for the experience of being a mother. You have to set yourself realistic targets and not expect to know things instinctively which can only be learned. The responsibilities of being a mother are only self-taught and there are few books which are adequate sources of information. Here are some do's and don'ts for new parents which you might find helpful.

THINGS TO DO

- Get as much help as you can from anyone, but try your partner first, then relatives, then dependable friends. Try to make them feel involved, to participate and share your responsibilities.
- Time on your own is an absolute necessity. Try to put aside some time each week which is entirely your own, when you can feel yourself to be a free, self-determinant and independent person with a life of your own. Enjoy yourself when you are away from the house and the baby. Work out a treat, a new hair-do, lunch with a friend, evening at the theater. Never fall into the trap of making motherhood the only reason for your existence.
- Try and get to know and become friendly with other couples who have successfully brought up children.
- Ask your family and experienced friends for advice and discuss your anxieties and your plans.
- Make sure that you get all your maternity benefits.

THINGS NOT TO DO

- Don't plan to sell your house and move just after the baby arrives.
- Don't try to keep up appearances; let them go.
- Don't over-burden yourself with tasks that are unimportant.
- Don't be the work-horse or confidant to friends and relatives during the first months after you have had your baby.
- Don't give up your own outside interests and hobbies; instead rearrange your schedules and cut out other responsibilities.

SPECIAL FEMALE PROBLEMS

Female complaints deserve a whole book to themselves rather than one chapter. Naturally, the primary criterion for including any condition is that it be specific to women, and will therefore concern the female genitals and/or reproductive tract. However, I have included venereal disease and cystitis because although they are not limited to women, they have a special significance for them. My other criteria for including a complaint, where so many had to be left out, are firstly that it is so common as to be almost universal, e.g. premenstrual syndrome, secondly that it can be deadly but is remediable if detected early enough, e.g. the female cancers, and thirdly that, despite evidence to the contrary, it is still generally considered by the medical fraternity to be neurotic in origin and therefore amenable to symptomatic treatment such as tranquillizers, sedatives and pain killers, e.g. dysmenorrhea.

In all these cases my aim is to give information which will allow a woman to take the initiative and act as her own advocate. The information can then be used to question the medical profession and allow her to be assertive with bureaucracy. Armed with knowledge, a woman will be able to exert leverage until she feels happy in her own mind about explanations and answers.

With diseases that are rarely discussed openly, like cancer, where women feel in the dark, fearful, and insecure, I believe it's necessary to have enough knowledge to take responsibility for early diagnosis, even prevention. There are people who say that information about cancer is alarmist – my answer would be no one has yet died of knowledge. Women die every day from cancer.

So often, women are under-informed about their options and are badly prepared for the outcome of cancer treatment. A typical example would be cancer of the breast. How many women ever discuss the various types of mastectomy with their surgeon? How many women are told prior to surgery that they will wake up from the anesthetic minus a breast? How many women are given psychological counselling prior to mastectomy to help them to cope with the emotional trauma of losing a breast? How many women are told about false breasts before surgery? The answer to all of these questions is precious few.

But all women can be. And all women should be. Many of us are intimidated by our illnesses and by our doctors. I hope this chapter will help you to come to terms with both. And then give you the courage to exercise your rights.

DYSMENORRHEA

For many women menstruation presents few problems. But for millions of women, menstruation is an incapacitating monthly torment. These women have *dysmenorrhea* – a Greek word which means painful menstruation and, in your terms, menstrual cramps. Some people, particularly men, and sadly male doctors, do not seem to take the subject seriously. Those who suffer with it know its real significance.

There are two types of dysmenorrhea, primary and secondary. Primary dysmenorrhea has no related disease background, e.g. endometriosis (see p. 290). Secondary dysmenorrhea, on the other hand, may have its cause in a pelvic infection, malformation or organ displacement, and has also been reported in association with the use of intra-uterine devices. Until recently, the cause of primary dysmenorrhea was unknown and it remained among the most widely observed and least understood complaints. Its symptoms had been noted and treated for thousands of years, yet not a single unifying theory of its cause had been postulated. Since time immemorial women have accepted menstrual pain as a natural sign of womanhood, to be borne without complaint. It has come to be accepted as the "curse" of womanhood: a punishment inflicted on all women for Eve's sin in the Garden of Eden, and because of this theory has been named "Eve's Curse."

Many classical theories of the cause of primary dysmenorrhea had at their core a large degree of female "neuroticism." The most commonly held theory (particularly in Victorian times) was that it was psychosomatic; dysmenorrhea was categorically labelled as such at the turn of the century, and this was because doctors noted that it appeared to be a symptom exhibited by hysterical women where there were possible marital difficulties or unsatisfactory child-parent relationships. The Victorian theory went so far as to postulate that it was a rejection of a woman's feminity and her marital and childbearing responsibilities. Such theories linger on still.

Incidence of dysmenorrhea

Although frequency varies widely from study to study and country to country, depending on the different definitions of the syndrome, the magnitude of the problem of dysmenorrhea is dramatically apparent to any student of the subject.

In the United States, for instance, it is estimated that about half the women of childbearing age suffer from dysmenorrhea and this results in the loss of 140 million working hours annually. A 1978 survey of 113 American patients seen in general practice showed a prevalence of dysmenorrhea ranging from 29% to 44% in any two-month period. Though the incidence of dysmenorrhea does decline after the age of twenty-five, there are women still suffering from incapacitating dysmenorrhea over the age of thirty-five and after several children. 10% of American female college students miss two or three days of class each month, and 20% of high school girls miss at least one school day annually because of dysmenorrhea.

Internationally, dysmenorrhea is a prevalent problem. In studies conducted in two Norwegian industrial companies from 1970 to 1971, 61% of the 234 women participating in the study experienced pain during menstruation. 28% had to stay in bed at least one day a month and 31% had to be absent from work due to menstrual cramps. Among 1200 women interviewed in France in 1978, 38% of all women reported painful menstrual cramps. 75% said the condition lasted one to three days and 67% of the 15–39 year old age group reported painful menstruation. Attitude studies conducted in 1979 among 351 women in Denmark and Sweden, revealed that 90% suffered from painful menstruation.

The social and economic implications of millions of women worldwide experiencing significant monthly pain may be impossible to estimate. Clearly dysmenorrhea is a common gynecological complaint and many women consider it so much a part of normal female functioning that they do not consult their physician for treatment.

Since most women do not believe a cure is possible for dysmenorrhea it is not surprising that so few seek medical attention for this condition. Low reporting figures are obtained from American general practice records: a 1976 study reported less than 0.5% − 1.4% of patient visits were for dysmenorrhea; only 1% of 4,216 female patients in a 1978 survey at the University of South Carolina medical school's general practice clinic had the diagnosis of dysmenorrhea.

The psychosomatic concept is still to be found in medical text books and is accepted by a large number of practicing physicians, and worse, by women. The usual recommended therapy is counselling or psychiatric help but that can be long and expensive and the value has not been proven.

Symptoms of dysmenorrhoea

Symptoms of primary dysmenorrhea follow a wide spectrum of complaints, from violent abdominal cramps, which occur just before menstruation, to intense suffering throughout the entire period with severe cramps, possible diarrhea, bladder distress, pelvic soreness, abdominal distention, painful breasts, depression, irritability, headache, backache, nausea, vomiting and fainting spells. Most often the pain is felt in the pelvic region but it sometimes radiates out into the flanks and back. Some women find that they are so incapacitated that they are unable to manage normal activities for the first 24 to 36 hours of each period.

In 1957 a pioneering study by V. R. Pickles of Sheffield University in England demonstrated that a rise in the concentration of a chemical called prostaglandin just prior to menstruation caused uterine muscle to go into spasm, and that spasm caused cramp-like pains. A particular prostaglandin, PGF_2 (alpha), was identified as the main cause of dysmenorrhea.

Research has shown that women who suffer from dysmenorrhea are biologically different from those who don't. Dysmenorrheic women produce excessive quantities of prostaglandin at the time of menstruation and this in turn leads to the symptoms listed above.

Treatment of dysmenorrhea

Doctors are now able to prescribe drugs known as prostaglandin inhibitors, or anti-prostaglandins, which work by inhibiting excess production of prostaglandin, thereby making dysmenorrheic women normal. The anti-prostaglandins successfully reduce or eliminate the pain and discomfort of dysmenorrhea. In carefully controlled studies, 70–90% of all women were relieved of all symptoms; others had partial relief. Furthermore, more than 70% of the patients who had previously had to stay at home or in bed could continue with their normal activities about the house or back at work.

When I complain to my doctor about period pains he tells me I should cope as best I can. What should I do?

Classical treatments like bed rest, heating pads and aspirin are not effective in treating dysmenorrhea. But doctors are now in a position to offer significant relief in the form of specific drugs. If you meet opposition from your family practitioner on this new treatment, ask for a referral to a gynecologist or change your doctor for a more sympathetic one.

I've heard that taking contraceptive pills can eliminate dysmenorrhea. Is this true?

Menstrual cramps are a direct result of ovulation – suppress ovulation (as some birth control pills do) and you eliminate cramps. However, not all women, nor doctors, are able to take or prescribe oral contraceptives for twenty-one days to treat symptoms which last for only a few, so it cannot be regarded as the ideal treatment.

EXERCISES FOR RELIEF OF MENSTRUAL PAIN

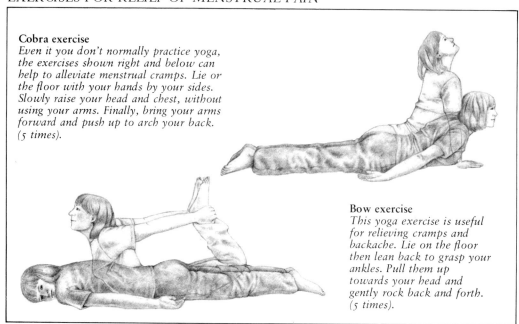

Cobra exercise
Even if you don't normally practice yoga, the exercises shown right and below can help to alleviate menstrual cramps. Lie or the floor with your hands by your sides. Slowly raise your head and chest, without using your arms. Finally, bring your arms forward and push up to arch your back. (5 times).

Bow exercise
This yoga exercise is useful for relieving cramps and backache. Lie on the floor then lean back to grasp your ankles. Pull them up towards your head and gently rock back and forth. (5 times).

OTHER MENSTRUAL PROBLEMS

Primary dysmenorrhea, or painful periods with no disease background, is primary among menstrual disorders, but there are several other conditions associated with the bleeding pattern which are also prevalent. Regular menstrual cycles are not universally the norm and most women have variable periods. Average cycles vary from 24–32 days and bleeding usually lasts 3–7 days with blood and tissue loss amounting to about 1 or 2 tablespoons. There are many factors which can contribute to unusual menstruation patterns and these include stress, malnutrition, chronic iron deficiency, blood diseases and even jet travel.

Vaginal bleeding that differs from the average normal pattern, especially if you are over thirty, should be reported to your doctor for investigation. Any bleeding after menopause, even the smallest amount, must be reported right away. If you are under thirty "unusual" menstrual patterns are quite normal, so only persistent problems such as heavy bleeding, cramps, signs of infection or inability to become pregnant should be reported.

Heavy periods (menorrhagia)

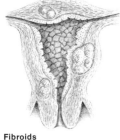

Fibroids

This condition not only includes heavy bleeding but also periods that go on too long, or those that recur too often. If total blood loss is very large, you may become anemic.

Common causes can include having thicker than usual endometrial tissue which, when shed, results in a heavier blood flow; having recently been fitted with an IUD, or possible dislodgement of one that has been in place for several years. Stress can also cause prolonged menstrual bleeding (when the source is removed, bleeding should clear). If there is increasing pain as well as bleeding, this could be due to *fibroids*–non-cancerous lumps of the uterus – which increase the bleeding surface. Consult your doctor for this, and also if the blood loss varies considerably throughout your periods, which can be a sign of hormonal imbalance.

Bleeding between periods (metrorrhagia)

Commonly known as "break-through bleeding," this is any vaginal bleeding or staining between periods (in 10% of women it occurs for 1 or 2 days at the time of ovulation). This is a frequent side-effect of the "pill," especially the minipill, and it usually occurs during the first few months, or if a pill is missed. This is because it takes a while for the hormones in the pill to completely control ovulation. Recently-fitted IUDs can also be responsible. If the bleeding is also heavy, you may have fibroids (see above).

No menstrual periods (amenorrhea)

There are two types of amenorrhea – primary, which means never having had a period, and secondary, which means a loss of periods for four months or more. Primary amenorrhea is often a familial characteristic or can be due to being underweight. Girls of fourteen who haven't menstruated (and who have no breast or pubic hair growth) should be investigated, or should normally-developed girls of eighteen who have had no periods.

235

Pregnancy is first suspected when there is lack of periods and this should be investigated first, especially if any drugs are likely to be prescribed. Stress is also found to have a connection. Severe changes in weight – both under and over – which may be related to hormonal imbalance, are a common cause, and another condition which suppresses hormonal production in the brain is the stoppage of birth control pills (amenorrhea can last up to a year).

Absence of ovulation, some chronic diseases (thyroid disease, anemia, tuberculosis), and certain drugs (tranquillizers, anti-depressants and anti-hypertensives) are other factors which can result in amenorrhea.

While some women welcome a loss of periods, others may find it a source of anxiety – especially if they want to conceive (see *Subfertility*, p. 172). Short periods of amenorrhea may be ended by a balanced diet, but medical assistance should be sought if it lasts for longer than six months or if you experience milk secretion. Certain drugs, including the pill, produce *prolactin* which stimulates milk production and suppresses ovulation.

PREMENSTRUAL SYNDROME

Once a month millions of women suffer incapacitating menstrual problems which can, and should, be cured.

It has been suggested by one gynecologist that premenstrual syndrome (PMS) is probably the commonest cause of marital breakdown. Three-quarters of a sample of over 500 women in a general practice survey in England complained of at least one premenstrual symptom. Other statistics show that crimes such as shoplifting are thirty times more common premenstrually.

This gives some idea of the extent and seriousness of a set of symptoms which knows no geographical, racial or social barrier and which, at any one time, affects an estimated one million women in England. It affects not only the happiness and health of the woman sufferer, but the health and happiness of her family as well. It is known, for instance, that the children of women who suffer premenstrual syndrome have more infections and more hospital admissions during the premenstrual period than at any other time of the month. And sometimes the personality changes that overtake women sufferers are so great, that they are unrecognizable to their nearest and dearest. Some husbands claim that they are married to a completely different woman.

Much of our knowledge about the premenstrual syndrome, about the wide spectrum of symptoms that may be exhibited in a seemingly unconnected way, and about the serious social and domestic, not to mention economic, implications has been generated by Dr. Katharina Dalton. All sufferers of premenstrual syndrome owe Dr. Dalton a great debt for her pioneering work in defining the syndrome, in drawing the attention of the medical profession to the condition, in forcing them to regard it as serious and eminently treatable, and for changing public opinion, not to mention women's minds, from regarding it not as a natural event which has to be suffered, but as an intolerable monthly occurrence which, in the majority of cases, is remediable.

Symptoms of the pre-menstrual syndrome

Mood changes

Most of us suffer from mood swings which cause little disruption to ourselves and others (see p. 306), but in the premenstrual period a happy, energetic, vivacious woman may become a sour, bitter, misanthropic person whose fits of temper, scolding, shouting and even physical violence reach catastrophic levels. 50% of all women experience severe mood swings at the time prior to menstruation.

The onset of mood swings is variable. In some women they begin gradually, the symptoms getting worse day-by-day but usually starting after ovulation, and occasionally lasting until menstruation occurs. Some women have described this as being "crazy for half my life."

In other women the mood swings are quite sudden and the sufferer may even be surprised at her own outrageous behavior which, under normal circumstances, she would find quite insupportable. Often it is a member of the family, usually the husband or mother, or an outside observer and, occasionally, a fellow employee or an employer who notices the onset of a mood swing. For some husbands the swings are so sudden and easily recognized that they rush to the calendar to confirm their worst fears.

For a number of women, the onset of menstruation seems to work like a charm. They describe the relief like a cloud lifting or curtains opening, and sometimes may find that their mood lightens a few hours before menstruation starts. Indeed, a woman may feel this signal and know that her menstruation is beginning.

Age and pregnancy tend to make the symptoms of premenstrual syndrome worse and also last longer. Indeed, premenstrual syndrome may be first diagnosed in the 30s after a first, second, or third pregnancy. Unfortunately, the symptoms tend to become severe in the years just prior to the menopause, making some women think that they have been going through the menopause for a decade or more. Fortunately, coming out of the menopause is very much like coming out of a storm: the fluctuating hormonal levels die back to a steady, though lower, state and one can look forward to an age of serenity.

Premenstrual Tension (PMT)

Premenstrual tension for some women brings them near to breaking point. Very often they have insight into their "loathsome" behavior; this can increase their feelings of self-disgust and make the symptoms worse. Premenstrual tension usually has three major components: depression; tiredness; irritability.

Depression This can vary from anything as mild as a feeling of moderate unhappiness to a depression which will be so severe that it affects all bodily functions. Premenstrual depression increases after the age of 36 and is more common among single women than married women.

I like Dr. Dalton's description of depression as a disease of loss. Loss of happiness, loss of interests, loss of enthusiasm, loss of energy, loss of sleep, loss of sexual arousal, loss of security, loss of adequacy, loss of the powers of concentration, loss of self-control, loss of the ability to stop crying, loss of appetite, loss of the ability to make decisions or to control one's behavior. There often may be a loss of insight and loss of your sense of perspective which prevents you from realizing that after menstruation you will return to normal.

One of the most serious complications of depression is suicide. In 1965 a team of doctors showed that there was a preponderance of successful suicides among women in the premenstrual period, and this finding has been confirmed in London, Delhi and Los Angeles where half of all women's attempts at suicide are made during the four days immediately before or during menstruation.

Tiredness Many women will admit that they lose the ability to think clearly and quickly and feel mentally dull and slow in the premenstrual period. They may feel a bit headachy or they may feel so tired that they are unable to get out of bed. Housewives quite often state that they feel so sleepy, for as long as ten days prior to menstruation, that no housework or proper cooking gets done at this time.

This tiredness can have an effect on productivity, and in one study of the weekly grades of schoolgirls at a boarding school, during the premenstrual week, it was found that there was an average drop of 10% compared with a rise of 20% during the week immediately following menstruation. This effect was also noted in examination results.

Irritability Very often it is the people around you during your premenstrual period who suffer most – such as your partner, children and co-workers. Irritability can be so severe that the least thing upsets you, you hate everyone, you shout at everyone, you pick quarrels at the slightest thing, everything gets on your nerves and you can only see the world through jaundiced eyes. Sadly, premenstrual irritability is more common among married women, so it is the husband who has to bear the brunt of this edgy, irrational, agitated, and hypersensitive behavior, sometimes for one week out of every four. Not surprisingly, many husbands get out and seek a divorce.

Irritability leads to aggressive behavior which can result in physical violence. There are reports of assault where a fit of temper has caused a woman to throw a rolling pin at her neighbor, a typewriter at her boss, or tried to bite off a policeman's ear. There are reports of baby battering, husband hitting and homicide.

The desire to drink alcohol is increased and, in parallel, alcohol has a heightened effect and there is an increase in the number of charges for being drunk and disorderly in otherwise well-behaved and respectable women.

A survey of 156 women prisoners in Britain showed that nearly 50% had committed their crime during or before menstruation and that 63% of these women had been suffering premenstrual syndrome. As early as the turn of the century, police in Paris had noticed that 84% of violent crimes were committed by women around the time of menstruation, and a similar study in New York showed that 62% of violent crimes were committed at this time.

Water retention

Water retention is characteristic of premenstrual syndrome whether or not you suffer other symptoms: what happens is that water accumulates in the tissues of the body during the fortnight prior to menstruation, leading to a gain in weight, a feeling of bloatedness, heaviness, soreness and enlargement of the breasts.

Weight gain By far the commonest symptom is weight gain, being on average 4–7 lbs (1.8–3.2 kilos), but it can be as high as 10–12 lbs (4.5–5.4 kilos), and weight gains of 14 lbs (6.5 kilos) have been recorded. All this weight is lost either just prior to menstruation, or when menstruation starts, or within two days of menstruation beginning, and may result in the output of as much as 9 pints (5.14 litres) of urine in one day.

Water retention results in an increase in blood pressure and also in the pressure inside the eyes as is shown on the following chart:

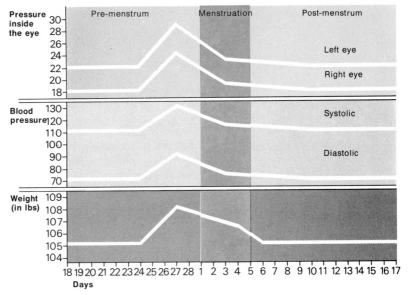

Breast changes Women commonly complain of soreness of the breasts, with enlargement necessitating wearing a bra of a larger size, and tender nipples. Just prior to menstruation, the breasts feel heavy and their consistency may become nodular. This should not be confused with the finding of a discreet lump which you are searching for on self-examination of the breasts (see p. 78). The breasts are stimulated by progesterone in the second half of the menstrual cycle and increase in size and soreness because of growing, dilating milk glands.

Other symptoms Fluid retention may show itself as a swelling of the fingers (you will find that you can't remove your rings), swelling of the ankles, and tightness of your shoes. Women who wear dentures may also notice that their gums swell and that their dentures no longer fit. Many women say that their skin becomes coarse and blotchy, their contact lenses no longer fit properly, and their hair becomes lank.

But water retention can cause more serious symptoms than these, particularly if water accumulates in an area that is not easily stretched, such as the labyrinth in the inner ear which controls our balance. An excess of fluid raises the pressure inside the inner ear and causes giddiness. In the eyeball it may cause severe pain, and in the rigid, bony skull, headaches. The widespread accumulation of fluid has been blamed for vague symptoms such as muscle and joint pains, and generalized rheumatic pains.

The majority of symptoms of water retention are, surprisingly, worse in the early morning after waking, especially in women who suffer from migraine or pain in the eyes, and asthma. Some women are woken in the night by a feeling of numbness in their fingers and hand, and a sensation of pins and needles down the arm. This is due to the nerve to the hand and fingers being constricted by tissues which pass over the nerve, and which become tight due to the accumulation of water (carpal tunnel syndrome).

Asthma seems to get worse around menstruation, probably due to water retention in the cells lining the small air passages in the lungs. The cause is not, therefore, necessarily allergenic and so patients do not respond to antihistamines or to inhalers or to drugs like sodium cromoglycate. Premenstrual asthma seems to reach its peak in women in their 30s and 40s.

Premenstrual rhinitis, hay fever and hoarseness are also quite common and are again related to fluid retention and are not responsive to antihistamines and cold remedies.

A loss of the sense of smell is thought to be due to water accumulating in the cells which pick up the sense of smell.

Cystitis and urethritis become more frequent premenstrually, and may be part of generalized pelvic congestion.

Joint and muscle pains are reported by some women in a well-defined monthly cycle, coming on just prior to menstruation and lasting a few days and then disappearing without treatment. There is quite often stiffness in the joints on waking which gradually disappears and the pain is thought to be due to the swelling of the cells in the joints and a spasm of the muscles around the joints. As these aches and pains are alleviated to a certain extent by the use of diuretics, it is thought that the cause is water retention.

Varicose veins may be painful only at the time of menstruation.

Headaches

Monthly headaches can take a variety of forms – migraine, sinus or tension – but they are very real and their periodicity is well established. Puberty, pregnancy and being on the pill can also trigger headaches and while premenstrual headaches often disappear at about the fourth month of pregnancy they return when the pregnancy is over. And, very often, women find their headaches become worse while on the pill or that they occur on the first or second day after stopping the course of oral contraceptives. On the bright side, the majority of women who suffer from headaches at or about menstruation will probably find that they cease when the menopause is over.

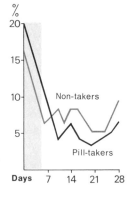

As can be seen from the graph, the percentage of women experiencing migraines increases around the time of menstruation. The incidence is even greater in women on the "pill".

SYMPTOMS OF PREMENSTRUAL SYNDROME

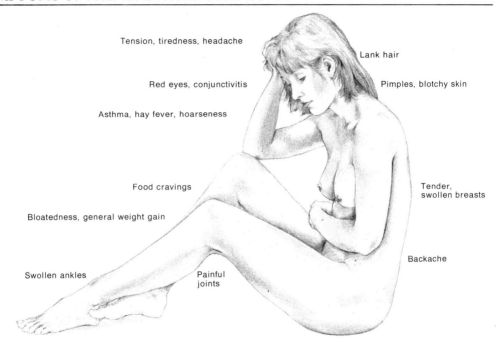

Tension, tiredness, headache

Lank hair

Red eyes, conjunctivitis

Pimples, blotchy skin

Asthma, hay fever, hoarseness

Food cravings

Tender, swollen breasts

Bloatedness, general weight gain

Swollen ankles

Backache

Painful joints

Skin blemishes

Slight pimpling occurs in almost all women in the days prior to menstruation but for some women acne can be a serious problem, along with boils, sties and attacks of *herpes labialis*. Women also notice that the skin becomes greasy and that blackheads become worse.

Conjunctivitis (red eye)

This often appears each month with menstruation and is not related to infection. Such an effect was noted as long ago as the sixteenth century.

Disorders of appetite

Food cravings and binges very often occur at the height of premenstrual tension, even in women who can diet strictly during the rest of the month. Many women report that they can eat enough for a week in just one meal.

Alcoholic bouts

These are fairly common. An American survey among female alcoholics showed that about 1 in 10 related an increase in their intake at the menstrual time, even when they were able to abstain at other times of the month. Metabolically speaking, alcohol is handled differently at the time of menstruation. It is broken down more slowly and therefore accumulates in the bloodstream, having a greater effect than at other times. Women find that they cannot hold their alcohol as well as they normally would.

Causes of premenstrual syndrome

Three important control centers are situated in close anatomical proximity in the hypothalamus at the base of the brain.

A change in any one of these centers can well have an effect on the other two, and these changes may be caused by chemicals and hormones but possibly even by electrical stimuli. Dr. Dalton suggests several factors which point towards a progesterone deficiency being the cause of the premenstrual syndrome. For instance:

● Premenstrual symptoms are only present when progesterone should be in the bloodstream. After menstruation, when there is no progesterone in the body, symptoms disappear.

● The onset of premenstrual symptoms is usually at a time when hormonal balance is disturbed, i.e. at puberty, after taking a hormonal contraceptive pill or after pregnancy.

● Frequently there is relief of premenstrual syndrome during pregnancy when progesterone levels in the bloodstream are very much higher.

● The keeping of temperature charts confirms that premenstrual syndrome sufferers rarely sustain a raised temperature.

● Women who suffer from premenstrual syndrome are biologically different from normal women in that they have lower progesterone levels in the second half of the menstrual cycle.

Some of the symptoms of premenstrual syndrome have been related to lower blood sugar levels, which does not refer to the common (but quite erroneous) condition termed *hypoglycemia*. Changes in hormone levels before or during menstruation alter your body's tolerance to sugar and raise the level of the baseline at which you feel symptoms of a low blood sugar. This means that your blood sugar level does not have so far to fall before the baseline is reached and you feel the effects. Many women have noticed that in the first half of the cycle they can go for five or even six hours without food whereas abstinence for the same length of time before menstruation would lead to a profound craving. If progesterone is given, this premenstrual alteration in blood sugar level is corrected.

Coping with premenstrual syndrome

Keep a chart

The first thing you should do is to start keeping a menstrual chart. You can devise your own or use one as illustrated. The point of keeping such a chart is so that the symptoms don't take you by surprise, so that they act as a record for your doctor, and so that you will be able to show the effect of treatment that your doctor gives you.

	1	2	3	4	5	6	7	8	9	10	11	12	13	14	15	16	17	18	19	20	21	22	23	24	25	26	27	28	29	30	31
Jan	hT	hT	hT	hT	HT	HT	HT	HM	hM	hM	M	M	M									T	T	T	hT	hT	hT	hT	hT	hT	hT
Feb	hT	HT	HT	HM	M	M	M	M										T	T	T	Th	Th	Th	HT	HM	hM	M	M			
Mar	M	M	M								T	T	T	Th	Th	Th	Th	Th	TH	TH	H	HM	HM	M	M	M					
Apr							T	T	T	T	Th	Th	Th	Th	Th	TH	TH	M	M	M	M										

h Mild headache   H Severe headache   M Menstruation   T Tension   Clear days

Talk about your feelings
Discuss how you feel, and why you think you do so, with your partner or other people close to you. Make sure that you are understood so that others may be able to help you. If you are strong enough, you may even confess during the bad times that you know you are behaving improperly. If not, admit to your knowledge and sadness about your periodic loss of control when you feel well again. If you have any fears about physical violence or attempted suicide, discuss them with your partner or with a close friend and, if at all possible, with your doctor. And while you are discussing them with your doctor, of course, ask for some form of treatment.

Note down the dates of your period
Mark in your diary the expected date of your next period and start keeping a diary that has a month to a page. In this way, you can avoid important professional or social engagements which fall at the time of the month when you are at your lowest. Professionally speaking, it is important that you don't give yourself difficult tasks or impose deadlines at a time when your productivity and efficiency are under par.

Tell your employer or personnel manager
An enlightened employer or personnel manager will be sympathetic to your problem and will try to arrange some sort of flexible work timetable, so that you are able to cope and they do not lose your services. If you suffer very badly from premenstrual syndrome, try to avoid night-shift work and, if possible, do not undertake a long flight which involves time zone changes. Both of these are very unsettling to your biological clock, let alone your menstrual clock.

Note down the times of your outbursts
Record any anger, aggression and panic or the onset of a migraine headache. Later, when you are calm, try and relate it to when you took food. You may find that there are long intervals between your meals resulting in low blood sugar levels; but you can avoid or alleviate future outbursts by making sure that you eat more frequently and avoid missing meals at these times.

Limit your fluid intake
From the fourteenth day after the day that you started to bleed, cut down on fluids but drink strong black coffee which acts as a diuretic.

Eat whole grain foods

To avoid constipation eat bran and lots of fresh fruit and vegetables, raw if possible. Reduce your sodium intake to cut down on bloating by avoiding salt and salty foods but do make sure that you eat foods that contain lots of potassium, such as green beans, jacket potatoes, seafood and peanuts to help reduce fluid retention.

Take alcohol in moderate quantities only

In the premenstrual period never mix the grape with the grain. Don't mix your drinks at all if you can help it, and don't drink on an empty stomach. Never drink and drive.

Try to take rests

Not all of us can do it, but if you possibly can, rest or nap in the second half of the cycle, and whenever you rest put your feet up. It isn't necessary to go to sleep, it is rest that is important, so just lie down in a darkened room with your eyes closed. If you drop off, all the better; sometimes five or ten minutes of sleep, or twenty minutes resting completely horizontal, can be enormously refreshing.

Consult your doctor

If you are at all worried or troubled by your symptoms, ask for treatment.

Progesterone therapy

Women who suffer a severe premenstrual syndrome are probably deficient in progesterone so it's worth taking progesterone on a trial basis, at least. Progesterone can be taken in several forms but not as tablets as it is insoluble by mouth. Two of the most popular forms are suppositories (inserted in the rectum) or pessaries (placed in the vagina), and they can be used interchangeably. If you are sensible, your doctor will very often give you permission to use an extra pessary or suppository when you feel tension building up, particularly if a migraine headache is threatening. But usually s/he will recommend that you only take up to four 400 mg in one day. While not readily available from American gynecologists, progesterone treatment has been found to be highly effective in Europe for severe cases.

Note the days that you take progesterone treatment on your chart, and also chart your symptoms, so that improvements can be seen clearly. The individual needs of patients differ and the dosage regimen should be tailored to specific needs. Sometimes progesterone is started immediately after ovulation and sometimes only a few days before menstruation is expected – in any event, it is essential that progesterone therapy starts four days before the symptoms are expected, so it is important for you to go along to your doctor armed with your symptoms recorded on a menstrual chart (see p. 242).

Progesterone is absorbed quickly from pessaries and suppositories and there is a rise in the blood level after about 20 minutes, but in most women the blood progesterone level is back down within 24 hours; in some it is even sooner. This means that some women need to use a suppository or pessary two or three times a day.

Progesterone is also given by injection, which lasts longer and only needs to be repeated on alternate days. Some women, however, need injections daily. Injections are usually reserved for very severe symptoms or desperate situations, such as when a marriage is breaking up or when children are being battered.

Progesterone implants can also be given. Once it is certain that you obtain relief from progesterone, in the form of pessaries, suppositories or injections, it proves a very convenient form of medication because it lasts for between six and eighteen months.

The risks from progesterone therapy are virtually nil. There are no contra-indications to its use and there have been no known risks of cancer. As is quite well known, progesterone is used for the treatment of some cancers, particularly breast cancer.

The synthetic forms of progesterone, for example, norethisterone and norethisterone acitate, may be partially effective in relieving the symptoms of premenstrual syndrome but are very much less effective than natural progesterone. In America, many gynecologists use Aldactone to treat PMS; it works by affecting water balance and it may have an effect on the hypothalamus.

A friend suggested taking vitamin B6 to help combat PMS – is this a good idea?

Some women find vitamin B6 (pyridoxine) does, indeed, relieve depression. The results differ in different women, and the vitamin tablets must be taken from 3 days before the expected onset of symptoms, through until the time when the symptoms would disappear (i.e. 1–3 days after the start of a period). Two 50 mg tablets is the recommended amount.

Can you recommend any exercises that might be useful?

Some women find relief through deep breathing and other relaxation techniques (see p. 43), but swimming is often ideal for lessening tension.

THE MENOPAUSE

Menopause literally means the cessation of monthly periods. "Climacteric" is the medical word used for the time during which menstruation begins to decline (it rarely occurs abruptly); menstrual regularity is at first disrupted, and then menstruation finally stops. Definitions like "the change of life" are to be deprecated because they imply that the menopause brings with it an irrevocable decline in lifestyle.

Of all the species in the animal kingdom, we are the only one which lives to any extent beyond our fertile life, and this is only possible because of our increased life expectancy. Menopause can occur at any time between thirty-five and sixty-five; in America the average is fifty. The menopause may, of course, be brought on by surgical intervention involving hysterectomy and salpingo-oophorectomy (see p. 295); when the ovaries are removed the menopause occurs artificially and prematurely. In the United States it is estimated that something like twenty-seven million women are over the age of fifty at any one time. Between a fifth and sixth of the population is in the menopausal age group and possibly suffering debilitating symptoms as a result of the hormonal changes which accompany the climacteric.

Attitudes to the menopause

Largely due to programming by the media, by teaching, and by example from older female relatives who consider menopause and its discomforts as natural, many women view menopause as something which has to be suffered and is beyond treatment. The unsympathetic attitude of a male-dominated medical profession encourages women to look upon menopause with fear and depression. Undoubtedly, some women have more problems than others, but many sail through menopause without even being aware that it is happening. The majority of women manage to cope with the menopause just as successfully as they have coped with menarche and with childbirth. While menopause undoubtedly marks the end of one part of a woman's life, it marks the beginning of another and you mustn't forget this. It is up to you to make sure that menopause is a beginning – it should be a time of looking forward and not a time of sadness and regret.

We can take an example from some primitive societies in which a woman is admitted to the ruling councils of the tribe, and assumes full responsibility as an elder, once she has stopped menstruating. It is usually older women, too, who hold positions of political authority, not only in the less developed areas but in western society as well.

Try and make sure that you do not view yourself and other women as over-the-hill just because you are over fifty. To do that you have to have self-respect and self-assurance. There is a certain serenity and maturity which comes from getting older and the knowledge that you are in a good position to contribute to society. I hope that an awareness and understanding of what is going on in your body during the climacteric will help to give you confidence and help to remove your fears. See also *Staying Youthful*.

Onset of the menopause

As the graph shows, there is some variation in the age at which menopause occurs: 50% of all women have their last period by the age of forty-eight, by the age of fifty-six, 99% have ceased menstruation, and by the end of their forties, most women have lost the capacity to bear children. Most women are safe in expecting that their periods will end around fifty. From medical records going back as far as the sixth century A.D., this has been the estimated age of menopause.

The actual age at which menopause occurs tends to run in families, and women tend to have early or late menopauses in similar patterns to their mothers. An early first period often means a late last period but there is no real way of estimating when your menopause will happen. There are tests, some simple, some complicated, which will tell you whether menopause is on its way. These tests reveal the level of female hormones in a woman's body. The simple one is to take a vaginal smear – examination under a microscope gives a maturation index which indicates the maturity of the vaginal cells, and this is directly linked to how much oestrogen there is in the body. A more complicated test can be performed on the blood or urine to tell you the level of pituitary hormone, but this is expensive, unnecessary, and is only performed as part of a more comprehensive hormonal analysis.

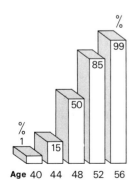

Percentage of women who will have experienced the onset of menopause at various ages

Bodily changes during menopause

Every month once menstruation begins the ovary responds to increasing levels of follicle-stimulating hormone (FSH) by ripening an egg follicle. A surge of luteinizing hormone (LH) liberates the ripe ovum by rupturing the follicle. The follicle first produces estrogen and then after ovulation it produces estrogen and progesterone. We now know that the ovary becomes resistant to FSH as menopause approaches and no longer responds with the maturation of an egg. Over thirty or forty years of menstruation the ovary becomes pretty well depleted of the ova that the female baby was born with. Occasionally the pituitary gland sends out very high levels of FSH which coaxes the ovary into functioning for a little longer, but eventually the ovary simply quits. The result is that levels of estrogen and progesterone swing in an irregular way, resulting in missed periods and scant periods (but never abnormal bleeding). Occasionally there are troublesome symptoms (see below). Your menopause can happen in any of the following ways:

● It is rare for your periods to stop suddenly but you may have regular periods right up to the day when you miss one and you will have no more.

● Much more commonly, you will continue to have periods for a few months and then you will miss a few, have a few more normal periods and go longer and longer between periods until they eventually stop.

● Your periods may simply become scantier and scantier and shorter and shorter until they eventually stop.

If you are under the age of fifty and do not have a period for twelve months, or if you are over fifty and don't have a period for six months, then it is more than likely that your periods have stopped for good.

It is never normal to have frequent heavy periods during the climacteric. Nor is the passage of clots normal. Bleeding in between periods or after intercourse should never be accepted, nor should painful periods. None of these are symptoms of a normal menopause and you must consult your doctor immediately should any of them occur.

Symptoms of the menopause

The sometimes chaotically-swinging levels of estrogen, progesterone and FSH can lead to many real and debilitating symptoms, and when estrogen and progesterone production have stopped completely, symptoms may continue due to a true hormonal deficiency.

By no means all women suffer symptoms of menopause but when they do there are three classical ones: hot flashes; night sweats; loss of lubrication in the vagina. These cause varying amounts of discomfort to their sufferers.

All of these symptoms have been attributed to low levels of estrogen in the bloodstream, which is also responsible for the gradual but inexorable loss of calcium and protein from the bones – a condition known as osteoporosis (see p. 250). Approximately 20% of women who don't take additional estrogen will develop this condition after menopause.

Hot flashes

These are just what the word suggests. The skin becomes suddenly suffused with blood and turns bright pink, the skin starts to sweat, and you feel very hot. (Sweating during the night is called "night sweats" and may or may not be accompanied by hot flashes just as hot flashes may not be accompanied by sweats.) Some women never have them at all, and only a very few are troubled with hot flashes for years. The majority of women have them quite severely for a year or so then they gradually taper off.

There seems to be a certain level of estrogen in the blood which is necessary for hot flashes to occur, because flashing is rare in pre-menopausal women and hardly ever happens after the periods have stopped. This "flashing band" of blood estrogen varies from woman to woman, some having a narrower band than others. Women suffer from hot flashes for a long time or for only a few months, according to the rate at which estrogen levels fall in the blood.

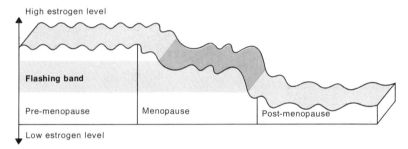

Night sweats

Some women have night sweats which stop them from sleeping and necessitate throwing off bed clothes and getting out of bed to cool off. They are nearly always severely disruptive to the sleep pattern and a woman suffering from continuous night sweats can become exhausted from lack of sleep. The main characteristic is profuse sweating, sometimes sufficient to change the bed clothes several times a night.

Vaginal changes

Thinning, dryness and soreness of the vagina can be among the most troublesome effects of the menopausal years and yet many women are too shy to discuss these complaints with their doctor. During your fertile years, the lining of the vagina is kept healthy, well-lubricated and plump by estrogen. As estrogen levels fall the vagina changes dramatically – not only do the cells of the lining become thin and dried out, but they become unable to protect themselves against invasion by bacteria, so an infected vaginal discharge may occur in menopausal women. These changes involve the urethra as well as the vagina and many menopausal women may suffer from cystitis or pain and burning when passing urine. If the symptoms are mistaken for a urinary infection, the careless administration of antibiotics can precipitate a thrush infection which only makes the vaginal problems worse.

As the vaginal cells are no longer able to secrete their normal lubricating mucus, sex can become difficult and there may even be pain with intercourse (*dyspareunia*). This discomfort on intercourse can lead to your reluctance to have sex, trying to avoid it and even shunning it, with the consequent deterioration of your relationship with your partner. Thus, indirectly, dyspareunia may lead to a loss of libido. There are, however, many women who report that their sexual desire increases during and after menopause.

You can help yourself with this particular sex problem by discussing it with your partner and explaining that it is a natural consequence of menopause. Ask for sympathy and understanding and as a practical step start to use a lubricating jelly. The best non-hormonal lubricant is KY jelly, which is used by surgeons and doctors to lubricate their vaginal instruments.

You can also get help from your doctor. Hormone creams, obtainable only by prescription, occasionally help with soreness or itching but do little to return the vagina to its former healthy state. This needs to be treated from the inside and this is best done with hormone replacement therapy (see p. 251).

Other physical problems

So many physical symptoms occur in menopause that many doctors talk about the menopausal syndrome. Symptoms which have been reported and attributed to menopause are dizziness, headaches, insomnia, fatigue, lack of energy, abdominal distention, digestive troubles (including pain, flatulence, constipation and diarrhea), also breathlessness ansd palpitation. All of these symptoms are not present at any one time, in any particular woman, but vary from day to day. It must be emphasized that many women do not experience any of them at all. Few of these symptoms have been proven to be directly caused by menopause, with the exception of backache and joint pains which are referrable to osteoporosis. However, spinal osteoporosis is four times more common in women than men.

Bone changes (osteoporosis)

During your reproductive years, estrogen is an important contributor to the healthy calcium balance and sturdy protein architecture of the bones. Studies performed under Professor Nordin at Leeds University, using special sensitive techniques, have shown that as the estrogen level falls in menopause so the bones thin, become weak and prone to fracture. This also gives rise to aches and pains in the bones and joints. A further important point of Professor Nordin's research has been to show how these bone changes can be arrested. Hormone replacement therapy (HRT) – estrogen and progesterone combined – can completely stop the weakening of our skeleton but it is neccessary to continue HRT if bone loss is to be abolished. If HRT is stopped, within six months the bones will be exactly the same as if you had never taken hormones. Estrogens cannot repair weakened bones but they can prevent the condition from getting any worse. HRT should be accompanied by calcium and vitamin D supplements. Calcium on its own without HRT is not effective. After the age of sixty-five, calcium and vitamin D alone are probably sufficient.

Emotional changes

For many women, emotional problems turn out to be the predominant symptom of menopause. Moodiness, tearfulness, irritability and depression are very common. Intellectual functions such as memory, decision-making, speed and accuracy may also deteriorate. A woman may find that she is more accident-prone than she used to be, generally less stable, and less sure of herself.

Quite independent of this, a fifty-year-old woman may be going through a personal crisis. Her children may have grown up and left home so she no longer feels needed by them, and teenage children or just-married children may bring problems of their own. If the woman hasn't continued a career, she may feel a useless member of society with no point to life or she may find her job boring and unfulfilling. She may find that her parents are becoming more dependent on her as they grow older and this becomes a heavy burden. She may find that her friends are beginning to suffer from serious illnesses and some may even die. These problems are not going to be removed by HRT or any other form of medical treatment. They will need to be worked out for themselves by each individual. However, this need not be done alone. Doctors may be willing to counsel on ways of coping with the mid-life crisis or recommend someone who is very experienced in this area.

Changes of lifestyle aside, there is quite a lot that can be done to relieve the psychological symptoms of menopause. Research has shown that menopausal anxiety and depression quite often do not respond to anti-depressants and tranquillizers alone. They may be prescribed, but only as supportive medication. Specialists in the field regard HRT as the mainstay of medication: the menopause is a hormone-deficient state and it is this deficiency that is mainly responsible for your emotional fragility.

When you visit your doctor to discuss your psychological problems, raise the subject of HRT if s/he suggests using tranquillizers or anti-depressants alone. If you have difficulty obtaining HRT for severe psychological or other physical symptoms, ask for a second opinion, or suggest referral to a gynecologist more sympathetic to its use.

Hormone replacement therapy

By no means all women have symptoms severe enough to warrant the use of hormone replacement therapy, and its use should never be regarded lightly. If used judiciously, and with care in the right patients, it carries a low risk and a high chance of success – but it should never be regarded as an elixir of youth.

It should never be used prophylactically and it should never be used to prevent symptoms. There is only one indication for hormone replacement therapy and that is menopausal symptoms that are severe and debilitating, particularly hot flashes, night sweats and vaginal changes.

Indiscriminate use of hormone replacement therapy is to be deprecated and the notion, started in America, that estrogens were the key to remaining female forever has done a lot more harm than good. First of all, they can't fulfill that promise.

251

Hormone replacement therapy, or HRT, requires the use of both estrogen and progestogen, while estrogen replacement therapy, or ERT, is limited to the single hormone.

Secondly, it was the use of *estrogen* replacement therapy as opposed to *hormone* replacement therapy that gained general acceptability, and the risks associated with the former are much greater than those associated with the latter. The United States is almost the only country where menopausal symptoms are treated with estrogen alone. In the United Kingdom, a combination of carefully measured doses of estrogen and progestogen is prescribed in a pattern which mimics a woman's own hormonal output during the menstrual cycle. Research has shown that estrogen and progestogen, used in combination, do not carry the risk of cancer of the uterus in the same way as estrogen replacement therapy only does. Indeed, exposure to a minimum of thirteen days of progestogen during a month's course of hormone replacement therapy creates a protective effect against cancer of the uterus in that it causes a monthly shedding of the endometrium and therefore does not allow cancerous or pre-cancerous changes to take place. This is the way hormone replacement therapy is advocated in the U.K. It does, however, carry the inconvenience of the monthly withdrawal bleeding.

The benefits of HRT are well known and well documented. Hot flashes, night sweats and dry vagina with accompanying problems are almost always relieved, sometimes within a few days. By allowing sleep, and removing anxiety and depression, HRT undoubtedly improves a woman's mental and physical state; in addition it arrests osteoporosis.

Risks of HRT

There is no clear evidence that estrogens, used in the doses suitable for replacement therapy, increase the risk of blood clotting or heart disease. Your doctor may consider that if you have had previous clotting problems, or high blood pressure, or if there is a strong family history of heart disease, you are not suitable for hormone replacement therapy.

There is absolutely no evidence to show any increase in breast cancer in women who take estrogen. However, women of fifty and over have a higher risk of breast cancer compared to younger women (see p. 263), so they should be especially careful to have regular breast checks done both by themselves and their doctors, and by mammography.

An increased incidence of cancer of the body of the uterus, associated with estrogen replacement therapy, has been found only in the United States, and the rate varied with the length of time that estrogens had been used. It dropped back to normal after discontinuing estrogen replacement therapy. In addition, the early studies which claimed to prove a cause-and-effect relationship between cancer of the body of the uterus and estrogen replacement therapy did not involve treatment with progestogen supplements. In the U.K. no association has been found between cancer of the uterus and the taking of cyclical estrogens with progestogen supplements for a minimum of thirteen days.

Medical evidence seems to suggest that gallstones are more common among women who take HRT.

Management of HRT

Before you start on HRT make sure that you are perfectly healthy and be aware of your full past medical history. There are several contra-indications to the use of HRT including: high blood pressure, past history of thrombosis of any kind, diabetes, chronic liver disease, etc. If you smoke, you will automatically fall into a higher risk group than women who do not. In addition, your doctor should examine you fully to make sure that you are physically fit. Your breasts should be examined and you should have an internal examination, a cervical and a vaginal smear.

Once you start taking HRT you should have routine, six-monthly checks with your doctor which should include a physical examination, analysis of your urine, measurement of your blood pressure and breast examination; have a smear test yearly.

The length of treatment with HRT varies among medical authorities, and some doctors are so prejudiced that they won't use it at all. Sometimes, however, it is necessary to treat the symptoms of the menopause for two or three years, though not always continuously; breaks are advocated. Contrary to the opinion of some doctors, hormone replacement therapy does not, to use their own words, simply put off the evil day. These doctors claim that when hormone replacement therapy is withdrawn, the symptoms return, and they may even return in a more severe form. As has already been explained, menopausal symptoms only occur when estrogen levels are in the sensitive band. Once they have fallen below these levels symptoms will cease. Hormone replacement therapy should be used as a treatment for symptoms while you are going through your sensitive band. You can stop taking them and your symptoms will not return when your estrogen levels have fallen below the symptom threshold.

Is there anything I can do to prevent hot flashes?

Don't drink hot liquids or eat curry and other spicy foods, and stay out of the sun and away from fires, is my advice to help prevent hot flashes; also avoid sudden changes of temperature. Whenever possible, wear several layers of clothing, rather than one-piece outfits – parts of which can be removed if a flash occurs.

Does being under stress make menopausal symptoms worse?

Severe and prolonged stress can greatly exacerbate menopausal symptoms and can result in complete loss of cycles. Even minor stress can provoke outbreaks of hot flashes and sleeplessness.

Is having a hysterectomy a necessary aftermath of menopause?

While it is true that most hysterectomies are performed on women past the age of fifty, this serious operation should never be performed except in certain very definite situations (see p. 294). However, changes in the tissue due to hormonal variations in menopause may make certain pre-existing conditions more severe, so that hysterectomy becomes the desired treatment. These conditions might include endometriosis, fibroids and recurrent pelvic infections.

VENEREAL DISEASE

A venereal disease is one which is transmitted by sexual contact. There are many of them but by far the commonest is gonorrhea. Before describing that I'd like to suggest some guidelines about the way you approach venereal disease.

● If you suspect that you have it or have had sexual intercourse with someone who has it, got to a VD clinic as soon as you can (5 out of every 6 women with VD have no symptoms).

● If you have any kind of sore on the genital area or lips that doesn't start to heal after a few days, consult a VD clinic.

● If your sexual partner has any discharge from his penis (by far the commonest symptom in men), or any sores on his genital organs, don't have intercourse with him.

● If you discover you have VD make sure you tell all your sexual contacts so that they can get treatment before infecting others and limit their own sexual activity until they've obtained treatment. During the late 1970s gonorrhea reached epidemic proportions, mainly due to the penicillin-resistant strain of the bacterium brought back by soldiers from Vietnam. Gonorrhea is most common in men and women under twenty-five who have many sexual partners. Over the last few years the infection has become less widespread, possibly because the use of condoms and spermicidal foams has increased and both have a protective effect.

Gonorrhea The 1 in 6 women who have symptoms complain of urethral discharge more often than vaginal discharge, pain and burning on passing urine, soreness and irritation of the perineum and possibly pain on passing stool because of rectal inflammation. By far the most serious aspect of gonorrhea, however, is the silent, chronic inflammation that may be grumbling away in the pelvic organs. The ovaries and fallopian tubes may be affected, sometimes becoming blocked and causing infertility. The gonococcus bacterium infects the lining of the vagina, cervix, urethra, rectum and throat. It dies very quickly if allowed to dry out so it's wishful thinking to suppose you can catch it from a lavatory seat.

Penicillin is the mainstay of treatment and in the slow-release, injectable form, only one dose is necessary. The organism should be cultured and tested for penicillin sensitivity. If it is resistant, tetracycline can be given by mouth as a four day course. If there is severe pelvic disease, antibiotics must be given intravenously.

Syphilis Syphilis is caused by a spiral-shaped bacterium which leads to the production of sores, called chancres. These usually appear at the site of sexual contact – the edge of the vagina, cervix, vulva, mouth or penis – and are hardened, red-rimmed and pimple-like, and usually painless. Syphilis has three stages and the first two are highly infectious. Primary syphilis occurs about three weeks after exposure, and the onset of symptoms can occur anywhere from 9–90 days. Only a small percentage of women who develop a chancre will notice it, and it will disappear within 2–6 weeks, even without treatment.

The second stage, secondary syphilis, occurs anywhere from one week to six months after the initial chancre heals. Symptoms include a rash, fever, sore throat, headaches, loss of appetite, nausea, inflamed eyes, and loss of hair. This stage can last from 3–6 months or even several years.

Tertiary syphilis may appear in 10–20 years and can result in heart disease, brain damage, spinal cord damage and blindness. About 1 in every 4 people not treated for secondary syphilis will eventually die or be incapacitated by it.

Treatment of syphilis is with penicillin or tetracycline, and both parties must be treated at the same time or re-infection is likely. If cured in the primary and secondary stages, permanent damage will be prevented. Since syphilis can be passed on to, and has dire consequences for, a developing fetus, all pregnant women are given a blood test for it within the first four months.

GENITAL HERPES

It is the herpes virus Type II which causes the genital infection; Type I causes cold sores around the mouth (see p. 116). Herpes Type II infection is very rare before women are sexually active. The average age for a primary infection is about eighteen years old, and for a secondary infection about twenty-five. The incidence of the virus is three or four times higher among the lower socio-economic groups, where antibodies have been found in a third of all sexually active people; in individuals who have a very high rate of sexual activity, the incidence of herpes Type II antibodies is almost 60%.

The herpes virus is transmitted during sexual intercourse when the virus is active in the surface layers of the skin, usually when blisters or raw areas of skin are exposed. Herpes infection, both around the mouth and the genital area, has a characteristic waxing and waning history. The virus lies dormant in the skin until it is activated by a rise in temperature, which may be due to another virus infection, or the rise in temperature at ovulation.

There is nearly always a prodromal phase to the appearance of blisters when the area of skin feels very sensitive to touch, painful, even ticklish. It is only if treatment is applied at this stage that the cold sore can be aborted. If treatment is not applied, blisters appear within a few hours. There are very few treatments which are effective against viruses, and so the development of the cold sore to a blister and then to a scab which finally dries up, usually takes ten to fourteen days, irrespective of the treatment used.

Genital herpes is extremely difficult to eradicate; the condition usually recurs until the individual has built up sufficient antibodies to kill off the virus. But there are one or two treatments that work. Idoxuridine, which is available on prescription, either in liquid, cream, or ointment form, should be applied as soon as the symptoms are felt within the skin, when it may be possible for it to prevent the blisters from erupting. Other research studies have shown that daily douches with Providone iodine solution will relieve symptoms in 90% of patients within a few hours and the relief may last for two or three days. Alternatively, healing seems to be speeded up when the skin is exposed to ultra violet light after it has been painted with Proflavine ("neutral red dye").

PELVIC INFLAMMATORY DISEASE – (PID)

This is a general term used for chronic inflammation of the pelvic organs. At one time the commonest cause was tuberculosis; now it is gonorrhea. Infections complicating the use of IUDs may also be contributory. Symptoms include abdominal or back pain, persistent cramps, vaginal spotting, tiredness, pain during or after intercourse, foul-smelling vaginal discharge, fever and chills.

Serious scarring of the ovaries and tubes is the most serious effect, quite often causing sterility in the long term. Other complaints include dysmenorrhea (see p. 232) and continuing pain during intercourse.

Many gynecologists would want to perform a laparoscopy to confirm the diagnosis, and would prescribe bedrest and a course of antibiotics. Unfortunately, the chronic infection may be very difficult to eradicate, especially if it has formed a walled-off pocket which antibiotics can't reach in high enough concentration to kill off the bacteria. Sometimes total hysterectomy is the only resort.

CYSTITIS

Cystitis means inflammation of the bladder. It is much more common in women than in men because women have a shorter urethra (which is the tube leading from the bladder to the exterior). Nearly all infections which reach the bladder are due to bacteria entering the urethra from the outside: they spread upwards from the vagina, the anus, or the skin of the perineum, and inflame the lining of the bladder.

Symptoms of cystitis

Only a sufferer from cystitis knows how debilitating, and occasionally agonizing, the symptoms can be; the irony is that a cystitis sufferer has warning, nearly every time, that the infection is about to begin, but repeatedly believes that it will get better on its own. You can pre-empt this by prompt action and it's important that you do because, if left to recur, cystitis becomes chronic and is then difficult to eradicate. The symptoms include:
● A severe dragging down pain, usually in the front of the lower abdomen, but quite often radiating up the flanks and into the back (if this ever happens get in touch with your doctor immediately because it may mean that the infection has ascended to the kidneys, and this is serious).
● The urgent need to pass urine frequently. The urgency may be so great that you start to pass urine before you reach the lavatory

but when you get there there may be very little urine to pass. This is a symptom of irritability of the bladder muscle due to inflammation of the lining; even drops of urine stimulate the irritable bladder to contract.

● Severe pain on passing urine. The pain may be at the beginning, when the bladder muscle starts to contract down on the inflamed lining, during urination or at the end, when the muscle squeezes the last few drops of urine out of the bladder.

● Having to get up several times during the night to empty your bladder.

● The passage of blood in the urine (this is always a symptom of an extremely severe inflammation of the bladder lining). The blood may be obvious streaks of red or, not so obvious, simply pale pink coloring of the urine. If you spot either of these things, save a specimen to take along to your doctor for examination and see her/him immediately.

Causes of cystitis Far and away the most common cause of cystitis is infection (usually the bacterium *E. coli*). This bacterium lives quite normally in the intestines and around the anus, and under normal circumstances it does not ascend the urethra to cause an infection – in fact it causes no problems at all. There is nearly always a predisposing factor which renders the urethra susceptible to infection and which causes multiplication of *E. coli* bacteria. Some

FEMALE-MALE GENITO-URINARY SYSTEMS

The female urethra, in contrast to the male's is short: only about $1\frac{1}{2}$ ins (4cm) in length compared to a male's 8 in (20cm). This, plus the urethra's proximity to the vaginal opening, means that bacteria can easily penetrate internally to cause infection.

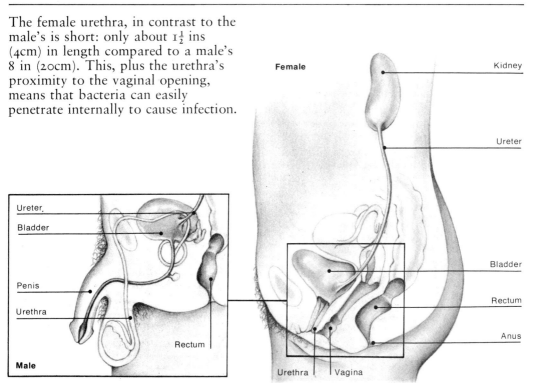

Female

Kidney

Ureter

Ureter

Bladder

Penis

Urethra

Rectum

Bladder

Rectum

Anus

Male

Urethra   Vagina

of the factors which may predispose to infection are as follows:
- Dirty toilet habits;
- A sudden increase in the frequency of intercourse – called "honeymoon" cystitis;
- If a catheter has had to be inserted into the bladder;
- A chronic infection of the cervix or the vagina;
- A prolapse of the front vaginal wall causing a hernia of the bladder down into the vagina (*cystocele* – see p. 291).

Of course there are causes of cystitis, other than infection, and these include:

An allergic reaction, say to a vaginal deodorant or an antiseptic or a chemical added to a vaginal douche.

Irritation of the urethral opening and the perineum by the obsessive use of soap, toiletries, substances that you put in your bath, e.g. antiseptics, or just from scrubbing too hard when you wash, or drying yourself too roughly.

Hormonal deficiency after menopause which cause dryness and thinning of the vagina and the perineum (see p. 248).

Vaginal irritation due to an improperly fitted diaphragm, the over-use of pessaries, careless use of spermicides, or leaving a tampon *in situ* for too long.

Mechanical irritation of the urethra from tights or tight jeans, or from jogging movements.

Preventing cystitis

Cleanse yourself thoroughly after going to the lavatory, particularly after passing feces. If you have a bidet, wash yourself gently, making sure that soap is simple and unscented – baby soap is a good one; see that none of the lather penetrates the vagina. Dry yourself very gently; pat dry, don't scrub dry. When you pass feces clean yourself by wiping from the front backwards. Never use antiseptics in your bathwater; never use vaginal douches.

Avoid wearing tights or tight trousers which put pressure on the perineal area, and wear cotton panties that are absorbent, not those made of synthetics. Sanitary towels are more likely to allow bacteria to thrive (they link the anus to the urethra) than tampons.

One of the best ways to stop bacteria multiplying in the bladder is to keep it flushed out by drinking plenty of fluids to make you pass a lot of urine. You should drink at least three pints of fluid a day and there is nothing better than water.

Treat an irritating, offensive vaginal discharge promptly by going to see your doctor for specific treatment immediately.

Self-help treatment

Take plenty of liquids
Drink a pint of water as soon as you feel the first twinge of symptoms. As *E. coli* don't thrive in alkaline urine, and our urine is usually acid, you can make it alkaline by drinking a teaspoonful of bicarbonate of soda in water or fruit juice. You should do this three times within 4–6 hours of your first twinges of cystitis (if you have heart trouble consult your doctor first).

Make some strong black coffee and drink two cupfuls if you can; caffeine is a diuretic and will make you pass urine to keep the bladder flushed out.

Fill a jug with water or diluted fruit juice and put it on your bedside table. Drink a glass of fluid every half hour if you can.

For pain relief
Dissolve a couple of soluble aspirin in water and take them straight away. The pain is sometimes relieved by heat so prepare two hot water bottles to lay on your abdomen.

Care of the perineum
Each time you pass urine attend carefully, but not obsessively, to your hygiene. Wash your hands carefully. With three or four cotton balls, rung out in warm water, wipe your perineum from the front backwards, once, and throw the cotton balls away. There is no need to use soap and water. In fact, the too-frequent use of soap and water will dry up the perineum and the vagina and will only make it more prone to infection. When you dry yourself, pat away the moisture gently, don't rub briskly.

Get medical help
Make an appointment with your doctor as soon as possible and pass a specimen of urine into a clean receptacle to take along.

You need a course of antibiotics from your doctor and you should take the full course even though the symptoms may disappear within thirty-six hours. A minimum course of antibiotics for mild cystitis would be five days, and seven to ten in the case of a severe attack. In chronic infections, your doctor may insist that you take antibiotics for three weeks or even six weeks. Do exactly as s/he advises.

Recurrent cystitis

If your cystitis proves to be intractable it is essential that you have a full hospital investigation to see whether or not there is any predisposing internal cause (such as a minor abnormality of the valve to the bladder or a small polyp on the bladder wall). In the hospital you may have a cystogram (X-rays of your bladder after it is filled with a radio-opaque substance) and an intravenous pilogram (the injection of a radio-opaque substance which is eventually excreted by the kidneys and shows up on X-ray).

If you find that cystitis recurs after intercourse, and your partner has a large penis, it may be due to mechanical bruising. Here are some of the things you can do to alleviate this:
● Ask your partner to be gentle;
● Try oral sex;
● Try out various positions until you find the one that is most comfortable to you, where penetration is not too deep but still satisfactory for both of you;
● Use a lubricating jelly so that penetration is aided, and painful or traumatic friction is minimized.
Don't keep your problem to yourself, discuss it with your partner. Almost certainly you will find him sympathetic and only too eager to put things right. You must involve him otherwise you may find that your cystitis becomes a barrier between you and causes you to reject sexual relations. Never allow this to happen.

BREAST CANCER

Breast cancer is the leading cause of death for women aged between thirty-five and forty-four. In America, 1 in 13 women will eventually develop breast cancer and 1 in 25 women will eventually die of it. 90,000 new cases are diagnosed yearly.

However, breast cancer is an eminently curable disease. We women are fortunate; the breast is almost unique in that it is virtually a separate organ stuck on to the chest wall. This means it is easy to get at and can be completely removed. The single most important way in which you can help yourself, and help your doctor and surgeon to cure your cancer, is to examine your breasts regularly, and if you feel anything suspicious, consult your doctor immediately. Whatever you fear – don't hesitate. Your chances of a cure are in your hands; take them.

If breast cancer is discovered before it has spread to the lymph glands under the arms, the patient has a 70% chance of being alive in ten years' time. If the cancer is caught after it has spread lymphatically, the survival rate drops to 30% ten years after treatment. The extent of the spread is very important, however, for if it is minimal, the success rate is a good deal higher than 30%, whereas if it is extensive, it can be much lower.

In general, the size of the tumor is a good indicator of the extent that it has spread. If it is larger than $2\frac{1}{2}$ inches (6.5cm), three-quarters will involve the glands; if it is less, only half will have spread to the lymph nodes. No more than 1 in 10 small tumors ($\frac{1}{4}$in/8 mm) will spread to the nodes. One thing we know for certain – the cure rate for cancer of the breast is directly related to its early detection. In areas where there are publicity campaigns to encourage self-examination of the breast or mobile screening programs to pick up very tiny tumors, cancers are being caught before they have spread, and survival rates are improving.

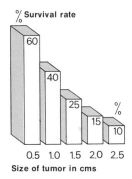

% Survival rate

The cure rate of the cancer depends on its size when detected and whether it has spread. The smaller it is, the more likely it is to be cured.

Factors linked to breast cancer

Race
If you are white, you run a higher risk than women of other races, and this is a pattern which prevails all over the world. The incidence in Latin races and Mediterranean countries is considerably lower, and lowest of all among black women. However, as black women climb the socio-economic scale and their lifestyles change, then their breast cancer incidence can be related to income and social status of the equivalent white women. If you are Jewish, you run a higher risk, though it depends on where your ancestors came from. If your parents or grandparents came from Europe, you are in a higher risk group than if your family came from North Africa or Asia.

Heredity
Breast cancer is not actually inherited in the way the color of your eyes and hair are, but there is a familial element. If your sister has developed cancer of the breast, then your chances are high, but if your mother had the disease your risk is slightly lower than with your sister. If both your mother and your sister have developed

☐ High incidence

cancer of the breast, then your risk is extremely high. Even an aunt or a grandmother on your mother's side with the disease puts you in a fairly high risk category. However, it is the age at which your relatives develop breast cancer that counts. If they develop it at the ripe old age of seventy, the risk would be low, but if they develop it prior to the menopause, the risk increases, and if they were younger than thirty, then the risk is high.

Previous breast disease
A past history of having benign breast disease – fibrocystic disease, chronic mastitis and benign lumps – seems to increase a woman's risk. Women who have a tendency to grow benign lumps may have a pre-disposition to develop malignant ones as well. A woman who stands the highest risk of developing breast cancer is the one who has already had cancer in her other breast.

Fertility
Women who have no children are at the highest risk, and those who have most are at low risk (see opposite). Women who have their first child after the age of 35 increase their risk, while women who have their first child before the age of 20 lower it.

Breast feeding
It is widely agreed that the more children you have, the less risk you run of developing breast cancer, and it may be that breast feeding your children contributes to this. More important than the number of children you have is the years of breast feeding that you undertake. The theory behind this hypothesis is that prolactin, the hormone which triggers milk production and which, under non-lactating conditions is thought to promote the development of breast cancer, loses its ability to do so when a woman nurses.

Diet and environment
There is an undoubted connection between a high intake of animal protein, saturated animal fats, and dairy produce of all kinds in the development of breast cancer. In Mormons, who eat little meat, incidence of breast cancer is lower than the rest of the population and is lowest among Seventh Day Adventists who are total vegetarians. Fat women undoubtedly run a higher risk of developing breast cancer than their thinner sisters. A combination of height and weight, or total body volume, is thought by scientists to be a contributary factor. Therefore, large women, including those women who are unusually tall or fat, or both, fall into a high risk category.

Environment does have a definite link with cancer, not only geographically speaking, but it is proven that women living in urban, rather than rural areas, run a higher risk. This may also be interrelated with diet.

Will taking the "pill" make me more susceptible?
There is no medical evidence either retrospective or prospective which establishes a cause-and-effect relationship between oral

RISK TABLE

Risk factors	High risk	Medium risk	Low risk
Cancer in the family	Self,sister, mother, maternal grandmother or aunts, maternal first cousins	Same factors as for high but lower incidence	None
Previous breast cancer	Past history of benign conditions of the breast	Same factors as for high but lower incidence	None
Gynecological and obstetric history	Early onset of menstruation No children First child after 35 Late start in sexual activity Late menopause	Same factors as for high but lower incidence	Late onset of menstruation First child before 20 Early sexual experience Early natural or artificial menopause
Race	Jews of European origin Non-Jews from Northern Europe Affluent Blacks	Middle income Blacks Latin Americans Southern European in origin	Jews from N. Africa/Asia Non-Jews from Finland Low income Whites/Blacks American Indians Orientals
Diet	Obesity Diet with high animal fat and dairy food content	Diet contains moderate amounts of animal fats and dairy produce	Vegetarian with low intake of dairy produce
Age	40 years or more	25–39	Less than 25
Environment	Large industrial cities	Medium sized cities	Small towns/rural areas

contraceptives and breast cancer. What does exist is animal data suggesting a connection between the administration of estrogens and breast cancer. This is questionable in its applicability to women taking the pill. Firstly, women do not metabolize hormones in the same way as rats, so results of experiments in rats cannot be directly applied to women. Secondly, no oral contraceptive contains estrogen alone. Progestogens are also present and there is no evidence that the combination is carcinogenic.

Are there any medical conditions which affect my chances?

An early onset of menstruation seems to increase the risk but having your ovaries removed before the age of thirty-five, or having an early natural menopause, considerably reduces the chance of developing breast cancer. The association of breast cancer and diabetes is well-documented, but some scientists would go further and say that there is a connection between breast cancer and those women who develop cancer of the salivary gland, or have an over-active thyroid gland (*thyrotoxicosis*).

Is one factor more important than the others?

Diet, obesity and environment, if changed, can push a woman into a higher or lower risk category. Japanese women, for instance, whose culture and diet and racial history confer on them a "protection" against cancer, move into a higher risk group if they go to live in America and take up indigenous eating habits, diets and way of life. In this case, environment seems to outweigh the racial factors.

263

Is there any way I can prevent it or find out if it is developing?

Consult the chart, below, on which factors place you in a high risk group, then do your best to eliminate or correct those factors, e.g. the sort of food you eat, how obese you allow yourself to become, even possibly where you opt to live. Of course you cannot change the aspects of your life which are not under control, e.g. family history or past personal history, or your racial origins, but you should take corrective steps wherever you can.

SELF TEST SCORE TABLE

Risk factors				Score
Age	20–34 years	35–49	50 years plus	
	10	40	90	
Race	Oriental	Black	Caucasian	
	10	20	30	
Family history	None	Mother, sister, aunt or grand-mother with breast cancer	Mother and sister with breast cancer	
	10	50	100	
Personal history	No breast cancer		Previous breast cancer	
	10		100	
Pregnancy	Became pregnant for first time before 25	Became pregnant for first time at 25 or after	Never pregnant	
	10	15	20	
			Total =	

Low risk below 100	Medium risk 100–225	High risk more than 225
Self examination of the breasts monthly	Self examination of the breasts monthly	Self examination of the breasts monthly
Annual check by doctor	Annual check by doctor	Examination by your doctor every six months
	Chest X-ray every two years	Mammography every 12 months

Practice regular self-examination of the breasts once a month at a convenient time, for example when you are going to have a bath. For a detailed explanation of the technique, see p. 78.

Go to the doctor every six months or, at a minimum, once a year, for manual examinations of your breasts. You must make certain that the doctor who examines you periodically is as expert as you, and doctors vary. The proper medical technique for breast examination has special requirements, and if you are not happy with the way your own doctor goes about examining your breasts, ask to be referred to a doctor who specializes in detection and treatment of breast cancer so that you are reassured that the manual examination is being carried out correctly (see p. 268).

If you fall into a high risk group, or you need the reassurance, there are certain technical investigations which can be done in the hospital in specialized departments. Such investigations would be mammography, thermography, and ultra-sound.

Investigative procedures for breast cancer

Mammography

A mammogram is a standard X-ray of the breast and shows up variations in consistency. Each time you have a mammogram you will be subjected to a standard dose of X-ray and therefore the frequency with which you have such an examination will not rest entirely with you. Your doctor or specialist should weigh the pros and cons of successive doses of X-ray and this procedure, in any case, is not recommended for those under fifty or without other symptoms.

Mammograms
These are standard X-rays of the breast which, when interpreted by a trained radiologist, reveal areas of calcification and increased densities indicating possible cancerous conditions.

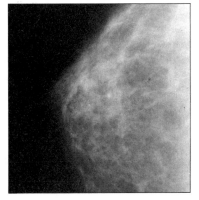

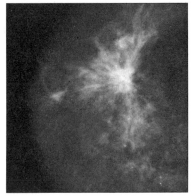

Normal　　　　　　　　　　**Abnormal**

Mammography
This painless procedure provides an X-ray picture of the internal breast structures. To have one done, you must strip to the waist and place your breasts in various positions under a cone-shaped device.

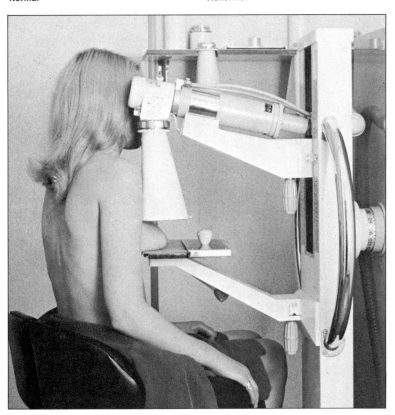

To have a mammogram done, you will be asked to strip to the waist and, using a cone-shaped device, the radiologist will ask you to pose in a variety of positions so that your breasts can be photographed from different angles (see p. 265). The films will be developed and examined by a radiologist specialized in the interpretation of mammograms. Mammography is most reliable for the examination of large breasts because they allow a greater degree of contrast for clear and more accurate X-ray pictures. However, the trained radiologist is able to pick out even small cysts and tiny tumors.

Xero-mammography requires different equipment from the standard X-ray machine which takes a mammogram, and in essence is a photocopying process for reproducing X-ray film. It is not necessarily more accurate than mammography; accuracy of interpretation seems to depend on the experience of the radiologist in whichever method is used.

Thermography

Thermography picks up "hot" spots, and in the case of breast cancer can pick up a "hot" cancer nodule through infra-red scanning. Any rapidly growing area of the body is hotter than the rest of it, and so a growing cyst or a tumor will show up on a thermogram as a more intense area of heat than the surrounding tissue. Thermography is by no means as accurate as mammography and should never be relied on alone. It should always be used as a supportive investigation to manual examination and mammography. It is, however, safer than mammography because it involves no X-radiation. To have one done, the patient undresses and holds her arms up in the air or stretched out from the body to allow the breast skin to cool. Photographs are then taken of the breasts from different angles with an infra-red camera.

Ultra-sound and aspiration of breast fluid

In a very few centers, ultra-sound (which produces a picture very similar to an X-ray photograph except that the patterns are produced by the echoes of sound waves which vary in intensity according to the solidity of the tissue that they bounce from) and aspiration of breast fluid for examination to detect the presence of malignant cells are only being used in the most advanced centers in the world, but nonetheless, these treatments give hope for the very early detection of breast malignancy or pre-malignancy.

Breast tumors   Tumors vary in their size, shape and type. Some are small, hard, well circumscribed and pea-like initially. Others may originate in a more diffuse cystic structure which is not as clearly defined and is somewhat more rubbery to feel. If a cancer develops in a lactiferous ductule (see structure of the breast, p. 141) then it may be difficult to feel it at all and you may only be alerted to its presence by a discharge from the nipple.

A rapidly-growing tumor will have somewhat different characteristics from a very slowly growing tumor. Cancers tend to spread in all directions. They therefore spread upwards and involve the skin, and this will show up in a certain way (see below). They may also spread downwards to involve the pectoral muscles and this will also give the tumor special characteristics.

For the purposes of positioning a cancer, the breast is divided into four quadrants – a tumor in the upper and outer quadrant is considered somewhat more dangerous than tumors in other areas because it can spread quickly through the lymphatic vessels, the lymph glands, in the axilla (armpit).

Breast changes   Cancer of the breast may exhibit any or all of the following features which you yourself can observe or feel if you practice regular self-examination of the breasts and which your doctor will be looking for when s/he examines your breasts (see p. 100).

A lump
The majority of cancerous lumps are hard. They are usually clearly defined and feel quite different from the "orange pip" consistency during the second half of the menstrual cycle.

Pain
The vast majority of malignant tumors are painless. If you have a painful tumor of the breast, the likelihood of it being malignant is very much reduced.

Skin involvement
If the tumor has involved the skin it will have sent up constricting bands to the skin which will tether it and pull small areas of the skin towards it. This gives the skin the classical orange peel appearance which is associated with breast cancer and becomes obvious when you raise your arms above your head.

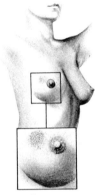

A pitted or "orange peel" appearance of the skin is a classical sign of breast cancer

Involvement of the underlying muscle
Similarly, the tumor may tether itself to the underlying muscle and therefore it will not be freely mobile. It will feel fixed to the chest wall.

Changes involving the nipple
If you are not pregnant and not lactating, you should consult your doctor immediately if you notice a discharge, crusting or bleeding from the nipple. Additional warning signs about which you should seek immediate advice would be scaling of the skin around the nipple, changes in the nipple texture and a cracked nipple for no reason.

Other changes
You may notice other changes in your breast which are not necessarily involved with cancer, but nonetheless require a visit to your doctor. These would include asymmetry of the breast, either in terms of appearance, feel or movement; a persistent ache, pain or tenderness in the breast which is not associated with the menstrual cycle; and a breast in which there is an area of heat, swelling and soreness.

Diagnosis of breast cancer

After questioning you on past, present, and family medical history, your doctor will carefully examine your breasts manually in very much the same way as you do when you examine yourself. The doctor should not squeeze, push or pull the breast tissue, but should examine it gently and carefully. Your doctor will examine your axilla for the presence of lumps (swollen lymph glands) and probably the area above your collar bone and your neck. S/he may include examination of your abdomen to feel whether or not the liver is enlarged. Whether or not a lump is detected in one breast, it is essential that the other breast is examined exactly the same.

If your doctor detects a lump, her/his first concern will be to refute the diagnosis of cancer. Doctors approach lumps in the breast as being malignant until proved otherwise, and will therefore probably act with great speed and efficiency and encourage you to see a specialist as soon as possible. This will probably be within 36 to 48 hours. Specialists who have the most experience with treatment of breast cancer are surgeons (who treat breast cancer with surgery), radiologists (who treat breast cancer with X-ray therapy), and chemotherapists (who treat breast cancer with anti-cancer drugs). The chances are that your own doctor will refer you to a surgeon for a first opinion.

Your surgeon will have three main aims: to find out whether your lump is malignant or not; to find out whether the tumor is rapidly growing or not; to find out whether or not it has spread, and if it has, to what extent. Most surgeons have a standard plan which they put into operation as the answers to the above three questions come in. Do not let the surgeon keep this plan private. Ask to be part of it. Find out about the various options and discuss each of them. While you need this expertise to decide which forms of treatment will give you the best chance in the long term, do not forget that you have a degree of freedom of choice about the treatment which is up to you to exercise.

The surgeon may take a few days to confirm what her/his medical acumen already suggests, and may order mammography and/or thermography, and – if available – ultra-sonic investigation. At the end of these investigations s/he will know, with a good degree of certainty, whether or not the tumor is malignant. This is peferable to treating a tumor hastily and perhaps performing an unnecessarily disfiguring operation.

Pre-operative investigative procedures

Fine needle biopsy

This is an almost painless procedure when a fine needle is inserted into the lump and a little fluid is aspirated. If the tumor is malignant, the malignant cells will be found in the breast fluid in 85% of cases.

In some cases, of course, the tumor is solid and it is very difficult to aspirate fluid. The next stage is to use a slightly larger needle which, when inserted into the tumor, removes a small plug of tissue which can then be examined microscopically. The widebore needle is slightly more painful than the fine one, but with a tiny injection of local anesthetic in the skin, it causes no more than mild discomfort.

Lumpectomy

A procedure which involves excision of the tumor if it is not too large or deeply embedded in the breast on an out-patient basis, without hospital admission. While waiting for the diagnosis from the pathology laboratory, you stay at home.

Breast biopsy

You are taken to the operating room and either the whole lump is taken out, or a small part of it. The specimen is rushed to the pathology laboratory, frozen, cut into small slices and examined under a microscope. While some doctors will operate immediately if the lump is found to be malignant, others believe that the condition of the cancer, whether it has spread or not (staging), must be ascertained first. A benign lump will generally be excised at the time of the biopsy.

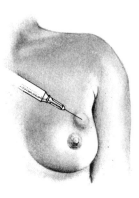

Fine needle biopsy

I've heard of some women going in for a breast biopsy and waking up without their breast. Can this happen to me?

Never allow yourself to be put in the position of going to the operating room without knowing for certain that your breast will be removed. The best centers treating breast cancer have devised pre-operative investigative techniques which provide the surgeon with enough information to decide on the malignancy of the tumor and it is therefore possible to discuss with your surgeon, well before any operation, the various options which you may take advantage of. You should put forward your views, and agree with the surgeon about the extent of the operation to be performed.

In this way you have an opportunity to adjust yourself to the physical and psychological realities of having a breast removed. If you are well prepared in advance for surgery, the chances are that you will make the best progress and have fewer psychological problems. If you are diagnosed to have cancer of the breast insist that you exercise these rights.

Is there any way to tell if the cancer has spread?

Other investigations should be performed to find out if the cancer has spread and to what extent. X-rays, of perhaps the whole skeleton, to look for bony metastases, liver function tests to see whether or not the liver is involved, and routine blood tests are the tests to be carried out. Some tumors of the breast are hormone-dependent and in specialized centers tests can be done to see whether or not the woman's hormonal status has a bearing on the treatment of her breast cancer. As a general rule, women of pre-menopausal age have tumors which are estrogen-dependent. In simple terms, this means that the growth of the tumor is encouraged by estrogens. The majority of tumors in the post-menopausal age group are not hormone-dependent. All of this information is gathered together to help the surgeon and his/her colleagues to form an individual plan for the individual patient to ensure the best treatment of the breast cancer, both in the short and the long term.

If I have cancer of the breast do I have to have my breast removed?

Strictly speaking, the answer is "No," but no matter how much you do not want to lose your breast, if your own specialist thinks it is necessary, then you would be unwise not to go along with that decision.

Centers that specialize in the treatment of cancer of the breast have certain standard procedures which they have found to give the best results, in their hands, for tumors of varying degrees of malignancy, and, quite rightly, they wish to adhere to the procedure which they know gives the best results for them. They have also studied the relative merits of different methods and different combinations of therapy (e.g. surgery + X-ray therapy, surgery + chemotherapy etc.) and will be able to explain to you the prognosis (the chances of being alive after a certain time, usually five years, or the chance of a cure) of each treatment regime. In your pre-operative discussions with your surgeon, make sure that you cover this ground. According to the stage of your disease, the surgeon will almost certainly opt for the treatment with the highest success rate, for that stage, at his center. This is the best advice you can yet, and it may involve mastectomy in some form.

Some centers have examined very carefully the comparative success of simple lumpectomy. That means taking out the tumors but leaving the rest of the breast intact, and treating or preventing spread with X-ray therapy or anti-cancer drugs. Clearly, anything more than lumpectomy is not justified if the cancer has already spread to various other organs of the body. At the other end of the scale, lumpectomy may be a valid option for a very small, early tumor, with adjunctive therapy of local X-ray therapy or chemotherapy to treat or prevent spread. If you fall somewhere in the middle, only your surgeon can advise you. What you should do is discuss the possibility of lumpectomy.

Available surgical techniques

There are seven different operations performed today for breast cancer although subcutaneous mastectomy is only available in the United States. There is some confusion about the names of these procedures; what is important, however, is the description of what each one involves. While all the operations demand the removal of some, if not all, the breast tissue, they differ most in the amount of underlying tissue, muscle and lymph nodes also removed.

Naturally, the greater the extent of the operation, the more mutilating the operation and the greater the amount of scarring. You should, however, try to discuss the scar itself as the surgeon may be able to alter the position of his incision.

Is any operation "better" than the others?

The Halsted and extended radical operations are by far the most mutilating and if your surgeon advises either of these you must make certain that you are aware of the post-operative consequences in terms of appearance, and discomfort. Many distinguished authorities insist that nothing as radical as a Halsted operation is justified, and that less mutilating operations give just as good success rates and fewer post-operative complications.

MASTECTOMY OPERATIONS

☐ Affected areas

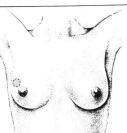

Lumpectomy, tylectomy and local excision
The whole lump is removed plus a little of the breast tissue surrounding the lump. After the operation your breast will not look very different from the way it did before.

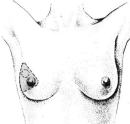

Partial mastectomy
In this operation the tumor, plus a sizeable amount of surrounding breast tissue, plus the overlying skin, plus some of the underlying tissue, are removed. Your breast may be somewhat smaller afterwards.

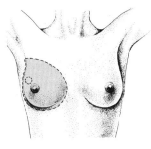
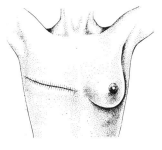

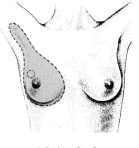

Total or simple mastectomy
The whole of the breast is removed, but the axillary nodes and the pectoral muscle are left untouched. The last lymph node in the breast itself (not the lymph nodes of the axilla) is routinely taken out to see if the cancer has spread to the axilla.

Modified radical mastectomy
The whole of the breast and the axillary lymph nodes are removed but not the pectoral muslces.

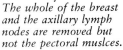

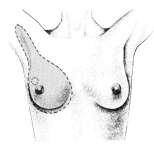
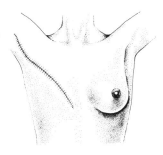

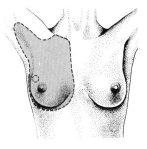

The radical or Halsted mastectomy
In this operation, which was perfected by Dr Halsted in 1894, all the tissues of the breast, axillary lymph nodes and pectoral muscles are removed.

Extended radical mastectomy
The breast, the axillary lymph nodes, the pectoral muscle and the internal lymph nodes of the breast are removed. To do this it is sometimes necessary to take out sections of the rib. Though rarely done, some surgeons even remove the nodes above the collar bone in the angle that joins the shoulder.

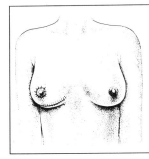

Subcutaneous mastectomy
The internal breast tissue is shelled out leaving the nipple and areola intact, and enough skin to accommodate a silicone implant, which is usually inserted several months later. The axillary lymph nodes may be removed. This surgery is usually only possible in centers where highly-skilled plastic surgeons work hand-in-hand with breast surgeons and is performed only on an individual patient basis.

Post-operative feelings
This incision will be sore, like a cut, as you would expect, but you may experience a burning sensation in certain parts of the scar. This will be due to the presence of drains which have been left there to draw out any fluid which may collect under the wound. They will probably be taken out on the third or fourth day.

You will most certainly have a sore throat due to the tube which was passed through your larynx to administer the anesthetic. It will probably have disappeared within 24 to 36 hours.

Your chest will feel rather tight over the area of the scar, as though your chest were being squeezed, and occasionally you may feel short, sharp jabs of pain over any part of the side of the chest which was operated upon. The amount and intensity of the pain vary considerably from woman to woman.

Because the nerves to the skin have necessarily been severed during the operation, you may find that as much as the whole side of the chest and also part of your upper arm, are numb. Be reassured, sensation will come back, but it will take several months to do so as the nerves grow. It will probably return initially, as tingling and pins and needles, but it may also be painful, so be prepared for it. You may also feel mild electric shocks in the skin as the nerves regrow.

If the wound is healing well, alternate stitches are usually removed between 7 and 10 days and then the rest between 10 and 14. After this, the wound will only need dry, antiseptic dressings. If all goes well you will probably be discharged during the second week post-surgery.

Are there any post-operative complications?

There is quite a controversy about the necessity to remove the axillary lymph nodes and many cancer specialists believe that the survival rates are no different if the breast only is removed and the axillary lymph nodes are left.

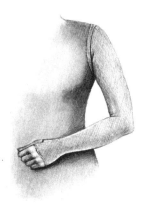

If the axillary lymph glands have been removed, *lymph edema*, or "milk arm," is usually a temporary, but in a very few women may be a permanent, post-operative complication. This involves swelling of the hand and arm up to the shoulder on the affected side. It varies from very mild edema, which cannot be seen but is only felt as a slight tightness, to a somewhat more severe state where it may be necessary to wear elastic bandages to settle down the swelling. In the worst cases, you may have to wear a post-mastectomy sleeve for the rest of your life. This sleeve is similar to an evening glove which reaches right up to the shoulder, minus the fingers, and is made of the same flesh-colored elasticized material as support stockings. Its action is to continually squeeze the arm to stimulate circulation and prevent fluid collecting.

In more radical operations, particularly the Halsted, some women may require skin grafts which are usually taken from the thigh. Grafting is very occasionally complicated by itching, infection, or rejection.

Very rarely, some women have limitation of shoulder movement which can usually be overcome by a course of physiotheraphy.

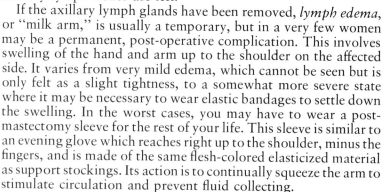

Physiotherapy   If you wish to regain your physical fitness fast, then it is vital to start exercising your muscles immediately. This is partly to strengthen the muscles of the arm that will do the job of the pectoral which has been removed, but it also stimulates the circulation of blood and lymph through the wound and therefore promotes healing.

POST-MASTECTOMY EXERCISES

Hair brushing
This is also effective in exercising your affected arm.

Wall climbing
Begin by standing close to a wall and reaching as high as you can with your unaffected arm. Make a mark.

With your toes and fore-head as close to the wall as possible, bend your elbows and place your arms against the wall at shoulder level.

Work both hands up the wall parallel to each other, until painful. Then work down slowly. Continue exercises until you are fully-extended.

Precautions
Don't ever allow the affected arm to be used for taking blood-pressure, for vaccinations, or injections of any kind. Take care when shaving under your arms, or when having a manicure.

How soon can I resume my normal routine?

Nearly all post-mastectomy patients are easily fatigued and you will quickly become exhausted if you try to fling yourself into your pre-operative domestic routine. Do not expect to be back to normal ·for several months. Most surgeons would say it takes something between four and six months to be feeling fit again. Do not be surprised if most areas that were affected by the surgery feel tender for some months, though the amount and intensity of the pain felt post-operatively varies individually. A very few women are pain-free and supple enough to be playing tennis in six weeks. In others it takes as long as a year for the feeling of tightness and numbness to disappear.

You can have sex as soon as you'd like to but you may find that your skin is just too sore for fondling for anything up to three months. The sooner you can resume relations with your partner, the soooner you will stop worrying about a loss of femininity.

Post-operative treatment

As part of your immediate post-operative treatment your surgeon may decide that you need to have a course of X-ray therapy and chemotherapy. During both radiotherapy and chemotherapy, a very close check is kept on your blood so that any ill-effects can be noted quickly.

The X-ray therapy is nearly always confined to the breast area and the armpits. What the radiologist is concerned to do is to give you a sufficient dose of X-ray to kill off any cancer cells which may remain in the area. The treatment is usually divided by time and dose, so that over a period of weekly visits you accumulate the dose of X-rays that is needed.

You may experience some reddening or even burning of the skin. Nausea and loss of appetite are also quite common. Weakness, fever, retching, swelling and pain, and occasionally baldness, will result from high doses. All side-effects should be reported to your radiologist who will adjust your treatment regime accordingly.

A wide range of anti-cancer drugs is available for your chemotherapist to choose from and they can be given by a variety of routes – as tablets or as injections into a muscle or into a vein. They are nearly always spread out into several doses over a period of time. Unfortunately, the effect of these drugs cannot be localized to the area affected and some of them have side-effects which affect the rest of the body, such as falling hair, which are disturbing. Some may affect the production of blood, and if you develop a sore tongue or a sore throat you should report these and any other side-effects to your chemotherapist immediately.

Follow-up examinations

Your first post-operative examination will probably be three months after your operation. At this time you will have a thorough manual examination of the chest and incision in the armpit, and of course, of your other breast and armpit, and your abdomen to detect any liver enlargement. You should tell your surgeon of any other abnormalities you have noticed so that s/he can perform appropriate tests.

Your second visit will probably be after six months and this time the manual examination will be accompanied by exhaustive tests on your blood and on the function of the various organs like liver and kidneys, and also X-rays of the chest, pelvis, skull and spine. A mammogram will be performed on your remaining breast. You will then probably be seen at three-monthly intervals up to a year, and the annual checkup will be as exhaustive as the one that you had at six months.

If anything untoward shows up as a result of these examinations or tests to suggest that the tumor has spread, then further special treatments will be considered. These might include:
● Further X-ray therapy if the spread is local.
● A course of chemotherapy described as above.
● If your tumor was shown to be hormone-dependent pre-operatively, then removal of your ovaries will be considered.
● The secretion of estrogens in any site in the body is controlled

by part of the pituitary gland and in some hospitals, this part of the pituitary gland is destroyed by special techniques.

● Estrogens are also produced by the adrenal glands and removal of these will be considered.

● Anti-estrogen drugs may be used to inhibit further growth.

Is there anything I can do to prepare myself emotionally for having a breast removed?

Many post-mastectomy women have admitted that the most difficult thing they have to cope with is the shock of waking up after the operation and finding that their breast has gone without having been warned of this eventuality prior to the operation. Not only can you avoid this trauma, but you can prepare yourself emotionally several days prior to the operation if you make certain, indeed, if you insist, that you have a full discussion about your mastectomy with your surgeon well before the operation is done. This discussion should include a frank approach to the fact that you have cancer and of the consequences.

Coping with breast cancer

For nearly every woman the major concern is "Will I die?", closely followed by "Will my partner still love me with only one breast and a hideous scar in place of the other?". The best possible advice that can be given about the first question is to go along and see your doctor as soon as you find a lump in your breast. It has been proven time and time again that by far the most important factor in curing breast cancer is the speed with which it is detected and then treated. As far as the second question is concerned, nearly all women find that difficulties with self-image and sexual attractiveness turn out to be of considerably less concern once they are real rather than imagined.

In the event, there will almost certainly be moments when you will have to be tough with yourself and force yourself to be realistic. Ask yourself questions like "who in her right mind can be concerned about being sexually attractive when she has cancer?". And, while you may care if your scar shows when you wear a bikini or a low-necked dress, you should be infinitely more concerned about whether you are strong enough to pick up your five-year-old child when s/he needs you. Though you may have episodic worries about what your partner will think when he sees you naked, you should also remember that if he loves you he will be more concerned about the fact that you have cancer than that your chest is lopsided. On this line of thought, your final backstop can be that if a man rejects you physically because you have had a mastectomy, he probably wasn't worth having in the first place.

If you are older (40+) you may find having a mastectomy is made particularly difficult if your relationship with your partner is already rocky. You may then view your condition as just one more thing that is driving your partner away from you. If you are menopausal, or have just gone through menopause, you may have pre-existing psychological problems which are only worsened by the added burden of having to cope with a mastectomy. Furthermore, your children are probably grown up and have left home, so their needs no longer act as a life force, nor can you gain direct support from them.

Young women with a family seem to suffer less, certainly from the point of view of their concern about their own attractiveness and their attractiveness to their partner. This is probably because they get a great deal of emotional support from their families and from the needs that their young children express.

Who can I turn to for help?

You will be serving your best interests if you express your anxieties and fears both to your own doctor and to your specialist. Both can help you. Your own doctor may decide to tide you over a difficult period by giving you a short course of tranquillizers and sleeping pills to help you sleep. He or she will be the best judge of when you can do without them. Your doctor and your specialist can put you in touch with psychiatrists and psychotherapists who can help you to adjust to this new and considerable stress in your life. You will find that social workers and welfare workers are at hand to help you rehabiliate your life, to get you over the initial difficult patches when you are not fit, by providing help in the home and other practical support. Best of all, your doctor or the specialist may put you in touch with other women who have had mastectomies, who have learned to come to terms with them and can give you tips on practical matters associated with the procedure. It is reassuring to see that such women are leading perfectly normal and well-adjusted lives. If they can do it, so can you. Added to this, many women find that their partners are more loving, understanding and sympathetic than ever before, and that as a couple they discover a closeness, particularly in their love-making, that did not previously exist.

How long will it take me to adjust to being without a breast?

It would be unrealistic if you did not expect it to take you some time to make the physical and psychological adjustments to losing a breast. Much of the work will have to be done by you, but you have your doctor, your specialist, your psychiatrist, your psycho-therapist, and your social worker, to help you. Do not forget your partner. He will also have to make adjustments, and you will be a support to each other if you do it together. Always discuss your anxieties with him. If he is willing, or if he feels the need, suggest that he gets involved in your discussions with your doctors and helpers, that for instance he attends your psychotherapy session with you, that he meets other women who have had mastectomies and, more importantly, their husbands. You could almost say that having breast cancer is a joint disease and you should handle it together as a couple.

Breast prostheses

There is quite a variety of breast prostheses available which can simply be fitted inside the bra, or you can have a bra specially made to incorporate the prosthesis. Materials are used which simulate the look, texture and feel of a normal breast. If you have nothing else, you should consider the possibility of temporarily

With a proper prosthesis a woman needn't feel her mastectomy is apparent, whether in everyday dress of even in a swimsuit.

stuffing your ordinary bra full of cotton when you are discharged from the hospital so that you are satisfied that your profile will at least look normal. Before being discharged from the hospital, however, your surgeon will almost certainly speak to you and, if not, you should raise the question with your surgeon of having a special prosthesis made. Most breast cancer units have special departments where these are individually designed and made. You will be given an appointment to visit this department where the

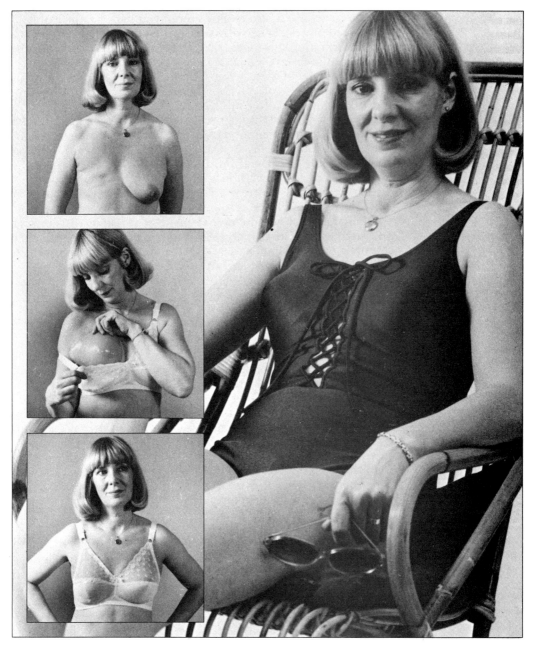

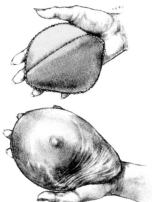

For swimwear

For general wear

Breast prostheses come in various sizes and materials and can be fitted to suit the individual.

various options open to you will be shown and discussed and you can make up your own mind as to what you will settle for.

If you are prepared to go further, you could have a breast prosthesis fitted underneath the skin by a plastic surgeon. This is easiest if you have opted for a subcutaneous mastectomy as this procedure will have been pre-planned, and the silicone implant will be fitted a few months after your mastectomy.

It is even possible to have your breast reconstructed from square one. The operation is rare, and few plastic surgeons are skilled enough to get good results. But should you find one (probably in the United States), s/he will take skin from another part of the body, form the substance of the breast from fat inside the abdomen and fashion a nipple from your ear lobe. In all honesty, the breast does not look entirely normal, but if you really want it, you can have a breast. The operation is rarely performed within four to six months after mastectomy.

It is very unlikely that your scar will be entirely invisible if you want to wear a swimsuit or décolletage. You can do something to help yourself if it really concerns you by telling your surgeon about it before the operation. It is up to the surgeon whether a horizontal or vertical incision is made, and although the surgeon's primary concern is to treat your disease efficiently, the surgeon will almost certainly be sympathetic to your concern. However, you may find that you do have to make concessions to your scar and wear clothes that hide it. The other alternative is to wear camouflage make-up. There is a special brand of make-up which has been designed to cover birthmarks and comes in a range of over fifty different skin tones. It is excellent for covering up scars.

CERVICAL CANCER

Cancer of the cervix is the most common malignant disease of the female reproductive organs, and is second in incidence only to cancer of the breast. An interesting epidemiological statistic is that in Great Britain the ratio of cervical cancer to uterine cancer used to be 6:1, and it is now 2:1 – this is partly because women are living longer, partly because it is diagnosed more frequently as the result of Pap smear tests, and partly because the disease is increasing in young women.

It is extremely important that every woman over the age of twenty seeks Pap smear tests every twelve months.

In the United States there are approximately sixteen thousand cases of cervical cancer each year and about seven and a half thousand of these women die, nearly always because routine Pap smear tests, which could have meant early detection and successful treatment, were neglected.

It is primarily a disease of young women and about 1% of all women between the ages of thirty and thirty-five have asymptomatic cancer of the cervix (that is, a cancer which has no obvious signs), discovered only on screening. The risk of it being present is especially high in the 25–34 age group.

Cancer of the cervix possesses one almost unique feature which separates it from most of the cancers in both sexes – it has a "pre-invasive phase" during which it grows but does not spread, before it becomes invasive. This means that if the cancer *in situ*, as it is called, is caught in the pre-invasive state, it can be completely cured by either cone biopsy in a young patient or hysterectomy if no more children are desired. The pre-invasive state may last several years and so, if a woman has regular Pap smears done, it is possible to pick up a pre-invasive cancer before it ever becomes truly malignant. Because very few pre-invasive cancers become malignant within twelve to eighteen months, annual smear tests would be ideal, though some medical authorities recommend them every two years and even some every five years.

This characteristic of cervical cancer is of crucial interest to both doctors and women. For doctors, it gives a sort of breathing space during which they have an opportunity to diagnose the cancer in an early stage while it is completely curable and to perform a relatively simple and minor operation to cure it. For patients, it means that rigorous annual checks will prevent the disease from ever reaching an advanced stage which requires radical surgical treatment, possibly followed by radiotherapy, with a lower chance of survival.

Factors linked to cervical cancer

Sexual activity
Sexual intercourse appears to be a major factor in the cause of cervical cancer: there is a very low incidence of cancer of the cervix in virgins, and the highest frequency is in those who have frequent sexual intercourse with many partners (cancer of the cervix is common in prostitutes). The disease is more common in women who begin sexual intercourse during adolescence.

There is a possible explanation of the role that sexual activity plays in the causation of cancer of the cervix. The lining cells of the cervix are most vulnerable during adolescence and the first pregnancy, and it is thought that frequency of intercourse during this period may initiate the cancer process. The inference is that there may be a carcinogenic component of seminal fluid which acts on the lining cells of the cervix to render them, after a latent period, cancerous. The cells lining the cervix are very special in nature. They have the ability to "ingest" sperm and other constituents of seminal fluid. Once the sperm or chemicals are inside these cells they may cause them to change their nature and become cancerous. Once this initiating process has begun there is very often a latent period of several years during which other factors may help the development of the cancer.

Racial and social groups
There is a low incidence of cancer of the cervix in Jews, Moslems and other religious groups, which may be explained by the influence of their religious beliefs on their sexual habits: for instance, abstinence during menstruation and pregnancy reduces the number of times that intercourse takes place; in addition, pre-marital and extra-marital intercourse are less common among these racial groups. There is an undoubted preponderance of the disease in lower socio-economic groups.

Venereal disease

I have seen it written that the herpes virus, now reaching epidemic proportions as a venereal disease, is thought to be a cause of cervical cancer. Most doctors would feel that the picture is not quite that clear; certainly cause and effect have not been proven. What has been shown is that women with blood antibodies for the herpes virus have a higher incidence of cervical cancer. However, it does not mean that any woman who has had herpes runs a high risk of cervical cancer. I would therefore disagree with the classification of cervical cancer as a venereal disease – one that can be transmitted through sexual activity – there is certainly no proof of that.

Risk groups for cervical cancer

Specific factors in lifestyle have not yet been identified as causes of cervical cancer although experts believe that environmental factors are of primary importance with this, as well as with many other types of cancer. However, studies of the rates of cancer of the cervix in different groups of women do provide some useful clues. We know that cervical cancer rates are lower in some women and much higher in others.

Do not make the mistake of over-interpreting the information on high and low risk groups of women. Remember that the list is relative and only suggests a slightly lower, or slightly higher, risk than average. As it happens, the overall incidence of cervical cancer is about 1 in 100,000 women between the ages of twenty and twenty-four and rises as you get older. So that at the age of forty-five to fifty-five the rate is about 50 per 100,000 and while it is reassuring to be in a low risk group, this doesn't mean that you can skip your annual Pap smear test.

HIGH RISK GROUPS	LOW RISK GROUPS
Women of low socio-economic state; Women who have had chronic genital infection with the herpes virus; Patients who attend venereal disease clinics; Prostitutes; Inmates of women's prisons; Protestant or Catholic women who rarely or never attend church; Black and Puerto Rican women; Mexican immigrant women; Women who took DES during pregnancy.	Women of high socio-economic status; Jewish women; Moslem women; Seventh Day Adventist women; Irish and Italian immigrant women; Virgins and celibate women; Protestant and Catholic women who regularly attend church.

Symptoms of cervical cancer

Unlike pre-invasive carcinoma, which is usually symptomless, true cancer of the cervix can usually be seen as an ulceration or a growth on the cervix itself when it is viewed directly during the vaginal examination with a speculum. By far the earliest sign is inter-menstrual bleeding (spotting or bleeding between periods), bleeding after intercourse, or post-menopausal bleeding. The blood usually comes from the ulcer on the cervix. Quite often the ulcer or the growth becomes infected, and this may cause an offensive vaginal discharge.

Investigative procedures for cervical cancer

Cervical (Pap) smear

Originally this involved collecting the fluid which lies in the upper back portion of the vagina by suction into a pipette. This "Pap" smear had the advantage of occasionally picking up cells from the vagina and the uterus as well as the cervix.

But now, the more effective way of obtaining cells from the cervix is to scrape its external opening with a wooden spatula during speculum examination – the cervical smear test. The cells which are collected on the spatula are then smeared on to a slide and stained in the usual way and examined under the microscope. Many women today call a cervical smear a Pap test, though this is not really accurate.

The results of your pap smear may be written as class I, II, III, IV or V. Class I should be interpreted as negative, class II as severe inflammatory changes, class III as mild abnormality of the cells, class IV as severe abnormality of the cells, and class V as malignant cells.

RESULTS OF PAP SMEAR TESTS

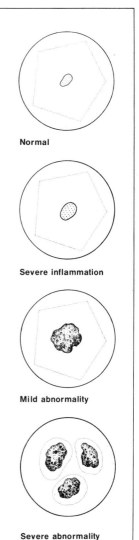

Negative or Normal
This includes mild inflammatory changes which are present in nearly all smears. Under a microscope cells are angular in outline with small nuclei in a clear cytoplasm.

Normal

Severe inflammatory changes
You may not have any symptoms but vaginal discharge or irritation is not uncommon. A repeat smear is sometimes recommended. The microscope will reveal a larger-than-normal nucleus in the cell.

Severe inflammation

Mild abnormality of the cells
A repeat Pap smear test will be asked for and may be necessary regularly every three, six or twelve months. The mild abnormality can revert to normal or persist for several years, in which case you should see a gynecologist for a complete examination. Alternatively the abnormality may become more severe. The nucleus, seen microscopically, is large with an irregular outline and contains heavy clumps and strands.

Mild abnormality

Severe abnormality of the cells
It means that you must have a thorough internal examination and possibly cone biopsy to remove the abnormal parts of the cervix (see p. 282). Severe abnormality of the cells may be due to pre-invasive or invasive cancer.

Seen under a microscope the cells are smaller, with irregular outlines and very large nuclei. Very course clumps and strands are unevenly distributed around them.

Severe abnormality

281

What will the result of my Pap smear test mean?

Your test will either come back as normal or abnormal. If it is the latter there is no need to panic. The first thing you should request is for the test to be repeated to make sure that there has been no laboratory error. Occasionally, when a woman has suffered from a chronic infection, the smears are questionable, as they are if they are taken too close – before and after – to menstruation. Also, the smear itself may have been badly preserved. False negatives, however, are very rare indeed and occur in less than 1% of patients. A positive smear *must* be followed by a biopsy of the cervix so that the extent of the malignancy can be fully assessed.

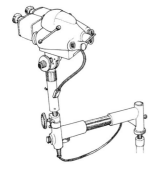

Colposcopy

This is a procedure whereby the cervix is examined in great detail. It is almost like looking at the cervix under a microscope, except that individual cells cannot be seen. The surface, however, can be seen in very great detail, as though you are looking at the surface of the moon with a telescope. In this way, doctors who are skilled at recognizing small areas of pre-invasive cancer can very precisely localize those parts of the cervix which appear abnormal.

During colposcopy it is possible for your gynecologist to take small specimens of the areas which s/he thinks appear abnormal to the eye and send them for examination to the laboratory. In this way it is possible to decide with some accuracy exactly how far the tumor has spread.

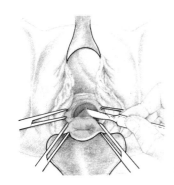

Punch and cone biopsies

Your gynecologist will almost certainly suggest this if colposcopy reveals that the cancer is pre-invasive or if the invasion is fairly localized.

Occasional target or punch biopsies may be taken from regions of the cervix which look abnormal. However, invasion of the deeper tissues and spread to the internal opening of the cervix cannot be excluded by any other method than cone biopsy. When the cone has been removed it is divided into blocks and these are sectioned very carefully so that the exact extent of the malignant tumor can be defined.

What are the risks associated with cone biopsy?

Heavy bleeding, during, immediately after, or about 10 days after surgery is a fairly common complication. Some rare long-term effects include cervical incompetence leading to premature delivery in subsequent pregnancies, and impaired fertility due to the removal of cervical mucus-producing tissue. Cervical scarring can occasionally lead to problems during labor and delivery in later pregnancies.

Does having a circumcised partner protect you against cervical cancer?

At one time it was thought so. Circumcision prevents the collection of *smegma*, a white cheesey substance which tends to accumulate in the loose prepucial skin of the penis, and this was thought to be carcinogenic – but this theory is no longer accepted.

STAGES OF CERVICAL CANCER

Very often doctors describe the clinical state of cancer of the cervix by stages which can be represented as follows:

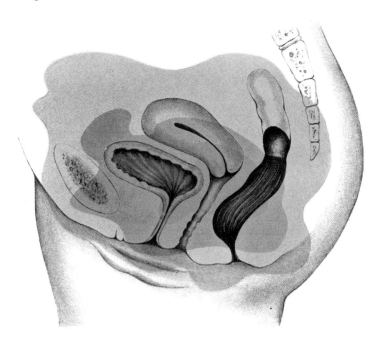

Stage 1
Pre-invasive cancer or cancer in situ.
Stage 2
Micro-invasive cancer (groups of malignant cells can be seen clustered together ready to invade the tissues).
Stage 3
Invasive cancer confined to the cervix.
Stage 4
Cancer extending to the upper two-thirds of the vaginal wall but not into the pelvis.
Stage 5
Cancer extending down to the lower one-third of the vaginal wall and extending into the pelvis.
Stage 6
Advanced cancer of the cervix with invasion into the bladder and/or rectum and beyond the pelvis.

Is there any way I can prevent cancer of the cervix developing?
The most important aspect in preventing cancer of the cervix is to have regular Pap smears. Medical studies have shown that the only way to improve the chances of a cure is to make the diagnosis early. The cure depends on the extent of the cancer when you first see your doctor. If you attend a gynecology or prenatal clinic you should have a Pap smear done as routine. You can help your daughters, too, by warning them of the dangers of sexual intercourse in early adolescence and coitus with several partners.

Treatment of cervical cancer
For invasive cancer of the cervix two forms of therapy – surgery and radiotherapy – have given equally good results, and different medical centers will use one or the other or a combination of both. Often the form of treatment chosen depends on the stage of the disease. In stages 4 and 5, for instance, palliative radiotherapy alone may be used, as surgical intervention cannot arrest the progress of the disease.

The news, however, is generally good. Even if the disease has reached an invasive stage the chances of it being controlled and reversed through surgery or radiotherapy or a combination of both, are excellent, particularly if it is caught in stages 1 and 2. After surgery, 90% of stage 1 cancers are cured five years after the operation. If radiotherapy is used for these same cases, 86% will be cured at five years after treatment has begun.

Surgical treatment

This is nearly always fairly extensive and involves removal of the uterus, the ovaries, the fallopian tubes, the upper half of the vagina and certain muscles and glands from inside the pelvis. The post-operative effects of hysterectomy are discussed elsewhere (see p. 296). Additionally, cryosurgery (freezing) can be used to eliminate abnormal cells as can electrocauterization, whereby intense heat is used to destroy the tissue. Complications following both procedures are rare.

Radiotherapy

This is the chosen treatment for nearly half the cases of cancer of the cervix. The aim is to deliver a fatal dose of radiation to the center of the cancer but also to cure those parts of the growth that are invading other areas. Quite often a radioactive palette is placed inside the vagina, or the cervical canal itself, and usually this is augmented with deep X-ray therapy to catch any spread to the outer parts of the pelvis. The cure rates for the various stages are shown in the table (left).

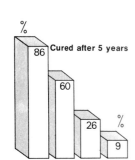

%

86	Cured after 5 years
60	
26	%
9	

Stage 1   2   3   4

If I have cancer of the cervix, do I have to have a hysterectomy?

The answer is "no" if it is in the pre-invasive state. Even so, the treatment of carcinoma *in situ* is different in different medical centers. Some doctors use a radical approach because they believe that the majority of cancers *in situ* will eventually progress to invasive cancer. They, therefore, feel that total hysterectomy is the treatment of choice. If, on the other hand, microscopic examination shows that cone biopsy has entirely removed the cancer, further treatment may be deferred, *provided* that the patient is followed up regularly with smears. In yet other medical centers with a more conservative attitude, few patients are treated by hysterectomy; the majority are given cone biopsies, repeat biopsies and regular smear tests.

What are my chances of having my cancer cured?

Your chances of curing frank malignant disease of the cervix is largely in your hands. You must have your annual Pap smear test done without fail, and if it is caught in the pre-invasive state there is absolutely no reason why you should not obtain a 100% cure. Even in stage 1 the chance of a 90% cure is extremely high. So if you take personal responsibility for the health of your own body and for preventing disease from developing, then there is no reason why you should fear cancer of the cervix. Even if your positive smear test does show the presence of cancer cells, and the chances are that if you had a negative smear test done twelve months earlier the cancer will still be in the pre-invasive state, then there is absolutely no reason why you should feel hopeless about your cancer. Discuss it fully with your gynecologist, explore all the methods of treatment, be co-operative and go into the treatment with a positive attitude. Welcome the interest and suggestions of your surgeon and look forward to a long, healthy and happy life.

UTERINE CANCER

In terms of your age, carcinoma of the body of the uterus is quite the opposite of cervical cancer. It is a disease of old women: 75% of patients are over the age of fifty and only 4% under the age of forty. Between the ages of fifty-five and sixty-four the incidence rises very steeply; in fact, it more than doubles from 15.9 cases per 100,000 to 36.6 cases. The increase in recent years is probably due to an increasing proportion of older women in the general population. There are thirty-seven thousand new cases of cancer of the uterus reported every year in the United States and about three thousand deaths.

Like cancer of the cervix, pre-invasive, pre-cancerous forms of the disease may exist for years or even decades before the condition becomes frankly malignant. Cancer of the uterus is found more commonly in women who have benign fibroids, and about half of all the women with uterine cancer are found to have latent diabetes.

Factors associated with uterine cancer

These are markedly different from cervical carcinoma. The incidence is highest among virgins; women who have no children; women of low fertility, possibly with hormonal imbalance and irregular menstruation; and women of the upper socio-economic groups.

One of the main anxieties that has been raised about estrogen therapy (when given without progestogen) is the possibility of increasing the tendency to develop cancer of the uterus. Reports supporting this hypothesis can be scientifically criticized on the grounds of biased patient selection, inadequate medical supervision, inappropriate hormone therapy and unclear descriptions of the uterine tissues examined.

So far there is no objective proof that there is a cause-and-effect relationship between estrogen treatment, properly given, and the development of uterine cancer. Indeed, one very large American study has shown that there are fewer cases of uterine cancer in women taking estrogen plus progestogen, than in the normal population.

Women in a high-risk category

The following women have a greater chance of developing uterine cancer; all should be on the lookout for the signs and symptoms:
- Women who are grossly overweight;
- Women who have a family history of uterine cancer;
- Women who used DES during pregnancy (see p. 289);
- Women with high blood pressure, diabetes, and fibroids;
- Women with estrogen-producing tumors of the ovaries;
- Women who have disturbed menstrual patterns with, for instance, long intervals between periods;
- Women with impaired fertility due to the lack of ovulation;
- Women with few or no pregnancies.

Symptoms of uterine cancer

By far the earliest and commonest sign of uterine cancer is abnormal vaginal bleeding, reported by about 80% of women with this cancer. Bleeding can be inter-menstrual (i.e. between periods), spotting, or very heavy and prolonged, either at period time or between periods. It may be a sign of the disease in post-menopausal women who stopped menstruating earlier.

As the cancer progresses it produces other symptoms, like cramping pain of the lower abdomen, somewhat similar to early labor pains; a feeling of pelvic discomfort and distention; and pressure in the lower part of the abdomen. It may cause bladder distress and the necessity to empty the bladder more frequently than usual. There may be bleeding after intercourse. Occasionally, a routine Pap smear may detect uterine cancer cells, but this happens in less than half of all the women who are found to have uterine cancer.

Forming a diagnosis
More often than not, the diagnosis is clinched after the suggestive symptoms have led to dilation and curettage (p. 197) of the uterine lining and malignant cells are found on microscopic examination of the scrapings.

Treatment of uterine cancer
The treatment, of choice, is total hysterectomy with removal of the ovaries and the fallopian tubes (see p. 295). In nearly all clinics, the surgical treatment is combined with radiotherapy, both before and after the operation. Most studies show that preparation of patients prior to treatment is very important: all the internal functions of the body should be checked, including the function of the kidneys and the bladder. It is important to take chest X-rays, to correct any anemia which may exist, and to eradicate any pelvic, uterine or cervical infections.

Occasionally, "extended" total hysterectomy is performed in which the top of the vagina is removed and the glands of the pelvis are dissected out. It is fairly routine to give four to six weeks of radio-therapy to all patients after hysterectomy.

If the cancer has spread to involve the pelvis, or distant sites in the body, then surgical treatment is obviously not suitable. Also it is extremely debilitating to give radiotherapy to wide areas of the body. In these latter cases, large doses of progesterone have given hopeful results and there have even been reports of complete disappearance of the primary cancer and secondary deposits in the vagina and the lung after high-dose progesterone therapy.

What are my chances of recovery from uterine cancer?
As with cancer of the cervix, prevention lies mainly with you. The likelihood of a thirty-five-year-old woman developing cancer is 1 in 70. And as with cancer of the cervix, the prognosis for a cure depends on the spread of the cancer at the time the patient seeks treatment.

The news is good. The overall cure-rate is as high as 90% when the cancer is localized to the lining of the womb itself. It is as high as 80% after five years if the cancer has only spread down to the muscle of the uterus. However, if it is embedded deeper than this, the figure is reduced to 40%. This means that if you spot any of the symptoms which are suggestive of uterine cancer you must seek help immediately.

OVARIAN CYSTS

The majority of growths in the ovary are benign. Doctors use the term *cystic ovary* to indicate the presence of a normal cyst in the ovary. The words "ovarian cyst," however, indicate a malignant growth. As a cyst expands, the ovarian tissue thins out and may eventually become a thin layer which completely surrounds the cyst. Some cysts have been known to grow up to 20 ins (50 cms) in diameter and are filled with a thick gelatinous material which very rarely escapes into the pelvic cavity.

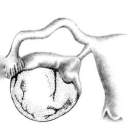

Occasionally, instead of bursting and releasing an egg, a follicle does not ovulate but continues to grow, accumulating fluid and producing estrogen.

Ovarian cells are primitive – they are the cells from which a baby grows and therefore they possess the potential to produce all the tissues in the body. It is quite common for hair, teeth, bone and cartilage to be found inside an ovarian tumor; teeth quite often show up on an X-ray of the abdomen.

A tumor of the ovary which is malignant is variable in size and is usually solid and firm, although there may be cystic areas in the center of the tumor. However, it may be impossible for a gynecologist to distinguish between a malignant and benign tumor simply by examining your abdomen or even by internal examination. Surgical removal will be required, whatever the type of ovarian cyst, and only microscopic examination of the cyst distinguishes a malignant from a benign tumor. The likelihood of the cyst being cancerous increases as you get older.

Symptoms of an ovarian cyst

Small ovarian cysts give rise to very few symptoms but as they get bigger, abdominal swelling may be noticed. When very large they may cause pressure, leading to breathlessness, bladder distress with frequency of urination, pressure on the veins of the legs causing varicose veins or swelling of the ankles, and intestinal or digestive disorders like vomiting and constipation.

Ovarian tumors very rarely cause vaginal bleeding unless they are producing estrogen. Then they may result in irregular bleeding and, in very young girls, precocious development of female sex characteristics such as the breasts and nipples.

Sudden severe pain is rare but does occur if an ovarian cyst grows on a stalk which becomes twisted, if there is a hemorrhage into the cyst, and if a large ovarian cyst ruptures. Alert your doctor immediately if you have an ovarian cyst and experience sudden pain. Infection in an ovarian cyst is now very uncommon.

Diagnosis of an ovarian cyst

The diagnosis of an ovarian cyst is suspected by feeling a large lump in the abdomen, but it can only be clinched by exploratory surgery. In some centers, a preliminary laparoscopy (the abdomen is opened and the ovary is looked at directly by the surgeon and the wound then closed, without intervention) or investigation with a fiberscope may be done by surgeons, according to their routine practice. Diagnosis of *malignancy* can only be made for certain if the tumor is biopsied and examined microscopically. Most surgeons would prefer to do this after complete removal of the ovary, rather than by taking a small specimen of the ovarian tissue during laparoscopy or during fiber optic examination.

287

Surgical procedure

Before you have any surgical investigation, make sure that you discuss the matter fully with your surgeon and decide upon a plan of action according to what s/he will find there at the operation. Exercise your rights to see your surgical and histological report when your operation has been completed.

For a benign tumor

If the tumor is benign your surgeon will almost certainly remove the tumor and leave the rest of your ovary in place. Your body will continue to secrete your female hormones and you will not experience an artificial menopause, requiring hormone replacement therapy, for several years. Cysts sometimes affect both ovaries and it may be possible, even if one tumor can't be dissected out, for your surgeon to remove only one ovary. The remaining one will maintain your normal hormone levels. Make sure that you discuss the possibility with your surgeon and ask her/him to do this if at all possible.

It is even possible for a surgeon to remove a substantial part of both ovaries but leave enough ovarian tissue behind so that hormone deficiency problems are avoided.

For a malignant tumor

If a diagnosis of ovarian cancer is made, your surgeon will remove not just the tumor but both ovaries, your uterus and fallopian tubes as well. There is the possibility, if the malignant tumor is small, and your surgeon can be certain at the time of operation (by performing freeze-dried section while the operation is going on and obtaining a rapid histological report to show that the tumor is confined to one ovary or part of an ovary) that the cancer is *slow growing*, that only the tumor and one ovary be removed.

What is the prognosis for these cysts?

The future outlook of treatment of the vast majority of ovarian growths is good; the surgical treatment of benign ovarian cysts is invariably curative.

But for those few women who do have malignant ovarian growths the prognosis is not so good. As with other cancers of the genital tract, the most important factor in the prognosis of the disease is the extent to which it has developed and spread at the time of treatment. If the growth is entirely confined to the ovary then the cure rate at five years after the operation can be higher than 90%.

What are the implications of having a radical operation?

If the surgeon removes your ovaries, fallopian tubes and uterus you will be unable to become pregnant, you will have an artificial menopause and may have to take hormone replacement therapy.

It is important to come to terms with these facts and, if necessary, ask your surgeon if you can speak to a psychotherapist or psychological counselor before the operation. Never have this operation performed without involving your partner in your thoughts, anxieties and any future implications.

Is a radical operation always preferred?

If you have a slow-growing type of ovarian tumour, a non-radical operation is one of the best options for you; it will leave your uterus and one functioning ovary intact which means that you may be able to become pregnant again in the future, and that your sex hormones will be produced normally. You will, in other words, be a "whole" woman, and a healthy one at that.

DIETHYLSTILBESTROL (DES)

Between 1940 and 1971, DES, an artificial estrogen, was used to prevent miscarriage in early pregnancy. In 1971 doctors working at Massachusetts General Hospital in Boston reported a significantly higher incidence of cancer of the vagina in the daughters of mothers who had received DES when carrying them, than in the rest of the population. Furthermore, 90% of these daughters had an abnormal growth of glandular tissue of the cervix and the vagina though, in most cases, this particular cell change did not progress to cancer.

More recently, there have been reports that between 75% and 80% of young women who were exposed to DES *in utero* may have abnormalities of the uterus as well, and it is possible that these women may have a higher incidence of incompetent cervix when they get pregnant than other women.

It is therefore essential that daughters of women who were given DES are properly monitored and followed up. So far, there are no strict guidelines as to how this should be done but there is no doubt that they should be referred to a gynecologist or obstetrician who is familiar with DES-induced changes, and that this should be done before puberty if possible.

A girl should be examined internally at about the age of fourteen (or whenever she starts to have menstrual periods). At that time she should also have biopsies of the cervix and the vagina and colposcopic examination.

Boys exposed to DES *in utero*, may also suffer genital abnormality such as cysts, small testicles and low sperm counts. However, a sufficient number of male children have not been followed for long enough to come to a reliable medical conclusion. But it is a good idea if there has been exposure to DES that an annual examination be undertaken.

Some recent medical reports suggest that women who took DES for threatened miscarriage may have a higher risk of developing breast cancer than ordinary women. They should follow the guidelines suggested for women falling into this risk category (see p. 263).

Almost certainly, the routine checkups on women who have taken DES, and children of both sexes who have been exposed to DES *in utero*, will change over the next few years so you should stay in touch with your family doctor, or with your gynecologist, so that you and your children can take advantage of any new preventive measures.

289

ENDOMETRIOSIS

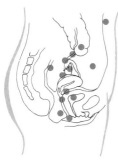

Endometrial implants can occur deep in the uterine muscle, on the surface of the uterus, on the ovaries, on the broad ligaments, or anywhere else in the pelvis. Sometimes they are found in the vagina and cervix, infrequently on the vulva and perineum, and rarely on the arm, leg and lung.

This has been called the career woman's disease, quite wrongly to my mind; it's not a consequence of having a career, nor do only women with careers suffer from it. It seems to me that this misnomer has arisen from incorrectly correlating two statistics: endometriosis usually starts in the late twenties; more women have careers in their late twenties than ever before.

The seeds of endometriosis are sown while a baby girl is developing *in utero*. Small nests of endometrial cells "stray" into the pelvis, ovaries, tubes and even the bladder. They form tiny cysts. With each period, they bleed with the rest of the endometrium, but there are no symptoms until the cysts become stretched and swollen. This may take ten or fifteen years.

The symptoms may be chronic lower abdominal pain, dysmenorrhea, dyspareunia and difficulty in conceiving if the tubes are involved.

Diagnosis can only be made for certain if the blood-filled cysts can be seen, i.e. at laparoscopy or by fiber optic examination. The cysts can be anything from pin-head size to the size of a walnut. There may be 1 or 2 or 100. They look dark-bluish purple and may be scattered over the pelvic organs.

Treatment is not always satisfactory, though courses of progestogens have been successful in some women. Some women find that they get benefit from the pill, though high dose ones give the best results and these are no longer advocated by doctors.

If there are only a few cysts, your gynecologist may suggest surgically scraping them off, but this is obviously impractical if the cysts are numerous. If the condition is extensive or your symptoms severe, your surgeon may recommend hysterectomy as a permanent cure.

PROLAPSE

A prolapse, or "pelvic relaxation" as it is sometimes called, occurs when the pelvic musculature becomes weakened and allows part of the pelvic organs to protrude or drop out of position. It is especially noticeable when intra-abdominal pressure is increased on coughing or straining at stool, or it occurs simply due to the downpull of gravity. The affected organs include the uterus, bladder, rectum and urethra; the uterus is the most likely one to collapse. The various types of prolapse include:

Urethrocele

This is a bulge of the lower front wall of the vagina which contains the urethra and, as this may irritate the urethral lining, it can often lead to frequency of urination.

Rectocele

This is a bulging of the front wall of the rectum into the rear wall of the vagina. Quite a lot of discomfort is experienced on moving the bowels and defecation may only become bearable if a finger is placed in the vagina to support the rear wall.

Cystocele
This is a bulging of the bladder into the upper front wall of the vagina, and is nearly always accompanied by bladder symptoms and possibly recurrent cystitis. Sometimes the bladder sags below the level of the urethral outlet which makes emptying the bladder extremely difficult. In such cases it may be emptied by inserting a finger into the vagina and elevating the sagging part.

Uterine prolapse
Due to loss of support from pelvic ligaments and muscles, the uterus can descend from the pelvic cavity into the vaginal canal. While there may be no discomfort from a uterus that has slipped partially into the vagina, low backaches and a slipping-down sensation are discernible in more serious cases. In addition, the cervix will prevent deep penile penetration during intercourse. First degree prolapse is when the cervix does not protrude beyond the vaginal opening; second degree prolapse is when the cervix begins to protrude from the vagina; third degree prolapse is when the entire uterus protrudes from the vaginal entrance.

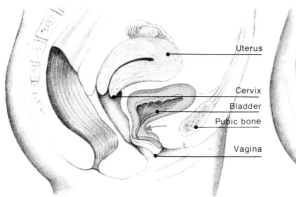

Uterus
Cervix
Bladder
Pubic bone
Vagina

Urethrocele

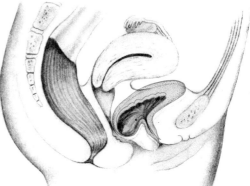

Cystocele

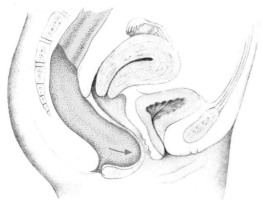

Rectocele

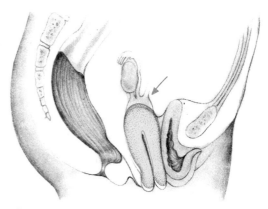

Uterine prolapse

Causes of prolapse

A prolapse is nearly always caused by injury to the pelvic floor muscles, or to the cervix and its supporting tissue, during delivery. The commonest causes are the consequences of child-bearing, such as too rapid a delivery, when a woman may tear the cervix by bearing down before it is fully dilated. If a baby has a very large head and the mother a small pelvis, and if the second stage of labor is prolonged, stretching and tearing may occur. It can also be caused by a forceps delivery if forceps are applied when the head of the infant is still very high.

Occasionally, the same conditions that produce hernias in men, such as strenuous physical or athletic activity, can produce them in women. Obesity, constipiation and chronic cough all aggravate the condition because they increase the intra-abdominal pressure and help to slacken the pelvic muscles even more.

Symptoms of prolapse

A woman with a prolapse nearly always feels tired and she may experience a dragging down sensation in the pelvis. This condition may be relieved, to a certain extent, by wearing a girdle and by resting whenever you can with your feet up.

Backache is also quite a common symptom. It is very important not to stand for long periods, to maintain good posture and to rest whenever you can.

The vagina may become so slack that both you and your partner may have difficulty in reaching orgasm due to lack of friction. In addition, you may find sexual relations uncomfortable because of the pressure from the descending organs.

One of the most troublesome symptoms of a prolapse is the uncontrollable escape of urine from the bladder which may occur at any time. It quite often starts as "cough incontinence," the leakage appearing because of a slight increase in intra-abdominal pressure when you cough. Leakage may become so bad that you have to wear special pads or napkins most of the time. This kind of incontinence is called *stress incontinence* and you should never ever let your symptoms reach the point where sanitary protection is necessary. You should consult your doctor long before then.

Treatment of prolapse

There are really only two ways of treating prolapse. The first is by conservative or mechanical methods, without any surgical intervention, and the second is reparative surgery.

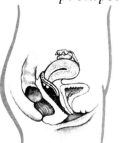

Hard rubber vaginal pessaries can be fitted to help support sagging pelvic organs.

Conservative methods

For older women, where the prolapse is not very severe, or where their infirmity makes a general anesthetic inadvisable, a ring pessary is usually placed in the vagina. It should not be worn for very long periods because it may erode thin, senile tissues simply by friction.

Surgical methods

Hysterectomy (the uterus is removed and the torn or stretched tissue replaced) is the usual surgery to correct this problem and can be tackled by the intra-vaginal or abdominal routes, depending on the severity of the prolapse.

A severe prolapse should be approached radically, and this must be done by abdominal surgery. Only certain forms of prolapse are amenable to surgery via the vaginal route, namely mild forms of prolapse where the uterus and cervix are still high and well supported.

The prolapse repair is a major abdominal operation and may take several weeks for full recovery. Discuss all the after-effects with your surgeon and make sure that you are psychologically prepared for the operation (see p. 296).

Do my chances of experiencing a prolapse increase with age?

I'm afraid that advancing age is one of the commoner causes of prolapse and if the pelvic musculature is weakened, it can only become worse in time, especially as your estrogen levels drop.

Does having an episiotomy prevent prolapse?

Contrary to popular practice, episiotomies are not effective in preventing prolapse as they do not affect the muscles which support the upper vagina and which are involved in the most common forms of prolapse – cystocele, rectocele or uterine prolapse.

Is there any non-surgical treatment I can try?

If your condition does not yet involve incontinence, you may be able to prevent it becoming worse by performing pelvic exercises (see p. 120), stopping strenuous activity, losing weight if you are fat, and stopping smoking – especially if you are coughing.

If you haven't yet completed your family you'll have to put off surgery anyway as a vaginal delivery rapidly undermines any plastic surgery repair of a prolapse.

HYSTERECTOMY

In the United States, 25% of all women aged fifty and over have had hysterectomies. Hysterectomy means surgical removal of the uterus, and other reproductive organs may be excised (see p. 294).

Very often, and particularly in the United States, hysterectomy is performed for no very good reason, such as the removal of small fibroids, and some American doctors even advocate routine hysterectomy once childbearing is over. They do this on the judgement that they are forestalling any risk of cancer. But many doctors in the United States, and most doctors elsewhere in the world, view this attitude as charlatanism. Some American doctors have suggested that hysterectomy should be a combined abortion and sterilization procedure for poor women with large families. But again this is generally disapproved of by the medical profession because hysterectomy within three months of conception is dangerous for the mother, and, secondly, very often impoverished patients cannot afford the hormone replacement therapy necessary to treat the resulting severe menopausal symptoms if the ovaries are removed.

Hysterectomy may be the end of your fertile life, but it does not have to affect your sexual life adversely.

Reasons for hysterectomy

Hysterectomy is absolutely necessary only when a life-threatening disease is diagnosed.

There are several clear-cut situations in which a hysterectomy is necessary; in each case the woman is suffering from a life-threatening disease:

● To remove cancer in the vagina, cervix, uterus, fallopian tubes and ovaries;

● To treat severe and uncontrollable pelvic infection;

● To stop severe, uncontrollable hemorrhage;

● In certain conditions affecting the intestines or the bladder, which threaten the life of the woman, and when it is technically impossible to deal with the primary problem without removing the uterus.

HYSTERECTOMY OPERATIONS

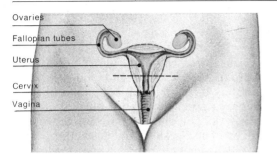

Total abdominal hysterectomy
This is removal of the uterus and the cervix through a horizontal incision in the lower abdomen. The fallopian tubes and ovaries are left behind.

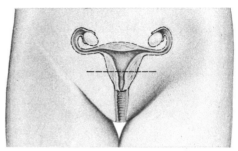

Total abdominal hysterectomy and bi-lateral salpingo-oophorectomy (complete hysterectomy)
This is removal of the uterus, cervix, fallopian tubes and ovaries through a transverse incision in the lower abdomen.

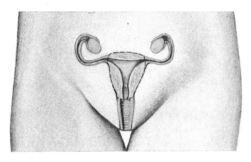

Vaginal hysterectomy
Removal of the uterus and cervix through an incision inside the vagina. The fallopian tubes and ovaries are left behind.

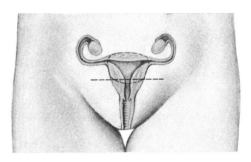

Sub-total hysterectomy
Removal of the uterus, but the cervix, fallopian tubes and ovaries are not removed. This operation is not done very often because the cervix on its own has no essential function. It is argued that it should be removed as a future cancer risk.

Elective hysterectomy

Some non-life-threatening conditions are considered grounds for hysterectomy, as long as there is full prior discussion with the patient and, if she is young, with her partner as well. It may be considered when alternative treatment for serious problems has been ineffective, or where the gynecologist knows from experience that present problems may become more severe in the future. If possible, emergency hysterectomy should be postponed as it carries a higher surgical risk than elective surgery. Here are some of the conditions in which elective hysterectomy may be justified:
● Extensive and very painful endometriosis;
● Large or multiple fibroid tumors (benign growths of the muscle of the endometrium);
● Injury to the pelvic muscular structure at childbirth which is severe enough to interfere with bowel or bladder function;
● Recurrent and severe attacks of pelvic infection;
● Vaginal bleeding that is so heavy that anemia results and it is impossible to control with hormone treatment.

The effects of hysterectomy

Whatever the reason that is given to you for hysterectomy make sure that you question your gynecologist closely so that you are satisfied in your own mind that it is necessary and that you want it and that your partner agrees with you. Hysterectomy is an irrevocable step. After it you are sterile. If the ovaries are removed as well, you will be menopausal after the operation. You may well suffer menopausal symptoms (see p. 248) and you will need hormone replacement therapy for a considerable period of time. Many women are concerned that they will put on weight after hysterectomy but this is a myth. You only put on weight if you eat excessively. A diet rich in proteins, fresh vegetables and fruit will help recovery and give you sufficient energy for you to undertake exercises to tone up flabby muscles. Other women are concerned about their sex drive. Research has shown that an equal number of women experience increased sexual desire as experience a diminution in sex drive.

Psychological effects of hysterectomy

A great deal of detailed research has been done on the after-effects of hysterectomy, mostly on American women, but the results are so dramatic and convincing that every woman should consider them before agreeing to a hysterectomy. Some of the conclusions which have been reached from the American studies are:
- While patients and gynecologists are extremely happy with the operation immediately after it is done, patients grow more dissatisfied with it as time passes.
- Patients are more likely to be dissatisfied with the operation if the ovaries are also removed because the tendency is to blame the operation for hot flashes, lethargy and obesity, and very often the patient is right to do this, suffering as she does from a true hormone deficiency. *Always* ask your doctor if it is absolutely necessary to remove your ovaries.
- Women who have hysterectomies are four times more likely to become depressed in the three years after hysterectomy than other women.
- Women who have had hysterectomies are likely to remain depressed for twice as long – on average two years – than women who have not.
- If you are under 40 when you have your hysterectomy you are especially liable to suffer from depression after the operation.
- Women who have had a hysterectomy are five times more likely to visit a psychiatrist for the first time than women who have not had the operation. The time you are most likely to seek your first consultation with a psychiatrist is about two years after the operation.
- By far the majority of women who seek psychiatric help following a hysterectomy are those who are given the operation for causes other than a serious or life-threatening condition. These statistics suggest that many hysterectomies are performed unnecessarily. In patients for whom the operation was absolutely necessary, serious or longterm psychiatric illness is less likely.
- Despite some unfavorable statistics, 41% of women are satisfied with the operation four years afterwards.

Recovery from a hysterectomy

A hysterectomy involves major abdominal surgery and like any other major operation it will take you some time to recover from it completely. You will almost certainly remain in the hospital for five or six days and then you will be expected to convalesce at home for about six weeks. To give you a timetable of the speed at which you should expect recovery I've drawn up the following chart:

TIMETABLE OF RECOVERY AFTER HYSTERECTOMY

Week 1
You'll be encouraged to get out of bed in one or two days. You may have pain and discomfort from wound. You may find urination difficult (tell the nursing staff), you may need an I.V. drip for 24/36 hours until you take solid food, then minor wind pains.

Week 2
Home at 7 to 10 days. Don't stay in bed but take it easy. No moderate activity e.g. walking ¾ mile for three more weeks. Can walk upstairs, sit in garden. Don't carry any weights or lift anything heavy.

Week 3
Gradually increase activities and take rest periods rather than rest most of the time and being active occasionally. Go to bed early.

Week 4
Start a few very gentle activities, walk around the garden, go for car rides. Try slowly making the bed to see if you can stretch a little (STOP IF ANY PAIN).

Week 5
Start moderate activity – going to the shops and doing light shopping, do light housework, walk the dog. Go to the hairdressers. Do gentle mobility exercises (see p. 38). Stop if you feel tired. Don't bend to the floor or lift.

Week 6
Start getting back to normal. Start doing routine housework. Do mobility exercises every day plus some strengthening exercises. You may still feel tired at end of day or even in the middle so rest with feet up for 15–20 minutes. Start bending gently but not to floor. Don't lift.

Week 7
You should be back to full normal activity. Continue exercises. Sexual intercourse safe and possible. Rest once a day with feet up.

Week 8
You can go back to work if it's sedentary. The rest of your life should be entirely normal. Don't bend to floor. Don't lift.

Week 9, Week 10
You can safely bend fully and lift.

What are the alternatives to a hysterectomy?

In certain cases where cell changes may be tending towards cancer, doctors have used successfully *cryosurgery* (freezing a section of tissue before removal) or laser surgery (the beam is focused on cells and destroys them). Cone biopsy (see p. 282) may also be sufficient for certain conditions of the cervix.

If fibroid tumors are a problem, a *myomectomy*, where the tumors alone and not the uterus are removed, can sometimes be performed. It is not a serious operation and the ability to bear children is preserved.

Should I get a second opinion before having a hysterectomy?

Definitely, yes. Hysterectomy is among the operations most often rejected by another doctor. One of the most frequently performed operations on women, it is often cited as a surgical abuse.

Will my sex life be affected?

A good proportion (10–39%) of women complain of sexual problems post-operatively. Although sex drive may not be affected, psychological problems due to the loss of fertility and loss of sensation upon the removal of uterus and cervix may be responsible for resulting sexual difficulties.

THREATS TO MENTAL WELL-BEING

There is no doubt that modern women are subject to more psychological strain than ever before. Paradoxically, we women have brought a good deal on ourselves and I feel strongly that we have to do a lot of work to extricate ourselves from the "Catch 22" we find ourselves in.

Don't misunderstand me; in many aspects of their lives women are pressurized as no human being has ever been pressurized – single-parents, working mothers with young children, battered wives confined to their homes by pre-school children, working mothers with divided loyalties and resentful husbands – all are stressed in a unique way, for either sex.

But one of the greatest causes of mental ill-health is a disparity between expectation and achievement, between make-believe and reality, between hope and actual result. Women have been made, by the more strident voices in the feminist movement and the media, to feel that if they don't enter successfully into a male-dominated world, if they don't make up for some of the imaginary lost time and play the field, if they don't feverishly fulfill every aspiration, then they're inadequate or a failure. Of course they're no such thing.

Happiness and mental well-being are not about playing out a fictitious role conjured up by journalists and authors. Happiness is about coming to terms with reality. One of the most important parts of that is learning what you want to do, deciding to do it to the best of your ability, and not feeling inadequate because it doesn't happen to coincide with what you think you *ought* to do. Forget what you ought to do. Learn to live with yourself. Most importantly, learn to love yourself for what you are, warts and all.

STRESS

Hospital admission figures for mental illness for women are double that of men.

Recently when I interviewed a leading authority on preventive cardiology, he said that to be alive and living in the Western world is about as stressful a form of life as you an think of. Human beings are not really very well designed to live under such conditions, for every aspect of Western life has an element of stress. Our society is success-oriented and the competitiveness and the desire to succeed which surrounds most of us in our working life is a stress we would rather be without. While the media has tended to concentrate on stress as it affects men, women have become increasingly susceptible to stress and its related illnesses. This is particularly true of working women, and research done during International Woman's Year (1976) proved that the hardest working person, and the one most liable to stress, is a full-time working woman, wife and mother.

There is quite a lot of evidence to show that a moderate degree of stress can be good for us – it improves performance, efficiency, productivity and many of us thrive on it. Indeed, there are some people who *need* stress and function at maximum efficiency when they are under stress. But they are rare. For most of us, if stress goes beyond a certain point, everything disintegrates and this can lead to both mental and physical illness. It is, therefore, very important for all of us to come to terms with what causes us stress, to recognize the part that it plays in our health or, conversely, ill-health, and finally to try and find out how we can get rid of it or cope with it.

Responses to stress

There is both a physical and an emotional response to stress. The physical one is dependent on hormones and constitutes the well known "fight or flight" reflex. It used to be thought that a woman responded differently in a physical sense to stress than a man; however, recent work in Sweden has shown that women have exactly the same hormonal response.

When we become stressed, the brain sends messages to the two adrenal glands which lie on the top of the kidneys. This electrical message is recognized instantaneously and the body begins to pump out adrenalin. The physical effects of adrenalin are those which we would all recognize:
- The blood vessels in the skin and internal organs constrict to make a large volume of blood available to the muscles of the body so that they are primed and ready to run;
- The heart begins to pound quickly so that the maximum amount of blood is being pumped round the body to make it ready for any kind of action;
- Simultaneously the rate of breathing increases so that our blood carries the optimum amount of oxygen for our muscles to work efficiently;
- Our blood pressure increases so that our essential organs become well supplied with blood;
- Our pupils enlarge so that we can see both what is frightening us and a route away from it, as clearly as possible;
- The blood sugar level rises steeply which makes available a large amount of energy which we will need to use if we either have to fight or flee.

Emotional response to stress is more individual and is affected by sex, cultural background, heredity, environment and by the ways in which we have been taught to deal with it. For instance, in most societies it is acceptable for women to become upset and cry while little boys are encouraged to face stress with a stiff upper lip and hold back the tears.

The "fight or flight" mechanism, although often called up, is rarely exercised. Most stressful situations (see right) cannot be

Normal pupil

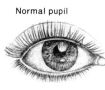

Pupil enlarged by fright

resolved by fighting or fleeing, yet adrenalin is pumped into the body which acts on it as previously described. However, even if we remain inactive, the adrenalin is not switched off. The body remains tensed for action which never comes. The resulting tension and frustration promote further stress – a vicious cycle worth breaking.

Causes of stress

The body's "fight or flight" reaction is triggered by many situations. Short-term stress, as occurs when we're stopped for speeding or have our house burgled, may happen only once and can be successfully dealt with at the time, unless it becomes habitual, see p. 304. Long-term stress is the result of certain events which occur in our lives, over which we have little or no control. Difficult working conditions, sexual and/or partnership problems, illness, involvement with the police, and death, especially if it is a close member of the family, are all situations difficult to cope with which can cause varying degrees of stress.

Stress scale
Two doctors, Dr. Thomas H. Holmes and Dr. Richard H. Rahe of the University of Washington in Seattle, designed a stress scale of 43 events which may occur to all of us and assigned to them a number of points out of 100 which indicated the degree of stress. According to Drs. Holmes and Rahe, when the points for a person in any twelve month period add up to a total of 150, then that person has about a 40% chance of illness. If the score is as high as 300, then the person has an 80% chance.

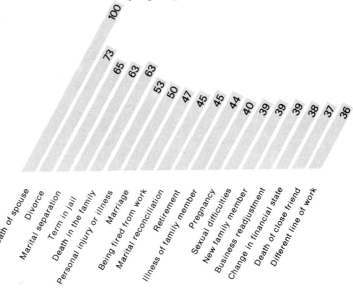

Personal score

Consequences of stress

As we have seen, stress calls forth strong responses from the body and if it is continuous or frequent, it can cause a large number of physical and mental illnesses. For instance, if the blood pressure remains raised for any length of time, this leads to damage of the arteries and possibly a heart attack. (However, illness usually occurs only when pressures are so great that a person is no longer able to cope; see chart, p. 301.) Certain classical conditions are stress-related – migraine headache is one of them and this may lead to dependency on analgesics in susceptible people. Skin conditions like eczema (dermatitis) and itching of the skin are also made worse by anxiety and stress. A group of disorders which doctors describe as "functional" have a background of stress and these include spastic colon, dyspepsia and duodenal ulcers.

Some major and life-threatening diseases are also linked to stress, such as severe, chronic high blood pressure, heart disease, peptic ulcers, arthritis, asthma and diabetes. It has even been shown that when people are under stress they are more susceptible to infection, particularly viral diseases, and some authorities claim that the development of cancer can be directly related to stress.

Certain stress-related problems are specific to women. These include menstrual disorders, pelvic pains, sexual difficulties, premenstrual retention of fluid, unwanted hair growth, disturbances of ovarian function leading to failure to ovulate. (This in turn leads to amenorrhea [lack of periods] and infertility.)

Symptoms of stress

Stress may lead to quite a list of symptoms which you yourself can interpret as the warning signs that your fuse wire is about to blow. Always remember that if you have any serious symptoms which you think are related to stress, go to see a doctor so that s/he can give proper treatment, if necessary. If the doctor feels your symptoms are emotional or psychological in origin, s/he can refer you to special clinics which will give you the help that you need.

Headaches	Insomnia	Menstrual disorders	Dry mouth	Tooth grinding
Stomach pains	Wanting to sleep	Pins and needles in	Sweaty palms	Compulsive eating
Chest pains	Diarrhea	the hands and feet	Cold hands	Muscle aches and pains
Palpitations	Constipation	Twitching eyelids	Skin rashes	due to muscle spasm

Dealing with stress

The "fight or flight" reaction prepares the body for action, not thought. Yet it is only by thinking through our difficulties that we can effect a resolution. A body pumped full of adrenalin is in a highly emotional state and one that is unable to produce rational thought – you cannot concentrate while the heart is thumping and the muscles are tensed to act. Therefore, try to distance yourself from the cause of the stress, gradually developing techniques of making it less important until finally you are able to think it through and make more permanent decisions about it.

The most important thing of all is that you cope with stress; it's much less important how you cope with it. It doesn't matter how eclectic you have to be, or how cranky some of your solutions seem to be. If they suit you and help you, go on doing them.

If stress can't be avoided, try one or all of the techniques discussed on the right.

METHODS TO HELP COMBAT STRESS

Dissociate
This means putting your worries out of your head. Some people have the facility for doing this more easily than others. If you find it difficult, persevere, because it is a trick that can be learned and brings great benefits. Try to ignore your problem for as long as possible. The longer you keep it at bay and remain calm, the more time there is for the body's fight and flight reaction to lessen, thereby reducing stress and anxiety. This simple mechanism makes it possible for you to approach the real problem and to deal with it in a calm, rational way instead of becoming very worked-up about it.

Have fun
Enjoy yourself; go out to dinner with a friend, or simply take the afternoon off to go shopping, or snatch a weekend away in the country. It's relaxing, restorative and gives you a chance to recharge your batteries. While you are having fun, and even after it, notice how most problems diminish in size.

Physical activity
Work off stress through any kind of exercise that you enjoy and are physically able to do. Physical activity of almost any kind counteracts the effects of stress and nearly always leaves you feeling more relaxed and rational about your problems. So you may find that jogging or a game of tennis or tackling a household chore (painting a wall, mopping the floor) relieves your tension.

If you are in good physical shape, and that means a regular diet and plenty of exercise (see p. 35), then you do have a better chance of coping with problems. You have greater resources to draw upon, greater resilience and greater staying power.

Relax
In order to neutralize the effects of stress on the body, have your own personal trick of drug-free relaxation, whether it's a series of special exercises to control muscles or breathing (p. 43), or a discipline such as yoga (p. 40), autogenic training or meditation (p. 44), learned from a qualified teacher. Learning to control your alpha waves or how to use a biofeedback machine (p. 45) to monitor relaxation are also useful, if unusual.

Get another opinion
Most problems which to us seem so overwhelming and individual are not uncommon. Getting advice from someone with experience in the situation, with no personal connection, can help to throw new light on the problem. Special groups like Weight Watchers and Alcoholics Anonymous are specially set up to deal with particular stressful situations. Clergymen and doctors can help put the poblem into perspective, and just talking things over can bring relief. A problem shared is a problem halved. While family and friends will often prove sympathetic and will willingly give advice, bear in mind that they are on your side and can often add fuel to an already flammable situation.

Look at the way you manage your time
Stress is often caused by mismanagement of time such as getting behind in our work or in household chores. It is important, therefore, to assign priorities to your tasks and do the important ones first. Look at the way you spend your time. If necessary, for a few days write down all of your activities, the relevance they have to sorting out your problem, and the result they achieved. At the end of this period it's quite astonishing to see how your time was spent – how much of it was wasted and how much of it was put to useful purpose. It's quite a lesson in itself just to undertake this exercise.

Scale down your expectations
Recognize your own limitations and take on only what you can accomplish in the time that you've allowed yourself. Realize that it isn't possible for you to totally control the world around you. Setting up and meeting realistic goals can lessen stress, while failing to live up to your expectations can bring it about.

You may feel that you can write better than Tolstoy and somewhere inside of you is a best-selling novel. Instead of struggling to reach a standard which most of us never attain, by all means write, and even try to have your novel published, but don't expect it to be as well received as Tolstoy, and don't expect it to be a best-seller. In other words, be realistic.

Withdraw
A more radical alternative is to cut yourself off from the situation that is causing you stress. If a relative is getting on your nerves, for example, try going away for a while. After all, out of sight is out of mind. Withdrawal, however, may involve substantial effort. If, for instance, you find that you cannot get on with your boss at work, you may have to change your job, or if you hate the house you are living in, you may have to consider moving to a new one, possibly in a new area.

Unnecessary stress Stress can be habit-forming, and, as such, it is often triggered without thought – for instance, just watching someone push ahead in line is enough to set the adrenalin flowing. Sometimes stress is caused by worries, which if not entirely imagined, often belong only to the future or to the past. Worrying about whether you will lose your job, for instance, is an example of a stressful situation which may be triggered by groundless fears. It is important to recognize such substanceless anxieties for what they are, for although the situation is imagined, the consequences are real. A stressful situation which occurred in the past, such as a domestic argument, can be recalled by the mind for the body to act upon. As you mentally recreate the situation, repeating what was said or done, your body reverts to a stressful state. It does not differentiate between a real or imagined situation. Therefore, the initial step is to discriminate between avoidable and non-avoidable stress.

What immediate action can I take?

Actually *taking* action is one of the best ways of coping with stress; doing something, doing almost anything. I have found one of the best ways to cope with stress is to start analyzing the problem on paper. You immediately begin to see written out in front of you the things that matter, the size of the problem and the scope of the solutions. It's an act which scales down the size of the stress-producing difficulty. By the time you have completed this analysis of what is causing you stress, you will have some action you have to do as soon as you stop writing, even if it's only to phone your mother or sister, or make a cup of coffee, or put on a record. So go ahead and do it.

First Begin by defining the problem clearly.

Second Write down as many optional solutions as you can think of, no matter how crazy they seem to be.

Third Select the most realistic two or three solutions to your problem.

Fourth Opt for one if you can.

Fifth Write down an action plan, taking into account each step you need to take to effect the solution.

Sixth Write down a timetable as to when you must complete each part of the action plan.

You now have a plan and a timetable. Follow it through, and you should feel less stressed. If you don't, you can always try one of the other options.

How can I cope with stress in the long term?

Although people can deal quite successfully with infrequent stress, long-term stress is a much more debilitating situation. Remember, there is no one magic technique to cope with stress although I have already pointed out ways of reducing it. A long-standing stressful situation can be relieved by immediate action but more far-reaching satisfaction can only be achieved with perseverance. If you are dissatisfied with your appearance, for instance, you can go out tomorrow and get a new hairdo, facial or make-up, but your unhappiness may be so great that you may have to consider psychiatric attention to learn to like yourself, or perhaps consider plastic surgery. Stress is an extremely personal phenomenon – both in its inception and in responses to it. Outside agents like pills or alcohol can never combat stress in the long-term, and they may lead to worse problems.

A degree of determination and will-power is necessary as well as an understanding of how you react in certain situations. It is important to exercise a good deal of control over your emotions to thrive in today's world.

Can I monitor stress in myself?

Asking yourself the questions listed below from time-to-time will prove beneficial in averting the harmful effects of stress. Be absolutely honest in answering the questions and see whether you have any of the symptoms (see p. 302). Discovering that you may be a candidate for stress is a sign that you should be considering some of the techniques set out earlier (see p. 303). If you are wise you will take action and start examining the stresses in your life and how you react to them as soon as the warning signs show, before letting them develop into serious physical or mental illness.

- Have any major stressful events occurred in the last six or nine months?
- Am I anticipating a stressful event?
- How do I feel mentally?
- How do I feel physically?
- Am I using alcohol or drugs to help me?
- Are my expectations in life too high?
- Am I satisfied with life in general?
- Do I feel in need of personal help – friends? – family?
- Do I feel in need of professional help – doctor? – social services? – psychotherapy?
- What short-term goals can I achieve?
- What long-term objectives can I set myself and attain?

ANXIETY

Anxiety is an experience closely related both to stress and depression. In fact, it can lead to stress and is an early symptom of depression. Anxiety is a fear reaction, and when it alerts us to situations we should take notice of – such as our children's welfare – it is a useful protective mechanism. However, when it occurs frequently, it can be dangerous. This is because anxiety, like stress, stimulates the adrenal glands to produce adrenalin. This substance makes the pulse quicker, the heart beat louder and the breathing shallower and more rapid. The whole body is in a state of tension – very jumpy and conscious of itself so that it's easy to concentrate on the quickening pulse and louder heartbeat. This in turn causes worry, and often we forget the original cause of the anxiety. We find problems, both real and imagined, swirl round in our brains and we are in no disposition to sort them out.

Treatment of anxiety This should center around helping to have as normal a routine as possible – eating a proper diet, drinking in moderation, getting plenty of fresh air and exercise, directing yourself outward by helping other people. Taking tranquillizers is not a good idea as they easily become addictive, at least in a psychological sense. If your anxiety is severe, this can be a terrifying experience and your doctor should always be notified. Psychotherapy can be of some help here.

Coping with anxiety Observe how your body works when it is anxious; in other words, *feel* your feelings. There is only so much adrenalin in your body that can be liberated at any one time and the worst panic feelings can subside in a few minutes. Once you've realized this try not to push your panic button again and release more adrenalin. Try to be still and wait. You'll need courage and patience. Help yourself by concentrating hard on something other than yourself and your problem. Study a picture or a pattern carefully; work through the details of it. Keep your mind off you.

Once your feelings start to come back to normal, take it easy. Stay calm. Continue what you were doing, slowly and without fuss. Don't rush yourself, take your time. Work towards a small achievable target and once you've reached that set another one, always achievable, and soon. Each small step forward will take you to your final goal which seemed so unattainable when you tried for it in one leap. Drift towards your target, don't battle your way there. If you fight you'll be pressing your alarm button and the frightening feelings will return.

You can break any unpleasant thought or feeling by closing your eyes and listening hard. Try it. Once you've learned this, your fears will subside. You're well on the way to being able to deal with life's stresses and to control your feelings. That self-knowledge is liberating.

Remember, your feelings can never harm you. Repeat it over to yourself until you believe it.

DEPRESSION

We all experience variations in mood – normal variations – and most of us have mood cycles or mood swings. We should expect them, we should learn to deal with them, and we should not be afraid when they occur. Just as we have a consistent temperature which is the result of our bodies automatically reacting to changes in the environment and putting into play certain responses to maintain it, so we have a certain emotional temperament which generally is on an even keel. However, most of us do experience bouts of especially good humor when something nice happens and bad humor when things don't go our way.

Apart from saying everyone at one time or another experiences mood swings, it is difficult to be very definite about their manifestation. Some people consider themselves "moody" and will experience frequent fluctuations in feelings, even throughout a single day. Other people are quite untemperamental and nothing seems to shake their steady humor. In some people the swings became quite pronounced and these people with exaggerated swings of mood are called cyclothymes. Cyclothymes have a typical build: they are the classical round, jolly person – the life and soul of the party one minute, and in tears the next. Generally the swings of mood, particularly the swings of depression, don't last very long and cyclothymes are happy-go-lucky people most of the time.

Changes in mood can arise slowly or be instantly produced, they can last a long time or just a few seconds and generally, once you become aware of these emotional swings, you should be able either to learn to preserve feelings of happiness and contentment, or to moderate feelings of unhappiness so that you don't become dragged down by negative emotions.

Real depression, however, doesn't have a lot to do with normal variation of mood. It is not a situation you can get out of without a lot of help. The experience of real depression is one of increasing worthlessness directed towards yourself and your environment. Such negative feelings can, in time, affect not only your self-image, but your ability to work, to carry on relationships with others, and even destroy your faith.

Vulnerability of women

"Learned helplessness," a major cause of depression, has a special significance for women. Whereas men generally attribute failure to effort and success to ability, women attribute failure to ability and success to chance. They are, therefore, caught both ways.

Although there has been much progress in alleviating depression through the use of drugs, women's physiology has made them much more vulnerable to this condition. Because they live longer than men generally, they suffer depression brought on by grief; because their hormones work cyclically, or cease at menopause, they are subject to depression brought on by hormonal imbalance, and because they bear children, they suffer not only from the effects of childbirth but from disruptions of the mother-child bond. While one in ten of the population will experience depression at least one time in their life, depressive illness is almost twice as prevalent in women.

Recent studies on increasing rates of depression in women have seen psychosocial factors as being strong determinants. The "learned helplessness" theory, in which women perceive failure as their fault and success as happenstance, has depression as a natural result. Furthermore, rising expectations, access to new opportunities, and efforts to improve women's social and legal standing, are now more often desired by women who are just as likely to have their aspirations unfulfilled. It is not only discrepancies between such aspirations and their satisfaction that lead to depression but conflicts also arise concerning women's "traditional" roles versus employment and recognition outside the home.

Factors affecting mood

Weather and hours of daylight
Your mood may be at the mercy of the elements. Prolonged cold, wet weather is inescapably depressing and most of us feel that things are better when the sun is shining and the temperature is equable and pleasantly warm.

The number of hours of daylight and darkness affect our mood, too. Countries near the Arctic circle, where the winter is protracted with almost six months of semi-darkness, have a higher incidence of depressive illness during the winter months than the summer months. In common with every living thing throughout the plant and animal kingdom, we and our moods are extremely sensitive to changes in the number of hours of light and dark. This probably accounts for the depression which may accompany jet-lag. Should we travel to a country where our regular routine of light and dark is disrupted, we may find ourselves in low spirits: a traveller to Helsinki in the summer months may find that there are no hours of darkness at all, and the startling experience of waking at 2 a.m. to bright sunshine can have a disturbing effect on mood, quite often resulting in depression.

Round the clock changes
Most of us feel a bit under par in the early morning. Our mood improves as the day goes on, coming to a peak mid-morning and again in the afternoon. These mood variations are directly related to the functioning of the adrenal glands and to the amount of cortisol, a hormone, which they produce. Cortisol not only normalizes many physiological functions it also helps to normalize our mood: the blood levels of cortisol rise after we wake and we become physically, intellectually and psychologically alert, and we begin to feel good.

Illness
Many quite common and, often mild, viral infections like flu, or more serious ones like hepatitis or glandular fever, can leave you feeling very low in spirits. What is more, this depression can last as long as six or nine months. The exact mechanism is not known but almost any virus can cause inflammation of the delicate coverings of the brain and the brain cells themselves (accounting for the severe headache pain behind the eyes, stiff neck and even vomiting during a viral illness) and so it is not a huge leap to postulate that viruses can penetrate brain cells and change their internal chemistry, particularly those body substances which regulate our emotional levels, such as 5-hydroxy tryptamine (5HT). Diabetes, anemia and nephritis are often accompanied by depression, and it may also be the aftermath of any severe illness or major surgery.

Hormones
There is a great deal of evidence that links estrogen and/or progesterone deficiencies, or relative lack of them, with depression. Premenstrual depression, post-partum depression and the depression of menopause are all related to lack of female hormones in the blood and all three conditions have symptoms in common. Premenstrual tension (see p. 237) and menopausal depression (see p. 251) can be corrected hormonally.

Post-partum depression has been attributed to changes in the level of circulating hormones. During pregnancy the levels are astronomically high compared to normal. As soon as your baby is

Isolation, boredom, frustration and resentment often affect mothers whose lives are entirely devoted to bringing up children. The highest rates of depression are among working class married women looking after young children.

born the hormone levels decline very steeply and this has a profound physiological and psychological effect (see p. 228).

Estrogens speed up the metabolism of certain chemicals in the body and in doing so use up vitamin B6, leaving the body relatively deficient in B6 for other purposes, such as the manufacture of 5-hydroxy tryptamine. It is thought that some cases of depression in women taking oral contraceptives are connected with low 5HT concentration and vitamin B6 deficiency.

As the result of this discovery it was suggested that depressed patients who were taking the oral contraceptive pill should be treated with vitamin B6. Some authorities even suggested pyridoxine should be added to oral contraceptives. Careful study, however, has shown that only women with rare and absolute vitamin B6 deficiency will benefit from vitamin supplements. Others will show no response, so the depression experienced in pill takers is only partly related to 5HT and to vitamin B6.

Personal experiences

Depression is also caused by emotional upheavals resulting from our social situation and relationships with others. The loss of a loved one, marital breakdown or partnership disturbances, an insecure job situation, children's adolescence and departure from home, even moving to a new neighborhood – all these and many more of our experiences can cause anxiety and stress leading to depression.

Other personal factors having a positive relationship with depression include having three or four children under 14 at home; lack of employment outside the home; and the absence of an intimate and loving relationship with a spouse or companion.

Different types of depression

Doctors generally divide depression into two types: "endogenous" and "reactive." Endogenous depression is a chemical upset or deficiency in the brain metabolism which is set off by biological changes in the individual. Doctors are still not able to say what triggers endogenous depression but they can treat it successfully with drugs. Reactive depression is a response to a particular situation, normally a loss – such as the death of a partner, a break-up of a relationship – or a reaction to a disease, illness, medication or hormonal imbalance.

The changes in mood which characterize depression can also be towards euphoria, in which case it is regarded as mania. A "manic-depressive" may go through periods when she alternately exhibits depression or mania or a mixture of both.

Symptoms of depression

Depression manifests itself in three areas:

Psychological

Mood changes shift in the direction of sadness, misery, gloom, blackness and then despair. There is a decrease in feelings of love and affection. Inferiority, inadequacy and uselessness are the most common feelings. Patterns of behavior can change radically, leading to shop-lifting, cheating and sexual aberrations.

In manic-depressives, however, without warning, this introspective depression may swing into a manic phase with agitation, aggression, over-excitability and wildness. The manic-depressive woman is particularly at risk as she may appear to be a nymphomaniac due to her increased sexual desire. In addition, deterioration in judgment can affect contraceptive measures, resulting in unwanted pregnancies. There are also some women who experience depression as a lack of pleasure rather than an abundance of misery, and these "smiling depressives," who require help as much as more normal depressives, may be unconvincing to their doctors.

Psychomotor activity
Thinking, attention, concentration and memory can deteriorate. A very depressed person may be silent, withdrawn and immobile; she exhibits a loss of vigor and interest in life; she is frequently untidy, apathetic and lethargic.

Physical manifestations
First, there is a lack of appetite and interest in food followed by reduced sexual activity and menstrual difficulties. Sleep patterns are severely affected and there is a loss of energy. Depression can also cause indigestion, abdominal distention, sweating and pain.

Consequences of depression

While depression as a mental illness is not usually permanently damaging or harmful to the individual, it puts great strain on the families and friends of the sufferer. At its worst it can lead to suicide. More women than men attempt suicide, and repeatedly, but luckily, they are less successful at it. However, the rate of successful suicides for women is increasing, especially in women over sixty.

Medical treatment of depression

Most serious forms of depression won't respond to self-help, especially if the circumstances responsible for the depression cannot be altered. You will have to ask for professional help.

In the first instance, your doctor may offer you support from a social or health worker who can talk through your problems and put you on the right road to finding a solution. You will find that unburdening yourself to a sympathetic ear can be a great relief.

Secondly, as depressed people are often sleepless, your doctor may give you sleeping pills to tide you over a bad spell until your sleeping pattern is re-established: no psychological illness can get better without sleep.

Furthermore, your doctor may prescribe anti-depressant drugs, which are powerful substances reserved for the treatment of severe depressive illness. The most commonly used anti-depressants are the tricyclic compounds, the mono-amine-oxidase inhibitors (MAOIs) and lithium salts. The tricyclics affect the mood of depressed people because they raise the levels of 5HT in brain cells. They may however take anything up to two weeks to have a measurable effect. The MAOIs are effective drugs in certain patients, but it is necessary to avoid taking other drugs at the same time and to avoid certain foods like meat extracts, lima beans, cheese, wine, beer, alcohol, yoghurt, etc. because the drugs may interact with the food and produce a rise in blood pressure. Lithium salts have recently been introduced for the treatment of manic-depressive illnesses, though their mode of action is not properly understood.

Really severe depressive illness may need specialist psychiatric help or hospital admission which can be arranged on an informal daily basis. While psychotherapy is directed towards growth of personality it often has the secondary result of reducing conflicts precipitating depression.

Electro-convulsive therapy (ECT) is still occasionally used for patients with very severe depression who do not respond to other treatments. Usually their cases are thoroughly examined by several doctors before the decision is taken to give ECT. Before the ECT is administered, the patient is sedated and then anesthetized so that she is unconscious before and during the shock therapy. An electrical shock then passes through the body and the brain for a few seconds. Usually ECT is given in a course of treatments which may do much to ameliorate depressive illness. Over the last decade ECT has fallen into disrepute because of the rather brutal effect it has on the patient, and it is becoming increasingly rare.

Self-help for depression

There are a few things you can do to offset depression which has not yet reached the form of a serious illness. Thinking about things or willing yourself to change them won't work, but keeping to as normal a routine as possible will help.

A sense of humor Very important – it not only helps to reduce feelings of unhappiness but may put things back into perspective.

Activity Any kind is important in that the pleasure of achievement can overcome any misery.

Work Tackling and finishing almost any job is a great boost to morale and brings a unique sense of worthiness – which is almost a miraculous antidote to depression. If you're up to it, try forcing yourself to tackle a job you've been putting off: the resulting satisfaction is the best treatment you can get – from anyone.

Indulgence Treating yourself can often lift the spirits but bear in mind that over-indulging in food or alcohol can lead to weight or dependency problems, and alcohol can deepen depression. Some people find being alone with a good book or a solitary walk or bath is comforting.

Company Being with other people can put your own problems in perspective and their good naturedness can often be catching.

Time and repentance Many depressive feelings wear off in time or can be alleviated by your making amends, if you feel you've inflicted hurt or damage.

Professional agencies (material relief, social security, marital or family guidance counselors, etc.) Getting help with the nuts and the bolts of life helps too, even if they are not the actual cause of your depression. Also the activity is distracting; talking to people soothes, smoothing out wrinkles boosts self-esteem. Knowing that others suffer similarly can also put your problems in perspective.

Music Found to be a mood elevator by most people.

Increased sexual activity If your depression hasn't dampened down your libido altogether, speak to your partner about your sex life: good, wholesome sex can make all aspects of life not only seem, but be, brighter.

Religion (confession and discussion) A kind of cleansing or even "purging of the soul" can be helpful to some people as long as it isn't used as an escape route from reality. But it can be a long-term support too.

Women's groups Lean on people, especially those who know how to help at a personal, practical level. Other women may be able to supply you with support and emotional bonds which can alleviate some of your dissatisfaction, unhappiness and loneliness.

How will I know when I need help?

Signs are an inability to handle situations others do with ease and the presence of severe symptoms which make ordinary life difficult. Suicidal feelings are present in extreme cases.

Is depression more common in older people?

It is far more prevalent in the second half of life and modern medicine has been directed at uncovering and treating depression in the elderly; some depression has been taken for senility.

PHOBIAS

A phobia is an overwhelmingly unreasonable fear of a situation. Most people suffering from a phobia are aware that they are behaving in an extreme manner but find it impossible to control their fear. When a person finds herself in her phobic situation, she may exhibit physical symptoms, such as shivering, sweating, rapid breathing, palpitations, feelings of sickness and even vomiting.

The word phobia comes from the Greek word *phobes*, which means panic, fear and terror. Phobias were described by the Greeks, but in the nineteenth century, the only phobia which was commonly described was hydrophobia, the fear of water, which is one of the symptoms of rabies. Nowadays, there is a long list of phobias, some of them well known, which we can identify with, others less common.

Acrophobia – fear of heights	*Brontophobia – fear of thunder*	*Mysophobia – fear of dirt*
Agrophobia – fear of open spaces	*Claustrophobia – fear of enclosure*	*Ophidiophobia – fear of snakes*
Ailurophobia – fear of cats	*Cynophobia – fear of dogs*	*Pyrophobia – fear of fire*
Arachnophobia – fear of spiders	*Equinophobia – fear of horses*	*Thanatophobia – fear of death*
Anthrophobia – fear of people	*Microphobia – fear of germs*	*Xenophobia – fear of strangers*
Aquaphobia – fear of water	*Murophobia – fear of mice*	*Zoophobia – fear of animals*

It is important to distinguish between behavior which is phobic and behavior which is only eccentric. A housewife who refuses to go beyond her front door is not necessarily ill; it is possible that she has decided to withdraw her labor because she feels that her role as a housewife devalues her.

313

Onset of phobias

There are certain trigger situations which may exacerbate phobias at particular ages. For instance, sudden loud noises or movements cause fear in very young infants. Fear of strangers generally occurs in toddlers. At a slightly later age, children become fearful of any object which moves towards them rapidly with a jerking or swerving movement; for example, snakes. Fear of animals usually starts in pre-school children. Fear of open spaces and social situations normally starts before adolescence, or after middle age. Fear of heart disease, cancer and death appear increasingly in later years.

Other fears which may occur at any time of life are fear of darkness, enclosed spaces or thunder. Very often a fear is related to an earlier distressing event, which has been forgotten. It is quite often founded on the absence or loss of loved ones, particularly if it occurred when seven or eight years old.

The phobic personality

There is said to be a personality which is predisposed to develop phobias, though I would advise you to interpret this loosely. Phobic people are said to be shy, timid, dependent and immature, but are dutiful, are usually reserved, with high ideals, and have the tendency to keep feelings bottled up. However, this description describes their personality when they are suffering from a phobia. Before their phobias began, they were usually socially outgoing and independent people.

Research has shown, however, that people who suffer phobias are different in one way from those who do not – the feeling of anxiety has a greater physical effect on them than on most other people. On a hypothetical scale we would find at one end people who experienced very few physical effects of anxiety – like increased heart rate, sweating and shaking, and at the other end, people who suffer from phobias and have profound physical symptoms from anxiety. Most normal people would be somewhere in-between.

Treatment of phobias

Most people feel that the easiest way to deal with their phobia is to avoid the phobic situation, and as a result greatly restrict their lives. (An agrophobic housewife who is terrified of open spaces, may become totally housebound, unable to make an outing to the local shops unless accompanied by a friend.) But there are many ways in which people who suffer from phobias can be helped:

Desensitization

Phobias are fairly common. A survey conducted in America in 1969 showed that 77 out of 1000 people suffered from some sort of phobia, but severely disabling phobias were estimated at only 2 per 1000.

Here the phobic situation is combined with a pleasurable experience, and it is one of the most successful ways of treating phobias. An example would be to give a child who has a phobia of cats an ice cream to eat, and gradually to expose her to a cat if she is enjoying herself. With adults, this form of treatment is usually accompanied by exercises in relaxation. Once you are completely relaxed, you will be asked to imagine increasingly unpleasant situations, which gradually approach your phobic situation. If you are working with a good therapist, you will be encouraged to chart your improvements, and to report your progress. Your efforts will be rewarded with praise and you will be given constant support. Very often, you may feel like having a friend with you, and the presence of a trusted companion can do a lot to help.

Modelling
This is a technique whereby the phobic person is exposed to the phobic situation, among people who are entirely fearless of it. The aim of this form of group therapy is that if it is repeated, the phobic person will imitate the fearless behavior of others.

Flooding
This encourages the patient to experience her phobic situation as vividly and as long as possible until it no longer arouses fear. It has been used successfully to treat such conditions as examination phobia and examination nerves.

Logotherapy
This involves exaggerating the phobic situation and the symptoms of the phobia instead of running away from it. It is felt that after the repeated discipline of facing the fears, the phobic person will stop being haunted by them.

Cognitive manipulation
This simply means telling yourself over and over again that you are not afraid, and, with some technical help, the hope is that you will stop being afraid. This sort of technique is as follows: a person who is afraid of snakes, hears her heart beat played back to her, and on seeing a snake, hears the heart rate increase markedly. She will then be told that her heart rate will not race when she sees snakes, and the next time she is shown one, a recording of a normal heart beat will be played. If the treatment is successful, the phobic person will have stopped avoiding snakes.

Besides these methods, hypnosis, meditation, and psychoanalysis have been tried to help cure people of their phobias. Whatever the form of treatment, it must be supervised by a trained and experienced medical practitioner. Whatever you do, don't think of a phobia as something which makes you different, inadequate or inferior, and therefore something you should keep to yourself and try to come to terms with on your own. An awful lot can be done to help you if you take advice and discuss your phobia frankly. The first step is to overcome your fear of admitting it. There are self-help groups for phobic people, and they usually have a high rate of success, so ask your doctor if there is one in your locality.

DEFORMITIES

One of the things that doctors have learned is that women who are emotionally disturbed by a disfigurement, no matter how unobtrusive it seems to others, must be taken note of. The truth is that hardly any woman with a disfigurement – be it spots, pimples, birthmarks, a large nose, shortness, tallness, large breasts, obesity

– escapes the psychological effect, whether the case is accidental as in a car crash, or surgical, such as the removal of a breast for cancer. Many who are born with one, such as a birthmark, are unable to come to terms with it emotionally, and need psychiatric help. It really doesn't help a woman one bit to say that her nose isn't such a bad shape, her breasts really aren't out of proportion with the rest of her body, or that her birthmark is barely noticeable when it is camouflaged with make-up. If it is real to her, her emotional disturbance will not improve until rectification of the disfigurement is attempted. I say attempted, because it is not always possible to completely get rid of it (see p. 348).

When you come down to it there are really only two ways to cope with a physical disfigurement: either you can discuss plastic surgery with your doctor and attempt to reconstruct your body to conform to your idea of aesthetic acceptability, or you can make mental adjustments to your own concept of what is acceptable to conform with your changed appearance. The former, of course, is much easier than the latter.

The reason why most of us have difficulty in making either adjustment – despite the brilliance of modern plastic surgery – is because we feel insecure about our physical imperfections. Through films and advertising in glossy magazines, we feel the pressure every day of an increasingly competitive world, where success seems to be more and more dependent on self image: success with boyfriends, success with work, success with other women, success at getting and keeping a partner. What we fear is that success will evaporate with the loss of self-image.

Just take a look around at all the couples who go on loving each other despite the pendulous breasts, despite the sagging waistline, and despite the bulging stomach. The difference is time. If the accumulated and gradual changes to our bodies occurred overnight, we would consider ourselves disfigured. Given ten years, however, we can grow accustomed to and even feel comfortable with disfigurement which in the short term seems appalling.

It is said that Brigitte Bardot thought she was ugly, and constantly needed reassurance about her physical appearance. At the other end of the scale, a friend of mine who had a mastectomy, was surprised and delighted to be told by her husband that she was the same delicious wife to him – with or without her left breast. That is the real world.

DEPENDENCY/ADDICTION

Using chemicals to alter the state of mind is as old as people themselves. As long ago as Biblical times the question was asked, how can we enjoy the benefits of drugs without risking dependency and addiction? Even then, people noticed and disliked the side-effects that were sometimes produced.

Dependence builds because with certain drugs repeated use leads to a change in the way the user reacts to the drug. The first change is that the ability of the user to choose when and where to take the drug is reduced; in other words, there is a loss of control over decision and a loss of autonomy. In extreme cases, as control is gradually lost, the life of the user may be completely given up to securing a supply of the drug and the use of it. Even after a period of abstinence there is a tendency to start using the drug again, even if the addict has been under-going treatment.

The word addiction derives from the Latin which means to be given over to a master, to be enslaved. The term has been used not just for the desire and need for drugs, but has been applied to any kind of substance-dependent behavior such as smoking and, more recently, has been applied to any pattern of behavior which stems from an almost uncontrollable desire. But it can be unrelated to drug taking – for instance, an addiction to gambling or card playing.

How dependencies arise

There are two main ways in which dependencies start. One has more to do with the personality of a potential addict than anything else, and the other has to do with the nature of the drug.

Personality problems

In the first instance, the user seeks out the drug in order to escape from situations which she feels are too painful to contemplate, even though they may be simply the realities of life to another person. This sort of user may seek out drugs in adolescence or earlier, and has been described as having an inadequate personality.

Young heroin addicts in New York have been described as having a profound sense of inadequacy and very low self-esteem. This is coupled with the inability to find satisfaction in work and in their personal relations with other people. Heroin is used, therefore, to reduce tension pleasurably and during the effect of the dose, at least, obliterate other needs.

Another study has described addicts as being hostile, depressed people who have difficulty in forming intimate relations with others. A typical relationship would be immature and dependent. Some researchers go as far as saying that psychopathy is the common denominator. Addicts, therefore, are seen as immature, lacking in moral responsibility, ready to exploit other people and demanding instant gratification of their needs.

However, it is well known that people with relatively normal personalities can "learn" to use drugs. Researchers believe that a psychopathic personality, adverse home background, or socio-economic conditions are necessary to account for dependence and relapse after withdrawal. A good example of dependence without personality disturbance can be seen with drugs like nicotine but, of course, it can also occur when patients take tranquillizers, sleeping pills or opium derivatives which are prescribed.

Drug characteristics

Recent studies have shown that with certain drugs such as the opiates, and probably with alcohol and barbiturates as well, biological changes occur with the first dose which lead to physical dependence (yet many patients are given opiates several times a day to relieve pain following surgery, and virtually none become psychologically dependent or addicted).

Why do some people seek out a drug even if it is prohibited by society and eventually cannot get along without it, while others seem to be able to stop using it with only minor difficulties even when they are physically dependent on it? How much can we attribute to the drug, to the individual and to the circumstances in which that person finds herself? Years of research have not brought answers to these questions. However, one of the patterns which has been revealed, is that there is an escalating history of drug use and dependence, and that different factors may have a different impact at different stages. Any one of four factors, psychological, sociological, biological and pharmacological, can affect initial use (experimentation), then whether the user will take the drug again (and become a casual or recreational user), then whether the user will escalate to heavy or intensive use or to compulsive use (addiction), or in the case of alcohol, alcoholism. The same question will have to be asked about what leads to relapse after a period of abstinence.

The reasons for relapse are complicated. It is possible that the addict becomes so used to treating the withdrawal symptoms which occur several hours after each dose of the drug with yet another dose, that the craving almost becomes reflexive. So the narcotic addict who is cured and feels no craving in the hospital may feel the need for a fix on returning to her home environment where she used to use drugs and had previously experienced the withdrawal symptoms.

Dependency versus addiction

The terminology of drug dependence is confusing. A person is said to be physically dependent on a drug when it has produced biological changes sufficient to cause withdrawal symptoms when the drug is discontinued; in other words it causes severe dependence syndrome. Drugs which do not behave in this way are said to cause habituation or psychological dependence. However, this is an over-simplified way of viewing the whole subject of dependence and addiction. Many drugs given repeatedly over a long period, produce physical dependence and a withdrawal syndrome, but the syndrome is not necessarily accompanied by the severe discomfort-anxiety, or marked desire to get more of the drug, which addiction and psychological dependence nearly always is. A drug which behaves in this way is *Imipramine* which is used to treat depression. If it is stopped after long-term treatment, the patient may suffer nausea, anxiety, difficulty in sleeping, and muscle aches and pains, but never a compulsion to start using the drug again.

Legal and "soft drugs"

Men are much more likely to use illicit drugs than women: only about 25% of cannabis smokers or takers of illegal drugs are women. However, women are the overwhelming consumers and mis-users of legal drugs such as tranquillizers and sleeping tablets, which not only result in dependency but often addiction as well.

Regarded as "minor tranquillizers," both Valium and Librium are intended to relieve anxiety without producing the drowsiness which characterizes barbiturates. However, cessation of prolonged regular use can occasionally produce withdrawal symptoms comparable to those of barbiturates: abdominal and muscle cramps, insomnia, anxiety, depression, convulsions, vomiting and sweating.

If taken within the first 42 days of pregnancy, both Valium and Librium can cause birth defects such as mental retardation, heart damage, deformities of joints and intestines, and deafness.

Problems resulting from excessive use of both these drugs include drowsiness, depression, altered sex drive, jaundice, constipation, skin problems and confusion. If taken in conjunction with alcohol, the effects can be lethal.

Cannabis, both in hashish and marijuana form, is an illegal drug but one that is quite often smoked socially. It is a depressant drug which slows reaction time, impairs co-ordination and may induce drowsiness. Its desired effect is a "high" or euphoria, but occasionally it can be unpleasant for the user.

Tolerance builds rapidly with this drug, so steadily increased amounts are necessary to produce effects. Prolonged use has been associated with damaged blood cells and severe psychological impairment.

While large numbers of women use the drug only intermittently without apparent harm, it is still a drug, and an illegal one, and I don't advocate using it – especially if you are pregnant or intend to have children.

"Hard drugs"

LSD (lysergic acid diethylamide), barbiturates, heroin and morphine are psychotropic drugs which alter your emotions and mental state; amphetamines (not literally "hard" drugs but used here to refer to their "abused" state) and cocaine are stimulants which produce feelings of alertness, energy and confidence. These drugs should never be used as they are *deadly* to a woman's health.

Side-effects include "bad trips" with extremely unpleasant experiences leading to mental disorientation, unconsciousness and coma, hepatitis (from dirty needles), high blood pressure, irregular heartbeat and even death – especially if combined with alcohol (see chart p. 71).

Treating drug dependence and addiction

Authorities working in the area of drug dependence have realized that generalizations can be made and applied to the treatment of any drug dependence: it is prevented or at least ameliorated by social support, and one mandatory component of treatment is directed towards social relationships and marital relationships, if the addict is married. The greatest difficulty with the smoker, the alcoholic, and the drug addict, is to avoid relapse. Coming off the drug for a few days or weeks is usually not very difficult, but relapse is frequently precipitated by a crisis such as depression, anger, failure and hopelessness. It becomes important, therefore, to help the addict to avoid such situations and support her through them if they occur. It is also known that the presence of the drug, regardless of what it is, can increase craving. The addict has the tendency to abuse more than one drug, and it is important to give up all dependencies at the same time otherwise slippage on one can lead to relapse on another.

The average medical practitioner is generally not well equipped to help addicts, but your family doctor will certainly be able to refer you to a hospital department which specializes in drug dependence and may even know of a self-help group.

Most addicts prefer the latter, because it involves mutual support, identification and shared experience, but also coping through involvement. In other words, helping others. This is very important to the addict, who was driven to her addiction very often by a feeling of hopelessness and a pointlessness to life. Conquering the addiction is achieved by becoming actively involved with the self-help group, attending meetings, holding official positions, helping others attending events, and generally being a samaritan.

Other self-help groups concentrate on training in self-control, training in social skills, training in relaxation, and training in self-assertion. All these things aim to teach the addict how to cope with her own personal problems. A group in the United States has had encouraging results with alcoholics by helping them to deal with social, vocational and marital problems. This group sets out to encourage the alcoholic to develop strong bonds with her community, by developing and practicing social skills, whether it be communicating with her partner, being interviewed for a job or just chatting to someone.

There are two methods of hospital treatment which are used by drug dependency programs. The first method involves a long period of hospital treatment, say up to three months, and the second a brief period, three weeks or less. The staff include doctors, psychiatrists, psychologists, social workers. Hospital treatment usually demands total abstinence from alcohol if you are an alcoholic, and the involvement in a drug withdrawal program if you are a drug addict. Medication is given to help you with withdrawal symptoms and depression. In addition there are group therapy sessions which will help the addict to face up to her own problems and there is usually psychotherapy from a psychiatrist or a psychologist. Controlled studies have been performed and patients have been followed up for two years – there were no differences at all between the two methods of treatment.

It is never easy, but it is possible to conquer drug addiction, and the chances of giving up a narcotic increase with time. In a study of heroin addicts in London clinics, it was found that one third were leading normal lives and were not on any kind of drug to excess. Some former drug addicts attribute their success in kicking the habit to a radical change in their lives – usually something good happening, often the formation of a new friendship. They also point to the importance of the love of someone who is special to them. Nearly all describe the turning point as the time when the reasons for changing became more powerful than the reasons they had for continuing.

ALCOHOLISM

Alcoholism, and alcohol-related problems such as arrests for drunkenness, liver cirrhosis mortality, and institutionalization due to alcoholism, are increasing rapidly among women. Moreover, the greatest amount of increase has been in younger women aged 30 and below – and ironically many of the factors involved can be attributed to the gains women have made in being "emancipated."

Physical reactions to alcohol

Your body contains 5–10% less water than any man's so that the same amount of alcohol will be more concentrated in your system and thus have a greater toxic effect on your body organs. With the same amount of alcohol, your blood will contain higher alcohol levels than any man and thus you will become more intoxicated more quickly. Therefore, it takes less alcohol, consumed over fewer years, to cause liver damage in women than men. In women a much shorter time elapses between early problem drinking and the development of physical illness.

Just being a female significantly predisposes to alcohol-related liver disease.

It has been found that female response to alcohol varies according to the menstrual cycle – there are higher alcohol levels during the premenstrual and ovulatory phases. The fact that variability exists has been thought to make women more cautious when drinking, so that they also fail to develop a high alcohol tolerance level. In addition to jeopardizing liver and heart function, causing brain damage and making you liable to many other disorders, alcoholism increases your chances of miscarrying, and of producing severely physically and mentally disabled children. Fetal alcohol syndrome (FAS) consisting of growth deficiency, abnormalities of the head and face, mental retardation and associated features such as abnormal heart and kidney development, has increasingly been diagnosed in infants of alcoholic mothers.

Causes of increased alcoholism

The reasons for the rising figures of female alcoholism are many, and they can be roughly grouped under such headings as economic, social and, probably most important, psychological.

Economic causes

At the simplest level, alcohol has become increasingly available to women, mainly due to their rising income level. Interestingly enough, it is younger women who earn the most money (one study proves that the average woman's income is the highest between the ages 25 and 29; the average man's is highest between 30 and 50), and manufacturers have been quick to exploit this both in the type of product they make and in their advertising. The real growth market in alcohol is wine, where women are the dominant purchasers and consumers. American surveys have shown the higher the income bracket, the more women drink (this is reversed in men). Alcohol is now sold in supermarkets, and other large stores, making it very easy for women to obtain it without provoking any comment.

ALCOHOL CONSUMPTION

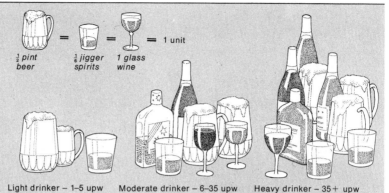

Alcohol consumption is presently measured in units per week. While 35 units per week seems a very large number, bear in mind that this represents only ½ bottle of wine and 2 half-pints of beer per day, for instance. One more drink and you're in the heavy drinker category.

¼ pint beer = ⅙ jigger spirits = 1 glass wine = 1 unit

upw – units per week   Light drinker – 1–5 upw   Moderate drinker – 6–35 upw   Heavy drinker – 35+ upw

Social causes

It has now become more socially accepted, even fashionable and approved, for women to drink not only at parties, but at bars. Where once it was frowned upon if women went to a bar, they now go in increasing numbers, not only with male escorts but with female friends, and, occasionally, alone.

More women work in occupations where free or cheap drink is readily available – such as at bars or clubs – where there exists a natural risk of increased alcohol consumption.

In addition, increasing numbers of women are working in professions which carry a high risk of contracting drinking problems: these include journalism, publishing, advertising and marketing; and more are in responsible positions such as management and personnel, where there is usually a great deal of stress – a prime cause of alcoholism. If a woman is also the breadwinner and mother and/or wife, these pressures increase.

As taboos have eased on women drinking in public, and drinking in groups, so have their "protective" function. When society placed strong inhibitions on behavior so that women were prevented from drinking, it also assured they could not be arrested, convicted or confined for drunkenness. Now that women are more "emancipated," they are afforded less protection by society against such behavior, and the crime rate for women has been rising accordingly. However, the easing of taboos has not been universal and those which remain strong still cause problems in other areas (see below).

Psychological causes

Drinking problems in women are due to a variety of psychological and psychosocial causes, including stress, reactions to specific life events, and difficulties over self-image.

As mentioned above, women are now prey to greatest stress as they enter more competitive work fields and take positions of higher responsibility. As the major increase in women's employment is among the married, the pressures of home and family, added to those of work, can make an intolerable burden. It has

been reported that women regard alcohol as a mood changer and tranquillizer and that they often drink for "escape" reasons. Therefore, with increasing stresses to escape from, it is not surprising that women are drinking more (they are also using more tranquillizers see p. 70).

It has also been shown that women tend to increase alcoholic consumption when faced with difficult life situations. Loss of any kind, including fertility (menopause), children (empty nest syndrome), divorce and separation, is heavily implicated in increased drinking, and does seem incontrovertibly part of modern life.

Threats to a woman's feminine role of mother, wife, homemaker and lover are closely associated with alcoholism. Feelings of inadequacy about performing these roles, brought on by society's changing and often conflicting views on what a woman's "true" role is, and how she should manage it, are further complicated by personal expectations of achievement and their continual unfulfillment, both at home and in employment. An example of this contemporary confusion is the "so-called sexual revolution" which allows women to be more sexually aggressive in initiation and enjoyment but has lead to worries about sexual adequacy and performance, which are exacerbated by prevailing double standards ("proper" sexual behavior is not universally agreed upon), and are likely to drive women to drink.

Treatment of alcoholism

The treatment of alcoholism in women is complicated by the double standards society applies towards them. Strong social sanctions exist against female drunkenness due to the importance, almost sanctity, of the wife and mother role, and these encourage women to be "secret drinkers." Most female alcoholics drink alone, frequently during the day, and tend to deny this solitary behavior. Women cover up the fact of their drinking more than men and this leads them to be regarded as untruthful.

There are three major sources of treatment:

Detoxification and related medical care
This is for the severely alcoholic woman who must recover from the acute effects of drinking before she can change her life in other ways. Medication and diet are adjusted for her condition, and she can be seen either as an in-patient or as an out-patient.

Therapy
A woman must come to terms with why she drinks and the problems arising from this, and counselling programs exist to help her. Individual group and family therapy are all available; if a woman has a permanent companion, it is very important that he be involved.

Female alcoholics consistently report that they often drink alone when they are at home. This is due primarily to society's negative view of women who drink heavily in public, and a lack of suitable or available drinking companions.

Alcoholics Anonymous
This voluntary association exists to help people who want to stop drinking. All members have been alcoholics and thus they are able to use their experiences to help alcoholics stop drinking, stay sober and rebuild their lives.

Are there any predisposing factors to alcoholism?

Research has shown that many women alcoholics have suffered emotional traumas in early life such as the loss of a parent and siblings and are more likely to have had alcoholic parents. In later life, they have a high rate of marital instability and psychiatric problems, and many have alcoholic partners.

Are particular types of women at special risk?

Women under mental stress such as unsupported mothers with young children, women who are at home all day or whose children are leaving home, women who have to compete a great deal with men at work, and lesbians who are still regarded as "socially unacceptable", stand a greater chance of becoming alcoholics. So, too, do those who suffer a great deal of physical stress, perhaps as the result of an abortion, post-partum depression, or menopause.

How will I know when my drinking has reached the "problem" stage?

You only have to answer "yes" to just one of the questions below to know that alcohol is affecting your life in a major way, and that you should do something about getting help:

● Has someone close to you sometimes expressed concern about your drinking?
● When faced with a problem, do you often turn to alcohol for relief?
● Are you sometimes unable to meet home or work responsibilities because of drinking?
● Have you ever required medical attention as a result of drinking?
● Have you ever experienced a black-out – a total loss of memory while still awake – when drinking?
● Have you had distressing physical and/or psychological reactions when you tried to stop drinking?
● Have you often failed to keep the promises you have made to yourself about controlling or cutting out your drinking?
● Are your children embarrassed to bring friends home because of your drinking?

BATTERED WIVES

Women have been attacked by all types of men with whom they have relationships – husbands, boyfriends, and even sons. There are frightening statistics coming out of the United States where it is estimated that as many as 50% of all women will be battering victims at some point in their lives. Various studies have shown that of 500 women represented in divorce actions in Brooklyn, New York in 1976, 57.4% claimed they had been physically assaulted for approximately 4 years by their husbands; 36.8% of divorcing wives in Cleveland (from a study of 600) reported physical abuse by their husbands; and in a study conducted across the United States, it was confirmed that a physical assault had occurred in 28% of all American homes during 1976. Because wife battering is not a pleasant subject many erroneous ideas have arisen about it.

To put the record straight:

● Few, if any, battered women are masochistic and enjoy or invite being beaten;

● It is not only lower class, but middle and upper class, women who are beaten;

● Women of every ethnic and religious background, including WASPs, are beaten;

● Women of high educational level and job status are beaten as well as uneducated ones;

● The majority of wife-beaters are professionally successful and are eminent members of their community;

● Batterers are often charming and loving and do not necessarily exhibit psychopathic personalities;

● Battering is not necessarily lessened during the lifetime of a marriage, or after marriage if it was present earlier.

The law does not recognize rape within marriage, but battering often is linked to sexual violence. Other forms of brutality described by wives include punching, kicking, the use of weapons, boiling water and even attempted strangulation. Battering is not only physical; it can involve humiliation and mental torture.

We tend to think that wife battering is a recent phenomenon, but it is not. It was first reported in the 1870s. However, it was only in 1971 that Erin Pizzey, an English woman, set up the first refuge for battered wives in London. Now, thanks to Erin Pizzey and women like her, a good deal has been done to make wife battering a public issue, and this has enabled women to talk about it, complain about it, and seek help through official avenues. It has also made society question men's behavior within marriage.

Why women tolerate violence

One of the commonest reactions to a woman who has suffered violence is that she must be in some part to blame: that her behavior has warranted physical violence from her husband, or that she was violent first. Many people conjecture that a wife would leave her husband if she did not feel some guilt about the situation. In point of fact, very few battered wives are in a position to leave their husbands – due mainly to economic reasons, but also because of social pressures and their own psychological make-up.

Economic difficulties

A woman with small children, totally dependent on her husband for money, is in no position to walk out – though he may at any moment. In many countries, the home is in the husband's name only, and if the wife leaves she will find it very difficult to find another one, especially if social security is her only means of financial support.

Social difficulties

A woman who leaves home with her small children runs the risk of having them taken into custody if they are considered "homeless." Many local officials believe that women should never leave their husbands, regardless of the provocation, and have been very slow in providing refuges for them. In court, women are often made to feel ashamed, guilty and even responsible for being battered.

Psychological difficulties

A woman who is battered invariably has a low self-esteem which can make her feel she deserves a beating. If she has children she often despairs of raising them alone. Usually such a woman has "traditional" feelings about the home and her place in it and goes out of her way to establish her husband as head of the family, even to her own detriment and powerlessness.

Characteristics of batterers

Men who beat their wives share several qualities with them: they have low self-esteem, they accept many of the myths relating to wife battering behavior, and they are traditionalists in the home with a strong belief in family unity and their wife's sex-role stereotype. Other characteristics include blaming others for their actions, pathological jealousy, dual personality, severe stress reactions, an aggressive use of sex, possible bi-sexuality, and a denial of the consequences of their violent behavior.

Other related factors include a military background, a history of childhood violence and ambivalent relationships with their mothers.

The cycle of violence

Some writers have recognized three distinctive and cyclically occurring phases in a wife-battering situation. At each stage, the wife's responses are insufficient to protect her from future violence. The first is a tension-building stage which may include some minor battering incidents. At this time the wife often tries to dampen down tension without confronting it directly, which indirectly encourages her husband to continue, while leaving her with a false sense of being in control.

Battering incident

Tension builds

Contriteness

The second stage is when an acute battering incident occurs. At this time, most women do not resist but act only to minimize the danger to themselves. Afterwards they tend to deny or rationalize the incident.

The third stage is one of kindness and contrite loving behavior on the part of the batterer. He *believes* he will never beat his wife again and promises this, and the wife wants to believe it, too. This last stage is, in effect, the most dangerous in terms of perpetuating the cycle, as the harmony and intimacy built up at this time tends to bond a woman closer to her husband.

Breaking the cycle of violence

Any woman who hopes that by staying in her marriage she will prevail over her batterer is indulging in fanciful thinking. The cycle of violence shows that the woman on her own is incapable of breaking it, and research shows that a batterer will seek help only after his woman has left, in the hope that he can get her back.

The first step, therefore, is for the woman or the batterer to leave. Once she is out of physical danger she will need help to develop feelings of self-esteem and competence. Certain services are available to help battered women and they include:

Erin Pizzey surrounded by some of the hundreds of wives and children who come to her shelter in England seeking refuge from violent husbands.

Refuges, safe houses, or shelters

Here a woman will find some assistance, even if it is just a place to sleep – an open-door policy usually guarantees that no woman or child will be turned away. Other women who have been battered in the past act as a support system for the victim while encouraging her to develop her own way of coping.

Legal and medical alternatives

The major law enforcement agency, the police, does not seem to be able to protect women from their husbands – the highly personal circumstances surrounding domestic violence are not conducive to social control. While the police may not be very effective in controlling wife battering (this is often because women, having little faith in them, do not call upon them, or if they do, battered wives often drop charges once pressed), legal protection is, however, available through restraining orders handed down by the court banning a husband from his wife. Medical treatment, as an out-patient in hospital emergency rooms is always available, but women should attempt to be admitted to the hospital – not only will their injuries be better treated, but they will have a means of refuge and witnesses to their condition.

Counselling and psychotherapy
To help battered wives overcome inherent feelings of inadequacy, psychiatric help is necessary to help them adjust motivation and aspiration levels, and to learn that they can control their behavior and thus affect what happens to them.

RAPE

Rape of women and children is growing at an alarming rate. Most cases of rape occur between people who know each other, making it difficult for the woman to prove that rape has taken place. Moreover, it often occurs in circumstances where the victim is unlikely to tell anyone about it or where she is not likely to be believed. In other words, any time a woman is in a compromising situation such as hitch-hiking or out alone.

This last situation, which says a lot about prevailing double standards in society, has further repercussions for rape victims. Even if the ordeal of rape is bad, going to the police and courts can be worse. Most rape victims find insensitivity and callousness, if not downright obstructiveness and disbelief, at all levels of the legal process – from police questioning, to the gynecological examination, to the questioning of prosecutor and lawyer. It is a brave woman who follows up a rape charge to the end; most women do not want every detail of their daily lives laid bare in court, or to deal with innuendos or implications about their sexual behavior. The present rape laws are designed to protect men from women, and quite innocent behavior on the part of women can be misinterpreted in a very sinister way against them.

It takes some time for victims to get over the anger, depression and vulnerability engendered by this aggressive crime. Time, emotional support and counseling will all be needed to resolve them.

The potential rapist
While it is impossible to generalize about the kind of man who rapes women, certain characteristics occur too frequently to be coincidental. Rapists very often dislike women and find their desire to intimidate and humiliate them difficult to control. Frequently they are described as immature, and are often known to be violent. Usually they believe that the only way they can achieve sexual satisfaction is through violence, and many have sexual problems such as impotence or an inability to reach orgasm. Very often rapists have been subjected to humiliation at some time in their lives and they feel they have to get rid of their resentment by attacking other human beings.

Alcohol is frequently connected with rape. One study in America revealed that 50% of rapists had taken alcohol before the rape, and 35% of them were actually alcoholics.

Avoiding rape
There are certain things that you can do to avoid being raped.
On the street
● Don't venture alone in areas where you know there has been trouble and where there are street gangs.

● If you suspect that someone is following you, walk out into the middle of the street where there are cars, and run.
● If you feel that you are being followed by a man and his behavior suggests that he may attack you, run into the middle of the street and start screaming. It is quite likely (though not certain) that when the man is faced with a crowd, he will not attack you.

By your car
● Never leave your parked car unlocked and park by a street lamp at night, if possible.
● Before you get into your parked car, look onto the back seat.

At home
● Have strong locks on your windows and doors; install and use a peephole.
● Never open your front door to a man who has come to do a job in your house without seeing his identity card.

Once attacked
● If you find yourself in a situation where you are being sexually assaulted, scream as loudly as you can and fight as hard as you can. Try to get a finger in the man's eye or pull your knee up sharply into his groin.
● On the other hand, if your assailant is armed, lack of resistance on your part may be necessary to save your life.

Being raped   Once you determine that resistance is useless or is likely to lead to more violence against yourself, do the following:
● Stay calm. Talk quietly and carefully to your attacker to remind him that you are human.
● Don't excite him further by answering leading questions about your feelings during rape – reply with a calm, factual statement about something else, i.e. "You're hurting my back."
● Concentrate on his features and clothing and on any regional accents or speech patterns or other identifying factors.
● Think about something concrete and routine – like what you are going to do about notifying the authorities once you're free.
● Try not to show any pain or weakness as it will only make him more violent.

CHECKLIST FOR POST-RAPE ACTION

1. If there is no one in the house, telephone a friend or relative who can get to you fairly quickly, so that s/he can give you support. Try to keep her/him with you all the time.
2. Report the crime to the police: if you feel you cannot do this, tell your nearest and dearest friend immediately, who may be able to persuade you to report the incident.
3. Contact your doctor and ask to see her/him as soon as possible or go to the hospital if s/he is not immediately available.
4. Do not take a bath. Take off the clothing you were wearing. Do not wash or change it, as doctors and police may want to examine it.

5. Try to remember every detail you can about the man who assaulted you. Keep a notepad by you and write down everything you can remember. Not just physical features, but perhaps a regional accent or peculiar words that the rapist used.
6. After you have made your report to the police, don't go home alone. Don't stay at home by yourself. Try always to have a friend with you or, if that is not possible, go and stay with friends or relatives.
7. There are rape crisis centers in many areas, or local women's groups who will give you advice. Contact one of them quickly.

Informing the authorities

When you have to report the case to the police it is almost certain to be embarrassing, so ask for your interview to be in a private room, and by a female officer if there is one at that police station. If at any time you think that your investigator is becoming offensive, don't be afraid to say so. *Always* have a second person with you while your statement is being taken.

If your case goes to trial, you will find it at the least embarrassing and, possibly, psychologically traumatic. However, all the questions which you can be asked either for the police report or in court must, by law, be confined to the rape incident, and questions into your private sex life are not permitted. Many women's groups have volunteers on call who will accompany rape victims to court. If you cannot get one of these women to accompany you, take a friend.

The legal definition of rape is contact between a penis and the vagina against the will of the victim. One of the most difficult things to prove is that there was force, particularly if there is no bodily injury. This is why you should contact your doctor as soon as you can after rape, so that s/he can perform a careful medical examination; the testimony may count in your favor in court.

Also by legal definition, fear of bodily injury is considered to be force, and you will have to prove that in court too. In other words, that you did not willingly engage in sexual activities.

The presence of sperm or semen in your vagina is considered to be very strong corroborative evidence. However, it is possible that your rapist did not ejaculate – 1 in 3 don't – and therefore the medical examination becomes crucial to see if there is any evidence of injury. It is very important for you to tell the doctor and the police if you think that the man didn't ejaculate.

● You will first of all have a general examination of your whole body, so that the doctor can describe bruises, redness, cuts, pain, and tenderness.

● Then you will have an internal pelvic examination, partly to look for evidence of injury and partly to take a sample of the vaginal secretions to see if there are any sperm present, or a chemical called *acid phosphitase* which is found in seminal fluid. This will be present in your vagina if the man ejaculated, but had no sperm.

● Ask if you can have tests done for gonorrhea, just in case your assailant had venereal disease.

● It is possible that your mouth and anus will be examined, to see if your attacker harmed these areas.

● If you are really concerned about VD and pregnancy, consult your doctor about the possibility of having prophylactic penicillin and a pregnancy test as soon as possible. You should also make sure that you have blood tests for syphilis.

● Don't let your doctor put you off by saying that the chances of your having caught VD or being pregnant are very small. Assert yourself and get your rights.

● Doctors are familiar with the use of the morning-after pill to prevent conception. You can discuss this possibility with the doctor. And if you find that your period is delayed, discuss with the doctor the possibility of having an abortion.

● Never leave the doctor's office without getting a name, address and telephone number, so that you can phone her/him back if any problems arise, and tell her/him that you will do so.

Your state of mind after being raped makes it quite difficult for you to think calmly and coolly about all the things that you should be doing and asking. Indeed, you may be so shocked that you cannot think straight or say anything. This is one of the reasons why it is very important to have a friend with you so that she can act as your advocate to ensure that nothing is forgotten and that everything is done.

Coping with rape The after-effects of rape are both physical and psychological. You may discover a vaginal discharge and you may have itching of the perineum – this could be due to an infection of moniliasis (thrush) or trichomoniasis (see p. 120). Quite often bruises and swelling and tenderness appear several hours after the rape. If they do so, go back to the same doctor who examined you to make sure that they are recorded. It is possible for slight tears to occur in the lining of the rectum, if your assailant involved this area. Sometimes they may bleed when you move your bowels. Make sure that you report this also to the doctor who examined you, even if some time has elapsed.

No woman who is raped does not suffer some sort of psychological after-effect, though it differs greatly. Some women are completely stunned, and others are quite calm. However, it is quite normal to suffer some anxiety which may go as far as hysterical behavior. It is also perfectly normal to be afraid of being left alone, even for a few minutes; it is normal not to be able to sleep, and it is normal to want to run away and hide yourself. With the help of friends and family, these feelings will pass more quickly than when alone. When choosing a friend that you want to stay with, choose the one who cares most about you, and not about the fact that you were raped. This is because many people have conflicting ideas about rape and they may give more attention to the incident than to your particular needs.

One of the best ways to help yourself is through women's groups and through rape crisis centers; this is because they are experienced in dealing with all the various reactions that a woman can feel after being raped. They will counsel you and give you comfort. They will seek legal advice on your behalf and they will help to get you through your serious psychological upsets. One of the most important things is that you get help and support from friends and sympathetic groups as soon as possible. This way you are giving yourself the best chance of coming through your rape experience without long-term psychological trauma.

Women's rape crisis centers say that one of the most helpful emotions for you to express after rape is rage, so get angry if you feel like it. They also point out that the least helpful emotion is guilt. Sympathetic and understanding friends, and qualified counsellors from rape crisis centers, can help you come to terms with both of these emotions.

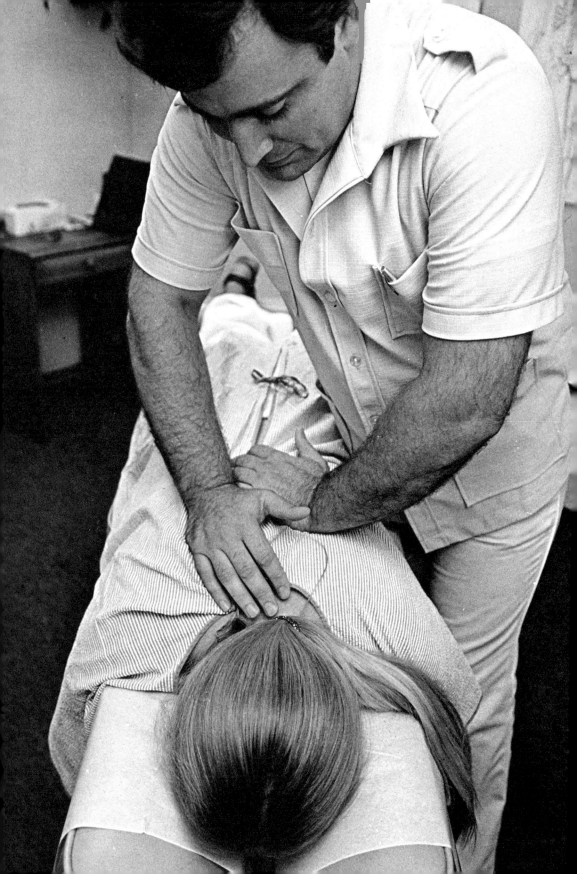

SPECIALIST HELP

The two main schools of Western medicine – orthodox and alternative – are still wary of each other's practices and attitudes. As a mainstream physician standing back I can see both points of view. There is much in unorthodox medicine that is mystifying to the traditionally trained physician. On the other hand, the results of alternative medicine must count for something. As long as they're not due to a natural remission (recognized in many chronic disorders such as rheumatoid arthritis or dermatitis), not due to the natural history of the disease in which improvement is common, for example migraine, nor any other factors which could contribute to a cure, they cannot be dismissed.

Specialist help straddles both schools. I'm very much in favor of an eclectic approach to health care and medicine, and it's my advice that you should not let current opinion, peer pressure or medical orthodoxy prevent you from trying something if you really feel like trying it. All I would suggest is that you find out as much as you can about any form of treatment before having it, that you retain a degree of skepticism, and that you analyze your expectations so that you can accept failure without too much discomfort.

The truth of the matter is that if you *believe* that a treatment will do you some good, then it probably will, but it may only be in your head. If, of course, your complaint has a psychosomatic element, then it will improve, but the improvement is not due to a direct medical effect. It's due to the fact that your attitude towards your condition has changed. This applies to most health spas and to most of the treatments, though not all, that you will receive there and to *all beauty clinics* (see chart on p. 344–347) unless it involves a specific proven treatment such as electrolysis, for the removal of unwanted hair.

Don't feel hidebound by tradition: specialist help is there to be taken advantage of and, as long as the claims aren't extravagant, then try new ways of taking care of your body. But beware of beauty clinics if you want any permanent result; almost the only guarantee is the feeling of having been pampered.

HEALTH SPAS

Health spas vary a great deal both in their attitude towards health and in the sort of treatment that they offer you. Many of them are devoted to one discipline; for instance, there are naturopathic health spas which believe in applying natural methods to promote fitness and health, such as meditation, hot baths, organically grown food, and massage. Others are osteopathic health spas, where the basic treatment is manipulation of the spine in the belief that the removal of pressure on nerves and the relaxation of muscles can have an effect on organs a long way from the spine (see p. 338). Yet others are nothing more than glorified hotels where you can pick and choose some semi-luxurious treatments, adhere to a diet during the day but go out on a binge at night.

The latter cannot be said to take the matter of health and fitness at all seriously but are really there as holiday hotels with all the amenities of a hotel resort and a few additional ones like massage, heat treatments and facials. For people who are more serious about their health there are genuine health spas, but they are few and far between and you have to search them out. They take health, fitness, diet and the care of one's body very seriously. Staying at one of these and taking advantage of the expert help which is available, not to mention the information which any of the consultants will readily give to help you, can change your attitude towards diet, towards exercise, towards keeping fit, towards maintaining your health, towards taking responsibility for your body and even towards changing your lifestyle for good.

You can almost determine how serious a health spa is about health and fitness by the length of time it suggests you stay there. Most good ones require a minimum stay of 3 or 4 days. They justify this on the grounds that it takes at least that length of time for their treatment regimens to have any effect. Frankly, I do not believe that this is a commercial ploy: the serious health spas in which I have stayed firmly believe it.

On the other hand, some of the more frivolous health spas offer bargain breaks/stays, or weekends and may even describe them as slimming sessions or simply a relaxing weekend. Most of their advertisements stress that a large number of treatments are crammed into a short stay (and may include body massage, saunas, yoga, facial massage, Slendertone treatment and jogging), and there is an emphasis on beauty rather than on health care.

In those clinics where the minimum stay is 4 days you will be received by one of the consultants as soon as you check in for your initial consultation with a member of the medical staff. This involves a fairly lengthy conversation about your health and past illnesses, your diet and your fitness. It's modelled on an orthodox medical interview but the consultant spends more time with you and goes into greater detail. There is not an orthodox medical examination, but at the very minimum your weight and blood pressure are measured. If your particular health clinic specializes in osteopathy or chiropractic you will have a full osteopathic or chiropractic examination to assess the health of your spine, muscles and joints.

The consultant will almost certainly ask what your expectations from your stay are, what you hope to gain, and what you hope to do. As a result of this, you will mutually agree on a desirable program which will be carried out each day and will include the sort of diet that you will eat and the various treatments that you will receive. The consultant will take care to explain the rationale behind the treatments and will be very happy to answer any of your questions. At the best clinics, a holistic approach is employed. In other words, the consultant is eager to consider all aspects of the body and its health, including your emotional and psychological health, social, domestic, and professional welfare.

Special diets

Nearly all naturopathic clinics consider nutrition a major factor in combating disease, and malnutrition or poor eating habits to be an important cause of disease. In no serious health spa is diet ever neglected.

You will be advised to spend the first 2 or 3 days on fluid. The consultant will explain that the theory behind this fasting is to allow "toxins" to be eliminated by the body and to give the digestive and other metabolic processes complete rest from having to handle food, thereby diverting energy used in digestion and metabolism to self-healing and self-curing body processes. To the best of my knowledge there is no medical evidence to prove this theory. The scientific definition of a toxin is a poison, and if you ask a consultant to explain which poisons will be eliminated from the body, you will be given a rather ill-defined reply. However, most naturopaths consider that the elimination of deleterious chemical substances from the body is the first step towards restoring your health.

During a fast you may experience unpleasant symptoms like a headache, a feeling of weakness, even faintness on standing, but true to their claims, these feelings usually disappear after 48 hours. At any time, of course, you can discuss your symptoms and seek assurance from your consultant.

A typical diet regimen in a health spa for the first days following a fast is usually made up of yoghurt, fruit, vegetables, honey, wheatgerm and small amounts of lean meat, chicken or fish.

Treatment baths

The commonest sort of *bath* is simply warm water in which any of a variety of "health-giving" substances have been dissolved.

Moor or peat bath
This is frequently used because it is said that peat has soothing properties and holds heat so it acts like a complete body poultice and helps to promote relaxation of the body when it is tired and tense. This sort of bath is used particularly for older people who are not fit enough to withstand the strong heat of steam cabinets.

Sitz bath
This is a special treatment which is used to tone up the muscles and organs in the abdominal and pelvic areas: it is said to improve circulation to these parts of the body. When I attended a health spa after an attack of hepatitis it was claimed that the sitz bath would help to improve the circulation to my liver. Medically speaking, I had little faith in this claim.

As the name would suggest, a sitz bath is a small bath in which you simply sit. First of all you sit with the lower part of the abdomen, buttocks and thighs in hot water and your feet in cold water. This opens up the blood vessels,

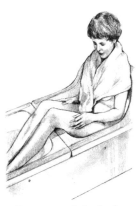

One type of sitz bath contains hot and cold tubs.

certainly of the skin of this area, and possibly of the internal organs, and improves the blood flow. After ten minutes or so, you change and sit in a sitz bath full of cold water. This does the opposite; it makes the blood vessels contract down and the blood is withdrawn from this area, and it is claimed impurities are drawn along with the blood into the rest of the circulation. In this way, blood is flushed in and out of the lower abdominal and pelvic area with alleged cleansing and toning results.

Massage   Most health spas include a massage regime as a standard part of treatment; they claim it releases tension, stimulates circulation and assists the elimination of toxins through the skin.

One thing should be clearly understood: massage does not help you to lose weight and it does not break down fat. The masseur or masseuse who works extremely hard may lose some weight, but you will not; nor does massage help to tone or strengthen muscles. It will almost certainly help you to relax and will probably make you feel good, but it sometimes uncovers a few aches and pains that you didn't have before. Massage stimulates circulation to the part which is being massaged and generally improves nourishment of the tissues and it may release emotional tension by breaking down muscular tension.

Massage may take some getting used to, particularly if the masseur or masseuse is strong and firm with you. I certainly found the first two or three times somewhat uncomfortable.

MASSAGE TREATMENTS

Massage is a means of releasing tension and stimulating circulation in the body. To prevent friction and facilitate the movement of the masseur's hands, either oil, talcum powder or cream is smoothed onto the body. The techniques used, and the order in which the masseur works on the body, are a matter of individual taste, but s/he will always work towards the heart to promote the return of blood. Whichever method of massage is used (see right), the movements should always be smooth and rhythmic; they may be firm but they should never be rough.

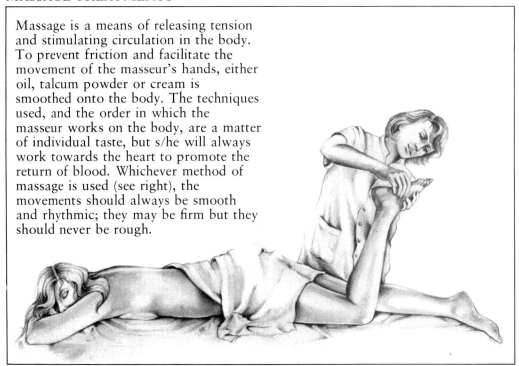

In so-called *Swedish massage*, the movements are carried out with energy and force. The strokes of the massage are long and heavy, particularly over the large muscle masses such as the calves, thighs and back, and your masseur may employ slapping movements with the side of the hand and firm downward movements with the cupped hand.

Other methods of massage may be used, such as *Shiatsu* (the forceful application of the thumb to specific points of the body with the object of stimulating particular nerves), water massage, as in whirlpool baths (jets of water in a special tub bombard the entire body), and neuro-muscular massage (fingertip pressure on specific motor points of muscles to relieve muscular tension).

Heat treatments

Health spas claim that these generalized heat treatments have two effects: the first is to increase the body temperature, thereby accelerating the elimination of toxins from the body, and the second is to make the body sweat. It is claimed that toxins are lost through the skin in sweat.

Sauna and steam bath
These are the most radical of the heat treatments and can raise the body's temperature several degrees, causing profuse sweating. They should not be undertaken by anyone who is medically infirm or who has a heart or chest condition. It is usually recommended that the first sauna or steam treatment last only a few minutes and can be curtailed at any time the patient feels unwell. In a sauna, you should lie down on a towel, in a steam cabinet you are sitting up. After each of these treatments, you are encouraged to have a cool, or cold, shower, and with the sauna you may return for several more minutes of heat. Exposure to the heat should be raised very gradually by only a few minutes each day.

Because body temperature is increased and the blood vessels in the skin are dilated, the pulse rate rises and the work done by the heart also increases. This improves the circulation and certainly after a few minutes of rest following a sauna or a steam treatment and a cool shower, there is a general feeling of well-being.

Hot blanket
This treatment consists of wrapping you in a specially-designed electrically-heated blanket so that gentle heat can be applied to the whole body.

Physiotherapy

A number of treatments are available for patients who either require specialized attention or simply need their muscles toned up to get into condition.

Exercise programs
There are a variety of gentle exercise programs which are designed to help people to loosen up arthritic joints, to strengthen damaged muscles, or possibly to improve breathing in people who have chest diseases. Many exercises may be carried out in warm water or heated pools.

Local heat

Local heat, quite often infra-red, is usually used to treat sore or uncomfortable parts of the body such as fingers, wrists, elbows, hips, shoulders, etc. Wax baths, when the hands are immersed and exercised in the melted wax, are used for the small joints of the hands. The hands may be wrapped in warm wax following the exercises to prolong the heat treatment.

Ultra-violet radiation

Ultra-violet radiation or sunlight treatment is used in a variety of forms, none of which does any good. One method which is advocated is a short burst of no more than a minute of a very narrow spectrum of ultra-violet radiation which kills off bacteria on the surface of the skin. There is absolutely no medical indication for this nor any benefit which can accrue.

Obtaining a suntan through ultra-violet radiation, by gradually increasing the dose day by day is to be deprecated. Ultra-violet radiation does nothing but harm to the skin (see p. 83), even though a tanned skin may be thought to be healthy in appearance.

Electrical stimulation (microwave)

Microwave is an electrical therapy which works on the same basis as a microwave oven. It promotes internal heat in a painful or uncomfortable part of the body by causing water molecules to vibrate and heat up.

Ultrasound

Ultrasonics use sound waves of very short wave length which penetrate to the deep layers of muscles and joints and create a vibration which in turn creates heat. Ultrasound may be of benefit in some conditions such as frozen shoulder, tennis elbow, strains and sprains.

Inhalation exercises

These are recommended for patients with chest conditions, and involve an exercise program performed daily to improve breathing. An instructor will demonstrate correct breathing and then advise and guide a patient as to how to go about achieving full inhalation and expiration. Quite often, steam inhalations, possibly combined with aromatic oils, are used to soothe and open up the air passages. These treatments are of possible value and certainly are good in terms of re-educating a patient about deep breathing if she normally only uses the upper part of her lungs.

Enemas and colonic irrigation

These two treatments are alive to the theory that it is necessary to help the body get rid of toxins and waste substances by cleaning out the intestines. There is no medical evidence to support that the body needs to do this. Even during fasting, when feces may not be rapidly transported along the intestines and expelled, there is nothing to be gained by washing them out. The theory of auto-intoxication, i.e. that poison may be absorbed from feces which stay in the intestine, has long been disproved.

Special classes   Nearly every health spa has classes in the afternoon which are not compulsory but which anyone can attend to learn the various ways of relaxation, yoga and meditation. A person specially trained in yoga may conduct classes for anyone who wishes to attend and will advise and teach you how to continue practicing after you have left the health spa. These treatment sessions are usually optional and most often take place in the late afternoon, at a time which is free from other treatment regimens. They normally involve attendance at hour-long sessions given by experienced practitioners.

Nearly every day a member of the staff or a visiting lecturer will give a seminar on a specific subject, such as stress control or nutrition, which is aimed at giving general advice on how to achieve and maintain health and fitness of the body.

What are the "real" benefits of staying at a health spa?

Nearly every health spa you will attend has a great respect for *rest* and sleep. Most have a notice that you can put on your door if you wish to sleep or rest and you will not be disturbed even though it means missing your treatment regimes. Of course, health spas are quite right to respect this desire to rest because who knows, it may be rest alone that makes you feel so much better. It may be catching up with a prolonged sleep debt, it may be slowing down the pace of your usual lifestyle, it may be simply lounging, relaxing and contemplating.

Because nearly all health spas are in beautiful country houses set in well laid out gardens in the heart of the country and are peaceful and quiet, you are *removed from stress* and in pleasant surroundings. This in itself can be therapeutic. There are no phones constantly ringing, no-one requiring your attention, no day-to-day problems to look after. Just this peacefulness alone may account for the feeling of well-being which for most people is the real result of staying in a health spa.

If you wish you can *learn new habits* by taking advantage of the various theories about diet, exercise, sleep, naturopathy, homeopathy, etc., which are taught or are readily available on asking at most health spas. If you are determined that you will change your lifestyle to accommodate them and you feel the benefits are rewarding, then, of course, you can use a visit to a health spa to start a retraining program for yourself, and when necessary, revisit the health spa to give your morale a boost and your determination a second wind.

Will staying at a health spa help me lose weight?

Don't expect to lose a lot of weight; weight loss is nearly always slight. This is because while you may eat less, your level of activity is also a great deal less than that which you generally undertake during your normal working life. There is a great deal of rest, there may be gentle walks through the grounds, but there are no activities which really use up energy, so while you consume fewer calories, you also use fewer calories. Any weight which is lost due to heat baths, blanket baths, saunas, steam cabinets or sweating, is put back as soon as one starts to take fluids because the body re-establishes its fluid balance by retaining all the liquid which it has lost through sweating.

Can health spas help cure disease?

While spas offer a variety of treatments which are claimed to be specifically designed for specific diseases, such as wax baths for arthritis, breathing therapy for asthma, and colonic irrigation and sitz baths for digestive problems, and while arthritis, asthma and digestive problems may be improved (though not necessarily due to these specific cures), most people will be sadly disappointed if they expect to see a radical change in an existing medical condition simply due to a stay in a health spa. Indeed, most health spas encourage the continuation of all conventional medicines while patients are staying there. On the other hand, some general changes in lifestyle, if taken seriously and practiced regularly, e.g. inhalation exercises for asthma or a high fiber diet for diverticulitis, can lead to improvement and possibly lower doses of orthodox medication.

Will I be more fit after a visit?

To increase your fitness you must exercise. You must exercise to improve the suppleness of your body and its joints, to increase the strength and mobility of your muscles and joints, and to improve the efficiency of your heart and lungs. This can only be done through an exercise regimen such as that given on p. 40. It cannot be done with massage, with electrical stimulation of the muscles, with gentle workouts in the gym or with other machines which make claims to spot reduce, that is take fat off the hips or thighs. These machines which pummel and vibrate the fat do absolutely nothing to remove fat pads.

BEAUTY CLINICS

While a dedicated health spa can contribute to making your life healthier in practical ways, beauty clinics cannot, and despite their seductive and over-stated claims, they cannot make any radical or even semi-permanent change in your appearance. If you are going to pay good money to go to beauty clinics, you should be very clear about what to expect. They may specialize in certain forms of treatment, indeed most do, though they will also offer a variety or a menu of skin treatments and possibly hair treatments from which you can choose. However, none of the procedures which they use (see p. 344–347) has ever been shown to have more than a transient effect. By transient I mean an effect which lasts at the very most a few days, possibly a few hours, and in many cases, no more than a few minutes.

There are several aspects of beauty clinics that form the basis of my distrust about what they are doing and the honesty of their claims. Cleansing of the skin forms the bedrock of all beauty clinic practices; not only is it emphasized, it is performed in many ways using a multiplicity of techniques and a great variety of different pieces of machinery. Indeed, the beauticians' interest in cleansing verges on the obsessional. This has no medical or physical rationale at all and to a dermatologist, like myself, it is difficult to understand, for the skin is a self-cleansing organ. Not only that, it has never been shown either physiologically or medically that there is any particular benefit in cleaning skin (see p. 81).

Very often we hear that the "pores" of the skin need opening up, cleaning and, to use a beautician's word, "refining." If by the pores of the skin the beauticians mean the sweat glands, and the sebaceous glands, then they are nearly always open. Furthermore, they cannot be blocked, not unless there is an underlying medical condition, such as acne – where they are blocked due to the secretion of a hormone inside the body, and the application of creams to the outside of the skin cannot unblock the sebaceous glands permanently in acne. They may have an effect lasting a few hours, but the exit from the sebaceous glands will reblock again simply because one cannot change the hormone levels in the blood by applying creams to the skin.

Another of the things that makes me most suspicious about beauty clinics, beauticians and cosmeticians is the language which they use. Much of the language is pseudo-scientific; it has no basis in medicine, in science, or indeed in the language itself. As already stated, I can find no medical explanation for words like re-energize, refine and revitalize when applied to the skin. It is just not possible to revitalize the skin, or any other organ for that matter. Revitalize means give new life; medicine knows no way of giving new life to any part of the body. The words are there to impress and to seduce, and to a certain extent bamboozle. To my mind this verges on dishonesty.

Nowhere in the advertising world are such exaggerated claims made as in the field of cosmetics and beauty. The astounding thing is that so many women accept them unproven and unchallenged. On many occasions I have attempted to obtain scientific data which would support the claims made by cosmetic firms. On no occasion has the data been sent to me. Having worked in the pharmaceutical industry and belonging to a profession where scientific proof of the efficacy of any medication is a basic necessity for its use, the lack of information about the efficacy of beauty products makes me highly skeptical about the basis for claims. For example, if a new and extremely expensive cosmetic claims that it will make you "look younger, longer," my two immediate questions to this statement are – "Younger than what?" "For longer than what?" The statement is empty without a comparison. The experiment to prove this statement would take many years, because what you would have to do would be to use the cosmetic on one side of your face and any other cosmetic that you use routinely on the other side of your face. At the end of several years you would see if there was any difference. The test has obviously not been performed and the claim is therefore an empty one. The cosmetic manufacturers know this but simply hope that women will continue to be fooled.

The most exciting part of your visit to a beauty clinic may be getting a new make-up because certainly a good beautician can give you make-up tips which can do quite a lot to change your appearance. A beauty clinic, however, is not necessarily the best place to get this advice. It is better to go to a make-up expert, someone who works professionally at making up the faces of models, or does work for television and films. A visit to a cosmetic house may give you this sort of advice.

Some beauty clinics do offer a service – to perform *electrolysis* which undoubtedly is effective for the removal of facial hair (see p. 84). The treatment may require several repeat visits because only a few hairs are treated at once, but it is a true cure.

"Beauty treatments" The following information on some of the treatments which are available at beauty clinics is my attempt to help you find your way through the maze of exotic-sounding treatments that you are offered. None of them is necessary and some can be harmful. However, you must decide whether or not you want to spend your good money on getting very little in return.

Many of the treatments involve some type of electrical apparatus, which is primarily beneficial in maintaining client interest rather than providing a lasting change in appearance. Don't be fooled into thinking they have a greater scientific basis.

Name of treatment and claims made for it	Explanation of what it does	What are you likely to get from it?	Instances when you should not have it

SLIMMING TREATMENTS

Electrical muscle stimulation (Slendertone)

Supposed to make the muscles work without your doing any work	By the application of pads through which an electric current runs, the muscle underlying the pad is made to alternately relax and contract	Very little other than a tingling sensation in the skin underneath the pad. If a muscle contracts without you doing any work you do not use up any energy. You will therefore not lose weight and it's very doubtful indeed whether the muscle will be toned up	If you have a skin complaint like dermatitis or psoriasis

Massage

Said to release tension, relax muscles, improve congestion	There are various forms of massage, e.g. Shiatsu (see p. 339 for more information)	For many people it may aid relaxation. It may improve the blood flow to the muscles and skin	None if it is gentle.

Sweating

Attempts to decrease body weight through water loss	By sweating a great deal you temporarily lose moisture and therefore lose as much as 4 lbs in weight if the sweating procedure is extremely rigorous	Loss of weight lasting only a few hours. The body reacts to the weight loss by retaining all the fluid you take in the next few hours to replace that you will have lost. One can feel weak due to the heat and in a thin or old person it can cause dehydration	If you have a weak heart, high or low blood pressure or if you are medically infirm and given to fainting

Name of treatment and claims made for it	Explanation of what it does	What are you likely to get from it?	Instances when you should not have it
Suction cupping			
Claims to help break down fat and aid weight loss. It is also said to improve lymphatic drainage	A rubber cup, connected to an air pump, is applied to the skin and a vacuum is created underneath the skin which sucks up subcutaneous fat into the skin	Nothing other than its psychological effect. Fat cannot be lost by any amount of massage or suction. Lymphatic drainage does not help weight loss	None
Wrapping			
Attempts to decrease body weight through water loss	Wrapping involves covering the body in cloths which may or may not be impregnated with lotions, gels or extracts which are usually vegetable or herbal	Same as sweating	Same as sweating

SKIN TREATMENTS

Brush cleansing			
The dead layer of cells is peeled off from the skin surface leaving it smooth and "cleaner"	The skin is cleansed by the use of a circulating brush. The brush may be replaced with a pumice block of a more abrasive effect	Your skin will certainly feel smoother but only temporarily. Dead cells reach the surface of the skin and you are back to square one in a few hours. It releases bacteria from the lower levels of the skin and therefore may increase the number of bacteria on the skin	If you have any form of skin complaint affecting the skin. Never ever have a cleansing routine like this performed in a beauty clinic if you have any spots
Skin peeling			
Claims to make the skin fresh, young, clean and more supple, and surface wrinkles may even be removed. In particular, "sallow complexions" and post-acne scarring are said to benefit	Fruit and vegetable extracts and abrasives remove dead cells and speed up the rate at which the skin loses dead cells	A clean, smooth skin which lasts at the most a few hours. It will not change a sallow complexion into a bright one; it will not affect acne scarring	If you have a skin disease, or if you have a sensitive skin or one, for instance, that burns easily in the sun, as the dead layer of skin acts as a necessary protection and should not be removed artificially
Facial massage			
Said to "increase the skin's capacity to function more efficiently"	The skin and muscles of the face are massaged in various directions, usually upwards and outwards; the direction is crucial to the beautifying effect of the treatment. There is a variety of more sophisticated massage procedures, including *Viennese* facial treatment which involves cleansing, massage, the use of high frequency electrical current (see below), a facial mask, skin toning and make-up. None of these procedures has any physiological rationale	A feeling of being pampered and possibly relaxed. Neither the skin nor the muscles of the face need massage. There is no better way of exercising the skin and muscles of the face than by normal activity such as talking, chewing, laughing, smiling	None

Name of treatment and claims made for it	Explanation of what it does	What are you likely to get from it?	Instances when you should not have it
Face masks			
Said to cleanse the pores, make the pores shrink, remove dead cells from the surface of the skin, increase blood flow to the skin	A face mask is applied to the skin containing such ingredients as honey, egg yolk, peach, avocado or glycerin. It is applied to the skin, allowed to dry and wiped away	A pleasant, relaxing interval without justification. Pores cannot be permanently shrunk, and the feeling of tightness that follows the removal of a face mask wears off very quickly	If you have a sensitive skin, eczema, dermatitis, or an infection of the skin, e.g. acne
Pressure spray toning			
Said to tone skin by increasing water content	A fine spray of water under pressure is forced on to the face, usually to remove a face mask	A psychological lift. Any water that enters the skin in this form will escape due simply to evaporation within about 20 minutes	None
Facial vacuum treatment			
Claims to improve the lymphatic drainage of the skin, the nutritional state of the tissue and helps to remove blackheads and oily secretions	Treatment with a facial vacuum may last from 3–5 minutes for cleansing and for 10–12 minutes for massage and drainage of the lymph vessels	A psychological benefit. It will cleanse and it may help to remove blackheads and oily secretions. It cannot improve the nutritional state of the skin nor can it help lymphatic drainage. This is done most efficiently simply by the force of gravity because all the lymph vessels of the face, head and neck drain down	If you have any form of skin disease
Ozone therapy			
Said to dry, heal and stimulate seborrheic skin, especially acne, and is beneficial to "disturbed and blemished" skin	Ozone, which is chemically related to pure oxygen with one more atom of oxygen in the molecule, is applied to the skin, usually in the form of steam	Psychological benefit. At one time it was thought that ozone had all sorts of medicinal properties. These have never been clearly defined let alone proved	If you have a very sensitive skin or skin disease

ELECTRICAL TREATMENTS

Audiosonic vibration			
Said to increase the circulation of the blood in the locality being treated, beauticians claim "that it can increase cellular activity" and so delay or arrest the development of wrinkles, lined skin and other symptoms of advancing age	The audiosonic vibrator may have a sponge or flat disc head which vibrates due to an electric motor	Psychological benefit only	None
Vibrator treatments			
Said to stimulate circulation and have a relaxing effect	An electric facial vibrator produces mechanical vibrations to simulate the effects of massage with the hands	You may feel relaxed after it and it may increase blood flow to the skin but no more than talking, chewing, eating, laughing	None

346

Name of treatment and claims made for it	Explanation of what it does	What are you likely to get from it?	Instances when you should not have it
Diathermy			
Used for removing unwanted facial hair	A fine wire or metal point, which becomes red hot when an electrical current is passed through it, is applied to the hair root to kill it	Permanent removal of unwanted facial hair	Where the treatment is for broken veins if the practitioner is not a medically qualified dermatologist (see p. 354)
High frequency			
Said to dry, refine and heal the skin and produce a germicidal effect on the skin's surface to reduce the production of sebum	A high frequency current is applied to the skin	You may get permanent scarring of the skin if this is used in inexperienced hands	If you have any skin disease

GALVANIC TREATMENTS

Iontophoresis			
Said that acidic substances have an astringent effect. There is a variety of treatments packaged pseudo-scientifically in ampules which beauticians use from 3–12 minutes to moisturize or normalize the skin	Galvanic current is used to introduce water soluble chemicals into the upper layers of the skin	Psychological benefit. Nothing can stay in the skin, not even an ion which is electrically pumped into the skin, because it is lost or shed in the skin cells within a few hours and in the case of water, a few minutes. The claim that frequent and regular prolonged courses of this treatment have a lasting effect on the skin are without foundation	If you have a skin disease
Disencrustation			
Said to remove blockages in the skin's surface oiliness and regulate secretions	There is special disencrustation fluid contained in ampules for use during iontophoresis. Many beauticians claim, however, that a simple solution of salt and water is as effective as the exotic ingredients contained in these ampules and indeed very often do use salt water on their client	Psychological benefit. The word "disencrustation" is a word entirely made up by beauticians: it has no scientific basis, nor can I find any true meaning for the word whatsoever; it is true pseudo-science	If you have a very sensitive dry skin or any form of skin disease

REGENERATIVE CELL THERAPY

Most extravagant claims of anything from curing diseases to putting off the effects of ageing	Cells from the organs of animals are injected into people for the treatment of specific organ complaints, for instance, if you have a liver disease then the liver cells from healthy animals are injected into you. Failures are claimed to be due to improper administration of treatment – not treatment itself	Psychological benefit at most. Despite exhaustive medical testing has never been proven to have any medical effect. It is extremely expensive	None

347

Can beauty clinics effect a permanent change in appearance?

No treatment offered in a beauty clinic can in any way permanently change the look or the nature of the skin you have inherited, because you have inherited it. It is as unchangeable as the color of your eyes. Nothing that a beauty clinic can do will make your skin less greasy or less dry than it is, all you can hope to do is to repeat procedures daily or several times daily that will mop up the excess grease or moisturize your skin.

Are there treatments which slow down ageing?

The very fact that there is a multiplicity of treatments offered by beauty clinics means that none of them works satisfactorily. There is nothing that a beautician can do to your skin, nor advise you to take, or give by injection, that will do anything at all to slow down ageing, either in terms of the appearance of the skin or the way the body functions. If people knew how to slow down ageing they would have the secret of life and they would be millionaires.

Can beauty clinics remove wrinkles?

The only way that wrinkles can be *removed* is by cosmetic surgery, nothing else, no matter how compelling the sales pitch. Various drying preparations can be put on the skin which make it contract and make wrinkles shrink. For a few hours, your wrinkles may look less, but anything which dehydrates the skin is bad for it and is to be deprecated and avoided. If you want to look especially good for special occasions, I would suggest this form of beauty treatment should be used sparingly and very seldom. If you can resist it, do so.

Do hormone creams have any value?

There are many preparations advocated by beauty clinics to be used on the skin, usually creams containing exotic ingredients, many of them containing hormones. None of these has been shown to have any more benefit to the skin than simple moisturizing cream. Furthermore, the concentration of medical additives such as hormones, e.g. placental extract, etc. (though again I am not sure what this means), is by law, necessarily low, for the law states that any medical substance which is applied to the skin in sufficient quantity to have a measurable clinical effect, can only be obtained by prescription. It follows, therefore, that if you buy something over the counter, the concentration of the medicament in the cream has to be so low that it has no measurable effect.

COSMETIC SURGERY

In the Western world, particularly in America, taking advantage of cosmetic surgery has almost become an inevitable part of getting older. With the cult of youth many women feel forced to try to maintain their youthful looks by artificial means. Cosmetic surgery will certainly reverse some of the effects of ageing and so has now flourished because there is a ready market. At one time, it was little discussed and was almost a taboo subject. Now most women boast about it and there is a great deal of publicity when someone like Betty Ford is able to change her appearance by a total facelift. The results, in most cases, are excellent. It is possible for a good plastic surgeon to completely change your appearance, not just of your face but of the actual contours of your body. However, it is necessary that if you are going to have cosmetic surgery you be well motivated because you will have to bear discomfort and you may be somewhat depressed after the operation when the effects are not immediately apparent. In addition, it is important that you are not having the operation for the wrong reasons: if you have serious psychological problems which affect aspects of your life other than your appearance, cosmetic surgery is not going to put them right. On the other hand, if you have suffered severe psychological stress as a result of some deformity, then the long-term benefits of cosmetic surgery are undoubted and will affect all aspects of your life including your relationships with other people, the way you do your job, and your self-assurance. You very often will feel more at ease with yourself and be more self-assured and, as a result of that alone, you will look better. For some people it amounts to starting a new life.

Choosing a cosmetic surgeon

Before you go into the actual business of seeking help by cosmetic surgery you should be aware that it is an extremely expensive business. A facelift costs upwards of $5000; pinning back protruding ears costs about $1500; removing drooping skin from your upper eyelids may cost you $600; breast reconstruction runs at least $5000. If you wish to have your whole body contour changed you can expect to make an outlay of many thousands.

First of all you have to find a good cosmetic surgeon and these are the things that you should look for or do:
● Get a good recommendation. The best possible recommendation is from your own doctor because s/he will be able to give you an objective professional opinion. Almost as good is a recommendation from a friend who has had cosmetic surgery, especially if you knew her before and afterwards. Never, ever, follow up an advertisement in a newspaper or magazine. Anyone who has to advertise their services cannot be that good because a good surgeon would have no need to advertise. Your county medical society may be able to supply you with the names of local surgeons.
● Be suspicious about a surgeon who will perform exactly the operation that you request without giving her/his professional opinion as to what you actually need. A good surgeon will advise you as to the operation that will bring about the best results for you and should make recommendations of what should be done.
● Be skeptical about a surgeon who is not realistic about the results of the operation. No good surgeon will give you 100% guarantee of success. S/he should also take some time to explain in detail exactly what the operation involves and what s/he is trying to achieve, and a realistic estimate of the chances of success.

● Be mistrustful of a surgeon who doesn't answer your questions in detail with drawings, pictures, and examples of her/his work, especially the before and after photographs.

● A good surgeon should take several photographs of your body or the part of your body that s/he is going to operate on, because s/he needs the photographs to study exactly how to make the correction and what s/he needs to do. If the surgeon does not, ask why not, and if you cannot get a good reason, move on to another surgeon.

● Never ever work with a surgeon whom do not establish a good rapport with. If you do not like the surgeon at your first visit, then you are unlikely to get to like her/him later on, so only entrust yourself to a surgeon with whom you strike up a good relationship from the very beginning.

Deciding on cosmetic surgery

Having cosmetic surgery is a two-way contract between you and the surgeon, and while the surgeon owes you services of a high standard, you owe it to her/him to have thought it out in some detail. Before you make a decision, here are a few points that you ought to think about:

● There are occasionally pre-conditions for some types of surgery such as being of a certain age, being as slim as possible, having completed your family, being unable to breastfeed subsequently and, if for breast augmentation post-mastectomy, that there is no indication that cancer has spread.

● The results of the operation may not be as good as you expect and in a very few cases may not be good at all, so that it does not work out exactly as you planned. In addition, there may be complications that delay your recovery and, of course, there are always risks associated with any operation even though they are often slight.

● All surgery carries some risk – the risk of a general anesthetic and of a subsequent chest infection, and very, very rarely, of dying – and you should be aware that you are having a serious surgical procedure which, except in a very few instances, is entirely unnecessary. In addition, the majority of patients who have cosmetic surgery are not young; their hearts and chests are less fit and healthy than younger women and it could be argued that they run greater risks with surgery and anesthetics.

● Immediately after the operation, it will be unpleasant. You will feel sore, there may be bruising, your skin may be swollen, there may be redness and discomfort or even pain for several days or weeks. You may be completely immobilized for a short time, or your activities restricted. If you are highly motivated to have the operation you can almost certainly cope with these temporary setbacks, but you must be prepared in advance.

● Some of the operations leave tiny scars behind them. A good cosmetic surgeon will be careful to hide the scar in natural skin lines inside the mouth or under the hair line, but occasionally they are still visible. If you have any concern about scarring you should talk in some detail to your surgeon about the chances of there being any present when surgery is completed.

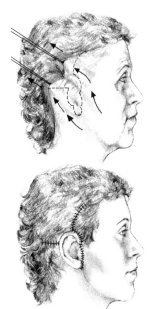

In a standard facelift the extraneous, loose skin is lifted off the face and pulled taut over the ear. It is then trimmed and stitched along the lines shown. The dramatic results of only half a facelift are shown, right.

Three frequently per- formed operations are shown here: in nose re- ductions excess bone, cartilage and tissue are removed, working from inside the nose so that no stitches are needed. Chins are built up with a plastic im- plant, working from inside the mouth, and breasts are augmented with an implant, in- serted into the breast through the fold.

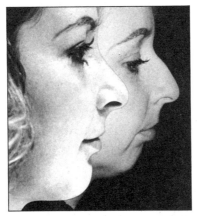

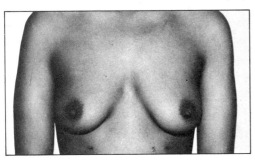
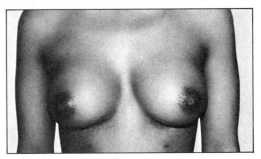

COSMETIC OPERATIONS

Operation	In/Out-patient Length of stay	Post-operative effects	Stitches removed	Results Recovery time
Blepharoplasty (removing bags under eyes and reshaping eyelids)	In-patient 3 days if possible	Sore and bruised eyes	48 hours	Very good 3 months
Rhinoplasty (reshaping nose)	In-patient 3 days	Sore, swollen nose, and bruising under the eyes	None	Excellent 6 months
Chin augmentation	In-patient 3 days minimum	Sore inside the mouth and a swollen chin	None	Excellent 3 months
Facelift	In-patient 3 days	Red, swollen face	Some after 5–7 days, the rest after 2 weeks	Generally good; should last 8 years Swelling goes down after 4 weeks
Breast augmentation	In-patient 3 days minimum	Bruising and tingling around the nipples; occasionally soreness	1 week	Very good 2 months

MEDICAL SKIN TREATMENTS

Any technique or treatment which is capable of altering the skin's appearance permanently, for example, up to a year, should be undertaken only by a medically qualified person, for instance, a dermatologist or a plastic surgeon. I am absolutely categorical in making this statement, the reason being that treatments which have such radical effects, have side-effects as well, and can damage the skin if the treatment is not properly performed. Only a person who is medically qualified has sufficient knowledge to make the acute judgement about how much and when the treatment can be given safely. If one of the following treatments is being offered by a non-medically qualified person, then do not have it; any of the following, if badly administered, can damage the skin permanently and have serious side-effects, including scars.

Chemical skin peeling

This can be done for medical or cosmetic reasons. The agent most commonly used by doctors is phenol which, when painted on the skin, causes coagulation, inflammation, swelling and peeling. Phenol may be absorbed through the skin and in large doses may harm the kidneys. It must, therefore, be used cautiously and infrequently and never applied over a large area. Usually used in small local areas for the treatment of acne scarring, or superficial complaints such as small spots and cysts, skin peeling treatment for cosmetic purposes may involve large areas in order to get rid of minor blemishes, fine lines and wrinkles, pit marks and scarring, and even treat discolored areas of skin and freckles. This process may soften the facial lines but does not stop the ageing process. The rejuvenating effect usually wears off within a year. The skin peeling agent may be an acid such as trichlorascetic acid, which produces a second degree burn and turns the skin a whitish grey color. A brown crust forms within 3–5 days and then drops off. The skin becomes pink and tight with fewer lines and wrinkles.

Beauty clinics offer skin peeling using fruit and vegetable extracts which have a transitory effect (see p. 345).

Cryotherapy

As does the treatment mentioned above, freezing kills the cells on the surface of the skin and is a satisfactory way of treating warts and age spots. It is sometimes also used to treat broken veins on the cheeks. Agents used include ethyl chloride, carbon dioxide snow (carbon dioxide gas which is solid), and liquid nitrogen. Liquid nitrogen is a very good treatment for warts and verrucae, when applied for 5–30 seconds in saturated cotton wool. Blisters in the surrounding skin may follow treatment if any of the freezing agent touches it.

Curettage

This means scooping something out of the skin, such as a wart, with a cup-shaped spoon with a sharp cutting edge and is very simple and very quick in experienced hands. The small cyst or wart should simply shell out of the skin, leaving the bed intact with no bleeding. A caustic agent such as phenol may be dabbed into the crater after the treatment of warts to prevent regrowth.

353

Dermabrasion Usually used to improve acne scars on the face or to treat large birthmarks, it may produce fairly good results for the treatment of stretch marks and fine lines around the mouth. First introduced in the 1930s, it has today achieved a high level of sophistication. Results on the face are generally good because the skin is well supplied with hair follicles and sebaceous glands which allow the skin to regrow quickly. Scarring is rare. Dermabrasion is usually done with high-speed rotary drill plus cooling techniques. You are usually sedated or tranquillized before treatment begins and the area to be treated is filled with cold packs and cleansed with soap and water and then with surgical spirit. Ears, nostrils and hair are carefully protected and the eyes covered with an ointment and a lead shield held by an assistant. The skin is frozen with a stream of cold gas and then the drill abrades the skin to the required depth. Great experience and skill are required to perform this correctly.

The area may bleed for 15–30 minutes after treatment and non-adhesive surgical dressings are used for 12–24 hours. Crusts form over the treated area and drop off 7–10 days later. The wound should be left dry and open after this; if necessary, the treatment can be repeated after about four weeks.

Electro-desiccation This involves killing the cells of the skin with an electrical current either by a spark which solidifies the skin, or by heat which coagulates it; in either case the skin cells shrivel. This procedure is usually used for the treatment of broken veins on the face and legs and is sometimes used for the treatment of warts. A valuable technique in the dermatologist's clinic, it can treat small skin tags, several of which can be removed in one treatment session without any anesthesia: skin tags are coagulated by the application of the fine metal electric desiccator needle for only a few seconds, and because the blood vessels are coagulated, there is no bleeding. The surrounding skin may become inflamed by the burning, and crusts may form which fall off in about two weeks. Scarring is rare.

In a beauty clinic, electrocoagulation or *diathermy*, is used to remove unwanted facial hair, see p. 347.

ALTERNATIVE MEDICINE

There is no reason at all why you should think that the only medicine available to you is orthodox medicine practiced by orthodox physicians. There are many other forms of alternative medicine which can give very good results in certain circumstances. Unfortunately, because the practitioners of alternative medicine do not always subject their methods, treatments and results to the objective scientific scrutiny which is the accepted norm in orthodox medicine, they tend to remain on the fringe and be viewed as eccentric by orthodox medical practitioners.

You, however, should view the whole of medicine as a menu from which you can choose the dishes which suit you and which bring you the best results. To my mind, any medicine which makes the patient feel better, relieves discomfort and gives a general feeling of well-being without doing any harm, and without depriving the patient of essential orthodox medical therapy, for instance, digitalis for heart failure, then that is good medicine, and the practitioners of such methods are practicing good medicine.

You should view your body in a holistic way. In other words, you should look at all aspects of your health and include domestic, professional, emotional and psychological aspects of your life as well as the physical aspects which may be the ones that first take you along to your doctor.

The following summary is not meant to be exhaustive. It by no means includes all the various types of medical practice which would fall into the general category of alternative medicine. Please use it only as an introduction.

Osteopathy

Founded by an American doctor, Andrew Sill in 1874, his original thesis was that the body had the ability to regulate and heal itself provided that its structure is sound and the blood and nerve impulses can move freely. The basis of osteopathy is manipulation, and it tries to rectify changes in the body which are considered harmful. Changes may arise as a consequence of poor posture, trauma, sudden movement or bad sleeping positions.

Osteopaths manipulate the vertebrae in the spinal column and it is claimed that by doing so, the nervous system resumes its healthy functioning and may improve the health of distant organs. Osteopaths also believe that relief of muscle spasm by manipulation cures illnesses caused by stress and strain on the bones, muscles and nerves of the spinal column. Two basic techniques are massage to relieve muscle spasm, and manipulative correction of dislodged bones in the spine. The latter technique involves gentle leverage of one part of the body against another, e.g. the chin against the neck to adjust the position of the vertebrae at the base of the skull. One of the few branches of alternative medicine with well-documented cures, this is gaining medical acceptance.

Homeopathy

Started in the eighteenth century by a German doctor called Samuel Hahnemann but first mentioned by Hippocrates, Hahnemann's theory states that the human body has a capacity to heal itself. Symptoms of a disease are a reflection of the body's unsuccessful struggle to overcome the disease which is threatening the body's own life force. The basic theory behind homeopathy is that a doctor should discover and remove the cause of the disease and then allow the body's own self-healing force to cure itself by stimulating it. One of the basic tenets of homeopathy is that the smallest effective dose of any medicine should be used. Side-effects are rare. Hahnemann used a special method of dilution and found that the greater the dilution of medicine, the greater the effect. Homoeopathic medicines are usually of animal, vegetable or mineral origin; natural, therefore, and not synthetic. Herbs and botanical medicines and some naturally-occurring drugs like morphine, cocaine, arsenic, sand, charcoal, salt, phenol and lead are used. Homeopathy is a holistic medicine and treats the whole patient, not just the symptoms and not just the disease. Many cures have been recorded by homeopathic methods and this is one of the branches of alternative medicine that should be accepted by orthodox medical practitioners.

Naturopathy

These are the basic beliefs in naturopathy:
- The patient must be treated, not the disease.
- The whole patient must be treated, not just a part.
- The disease's cause must be removed before healing can occur.
- A disturbance of the body's natural life force causes disease.
- The true healer is the patient's life force, in other words, it is nature's healing power that cures.
- In order to cure itself the body has to go through a healing crisis; the life force cleanses the body by eliminating toxins or poisons.

Naturopaths believe that the potent drugs used by orthodox physicians, while having a superficial effect, actually drive the disease deeper in the body, leaving behind a chronic disease for the future. A natural diet and attention to nutrition are the mainstay of naturopathy. Fasts are advocated. Dietary constraints such as the elimination of refined foods, too much red meat and animal fat, and the inclusion of semi-digested foods such as yoghurt and natural foods like honey and bran are advocated. Food should be organically grown and unprocessed and, if possible, uncooked.

Naturopathy is also holistic and depends on the patient adopting the right attitude of mind. All forms of relaxation exercises, yoga, meditation, and psychotherapy are encouraged. Naturopaths also believe in breathing exercises and body exercise to keep muscles, bones and joints toned up and supple.

Acupuncture

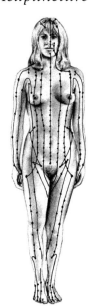

This simply means to pierce with a needle. It started when it was noticed that Chinese soldiers wounded in battle by arrows recovered, not only from the arrow wound, but from other ailments at some distance from the original wound as well. The theory of acupuncture is that life forces flow down energy channels along lines called meridians which are quite different from the lines followed by the nerves. The practitioners of acupuncture believe that this life force is interrupted in disease: if health is to be restored and maintained, the energy flow must be re-established. This is done by placing a copper, silver or gold needle in the meridian which is believed to be interrupted. The needle is inserted superficially in the flesh and should be painless. It is thought that the needle sets up some kind of an electrical current along the line of the meridian which re-establishes the life force which then affects the central nervous system and a distant organ such as the liver, kidneys, heart or lungs, stomach, bladder, etc. In the East, acupuncture is simply one of an array of medicines which are used by practicing physicians. The 10-minute session in private consulting rooms, as is practiced in the West, is frowned upon by Eastern acupuncturists. There are many well-documented cures of diseases by acupuncture: films exist of open cardiac surgery being performed – apparently only under anesthesia induced by acupuncture. It cannot be ignored though we do not know how it actually works.

You may choose to try an alternative treatment, such as acupuncture, especially if you've found traditional medical remedies for your problems unsuccessful. Acupuncture is used to treat various ailments, from migraines to asthma, and is even used for anesthesia.

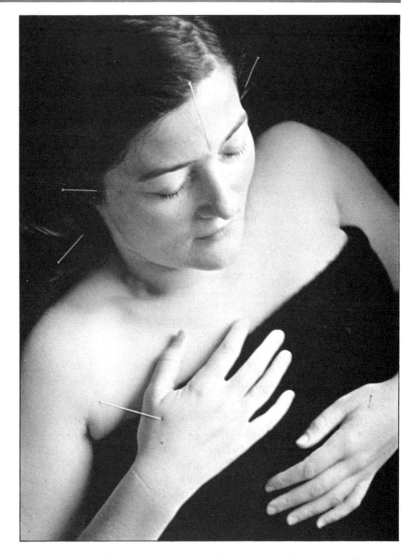

Chiropractic   Meaning literally "to practice with one's hands," it was founded by Daniel Palmer in the United States in the 1890s. Chiropractic, like osteopathy, treats diseases by manipulation of the spinal cord, thereby affecting the spinal nerves which branch out from it and supply all other parts of the body – skin, bone, muscles and internal organs, segmentally. Basic theory is that by manipulating a particular vertebrae and stimulating that spinal nerve, the health of muscles and organs which receive that nerve supply can be influenced. An example would be the liver, which is supplied by the nerves from the middle chest vertebrae. Manipulation is different from that in osteopathy. It is done with short, sharp thrusts which are intended to "spring" the bone into place. Very often the movements are sudden, downwards and upwards, and require great precision in placing the hands, timing, and directing the thrust of the movements.

357

Herbalism

Greater stitchwort

Eyebright

Herbalism is one of the oldest forms of medicine known to people. Herbal medicines are usually handed down as recipes through families, many having their own special remedies and tonics. Herbal treatments survived in an entirely hit-or-miss way, it being noted over the years that particular herbs had particular properties and could help particular diseases. In the beginning, like-cures-like was the basic theory behind herbal remedies: for example, yellow plants were used to cure yellow jaundice; plants with heart-shaped leaves were used to treat heart disease.

Plants may take their names from their medical application, e.g. heartsease, liverwort, eyebright, spleenwort, bloodstone (which is supposed to stop bleeding). Literally hundreds of herbs are listed in herbal medical textbooks and the list of cures is startling, including anemia, asthma, bladder trouble, "female troubles," insomnia, acne, sleeplessness, somnambulance, headaches, etc.

Hypnosis

Hypnosis literally means "a temporary condition of altered attention, the most striking feature of which is increased suggestibility." It is similar to sleep, but the body retains its tone, and the muscles don't relax completely as in sleep. It is a state in which people keep most of their faculties but, as they are deprived of full consciousness, accept and act on suggestions made by the hypnotist. Practitioners of holistic medicine say that hypnosis should only be used as an adjunct or part of another type of alternative medicine. They generally disapprove of the use of hypnosis for symptomatic cures e.g. to help give up smoking, to conquer drug addiction or cure obsessive eating. In this instance, hypnosis is being used to treat the condition superficially and is not reaching the root cause. Hypnosis should be used as a method for disciplining the mind and body and one of its best applications is to help people control anxiety and cope with stress. People who are highly suggestive to a hypnotic trance exhibit startling effects when hypnotized. For example, a person under hypnosis when told that a burning match will be placed on her hand, will pull her hand back quickly, as though burned, and the hand will become red and swollen when it is touched with a pencil. When the hypnotic trance is over, the hand still feels as if it has been burned.

Aromatherapy

Fairly new in terms of wide practice, though its roots go back for centuries, pleasant smells have always been associated with holiness, e.g. the burning of incense during religious ceremonies. Sweet, pleasant smells are supposed to appeal to our better senses and to be relaxing and tranquillizing. Our sense of smell is very well developed and we react to an odor within split seconds, though the reaction is often idiosyncratic – an example would be vomiting within seconds of smelling something offensive. Given that an offensive smell might cause this profound physical effect, it seems logical that a pleasant smell might have the opposite effect. Aromatherapy suggests that aromatic oil essences such as musk, damask, or sandalwood can be combined to suit a patient's personality and produce a desired effect. The aromas are smelled or inhaled and are sometimes rubbed into the skin in oils and creams. It is claimed this therapy brings about mood changes according to the ingredients used. One mixture tranquillizes, another mixture excites. It is suggested that tranquillizing aromatherapy may relieve tension and anxiety, and improve relaxation. It is therefore sometimes used for the treatment of headaches and high blood pressure. Mood-heightening aromas are said to increase efficiency and bring about a positive attitude towards life. Aromatherapy ignores the fact that the sense of smell becomes exhausted within minutes; this is a physiological fact. It is therefore difficult to see how the therapy can go beyond the initial impact of the first few sniffs.

Reflexology This theory works on the basis that the whole of the body is represented in a map on the sole of the foot, the nerve endings in the sole corresponding to different organs. These sites were charted hundreds of years ago in China and Tibet and have been used for healing purposes. It is said that diseases show up as small crystalline deposits on the sole directly in the area of the skin corresponding to the distant organ. By means of fine pressure over small areas, these deposits are broken down and reflexly restore the circulation of blood and vital energy forces to the organ concerned and so promote healing. There is a special reflex roller on sale, along with a map of the sole of the foot, which can be used by the patient herself to assist reflex massage – if you believe in it. I personally do not. There is no objective scientific evidence to support the theory.

Gerovital therapy Invented in 1956 by Dr. Ana Aslan working in Rumania, first reports were of treating old and ageing people with a substance known as H3, claiming that improved concentration and perception, and general retardation of the ageing process were achieved. Hair regrew, heart complaints like angina and high blood pressure were relieved, joint stiffness disappeared and skin diseases were cured. Dr. Aslan concluded "that H3 reduces the biological age of the individual below its chronological age." H3 therapy became very popular and widely used throughout Europe, and special clinics which practiced gerovital therapy were set up. Many studies have been done in England, Canada and the United States but have failed to support any of the extravagant claims which were made at the introduction of the therapy. Studies in England could find no difference between two groups of patients, one of which was treated with Gerovital H3 therapy and the other with injections of sterile water or saline. The only constant effect of the drug turned out to be the induction of euphoria. The euphoric effect can be explained because H3 inhibits the production of a chemical called monoaminoxydase. There are high levels of this chemical in the elderly and the depressed. The only conclusion to draw is that there is no justification for using Gerovital H3 in clinical practice as a rejuvenating agent. Anyone who does so is ignoring the scientific data and is paying for an expensive treatment which has no more effect on the ageing process than a placebo.

PSYCHOLOGICAL THERAPIES

Below I set out some of the psychological treatments available, and there are some general points to bear in mind about them:
- You should seek referral through your family doctor but if s/he is reluctant you can by-pass her/him.
- They all bring a degree of self-knowledge which nearly always has benefits, but some may have problems – be prepared for them, and be prepared to find yourself and your lifestyle changing.
- View them as a genuine form of self-help in that most forms of therapy aim to make you self-reliant and self-assured. They may not be able to "cure" you, just simply help you to help yourself.

Psychoanalysis

When Freud noticed that by encouraging a patient with a nervous disorder to talk openly, and by observing pauses, emphases, and avoidance of subjects, he could trace the source of her/his emotional disturbance, psychoanalysis was born. If the patient was further encouraged to recall or relive the incident which had triggered off the disturbance the illness often improved; psycho-analysis could therefore claim to be a useful therapeutic tool.

Psychoanalysis in its purest form is inevitably lengthy and therefore expensive. It is not uncommon for a course of therapy to demand daily attendance at the analyst's office for several years. An acceptable minimum might still involve two or three visits a week for more than a year.

One of the reasons why psychoanalysis is so protracted is that the analyst and the patient join in a contract to explore every aspect of the patient's feelings in a close intimate way in order to understand all facets of the patient's life as far back as the patient can remember. As a result, the analyst will attempt to interpret the patient's personality, motivations, inadequacies, and symptoms, and relate them to family, personal, social and professional relationships. Such a complex exploration is necessarily long.

The aim of psychoanalysis – and every other form of psycho-logical treatment – is to help the patient to have insight into her-self. In doing so, it attempts to explain the underlying reasons for her disturbance and symptoms. Once explained, the technique then builds in a positive way to support the patient while she faces her difficulties and copes with them.

Psychotherapy

Psychotherapy is an extremely important form of medical treat-ment because it gives help to a patient suffering from a fairly severe mental illness (though not severe enough to warrant hospital admission), on an out-patient basis. It rarely means attending a psychiatric clinic and therefore a mother can stay at home, and an employed woman needn't be absent from her job.

As with most other forms of psychological treatment, psycho-therapy must cover all aspects of the patient's life. It is useless to embark on a course of psychotherapy if you are not prepared to candidly explore your feelings and accept the involvement of your psychotherapist in the intimate details of your problems and in forming a treatment plan.

In the broadest sense, psychotherapy is useful for managing any illness which has a psychological component, the commonest being an inability to adjust to stress. As just being alive in the twentieth century is stressful, most of us would probably be better off for having psychotherapy.

While an almost standard group of illnesses heads any list of psychosomatic conditions e.g. overeating and obesity, chronic anxiety, depression, insomnia, anorexia nervosa, sex problems, dermatitis, there are others which can be life-threatening e.g. high blood pressure, asthma, peptic ulcer. There is no standard form of psychotherapy for a particular ailment; rather, the therapy is tailored to the patient's personality and the therapist's method.

One of the commonest syndromes a psychotherapist has to treat is a patient's intolerance of her own weaknesses. A woman often suffers from conflicts arising from the realization of what she is, compared to what she thinks she ought to be. Since what a person is is very difficult to change, the therapist's goal becomes to change the patient's concept of herself, to teach the patient to accept and respect herself as she is and not conform to a mold.

It may take time, but if a therapist can achieve this change in perception, anxiety, tension and physical illness may resolve.

Group therapy
There are many forms of group therapy but all rely on one basic premise; they set out to help individuals to take well-defined steps towards being able to deal with their problems alone. There are usually four steps. The first is discovery of what the real problems are, then to rationalize them, further to adjust to them, and finally to cope with them.

Whatever the form of group therapy, this step-by-step progress is facilitated by the presence of others. It may be possible to identify with another group member and share experiences. It may be possible to assess behavior in others as irrational when it's difficult to recognize and admit to the same thing in oneself when alone.

In group therapy, members use the group as a crutch, a cathartic and an instrument to work through their own difficulties. With successful group therapy, however, the patient ceases to be dependent on the group and has the confidence to face life alone.

Group therapy started just after World War II with small groups of 6 or 8 people, all of whom were strangers, under the direction of a therapist. Their common link was the inability to deal with the stresses in their lives. In a way, the group relied on the theory that several heads are better than one and worked out the causes of tension, subsequent behavior and suggestions for future actions of each member.

Encounter group therapy arose in the 1960s and demanded complete openness of behavior even, or rather especially, in areas of human relationships that were considered "forbidden," and the preparedness to follow any impulse be it to touch, caress, stare, scream, undress, etc. – the aim was to liberate repressions. They still exist, but are no longer as popular as they were.

LIFESTYLES

The very inclusion of a section on lifestyles suggests that you have a variety of options that you can take up, and, indeed, you have. Unfortunately, a great number of women are not aware of the options, or of the freedom to choose; others are not prepared to take the initiative, and still others feel that their freedom is curtailed by pressure from family and society. For most of us, the first obstacle that we have to overcome is our own diffidence. Most of us are content to be pushed, shoved and molded into one of life's clearly defined streams; most of us, whether we feel comfortable about it or not, take on the role that others expect us to. Stop thinking that way *now*. It's your life and it's your attitudes and your happiness that count. Though you cannot entirely ignore them – your parents' attitudes and hopes for you, your teachers' guidance and the pressure from your peers – these things count for very much less. In choosing your lifestyle you have to stand up and be counted – more important, you have to be accountable to yourself. If you are not, you will never achieve lasting happiness.

ADULT MILESTONES

Most books on growth and development stop at the teenage years – it's as though at eighteen we become static and unchanging. This is far from the truth. It's just that the physiology of physical growth, which for both men and women halts, for the main part, around seventeen or eighteen, has over-shadowed (cancelled out) intellectual and emotional development. All of us over the age of thirty know that the real growth period for us as people only begins after the age of eighteen, and that the achievement of true happiness may take another three decades of hard work.

Eighteen usually means legal adulthood, and society behaves as though we become adults overnight. Quite the reverse is true. Just like children who go through learning spurts when new skills are required, when physical and emotional difficulties are overcome, when great masses of information seem to be absorbed in a short time, when a sudden shaft of light appears that makes everything seem clear, or makes unconnected pieces fit together, so do adults. What is more, these learning spurts are usually just as painful for us as they are for the small child who, for instance, is trying to learn how to use a pair of scissors or is going through the frustration of first learning to share with others. We adults have "milestones" just the same as children. Very often they come upon us with no warning. Quite often, they are protracted – sometimes more protracted than in childhood. We therefore take longer to pass through them, and sometimes the passage is extremely painful. However, it is always a learning passage, and when we emerge at the other side we are nearly always more mature, stronger and better for having been through the experience. Just like children, successfully passing a milestone requires adjustments, sometimes radical changes, and, very often, the taking up of a new lifestyle.

Many of us, meeting a crossroads in our lives, at whatever age, think that we are alone, that our problems have never been faced before, that a way out through the maze of tensions and anxieties has never been found, and that we are experiencing this particular kind of difficulty for the first time. Well, we are not. You can be pretty sure that whatever crisis you come up against in your life, someone else has been through it too, and, what is more, they have survived. And you can survive as well.

Scientific studies have shown that there are fairly well-defined patterns of development that most adults go through while reaching the comparatively calm waters of middle age. Middle age, if it is defined as the time when we have come to grips with our inner yearnings, have chosen the lifestyle that fulfills them, and are feeling pretty content, stable, and happy with life, does not occur at any particular "age." Rather, it occurs at the end, as the final act, of a long line of intellectual and emotional milestones which have been successfully negotiated. It follows that these milestones, which most of us have to go through, occur at different times: according to our social status, according to parental pressure, according to education, according to prolonged training in a profession, according to the age at which we get married (if we get married), according to the wishes and needs of our partner, according to whether we have children or not, according to whether we have a career or not, and lastly, probably most importantly, according to how courageous we are. But whatever the time, the latter may be the most important, since going through a period of self-analysis, choice, and possibly change of lifestyle requires courage, so brave you must be.

Studies, mainly done in America, have shown that at certain ages (within a band of five to seven years), most people begin questioning the things around them, begin questioning their values and those of their peers. They start reassessing what they are doing and the direction that their life is taking. They may decide that the path they are on is not the only one and that there are alternatives. Having considered the alternatives, they may decide that another path is preferable to the one on which they are travelling, and if they greatly prefer an alternative, they may have to make the decision to change. Having made the decision they will then have to act upon it, and the actions may result in eruptive changes in lifestyle, which may include:

- Going to live with someone;
- Redefining companionship rules with your partner;
- Separation or divorce from your partner;
- Deciding to have children or deciding to have no more children;
- Putting your career before your marriage;

- Giving up your job to look after your family;
- Changing your career completely;
- Going to live in another part of the country.

Milestones in adult life have something very crucial in common with milestones in children: the milestones are particular to the individual. No-one else approaches them at exactly the same age, in exactly the same way, in exactly the same environment (just as you've been counselled in all the books on child development, you should not compare how your child is doing with a neighbor's child). Similarly, you may reach your milestone several years ahead of or behind other people that you know. On the other hand, milestones in adult life are very different from those in childhood. Childhood milestones usually appear suddenly and may be faced, mastered, dealt with and be over, in a matter of days. Adult milestones are rarely like this. They usually take a long time in coming. They may even creep up on you without you being aware of them. They may simmer away at the back of your brain for several months before they crystallize into a recognizable form. And it may take a sudden event to make you realize that you have a milestone to cope with such as you or a friend contracting a serious illness. Something dramatic may occur in your partner's life, like a sudden senior promotion which has implications in it for you. You may have a love affair. One day you may just suddenly wake up and find that your children no longer need you. This sudden event serves to bring your nagging doubts into focus and for the first time you see the need to really start thinking about the future implications of what you are doing.

It's important to think of milestones as being dynamic and not static; they move across time. They are not individual photographs taken at one particular moment which is frozen for ever. It is better to think of them as a collection of snapshots in an album, each page recording different events, changing attitudes, switching priorities, determining preferences, making choices, taking decisions and carrying out actions. Milestones, therefore, are much more like a full-length film than a film clip. It's also useful to remember that reaching a milestone and passing through it often necessitates building a new structure for your life. However, some claim that this structure can rarely last longer than seven or eight years. It's comforting to know that science has legitimized the seven year itch!

Although an outer change may precipitate a milestone, it is always initiated by an inner impulse, and for many people there are four areas of perception that are constantly undergoing change (though not always at the conscious level):

- The first is the relationship of oneself to others;
- The second is how secure or insecure we are feeling;
- The third is our perception of how much time we have left – does life seem to stretch ahead of us endlessly, or are we beginning to feel intimations of mortality;
- The fourth area is our instinct or gut sensation about whether we are really alive and growing and developing, or whether we are stagnating and becoming stale.

Even though the milestone brings with it periods of indecision, insecurity, tension, and unhappiness, you should have a positive attitude towards it because it results in growth, and growth is all important, no matter what the cost. It is much, much better to start a new life at forty, than to continue in an old, stale, and unsatisfying one.

Your choice of lifestyle not only influences your role in the future, it will also influence the time and the nature of your subsequent milestones or "crises." For instance, say you are twenty-three and have always had your heart set on marriage. Your partner is chosen, and you have decided on the date, but you are having doubts; if you decide to go ahead and marry, then certain things will automatically follow. In fact, there is a decision tree spreading out in life ahead of you as the result of which choice you make.

Age 18: belief in being happy = being married		
Doubts but get married	23	Doubts and don't get married
Not very happy but resigned	25	Not very happy but get over it
Frustrated, discontented and feel a loss of love for partner	27	Pursue career, meet new people
Need for change; crisis	29	Need for partner grows stronger; begin to seek partner
Separation, divorce, unhappiness	32	Find partner and happiness

At each of the branches on the decision tree you may find yourself going through a lifestyle crisis. The sort of choices you make will depend on many factors: your own personality and what you want out of life; what you think your parents are expecting of you; what your teachers have told you you are capable of; what you yourself think you are capable of; what you desire most; what you think will make you most happy; possibly what you think will make others happy; what your friends of the same age are doing; what you know most of your friends believe to be the right thing to do at this time. Ultimately, your choice will depend on your ability and desire to conform or not to conform. If you are going to conform and you know inside yourself that this is not what you truly want, beware, because your crisis will simply re-emerge in the future – possibly five, possibly seven, years later. If you decide that you wish to take a non-conformist line and are certain in your heart that it will bring you most happiness, then go ahead and do it. In the end, all you have got to march to is the beat of your own drum, so march to that. You may as well start marching to it from the beginning. At the very least, the milestone will have been faced, coped with; you'll be through it, and you'll be free to go on to the next stage of intellectual and emotional development. You will be those few years ahead of the person who decided on the opposite choice. You will have lowered your handicap towards happiness.

Knowing that it is only you who are in control of the runaway engine that is your life, and that the choices you make during your milestones will fashion the rest of your life, it may help you to negotiate the rapids if you have some idea of what the various decades might have in store for you.

The twenties Compared to the stormy adolescence which has preceded this decade, the twenties are stable, full of activity and very exhilarating. We are largely concerned with manipulating the external world around us. We want to find out how to make things work for us. We want to plan how our future goals and objectives may be met. We want to know where to start, who will help us, how to go about tackling new challenges. We are also very concerned with relationships with other people: most of us are concerned to find a degree of intimacy and permanence in a relationship with another person, while at the same time, doing our best not to lose our own identity. (Typically, the statistics favor settling down, as nine out of ten women get married at this time and also go on to have two or three children.)

During the twenties, most of us are at first guided by what we think we *should* do – and this we base on what we think our family expects, on what we think society expects, and on what we think our peers expect. Often we feel pressured about what we think we should do.

One of the most painful aspects of the twenties is that we believe that whatever decisions we take are irrevocable. They certainly are not, as you will see. On the one hand we will feel that we are pulled in the direction of making strong commitments and being in patterns for life. On the other hand we will find ourselves not wishing to be locked in forever to a particular lifestyle.

367

Many people find that the way between these two opposing forces is to explore and experiment, and keep any structure impermanent, tentative and reversible. So the twenties for most of us offer two different life patterns: on the one hand, some of us decide to make strong commitments and to be locked into certain future events; others of us decide on the most transient and easily-changeable patterns. What is common to both groups is that we firmly believe the pattern we have chosen in our twenties is the pattern we are going to follow for the rest of our lives. We believe it is the only way. It isn't, of course.

The thirties One of the commonest changes that occurs as we enter the thirties is the complete negation of the life we so carefully built in the twenties. Both men and women commonly express the feeling that life is too narrow and restricted – we long to break out. While we may agree that the choices we made in our twenties fitted us perfectly, the fit in our thirties is a long way short of perfect. Many people feel that new choices have to be made and commitments have to be adjusted or altered. Very often this drives us to make great changes, create turmoil and sometimes crisis. At one and the same time we may feel that we have hit rock bottom, but nevertheless we feel an irresistible urge to break free.

This may mean that a single woman finds herself trying hard to find a partner. It may mean that a woman who chose to put motherhood first, and who was quite content in her twenties to stay at home with the children, is now becoming frustrated and impatient with domestic life, and wants to break into the outside world and take on a new job. It may mean that a happily-married couple, who had decided that children were excluded, begin thinking about starting a family, and almost everyone who has been married for 6–7 years starts to feel somewhat discontented.

The thirties also bring a strong desire to make a social contribution. We find ourselves saying there's got to be something more to life than this, and so men and women look around for ways in which to expand their personal lives, besides simply developing themselves professionally.

At the age of thirty-five many of us reach a crossroads. Most of us carry around the time limit of three score years and ten and realize we have reached the half-way stage. For the first time, we believe that time is not infinite. We may even physically feel the loss of youth. We ache more after a tennis game, we are breathless after running up the stairs, and we get tired much more quickly. Many of us find we are seriously re-examining the purpose of our lives and we begin to re-evaluate how we may spend our resources from now on.

Many women reach this inner crossroads earlier than men. At the age of thirty-five women often stop and completely re-appraise their lives from every point of view. Many a woman feels that this is her last chance and has an urgency to review the options which she deferred or decided against, and compare them with those which she chose to take up. In many cases, self-appraisal is prompted by a sense that age is biologically creeping on, and she puts a great deal of energy into looking for a new future. The sensation that time is running out makes her more assertive and more courageous. She is prepared to take up challenges that she felt she was not strong enough to take up before this time.

It's at this point that women may decide on really radical changes of lifestyle involving divorce, picking up the threads of an old career, switching from an old career to an entirely new one, setting up a new household with a new partner. It is a crucial time for most women. If you really feel a deep inner drive to have a change then you must take all the time and energy necessary to work out how it can be achieved. Making the change will ensure your future growth and development. Not making the change can only result in one or two unhappy outcomes. If you resign yourself to no change when you really want it, then you will become resentful, frustrated and eventually dissatisfied and stale. Worst of all, you will not grow or develop any further. Secondly, you may be putting off the day when the pressure re-emerges and you will have spent several years of great unhappiness, and possible ill-health, trying to come to terms with the decision you know you have to make.

The forties

The crossroads that many people reach at the age of thirty-five may not be reached until the age of forty and for everyone it takes two or three years before life re-stabilizes. The mid- and late forties, therefore, can be looked forward to as a period of equilibrium when the major problems of life and one's place in it, and the adjustments one has to make to feel at one with oneself, have been sorted out and life becomes fulfilling, satisfying and, for the first time, contented.

However, you will either feel renewed or resigned, according to the choices you made at your crossroads. If you refuse to make any changes, then your sense of staleness will only progress into resignation and a feeling of worthlessness. You will not be growing and you will not be developing – you will be standing still. What happens is that the things in your life which have made you feel safe, and which have supported you, will be withdrawn. Your children will grow up and leave you, your partner will develop faster than you and grow away from you, your career will become less satisfying and will merely become a job which has to be done. What is more, each of these events will gradually become less and less tolerable and your crisis will probably emerge again around the age of fifty, and, be assured, it will hit you much harder than it did around thirty-five or forty.

If on the other hand you faced up to your thirty-five-year-old crossroads, made the necessary choices, adjustments and changes, you will have found a renewed sense of purpose, and from within yourself a drive and energy to build a satisfactory lifestyle, and the sure knowledge that you are looking forward to the best years of your life. For most people who are prepared to take on this difficult passage, personal happiness soars. A self-confidence which you had never suspected emerges, and you can take on problems and difficulties calmly and rationally. You become less

possessive about your children, you become less possessive about your partner, you find yourself warming and mellowing towards life and other people. Friends become important, you carve out a little niche of privacy in your life which is crucial to all of us. Priorities suddenly become very clear and decisions much easier to take. You know what the score is and life may suddenly become very pleasurable and very comfortable.

The fifties   The fifties are a time when, once again, people take stock of their lives – mainly because it becomes impossible to ignore the deterioration of one's physical and mental capacities (such as loss of stamina and strength, as well as sight, hearing and memory), and we all become much more aware of the finiteness of life. For women, menopause is undoubtedly the period's most significant biological and psychological event.

Psychologists have remarked on a gradual reversal in roles of married men and women in the fifties. As thoughts turn continually from business (in preparation of a partner's retirement) to social and leisure matters and men begin to lose some of the dominance attendant upon being "higher up" in business and social circles, women are likely to be seeking self-expression in and mastery of areas outside the home.

Many of us, if we haven't worked, express a desire for having done so, and if we can't exhibit creativity and competence at some work, we often become more aggressive at home. Our last child leaves home at this time and we may look forward to a "second honeymoon" situation with our partner, but we are quite often likely to be disappointed in this, as he may react badly to this shifting of roles.

The fifties are crucial for health considerations. As we become more aware of the physical changes in ourselves, we also become concerned about the declining health of our partners, and tend to be beset by worries about a possible future financial and physical dependency on our family and community. We also worry about retirement – if not our own, then certainly our partner's – and its effect on our lifestyle. Usually, too, we are faced with familial problems in the form of aged parents. It is almost exclusively the role of women to provide this care, and the constant attention it necessitates from us usually puts a great strain on our relationship with our partner and children, creates havoc with our working life, and places us under great physical and psychological stress. Moreover, those of us who had children late often experience difficulties with our children as well.

During the fifties the pace of life at which we work and enjoy our leisure (including sexual activities) generally slows down. Our increased physical awareness leads to increased personality awareness and we become more reflective. We continually re-examine our priorities and become more tolerant of our own abilities and those of others; our outlook becomes increasingly mellow and philosophical and by the end of our fifties, if we've managed to remain married, we're often closer to our partner than at any other time. One of the reasons for this may be the presence of grandchildren. Being a grandparent is one of the most satisfying roles the fifties has to offer, and the love of grandchildren can bring both partners and children closer together.

The sixties The most dramatic change in this decade is the rate at which adverse changes in biological, social and psychological factors take place. The greater proportion of people in this age range become physically ill, emotionally disturbed or functionally less competent. The acceleration is sharp. There is a decline in our physical and mental capabilities, including such obvious things as appearance, stamina, speed and sexual vigor. These changes limit the nature and scope of activities that are now open to us and the overwhelming factor which determines the quality of our life is whether or not we remain in good health. Many women do, however, retain a high level of biological and intellectual competence in terms of having important positions in social affairs and at work, simply because many of the skills we now possess are the result of long experience.

Both at home and at work there is the tendency for us, now that we are nearing, or at, retirement, to be disengaged from the mainstream of social and professional activities. Indeed, some of us disengage ourselves by handing over responsibilities, shedding workload, creating deputies, selling a large house and buying a smaller one, paving over our garden, in order to prepare for the next stage of our life which will lay much greater emphasis on leisure time and reduction of living costs. On the other hand we tend to become more involved with personal relationships, particularly with family, with neighbors and with like-minded people, i.e. religious or racial groups. Many of us rise to hold senior positions in social organizations, especially if the duties entail little physical activity, but are mainly ceremonial and ritual.

Many of us find it difficult changing from being an economically productive person to an economically non-productive one with a dependent status. It is made harder because society makes the cut-off point dramatic, and it is rapid. There is little time for adjustment if we don't prepare for it.

Retirement will mean different things to us depending on our health and fitness, our socio-economic status, and our psychological make-up. For most of us, however, retirement means no longer continuing with our main professional job. This brings a number of basic changes in our lifestyle: for instance, in our daily activities, social contacts, professional contacts and standard of living. But, if we prepare well, we can better adjust to such radical change. However, during this time, the cumulative effects of ageing, with the greatly increased chances of disease, slow recovery and disability, almost force a person to leave behind some social activities and interests simply because the physical and psychological demands are too great. We would be unwise to fight this natural tendency.

The seventies "plus" This age is largely defined by our ability to cope with the everyday affairs of life without help; our chronological age is probably more arbitrary at this time than at any other, since individual differences, due to states of health, are enormous. If we are married or living with someone we are better off than those women living alone, usually because of the mutual support that is provided for each other. At this time we normally become disengaged from all professional and most community activities and rely more and more on a social life involving our close family, friends and peers. Such activities can be a source of continuing pleasure, especially if we feel our past experiences are worthwhile to others.

In Western society the life expectancy for a woman is seventy-five (for a man, sixty-nine), but for those women who have reached this age, there is a further expectation of about ten years. As we age we become ever more philosophical, and most of us fear death less when we're seventy, than at thirty. We become increasingly inward-looking and egocentric, perhaps as a way of understanding ourselves and making sense of our lives. We often cling to old friends, and to our partners if we're still married, and their deaths can be our greatest stress. Our biggest problems are

remaining well, independent and capable. To keep mentally alert it is necessary to stay active; we can continue to enrich and renew our minds, even at a slow pace. It is often society's expectations about the quality of older people's lives, rather than our own, which determine the amount of zest we bring to our old age.

This really is the part of life which leads up to death and, medically speaking, it is the final stage in the breakdown of the physiological functions necessary to sustain life itself. We usually die through some kind of terminal illness – whether it is medically obvious or obvious to us as individuals or not – or through a simple accumulation of the deterioration which is taking place in every part of the body so that it can no longer go on functioning and literally gives up the ghost, or through violence and other un-natural causes. It is fairly obvious from statistics that the major reasons for dying are those due to the steady accumulation of illness which the body cannot throw off and which gradually completely erode the living process. It is such disease in the heart and the brain which is the major cause of death. Heart disease causes 1 in 4 of all deaths and strokes cause nearly a sixth of all deaths. Cancer kills more than 1 in 10 people and bronchitis 6 out of every 100.

LIFE CHOICES

No matter how many ways you try to permutate them, there aren't really that many choices open to women – for most of us, basically only three:
- Marriage and family
- Work
- Both together

You may be one of nature's natural mothers. You may have been a domesticated daughter. Your heart may be set on marriage, a home and a family. But it's worth knowing a few home truths about marriage as far as women are concerned before you make your final decision (see pp. 379 to 384). Many women view marriage as a career. Not only that, many women view marriage as their *only* career. Once you become married and have children, it *will* be your only career unless you mark out the ground rules first with your partner. Sadly, the statistics show that very few women are happy and healthy when marriage is their only career. In fact, they say the opposite. Married women are not only less healthy and happy than their unmarried sisters, they are less healthy and happy than married men who have never perceived marriage as a career, far less their only career. It is therefore worth considering alternatives.

Maybe if you have a high energy level, you are well organized and you are quite happy handling several balls in the air at once you may be able to combine work and marriage. This, however, is a very tough option, and not many women succeed at it and remain healthy, happy and stable. Nonetheless, it is worth considering (see pp. 404 to 409).

And then, of course, you may be one of those women who eschews marriage altogether and puts her career first. That's fine, and many women have achieved happiness doing just that. It simply means that your milestones will be somewhat different and possibly fall at different times from the woman who exercised the other two options and it may be at a future time in your development that you change your option and go for one of the other two (see pp. 401 to 404).

If these options seem limited, take heart. Women have been forced to choose from this limited menu for some time – since Victorian times in fact. The only change in our social mores, in fact, is the loosening up of the interpretation of "marriage." Nowadays for the word "marriage" we can substitute the phrase "lasting relationship" which has all the implications of marriage, but not the formalized vows. If you are thinking that opting for a lasting relationship is another way of keeping your options open, you are only fooling yourself because the majority of us reach a point in our lives where we realize that we cannot live alone, or, alternatively, that we cannot face the prospect of a future lived entirely alone. One has simply deferred the option of marriage in the true meaning of the word.

While you should always view the future with the belief that you can change your life pattern and your lifestyle if you wish to – it's a woman's prerogative to change her mind, historically at least – it would seem that there are several well-defined lifestyles that women have chosen to lead in the past. Remember that these life patterns are historical, and there is no reason why they should not change in the future, but they are the only ones that we have at our disposal at present.

The care-giver
This is the woman who marries around the age of twenty and who has no aspirations beyond the role of wife and mother.

The chooser
In their twenties, these women choose between marriage and children or career and achievement. The first defers professional achievement; she marries and starts a family. Unlike the care-giver, she always intends to pursue her career at a later date. The second defers a family. She certainly puts off motherhood and she may even put off marriage as well. This is with the specific aim of spending six or seven years completing her career development.

The integrator
This is a woman who tries to combine everything in her twenties. She tries to integrate marriage, motherhood and a career.

Please remember that these are descriptive labels. They do not mean that they are the only options open. What is more, no woman makes a choice at a given time. In other words, these life patterns are dynamic and they move *through* time. We have arranged them in chart form so that you can scan them at a glance.

PREDICTABLE EFFECTS OF ADULT MILESTONES ON LIFE "CHOICES"

	18–22	22–28	28–32
Enough scientific studies have been done to enable us to predict what problems women will face at particular stages of their lives (milestones) according to their "choice" of lifestyle. This chart traces what commonly happens to women in four specific situations. The word "choice" is used advisedly; no matter how we arrive at our lifestyle, the outcome is the same.	*The time when strongly influenced by ideals formed in the "teens" and having left school and/or one's family we explore the necessary paths to independence and adulthood.*	*The time when we have to establish ourselves as productive members of society and put our ideas about lifestyle into practice.*	*The time when having become established in a certain pattern, we begin to experience doubts about the "rightness" of our lives which often lead to a growing disillusionment.*
Marriage as a Career	She enters maturity dreaming of the "ideal" husband without having many goals for herself. She seeks to secure for herself a happy domestic life, thus avoiding the decisions she should be making for the future.	She is very happy during this time establishing a household and producing babies. She is dependent on her husband's and babies' continuing need for her. Her world is very much defined as wife and mother – "a good thing to be."	Her enthusiasm for being a housewife diminishes as she finds it less fulfilling than she'd supposed. Her children are becoming more independent and need her less. Her husband wants her to show more interest in the world outside the home (where previously he wanted a homebody, now he wants adventure and intelligent conversation).
Family before a Career	She chooses marriage and children as her primary role, with a career second. She plans to work until her husband is established, then have children and return to work at some later, unspecified time.	Having postponed a career, she willingly leaves her job for home-making and babies. Since a career is very much a possibility she uses her free time to keep up with her work. This period of her life is quite happy.	She begins to feel frustrated and impatient with domestic life and makes a concerted effort to reshape her life to allow herself time to devote outside the home. Although she wants to go back to work she finds it difficult to ignore her family responsibilities. Her mate feels "unsettled" about changes in his homelife and this discourages her further.
Family and a Career	She approaches adulthood with the desire for both a career and children. She is convinced that it is possible to combine marriage, career and children.	She spends most of her time during this period establishing herself at her job. She is less "settled" than those who chose marriage as their primary goal and is not so quick to have children although a sympathetic and supportive mate is very important to her.	She has her children and spends most of her time during this period trying to fit in work and managing her home. She has two jobs to her mate's one. She doesn't have much time to think about herself or give any one thing her undivided attention. She is torn between domestic life and work and she feels guilty about her lack of attention to both.
Career	She has a definite career in mind and pursues this with great singlemindedness and a clear sense of direction. She has strong expectations of achievement.	She identifies quite strongly with her work and with any "mentors" which may be involved. Being successful at work reinforces her decision to place it before a family. If she does get married, the marriage is deemed secondary to her career.	She works hard throughout the period but towards the end begins to realize that her career opportunities may be limited and that being successful in a man's world is increasingly stressful. She questions both her self-confidence and her belief in the people around her who have influenced her.

32–38	38–45	45–55	55 +
The time when having achieved many of the goals envisioned in the early 20s, we make a re-assessment of choices that may result in radical changes in lifestyle.	*The time when approaching middle age leads us to reconsider our past and future achievements as well as our commitments to career and family.*	*The time when physiological changes resulting from menopause are often accompanied by psychological disturbances related to premonitions of mortality.*	*The period when time stretches ahead and lack of familial responsibilities causes us to come to terms with how we've spent our lives and what we may still possibly accomplish.*
She experiences a rude shock during this period. Not having developed her own identity, being someone's wife or mother has become an unattractive, low-status situation. Her husband and children need her less. In fact, he urges divorce while she considers having another baby to "reinstate" herself.	She weathers the previous marital crisis but finds her adolescent children and a husband beset by worries about his future difficult to cope with. He still considers divorce as a real possibility. She tries to work but she has neither the training nor the confidence and she finds that continuing disappointments and feelings of uselessness lead to depression.	As she has not made significant strides outside the home, this period is particularly agonizing and fearful. Biological changes scare her. With her children grown she feels at last able to do something outside the home but she hasn't moved away from home-making and she has no confidence or skills, so the task of finding work is doubly hard.	As she has filled her life with home-making and little else, her lack of growth means that she has little in common with her husband and their relationship by this time can be a hollow one. Staying together for the "sake of the children" is no longer necessary and she is often abandoned for another woman or a deeper interest in his work.
She returns to work with ambivalent feelings about her capabilities, and anxieties about family responsibilities. She requires a great deal of support from her family which they may not be able to give as they resent having to readjust to her new independence and their increased responsibilities about the house.	Her hardest problems now center around her mate. She is branching out in the world while he is becoming introspective about what he is doing. He may be more interested in having a "family" life while she wants to put more effort into work.	"Menopausal" reactions in herself and her mate prove difficult to deal with. Although she finds work rewarding, it is difficult to manage it successfully along with housekeeping and coping with a husband who may want more of her attention.	Having taken up work much later than her mate she still has plenty of enthusiasm and energy for working while she finds his career commitments becoming less. Her regained confidence often leads to a loss of self-esteem on his part.
She has to establish a routine of shared domestic responsibilities with her mate which may be in conflict with his perception of his career commitments. Worries about child care inhibit her satisfaction with her work.	Her children are now older and the shared work pattern fully established so she and her mate find their life easier than before. However, renewed interest and involvement in their separate careers may cause them to grow apart.	She and her mate will be experiencing many of the same problems as regards their career experiences but they may not be able to give each other the support they need. If she's especially successful at work she may find it brings added stress.	Both she and her mate having achieved similar high levels of success at their jobs are better able to convert their skills to activities which will interest them throughout retirement. They regard this period as an opportunity to do things together they hadn't had time for earlier.
She searches for her own happiness as opposed to career satisfaction. She has achieved the business goals she has set for herself but feels empty. She changes jobs, gets married, or divorces the husband she already has – a declaration of self-importance. If she remains married, she thinks about having children.	For her and the men around her, this is a difficult period – the stresses in their respective lives may be similar yet they are unable to provide support for each other. She feels the lack of children greatly and may have them at this time. If she does, she will find juggling her career and children particularly difficult and strenuous.	If she hasn't had children she may panic as menopause sets in. To offset some of the feelings of ageing she throws herself further into her work. However, achievement at work is often accompanied by self-doubts and social problems resulting from society's disapproval of women having serious careers.	Having worked most of her life she often suffers from career fatigue and is keen to retire. She may put her skills to work in a voluntary capacity or spend her retirement on activities she hadn't had time for earlier. She may build up a new domestic relationship.

MARRIAGE

Many of us are brought up with the idea that marriage will be a pinnacle in our lives, that it's a goal worth striving for, and that once achieved it will automatically make us happy. Many of us are so well programmed that we go on believing that (and behaving as though it were true), even though the evidence before our eyes, and the unhappiness we are experiencing, say the reverse. Unfortunately, most of the statistics say the reverse, too.

In one sense, marriage can be looked upon as a mechanism for controlling sexual behavior; this has concerned most societies throughout history and continues to concern our present one. Our society is no different from any previous one in that it subscribes to the religiously-based belief of the relationship between sexual control and social stability. Marriage is a very efficient device for controlling the sexual behavior of women in that it implies lifelong fidelity to one partner. In view of the future discussions of this chapter, it is worth emphasizing the truism that social convention places no such control on the sexual behavior of men within marriage. In this context it also has to be stated that most of the "natural laws" of marriage militate against women. Indeed, the authority of the husband is backed both by law and by religion – almost all religions, including Christianity, Judaism and Islam. Furthermore, a wife is not entitled to payment for household work (in the United States, for instance, there are some states where payment is expressly denied; in other states, the husband is in control of his wife's earnings, and in four states the husband's consent and court approval are required if a wife wishes to start a business of her own).

As long ago as the nineteenth century it was noted that the ideals expressly stated as democratic freedoms did not apply in relationships between husbands and wives. Indeed, to back this up, studies have been carried out which show that 75% of all men *perceive* that they have more power than their female partners. The terrifying corollary to this is that about the same number of women perceive that they have less power than their male partners.

In summary, therefore, when a woman enters into marriage, she enters a union into which male authority has been built and ratified by religious, legal, moral and traditional means.

His and her marriages

It is not surprising then that men and women have different ideas of what marriage constitutes. Researchers show that these different views of marriage go further than the sexes, they actually penetrate individual marriages. In other words, within the same marriage, a husband and a wife can have different views of their marriage. There is the husband's version of the marriage and the wife's version of the marriage, and they rarely tally. Researchers have described these as "different marriages" within the one marriage. It has been shown that the husband's and wife's view of the sort of sexual relationships, and the frequency of sexual relationships, differs; they have a different view of how much they share problems; how much they talk to one another; the degree of companionship they share; the way decisions are taken; even down to who does the household tasks. When husbands and wives describe different views of who pays the bills and who mows the lawn, then their perception of marriage is self-evidently and basically different.

Marriage is undoubtedly good for men. Although physically in no better health than the unmarried man, the married man enjoys far better mental health. What is more, being married is an asset to a man's career and may increase his earning power. In plain terms, it pays men to be married, and a classic study of suicide showed that marriage has a measurable salvaging effect on men. Unmarried men have a much higher suicide rate than married men; in the United States it is twice as high. The value that most men place on marriage is shown by the fact that most divorced and widowed men remarry, and remarry fairly quickly after finding themselves without a partner.

Sadly, none of the research has shown that women benefit from marriage in the same way as men and there is a great deal of sociological research which shows that women are unhappy with their marriages. A study in a population of couples who were having marriage counselling showed that more of the wives than the husbands felt they were unhappy during the first year of their marriage. What is more, the unhappiness did not seem to be alleviated, because they also felt unhappier than their husbands during subsequent years. The wives also saw more problem areas than their husbands, sometimes twice as many. However, despite the wives' dissatisfactions, a large proportion of married women paradoxically considered themselves and their marriage to be happy. It seems as though the wives had been indoctrinated to believe that marriage was "happy" regardless of its quality, and came to accept the inferior quality of their marriage as the definition of a happy one.

The physical health of married women is worse than that of married men, and their mental health is far worse. More married women than married men felt that they were:
- About to have a nervous breakdown;
- Experiencing more psychological and physical anxiety;
- Having feelings of inadequacy about their marriage and themselves;
- Unable to make the adjustments necessary for a happy marriage.

Several studies have shown that married women exhibit more symptoms of mental distress than married men:
- They have more phobic reactions;
- They suffer attacks of depression more often;
- They take a passive behavior pattern more often (the easy way out);
- They exhibit the symptoms of mental ill-health more often than men, e.g. nervousness, inertia, insomnia, trembling of the hands, nightmares, fainting, headaches and palpitations.

Furthermore, this comparison remains just as unfavorable if it is made with unmarried women. So the symptoms are not due to sex, but to marriage. The cost of marriage to women, as opposed to the benefits of marriage to men, is shown by the fact that unmarried women are in far better physical and mental shape than are unmarried men.

This is not helped by the fact that there is in most marriages what one writer has termed "the marriage gradient." This means that there is a tendency for men to marry women slightly below themselves in terms of age, education and occupation. This automatically confers on the husband a degree of superiority and gives the wife someone to "look up to" (which in itself confirms the husband's idea that he is superior to his wife).

The idea that marriage is *a shock* to most women is not new. Marriage itself introduces serious disruption into the lives of most women which, at any level, for even the strongest of women, may be genuinely hazardous to her emotional health. Many of these disruptions, changes and discontinuities are taken for granted: marriage does not turn out to be the romantic honeymoon that the girl thought it to be, and she may even become disenchanted with marriage; it may become quite a strain to keep up the effort she has made to be always on her best behavior during the pre-marital period; it is also an effort to keep up daily appearances. A woman can no longer please herself as she could when she was self-determinant and lived in her own place and kept to her own timetable; if she lived at home, her mother almost certainly catered to her; now she has to cater to someone else.

Perhaps the worst shock of all may be to find out that her husband is not the knight in shining armor that she thought him to be. He comes down to life size. He's really not as strong as she thought, not as protective as she thought he might be, and not her intellectual superior. Realizing that her husband is not omniscient, infallible, and indefatigable is sometimes such a shock to a woman that she will not readily accept it, and, therefore, adds to her own burdens by working extremely hard to maintain her ideal image of her husband, and also bolstering his own image of himself as such.

One of the most difficult shocks for women to deal with, however, is that marriage *per se* confers on her a lower status than she enjoyed before marriage. Legally, a married woman has fewer rights than a single woman, as her legal status is lower than that of her husband. Indeed, a married woman loses a number of legal rights when she marries. Mentally she finds that she is having to make many adjustments, in fact more than her husband, to make her marriage work, because very few women have a fail-safe position to fall back on. They make this extra effort without realizing that they are compounding the imbalance within the marriage. So she not only makes adjustments, she makes concessions, submissions, she changes her level of expectations to suit her husband's wishes, and, what's more, she very often does this without protesting. So she finds herself adjusting to her husband's expectations of her, and fitting into the mold that is dictated by her husband. Women truly reshape themselves for their husbands, an effect which has been described as the "Pygmalion effect." Husbands do this to a much lesser extent. As time goes on, many women become numbed to the fact that they are making changes because some of them are extremely subtle. One of the most subtle being the loss of sexual identity, for in becoming married, women move from the status of being truly female to that which is nearer neuter. Many women past their twenties, imagine themselves to be less sexually attractive, some even sexless. This neutralizing heightens when their sexuality becomes muted, or they themselves mute their sexuality through motherhood.

Exaggerated though it may sound, many women find themselves "dwindling into wives." Their inferiority, both in their marriage and in the outside world, is confirmed by the acceptance of the low status of motherhood, housework and domesticity. What is more, a housewife's job is a dead-end job with no promotion. Household duties rarely seem to challenge her capacities, so it's very hard for a woman if she is a housewife. Conversely, because her husband's work outside of the home is specialized and detailed he alone continues to grow and develop, and in many cases outgrows his wife and leaves her behind, and husband and wife may steadily grow apart.

Egalitarian marriage

In view of the unhappiness, psychological distress and mental illness experienced by married women, it is hardly overstating the case to say that wives are *driven mad* by marriage and their roles. At the very least, marriage for all women is a significant stress, and for many, the stress is sufficient to cause sickness. Given all of these negative aspects of marriage, the future of marriage must surely mean significant changes in the marriage contract to ameliorate and equalize the woman's position.

The first step, however, is to change the attitudes of women themselves. Women who have taken up passive, dependent roles will always fare badly. They are vulnerable and easily exploitable, not just inside of marriage, but outside too. It is necessary for them to be trained or to train themselves to be more assertive and less easily molded. These changes will help them not only within marriage but will be greatly to their advantage in all their relationships with the outside world.

For marriage to change in the future, both sexes must discard the image of a woman as docile and manageable, with few inclinations beyond the domestic. In doing so, women will have to take on the responsibility of accepting that they no longer have the right to be supported for all of their lives.

So marriage in the future is quite a challenge for women and it means that they will have to start thinking about the future very early in life. If a woman is no longer to have financial support from her husband, whether married (or divorced), then she will have to start thinking about her career during her school years. She will have to think in terms of life-long work and map out her future career development, because in order to take up equal status with her partner in marriage, she is going to need the confidence which derives from the sure knowledge that she can get on perfectly well without him – the knowledge that not only can she get along without her husband, but that she and her children will be independent.

These are severe demands that will be made of women if marriage is to change for the better in the future. It means that opportunities will be made available for women in exactly the same way as they are for men, and they must be freed from the handicaps of sexual discrimination in any area.

So women are going to have to work towards a new conception of marriage – egalitarian marriage – marriage which is based on a relationship between equals. This concept is fairly new but not that new; it's been around for a few decades. It is talked about widely but it is hardly ever found in practice, and while there is a trend towards equalizing marriage, there is very little research which shows that there is a real increased equality between husband and wife. This is possibly because there is a basic misunderstanding about what equality means. What it certainly does not mean is role reversal: that is that men must stop being dominant and women must become dominant, and that women must stop being subservient and men must become subservient. Equality means that we must stop thinking in terms of sexual polarity, and think of men and women purely as human beings and not stereotypes. It means that we must think of the roles of husbands and wives in terms of their personality, temperament, talent and predilections and that we must come to accept that the role of husband may well overlap with the role of wife, and vice versa. This would be a truly egalitarian marriage.

Yet a further property of the egalitarian marriage is a change of style. This is not to be confused with a change of power: traditionally the husband has greater power than the wife, but in certain marriages which are wife-dominated, this is reversed. Achievement of equality does not necessarily mean a shift of power; it means a change of behavior. The woman no longer dissembles, she no longer accepts without question, she no longer acquiesces without protest, she begins to express her views openly, she begins to state her preferences assertively, she begins to show her own personality.

Marriage also promises a change in terms of the wife's achievement. In the past, wives have enjoyed most of their recognition indirectly through their husbands. This reflects the commonly-held view that a wife cannot achieve very much in her own right in terms of becoming a great lawyer, a good doctor, or an efficient business executive, but she can do so through her husband. Women must become more motivated by achievement; they should be less willing to settle for less, they should not be prepared to accept a slower pace, and they should not stop at a lower level of achievement than men. Women will gradually stop wanting to be simply the woman behind every successful man and will want success for themselves.

This is not to say that egalitarian marriages do not need a bit of maneuvering – most successful ones do not take the wife's achievements blatantly into the home. A marriage may founder if a career wife insists that her husband treats her as a successful professional. What is more, she may become very boring and it would be quite wrong for a wife to expect her husband to treat her with the formal respect and deference that some of her junior colleagues may. A successful woman is still a wife, and her husband is entitled to her love. So it would be plain bad management for a successful wife to throw her weight around at home. It's as well to remember that being a boss on the job doesn't automatically entitle a woman to be a boss at home.

SINGLE WOMEN

Until the 1970s, being a single woman was synonymous with being a neurotic spinster, then, a decade ago, this stereotype was attacked by both men and women. Growing pressure to lower the birth rate serendipitously coincided with the birth of the women's liberation movement: the demolition of the idolatry of marriage, started in the 1960s by the first of the feminists, was completed, and women in general seemed to be caught up in the excitement of both new opportunities and new lifestyles. All of this helped to upgrade the status of the unmarried woman.

The trend today is to glorify the single woman: that is, the *successful* single woman. Far from being a creature to be pitied and patronized the single woman is emerging as the great new glamour girl of our times. She is glamorized in terms of her worldliness and *savoir faire*, her independence, her highly-tuned intellect, and her personality, which allows her to compete successfully in a masculine world. The reality, as most single women know, is a good deal less glamorous than this, while being a lot more satisfactory than commonly perceived. And practically speaking, most women should plan on being single for a considerable part of their lives, because even if they marry they spend at least their last 13 years as a widow.

Many women see non-marriage as the simplest, if not the ultimate, way of achieving autonomy. In the early days of the feminist movement, women were encouraged to live alone and free so that they could be in control of their own lives. They were encouraged to abstain from marriage as a political action. It was said that before one could achieve self-confidence, one had to reject marriage as a relationship which offered women few possibilities and few options.

Political ideals such as these are only one of the reasons why women are choosing to be single. While many women opt for the unmarried lifestyle because they really believe that it is the only way they can enjoy complete freedom and fulfill their potential, others who once considered marriage as a social convention now muster sufficient courage to abstain from marriage – especially since society no longer seems to demand it – and the availability of more efficient birth control erases the need to seek respectability in wedlock. There are women who feel that they are not suited for the discipline of living with another person and who are now able

to declare that they simply feel a lack of aptitude for marriage. Also, some women are unwilling to assume the responsibility of marriage. Many women now perceive that they are very often driven into unequal marriages. The unmarried woman is often in the upper echelon of women, and if she marries herself off to the inferior kind of man (who tends to be left on the shelf), she is bound to find it an experience which brings her down. In addition to some element of choice, rising divorce rates, and uncertain economic conditions have also swelled the ranks of the unmarried.

Being single can have very definite advantages: there's greater opportunity for self-expression and self-realization, and a far larger amount of personal freedom. It can be very exciting and fulfilling, but there are plenty of problem areas. The major ones include housing, finance, social activities and emotional fulfillment – and all these are adversely affected by the fact that women are traditionally poorly paid.

Making the most of being single means being able to provide yourself with the kind of environment which will enable you to grow. This does not mean developing in isolation, but having a rich social life and a number of varied interests. Single women often find emotional fulfillment and sexual satisfaction hard to achieve, most often because of lack of opportunity. It is, therefore, important that you develop a degree of initiative and extroversion in order to develop relationships with people in groups. Joining a social club or evening class as well as becoming involved in community and volunteer work, are all useful for meeting new people. Finding separate accommodation from your parents will aid in developing an independent social and emotional life, although living with others, in communal form, is often the best way to begin to set out on your own.

Communes offer a variety of lifestyles. They can consist of a group of people of both sexes, or either sex, who will form and dissolve relationships without being seriously committed to one another (or if there is a commitment, it may be simply implicit and understood but rarely formalized). Some communes include married couples who stay true to their monogamous relationship, but others go so far as to discourage marriage and any form of pairing off, believing that everyone is committed to everyone else.

The commune is a loose, open household. It's a pattern of living and a lifestyle that may have a bright future as it provides a very happy, satisfying and rewarding way of life for many people who find our present society unacceptable, and who are not prepared to commit themselves to long-term relationships, who shrink from intimacy with another person, who really feel the need to be surrounded by several people rather than one. Communes also offer a half-way house to those people who wish to leave home and don't feel ready to set up a household of their own. Communes, however, can sometimes be hard on women, especially if they are designed and led by men, because they may find that their activities are confined to household chores. Yet another option for the single woman is a co-operative household where everything is shared: the finances, the responsibility, and the chores, but there is no formal marriage. Since there is an increasing tendency for single women to have children, both the co-operative and communal situations offer more stable environments.

The long-term happiness of a single woman largely depends on how well she deals with her social and emotional problems; naturally, some of this is easier if she has chosen and not had singledom thrust upon her. Success at work, wide-ranging intellectual and social interests all contribute to a satisfactory life.

The divorcée

Divorce is something which increasingly may affect us all. Over the past twenty-five years the divorce rate has risen steadily, and now about 1 in 3 marriages in America end in divorce within fifteen years. There were one million divorces in 1975. Divorce laws have become less strict, but this has made only a minor contribution to the rising divorce rate.

The leap in the divorce rate has occurred since 1945, and it is probably due to two things: life expectancy for most of us is greater and many of us are having our last child earlier. For most marriages, this means that there is probably twenty years of life ahead of couples when their last child has grown up and left home. In earlier times, this part of life was probably non-existent, but it has done a good deal to transform our attitudes towards marriage. It has created in many the desire to use the post-parenthood phase for activity and enjoyment, particularly as people are now young enough to do so. This has created questions about marriage itself, and whether or not a failing marriage should be kept alive once the reason for holding it together, the children, has gone. Many people are now opting to face the future more honestly and to dissolve their marriages.

There is a fairly high incidence of divorce among people in their twenties and early thirties, and more than half the people who get divorced admit that marital problems started within two years of being married. This suggests that the partners were incompatible from the start. The other kind of divorce results from a marriage which fails because the partners grow apart and become incompatible over time. Statistics show that the majority of couples separate between their first and fourth anniversaries, and divorce usually follows two years later.

In recent years, there has been a tremendous increase in the number of divorce petitions filed by women, and very often the possibility of divorce is first mentioned by wives. One researcher has shown that the chain of events follows a set pattern in which the wife first mentions divorce, the husband decides that he would like a divorce, and behaves in a way which forces his wife to ask for one.

There are certain groups of women who seem to run a higher risk of divorce than others:
● Women who prefer their father to their mother are slightly more prone to divorce;
● Women who are only children tend towards divorce;
● Women of the lower socio-economic groups.
The marriages that run into trouble are those which were opposed by parents, and those between couples who had previous break-ups before they got married. There are more divorces in couples who have short courtships than those who take proper honeymoons. Shotgun marriages have always had a poor prognosis and they still do. More divorcées had conceived children before getting married than women who remained married.

Paradoxically, infertility and early fertility seem to make divorce more likely, because divorce is twice as common in couples who had children very early in their marriage.

The greatest protection against divorce seems to be good communication between partners. Geographical separation, an unwillingness to talk about yourself, an inability to interpret your partner's needs, and, most important of all, the absence of a common language can all threaten this. Success in marriage often depends upon a shared culture.

However, the most important recent change in our attitude towards divorce is that women are increasingly turning to it as an option to change their lifestyle. Women expect a great deal more from their marriage than they used to. Women are becoming more and more aware that they benefit much less from marriage than their partners do. The marriage, therefore, has to live up to higher demands to justify a woman staying in it than it did previously. Equal job opportunities, sound economic and financial status have made women more likely to choose this option when their marriage turns sour.

A divorcée has many difficult adjustments to make after she has left her partner, but one of the things that she seems to find easy is re-marriage. Nearly half of all divorcées marry again within a year of their divorce, and 75% of them find a new partner within three years. It would seem that whatever reservations we have about marriage, it seems to be the lifestyle which suits most of us, and even several divorces are unable to turn some people off marriage completely. The bitter truth is that while many do not remember marriage fondly, they find being divorced even less palatable.

One of the major consequences that faces any divorced woman is less social contact with others. Divorcées as a rule are an embarrassment to their married friends, and many new divorcées find friendly support lacking at a time when they need it most, because friends wish to avoid embarrassment. Initially, at least, divorcées may find that the majority of single people around them are much younger, and they no longer want to do the things young single people are doing. Because of a lack of common interest, they may become insecure about their attraction for the opposite sex and begin to doubt their ability to ever compete again.

Despite the disappearance of the social stigma attached to divorce, divorcées are still subject to great stresses and strains in simply managing their everyday lives, because of logistical problems, because of loneliness, because of financial difficulties, not the least being acrimonious arguments between lawyers about alimony, because of insufficiently good support for the children, because of possible housing problems and problems at work. Divorcées have a higher suicide rate than married people, and they are also more prone to mental and physical illness. There is no doubt that the short-term effect of getting divorced is traumatic and can touch every aspect of our lives in terms of stress. However, the overall picture is good and very encouraging. The majority of divorcées recover very quickly. The first year is the worst, but research has shown that after two years, only 1 in 4 divorced women feel that their divorce was a mistake.

While more than half of teenage marriages end up in divorce, it would seem to be worth hanging on if possible until you are fifty, when attitudes become much more positive. Marriages seem to improve when children have left home, and people become happier about their marriages at the same time. Despite the rising divorce rate, even in the thirty-five to fifty-four age group, 82% of women are married, and the majority of them are in stable, long-term first marriages. This can be a time when partners draw closer and the marriage may become more harmonious. Many arguments between partners just don't happen any more because the children have left home.

As far as women are concerned, an unhappily married woman may decide that she will simply stick with the marriage, because her chances of finding another husband are much slimmer once she has reached menopause. She is afraid that she will no longer be attractive to men and so becomes resigned to her marriage and decides to grin and bear it.

There is a rule among horse riders that after a fall you must climb back onto the horse immediately; a similar rule should apply to divorce. Emotional upsets are unavoidable, and it may take you some time to get over the shock and insecurity, but you really must try to resume a normal social life as soon as you can. In most places there are divorcée clubs where you can get together with people of a similar age and similar circumstances, who can share your experience and show sympathy towards your predicament. If possible, you should try to have occasional dates and participate in whatever sort of outings your club arranges. It is important to realize that you are not unique. There are lots of other people who have gone through a similar experience to yours and life can go on in the single or in the remarried state. Indeed it might be a great deal better. Contact with people who have been through the same experience as you will help your wounds to heal.

You will be making a fatal mistake if you think that divorce will end all your problems, or that it will bring a life of pure excitement and glamour. Don't fall into the trap of letting fantasies take the place of reality. Don't become someone who is desperately searching for lost youth. Be realistic about your expectations and your lifestyle. Be astute and calm about assessing your future life. It may be mundane and ordinary, but there are many pleasures to be had from that kind of lifestyle. You can probably live quite happily with a few friends helping with your children and your grandchildren, and the odd trip or holiday, being with friends or visiting friends. It doesn't sound so exciting, but many other people are not as fortunate.

One of the most problematical areas of any divorce, is in ensuring the happiness and security of the children. Very often children are the real victims of divorce. For many of them their worlds fall apart. After all, the two people they love most in the world have separated, and life may never be quite the same again.

Just as for you, life has to go on for them, too. They have to cope with their own problems, go to school, face their friends, and try to understand the emotional conflicts between their parents which they often find bewildering.

One of the arguments against parents patching up a failing marriage is that children always seem to know when something is wrong and find it deeply disturbing. One of the aspects of a failing relationship between parents is non-cooperation: the parents don't hit each other, or throw things, but they do small things to annoy each other, like leaving things undone or not listening. In these circumstances, children feel helpless.

It probably never occurs to most couples who are in the midst of a disintegrating marriage that their child very often is suffering terrible pangs of guilt, and is feeling that it is actually his/her fault that the marriage has failed or that the parents are fighting. Even when they are reassured that it is not their fault, children still commonly feel fear, embarrassment, and insecurity.

One of the things that children unanimously agree on is that they should be informed about the intent to divorce immediately. Here are some of the other vital points that children feel they ought to know:

- That the parents don't love each other but that they still love their children;
- That life may be very hard before a settlement is reached;
- Where they are going to live after the divorce;
- How often will they see their parents;
- Why the parents are splitting up; this may not be advisable if the reason is a love affair.

Nearly all children agree that it is better for warring parents to split up than for them to stay together for the sake of the children, and they also agree that while they may think it is the end of the world when the divorce happens, it is very much better once parents are parted. A divorce is very hard and painful for children at times, but it is a great deal less painful once they have coped with it and it is behind them.

Custody of the children

It is only ten years since it was very rare for a custody judge to award the full-time care of the children to the husband. This is no longer a rare event. Judges now take note of what the evidence unequivocally proves, and that is that either parent is equally suited to look after the children, given that they are good parents. The sex is irrelevant. Women can therefore no longer rely on their sex as a guarantee of getting custody of the children.

Judges view each partner on her/his merit, and will select who is, in their opinion, the better parent to look after the children. This mainly applies when children are under the age of twelve. After that age, judges very often ask to see the children in private so that their own preferences of which parent they would like to live with can be taken into consideration, and these views will weigh very heavily with the judge. Over the age of about sixteen, of course, the child can decide for her or himself with which parent s/he lives, regardless of the judge's decision. The parent who has her children's best interests at heart, will, of course, go along with the desire of the children regardless of her own.

Bonding of mothers to children is very often used as an excuse for long and bitter custody cases, because a woman simply will not give up what she considers her inalienable right to cling onto her children. If there is a clear-cut case that she is not fit to look after the children, this simply causes unhappiness to everyone, including the children who should be her first consideration.

Custody of the children, of course, need not always be decided by a court. One would hope that two mature adults could decide on this sensitive issue without having recourse to the law, and many do. What must go hand-in-hand with custody of the children is the financial support of them, and it may be this side of the matter which is problematical. A greedy woman may well use the children as an excuse for higher alimony than is reasonable, and a husband would be quite right to fight this. On the other hand, many independent women refuse to have necessary financial support for their children when parting from their husband has been a bitter experience. What is needed is a well-thought-out and amicable financial arrangement based on immediate and future needs with both partners' earning power as the basis.

If the custody of the children does go to court, the judge will also make a ruling on the amount of money that the husband must supply for the support of the children. Resist the temptation to be greedy: judges can see through it easily and will have no hesitation in reducing the amount that you ask for.

Part of your custodial responsibilities is to allow access to the children's father. If it is decided out of court, the arrangements will simply be a matter of convenience for you and your husband, at a frequency that you both consider reasonable; "reasonable access" by many judges is considered to be alternate weekends and half the school holidays, so you could use that as a basis.

Research has come out strongly on the side of children having one home. It is known that they are unsettled by not having a single base to relate to. You should, therefore, never agree to the children spending half their lives in your partner's home and half in yours; certainly a judge would never allow it. It is essential that they live most of their lives, attend schools and make friends around one home base and see another as a place to visit. Regardless of who gets custody of the children, resist the temptation to compensate for absences by being over-indulgent with regard to presents, freedom and lack of discipline. Children are very sensitive to this and will beat you at your own game. As they get older, all that will happen is that you will lose their respect. If they love you, they will be made very uncomfortable if you make a fool of yourself. If they don't love you you can't buy their love.

It is very difficult to accept that firstly you may lose your children to the partner you have divorced, and secondly if your husband is re-married or living with someone, that they will rely for most of their daily care and love on another woman. Indeed, you may never come to terms with it inside of yourself, but it is essential that at least you behave as though you have come to terms with it. You will only cause greater conflict, unhappiness, confusion and insecurity for your children if you refuse to accept their stepmother. You will be judged by the ultimate test anyway, and that is that if you are as good a mother as you think you are, your relationship with your children will not be impaired by the presence of a stepmother. If she is a good stepmother, then you ought to be happy for your children because they have a third caring adult to supply them with needed affection and love.

Alimony

There are few countries in the world which are prepared to contemplate the enormous sums of alimony that are awarded in the United States. Alimony should cover enough money for you to continue to live the sort of life you were enjoying before you divorced your husband, and so that your children can do the same. Your own earnings, however, will be taken into consideration, and it is only right and proper that they are.

In the case of alimony it seems to me that many women want to have their cake and to eat it, too. On the one hand, they are the strongest protagonists of equal opportunities, an equal economic and financial status for women, and on the other, they demand large sums in alimony. The two actions are just not compatible. They are not compatible with any feminist philosophy, nor should they be with a woman's concept of what her position, and the position of other women should be in society. Women cannot be responsible and irresponsible at the same time.

Another part of the alimony agreement will be the splitting up of property and worldly goods. In most countries a wife (whether the property is owned jointly or not) is liable to half her husband's assets by law, and your legal counsel will not be slow to point this out to you. In the United States, these rights to claim half the assets of the husband have been extended from the legal wife to the living-in partner by means of a couple of test cases.

Many women are unaware that their legal costs, for the divorce and custody of the children as well as splitting of the husband's assets, are borne by the husband in certain countries. Without this knowledge, many women hesitate to take on what might be a protracted legal battle, because they feel that they cannot afford the legal costs. Be sure to discuss this whole matter with your legal advisers, to see whether or not the law of your country allows you to claim your costs from your husband.

It has to be said that most legal systems now consider marriage partners equal, which means that on the one hand the wife now can gain access to half her husband's assets, but what you must not forget is that your husband has the right to half of yours.

Being a single parent

Some women become a single parent unexpectedly through widowhood, an unexpected pregnancy or a divorce, but an increasing number are opting to bring up children alone by choice. When a woman finds herself with a partner who is not prepared to share the responsibility of bringing up a child she may decide to do it alone, and there is no reason why a woman who does not feel that she can sustain a long-term relationship with a partner should be denied the experience of motherhood, and some women, who by the age of 35 have not yet established a stable long-term relationship, may make an active decision to become pregnant and bring up their baby by themselves. Whatever route a woman becomes a single parent by, there are inevitable problems.

By far the biggest and most common problem is financial. The only way to solve this problem is to have a job, and you probably need a full-time job to provide enough funds to house and support yourself and your child. This, in turn, raises the second great area of difficulty for you – finding someone to take care of your child for most of the day. Very few single women are earning enough to pay for full-time help, and very few employers provide a day-care center at work, so you will have to find some other suitable form of child care.

Day-care centers which meet federal standards are usually too expensive to provide care during the entire time a full-time work-

ing mother must be away from her child. Also, many of these centers and (nursery schools as well) are inconvenient: relatively few of them are open either side of nine-to-five, and they will usually refuse to accept a child who may be even slightly unwell. In addition, there are usually transportation problems in getting to the center, both financially and in terms of time.

Therefore, family care by a sitter in your home or in her/his is often the best alternative. Such people are licensed, at a ratio of one supervising adult to six children, and you can usually find them through advertisements or recommendations by friends. A single woman with a baby has so many difficulties to contend with in life that it is important to find a baby-sitter whom you like and trust and know will give your child the love and care s/he requires during your working hours.

Many single parents opt to stay at home and give their children full-time care and rely on funds from the government as their source of money. However, the payments are minimal and will mean that you have to lead a fairly spartan life. There will be very little money left over for everyday expenses such as new clothes, baby equipment, even bus fares. You may not even be able to afford a babysitter, and this may increase your isolation. Any money that you earn will be deducted.

One of the ways of lightening your financial burden is to find someone to share accommodations with you. Besides halving many of your expenses, you will also have company.

In most communities there are groups which give support to single parents. Members will advise you on the best baby-sitters in the district and will help with babysitting chores, so that you can have free time on your own. They will give you reassurance and guidance on bringing up your baby, and they will put you in touch with people in a similar situation to yourself.

One of the most important ways in which these groups can help you is to advise on and to show you how to deal with government agencies and bureaucracies. There is quite a lot of red tape, but most of these groups have taken the trouble to get to know the system and work it efficiently. They can save you a great deal of time, effort, energy, and heartache, if you take advantage of their experience and expertise.

Most single women are concerned that there is no father figure in their children's lives. While it is very nice for both of you if there is a man in your life who can be one, there is no need for you to encourage a liaison simply to provide a surrogate father for your child. Research has shown that a baby needs neither parent, only a caring adult. Your child will do just as well with you as a loving mother as s/he would with you and a father figure.

Homosexuality

The sixth demand of the women's liberation "charter" goes thus: "We demand an end to the discrimination against lesbians, and the right of every woman to a self-defined sexuality."

Lesbians, probably more than male homosexuals, have been stereotyped by heterosexual society. Some people try to explain lesbianism in behavioral terms, describing lesbians as masculine, over-assertive, extremely ambitious. Others try to describe them in chemical terms, explaining their lack of heterosexuality as a hormone deficiency; yet others feel that the roots of lesbianism are in the childhood environment, and believe that lesbians, in the main, come from unhappy, unbalanced homes. Others see them as mentally ill or perverted. These pejorative descriptions have driven lesbians underground, and it is only with the alliance of the women's liberation movement, that lesbianism has been seen as an acceptable optional lifestyle of women, and that they have been able to come in out of the cold.

It may take a woman some time to realize that she is a lesbian, brought up as she has been with the traditional ideas that lesbianism is unnatural. Lesbianism very often does not occur overnight but, more often, as the result of a gradual change in attitude towards heterosexual relationships and the standards of a heterosexual society, or a gradual realization that relationships with men are unsatisfactory and therefore a lifestyle in which a heterosexual relationship is implicit will prove to be not only unpleasant but impossible.

For that reason, many women only come to realize that they are truly lesbians part-way through their lives, when they are already married and have children. It is only with maturity, experience, and growing self-confidence that they are capable of revealing that their marriage and lifestyle is unsatisfactory, and that they are no longer prepared to go on making concessions in so important an area of their lives.

Many social factors conspire against lesbians admitting their homosexual predilections: it may be very hard for a lesbian to declare herself if she is working in an environment where heterosexuality is considered the only acceptable norm; parental attitudes may preclude honesty. The majority of women, when they are young, are highly sensitive to peer and societal pressures.

Once a lesbian has "come out," she will be subject to the enormous pressures which any homosexual is subject to in a primarily heterosexual society. It is not surprising, therefore, that lesbians gather together in communes for added strength, and confine their social activities to places where gays are readily accepted. This in itself keeps them isolated and prevents integration with the rest of society.

Lesbianism does not solely imply a sexual preference for women – it is much more a matter of lifestyle. The majority of lesbians claim that sex occupies an important but small part of their lives. Much more important is contact with women, living with women, and planning a lifestyle that is built around openness and freedom in any sort of relationship between women.

In the early 1980s this lifestyle has not yet been legitimized on a wide scale and any lesbian must expect to meet prejudice, however unfair it may be. To my mind, the best way to cope with prejudice is to be honest, open, and forthright about the subject, and to resist the temptation to take the easy way out and be covert about it. The more lesbianism is discussed, the more lesbians show themselves to be useful, successful members of society, the more integrated lesbians become with society, the more easily this lifestyle will be generally accepted. It must be almost impossible for any woman with self-respect to condemn at least half of her life (her private life) to a clandestine status. For most women this would be a crushing blow to their dignity.

If you feel fairly certain that you have lesbian tendencies, or if you are undecided and simply wish to explore the possibility so that you can make up your mind, the easiest way to do so, is to join a lesbian club. Not surprisingly, they don't advertise, but in most localities it is not difficult to track one down by making judicious inquiries among your friends, some of whom may have male or female homosexual contacts. If your initial contacts confirm that you do wish to lead the rest of your life as a lesbian, then you will have to make radical changes in your lifestyle, especially if you are married. You may have to face the fact that your marriage will break up and that many of your relatives will revile your actions.

There is, however, no reason whatsoever that you should give up your children. Even if your marriage ends in divorce, the judgement on custody may come out in your favor, but be prepared for the law courts to be one area of life where you will meet prejudice. There is no need, however, for you to accept a custodial judgement against you if you feel it is done because of bias. Fight the case. However, you may have to change your job, as some employers and large institutions such as government offices are reluctant to employ lesbians and can make life very uncomfortable for you. In such a case you may find yourself gravitating to one of those professions where homosexuality is "accepted" such as the theatre and the arts.

Parenthood for lesbians is fraught with difficulties. They are in the constant watchful eyes of heterosexual mothers, teachers and possibly social workers. A lesbian mother finds herself surrounded by people who are only too ready to criticize her actions and blame her lifestyle if anything goes wrong in the bringing-up of her child. Furthermore, a lesbian mother may be well aware of the pain that society inflicts on her children: the criticisms of other children, the reflected bias of adults, and the conflict that any child must feel in being able to describe her/his mother's lifestyle and relationships honestly. She may even feel that she is creating uncertainty and confusion in her child's mind by living out one lifestyle when most school activities and the media reflect the heterosexual norm.

If possible, lesbian mothers should seek out lesbian groups, all of whom are concerned to help guide and support lesbian mothers. The likelihood is that you will meet other lesbian mothers at meetings of the group, and so you will be able to introduce your children to other children of lesbians. For children, the realization that they are not in a unique position in having a lesbian mother is of the greatest importance, and you should strenuously solicit opportunities to do this. One of the best ways of ensuring that future generations accept the lesbian lifestyle as part of the norm, is to educate your children to this point of view. Though they may choose a different lifestyle themselves, they will act as the most potent protagonists of your cause.

MOTHERHOOD

Nowhere is ambivalence about the role of the modern woman more clear-cut than in the conception of a mother; the growing emancipation of women hardly touches the universal acceptance that it is mothers who remain responsible for the care of children.

The media have done nothing to mitigate the duality of a mother's role: on the one hand, advertisers present motherhood as a glamorous activity; on the other hand, most of the blame for something going wrong with the baby is laid at the feet of the mother. Even though research has not been able to find evidence to support statements that the children of working mothers are less well off than those whose mothers stay at home, pressure is still brought to bear on the mother that maternal deprivation will harm her children. As Margaret Mead suggested in 1954, this was "a new and subtle form of anti-feminism in which men – under the guise of exalting the importance of maternity – are tying women more tightly to their children . . ." As it happens, the 1980 mother probably spends more time with her children than her mother did.

Very often, children and motherhood bring isolation, confusion and insecurity to many women. Despite all the joys of motherhood which are described in baby books, it can be a time of great loss of confidence to many young women. Many women feel that they are not particularly good at motherhood, and feel failures as mothers. They don't know when the baby has been fed enough, or why it is crying, or whether it is warm enough. This undermines their self-confidence and they often wonder if they will ever do anything properly again. If a woman feels that she is a failure as a mother, she may begin to feel that she is a failure as a person too, and from this time onwards she may begin to feel lonely and isolated. Undoubtedly, one of the loneliest people in the world can be the mother of children who are under school age. For many mothers, lack of help with the children, and reservations about leaving the children in the care of anyone but a relative, means that they spend their leisure time at home, very often with little more than television to divert them.

One of the most important aspects of motherhood, and one which is rarely discussed, is that every individual varies in her attitude towards it and her capacity to handle it. This is nothing to do with being a good mother or a bad mother. There is no such thing. A mother is what you are if you choose motherhood – you will then have your own style of doing it. Many of the different approaches of women to motherhood depend a great deal more on stamina and temperament than whether they feed the baby on time and change the diaper as soon as it is soiled. Some women will feel instant mother love for their child at birth. Others may be quite frightened by the absence of this bonding, though there is no reason to be so. Some women feel that being a mother is one of the most thrilling experiences and greatest privileges that they will ever enjoy, but it is easy to find others who will only be able to describe the exhaustion and boredom they experienced in bringing up small children.

Giving up work may not be resented at all by some women but others can find it quite frightening because they cannot resolve the competing demands of child-rearing and the desire for self-fulfillment. Living in a society which sees women primarily as mothers, who are expected to view motherhood with joy, and "non-mothering" women as perverse and deviant, denies and helps to suppress a woman's right to approach motherhood any way she wants to – if she wants to.

For many women one of the hardest parts of motherhood is mothering. More and more women come from small families, and the opportunities for gaining experience with babies and small children are few. In fact 4 out of 5 women have had no experience with babies of any kind when they have their first child.

In terms of motherhood, the luckier woman would appear to be a girl who comes from a fairly large family where, from an early age, she has been helping out with bringing up the children, and this familiarity helps enormously when it comes to having her own babies. Even so, many women feel that it is different when you have your own, and you do worry more.

For most women the birth of the first child seems to be a major psychological turning point. While the majority of mothers have no previous experience with babies, they find that their partners, doctors, parents, and child experts of all kinds feel that they ought to know what to do. As they can't live up to these high standards, many women feel as though they have failed, not just as mothers, but as persons. Very often, this feeling of inadequacy is aggravated for the professional woman who is constantly aspiring to an active intellectual life.

Women lower down the socio-economic scale, even though they have had more experience with babies, may suffer more from their first taste of motherhood. The working class wife hopes and expects to find her main source of satisfaction, indeed, her reason for living, in her family. Motherhood is one of the things that she most wants. If motherhood brings with it confusion, anxiety and a feeling of muddling through (as it does for most of us), then this particular woman can find that the very reason for her existence is seriously undermined, with subsequent frustration.

Motherhood in the 1980s brings with it two pressures which are age-old: the first is the desire to give the children a better life and greater happiness than you had when you were a child; the second is to try to avoid some of the problems with your own children that you experienced with your parents. However, there is no evidence to suggest that we are getting any better at parenthood and child-rearing than previous generations. Peer pressures are also unrelenting, and seem to have at least as great an effect on a growing child's behavior as anything s/he is taught in the home, and mothers certainly, if not fathers, have new stresses and difficulties to deal with, so while old problems may be conquered, new ones are constantly presenting themselves.

One thing is certain: if you wish your daughter to grow up to be liberated, and if you wish to protect your daughter from some of the bad experiences which you had during your own adolescence, then you have to start very early. In fact, you have to start in the cradle. Encouraging a girl to grow up with liberated ideas doesn't start with a talk about equal opportunities the first time she goes along to a job interview – it has to do with creating expectations from the word "go"; it has to do with participation in boys' activities as well as girls'; it has to do with instilling self-confidence and self-assurance; it has to do with showing your daughter the possibilities in life, the various options, and making sure that she scrutinizes her actions very carefully before making a decision.

One of the greatest favors you can do for your daughter is to teach her to be critical and skeptical of what people are saying and doing around her, and to be her own person and have the strength of character to do what she wants to do. From a fairly early age, you can encourage her to be responsible and to make sound judgments. This is, by far, the best way to prepare her for life, and to protect her from life if she needs it. You have succeeded if you don't need to protect her, but if she's able to protect herself.

Hardly any parent negotiates the choppy waters of her child's adolescence without friction – so be prepared for it and don't consider that you have failed as a mother if you encounter it. I have learned that there really is only one essential thing that you must do, and that is to keep the channels of communication open. You should never be the one to close them. Furthermore, you should do whatever is necessary to keep them open.

One of the best ways of mitigating the feelings of isolation, boredom, frustration, and resentment which affect mothers entirely devoted to bringing up children is to ensure that you have some time of your own to do whatever you please on a regular basis; there is absolutely no reason why you cannot have some time to yourself. Long before the birth of your first baby, there should be an agreement with your partner that you need some independent time; both of you will be much better off if you have it, and as a bonus, you will probably be a better mother.

If you possibly can, you should keep a stipulated day and time which everyone in the household understands and accepts is yours, and keep it sacrosanct. It may be that you choose every Tuesday afternoon to have your hair done, to go round the shops or museums and to meet a friend for lunch; or every Thursday evening you attend yoga class and then go out to dinner and drinks with your friends; or it may be that you want to take up a hobby, perhaps painting, and you will attend night classes at the local school, and then have some time during the week where you can go off and paint. It can be anything that you want to do which will give you satisfaction. The important thing is that you have time to and for yourself. It is an important need of every human being, and especially of a mother who feels that her time belongs to everybody else, and that she is being pulled in too many directions a lot of the time. Make arrangements with your partner or with a friend to look after the family, go off and enjoy yourself, and have no feelings of guilt. All you are doing is exercising one of your rights as a mother.

WORKING WOMEN

Women who work are almost certainly under the same stress and strain as men – indeed, married women and single mothers who work are subject to a much greater strain than married men. Such women workers have not only to get themselves and their families up in the morning, but then have to deal with the traffic jam on the way to work, very often struggling with heavy packages on public transportation, and, in addition, shoulder all the worries and burdens about a difficult boss, deadlines, promotion (just as any man does during his working day), and then she has to go home, and either keep her problems to herself or take them out on her family.

Furthermore, working women suffer from the same illnesses as working men, to the same degree: illnesses such as heart attacks, high blood pressure, alcoholism, and peptic ulcers have a similar incidence in working men and women. When women enter middle management, they are subject to exactly the same stresses as men, and suffer the same high levels of stress-related illnesses.

It is possible that women working alone in primarily male organizations may be subject to a great deal more stress than any man. Current research has revealed that "lone" women are subject to great psychological pressure. In such a work situation, a woman is seen as an outsider and one who is different from the rest. She, therefore, not only feels, but actually is, under pressure and scrutiny all the time. Her position can be likened to the first black mayor in America or the first woman on the stock exchange (the first person, whoever they are, in whatever position, will probably suffer greater anxiety and tension at her job than anyone second or third in position).

In addition to all that, most working women have extra burdens – they have to see the children off to school, clean the house, do the shopping, see to the laundry, cook all the meals, supervise the children doing their homework, attend school functions, oversee the children's outside activities, care for each member of the immediate family and perhaps aged parents as well – all this and manage to do the work at the office and hold down the position successfully. Such responsibilities are an unbearable burden for anyone of either sex, and it is no wonder that more women than men take tranquillizers and sedatives, or practice yoga or try psychotherapy to deal with their problems.

These problems are rarely self-inflicted. Contrary to masculine myths, the majority of women work because they have to and not because they want to. They may have to because one salary today is rarely sufficient to keep up a family's living standards; they may have to because they are self-supporting or have been left alone, and have to keep themselves and possibly several children. Their are countless reasons why women have to work, but regardless of the reason, women are under a great deal of stress, and generally more stress than men.

In one way, however, women seem to handle stress better than men, when they are both exposed to the same trauma. While women who are in middle management are equally as harassed as the men, and pay a considerable price in terms of menstrual problems, irregular menstruation, dysmenorrhea, inability to conceive, miscarriages (conditions mainly to do with female physiology), they react more emotionally, and are allowed a great deal more leeway in expressing their pent-up emotions than men, and in the long run are probably better off in terms of mental as well as physical health.

Since the early 1960s women have achieved greater equality of opportunity. With the advent of the oral contraceptive pill and the freedom from unplanned pregnancies, coupled with greater availability of abortion on demand, women could counter arguments of employers that they might get pregnant at an awkward time and that they might leave their jobs and, perhaps, might not return. What woman then had to contend with was not the struggle to get a job in the face of male competition, but to cope with the stresses of getting to the top, because many women are natural leaders, good managers, with brains at least as able as men, and find it quite easy to ascend to managerial and supervisory roles.

However, there is a very high cost to rising to the top, and many men as well as women refuse to take on the burden. Many companies move their employees at intervals, and moving is traumatic, not just for the employee, but for members of her family as well. Few women are prepared to contemplate moving their children from school to school, and although it happens more frequently than in the past, most men are unwilling to find a new job in their partner's new location.

In this respect, a woman is no different from a man. Research has shown that a man's stability in his job relies very heavily on stability in his home environment, and men suffer greatly from just the same stresses as women, including moving locations, family problems, illness in the family, a traumatic divorce. In such circumstances a man's performance suffers noticeably, and so all the same criticisms can be levelled against men employees as well as women.

Very often, feminine women find it very difficult to be happy in masculine jobs. Feminine women are psychologically and sociologically inclined to be conciliatory and nurturing. This sort of woman, while she makes an excellent supervisor, may not be entirely happy in a leadership role which calls for certain aggressive, assertive and masculine qualities. She is, therefore, called upon to be masculine/feminine. There are women graduating every day in professions which have been traditionally thought of as masculine – for example, law, business administration, architecture, medicine, etc., and the future is very bright for them indeed. But progress up the professional ladder may cost a great deal in anxiety, tension, and illness for women who find it difficult to accept their androgynous role. Women who have been brought up to fulfill a feminine role, and are then thrust into masculine work, probably pay the greatest price of all and suffer most from psychological disturbances.

The assertive, aggressive woman has most probably been a

tomboy all her life, possibly with male interests. This is not because she is emotionally more like a man. She may be a tomboy because her parents might have always encouraged her to work and fulfill her ambitions in a male occupation, and while she may succeed and grow up to be a lawyer or a doctor, her parents may have not done her a great service. Studies have shown that women who work continuously in their jobs die at approximately the same rate as men in the same jobs.

There is no doubt that many women who feel that they have to adopt male standards of pushiness, hard work, aggression, and application to achieve success are not only making it difficult for themselves but they may be making themselves unhappy. Such behavior is difficult for most women because they are not only acting unnaturally in being overly assertive, they are actually suppressing those qualities which may be most useful in a senior position. The participatory, nurturant management style has been shown to produce excellent results, and this is exactly the style which comes easily to most women. Women must, therefore, be careful not to fall into the male trap. Women who are reaching the corporate board room directorships, senior managerial roles, places on executive councils, do not have to work and behave as men do. The age-old proverb that a professional woman has to think like a man, act like a lady, and work like a dog, could not be less true. Women can be just as successful as men while behaving in a way which is naturally a part of their softer, feminine nature. They can retain their femininity, indeed, they are missing an opportunity if they do not use their femininity as a managerial tool, and they should feel perfectly comfortable with the thought that they have to sacrifice no femininity whatsoever in order to succeed in a man's world.

One of the worst mistakes that women make, is to use sexual discrimination as a lever in obtaining equal opportunities. They are quite right, of course, to get what they deserve, but very often it seems to be on sex and not on merit. One of the qualifications for any job is that you get on well with your associates and the other criterion is performance.

It doesn't have to be sex discrimination which prevents a woman getting on; it does not have to be a male boss who prevents a woman being promoted because of her sex. After all, nearly every successful woman executive has been promoted to her position by a man, so some of them are on our side. No, I am afraid the truth is that women employees who behave badly have only themselves to blame. It is they who are preventing their own promotion.

Working mothers
At the beginning of the century, most women who worked were single. At present, in the United Kingdom, there are nearly six million working women, and half of them are married. Many studies have been done to find out the reason why married women work, and the conclusion is that financial motives are the most important. However, more often than not the financial need is not one of necessity – a woman makes the decision to work to raise the standard of living of the family. The second most important reason for working appears to be a combination of loneliness and boredom.

Amongst middle class women there is another factor, because nearly 7 out of 10 women have been trained to do a particular job or enter a profession, or at least to qualify for positions in business or service organizations. Only 1 in 10 have not been trained for a role other than a wife or mother. Well over two-thirds of women who have trained, intend to take advantage of their training when they return to work after having a family. This shows very clearly that women no longer see their lives as being dominated in the long-term by the role of wife and mother.

Even today, the pattern of work for most women is to work until marriage, to work after marriage, and then to stop when the children are young. By far the commonest reason for stopping work is that women feel it is wrong to leave the children, even though three-quarters of all women who are at home, would like to be working.

Despite domestic pressures from husbands, social pressures from family and neighbours to stay at home and look after the children, more than a third of women continue to work when they have young children. Women with training find it easier to arrange part-time work which can fit in with the needs of their children and family; working class women without training are much less successful at combining work with demands of the home and family.

Many women go out to work because of an intellectual need. They find being at home all day very boring, frustrating and quite often "inferior". Some women complain of boredom, others are just fed up, and are angry and resentful of the sense of wasted time.

Once they have worked, very few women are prepared to say that they will not return to work at some time in the future after having a family. Indeed, the majority of women regard this as automatic, and feel no need to give reasons for doing so, because it seems a natural part of their lives. Many women consider it so natural, that if they were prevented from working at a later date, they would feel both deprived and trapped. They feel that they haven't stopped working, they have merely taken a short interval.

There is no doubt that if a wife is to make a success of her job, then she needs the support of her partner, and contrary to popular belief, studies show that 60% of husbands approve of their wives working. The number of husbands who do not want their wives to work increases as they descend the socio-economic scale. About 40% of working class husbands are opposed to their wives working. This means that about a third of all working class wives who work, are working despite their husbands' views.

In a way, the working-class working wife is the greatest credit to her sex, because despite lack of education, lack of training, and limited employment opportunities, as well as greater social and domestic pressures in which they are more dominated by their roles of wife and mother, they still go out to work.

When questioned, most working mothers admit to feeling guilty for leaving their children alone, when to their own minds they should be at home looking after them. A rather surprising finding is that women feel less guilty about leaving their children alone if they have to work for financial reasons or because they are divorced, widowed, or are a single-parent family. The research would indicate that a mother who is in fairly comfortable financial circumstances, and gains a great deal of satisfaction and intellectual stimulation from her job, feels more guilt, because by feminist standards, this kind of woman would be the most fulfilled, not to mention the most useful member of society. However, it would seem that women cannot easily shake off traditional concepts of a woman's role; men find it much easier to separate their roles at home and at the office.

In lucid moments, guilt does seem to be a non-affordable luxury. As a satisfied middle-class working mother, even if you

have sorted out the reasons for why you work – be it self-fulfillment, an intellectual or psychological need, money to be independent, fame if you are egocentric – there really are no rational reasons for feeling guilty. Overcoming the feeling, however, is not so easy. I have tried to rationalize my own guilt in several ways: when my children were being dealt the cards of life, I was the card they drew, and they are stuck with me; I am not the best mother in the world, nor am I the worst – they have to make the best of it just as I do. I would be a pretty awful person to live with if I didn't work – I have no doubt I would be resentful, to a certain extent bitter, and I am sure these feelings would be reflected on the children. I am a more interesting wife. My husband has to eat at irregular times, he has to share the housework and the chores and looking after the children, but at the same time we can have a conversation on almost any subject at the level of peers. We mutually respect what the other is doing, and the other's privacy. We have a very adult relationship. I have no doubt that our relationship would not be as healthy, nor would it work so well if I were not working, mainly because he would be my main source of interest, and inevitably I would feed off him. This would be unhealthy for both of us. The contribution that I am able to make to the family finances brings a great deal of satisfaction, and the fact that I am free to make arrangements and buy things for the family, independently of my husband, benefits us all.

However, some of the guilt remains, and I feel that the 1980s woman will really have achieved only psychological equality when she finally takes off the burden of guilt which most of us carry around for being working mothers. She has to come to terms with the fact that she cannot be all things to her children or her partner. Very often one of the worst stresses that a working mother has to deal with is that she is conscious of falling short in all the areas of her life. She is not quite as good a mother as she would wish to be; she is not as good a wife as she knows she could be; she doesn't perform her job as efficiently as she is capable of. In other words, her whole life is a series of compromises. It takes a great deal of mental adjustment to live with this knowledge of second-rate performance in all departments as well as the guilt.

However, it seems to me that it is perfectly reasonable in that situation to decide what are the most important things in your life, and to spend most of your energy seeing that those are taken care of first of all.

Top of your list has to be adequate care of the children, and therefore you will need help. You should be fairly unscrupulous about getting help – by that I mean that you should get the best help that you can afford. Very often in a low-income family, the best help is in the form of relatives if they live near enough. Members of the family, given that they care for children, are the people you can most easily trust with your children. It is also good for the children in that it helps to extend the nuclear family. If you are not one of the lucky mothers that can afford to have a live-in person to help with the children, then you will have to resort to a someone, who, if well chosen, can be a perfectly adequate substitute for you. But if not, s/he can have a deleterious effect on your child's mental and physical well-being, so it is worth spending some time and investigating this person thoroughly. By far the best way to find a good "mother's helper" is through the personal recommendation of a friend.

Whatever your lifestyle, however, it is essential that you have good help with the children. It is essential that in your absence there is a caring adult to look after them. I well remember giving a lecture to a group of men and women in which I mentioned that I was back in the office five days after having my second son, and I was accused by one of the women of having abandoned my children. This seemed very puzzling to me as I had abandoned them only to the care of a very loving father. Why was he not as good a person to look after my baby as I was? Of course he was, and my baby suffered not one bit.

Indeed, research has shown that babies don't need parents at all. What they need are caring adults. Furthermore, they don't need more than one. This information may reassure you about the possible guilt you feel about leaving your baby in the hands of someone who is not a parent. As long as the person you choose has your baby's welfare at heart, is a naturally loving and giving person and is concerned to make your baby's life varied and interesting, as well as looking after her/his basic needs, your child will come to no harm at all.

Studies performed several years ago have shown that the children of working mothers, as long as they are well cared for in her absence, do not suffer intellectually, emotionally, mentally or physically. A group of children who were studied for the effects on their development of having a working mother were found to be no different from the control group, whose mothers stayed at home and looked after them.

It would be reasonable for the second priority on your list to be your partner, and for many working women, it probably is. However, a larger number than would like to admit put themselves before their partners. This is inevitable, and if you do, you should not feel guilty about it. A woman who has to pursue her career actively, and is keen to succeed and ambitious to achieve promotion, has to devote so much of her energy towards that end, that her reserves will only stretch to looking after the children, and her partner, though she loves him, and though she wishes whole-heartedly to be a good companion, must necessarily in some people's eyes be neglected. This depends a great deal on the attitude of the man and his expectations, of course, but most reasonable women, who have established a standard in their own minds for the way reasonable mates ought to behave, will feel that they are falling short.

The reason for this is that to succeed in a competitive world, women have to be more selfish, more self-indulgent and more self-centered than they feel a reasonable woman ought to be. To come to terms with this rather unpleasant knowledge, one either has to decide that it doesn't matter, and get on with it anyway, or to come to a mutually-agreed *modus operandi* with your husband, accept that it is a concession you have to make, and live with the guilt that you may feel.

The majority of women don't have a natural tendency to act selfishly. Biologically, they put their children and their mates before themselves. But another paradox for the working mother is that she has to place herself higher on her list of priorities than is her natural inclination, and this is yet another inner struggle that she has to contend with. One fact is fairly plain, however, and that is that if you wish to climb the ladder you are going to have to be selfish about your desires. Perhaps more selfish than you would like to be.

As a working mother, there is no way that you can be all things to all people in your life, and it is essential that you don't try to cover the water front, otherwise you will simply be spreading yourself too thinly. You will have to live with the house not being as clean as you would like it, the children not getting all the care and attention that you would like them to have, the meals quite often being out of a can, or not quite as nutritious as you know is best, and many things seeming to get done at the last minute. You are just going to have to accept those things, so there is no use pining about them. They are a fact of life for the working mother.

One of the things you can do, of course, is to involve your family in your problem. Your problem is that you need helpers. There is no reason at all why children, as soon as they are capable, cannot help you with many of the tasks that you perform. Children are extremely happy to feel needed and will gladly set tables, fetch and carry, help with the shopping, run errands, and generally save you quite a lot of time if you make them a member of your team. In fact, it is only a fair trade. The children benefit a great deal from the fact that you are working, and therefore it is only just that they help you out with some of your chores in the house. That goes for your partner too.

One of the things that you can look forward to is that in your forties, you will have the freedom to increase your interest in your work. Research has shown that work becomes more and more important to women from one decade to another. In one survey, money was the most important factor in a woman's life during her thirties. Work overtook that priority at forty, and by the time she was fifty, work ranked alongside friends. This statistic is not a reflection that women who have not been working start or go back to a job in their forties. Even women who have been working throughout the time of having their family, begin to take a greater interest and invest more energy in their work as they approach the time when their children will grow up and leave home. The research showed that the reason why a woman regards this period as the prime of her life is because she sees freedom from daily responsibilities added to the knowledge that she is wiser, and these two things are what a woman relishes most. As a consequence you can look forward to giving your job greater commitment than you are able to at any other part of your life, with the corresponding satisfaction that this will bring.

STAYING
YOUTHFUL

A glance at the people you know will show that hardly anyone looks, behaves or is capable of acting the same way at a given age – they are as young as they feel, irrespective of how old they are. Our chronological age is, at best, a marker of how long we have been alive; more important is our functional age, which reflects how well our body copes with problems and circumstances, regardless of actual age.

Some women, however, view the years from fifty onwards as a period of decline into the grave, a time when they lose their youthfulness, beauty and vigor. What they fail to see is that frailty and old age do not necessarily go together, as long as you take a *positive* attitude towards getting older. Although we do not know exactly what causes ageing, we do know what ensures a healthy and productive elderly life: self-esteem is one of the most important elements in staying young, and a good diet and regular exercise are the two complementary factors.

Bear in mind that the later years in life bring their own kinds of achievement. With children out of the home and the major domestic burdens lightened, women at last can and do embark on public life and vocational training in many fields. They become eligible for jobs carrying high social status, such as those in law and government, which are rarely taken up before middle age. Indeed, authority, esteem and the approbation of peers seem likely to reach their peak in middle age. And it is not only in professional life that advanced years have advantages. Very often, the experience and wisdom of middle age make it easier to cope with the normal demands of everyday life. Even physical activities like driving are modified by experience, and by the time most women have reached middle age they have found their "psychological niche." This means that they have adjusted to the demands of their lifestyle and reduced them to a regular routine that they feel both relaxed and happy with.

It is often said that women do not reach their sexual peak until they are in their forties. This is not because they are experiencing anything different, in a physical sense, but they are in an emotional sense. Many women find that the self-confidence and self-knowledge attained in the decades after forty can achieve expression sexually, as well as in other ways.

THE AGEING PROCESS

As the body ages there is a gradual decline in function (as you will discover below), but the most obvious effects of ageing can, to a large extent, be controlled by enjoying a healthy diet, regular exercise and, above all, by keeping yourself mentally alert. Some Japanese research has, too, shown that an active mind is one of the most powerful counterbalances to ageing.

Effects of ageing on the body

Dowager's hump
Calcium loss in older women may lead to vertebrae collapsing, resulting eventually in a rounded back.

The skeleton
Although there is no growth after full adult height has been reached in the late teens, the bones of the body are affected by age. Almost all women over the age of 60 have some detectable form of arthritis or inflammation of the joints. In *osteoarthritis*, which mainly affects the lower back, hips, knees, ankles and feet, the cartilage between the joints erodes and this leads to a thickening of the two bone ends. This results in the classic symptom of bony lumps. Post-menopausal women may find that their hands are especially affected by a thickening or mis-shaping of the last joints of the fingers, known as *Heberden's nodes*.

1 out of 4 post-menopausal women will experience the effects of *osteoporosis* – a gradual thinning and softening of the bones caused by loss of calcium and protein. This is sometimes linked to the thinning and flattening of the vertebral discs of the spine, a gradual curvature of the spine and loss of height.

The muscles
Maximum muscle strength is normally reached around the age of 25–30. After this age, there is a gradual reduction in the speed and power of muscle contractions and also a decrease in the capacity of a muscle to sustain effort. There is less elasticity in the muscle and an increase in non-elastic fibrous tissue. The number of muscle fibers and the amount of protein in the muscles steadily decreases.

The skin
The skin's remarkable elastic properties are due to the presence of collagen. With age, however, the collagen becomes less capable of stretching, and wrinkles and sagging result. There is a general loss of bloom, and the skin becomes thin and blotchy. Small veins

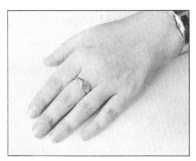

24-year-old hand

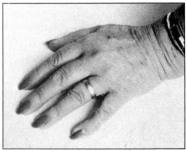

65-year-old hand

appear on both face and legs, and in advanced old age, skin takes on an almost transparent quality, with no elasticity left at all. New collagen forms more slowly as we get older, and is less capable of retaining water. The appearance of brown, so-called "age" or "liver" spots, occurs during middle age.

Fewer calories are needed to maintain weight as we get older so most women find that they put on weight unless they adjust their food intake to physical requirements. With increasing age, however, this fat tends to disappear, as does muscle bulk, leaving folds of inelastic skin and wrinkles.

The heart

After the age of 55 the heart may beat more slowly than the normal 72/min, and it may also become more irregular. Blood pressure often rises above the normal 120/80, and this may in turn cause the major arteries to increase in diameter. The smaller arteries, however, may narrow and their walls thicken because of calcified deposits of fat; blood clots may result. From the age of 60 onwards, heart disease is the major cause of death. The increased risk is caused not only by the narrowed walls of the blood vessels, which impair blood flow, but also by smoking, overeating, too much salt, lack of exercise and, to an extent, stress.

The kidneys and sex organs

The working order of the kidneys deteriorates as the number of functional kidney cells decreases with age. The kidneys are also affected by ageing in other organs. For example, if the blood vessels entering the kidneys are affected by *arteriosclerosis*, the kidney tissue will be undernourished, and will "age" in consequence.

Weakening of the pelvic floor muscles can result in a prolapsed womb or incontinence. There is a drying up of the vaginal secretions both during and after menopause, and the vaginal walls become thinner and may atrophy.

The brain and nervous system

Throughout life the nerve cells of the brain die off, and because they are not replaced, the brain becomes lighter as it ages. Brain weight is a crude measurement of the number of intact nerve cells present, and on average a 20-year-old brain will weigh 1250 grams; an 80-year-old brain, 1125 grams. The regenerative powers of divided or injured nerves diminishes; the reaction time of the autonomic nervous system, which controls our internal physiological functions, and the speed at which electrical impulses are passed down the nerves, tends to be slowed down.

The eyes and ears

The lens of the eye becomes more opaque and less elastic as we grow older. These changes, in conjunction with changes in the ciliary muscles which control lens movement, mean that the eye ceases to accommodate efficiently with consequent loss of visual acuity. The diameter of the pupil gets smaller, restricting the amount of light entering the eye. The iris fades in color; the cornea thickens and becomes less transparent. There is also a tendency for the intra-ocular pressure to increase as the eye ages.

Most adults suffer some hearing loss as they get older but it is gradual, and the degree of impairment varies. Initially, hearing loss is greater for high tones than for low ones, and eventually very high tones may be completely lost. Impacted ear wax can also be a problem for elderly women.

Digestion

Although many digestive complaints arise later in life, there is a high probability that their cause is psychological rather than any actual deterioration of the digestive system. A single woman, for example, may not want to cook for herself alone. Less saliva and digestive juices may be secreted because of a lack of arousal, caused by a poorer sense of smell and taste.

Metabolism

With age, the metabolic rate declines, partly because of reduced thyroid function, and partly because the total number of cells requiring nourishment is reduced.

The body is no longer able to respond efficiently to rises or falls in temperature – it doesn't sweat efficiently, nor does it shiver properly. This inability of the body to regulate temperature properly and the corresponding reduced awareness of cold lead to a severe risk of *hypothermia* – a common condition in the elderly, where body temperature drops to a dangerously low level. The person often fails to realize what is happening and eventually becomes unconscious.

The body is less able to move minerals like sodium, calcium and potassium around and this leads to a build-up in the cell structure which interferes with the normal functioning of the body.

I know that heart disease is a major killer of men; is this true for women, too?

Heart disease is uncommon in pre-menopausal women (probably due to hormonal influence; see below). After menopause, however, the incidence becomes equal to that in men.

Do estrogens prevent coronary thrombosis in menopausal women?

It is thought that female hormones have a protective effect prior to menopause, and there is suggestive evidence, but no proof, that hormones after menopause will prevent heart disease. However, the best way to prevent the disease is to have a healthy diet and to take regular exercise.

Is increasing forgetfulness, especially about things which have occurred in the past couple of days, a sign of senility?

Recent memory does deteriorate with age, but not usually until the sixties. Forgetfulness probably means you are under stress and have more than anyone could normally be expected to remember. Take the pressure off yourself by making lists; have note pads all over the house.

Is having to hold a book further and further away a sign of ageing eyes?

Not ageing eyes, but of a gradual change in the shape of the eyeball and the lens, caused by the muscles in the eye. If they elongate the lens you will have to hold the book further away to focus; if they flatten it you will have to do the opposite. If the shape of the eyeball flattens or elongates, the same things will happen.

Is losing part of what people say always a sign of deafness?

No. It probably means that you are preoccupied with another thought. This happened to me recently with my mother and I apologized, saying that I was distracted with a small problem. "You always are," she retorted.

Is it true that vitamin D helps prevent the thinning of bones?

Yes, but only over the age of sixty-five. Before that it is mainly estrogens that help, plus a balanced diet.

Is there any way of avoiding "dowager's hump"?

Yes, eat a good diet, rich in calcium and protein (see p. 20), and take vitamin D supplements if you are over the age of sixty-five. Pay attention to posture and keep exercising.

Does exercise prevent the kind of loose skin often seen in elderly women?

No. That's due to loss of collagen (see p. 412), but well-toned muscles do help to keep the skin taut and firm so make sure you exercise regularly and maintain a good posture.

MAINTAINING FITNESS

As we age it becomes increasingly important to exercise regularly, and there are two major reasons for this: mobility/suppleness and heart/lung strength.

Mobility is the key to a youthful old age and the phrase "use it or lose it" is not far from the truth, as muscles which are not used will deteriorate. If a woman is fit she will suffer less from the stiffness and muscle weakness associated with old age. Indeed, one of the dangers of an inactive old age is the vicious circle of inertia that can be established. Take, for example, the case of an unfit woman who becomes increasingly stiff as she ages. She simply puts this down to growing older, and because she finds it difficult to move her limbs easily, gives up and becomes progressively immobile. What she fails to realize is that if she made the effort to use her limbs and keep them supple, the grosser disabilities of ageing would not occur.

The second important reason for exercising is the greatly improved efficiency of the heart and lungs, which in turn benefits the individual's stamina, circulation and resistance to disease. This general enhancement of health is obviously desirable, and even if you have never taken regular exercise, there is nothing to prevent you starting now (it is, however, sensible to see your doctor first for a checkup).

The types of exercises which are desirable can be divided into warm-up exercises, mobility or suppleness exercises, and aerobic or heart-lung exercises.

Warm-up exercises

Before vigorous exercise, it is essential to loosen up the body to avoid any unnecessary strain. As the body warms up, the blood vessels of the limbs gradually dilate, allowing the body to meet the increasing demand for oxygen that comes with aerobic exercise. Warm-ups should be done for 5 minutes before gentle exercise and 10 minutes before more strenuous types.

Spine-stretch (10 times)
Stand with your feet slightly apart and stretch up. Bend your knees, swinging your arms down and back. Swing arms up again and arch back.

Waist-stretch (10 times)
Stand with your feet apart and stretch up. Keeping legs straight, swing left arm over your head, sliding right arm down your leg. Repeat with other side.

Knee-clasp (10 times)
Stand up straight, with your feet apart. Bend one knee and bring it up tightly into your chest. Then repeat with the other leg.

Aerobic exercises

The ability of the body to function well depends on the soundness of the heart and lungs, and it is therefore essential to keep them in good working order. Sports like running, tennis, skiing and swimming both condition the muscles and improve the endurance and strength of the heart and lungs. This is especially true of swimming, which is an ideal sport for older women to take up because the body's weight is comfortably supported in the water, and no undue tension is exerted on the limbs.

THE BENEFICIAL EFFECTS OF EXERCISE

Activity	Endurance	Strength	Mobility	Activity	Endurance	Strength	Mobility
Climbing stairs	●●	●●	●●●	Running	●●●	●●	●
Digging garden	●●	●●●	●●	Squash	●●	●●	●●●
Horse riding	●●	●	●	Swimming	●●●	●●●	●●●
Housework	●	●	●●	Tennis	●●	●●	●●
Jogging on the spot	●●	●	●	Walking quickly (1 hr+)	●●	●	●

●●● Very effective   ●● Moderately effective   ● Very little effect, if any

MOBILITY AND SUPPLENESS EXERCISES

If the idea of vigorous sports such as tennis, squash or jogging does not appeal to you (see left), there are certain beneficial "on-the-spot" exercises which you can do (see p. 38). They not only improve suppleness but also sharpen mental and physical responses and improve appearance. If, however, you've let yourself get badly out of condition, or if you suffer from arthritis, the exercises below make an ideal alternative.

Ankle mobility
Cross your legs and slowly draw out a circle with your toe. Repeat with your other foot.

Leg mobility
Slip a scarf under your foot and gently try to pull your toe up. Repeat with the other foot.

Waist mobility
Sitting back in your chair, twist round to put your elbow on the chair back. Repeat with the other side.

General posture
Sit well back in your chair and pull yourself up straight, chest out, head up.

Foot mobility
Flex each ankle by pulling up your toe first and then your heel.

Neck mobility
Let your head fall forwards; pull it up slowly. Let it fall to the side, then pull it up again.

Arm muscles
This exercise is designed to combat flabbiness under the arms. Hold two weights (or heavy books) over your chest then slowly swing them out to your sides. Repeat, but never strain yourself.

ADAPTING DIETS

Many women find that their weight gradually increases as they age, and that this becomes especially noticeable during the post-menopausal period. The major reason for this increase is that the metabolic rate slows down as we mature, and that by the age of about 55, fewer calories are required daily just to maintain body weight. So, even if you continue eating what you usually do (and no more), it will still be too much and you will have to cut down. A secondary factor is the lack of regular exercise common to middle-aged and elderly women.

How can this weight increase be resolved? Simply, you have to eat less and take more exercise. This, however, is easier said than done since the body's nutritional needs remain the same, despite the fact that it should take in fewer calories. This means, in effect, that you've got to find all that the body requires to function well in fewer calories, and it is especially important for older women that their diets contain adequate amounts of protein and vitamins. The thought of counting up and calculating the precise nutritional versus caloric value of food is too taxing for most women, so the best idea is to choose your balanced diet as on pages 20–26.

A common problem among many older people, especially when they live alone, is that all interest in food is lost, though there may be nothing wrong with the digestive system, teeth or taste buds. This is a very worrying syndrome because of the risk to general health. An effort *must* be made to eat and an interest in food should, at all costs, be rekindled. What you must not do is cut out meals, or rely on biscuits and cakes to keep you going. If, for example, you cannot face the idea of cooking a meal for yourself, arguing that the amounts used are wasteful, then try cooking in large batches so that you freeze three portions for later use, and eat one at the time of cooking. Also, try experimenting with different food styles – vegetarian, Chinese, Indian – to prevent monotony and to tempt the taste buds.

Some women find that they cannot manage to eat three main meals a day. If you find this, try taking five or even six small meals at regular intervals instead, so that the nutritional load is spread.

Another eating habit which should be carefully watched is the liberal use of salt. As mentioned on page 24, high salt intake is closely linked to hypertension and heart disease, and should therefore be discouraged; stop adding salt to food.

Calorie needs

Age	
5	1700
15	2300
25	2200-2700
45	2200-2500
60	2000

Our calorie requirements vary according to both our age and how active we are. As can be seen, the number of calories we need in order to function well declines with age.

MAINTAINING APPEARANCE

Many women are upset by the effects of ageing on the face and body, sometimes to the extent that they no longer make any effort to help themselves. There can be few things as depressing as looking in the mirror and hating what you see, but on the other hand if you look in the mirror and *like* what you see your whole outlook and demeanor will improve. This positive sense of self-esteem becomes increasingly important in old age, and looking after your appearance is one of the best ways of achieving this. The beneficial effects of a good diet and regular exercise on appearance will be further aided if you dress well and take good care of your skin and hair.

Thinking anew about your figure

Before you buy any new clothes, think first about your body: a trim and healthy figure is one of the most important factors in maintaining a youthful appearance, so if you see rolls of flesh when you stand in front of the mirror, make the effort to diet, and start taking regular exercise, *now.*

The female body has certain key points which indicate a youthful figure: the bustline, the waistline, the back and the buttocks. If your figure is not in perfect shape, you should watch these key points, and dress accordingly. Your bustline should be midway between your shoulder and your elbow, and it should be kept there with a wired bra if necessary! If you are overweight make sure your bra does not cut into your back, producing folds.

On the other hand, you should make the most of your best points: if you have a nice bust, show it; if your waist is attractive, wear clothes which accentuate it; if you have good legs make sure that they are seen by keeping hemlines relatively high, and by wearing attractive shoes.

Choosing the right clothes' style
It is impossible to give definitive advice on what to wear. Not only will you have developed your own sense of style, but more important, fashions will be constantly changing. It is, however, necessary to keep abreast of current fashion trends if you want to avoid looking dowdy. Therefore, incorporate colors and styles which flatter you into your wardrobe, but avoid the more exaggerated and transitory styles, which will probably not suit you. Keep well away from matronly styles with indistinct outlines and anything that could be classified as "safe," and don't choose stiff or sturdy fabrics because they will make your body look rigid and unsupple. If you are short-waisted, avoid looking dumpy by choosing clothes which conceal the waist. Ideally you should dress in one color from top to toe. If your buttocks are too big, disguise them with long tunics, jackets or overblouses, and avoid any

tightly-fitting skirts or trousers. By keeping pace with the overall trends you will not only be better dressed, but will feel more youthful and up-to-the-minute.

Shopping for clothes

Some women hate shopping, and this dislike is unlikely to disappear as you get older! You can, however, alleviate this by shopping early in the morning, when the shops and changing rooms are empty. Similarly, when you find a style that suits you, buy it in a number of colors. If you find, as some women do, that your sense of color deteriorates as you get older, either take a friend with you, or ask the advice of an assistant. Another disability which affects some women with age is a slight stooping, and any clothes bought should accommodate this.

Renewing your make-up

In my opinion, no feature on a mature face should be without make-up, and the older you get, the more subtle and refined this make-up should be.

If you haven't changed your make-up in the last twelve months, then you should start experimenting now. Look through glossy magazines and study how the models make up their eyes and mouths, paying close attention to how they shade and contour their faces. Then, without trying to copy any one of the pictures, work out for yourself what the essence of the "season's" look is. Jettison all your old make-up ideas and try out these newly-discovered ones.

If necessary, go to a make-up expert (*not* to a salon attached to a cosmetic manufacturer). He or she will show you how to make the most of your face – how to capitalize on your best features and conceal your faults, neither of which should require layers and layers of make-up. In order to make you up the expert will use a particular brand or range of cosmetics, and will probably give you the option of buying them. Do not be pressured into buying what is offered. If you think you can buy the same, or similar, goods more cheaply elsewhere, do so. And remember, the whole purpose of the exercise is to enhance your face and personality – if you're not happy with the results after a few trials, scrap the idea, and find something that *does* suit you. Be positive – if you look good, you'll feel good!

The face

Skin is prone to dryness as it ages, and for this reason a rich moisturizer should be used daily. Before you put on any make-up, first apply a film of moisturizer, smoothing it over your face with either a dampened sponge or your fingertips. Then use a moisturized, beige- or peach-toned foundation which should be one shade lighter than your own skin color. This lightness will help to reflect the light and minimize the effect of the lines. Dust over the foundation using a minimum of powder. If the powder is applied too heavily it will clog up any wrinkles and make them seem more obvious than ever. Never repowder during the day; simply blot any moisture dry with a tissue or cotton.

The well-known American actress Lauren Bacall has been making movies for almost 40 years, and at the age of 56 starred in a Broadway musical.

Try to avoid any complicated shading or highlighting. They require practice to put on well, and can look very unnatural on a slightly wrinkled face. What you should concentrate on, instead, is enhancing color with blusher. Choose a rather tawny, apricot shade (never pink) and place it just on the high point of the cheekbone; never use too much blusher on the first application, you can always add more later. Gently smooth it upwards and outwards towards your temples.

If you *do* want to try shaders and highlighters, start with your cheekbones. Use a slightly darker make-up stick than your foundation to draw a triangle under each cheekbone, with its point winging up towards your ear. Blend the color smoothly into the rest of your make-up, and make sure that no ugly streaks have been left. Then, take a light cream shadow-coverer (not the stick variety, which is much too heavy), and apply this underneath your eyes (even if you have few bags), over your upper lid and the whole of your brow area. To disguise laughter lines, and brow or lip wrinkles, use light cover with an eyeliner brush to carefully paint in the lines, working the make-up well into the creases, which should then be set with powder. Cover any areas of broken veins with a green-tinted moisturizer, and follow this with a beige foundation.

Hair
Your hair is an important factor in your appearance. Keep your hairstyle soft and if you do dye it, keep the color subtle.

Highlights
Use blusher on your cheekbones instead of highlighter and shadow – the effect is much more attractive.

Lips
Choose a lipstick which suits your coloring then powder your lips before applying to minimize running.

Eyes
Keep your make-up up-to-date by adapting new trends to suit your own preferences.

Wrinkles
These are a natural effect of ageing, but if they really worry you, work in a light foundation to help lighten the shadows.

Neck
Don't put foundation on your neck; just make sure that there is no line of foundation under your chin.

The eyes
Nothing marks a woman's age quite like her eye make-up. In any crowd of women it is usually possible to guess the age of about half of them by the make-up they wear on their eyes – it probably

hasn't changed for 25 years. What you *must* do is keep abreast of current trends, adapting them if necessary to suit your features. There are, however, some general guidelines to follow. Subtle, neutral shades like sludgy greens, greys or browns are the most flattering for ageing eyes. Very dramatic colors like purple or blue, and all frosted shadows, should be avoided because they emphasize wrinkles. Apply the shadow in the most fashionable way – whether it is just to the outer corner, or lightly smudged underneath – but avoid caking it on the upper lid, as this only draws attention to wrinkles. You may want to use eyeliner along the top lid to define your eyes, but avoid kohl pencils because they will look too heavy. Use non-run mascaras (in case your eyes "weep" a bit), in brown or grey; only use black if you are naturally very dark.

Many women dislike the idea of false eyelashes, but I feel that they are the greatest beauty aid a middle-aged woman can have because they enlarge and enhance the eyes. They don't have to be dramatic, in fact they should be almost invisible when you have them in place. Always wear brown eyelashes, never black ones because they are too heavy and harsh looking. Start off with thin, longish ones and attach them with the best glue available (even if it is expensive). Carefully trim them when they are in position. Ignore advice to mascara the false eyelashes with your own; this only makes them clog and look ageingly artificial.

The mouth

As we get older our mouths start to lose definition, and gradually acquire a fine network of lines which invariably cause lipstick to "bleed." The best way to make up your mouth to avoid these problems is to carefully outline the lips with a lip brush, which will give the mouth a more generous and precise shape. Blot the outline with a tissue, smile with your lips shut, and then pat with powder. Fill in your mouth with a lightish shade (dark shades are ageing) that best suits your own coloring.

Outlining the mouth
Choose your lipstick according to your own coloring, then use a lip brush to carefully outline your mouth shape. Blot carefully with a tissue.

Powdering the mouth
Smile, keeping your lips shut, and very carefully powder your mouth and surrounding skin to prevent lipstick running. Fill in lip shape.

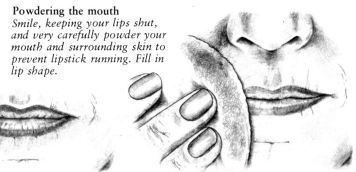

Skin and hair care

As we have mentioned, your skin may well become very dry as you get older, so frequent applications of moisturizer and body creams are advisable. This may already be part of your established routine; if so, you should continue with it. Try not to bathe too frequently, and put some oil in the bath when you do.

Wrinkles are a natural result of ageing, but despite this some women opt for cosmetic surgery to relieve the most obvious effects (see p. 348). Although the operations are not permanent, the majority of women who have surgery consider the results, for the few years that they last, adequate enough reason for considering it. Careful use of make-up, although not as dramatic as surgery, is nevertheless a suitable alternative which women should consider.

While temperate climates are good for general health, too much sun is not (see p. 83). Wear a hat if necessary and apply a PABA (para-aminobenzoic acid) sun-barrier cream to cut out the most harmful effects whenever the sun is strong.

Be meticulous about foot hygiene and care. Get rid of all thick, dead skin weekly, after your bath, or alternatively have a pedicure. Similarly, look after your hands as much as your job, hobbies and family allow. Whenever you have any washing or dirty jobs to do, wear protective gloves, lined with a cheap pair of cotton gloves soaked in hand lotion, and keep tubes of handcream in your office, car and kitchen.

You will probably have been dealing with body hair throughout your adult life and you should continue doing this by waxing, electrolysis, shaving or plucking (see p. 84).

Keep your hair in good order. If you can't run your hands through it and still look good, then it needs cutting, shaping or restyling. As long as your hair is fairly thick, you will look younger if it is unpermed and loose, in an unlacquered style that moves freely. If, however, you have thin hair your hairdresser may suggest a light perm to give it body, but whatever you do, keep away from old-fashioned styles and harshly-colored dyes.

SEX AND OLDER WOMEN

It is an all too common myth, especially among younger people, that the middle-aged and elderly cannot, or do not, enjoy making love. But your emotional needs do not necessarily change as you get older, and this applies to sex as much as anything. Indeed, an active sex life is an important factor in maintaining self-esteem and self-confidence – and it strengthens the emotional bond between a woman and a man, no matter what their ages.

Studies show that women have a more stable sex drive than men, and one that is less susceptible to the effects of ageing. It has been revealed that even women over sixty-five seek out, and respond to, erotic encounters, have erotic dreams, and continue to be capable of orgasms, even multiple ones. By far the most important factors influencing the sexual behavior of an older woman are the opportunity for regular sexual activity and the availability of a partner.

Enhanced sexual expression

For some couples, middle age may be the time when they discuss their own needs and preferences more openly, and this in itself can result in an improved sexual relationship. Many women, once the demands of childbearing and other domestic matters have lessened, find they have the privacy, and time and energy to invest in themselves and their mates – they often experience a revival of sexual interest as part of an awareness of the varied possibilities of their mature years.

Kinsey showed that the proportion of women experiencing orgasm rises steadily through the years. Other studies have shown that once women are no longer capable of having children, sexual desire and activity increases.

Sexual difficulties

Problems with sex in later years fall into two major categories: social and physical. Unfortunately, the social difficulties are the most significant, as well as the hardest to overcome. Psychological difficulties often result as a response to these problems.

Social preclusions

As I said above, the most important factors affecting long-lasting sexual activity for women are the opportunity to have sex and the availability of a partner. Widowhood and divorce increase the "pool" of unattached women in the fifties-and-over age group (at ages 54–64 there are 80 men to 100 women; at ages 65–75 there are 72 men to 100 women; at age 75 + there are 63 men to 100 women), and, unfortunately, remarriage is not as likely for older divorced and widowed women as it is for men. A double standard of ageing exists, so that while men at 50 may be still as sexually and socially eligible as they were at 25, women are not, and it is very difficult for an older woman to develop a new sexual relationship.

In addition to this lack of opportunity, older women, both married and not, tend to curb their sex life even further by being ashamed or embarrassed by their ageing body. Social conventions about "dirty old women" and "sex-starved spinsters" cruelly inhibit women from seeking out sexual partners and restrict the enjoyment of their sexual behavior. Older women often feel resentment of the freer sexual behavior of younger ones and, quite rightly, inwardly rage at the limitations on their sex lives.

Physical considerations

Progressive thinning of the vaginal walls and drying out of the mucus membranes, with resulting loss of lubrication, are the main physical difficulties women have to contend with; intercourse often becomes painful. Sometimes women experience a burning sensation after sex, caused by irritation of the bladder and urethra. Orgasm can be complicated by painful uterine contractions.

Bear in mind that physical difficulties in sex also depend on your partner's performance. While the frequency and intensity of women's orgasms are reduced, they still remain capable of them; men as they age become less capable of erections and if they do have them, tend to climax sooner.

Psychological difficulties

Maintaining happy sexual relationships in later life is just as important, and as difficult, as in earlier years. Indeed, just as many women reach and enjoy their sexual maturity, their partners' are declining. Now the problem arises of women trying to satisfy their sexual needs without making their mates feel sexually incompetent or impotent. Many women find that once their partners' sexual needs diminish and their demands on them decrease, that they become more aware of their own sexual rhythms and desires. In effect, just as women feel ready, able and willing to take the initiative, they are forced to tread carefully and play down these sexual feelings in order to bolster their mates. Frustration, at the very least, and often anger is the result. Such anger, of course, easily carries over into other areas of the marriage, resulting in disharmony.

Keeping sex good

The best way to ensure a satisfying, continuing sex life is to have frequent sex. Many women, especially those who have regular intercourse – about once or twice a week – maintain a healthy vaginal condition into advanced old age. Since orgasm increases the vascular supply to the vagina, and responses in intercourse stimulate vaginal muscles, even an ageing vagina will continue to be sufficiently lubricated and elastic. Gentle arousal, of course, should also be employed as rough caresses can irritate sensitive areas. If dryness continues to be a problem, the use of lubricating creams, such as KY Jelly, can be very beneficial. Hormone replacement therapy (HRT) has also been successful in alleviating these complaints (see p. 251) but should not be used for that sole purpose.

Both for women with partners, and those without, masturbation is an important form of sexual release; it has also been shown to be healthy for you as it increases lubrication and diminishes vaginal pain due to dryness. Whether masturbation has been continuous, or whether it is taken up again on the loss of a partner, it is an ideal sexual activity – an easy way to orgasm – and one that is guaranteed to prolong your love life. Masturbation provides great scope for sexual pleasure at all times.

While it may be frightening to seek sexual response, especially if you've been living a celibate life for a while, it is often the idea more than the reality which is difficult to handle. Remember, sex is both normal and natural, and you should use all the reserves of your past experience, compassion and, maybe, humor to back you up in your search for a long and healthy sex life.

RETIREMENT

The one event which will change your life most profoundly in later years will be retirement – whether it is your own or your partner's. This change is often accompanied by depression and a sense of inadequacy, but it is usually the prospect of retiring rather than retirement itself that causes this. Don't, however, think that you will escape without temporary depression or anxiety – you will probably experience both of these – but studies have shown that if you are healthy, with reasonable financial resources, and have planned for your retirement, then you will adapt both quickly and completely to your changed circumstances. This preparation is now widely recognized as a real need, and is catered to by many firms and voluntary organizations.

To make the most of your retirement you will have to acquire new skills, new attitudes, new interests and, in some cases, new relationships, but you will only succeed if you approach it in a positive state of mind, with energy, resolve and determination. It will help if you share the responsibility of planning with your partner; if you are single and feel that you need help, either join up with another single woman or seek help from family, friends or a specialist organization.

It may also help to think of the years ahead in terms of possible problem areas, and to see what the most suitable solutions to them are. Whatever the situation, it will help to look at it in terms of how it can be made to work for you, and how it can eventually enrich your life.

Your partner's retirement
Whether or not you, yourself, have retired, it may be necessary to act as an emotional prop if your partner is unable to come to terms with his own retirement. Encourage him to talk about it, and to see the positive aspects of it; if you also work, plan out retirement for both of you.

Money
Your income and assets will provide for your material well-being, so make sure that you are well-prepared, financially, for retirement. If necessary, see your bank manager and discuss with him how best to invest or save your money. And once you have retired, use your money sensibly: never buy ready-prepared meals; buy, instead, low cost cuts of meat, own-label goods and fresh vegetables; avoid special diet foods; save and use all food coupons; keep your eyes open for bargains – whether in food or clothing; book your holidays well in advance, and take full advantage of all reduced fares on all forms of transport.

Moving
For some people, retirement is the ideal opportunity to make a break and move elsewhere, but it is a decision which should be well-considered beforehand. If, for example, you do want to move, make sure that you know enough people in the new town for social contact. Check, beforehand, that there are facilities for your favorite hobbies or sports; make sure that the shops are easily accessible, and guarantee that you do, indeed, like the area, both day and night. These suggestions may seem pedantic, but with your increased leisure time, it is doubly important that you enjoy your surroundings and are able to make the most of them.

Social relationships
If possible, continue some of your earlier working activities or social relationships with old colleagues. This will help you feel a sense of belonging and participation, and will avoid the traumatic,

sudden withdrawal of all your professional relationships. At the same time, make use of any new contacts that you have – join clubs, if that suits you – but don't become isolated.

Leisure time

Now, more than at any other period in your life, your time really is your own, but you must plan and make proper use of it. There is no truth in the adage "You can't teach an old dog new tricks," so, if you feel like going to day or evening classes to learn something unusual, do so. You can only benefit from the fact that your brain is being kept alert; indeed you will feel a sense of achievement, usefulness and happiness. To enable you to make the most of all the new opportunities for social activity and travel, make sure that you attend to your diet, physical fitness and health.

Finding another job Some women find that although they enjoy their new-found leisure time, what they really want is another job. The idea of finding a job is an admirable one as it may restore any lost sense of self-esteem and will keep the mind alert. If you have both the business acumen, and financial backing, you may decide to start up a new business. Alternatively, you may decide against this kind of responsibility and opt, instead, for a part-time job in a local business or shop. If this is the case, then advertisements in the local stores or newspapers are an ideal means of finding such jobs. The only reservation would be if the job became too taxing or tiring, in which case it should be stopped or at least curtailed somewhat.

Travel The period after retirement is an ideal one for travel as it is possible to journey at off-peak times, and make full use of any fare concessions. If you feel like travelling – whether in your own country or abroad – it is an ideal way of not only "broadening the mind," but also of meeting new people in new situations. What you must do, however, is make a plan well before you start, taking the advice of a travel agent if necessary. Make sure that you choose the travel arrangements which suit you best – do you want, for example, to have everything organized for you, from flights and rooms to tours and restaurants, or would you rather buy an open-ended ticket and explore? Avoid travelling alone if you can. Not only is it more fun going with someone else, but should there be any trouble, it can be a great help to have someone there to help. If you take regular medication, or if you have any allergies, keep a note of them in your wallet or on a medallion around your neck or wrist.

WIDOWHOOD

It is physiological fact that women live longer than men, and that the majority will therefore experience widowhood (about 2 out of 3 women over the age of sixty-five are unmarried and most are widows). But, once again, the situation can be greatly relieved if both partners discuss the eventuality of one or the other of their deaths, and make plans accordingly. Interestingly, studies have shown that widowhood is less traumatic for women than men.

The stages of grief The expression of grief is individual to each woman. but it is a necessary process if you are to once again cope mentally and physically with life's demands. There are three recognized stages and each one is characterized by a particular attitude.

Stage 1 – numbness
This is the pervading feeling during the first terrible days and it enables one to get through the funeral arrangements, the family gatherings, and the initial applications for pensions and insurances. It very often happens that the reality of death does not penetrate completely at this time and many women continue to behave as though their partner was still alive – shopping and cooking for two,

for instance. There is nothing unusual or abnormal in this. This particular stage, for most women, can last anywhere from three days to three months.

Stage 2 – depression
Some time after the death of her partner, when the numbness wears off, a woman begins to perceive an emptiness in life, and the future seems filled with dread. It is especially difficult for her if she is not working, or has few outside interests or friends, as her partner would have been central to her life. Now that he is dead she is overwhelmed, and often experiences feelings of panic and frenzy. Moreover, she may blame herself for his death, and expressions of guilt will be to the forefront of her thoughts and speech – "If only I'd. . ." becomes her regular refrain.

The death of a partner is the most traumatic event that a woman is likely to experience and most bereaved women develop some depressive illness. Anxiety symptoms which express themselves in physical terms may also be produced; illnesses such as colitis, diverticulitis, gastritis and mental disorders are not uncommon, nor is attempted suicide. Research has also shown that bereavement may result in an increase in alcohol, tranquillizer and drug intake, insomnia, malaise, agitation and tearfulness.

Stage 3 – acceptance
Hopefully within 1–2 years of bereavement, a woman will have accepted her partner's death and have begun to make positive plans for the future. This is a gradual process – pain and grief ebbing, while enthusiasm and interest once again begin to flow. One can't expect a smooth transition, but gradually positiveness should triumph over despair.

Coping with bereavement
When a death occurs there will be various kinds of difficulties and problems that you may encounter, and you need to set out plans for coping with them, and for asking for help if needed.

Funeral arrangements
Should your partner die, you will find it easier to stay with a friend or relative for the initial period, no matter how alone you want to be, and let someone else make the arrangements. If, however, it upsets you to leave your home, then ask someone to stay with you. If there is no one you can call on, there are many things you will have to see to yourself.

Once you have received a certificate of death from a doctor (if your partner has died in the hospital this will be taken care of automatically, but if death occurs at home you must call in a doctor), you can then arrange for burial or cremation. While it will be extremely difficult to discuss such arrangements yourself, you may have to contact several firms before you can agree on the procedure and price. Funerals are usually more expensive than expected, so make sure you have the funeral director discuss the various options and itemize all the costs. Normally you won't be billed until some time afterwards.

Financial and legal considerations

You may be entitled to government grants, not only covering expenses immediately after your partner's death, but also in the long term, and for any children or other dependents. It is, therefore, important that you get in touch with your local government department immediately. It is vital, too, that you be aware of your partner's insurance provisions, and contact the firm or his attorney immediately; in addition to life insurance he may have policies which cover funeral expenses and mortgage payments. Make yourself aware of the provisions of any will as they may concern his wishes and any bequests that he wanted.

Emotional support

One thing all grieving women have in common is the need for support from friends and relatives. Unfortunately, bereavement may drive us into such a state of apathy that we are unable to do anything for ourselves, and are therefore completely unable to seek support. Moreover, while everyone knows that a widow needs support, it may be very difficult for them to give it because widows are usually introspective or very boring because they only have one topic of conversation. They may also be extremely bad company because of tearfulness and depression. Relatives, for instance, are not necessarily able to overcome their own reactions to a death, and may impede the recovery process by avoiding discussion of it and other matters that they fear may be upsetting. The best support, therefore, may come from a self-help "widows" group.

It is rare for a woman to seek support from such groups when she is in the depths of grieving. The realization that you need support is very often a sign that you are on your way back to mental health and stability. Therefore, one of the most important acts of friendship that a relative can do for someone who is grieving is to ensure that they do go along to an occasional group meeting.

Medical help

For some widows, medical help becomes a necessity when depression, apathy, and lethargy obstruct any chance of recovery. If the bereavement coincides with menopause, there may be physical reactions as well. A doctor and/or psychiatrist may be able to treat you with drugs to clear some of these symptoms and increase the chances of recovery.

Self-help for bereavement

- Expect many confused and confusing emotions. Shock, disbelief, denial, followed by grief and depression, even rage, are all normal and healthy. Failure to work through grief and mourning can produce neurotic symptoms and psychosomatic illnesses. Mourning lasts for a variable period but, in time, must be put aside so that you can get on with life.
- Do yourself a favor by setting a limit as to how long you allow your initial grieving period to go on. Most people need at least six to twelve weeks, but you really should try not to let yourself go beyond that. This is not a hard and fast rule, and it will take you a much longer period to adjust to the loss of a very loving partner.

431

- Don't spurn friends and relatives who are usually only too keen to help and support you, if only for short periods such as a week or ten days. Do accept their invitations to visit for such a time, but don't outstay your welcome.
- After a period of grieving it may be necessary to push yourself to go into the community and meet new people in order to avoid excessive depression. You should avoid retiring to a strange town where it will be difficult to meet new people; instead, you should stay within travelling distance of friends and relatives. If you find yourself becoming lonely, make the effort to meet people (of whatever age). One of the best ways to do this is to join a group or social club that caters to one of your special interests and to really get involved in the working of it.
- If, however, you become severely depressed, despite talking the subject over with family and trying to overcome it yourself, then *do* seek medical help, and do not refuse it if a friend calls a doctor in on your behalf. Should you be under medical supervision never stop taking anti-depressants without permission and remember, if at any time you contemplate suicide, contact someone first – in the majority of depressions, the symptoms can be relieved with time, medical treatment, or both.
- Expect great demands to be made of you and you will need to have the traditional stiff upper lip in order to get back to anything like a normal way of life, and also to feel as normal as you did before you lost your partner. It isn't easy, it will take time, and you should be realistic with yourself. Nonetheless, in the fullness of time you will manage it.

EMOTIONAL ADJUSTMENT

Growing older involves a process of disengagement – a gradual withdrawal from certain aspects of your life including your work, your colleagues, various social activities and sports. Some women, of course, resist the pressure put upon them to reduce their commitments, to get rid of responsibilities and to do less work, but even though they fight the process all the way, disengagement is bound to come, simply because you will neither have the physical nor the mental strength to do what you did when you were young. It's as well, therefore, to meet disengagement in a positive way, to look forward to it and to plan for it. Regard it as a renewal of other sorts of activities, especially those involving the family, friends and neighborhood, and bear in mind that while the net effect may be a shrinkage in the range of your activities, the quality of them will almost certainly increase. There is also the added bonus that you will be less involved in the stresses and strains of professional and social engagements and commitments.

Attitudes towards ageing Your psychological attitudes towards ageing will affect your behavior as you grow older. It has been shown, for example, that if you have a balanced, positive attitude towards ageing your later years are much more likely to be both pleasant and fulfilled; with a negative approach the reverse is true. As we have stressed throughout this chapter, you should aim to develop a sense of continuity in your life, learning from earlier patterns of behavior and past mistakes. You should accept the fact that you are getting older and that you will die, but nevertheless be contented in your personal activities and relationships and financial security. Read through the following categories and compare the opinions with your own on your life, your work and the people around you. Being aware of a negative attitude is the first step towards correcting it and you should use the advice given in the chapter, and throughout the book, to help work out any problems.

The constructive attitude
This is invariably the attitude held by an intelligent and well-adjusted woman who is happy in both her personal and professional life. She has a fairly high sense of self-esteem and is satisfied with her achievements, while never losing sight of her failings. She is self-assertive without being aggressive, and is neither inhibited nor uncontrolled. Accepting the facts of old age, she looks back at the past with few regrets and overall approval, and looks forward to the future with optimism and anticipation.

The passive attitude
A woman with this outlook is generally happy in her personal life but is of a rather self-indulgent nature, relying on others to provide both material and emotional support. She looks forward to old age, not because it means a new start in life, but because it means retirement from work – which she never enjoyed.

The defensive attitude
This is an attitude taken by a woman with an immature attitude towards ageing. She tends to be emotionally cold, neurotic and very conventional, with a compulsive attitude towards work. While she will probably have prepared, financially, for old age, she will not be well-adjusted, emotionally, to the idea of it. She sees few advantages to old age and envies the young.

The hostile attitude
A woman with this approach will be aggressive and competitive, and will tend to blame others for her own failures. She hates the idea of getting older and sees age only in terms of a mental and physical deterioration culminating in death, which she fears. As a result she throws herself into work in an attempt to put off the day of retirement. She dislikes the young because of her envy of them, and faces old age with feelings of pessimism and anxiety.

The self-hating attitude
This is an extension of the hostile woman's approach to old age. Such women are highly critical of themselves, and have no desire to live their lives again. They don't envy young people and tend to look forward, instead, to death, which they regard as a welcome release from a second-rate existence.

USEFUL ADDRESSES

There may be occasions when you feel that you want advice and guidance on a specific problem, but you may be unsure whether an organization exists to help you. To make this easier for you, we've included a selection of addresses relevant to the various chapters in the book. Don't be put off by the fact that many of them are of the head office. Not only may they be able to help you from a distance, but they may be able to put you in touch with a group or organization nearer to you.

BEING A WELL WOMAN

OFFICE ON SMOKING AND HEALTH
Park Building Suite 1–58
12420 Parklawn Drive
Rockville, Maryland 20857

AMERICAN MEDICAL ASSOCIATION
535 N. Dearborn St.
Chicago, Illinois 60610

(DESAD PROJECT)
NATIONAL CANCER INSTITUTE
(Office of Cancer Communication)
Bethseda, Maryland 20014

PRESIDENTS COUNCIL ON PHYSICAL FITNESS AND SPORTS
7th and D streets S. W.
Washington D.C. 20202

EPILEPSY FOUNDATION OF AMERICA
1828 L Street NW
Washington DC 20036

AMERICAN DIABETES ASSOCIATION
600 Fifth Avenue
New York, New York 10020

ALCOHOLICS ANONYMOUS WORLD SERVICES INC
Box 459
Grand Central Station
New York, New York 10017

OVEREATERS ANONYMOUS
1246 La Cienega Blvd
Suite 200
Los Angeles, California 90035

TOPS (TAKE OFF POUNDS SENSIBLY)
4575 South 5th St.
P.O. Box 07489
Milwaukee, Wisconsin 53270

SOCIETY FOR NUTRITIONAL EDUCATION
2140 Shattuck Avenue
Suite 1110
Berkeley, California 94704

AMERICAN HEART ASSOCIATION
7320 Greenville Avenue
Dallas, Texas 75231

NATIONAL WOMEN'S HEALTH NETWORK
1302 18th Street N.W.
Suite 203
Washington, DC 20036

DAY-TO-DAY CARE

AMERICAN DENTAL ASSOCIATION
211 E. Chicago Avenue
Chicago, Illinois 60611

AMERICAN MEDICAL ASSOCIATION
535 North Dearborn Street
Chicago, Illinois 60610

NATIONAL INSTITUTE OF ALLERGY AND INFECTIOUS DISEASE, NIH
Allergic Diseases Section
Room 11 N.246–Building 10
Bethesda, Maryland 20014

SIGHT IMPROVEMENT CENTER, INC.
25 West 43rd Street
New York, New York 10036
(Information on contact lenses)

AMERICAN PODIATRY ASSOCIATION
20 Chevy Chase Circle, N.W.
Washington, D.C. 20015

AMERICAN SOCIAL HEALTH ASSOCIATION
1740 Broadway
New York, New York 10019

NATIONAL SOCIETY FOR THE PREVENTION OF BLINDNESS, INC.
79 Madison Avenue
New York, New York 10016

FERTILE LIFE

AMERICAN FOUNDATION FOR MATERNAL AND CHILD HEALTH
30 Beekman Place
New York, New York 10022

INTERNATIONAL CHILDBIRTH EDUCATION ASSOCIATION
P.O. Box 20852
Milwaukee, Wisconsin 53220

NATIONAL GENETICS FOUNDATION
250 West 57th Street
New York, New York 10019

NATIONAL FOUNDATION – MARCH OF DIMES
P.O. Box 2000
White Plains, New York 10602

PLANNED PARENTHOOD FEDERATION OF AMERICA
810 Seventh Avenue
New York, New York 10019

RESOLVE INCORPORATED
P.O. Box 474
Belmont, Massachusetts, 02178
(Infertility counseling)

MATERNITY CENTER ASSOCIATION
48 East 92nd Street
New York, New York 10028

AMERICAN COLLEGE OF NURSE-MIDWIVES
1012 Fourteenth St, NW
Suite 801
Washington, DC 20005

LA LECHE LEAGUE INTERNATIONAL, INC
9616 Minneapolis Avenue
Franklin Park, Illinois 60131

NATIONAL ABORTION COUNCIL
120 West 57 Street
New York, New York 10019

NATIONAL ABORTION RIGHTS ACTION LEAGUE
706 7th Street, S.E.
Washington, D.C. 20003

UNITED INFERTILITY ORGANIZATION
P.O. Box 23
Scarsdale, New York 10583
Hotline (914) 723-1687

NEW YORK FERTILITY RESEARCH FOUNDATION, INC.
123 East 89th Street
New York, New York 10028

H.O.M.E. (HOME ORIENTED MATERNITY EXPERIENCE)
511 New York Avenue
Tacoma Park
Washington, DC 20012

AMERICAN ACADEMY OF HUSBAND-COACHED CHILDBIRTH
P.O. Box 5224
Sherman Oaks, California 91413

CESAREANS/SUPPORT, EDUCATION AND CONCERN
66 Christopher Road
Waltham, Massachusetts 02154

SPECIAL FEMALE PROBLEMS

BREAST CANCER ADVISORY CENTER
9607 Kingston Road
Kensington, Maryland 20795

NATIONAL WOMEN'S HEALTH NETWORK
1302 18th Street NW
Suite 203
Washington DC, 20036

WOMEN IN MIDSTREAM
University of Washington YWCA
4224 University Way NE
Seattle, Washington 98105

THE NATIONAL CANCER INSTITUTE
Bethseda, Maryland 20014

THE REACH TO RECOVERY PROGRAM AMERICAN CANCER SOCIETY
777 Third Avenue
New York, New York 10017

VD CLINICS
Contact your local city or county health dept.

DES-ACTION
P.O. Box 1977
Plainview, New York 11803

CENTER FOR PREVENTION AND CONTROL OF RAPE
NATIONAL INSTITUTE OF MENTAL HEALTH
5600 Fishers Lane
Rockville, Maryland 20852

NEXUS
P.O. Box 176
Garden City, New York 11530
(offer service for newly separated,
divorced or widowed women – "provides
a haven after breaking up and helps her
in her new lifestyle.")

SINGLE PARENT RESOURCE CENTER
10 West 23rd St
New York, New York 10010

SINGLE PARENT PROJECT
5715 Lindo Paseo
San Diego, California 92115

NATIONAL ASSOCIATION FOR MENTAL HEALTH
1800 North Kent Street
Arlington, Virginia 22209

DIALOGUE HOUSE
45 West 10th Street
New York, New York 10011

THE COLORADO ASSOCIATION FOR AID TO BATTERED WOMEN
P.O. Box 136
Colorado Women's College
Mountview Boulevard and Quebec
Denver, Colorado 80220

THE CENTER FOR WOMEN'S POLICY STUDIES
2000 P Street N.W.
Washington, DC 20036

SIECUS (SEX INFORMATION AND EDUCATION COUNCIL OF THE UNITED STATES)
1855 Broadway
New York, New York 10019

SPECIALIST HELP

AMERICAN SOCIETY OF PLASTIC AND RECONSTRUCTIVE SURGEONS
29 E. Madison, Suite 800
Chicago, Illinois 60602

AMERICAN ACADEMY OF FACIO PLASTIC AND RECONSTRUCTIVE SURGERY
70 W. Hubbard St.
Suite 202
Chicago, Illinois 6061D

AMERICAN OSTEOPATHIC ASSOCIATION
212 East Ohio St
Chicago, Illinois 60611

AMERICAN CHIROPRACTIC ASSOCIATION
2200 Grand Avenue
Des Moines, Iowa 50312

LIFESTYLES

SISTERHOOD OF BLACK SINGLE MOTHERS
P.O. Box 155
Brooklyn, New York 11203

NATIONAL FEDERATION OF PARENTS AND FRIENDS OF GAYS
P.O. Box 24528
Los Angeles, California 90024

SINGLE PARENT RESOURCE CENTER
10 West 23rd Street
New York, New York 10010

SINGLE PARENT RESOURCE CENTER
3896 24th Street
San Francisco, California 94114

SINGLE PARENT PROJECT
5715 Lindo Paseo
San Diego, California 92115

NEXUS
P.O. Box 176
Garden City, New York 11530
(offer service for newly separated, divorced or widowed women – "provides a haven after breaking up and helps her in her new lifestyle.")

MARRIAGE ENCOUNTER NATIONAL OFFICE
5305 West Foster Avenue
Chicago, Illinois 60630

STAYING YOUTHFUL

NATIONAL COUNCIL OF SENIOR CITIZENS
1511 K Street NW
Washington, DC 20005

AMERICAN ASSOCIATION OF RETIRED PERSONS
1909 K Street NW
Washington, DC 20006

THE GRAY PANTHERS
3700 Chestnut St
Philadelphia, Pennsylvania 19104

NATIONAL COUNCIL ON THE AGEING
1828 L Street NW
Washington, DC 20036

US ADMINISTRATION ON AGEING
US Dept of Health, Education and Welfare
Social and Rehabilitation Services
Washington, DC 20201

WOMEN IN MIDSTREAM
University of Washington YWCA
4224 Union Way, NE
Seattle, Washington 98015

All addresses were correct at the time of printing

Index

V

W

X

Y

Z

Acknowledgments

Managing Editor	Amy Carroll
Art Editor	Denise Brown
Editor	Fiona MacIntyre
Designer	Derek Coombes
Art Director	Debbie MacKinnon

Dorling Kindersley would like to thank the following for their assistance: British Dental Health Association; Jan Croot; Dr Elizabeth Hudson; Dr O.A.N. Husain; June Kenton; Philip Kerland; Dr Patricia Last; Wendy Morgan; Sandra Schneider; Dr A. Singer; Ken Westall/Harley Street Clinic.

Illustrators
David Ashby
David Baird
Giovanni Caselli
Alicia Durdos
Carol Johnson
Elaine Keenan
Patricia Ludlow
Brian Sayers
Kathy Wyatt

Photography
Daisy Hayes
Anthea Sieveking

Photographic Services
Ron Bagley
Negs

Typesetting
Servis Filmsetting Ltd

Lithographic Reproduction
Repro Llovett, Barcelona

Photographic Sources
Key t = top; b = bottom; c = center;
l = left; r = right
Aspect 55; 378
Barnaby's Picture Library 158
Michael Boys 1; 87; 95; 139
British Dental Health Association 115
BUPA 265
Camera Press 18; 33
Clairol 93; 98l
Cornell Medical Center, New York 168
Daily Telegraph 357
Richard & Sally Greenhill 11; 13; 308; 314; 334; 362
Sally Hansen 125
Harley Dean Clinic, London 352
Harley Street Clinic 230
Daisy Hayes 69; 260; 324; 412
Dr O.A.N. Husain 58
Carolyn Johns 219
Philip Kerland 113
Kobal Collection 161
Paolo Koch/Vision International 19
Andrew de Lory 2 (except bl); 9; 367; 385; 398; Cover (except bl; br)
Mayotte Magnus 329
Pictor 298; 393; 410; 428
Pountney Clinic 352
Rex Features 351; 420
Science Photo Library 98c; 98r
Anthea Sieveking/Vision International 2bl; 201; 277; 406; 416; 417; Cover bl; br
Slimming Magazine 31
Spectrum Colour Library 373
Tony Stone Associates 136; 156; 370
Women's National Cancer Control Campaign 59
Zefa UK Ltd 76; 225; 246; 294; 403